Lecture Notes in Computer Science 14353

Founding Editors

Gerhard Goos

Juris Hartmanis

Editorial Board Members

The series Lecture Notes in Computer Science (LNCS), including its subseries Lecture Notes in Artificial Intelligence (LNAI) and Lecture Notes in Bioinformatics (LNBI), has established itself as a medium for the publication of new developments in computer science and information technology research, teaching, and education.

LNCS enjoys close cooperation with the computer science R & D community, the series counts many renowned academics among its volume editors and paper authors, and collaborates with prestigious societies. Its mission is to serve this international community by providing an invaluable service, mainly focused on the publication of conference and workshop proceedings and postproceedings. LNCS commenced publication in 1973.

Mohamed Sellami · Maria-Esther Vidal ·
Boudewijn van Dongen · Walid Gaaloul ·
Hervé Panetto
Editors

Cooperative
Information Systems

29th International Conference, CoopIS 2023
Groningen, The Netherlands, October 30 – November 3, 2023
Proceedings

 Springer

Editors
Mohamed Sellami ⓘ
Telecom SudParis
Evry, France

Maria-Esther Vidal ⓘ
Leibniz University Hannover
Hannover, Germany

Boudewijn van Dongen ⓘ
Eindhoven University of Technology
Eindhoven, The Netherlands

Walid Gaaloul ⓘ
Telecom SudParis
Evry, France

Hervé Panetto ⓘ
University of Lorraine
Vandoeuvre-les-Nancy, France

ISSN 0302-9743   ISSN 1611-3349 (electronic)
Lecture Notes in Computer Science
ISBN 978-3-031-46845-2   ISBN 978-3-031-46846-9 (eBook)
https://doi.org/10.1007/978-3-031-46846-9

General Co-chairs and Editors' Message for CoopIS 2023

The 29th International Conference on Cooperative Information Systems (CoopIS 2023), held October 30 – November 3 in Groningen, The Netherlands, serves as a significant milestone in the ongoing series of annual conferences that began in 2002 in Irvine, California. The conference subsequently traveled to various locations, including Catania, Sicily in 2003; Cyprus in 2004 and 2005; Montpellier, France in 2006; Vilamoura, Portugal in 2007 and 2009; Monterrey, Mexico in 2008; Heraklion, Crete, Greece in 2010 and 2011; Rome, Italy in 2012; Graz, Austria in 2013; Amantea, Italy in 2014; Rhodes, Greece in 2015, 2016, 2017, and 2019; Valletta, Malta in 2018; and Bozen-Bolzano, Italy in 2022. The CoopIS 2023 conference in Groningen further solidifies the significance of this series.

Cooperative Information Systems (CISs) play a pivotal role in fostering collaboration among individuals, organizations, intelligent devices, and complex systems. By delivering adaptable, scalable, and intelligent services, CISs extend their benefits to enterprises, public institutions, and user communities. This dynamic enables seamless interaction, information sharing, and collective efforts even across physical constraints. The realm of CISs amalgamates insights from diverse computing domains, including distributed systems, coordination technologies, collaborative decision-making, enterprise architecture, business process management, and conceptual modeling.

Recent times have witnessed the emergence of pioneering technologies such as Cloud Computing, Service-Oriented Computing, the Internet of Things (IoT), Linked Open Data, Knowledge Graphs, Semantic Systems, Collective Awareness Platforms, Blockchain, and Hybrid Artificial Intelligent Systems. These innovations collectively set the stage for the evolution of the next-generation CISs.

As we venture into crafting these advanced CISs, there arises a call for research in several directions. Firstly, there is a need to explore the practicality and application of the aforementioned innovative technologies. Secondly, strategies must be devised to construct CISs that cater explicitly to the diverse stakeholders inherent in developing socio-cyber-physical systems. Lastly, it is imperative to develop modeling techniques that can comprehensively articulate and analyze the multifaceted dimensions of these cohesive systems.

This 29th edition was collocated with the 27th edition of the Enterprise Design, Operations and Computing (EDOC) conference, and its guiding theme was *Human-centric Information Systems*. Just like in previous iterations of CoopIS, the organizers aimed to foster this cross-fertilization through a compelling lineup of keynote speakers representing both academia and industry. We take great pride in presenting this year's distinguished speakers:

– Boualem Benatallah, Dublin City University, Ireland (CoopIS keynote)
– Fabio Casati, ServiceNow, California, USA (CoopIS keynote)
– Coral Calero Muñoz, University of Castilla-La Mancha, Spain (EDOC keynote)
– Jerker Delsing, Luleå University of Technology, Sweden (EDOC keynote)

We have succeeded in crafting a high-quality conference program for this year's edition. A comprehensive pool of 100 papers was received and subjected to a rigorous review by the CoopIS Program Committee, maintaining the highest professional standards. Each paper underwent evaluation by a minimum of three referees, with mediated email discussions in cases where assessments significantly differed. Following this meticulous process, a total of 21 submissions were chosen as regular papers, while an additional ten were selected as work-in-progress papers. Reflecting the global scope of CoopIS, the authors of these accepted papers originate from diverse nations across the world.

We extend our heartfelt gratitude to all those who played a pivotal role in ensuring the success of CoopIS 2023. A special mention of appreciation goes to the EDOC 2023 organization committee for their invaluable assistance in orchestrating CoopIS 2023. Our sincere thanks also extend to the authors whose research papers enriched the conference, the dedicated PC members, and the additional reviewers, who diligently evaluated the submissions, providing authors with invaluable insights.

October 2023

Mohamed Sellami
Maria-Esther Vidal
Boudewijn van Dongen
Walid Gaaloul
Hervé Panetto

Organization

General Chairs

Hervé Panetto   Université de Lorraine - TELECOM Nancy,
France
Walid Gaaloul   Institut Polytechnique de Paris - Télécom
SudParis, France

Program Committee Chairs

Maria-Esther Vidal   Leibniz University Hannover and TIB-Leibniz
Information Center for Science and
Technology, Germany
Boudewijn van Dongen   Eindhoven University of Technology,
The Netherlands

Proceedings Chair

Mohamed Sellami   Institut Polytechnique de Paris - Télécom
SudParis, France

Demo Track Chairs

Nour Assy   Bonitasoft, France
Felix Mannhardt   Eindhoven University of Technology,
The Netherlands

Publicity Chairs

Slim Kallel   University of Sfax, Redcad, Tunisia
Gabriela Ydler   Leibniz University Hannover, Germany
Zhangbing Zhou   China University of Geosciences, P.R. China

Program Committee

Joao Paulo Almeida	Federal University of Espirito Santo, Brazil
Abel Armas Cervantes	The University of Melbourne, Australia
Nour Assy	Bonitasoft, France
Ahmed Awad	University of Tartu, Estonia
Banu Aysolmaz	TU Eindhoven, The Netherlands
Eduard Babkin	State University, Russia
Sylvio Barbon Junior	University of Trieste, Italy
Ingmar Baumgart	Karlsruhe Institut of Technology, Germany
Salima Benbernou	Université Paris Descartes, France
Mario Luca Bernardi	University of Sannio, Italy
Uwe Breitenbücher	Reutlingen University, Germany
Carlos Buil Aranda	Universidad Técnica Federico Santa María, Chile
Cristina Cabanillas	University of Seville, Spain
Paolo Ceravolo	University of Milan, Italy
David Chaves-Fraga	Universidad Politécnica de Madrid, Spain
Richard Chbeir	Univ. de pau et das pays de l'Adour, France
Saoussen Cheikhrouhou	University of Sfax, Tunisia
Diego Collarana	Fraunhofer FIT, Germany
Carlo Combi	Università degli Studi di Verona, Italy
Marco Comuzzi	UNIST, Republic of Korea
Silvia Inês Dallavalle de Pádua	Universidade de São Paulo, Brazil
Johannes De Smedt	KU Leuven, Belguim
Adela Del Río Ortega	University of Seville, Spain
Claudio Di Ciccio	Sapienza University of Rome, Italy
Chiara Di Francescomarino	Fondazione Bruno Kessler-IRST, Italy
Rik Eshuis	TU Eindhoven, The Netherlands
Marcelo Fantinato	University of São Paulo, Brazil
Luciano García-Bañuelos	Tecnológico de Monterrey, Mexico
José González Enríquez	University of Seville, Spain
Irlán Grangel-González	Bosch Corporate Research, Germany
Daniela Grigori	University Paris-Dauphine, France
Georg Grossmann	University of South Australia, Australia
María Teresa Gómez López	University of Seville, Spain
Önder Gürcan	NORCE, Norway
Mohand-Saïd Hacid	Université Lyon 1, France
Lazhar Hamel	ISIM Monastir, Tunisia
Anett Hoppe	Leibniz Universität Hannover, Germany
Stijn Hoppenbrouwers	HAN, The Netherlands
Stefan Jablonski	University of Bayreuth, Libanon
Andrés Jiménez Ramírez	University of Seville, Spain

Slim Kallel	University of Sfax, Tunisia
Dimka Karastoyanova	University of Groningen, The Netherlands
Dimitrios Katsaros	University of Thessaly, Greece
Kais Klai	Université Sorbonne Paris Nord, Paris, France
Matthias Klusch	DFKI, Germany
Maria Leitner	University of Vienna, Austria
Henrik Leopold	Kühne Logistics University, Germany
Francesco Leotta	Sapienza Università di Roma, Italy
Mario Lezoche	University of Lorraine, France
Jiangang Ma	Federation University, Australia
Samira Maghool	University of Milan, Italy
Amel Mammar	Télécom SudParis, France
Felix Mannhardt	TU Eindhoven, The Netherlands
Rabia Maqsood	FAST - NUCES, Faisalabad Campus, Pakistan
Raimundas Matulevicius	University of Tartu, Estonia
Philippe Merle	Inria Lille - Nord Europe, France
Nizar Messai	Université François Rabelais Tours, France
Sellami Mokhtar	Liris UCBL, France
Alex Norta	Tallinn University of Technology, Estonia
Selmin Nurcan	Université Paris 1 Panthéon-Sorbonne, France
Hajo A. Reijers	Utrecht University, The Netherlands
Manuel Resinas	University of Seville, Spain
Sonja Ristic	University of Novi Sad, Serbia
Michael Rosemann	Queensland University of Technology, Australia
Flavia Santoro	Rio de Janeiro State University, Brazil
Fatiha Saïs	Paris Saclay University, France
Michael Sheng	Macquarie University, Australia
Pnina Soffer	University of Haifa, Israel
Jacopo Soldani	University of Pisa, Italy
Nick van Beest	CSIRO, Australia
Han van der Aa	University of Mannheim, Germany
Sebastiaan van Zelst	RWTH Aachen University, Germany
Georg Weichhart	PROFACTOR GmbH, Austria
Karolin Winter	Technical University of Munich, Germany
Guido Wirtz	University of Bamberg, Germany
Moe Thandar Wynn	Queensland University of Technology, Australia
Jian Yu	AUT, New Zealand
Zhangbing Zhou	China University of Geosciences, P.R. China

Additional Reviewers

Imen Abdennadher
Drissi Amani
Robert Andrews
Sowelu Avanzo
Iris Beerepoot
Khouloud Boukadi
Francesca Bugiotti
Ana Rocio Cardenas Maita
Caio Coneglian
Irene Bedilia Estrada Torres
Ghareeb Falazi
Evangelia Fragkou
Moshe Hadad
Mubashar Iqbal

Aleksandr Kormiltsyn
Antonio Carlos Meira Neto
Chao Pan
Tobias Pfaller
Saurav Prakash
Gianluca Quercini
Mirela Riveni
Diana Carolina Roca Arroyo
Sareh Sadeghianasl
Salma Sassi
Ratan Sebastian
Sana Sellami
Judith Stanja
Athanasia Zacharia

CoopIS 2023 Keynotes

Conversational AI Enabled Services: Opportunities, Risks and Directions

Boualem Benatallah

Dublin City University, Ireland

Short Bio

Boualem Benatallah is a full professor of computing at Dublin City University (DCU, Ireland) since Jan 2022. He is a fellow of the IEEE. His main research interests are developing fundamental concepts and techniques in Web services middleware, business process automation, quality control in crowdsourcing and AI-enabled services, automated and crowdsourced training data curation, conversational cognitive services, and context-aware and compositional task-oriented conversational services. He has published more than 300 refereed papers including more than 100 journal papers. Benatallah has been general and PC chair of a number of international conferences. He has been a guest editor of several special issues for reputable international journals. He is a member of the steering committee of ICSOC (Int. Conference on Service Oriented Computing) conferences. He is a member of the editorial board of numerous international journals including ACM Transactions on Web, IEEE Transactions on services computing, and ACM Computing surveys. He supervised over 36 research (including 32 PhD and 5 Masters by Research) students to completion as principal or joint supervisor. Benatallah has had over 21 years as a senior lecturer, associate professor, full professor and then Scientia professor at UNSW Sydney (Australia) before joining DCU.

Talk

Conversational AI-enabled augmentation and integration promises to transform services and processes through data-driven automation and insights. Nonetheless, despite the early adoption, conversational AI-enabled service and process management technologies are still only in their preliminary stages of development, with several unsolved challenges stemming from a lack of computational abstractions and models to reason about ambiguity, composition and quality aspects that are inherent in data-driven processes. We will revisit abstractions, concepts, and techniques in data-driven service models and middleware. We will discuss synergies between intent-based composition, composition synthesis, robotic process automation and other technologies as a step forward to scale conversational AI services enablement. We will also briefly discuss quality control in training data curation and AI-enabled software services.

Responsible Enterprise AI in the ERA of Powerful Models

Fabio Casati

ServiceNow, USA

Short Bio

Fabio Casati is a Principal Machine Learning Architect at Servicenow as well as technical lead for the AI Trust and Governance group in servicenow research. Fabio focuses on designing, architecting and deploying AI-powered workflows for enterprise customers. On the research side, he is working on AI applied to workflows and on quality in AI. Previously he was Professor at the University of Trento. In that role, he started research lines on crowdsourcing and hybrid human-machine computations, focusing on applications that have direct positive impact on society through tangible artefacts adopted by the community. Prior to that, he was technical lead for the research program on business process intelligence in Hewlett-Packard USA, where he contributed to several HP commercial products in the area of web services and business process management. He co-authored a best-selling book on Web services and is author of over 250 peer-reviewed papers and dozens of patents.

Talk

Companies are devoting significant effort -and budget- into powering their processes with AI. The trend and enthusiasm towards AI-powered processes has skyrocketed in recent months with the advent of powerful large language models (LLMs), that open new possibilities and drive users interest and expectations. Leveraging the benefits of AI in an enterprise context however is far from trivial. AI are still probabilistic systems that operate in somewhat mysterious ways, often with a business value that is hard to measure, that may fall into major blunders, and that may be harmful to people of not used properly. The distance that still exists between the power of modern AI and the impact it has had so far on the enterprise is surprising to many, given that recent models report super-human performance in many tasks seemingly related to what AI is asked to do in the enterprise.

In this talk I will present some of the reasons for the disconnect between the (perceived) quality of AI services on one side, and the transformational impact they can have on AI-powered enterprise processes on the other. I will focus specifically on two key challenges. The first is the way we measure and communicate the quality of AI services: the way many companies approach this problem is fundamentally wrong, and this leads to wrong process design decisions and to an improper use of AI in business processes.

The second is that AI service and technology providers often focus on the benefits of AI services once in production, but underestimate the importance of simplifying the journey that process owners have to follow to get there, the perceived risk - or lack of trust - in AI, and how difficult it is to create and use good benchmarks. I will present concrete examples of all these issues, and show (i) how we can rethink the notion of AI quality in enterprise processes and (ii) how we can simplify the journey to quality, useful and deliver trustworthy AI-powered processes.

Contents

Process Modeling

Process Analytics

Human Aspects and Social Interaction in CISs

Work in Progress (WIP) Papers

Knowledge Engineering

Enhancing Fairness and Accuracy in Machine Learning Through Similarity Networks

Samira Maghool$^{(\boxtimes)}$, Elena Casiraghi , and Paolo Ceravolo$^{(\boxtimes)}$

Department of Computer Science, Università degli Studi di Milano, Milan, Italy
{samira.maghool,elena.casiraghi,paolo.ceravolo}@unimi.it

Abstract. Machine Learning is a powerful tool for uncovering relationships and patterns within datasets. However, applying it to a large datasets can lead to biased outcomes and quality issues, due to confounder variables indirectly related to the outcome of interest. Achieving fairness often alters training data, like balancing imbalanced groups (privileged/unprivileged) or excluding sensitive features, impacting accuracy. To address this, we propose a solution inspired by *similarity network fusion*, preserving dataset structure by integrating global and local similarities. We evaluate our method, considering data set complexity, fairness, and accuracy. Experimental results show the similarity network's effectiveness in balancing *fairness* and *accuracy*. We discuss implications and future directions.

Keywords: Machine Learning · Fairness · Similarity Network

1 Introduction

Machine learning (ML) utilizes statistics and optimization algorithms to uncover relationships, patterns, and potential latent associations within sample features and their categorization. The application of ML to a huge volume of data may create an illusion of fairness because the learned model simply reflects what is observed in a domain. As a matter of fact, any dataset embodies the bias generated in the social context that originated it and may suffer from basic quality issues [30]. As an example, several papers using ML techniques on data from US hospitals have documented the highest age-adjusted infection rates and risk for Hispanic/Latino immigrants or other minorities [6,32], which may push ML algorithm to reinforce healthcare disparities. ML algorithms, while powerful in many domains, require caution when applied to datasets with *privileged/unprivileged* groups showing social bias. When *sensitive* features differentiate these groups, the model may incorrectly prioritize these features, resulting in a biased and unfair classifier. Instead of learning the proper classification rules, it mirrors the social patterns based on sensitive features.

M. Sellami et al. (Eds.): CoopIS 2023, LNCS 14353, pp. 3–20, 2024.
https://doi.org/10.1007/978-3-031-46846-9_1

One common approach to achieve fairness involves altering the data distribution or representation in the dataset [26], such as balancing groups [11] or removing sensitive attributes [2]. However, it worth to mention that these steps can potentially impact the prediction accuracy of the algorithms and their ability to uncover hidden relationships, patterns, and latent associations within the data. For this reason, the literature recommends striking a balance between fairness and accuracy by carefully considering the specific context, domain expertise, and the potential consequences of altering the data [11,22,41]. Additionally, researchers developed techniques, such as fairness-aware learning algorithms, that take into account fairness metrics during model training to achieve a better balance between fairness and accuracy [25].

In this paper, we present a novel solution to effectively tackle the delicate balance between fairness and accuracy. Our approach revolves around leveraging a comprehensive representation of the relationships and patterns within a dataset, allowing for the seamless integration of fairness-oriented modifications. Central to our method is the creation of a *similarity network* (a.k.a. graph) where node i represents the ith instance in the dataset and two nodes are connected by a link (edge) if they are "similar enough". While integrating all the dataset instances, the similarity network attends to capture the dependencies among various data-views and groups in the dataset. At the same time, it ensures that a classifier does not become overly reliant on a limited set of features to segment the data space. To effectively capture both the global and local structure of the dataset we used the similarity-computation method proposed by the Similarity Network Fusion (SNF) method [40], which has shown its promise in the biomedical field. Specifically, we aim to explore how adjusting the resolution of pairwise node similarities can provide more clear insights into the relationship between dataset complexity and model fairness. To evaluate the level of bias (fairness) imposed by protected features in the system, we calculate the *Equal opportunity* and *Equal mis-opportunity* metrics that are proposed considering privileged and unprivileged groups. The privileged groups often are defined by sort of social norms regarding the common features that may separate instances into groups with/without protected features, respectively. The definition of a privileged group composed of instances with protected features, not only requires finding the important features playing a role in a predictive model but also involves identifying the discriminative power of those features. To this aim, taking advantage of model explanations/interpretation, by e.g. computing SHAP values [24] or LIME [34] explanations allows the designer to effectively identify the impact of group membership in defining predicted outcomes.

More specifically, this paper is structured as follows. In Sect. 3, we introduce similarity measurements, discuss the use of kernels, and hyperparameter tuning. Section 3.6 discusses the limitations of standard classification metrics and the importance of considering the complexity of the addressed domain. Section 3.6 explores quantifying classification problem difficulty. Section 4 presents experimental results, including dataset description, preprocessing, similarity measures, and evaluation metrics. Section 5 offers final remarks. Section 6 concludes the paper, highlighting achievements and challenges.

2   Background and Related Work

ML fairness aims to prevent the models from systematically disadvantaging or discriminating against individuals based on their group membership. The goal is to create equitable outcomes and prevent any unjust treatment of individuals based on their association with a particular group. In [33] an insightful categorization of *measures* for assessing fairness is proposed. It distinguishes between methods assessing group or individual fairness, based on predicted outcomes, the ratio between predicted outcomes or probabilities and actual outcomes. Different measures verify different *fairness criteria* [4]. Selecting the appropriate measure requires considering the relevant legal, ethical, and social context [4].

The pervasive debate on the *accuracy-fairness* trade-off in ML is extensively documented in the literature. The pursuit of heightened fairness often entails a trade-off with accuracy [20]. Classifiers with fairness constraints typically (but not necessarily) exhibit lower accuracy compared to classifiers focused solely on maximizing accuracy. This trade-off has been rigorously examined from both theoretical [7] and empirical [12,27] perspectives. Fairness-aware algorithms aim to achieve higher fairness without significantly sacrificing accuracy or other utility measures [39].

Fairness-aware methods can be categorized as *post-processing* [17,36], *in-processing* [8,9], and *pre-processing* [10,14]. Post-processing methods focus on adjusting the predictions of an ML model to meet fairness constraints without modifying the model itself or the training data. In-processing methods incorporate fairness constraints during the training process by adding them to the model's loss function, often leveraging Lagrange multipliers for optimization. These methods tend to achieve a better trade-off than post-processing methods. Pre-processing methods address bias in the training data by modifying it to create a more "fair" dataset. Unlike post-processing and in-processing methods, pre-processing methods are model-agnostic, offering simplicity and stability. They do not require complex approximations, making them more practical to use. In recent literature, there has been a growing emphasis on integrating transparency into fairness-aware methods [21]. Transparency enables stakeholders to comprehend the decision-making process, the factors involved, and any potential biases, fostering trust and confidence in the system. Explainable ML methods play a crucial role in assisting designers in verifying the system's biases, and this is particularly relevant for fairness-aware algorithms. Regarding the data set transparency, measuring the level of difficulty of a classification problem could be a clue in finding the data set characterization domains that may challenge a predictive problem [18]. Mainly, these measures are categorized as "Feature-based", "Linearity", "Neighborhood", "Network", "Dimensionality" and, "Class imbalance" measures. In [23], some of the best measures for the data complexity induced by label noise imputation [13] are described, with an emphasis on those with low correlations between each other. In [13], the authors observed low correlation values between the fundamental complexity measures of [18] and graph-based measures, underscoring the relevance of exploring this alternative representation of the data structure. Furthermore, it substantiates the assumption that, when using graph-based models, the prediction problem remains stable even in the presence of noise.

Data heterogeneity presents another challenge, leading to inaccurate, poorly interpretable, and biased models. Heterogeneous data often comprises features with varying degrees of relevance and importance for the machine learning task. Some features may offer substantial information, while others may introduce noise or irrelevance. Inadequate handling of these disparities can result in models that focus on irrelevant or noisy features, leading to diminished generalization and biased predictions. Network structures have been commonly employed to enhance transparent data representation across various application domains. In [29] and [13], authors represented the dataset as a graph to extract statistical measures characterizing complex networks. Another example is label propagation [5]. In [42], the authors introduced the label propagation algorithm, which relies on the ϵ Nearest Neighbor (ϵ-NN) classification algorithm. Here, two nodes are considered neighbors if their distance falls below a threshold value, ϵ. While effective, this algorithm's performance hinges on a crucial parameter, ϵ, which must be carefully chosen to strike a balance between complexity reduction and information retention. Similarity Network Fusion (SNF) is a technique, originally introduced for multi-omics data fusion, to enhance the analysis and understanding of complex data [40]. Kernel functions (e.g., *Scaled-exponential Kernel*, *Diffusion kernel* [37] and *Random Walk kernel* [38]) serve as a fundamental component in similarity-based techniques like SNF by enabling the computation of pairwise similarities in a higher-dimensional non-linear space [35]. The choice of kernel and its associated parameters can significantly impact the performance and capabilities of the algorithm, making kernel selection and tuning an important aspect of machine learning model development. For example, using the scaled-exponential kernel to compute a global and a local similarity network for each view, SNF leverages the local similarity to guide a diffusion process across views, where the global view-similarities between two nodes (points) in the network are merged - to create an integrated similarity - if they have intersecting local neighborhoods within the different views. Consequently, the similarities between points that are neighbors (or distantly related) across multiple data views are reinforced (or diminished) in the integrated similarity network.

In our approach, inspired by SNF, we harness kernels for similarity networks to craft a pre-processing method. This method allows us to strike a favorable balance between fairness and accuracy in a model-agnostic and transparent manner. By connecting similar dataset instances, our network create a latent feature space that captures grouping patterns and latent associations within the dataset. This latent feature space ensures that, a classifier is not influenced by a limited set of features, eliminating the risk of segmenting the data space using sensitive features.

3 Material and Methods

Our experimental design aims to explore solutions that address the trade-off between accuracy and fairness while preserving the structure of a given dataset. We have chosen to focus on a pre-processing method due to its practical applicability across different scenarios and technological stacks. In the following sections, we will explain the procedure we followed.

First, we prepare the dataset by excluding unnecessary features and appropriately handling missing values. To avoid biases in favor of larger values, we normalize the data. Since our dataset is exploited to solve a classification problem, we specify the target labels. Our primary objective is to investigate the capability of similarity networks in enhancing machine learning tasks. To achieve this, we propose two approaches for measuring similarity. These approaches map instances from the feature space to a latent space. To capture latent groups and relationships in the dataset, we fine-tune the quantified similarity using kernels. Moving on to evaluation metrics, we consider the accuracy of our machine learning model, which is assessed using the F1 score. In addition to accuracy, we prioritize transparency to ensure the interpretability of the model's output. To gain further insights into the classification difficulty faced by the model, we employ classification complexity measurements. Toward the end of the evaluation process, we attempt to quantify the fairness in the results of our predictive model. For this purpose, we suggest two indicators: *Equal opportunity* and *Equal mis-opportunity*. These indicators aid in quantifying the fairness across instances belonging to distinct demographic groups.

3.1 Dataset

In order to demonstrate the proposed methodology, we used a public data set of the Curriculum Vitae (CV) of 301 employees[1] which contains both numerical and categorical features such as State, Zipcode, Age, Gender, Marital Description, Citizen Description, Hispanic/Latino, Race Description, Reason For Terminating the job, Employment Status, Department, Position, Payment, Manager Name, Employee Source, Performance Score, and, Work experience.

3.2 Dataset Preparation

We initiate the experiments with dataset preprocessing, considering normalization and handling of incompleteness. More specifically we executed:

1. **Data Exclusion**: Any feature or data point containing missing values exceeding 30% of all values is excluded from the dataset. Additionally, the Name and ID Number of employees are removed from the dataset as they do not contribute useful information.

---

[1] https://rpubs.com/rhuebner/hrd_cb_v14.

2. **Normalization**: All numerical features are normalized using min-max scaling.
3. **Data Imputation**: We employ the *Iterative Imputer*[2] algorithm, inspired by the R MICE (Multivariate Imputation by Chained Equations) package[3], for filling in missing values. This algorithm generates multiple imputations for multivariate missing data. It follows the Fully Conditional Specification approach, imputing each incomplete variable with a separate model. The MICE algorithm can handle various data types, including continuous, binary, unordered categorical, and ordered categorical data.
4. **Payment Categorization**: Given that the payment rate is a continuous value in the dataset, but our objective is to address a classification problem, we categorize the `Payment` using automated bin selection. This method determines the number of categories based on maximizing instances within a bin. Consequently, the number of bins varies according to the data distribution, potentially resulting in a multi-class classification problem.

3.3 Similarity Measurements

Graph construction from datasets based on instances' similarities can be implemented using various mechanisms to measure similarity values. In this paper, we consider two methods for calculating data point similarity and quantifying it to build the weighted network $\mathcal{N} = (\mathbf{V}, \mathbf{E})$, where $\mathbf{V}$ corresponds to the network nodes (vertices), and $\mathbf{E}$ to the links (edges) among them.

1. **Average Normalized Similarity**: According to [1,15], when data is represented by features with homogeneous numeric types, pairwise similarity is generally quantified by Pearson correlation, cosine similarity, or the inverse of the Euclidean distance. Otherwise, when the data points are represented by features with heterogeneous types, the *Gower distance* ($\mathcal{GD}$) is often used [16]. More precisely, if $\mathbf{a}$ and $\mathbf{b}$ are the values of the variable g for data points $\mathbf{a}$ and $\mathbf{b}$, and if $\mathbf{G}$ is the set of all values for the variable g (e.g., age), the (potentially normalized) similarity between points $\mathbf{a}$ and $\mathbf{b}$ according to feature g is computed as:

$$S(a, b, g) = 1 - \frac{abs(a - b)}{max(G) - min(G)} \tag{1}$$

if g has a numeric type, or by:

$$S(a, b, g) = I(a == b) \tag{2}$$

if g has a categorical type, where $I(x)$ is the indicator function that returns 1 if the logical expression x is true (other similarity measures may be used depending on the problem at hand). For a set of k variables $\mathbf{G} = \{g_1, g_2, ..g_k\}$,

---

[2] https://scikit-learn.org/stable/modules/impute.html.
[3] https://search.r-project.org/CRAN/refmans/mice/html/mice.html.

the Gower similarity S' between two patients **a** and **b** is then defined as the average of the (normalized) similarities for each of the variables:

$$S'_{a,b} = \frac{\sum_{i=1}^{k} S(a, b, g_i)}{k} \tag{3}$$

2. **Using NLP in Similarity Measurement:** As a second approach for measuring similarity, we leverage Natural Language Processing (NLP) to construct the similarity graph of data points. Using this technique, agents are embedded in a latent space, considering the similarity of their features in the real space.

   In this approach, feature vectors are created for each node as a tokenized document and then transformed by an embedding algorithm into a low-dimensional space. The *word2vec* [28] algorithm employs a shallow neural network to learn word-associated features from a large corpus of text, resulting in a set of low-dimensional vectors assigned to each word. In this way, similar nodes are mapped closer in the latent space. Using the Gensim[4] package for node embeddings, the similarity of two node instances (i.e., nodes representing data points **a** and **b**), featuring their characteristics in the original dataset, is computed using cosine similarity.

3.4 Similarity Tuning by Kernels

Given all the pairwise similarities between points in our dataset, the definition of a similarity network requires choosing the value of the ϵ parameter (see Sect. 2) that defines the existence (non-existence) of links between points. Selecting the proper threshold value is a crucial task that surely affects the algorithm's performance. Moreover, this choice may also introduce unfavorable biases to the model; indeed, too small values could easily result in too sparse networks, i.e. networks composed of many connected components (subgraphs), while too large values would increase the network connectivity, resulting in spread information and impacting on the computational cost required to leverage this graph data for further analysis. To address this issue, kernel matrices that are able to capture the topological characteristics of the underlying graph may provide a solution. Edge weights are represented by an $n \times n$ similarity matrix **W** where **W(a, b)** indicates the similarity between data points **a** and **b**. Hereafter, we denote $\rho(\mathbf{a}, \mathbf{b}) = 1 - \mathbf{S'(a, b)}$ as the distance between data points, as computed by one of the similarities described in Sect. 3.3. Initially, we use a scaled Exponential kernel (Ek) to determine the weight of the edges:

$$W(a, b) = exp(-\frac{\rho^2(a, b)}{\mu \epsilon_{a,b}}), \tag{4}$$

where according to the [40], μ is a hyperparameter that can be empirically set and $\epsilon_{a,b}$ is used to eliminate the scaling problem by defining:

---

[4] https://radimrehurek.com/gensim/models/word2vec.html.

$$\epsilon_{a,b} = \frac{mean(\rho(a, N_a)) + mean(\rho(b, N_b)) + \rho(a, b)}{3}, \quad (5)$$

where $mean(\rho(a, N_a))$ is the average value of the distances between a and each of its k NNs. The range of $\mu = [0.3, 0.8]$ is recommended by [40].

In the next step, the kernel matrix $\mathbf{K}$ is derived from the similarity matrix $\mathbf{W}$. To this aim, we used the Random Walk kernel (RWk) which is calculated as:

$$K = (m - 1)I + D^{-\frac{1}{2}}WD^{-\frac{1}{2}}, \quad (6)$$

where $\mathbf{I}$ is the identity matrix, $\mathbf{D}$ is the diagonal matrix with elements $d_{ii} = \sum_j W_{ij}$ and m is a value greater than 2. A p-step random walk kernel can be achieved by multiplying $\mathbf{K}$ by itself for the p times. RWk has the effect of strengthening (diminishing) similarities that were already high (low) in the input matrix $\mathbf{W}$, therefore highlighting only the relevant information.

3.5   Analytical Task and Evaluation Scenarios

Considering a predictive task based on the dataset, we propose implementing a classification model to predict the payment levels of employees. To facilitate the analysis, we explore various scenarios, differing by dataset representation, as it follows:

1. **Original data set**: this is the dataset after preprocessing and categorization of payments into *Pay rate* levels.
2. **Balanced data set**: a preprocessed dataset where we have addressed class imbalance in the *Pay rate* levels.
3. **Data set with balanced groups**: a preprocessed dataset that is balanced considering protected features for discriminated groups. In our experiment we balanced by the `Gender` and `Hispanic/Latino` features.
4. **A similarity network** leveraging the Gower distance and *word2vec* algorithm, which for simplicity we call $\mathcal{SGD}$ and $\mathcal{SCW2V}$ respectively in the rest of this work.
5. **A similarity network** created by the $\mathcal{SGD}$ and $\mathcal{SCW2V}$ mappings followed by Ek.
6. **A similarity network** created by the $\mathcal{SGD}$ and $\mathcal{SCW2V}$ followed by Ek and RWk.

3.6   Evaluation Metrics

To assess the equilibrium between accuracy, fairness, and complexity, we employ a range of evaluation metrics in our analysis.

1. **Accuracy:** Among the standard metrics evaluating the predictive algorithms, we can mention, the F1 score, Accuracy, and Recall [19]. In this paper, considering the number of levels of payment contains in our dataset, we choose the weighted form of these metrics [3].

2. **Transparency:** Regarding the model output transparency and explainability, we adopted the SHAP algorithm [24]. Leveraging this algorithm we can interpret how a model predicts a label based on the data set features.

3. **Classification Complexity measures:** Considering the fact that these metrics do not provide a full insight into the level of complexity of a classification problem that an algorithm has to deal with, we need to investigate whether the failure to distinguish different classes of the data set is caused by the incapability of a model in taking into account the crucial factors, or the data set intrinsically does not allow a sharp separation between classes. In simple words, we need to see how a classification problem is complex in nature and if some of the features play a more effective role than others. A classification model may bring up a highly accurate model by considering sensitive features during classification. In this regard, we highlight that, if a class is distinctively separated by a subset of sensitive features, this could be a sign of biased or discriminative behavior imposed on the system (data set or model or both). For this purpose, in the following section, we proceed with measuring the complexity and studying whether investigating the intrinsic characteristics of the data set could be helpful in improving the explainability of classification problems. We examine these measurements for different representations of graphs using different kernels to figure out how the kernels could change the complexity and accuracy of a model. According to [23], classification complexity measures could be categorized as follows:

   Feature-based measures characterizes the discriminative power of the available features; F1, F1v, F2, F3, F4 belong to this category.

   Linearity measures try to quantify whether the classes can be linearly separated. From this category we can name L1, L2, L3.

   Neighborhood measures which characterize the presence and density of the same or different classes in local neighborhoods; N1, N2, N3, N4, T1, LSC are defined for this purpose.

   Network-based measures extract structural information from the data set by modeling it as a graph and measure the Average density of the network (Density), Clustering coefficient (ClsCoef), Hub score (Hubs).

   Dimensionality measures, which evaluate data sparsity based on the number of samples relative to the data dimensionality; measures in this category are, for example, T2, T3, T4.

   Class imbalance measures consider the ratio of the number of examples between classes. C1 and C2 quantify the class imbalances.

4. **Fairness:** To examine the presence of bias in the system (both in the dataset and the model), we follow a three-step approach. (i) We consider complexity measures to assess whether the dataset is heavily characterized by specific features, which might manifest as high values in the feature under analysis. (ii) By analyzing the most significant features identified by a classifier, we monitor whether these features correspond to sensitive attributes. (iii) We employ SHAP (SHapley Additive exPlanations) values to gauge feature importance and to understand how distinctively each feature influences the model's output.

In the final stage, to quantify whether these features introduce bias into the system, we distinguish between privileged and unprivileged classes, based on specific feature values related to sensitive attributes. The privileged class comprises instances with protected or sensitive features, such as race or gender, that may play a role in achieving favorable outcomes. For instance, a privileged class could be defined by attributes like Race: *white*, Marital status: *married*, and Gender: *male*.

In evaluating fairness, we explore whether privileged and unprivileged groups have **Equal Opportunity** (Eq. 7) and **Equal Mis-opportunity** (Eq. 8) in the model's predictions [31]. This can be computed by:

$$Pr(Y' = 1 \mid s = 1, Y = 1) - Pr(Y' = 1 \mid s = 0, Y = 1), \tag{7}$$

$$Pr(Y' = 1 \mid s = 1, Y = 0) - Pr(Y' = 1 \mid s = 0, Y = 0), \tag{8}$$

where Y represents the ground-truth label, Y' denotes the predicted label, and s is a binary indicator distinguishing privileged ($s = 1$) and unprivileged ($s = 0$) groups. Consequently, *Equal Opportunity* assesses the equality of True Positive (TP) rates, effectively measuring the equality of recall values for privileged and unprivileged groups. In contrast, *Equal Mis-opportunity* focuses on accuracy, specifically the False Positive (FP) rate, and aims to ensure it is equivalent for privileged and unprivileged classes. In practice, these measures evaluate whether the classifier's outputs for privileged and unprivileged classes tend to assign fair labels to each class. Therefore, the closer the results of Eq. 7 and Eq. 8 are to zero, the fairer the model's treatment of sensitive features.

4   Experimental Results

In order to verify the applicability of our proposed methodology, we implemented an experimental analysis following the steps discussed in Sect. 3.

4.1   Building the Similarity Network

Initially, using the CV data set, the similarity of each applicant's features compared to other applicants is calculated as Eq. 2. Since our data set contains more than 5 features from both numerical and categorical types, we use Gower distance ($\mathcal{GD}$), and for defining the similarity we calculate $\mathcal{SGD} = 1 - \mathcal{GD}$.

To construct an adjacency matrix containing weighted links among all applicants as nodes, the average similarity of all features (Eq. 3) is considered. Secondly, we try to measure the similarities based on the *word2vec* algorithm for embedding the features in a latent space. Using this method we find the cosine similarity between embedded instances calling by $\mathcal{SCW2V}$.

Having the similarities of instances we leverage the kernels for mapping the similarity values. For this purpose firstly we use the scaled exponential kernel,

Ek, that is discussed in Sect. 3.3 in Eq. 4 as one representation of the dataset. Later, we use the Random Walk kernel, RWk, as the second representation using Eq. 6 while taking into account the different number of steps a random walker can take in exploring the neighborhood.

4.2   Analytical Tasks and Evaluation Metrics

To evaluate the ability of our approach in leveraging the graph representation, the impact of the kernel matrix in capturing the main characteristics of the dataset, keeping the explainability of the output effective, we considered the following points:

I) We implemented 10-fold cross-validated classification models using Random Forest (RF) and XGBOOST to predict the *Pay Rate* categories. The weighted F1 score of the classifiers in four scenarios is presented in Table 1. The first row displays the performance of the classifiers on the preprocessed original dataset. The second row on the class-balanced dataset. The third and fourth rows demonstrate the results for balanced groups, differentiated by protected features, such as gender and ethnicity. Additionally, we evaluate the classifiers' performance on the similarity graph using $\mathcal{SGD}$ and $\mathcal{SCW2V}$. Finally, we apply both classifiers to the mapped similarity graph using kernels, Ek (Eq. 4) and RWk (Eq. 6). Since this is a multi-class classification problem, we consider the F1 weighted score to avoid bias in the evaluation of the output in favor of the highly populated class.

II) In Fig. 1, taking into account the complexity level of classifier domains, we plot the diagram of *mean ± standard deviation* of complexity metrics, represented by error bars, for three data set representations: the *Gower similarity* network calculated from $\mathcal{GD}$, followed by Ek similarity network and similarity network representation using RWk, taking steps from 1 to 5. Figure 1 consists of sub-figures a) feature-based, b) linearity, c) neighborhood, d) network, e) dimensionality, and f) class imbalance measures of complexity, respectively.

III) To calculate fairness metrics, we need to consider binary classification. For this purpose, we categorized the *Pay Rate* into two levels. The results of calculating the metrics are displayed in Table 2. Furthermore, in Fig. 2, we considered **Gender** and **Age** as two discriminative features, defining the privileged class as **Gender**: *male* and **Age** $\leq$ *40*, while considering the remaining instances as an unprivileged class.

5   Discussion

In this paper, we focus on introducing a fairness-oriented workflow for predictive ML models. For this purpose, taking into account different strategies used for the dataset representations and the level of complexity of these representations, we evaluate the trade-off between the accuracy and fairness of a predictive model.

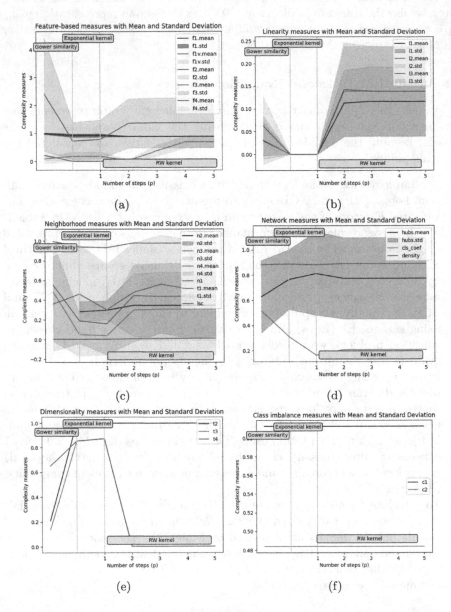

Fig. 1. The complexity measures of the classification problem for different representations of similarity network, Gower similarity network calculated from $\mathcal{GD}$ followed by Ek similarity network and similarity network representation using RWk kernel taking from 1 to 5 steps. In a) the feature-based, b) Linearity, c) Neighborhood, d) Network, e) Dimensionality and, Class imbalance measures are depicted respectively.

Table 1. The mean ± standard deviation of f1 weighted score for 10-fold Cross-validated data using XGBOOST and RF classification algorithms on the CV data set considering original and class-balanced data set; on balanced group data set respectively gender and ethnicity; and different representations of the dataset; similarity network using SGD and $SCW2V$, mapped data by the Ek and, RW kernels.

Dataset representations	Random Forest	XGBOOST
Original data set	0.666 ± 0.056	0.680 ± 0.059
Original data set with balanced classes	0.842 ± 0.038	0.817 ± 0.046
Original data set with balanced protected feature (gender)	0.700 ± 0.071	0.686 ± 0.067
Original data set with balanced protected feature (ethnicity)	0.783 ± 0.049	0.777 ± 0.055
SGD	0.944 ± 0.039	0.938 ± 0.034
Exponential kernel of SGD	0.921 ± 0.039	0.926 ± 0.048
Random Walk kernel of SGD	0.888 ± 0.055	0.907 ± 0.051
$SCW2V$	0.878 ± 0.036	0.878 ± 0.046
Exponential kernel of $SCW2V$	0.862 ± 0.041	0.876 ± 0.043
Random Walk kernel of $SCW2V$	0.857 ± 0.046	0.864 ± 0.042

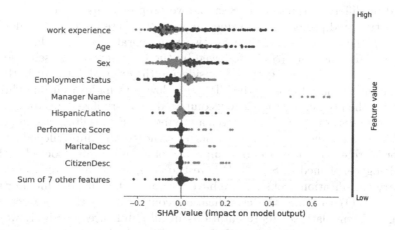

Fig. 2. The most important features using SHAP values, extracted from the RF classifier predicting the pay rate.

Table 2. Fairness metrics, true positive rate (recall) and False positive rate calculated for privileged and unprivileged groups. The metrics are reported for three different data sets representations after implementing RF for predicting Pay Rate.

Data set presentations	Classes	True positive rates	False positive rate	Equal Opportunity	Equal MissOpportunity
Original (Tabular) data	Privileged group	0.250 ± 0.335	0.0769	0.3	0.17
	Unprivileged group	0.259 ± 0.197	0.2432		
SGD	Privileged group	0.756 ± 0.225	0	0.2	0.027
	Unprivileged group	0.942 ± 0.078	0.027		
Similarity network (Ek)	Privileged group	0.600 ± 0.207	0	0.2	0.02
	Unprivileged groups	0.841 ± 0.088	0.02		

As mentioned in Sect. 3.5, we tested classifiers predicting the *Pay Rate* level of the employees described in our dataset, in 5 different data representation scenarios: I) Original data set, II) Original data set with balanced classes, III) Original data set with balanced groups (Gender and Hispanic/Latino), IV) similarity networks features using $\mathcal{SGD}$ and $\mathcal{SCW2V}$. According to Table 1, if improvements can be obtained by balancing the classes and protected groups, the implementation of the similarity network, in all representations, provides more increase in the F1 score for both XGBOOST and RF. This demonstrates our approach is positively impacting accuracy.

In continuation, as discussed in Sect. 3.6, we aim at measuring the effectiveness of features in the classification problem. In Fig. 2, we present the most important features along with their corresponding SHAP values. It is worth mentioning that in some cases, such as Work experience in this dataset, the features are important for the classification problem but we don't expect they can have a potential impact on discrimination. Conversely, features like Gender, Age, and Hispanic/Latino have this potential. We then decided to exploit them in evaluating the fairness achieved by the different scenarios. Evaluating the fairness achieved by different scenarios, in Sect. 3.6 we proposed Eqs. 7 and 8, as quantitative metrics and presented the values in Table 2. These metrics are calculated initially on the original data, then for two representations of the data set: the Gower similarity network ($\mathcal{SGD}$) followed by the Ek mapped representations on privileged and unprivileged groups. Considering the original data, for both privileged and unprivileged groups, the TP rate is low with high variation, while the FP rate for the privileged group is low compared to unprivileged group. Creating a similarity network by $\mathcal{SGD}$ and later applying the Ek resulted in a larger TP rate while fewer values for FP rate in both privileged and unprivileged groups.

In order to explore the level of complexity of a dataset, we proceed with the methodology explained in Sect. 3. Where the complexity measures are defined for binary classification problems, we have leveraged the One-Vs-One multiclass strategy (OVO) to study the classification complexity of the data set. Considering different data set representations in all sub-figures of Fig. 1, we have annotated three main regions by $\mathcal{GD}$, Ek, and RWk for five steps that a random walker may take to explore the locality. Each sub-figure represents one of the six domains of classification complexity measurements that we earlier mentioned in Sect. 3.6. In Fig. 1a, the feature-based complexity measures are depicted in order to evaluate the discriminative power of the existing features in the dataset. If there is at least one very discriminative feature in the dataset, the problem can be considered simpler. Herewith, the higher values indicate more complex problems. The presence of discriminative features among the most important features increases the possibility of bias in the modeling. As presented in Fig. 2, discriminative features such as gender and race are playing roles in the predictive model, which could be a sign of bias in the original data set. While in the first and third regions, the mapped dataset by $\mathcal{SGD}$ and RWk, show high values. Data representation using Ek shows small values of complexity. This could be interpreted as the Ek effect in discriminating some features in the data set that decrease the complexity level while increasing the performance of the model (Table 1). Using RWk similarity network removes the focus of the data set on the few features in classification by showing a higher level of complexity for those feature-based measurements as expected while still resulting in an acceptable performance. Here, there is a trade-off in dealing with a classification problem for keeping or excluding sensitive features. Regarding the linearity measurements of the classification complexity, L1, and L2 report if the data are linearly separable. From Fig. 1b we can see the more steps the random walker traverses the similarity graph, the more difficult is to linearly classify the classes as we expected before. A similar pattern to the feature-based domain is represented for the Linearity and Neighborhood measurements domains Fig. 1c. Network measures (Fig. 1d), which extract structural information from the data set by modeling it as a graph, show low dependency on the graph representations in "hub" and "density" values while showing a drastic decrease in the clustering coefficient values using kernels. Due to the fact that clustering effect in a network could be a reason for bias to specific features and decreasing this value is a sign of unbiased in kernel representations. Dimensionality measures (Fig. 1e) reflect the data sparsity. If there are many predictive attributes and few data points, they will be probably sparsely distributed in the input space. Therefore, lower T2 values indicate less sparsity and therefore simpler problems. Implementation of the similarity network increases the T2 since the features are mapped into the latent space and rather than classifying by few features in real space, more features from latent space are playing a role. On the other hand, T3 which is defined with a Principal Component Analysis (PCA) of the dataset and instead of the raw dimensionality of the feature vector (as in T2), it uses the number of PCA components needed to represent 95% of data variability and decreases with new representations. T4 also decreases. It gives a rough measure of the proportion of relevant dimensions for the dataset. The larger the T4 value, the more of the original features are needed to describe data variability. This indicates a more complex relationship between the input variables. Therefore, in this sense, using the similarity network seems promising in decreasing the feature-independent complexity of the problem. Considering the class imbalance domain of complexity measurements, Fig. 1f clearly demonstrates that the data set is imbalanced and the issue is persistent even with changing the data set representation, as expected.

The results we obtained from comparing the complexity levels across different scenarios unveil that harnessing data representation through a similarity network leads to enhanced accuracy and fairness. This improvement can be attributed to the network's superior ability to capture the dataset's organizational structure across multiple dimensions. On one hand, the high-dimensional space constructed by the similarity network effectively organizes the data, positively influencing accuracy. On the other hand, it diminishes the reliance on a limited set of features for this organization. Consequently, it prevents classifiers from leaning too heavily on a restricted set of features and mitigates the undue influence of a handful of features on the predictions they generate.

6   Conclusion

In this paper, we have focused on the applicability of graph representations of data sets in exploring the relevance of the complexity and fairness of an ML system, containing both the data set and the model used. By training classifiers using the weighted links of nodes derived from similarity networks as features, we observed notable improvements in weighted F1 scores across various forms of graph representations when compared to the original dataset. While our work has yielded valuable insights, it is important to acknowledge two primary limitations. Firstly, we conducted our experiments exclusively on a single public dataset, which implies that our findings may exhibit some degree of dependency on the specific problem under investigation. Future research endeavors will focus on corroborating our conclusions through experimentation with diverse public datasets. Secondly, our analysis in this paper leaned more towards complexity measures and had a comparatively limited focus on fairness metrics. Subsequent research will aim to strike a balance between these aspects and bring to light their shared and complementary insights.

References

1. Abdel-Megeed, S.M.: Monte Carlo study of psychometric effects of scaling levels on the pearson product moment correlation coefficient (1984)
2. Agarwal, A., Agarwal, H., Agarwal, N.: Fairness score and process standardization: framework for fairness certification in artificial intelligence systems. AI Ethics **3**(1), 267–279 (2023). https://doi.org/10.1007/s43681-022-00147-7
3. Aurelio, Y.S., De Almeida, G.M., de Castro, C.L., Braga, A.P.: Learning from imbalanced data sets with weighted cross-entropy function. Neural Process. Lett. **50**, 1937–1949 (2019). https://doi.org/10.1007/s11063-018-09977-1
4. Barocas, S., Hardt, M., Narayanan, A.: Fairness and Machine Learning: Limitations and Opportunities. fairmlbook.org (2019). http://www.fairmlbook.org
5. Bellandi, V., Damiani, E., Ghirimoldi, V., Maghool, S., Negri, F.: Validating vector-label propagation for graph embedding. In: Sellami, M., Ceravolo, P., Reijers, H.A., Gaaloul, W., Panetto, H. (eds.) CoopIS 2022. LNCS, vol. 13591, pp. 259–276. Springer, Cham (2022). https://doi.org/10.1007/978-3-031-17834-4_15
6. Casiraghi, E., et al.: A method for comparing multiple imputation techniques: a case study on the US national COVID cohort collaborative. J. Biomed. Inform. **139**, 104295 (2023)
7. Corbett-Davies, S., Pierson, E., Feller, A., Goel, S., Huq, A.: Algorithmic decision making and the cost of fairness. In: Proceedings of the 23rd ACM SIGKDD International Conference on Knowledge Discovery and Data Mining, pp. 797–806 (2017)
8. Cotter, A., et al.: Training well-generalizing classifiers for fairness metrics and other data-dependent constraints. In: International Conference on Machine Learning, pp. 1397–1405. PMLR (2019)
9. Cotter, A., et al.: Optimization with non-differentiable constraints with applications to fairness, recall, churn, and other goals. J. Mach. Learn. Res. **20**(172), 1–59 (2019)

10. Dwork, C., Hardt, M., Pitassi, T., Reingold, O., Zemel, R.: Fairness through aware-ness. In: Proceedings of the 3rd Innovations in Theoretical Computer Science Con-ference, pp. 214–226 (2012)
11. Fish, B., Kun, J., Lelkes, Á.D.: A confidence-based approach for balancing fairness and accuracy. In: Proceedings of the 2016 SIAM International Conference on Data Mining, pp. 144–152. SIAM (2016)
12. Friedler, S.A., Scheidegger, C., Venkatasubramanian, S., Choudhary, S., Hamil-ton, E.P., Roth, D.: A comparative study of fairness-enhancing interventions in machine learning. In: Proceedings of the Conference on Fairness, Accountability, and Transparency, pp. 329–338 (2019)
13. Garcia, L.P., de Carvalho, A.C., Lorena, A.C.: Effect of label noise in the complex-ity of classification problems. Neurocomputing **160**, 108–119 (2015)
14. Ghazimatin, A., Kleindessner, M., Russell, C., Abedjan, Z., Golebiowski, J.: Mea-suring fairness of rankings under noisy sensitive information. In: Proceedings of the 2022 ACM Conference on Fairness, Accountability, and Transparency, FAccT 2022, pp. 2263–2279. Association for Computing Machinery, New York (2022). https://doi.org/10.1145/3531146.3534641
15. Gliozzo, J., et al.: Heterogeneous data integration methods for patient similarity networks. Briefings Bioinform. **23**(4), bbac207 (2022)
16. Gower, J.C.: A general coefficient of similarity and some of its properties. Biomet-rics **27**(4), 857–871 (1971)
17. Hardt, M., Price, E., Srebro, N.: Equality of opportunity in supervised learning. In: Advances in Neural Information Processing Systems, vol. 29 (2016)
18. Ho, T.K., Basu, M.: Complexity measures of supervised classification problems. IEEE Trans. Pattern Anal. Mach. Intell. **24**(3), 289–300 (2002)
19. Japkowicz, N., Shah, M.: Performance evaluation in machine learning. In: El Naqa, I., Li, R., Murphy, M.J. (eds.) Machine Learning in Radiation Oncology, pp. 41–56. Springer, Cham (2015). https://doi.org/10.1007/978-3-319-18305-3_4
20. Kleinberg, J.: Inherent trade-offs in algorithmic fairness. SIGMETRICS Perform. Eval. Rev. **46**(1), 40 (2018). https://doi.org/10.1145/3292040.3219634
21. Lepri, B., Oliver, N., Letouzé, E., Pentland, A., Vinck, P.: Fair, transparent, and accountable algorithmic decision-making processes: the premise, the proposed solu-tions, and the open challenges. Philos. Technol. **31**, 611–627 (2018). https://doi.org/10.1007/s13347-017-0279-x
22. Liang, A., Lu, J., Mu, X.: Algorithmic design: fairness versus accuracy. In: Pro-ceedings of the 23rd ACM Conference on Economics and Computation, pp. 58–59 (2022)
23. Lorena, A.C., Garcia, L.P., Lehmann, J., Souto, M.C., Ho, T.K.: How complex is your classification problem? A survey on measuring classification complexity. ACM Comput. Surv. (CSUR) **52**(5), 1–34 (2019)
24. Lundberg, S.M., Lee, S.I.: A unified approach to interpreting model predictions. In: Advances in Neural Information Processing Systems, vol. 30 (2017)
25. Mary, J., Calauzenes, C., El Karoui, N.: Fairness-aware learning for continuous attributes and treatments. In: International Conference on Machine Learning, pp. 4382–4391. PMLR (2019)
26. Mehrabi, N., Morstatter, F., Saxena, N., Lerman, K., Galstyan, A.: A survey on bias and fairness in machine learning. ACM Comput. Surv. (CSUR) **54**(6), 1–35 (2021)
27. Menon, A.K., Williamson, R.C.: The cost of fairness in binary classification. In: Conference on Fairness, Accountability and Transparency, pp. 107–118. PMLR (2018)

28. Mikolov, T., Sutskever, I., Chen, K., Corrado, G.S., Dean, J.: Distributed representations of words and phrases and their compositionality. In: Advances in Neural Information Processing Systems, vol. 26 (2013)
29. Morais, G., Prati, R.C.: Complex network measures for data set characterization. In: 2013 Brazilian Conference on Intelligent Systems, pp. 12–18. IEEE (2013)
30. Naeem, S.B., Bhatti, R., Khan, A.: An exploration of how fake news is taking over social media and putting public health at risk. Health Inf. Libr. J. **38**(2), 143–149 (2021)
31. Oneto, L., Chiappa, S.: Fairness in machine learning. In: Oneto, L., Navarin, N., Sperduti, A., Anguita, D. (eds.) Recent Trends in Learning From Data. SCI, vol. 896, pp. 155–196. Springer, Cham (2020). https://doi.org/10.1007/978-3-030-43883-8_7
32. Ormiston, C.K., Chiangong, J., Williams, F.: The COVID-19 pandemic and hispanic/latina/o immigrant mental health: why more needs to be done. Health Equity **7**(1), 3–8 (2023)
33. Pessach, D., Shmueli, E.: A review on fairness in machine learning. ACM Comput. Surv. **55**(3), 1–44 (2022). https://doi.org/10.1145/3494672
34. Ribeiro, M.T., Singh, S., Guestrin, C.: "Why should i trust you?" Explaining the predictions of any classifier. In: Proceedings of the 22nd ACM SIGKDD International Conference on Knowledge Discovery and Data Mining, pp. 1135–1144 (2016)
35. Schölkopf, B.: The kernel trick for distances. In: Advances in Neural Information Processing Systems, vol. 13 (2000)
36. Singh, A., Joachims, T.: Fairness of exposure in rankings. In: Proceedings of the 24th ACM SIGKDD International Conference on Knowledge Discovery & Data Mining, pp. 2219–2228 (2018)
37. Smola, A.J., Kondor, R.: Kernels and regularization on graphs. In: Schölkopf, B., Warmuth, M.K. (eds.) COLT-Kernel 2003. LNCS (LNAI), vol. 2777, pp. 144–158. Springer, Heidelberg (2003). https://doi.org/10.1007/978-3-540-45167-9_12
38. Sugiyama, M., Borgwardt, K.: Halting in random walk kernels. In: Cortes, C., Lawrence, N., Lee, D., Sugiyama, M., Garnett, R. (eds.) Advances in Neural Information Processing Systems, vol. 28. Curran Associates, Inc.   (2015).   https://proceedings.neurips.cc/paper_files/paper/2015/file/31b3b31a1c2f8a370206f111127c0dbd-Paper.pdf
39. Tizpaz-Niari, S., Kumar, A., Tan, G., Trivedi, A.: Fairness-aware configuration of machine learning libraries. In: Proceedings of the 44th International Conference on Software Engineering, pp. 909–920 (2022)
40. Wang, B., et al.: Similarity network fusion for aggregating data types on a genomic scale. Nat. Methods **11**(3), 333–337 (2014)
41. Zhang, T., Zhu, T., Gao, K., Zhou, W., Philip, S.Y.: Balancing learning model privacy, fairness, and accuracy with early stopping criteria. IEEE Trans. Neural Netw. Learn. Syst. **34**(9), 5557–5569 (2023)
42. Zhu, X.: Semi-supervised learning with graphs. Carnegie Mellon University (2005)

Considering Vocabulary Mappings
in Query Plans for Federations of RDF
Data Sources

Sijin Cheng(✉) ⓘ, Sebastián Ferrada ⓘ, and Olaf Hartig ⓘ

Department of Computer and Information Science (IDA), Linköping University,
Linköping, Sweden
{sijin.cheng,sebastian.ferrada,olaf.hartig}@liu.se

Abstract. Federations of RDF data sources offer great potential for
queries that cannot be answered by a single data source. However, querying such federations poses several challenges, one of which is that different
but semantically-overlapping vocabularies may be used for the respective
RDF data. Since the federation members usually retain their autonomy,
this heterogeneity cannot simply be homogenized by modifying the data
in the data sources. Therefore, handling this heterogeneity becomes a
critical aspect of query planning and execution. We introduce an approach to address this challenge by leveraging vocabulary mappings for the
processing of queries over federations with heterogeneous vocabularies.
This approach not only translates SPARQL queries but also preserves the
correctness of results during query execution. We demonstrate the effectiveness of the approach and measure how the application of vocabulary
mappings affects on the performance of federated query processing.

1   Introduction

RDF federations play a crucial role in facilitating integrated access to distributed
data, allowing users to query and retrieve information seamlessly from multiple
sources. By leveraging federations, users can harness the collective knowledge
stored in the various independent federation members, enabling applications such
as semantic search, data integration, and knowledge discovery. Despite the use of
International Resource Identifiers (IRIs) in RDF to universally identify individuals, concepts, and predicates (e.g., ex:Bob, schema:Person, foaf:knows),[1] the independent datasets may employ their own local vocabulary, using different IRIs to
refer to the same things (e.g., foaf:Person, schema:knows). Hence, queries expressed
in a global vocabulary, which encompasses terms from multiple sources, will fail
to retrieve meaningful results when executed against federation members with
differing local vocabularies. For instance, a query requesting entities of type
schema:Person cannot retrieve entities of the equivalent type foaf:Person.

Vocabulary heterogeneity is further a problem when considering more complex queries that need to compute joins among the data in the federation members, when each federation member has its own unique vocabulary, or when the

---

[1] When writing concrete IRIs using the usual shorthand notation with prefix names
such as ex:, we use the prefix names declared at http://prefix.cc/popular/all.sparql.

© The Author(s), under exclusive license to Springer Nature Switzerland AG 2024
M. Sellami et al. (Eds.): CoopIS 2023, LNCS 14353, pp. 21–40, 2024.
https://doi.org/10.1007/978-3-031-46846-9_2

relationship among the IRIs used in the different datasets is more intricate than a one-to-one equivalence (e.g., subclasses, unions).

Despite the availability of many well-understood and well-performing ontology alignment approaches and corresponding tools, there is very little research on using the resulting mappings for integrated querying of multiple RDF datasets. The few related works [10–12] describe rather ad hoc methods for query translation, either not providing a thorough formal treatment, not showing clear query planning methods, or not introducing result reconciliation. In contrast, our work in this paper is the first to provide a systematic and formal approach to consider mappings among the vocabularies when processing queries over federations.

First, we define what the expected result of a query in a vocabulary-aware setting is; then, we introduce a new query plan operator to translate solutions from a local to the global vocabulary; and finally, we introduce an algorithm that produces correct, vocabulary-aware query plans. We evaluate our approach in federations with different vocabulary mapping scenarios. Our experiments show that there is no overhead in planning time when considering vocabulary mappings; however, it takes slightly longer to execute the queries than in a baseline scenario with materialized mapped data.

2   Related Work

The problem of achieving semantic interoperability across RDF data sources is a topic of research since many years. Various approaches have been proposed to address this challenge from different angles, including a focus on methods for representing vocabulary mappings [3,14], discovery of correspondences and mappings between different RDF graphs [6,9] and between their ontologies [7].

Our work relies on such ontology/vocabulary mappings to enable users to issue queries using a unified vocabulary over federations of RDF data sources with heterogeneous vocabularies, thereby facilitating seamless retrieval of results from multiple sources. While most work on SPARQL query federation engines has introduced various approaches to process queries over multiple RDF data sources (e.g., [2,4,15–17]), these engines are only capable of processing queries that directly use the vocabularies as used by the data sources, assuming that the user knows for each federation member what classes and properties it uses.

A few exceptions exist: Wang et al. introduce an approach to consider instance mappings when executing SPARQL queries over federations of SPARQL endpoints [18]. Joshi et al. describe a system called ALOQUS that considers both instance and vocabulary mappings when executing SPARQL queries over federations of SPARQL endpoints [10]. However, in contrast to our work in this paper, there is no clear definition of what exactly the query result is that the authors would consider correct and complete. Moreover, Joshi et al. do not provide any information about the types of vocabulary mappings considered and how exactly the mappings are used to rewrite (sub) queries.

Makris et al. also explore the use of vocabulary mappings and instance mappings in SPARQL query rewriting for accessing federations of RDF data sources [11,12]. Their approach supports a wide range of mapping types, covering classes, object properties, datatype properties, and individuals. Compared to our method, however, their approach is concerned only with defining how to rewrite a given SPARQL query into a set of SPARQL queries which may then be used to access the federation members, without considering the treatment of vocabulary mappings during result reconciliation, without formally defining the expected query results, and also without providing any evaluation to assess the effectiveness and performance of the approach. In contrast, our approach is explicitly embedded into the query planning and query execution processes.

3 Preliminaries

As is usual for papers about RDF and SPARQL [13], we assume four pairwise disjoint, countably infinite sets: $\mathcal{I}$ (all IRIs), $\mathcal{B}$ (all blank nodes), $\mathcal{L}$ (all literals), and $\mathcal{V}$ (all query variables). An *RDF triple* is a tuple $(s, p, o) \in (\mathcal{I} \cup \mathcal{B}) \times \mathcal{I} \times (\mathcal{I} \cup \mathcal{B} \cup \mathcal{L})$. A set of such triples is called an *RDF graph*. As for SPARQL, the major component of every SPARQL query is its *graph pattern* [13], where the most basic type of such a graph pattern is a *triple pattern*, which is a tuple $(s, p, o) \in (\mathcal{V} \cup \mathcal{I}) \times (\mathcal{V} \cup \mathcal{I}) \times (\mathcal{V} \cup \mathcal{I} \cup \mathcal{L})$. Other forms of graph patterns considered in this paper can be constructed recursively by combining two such patterns, P_1 and P_2, using the operator AND or UNION [13]; i.e., $(P_1 \text{ AND } P_2)$ and $(P_1 \text{ UNION } P_2)$.

To formally abstract the concept of a federation, we use the following definition, which slightly adapts the notion of a federation as defined in our earlier work [5]. The main difference of this adaptation is that, for the sake of simplifying the discussion in this paper, we focus only on federations of SPARQL endpoints.

Definition 1. A **federation member** *fm* is a SPARQL endpoint. A **federation** *fed* is a tuple (M, g) where M is a finite and nonempty set of federation members and g is a function that maps every federation member $fm \in M$ to an RDF graph (which is considered to be the graph that *fm* provides access to), such that the graph of every member $fm \in fed$ uses a disjoint set of blank nodes; i.e., $\text{bnodes}(g(fm)) \cap \text{bnodes}(g(fm')) = \emptyset$ for every other member $fm' \in M$.

4 Vocabulary-Aware Formalization of Queries

This section defines an evaluation semantics for using SPARQL graph patterns as queries over federations in which the data of the federation members is captured based on RDF vocabularies that may be different from the vocabulary used in the queries. This semantics considers mappings between the global query vocabulary and the vocabularies used locally at the federation members. We begin by introducing formal abstractions of vocabularies and vocabulary mappings.

4.1 Vocabularies and Vocabulary Mappings

For the purposes of the work in this paper, the relevant aspect of the notion of an RDF vocabulary is that it introduces two disjoint sets of IRIs; namely,

IRIs that denote properties and that can be used in the predicate position of triples, as well as IRIs of classes, as can be used in the object position of triples that have rdf:type as predicate. Hence, we abstract the notion of a vocabulary formally as a pair of such sets of IRIs. That is, a *vocabulary* v is a pair $(\mathbb{C}, \mathbb{R})$, where $\mathbb{C} \subset \mathcal{I}$ is a finite set of IRIs of classes and $\mathbb{R} \subset \mathcal{I}$ is a finite set of IRIs of properties, and we assume that $\mathbb{C}$ and $\mathbb{R}$ are disjoint; i.e., $\mathbb{C} \cap \mathbb{R} = \emptyset$.

Given this notion of a vocabulary, we can now define formally what it means for an RDF graph or a graph pattern to be expressed in terms of a vocabulary.

Definition 2. Let $v = (\mathbb{C}, \mathbb{R})$ be a vocabulary. An RDF graph G **is expressed in terms of** v if, for every triple $t = (s, p, o)$ in G, it holds that i) $p \in \mathbb{R}$ and ii) if p is the IRI rdf:type, then $o \in \mathbb{C}$. Similarly, a SPARQL graph pattern P **is expressed in terms of** v if, for every triple pattern $tp = (s, p, o)$ in P, it holds that i) $p \in \mathbb{R}$ or $p \in \mathcal{V}$ and ii) if p is the IRI rdf:type, then $o \in \mathbb{C}$ or $o \in \mathcal{V}$.

Mappings between vocabularies are then defined as follows.

Definition 3. Let $v = (\mathbb{C}, \mathbb{R})$ and $v' = (\mathbb{C}', \mathbb{R}')$ be vocabularies. A **vocabulary mapping** VM from v to v' is a finite set of *mapping rules* where each such mapping rule r is an expression of one of the following five forms.

RuleType1: $c \equiv c'$ is a mapping rule if $c \in \mathbb{C}$ and $c' \in \mathbb{C}'$.
RuleType2: $c \sqsubseteq c'$ is a mapping rule if $c \in \mathbb{C}$ and $c' \in \mathbb{C}'$.
RuleType3: $c_1 \sqcup \ldots \sqcup c_n \equiv c'$ is a mapping rule if $\{c_1, \ldots, c_n\} \subseteq \mathbb{C}$ and $c' \in \mathbb{C}'$.
RuleType4: $p \equiv p'$ is a mapping rule if $p \in \mathbb{R}$ and $p' \in \mathbb{R}'$.
RuleType5: $p \sqsubseteq p'$ is a mapping rule if $p \in \mathbb{R}$ and $p' \in \mathbb{R}'$.

Notice that, by design, the IRIs of the source vocabulary are on the left-hand sides of the mapping rules, whereas the IRIs of the target vocabulary are on the ride-hand sides. Notice also that the syntax of these rules resembles the syntax of terminological axioms of Description Logics, and so does their semantics. To define this semantics we introduce the following function which specifies the result of applying such rules to individual RDF triples.

Definition 4. Let $v = (\mathbb{C}, \mathbb{R})$ and $v' = (\mathbb{C}', \mathbb{R}')$ be vocabularies, let VM be a vocabulary mapping from v to v', and let $r \in VM$ be a mapping rule in VM. The **application** of r to an RDF triple $t = (s, p, o)$, denoted by $\mathsf{apply}(r, t)$, is an RDF triple that is defined as follows, depending on the form of r.

1. If r is either of the form $c \equiv c'$ or of the form $c \sqsubseteq c'$, with $c \in \mathbb{C}$ and $c' \in \mathbb{C}'$, and p is the IRI rdf:type and $o = c$, then $\mathsf{apply}(r, t) = (s, \text{rdf:type}, c')$.
2. If r is of the form $c_1 \sqcup \ldots \sqcup c_n \equiv c'$, with $\{c_1, \ldots, c_n\} \subseteq \mathbb{C}$ and $c' \in \mathbb{C}'$, and p is the IRI rdf:type and $o \in \{c_1, \ldots, c_n\}$, then $\mathsf{apply}(r, t) = (s, \text{rdf:type}, c')$.
3. If r is either of the form $p' \equiv p''$ or of the form $p' \sqsubseteq p''$, with $p' \in \mathbb{R}$ and $p'' \in \mathbb{R}'$, and $p = p'$, then $\mathsf{apply}(r, t) = (s, p'', o)$.
4. In all other cases, $\mathsf{apply}(r, t) = t$.

Example 1. If r is the mapping rule foaf:Person $\equiv$ schema:Person and t is the triple (ex:Bob, rdf:type, foaf:Person), then $\mathsf{apply}(r, t) = $ (ex:Bob, rdf:type, schema:Person).

For the purpose of defining the aforementioned evaluation semantics, we broaden the application of mapping rules both from individual triples to whole RDF graphs and from individual mapping rules to whole vocabulary mappings:

Definition 5. Let v and v' be vocabularies, and let VM be a vocabulary mapping from v to v'. The **application** of VM to an RDF graph G, denoted by $\mathsf{apply}(VM, G)$, is the RDF graph returned by Algorithm 1 for VM and G.

Example 2. Consider the vocabulary mapping $VM = \{\mathsf{foaf{:}knows} \equiv \mathsf{schema{:}knows}, \mathsf{foaf{:}Person} \equiv \mathsf{schema{:}Person}\}$. Then, $\mathsf{apply}(VM, G) = G'$ for G and G' as follows.

$$G = \big\{(\mathsf{ex{:}Bob}, \mathsf{rdf{:}type}, \mathsf{foaf{:}Person}), \qquad G' = \big\{(\mathsf{ex{:}Bob}, \mathsf{rdf{:}type}, \mathsf{schema{:}Person}),$$
$$(\mathsf{ex{:}Bob}, \mathsf{foaf{:}name}, \texttt{"Bob"}), \qquad\qquad (\mathsf{ex{:}Bob}, \mathsf{foaf{:}name}, \texttt{"Bob"}),$$
$$(\mathsf{ex{:}Bob}, \mathsf{foaf{:}knows}, \mathsf{ex{:}Eve})\big\} \qquad\quad (\mathsf{ex{:}Bob}, \mathsf{schema{:}knows}, \mathsf{ex{:}Eve})\big\}$$

Algorithm 1: Applies a vocabulary mapping VM to an RDF graph G.

---
1   $G' \leftarrow \{t \in G \mid \mathsf{apply}(r, t) = t \text{ for all } r \in VM\}$;
2   **while** there exists $r \in VM$ and $t \in G$ with $\mathsf{apply}(r, t) \neq t$ and $\mathsf{apply}(r, t) \notin G'$ **do**
3 | add $\mathsf{apply}(r, t)$ to G';
4   **end**
5   **return** G'

Note 1. By Definition 5, every triple of G that is translated to a different triple is not present anymore in the resulting RDF graph. In contrast, triples for which none of the mapping rules in VM has an effect are kept as they are (cf. line 1 of Algorithm 1). For instance, $(\mathsf{ex{:}Bob}, \mathsf{foaf{:}name}, \texttt{"Bob"})$ in Example 2 is such a triple.

Note 2. In some cases, applying a vocabulary mapping to an RDF graph has no effect at all. For instance, for the empty vocabulary mapping $VM_\emptyset$, it holds that $\mathsf{apply}(VM_\emptyset, G) = G$ for every RDF graph G. Similarly, given a (non-empty) vocabulary mapping VM from a vocabulary $v = (\mathbb{C}, \mathbb{R})$ to $v' = (\mathbb{C}', \mathbb{R}')$, if an RDF graph G does not use vocabulary v (i.e., none of the triples in G has any of the IRIs of $\mathbb{R}$ as its predicate and none of the triples with predicate $\mathsf{rdf{:}type}$ has any of the IRIs of $\mathbb{C}$ as its object), then it holds that $\mathsf{apply}(VM, G) = G$.

Given our definitions of vocabularies and vocabulary mappings, we can now introduce a vocabulary-aware view of a federation. To this end, we augment the notion of a federation (cf. Definition 1) with a so-called *vocabulary context* that establishes a global vocabulary in terms of which the federation can be queried.

Definition 6. A **vocabulary context** cxt for a federation $fed = (M, g)$ is a pair (v_G, vm) where v_G is a vocabulary (considered as the global vocabulary) and vm is a function that maps every federation member $fm \in M$ to a vocabulary mapping from some vocabulary v_{fm} (considered to be used by fm) to v_G.

We emphasize that different vocabulary contexts may be used for a federation, which makes it possible to query a federation from the perspective of different global vocabularies (as long as the relevant vocabulary mappings are available in a corresponding vocabulary context). Moreover, notice that the notion of a vocabulary context also captures cases in which some federation members directly use the global vocabulary. In such cases, the function vm of the corresponding vocabulary context simply assigns the empty vocabulary mapping to these federation members. Also, if multiple federation members share a common vocabulary that is not the global one, they can be assigned the same vocabulary mapping for that shared vocabulary.

In the remainder of this paper we assume that the federation members contain only instance data rather than statements about their vocabulary terms. Formally, we capture this assumption as follows: Given a federation $fed = (M, g)$ and a vocabulary context $cxt = (v_G, vm)$ for fed, we assume that, for every triple $t = (s, p, o)$ in the RDF graph $g(fm)$ of every federation member $fm \in M$, it holds that i) $s \notin (\mathbb{C}_{fm} \cup \mathbb{R}_{fm})$, ii) if p is not the IRI rdf:type, then $o \notin \mathbb{C}_{fm}$, and iii) $o \notin \mathbb{R}_{fm}$, where $v_{fm} = (\mathbb{C}_{fm}, \mathbb{R}_{fm})$ is the vocabulary used by fm (i.e., the vocabulary that the vocabulary mapping $vm(fm)$ maps to).

4.2 Vocabulary-Aware Evaluation Semantics

At this point, we have all the necessary elements to define the vocabulary-aware evaluation semantics of SPARQL patterns over federations. Informally, the idea is to define the result of a SPARQL pattern to be the same as the result of evaluating the pattern over the (virtual) union of the RDF graphs of the federation members in a global-vocabulary view of the queried federation. Formally, we define this view and the resulting evaluation semantics as follows.

Definition 7. Let $fed = (M, g)$ be a federation and $cxt = (v_G, vm)$ be a vocabulary context for fed. The cxt-**based global-vocabulary view** of fed is the federation $fed' = (M', g')$ such that $M' = M$ and, for every federation member $fm \in M$, it holds that $g'(fm') = \mathsf{apply}(vm(fm), g(fm))$.

Definition 8. Let fed be a federation, $cxt = (v_G, vm)$ be a vocabulary context for fed, and $fed' = (M', g')$ be the cxt-based global-vocabulary view of fed. The cxt-**based evaluation** of a SPARQL graph pattern P over fed, denoted by $[\![P]\!]_{fed}^{cxt}$, is a set of solution mappings defined as $[\![P]\!]_{fed}^{cxt} := [\![P]\!]_{G_{union}}$ where G_{union} is the RDF graph $G_{union} = \bigcup_{fm \in M'} g'(fm)$, and $[\![P]\!]_{G_{union}}$ is the evaluation of P over G_{union} as defined by Pérez et al. [13].

Example 3. Consider a federation $fed = (M, g)$ with a single federation member fm such that $g(fm)$ is the RDF graph G given in Example 2, and let tp be the triple pattern $(?s, \text{schema:knows}, ?o)$. Notice that the IRI in this triple pattern does not occur in the graph of fm. Hence, using this triple pattern directly as a query over the federation would result in no solutions mappings. In contrast, consider $cxt = (v_G, vm)$ as a vocabulary context for fed such that $vm(fm)$ is the vocabulary mapping *VM* of Example 2. Then, the RDF graph of *fm* in the *cxt*-based global-vocabulary view of *fed* is RDF graph G' in Example 2 and, thus, the query result is $[\![tp]\!]_{fed}^{cxt} = \{\mu\}$ with $\mu = \{?s \rightarrow$ ex:Bob, $?o \rightarrow$ ex:Eve$\}$.

Example 4. Still considering the federation and the vocabulary context of Example 3, assume now that the triple pattern $tp' = (?x,$ rdf:type$, ?t)$ is given as a query over the federation. The query result in this case is $[\![tp']\!]_{fed}^{cxt} = \{\mu'\}$ with $\mu' = \{?x \rightarrow$ ex:Bob, $?t \rightarrow$ schema:Person$\}$.

5   Vocabulary-Aware Query Plans

While the query evaluation semantics in the previous section defines the expected query results to be produced by a vocabulary-aware federation engine, we now establish a formal foundation to consider vocabulary mappings when creating query execution plans in such an engine. To this end, we build on FedQPL, which is a formal language to represent logical plans for queries over heterogeneous federations [5]. The basic idea of our approach is as follows: Given a FedQPL expression that represents a logical plan for a query expressed in terms of the global vocabulary, rewrite this expression into a FedQPL expression that represents a vocabulary-aware plan. In such a plan, requests to federation members are expressed in terms of the vocabularies used locally at these federation members, and the results retrieved via such requests are translated back to the global vocabulary. The latter is necessary to correctly join intermediate results from federation members with different local vocabularies and also to eventually present the overall query result in terms of the global vocabulary. To capture such a translation of intermediate results explicitly in logical plans represented by FedQPL we extend FedQPL with a new operator called l2g.

5.1   Vocabulary-Aware Extension of FedQPL

The following definition specifies our extended syntax of FedQPL.

Definition 9. Let *fed* $= (M, g)$ be a federation and *cxt* $= (v_G, vm)$ be a vocabulary context for *fed*. A **FedQPL expression** for *fed* and *cxt* is an expression φ constructed from the following grammar, in which req, gpAdd, join, union, mj, mu, l2g, (, and) are terminal symbols, *fm* is a federation member in M, P is a graph pattern, *VM* is a vocabulary mapping in the image of *vm*, and Φ is a nonempty set of FedQPL expressions (constructed recursively from the same grammar).

$$\varphi ::= \quad \text{req}_{fm}^{P} \quad | \quad \text{gpAdd}_{fm}^{P}(\varphi) \quad | \quad \text{join}(\varphi, \varphi) \quad | \quad \text{union}(\varphi, \varphi) \quad |$$
$$\text{mj}\, \Phi \quad | \quad \text{mu}\, \Phi \quad | \quad \text{l2g}^{VM}(\varphi)$$

Before focusing on the new operator (l2g), we briefly describe the other operators of FedQPL: req captures the intention to request the result for a graph pattern from a federation member. gpAdd captures the intention to interact with a federation member to obtain solution mappings for a graph pattern that are compatible with the result produced by the given subplan and, then, join these solution mappings into this result. join and union capture the intention to join, respectively union, the results of two subplans within the federation engine (i.e., without interacting with any federation member); mj and mu are multiway variants of join and union, respectively. For more details, several examples, and the formal semantics of these operators, refer to our earlier work on FedQPL [5].

The new operator is then meant to capture the application of a given vocabulary mapping VM to every solution mapping produced by the subplan. To define the semantics of this operator formally, we first introduce the corresponding notion of applying vocabulary mappings to solution mappings.

Definition 10. The **application** of a vocabulary mapping VM to a solution mapping μ, denoted by $\mathsf{apply}(VM, \mu)$, is a set of solution mappings obtained by performing Algorithm 2 with VM and μ, where $\mathsf{apply}(VM, u)$ in line 5 is:

$$\mathsf{apply}(VM, u) = \{x' \mid u \equiv x' \text{ is a mapping rule in } VM\} \cup$$
$$\{x' \mid u \sqsubseteq x' \text{ is a mapping rule in } VM\} \cup$$
$$\{c' \mid c_1 \sqcup \ldots \sqcup c_n \equiv c' \text{ with } u \in \{c_1, \ldots, c_n\} \text{ is in } VM\}.$$

Example 5. Consider the vocabulary mapping $VM = \{$foaf:knows $\equiv$ schema:knows, foaf:knows $\equiv$ ex:acquaintedWith, ex:Student $\sqsubseteq$ schema:Person$\}$. For the solution mapping $\mu = \{?x \rightarrow$ ex:Student, $?y \rightarrow$ foaf:knows$\}$, we have $\mathsf{apply}(VM, \mu) = \{\mu_1, \mu_2\}$ with

$$\mu_1 = \{?x \rightarrow \text{schema:Person}, ?y \rightarrow \text{schema:knows}\} \text{ and}$$
$$\mu_2 = \{?x \rightarrow \text{schema:Person}, ?y \rightarrow \text{ex:acquaintedWith}\}.$$

We are now ready to extend the definition of the semantics of FedQPL to cover expressions that contain the new operator. Since the original definition is

---

Algorithm 2: Applies vocabulary mapping VM to solution mapping μ.

1 $\Omega \leftarrow \{\mu_\emptyset\}$, where $\mu_\emptyset$ is the empty solution mapping, i.e., $\mathrm{dom}(\mu_\emptyset) = \emptyset$;
2 **forall the** $?v \in \mathrm{dom}(\mu)$ **do**
3 $\quad$ $X \leftarrow \emptyset$; // initially empty set of RDF terms, to collect new bindings for $?v$
4 $\quad$ **if** $\mu(?v)$ is an IRI $u \in \mathcal{I}$ **then**
5 $\quad\quad$ $X \leftarrow \mathsf{apply}(VM, u)$, where $\mathsf{apply}(VM, u)$ as in Definition 10;
6 $\quad$ **if** X is empty **then**
7 $\quad\quad$ $X \leftarrow \{\mu(?v)\}$;
8 $\quad$ $\Omega \leftarrow \{\mu' \cup \{?v \rightarrow x\} \mid \mu' \in \Omega \text{ and } x \in X\}$;
9 **return** Ω

based on a recursively-defined evaluation function [5, Definition 6], our extension in this paper consists of adding a new case to this recursive definition.

Definition 11. Let *fed* be a federation, *cxt* be a vocabulary context for *fed*, and φ be a FedQPL expression for *fed* and *cxt*. The **result produced by** φ, denoted by $\mathsf{sols}(\varphi)$, is a set of solution mappings that is defined as follows.

1. If φ is of the form $\mathsf{l2g}^{VM}(\varphi')$, then $\mathsf{sols}(\varphi) := \bigcup_{\mu \in \mathsf{sols}(\varphi')} \mathsf{apply}(VM, \mu)$.
2. If φ is of any other form, then $\mathsf{sols}(\varphi)$ is defined as in [5, Definition 6].

Example 6. Consider federation *fed* of Examples 3–4, which consists of a single federation member *fm* with the following RDF graph G (as given in Example 2):

$$G = \big\{ (\mathsf{ex{:}Bob}, \mathsf{rdf{:}type}, \mathsf{foaf{:}Person}), (\mathsf{ex{:}Bob}, \mathsf{foaf{:}name}, \texttt{"Bob"}), (\mathsf{ex{:}Bob}, \mathsf{foaf{:}knows}, \mathsf{ex{:}Eve}) \big\}.$$

Moreover, consider the FedQPL expression $\varphi = \mathsf{l2g}^{VM}(\mathsf{req}_{fm}^{tp'})$ where the vocabulary mapping $VM = \{\mathsf{foaf{:}knows} \equiv \mathsf{schema{:}knows}, \mathsf{foaf{:}Person} \equiv \mathsf{schema{:}Person}\}$ is the same as in Example 2 and the triple pattern tp' is $(?x, \mathsf{rdf{:}type}, ?t)$. Notice that the req operator in φ issues this triple pattern to be executed locally at the federation member *fm* and, thus, produces the following result: $\mathsf{sols}(\mathsf{req}_{fm}^{tp'}) = \{\mu\}$ with $\mu = \{?x \to \mathsf{ex{:}Bob}, ?t \to \mathsf{foaf{:}Person}\}$. The $\mathsf{l2g}$ operator then lifts this result to the global vocabulary: $\mathsf{sols}(\varphi) = \{\mu'\}$ with $\mu' = \{?x \to \mathsf{ex{:}Bob}, ?t \to \mathsf{schema{:}Person}\}$.

While the semantics of FedQPL defines the result that a plan represented by a FedQPL expression produces, it also needs to be shown that this result is indeed the expected result for the query for which the plan has been created. If that is the case, we say that the expression is *correct*. Formally, we define this correctness property for our extended version of FedQPL expressions as follows.

Definition 12. Let P be a SPARQL graph pattern, *fed* be a federation, and *cxt* be a vocabulary context for *fed*. A FedQPL expression φ for *fed* and *cxt* **is correct for** P if it holds that $\mathsf{sols}(\varphi) = [\![P]\!]_{fed}^{cxt}$.

Example 7. By comparing Examples 4 and 6, we observe that $\mathsf{sols}(\varphi) = [\![tp']\!]_{fed}^{cxt}$. That is, the result produced by the FedQPL expression φ in Example 6 is the same as the result expected for triple pattern $tp' = (?x, \mathsf{rdf{:}type}, ?t)$ over federation *fed* $= (\{fm\}, g)$ in vocabulary context *cxt*, where *fed* and *cxt* $= (v_G, vm)$ with $vm(fm) = VM$ as in Example 6. Therefore, φ is correct for tp' over *fed* in *cxt*.

Algorithm 3: Given a source assignment φ and a vocabulary context $cxt = (v_G, vm)$, both for the same federation fed, this algorithm rewrites φ into a vocabulary-aware FedQPL expression for fed and cxt.

---

1 **if** φ is of the form req_{fm}^P **then**
2 $\quad$ $VM \leftarrow vm(fm)$;
3 $\quad$ $P' \leftarrow \mathsf{apply}(VM, P)$, where $\mathsf{apply}(VM, P)$ as in Definition 13;
4 $\quad$ **if** $P' \neq P$ **then** $P' \leftarrow (P \text{ UNION } P')$
5 $\quad$ **return** $\mathsf{l2g}^{VM}\big(\mathsf{req}_{fm}^{P'}\big)$;

$\quad$ // If φ is not of the form req_{fm}^P, then it is either of the form $\mathsf{mj}\,\Phi$
$\quad$ // or of the form $\mathsf{mu}\,\Phi$ (because it is a source assignment).
6 $\Phi' \leftarrow \emptyset$; // initially empty set of FedQPL expressions
7 **forall the** $\varphi_i \in \Phi$ **do**
8 $\quad$ $\varphi_i' \leftarrow$ result of Algorithm 3 for φ_i and cxt;
9 $\quad$ $\Phi' \leftarrow \Phi' \cup \{\varphi_i'\}$;
10 **if** φ is of the form $\mathsf{mj}\,\Phi$ **then return** $\mathsf{mj}\,\Phi'$; **else return** $\mathsf{mu}\,\Phi'$

Example 8. Consider the triple pattern $tp = (?s, \mathsf{schema{:}knows}, ?o)$. For the same federation fed and vocabulary context $cxt = (v_G, vm)$ as in the previous examples (Examples 6 and 7), Example 3 shows that the expected result of tp is $[\![tp]\!]_{fed}^{cxt} = \{\mu\}$ with $\mu = \{?s \to \mathsf{ex{:}Bob}, ?o \to \mathsf{ex{:}Eve}\}$. It is not difficult to see that the FedQPL expression $\varphi' = \mathsf{l2g}^{VM}\big(\mathsf{req}_{fm}^{tp''}\big)$ with $tp'' = (?s, \mathsf{foaf{:}knows}, ?o)$ produces the exact same result and, thus, is correct for tp over fed in cxt.

Observe that the triple pattern tp'' in the FedQPL expression φ' of Example 8 is a version of the given triple pattern tp translated to the local vocabulary of the queried federation member. In contrast, for the FedQPL expression in Example 7 such a translation of the given triple pattern (tp', in this case) was not necessary. In the following, we introduce an algorithm to create *correct* vocabulary-aware plans represented as FedQPL expressions.

5.2   Creation of Vocabulary-Aware Query Plans

Our algorithm for creating a vocabulary-aware logical plan is designed based on the assumption that the query engine has already created an initial logical plan for the given global query, which is expressed in terms of the global vocabulary. In particular, we assume that this initial logical plan is the output of the source selection & query decomposition step, which is the first major query processing step in a query federation engine [1,17].[2] As shown in our earlier work [5], the output of existing source selection & query decomposition approaches can be captured by a fragment of FedQPL that consists of only three operators: req, mj, and mu. We call the FedQPL expressions in this fragment *source assignments* [5].

---

[2] Taking into account vocabulary mappings also during source selection is an orthogonal problem that we consider out of scope of our work in this paper.

Algorithm 4: Applies vocab. map. VM to triple pattern $tp = (s, pr, o)$.

1   $NewPreds \leftarrow \{p \mid r \in VM$ s.t. r is of the form $p \equiv p'$ or $p \sqsubseteq p'$, with $p' = pr\}$;
2   **if** $NewPreds$ is empty **then** $NewPreds \leftarrow \{pr\}$

3   $NewObjs \leftarrow \{c \mid r \in VM$ s.t. r is of the form $c \equiv c'$ or $c \sqsubseteq c'$, with $c' = o\} \cup$
       $\{c_1, \ldots, c_n \mid r \in VM$ of the form $c_1 \sqcup \cdots \sqcup c_n \equiv c'$, with $c' = o\}$;
4   **if** $NewObjs$ is empty **then** $NewObjs \leftarrow \{o\}$

5   $NewTPs \leftarrow \emptyset$;   // initially empty set of triple patterns
6   **foreach** $pr' \in NewPreds$ **do**
7   **foreach** $o' \in NewObjs$ **do**
8       $NewTPs \leftarrow NewTPs \cup \{tp'\}$ where $tp' = (s, pr', o')$;

9   $P' \leftarrow$ combine all triple patterns in $NewTPs$ into a UNION graph pattern;
10   **return** P';

Consequently, the main input to our algorithm in this section—see Algorithm 3—is such a source assignment in which the graph pattern of every req operator is expressed in terms of the global vocabulary. Another input is a vocabulary context for the federation considered by the given source assignment.

Then, the algorithm rewrites the given source assignment recursively while keeping the overall structure of mj and mu operators exactly as given within the source assignment (lines 6–10 in Algorithm 3). Hence, the only thing that the algorithm actually changes are the req operators. Each such operator is replaced by a subplan consisting of a new req operator with an l2g operator on top (lines 1–5). The vocabulary mapping of this l2g operator is the one associated with the federation member of the replaced req operator (line 2), and the graph pattern of the new req operator is obtained by translating the graph pattern of the replaced req operator (line 3) and, then, combining the translated pattern with the original one (line 4). While we shall discuss the reason for the latter step later (cf. Note 3), the translation of graph patterns (line 3) is defined as follows.

Definition 13. The **application** of a vocabulary mapping VM to a graph pattern P, denoted by apply(VM, P), is a graph pattern determined as follows.

1. If P is a triple pattern, then apply(VM, P) is the graph pattern that is obtained by performing Algorithm 4 with VM and P as input.
2. If P is a basic graph pattern $B = \{tp_1, \ldots, tp_n\}$, then apply($VM, P$) is the graph pattern $(tp'_1$ AND $\ldots$ AND $tp'_n)$ where $tp'_i =$ apply(VM, tp_i) for $1 \leq i \leq n$.
3. If P is of the form $(P_1$ AND $\ldots$ AND $P_n)$, then apply(VM, P) is the graph pattern $(P'_1$ AND $\ldots$ AND $P'_n)$ where $P'_i =$ apply(VM, P_i) for $1 \leq i \leq n$.
4. If P is of the form $(P_1$ UNION $\ldots$ UNION $P_n)$, then apply(VM, P) is the graph pattern $(P'_1$ UNION $\ldots$ UNION $P'_n)$ where $P'_i =$ apply(VM, P_i) for $1 \leq i \leq n$.

Example 9. Consider the triple pattern $tp = (?s, \text{schema:knows}, ?o)$ and the vocabulary mapping $VM = \{\text{foaf:knows} \equiv \text{schema:knows}, \text{foaf:Person} \equiv \text{schema:Person}\}$, as in Example 8. Then, by Definition 13, it holds that apply(VM, tp) is the triple pattern $(?s, \text{foaf:knows}, ?o)$ which, unsurprisingly, is the same as tp'' in Example 8. In contrast, for $tp' = (?x, \text{rdf:type}, ?t)$ in Example 7, apply$(VM, tp') = tp'$.

Example 10. For the vocabulary mapping $VM' = \{\text{ex:Student} \sqsubseteq \text{schema:Person},$ $\text{ex:Professor} \sqsubseteq \text{schema:Person}\}$ and the triple pattern $tp = (?x, \text{rdf:type}, \text{schema:Person})$, we have apply$(VM, tp)$ $=$ $\big((?x, \text{rdf:type}, \text{ex:Student})\ \text{UNION}\ (?x, \text{rdf:type},$ $\text{ex:Professor})\big)$.

While Examples 9–10 focus on translating graph patterns, the following example illustrates our main translation algorithm for a whole source assignment.

Example 11. We continue with the previous example (Example 10) in which the triple pattern tp is assumed to be expressed in terms of a global vocabulary. Now, consider a federation fed with a federation member fm that uses the corresponding local vocabulary; i.e., a possible vocabulary context for fed associates fm with the vocabulary mapping VM' of Example 10. Assume furthermore that fm has been identified to be the only member of fed that may have data to produce a nonempty result for tp. Hence, we have the single-operator expression req_{fm}^{tp} as the source assignment for executing tp over the federation. Algorithm 3 can then be used to rewrite this source assignment into a vocabulary-aware plan, which creates the FedQPL expression $\text{l2g}^{VM'}(\text{req}_{fm}^{P''})$ where P'' is the graph pattern $\big((?x, \text{rdf:type}, \text{schema:Person})\ \text{UNION}\ P'\big)$ that contains $P' = \big((?x, \text{rdf:type}, \text{ex:Student})\ \text{UNION}\ (?x, \text{rdf:type}, \text{ex:Professor})\big)$ from Example 10.

Note 3. Notice that the UNION pattern P'' in Example 11 contains the given triple pattern tp in addition to the pattern P' that resulted from translating tp based on the vocabulary mapping VM'. Combining the translated pattern with the original pattern in this way is the effect of line 4 in Algorithm 3. Adding the original pattern is necessary to guarantee complete query results in cases in which a federation member uses a term of the global vocabulary even if, according to the vocabulary mapping for this federation member, there is a corresponding term in the local vocabulary of the federation member. As a simple example that illustrates such a case, assume that the RDF graph of federation member fm of Example 11 is $G = \{(\text{ex:Bob}, \text{rdf:type}, \text{schema:Person})\}$. Recall that the vocabulary mapping for fm is $VM' = \{\text{ex:Student} \sqsubseteq \text{schema:Person}, \text{ex:Professor} \sqsubseteq \text{schema:Person}\}$. Hence, fm uses the global IRI schema:Person even if, according to VM', there are two corresponding IRIs in the local vocabulary of fm. Nonetheless, by Definition 8, the expected result for the triple pattern $tp = (?x, \text{rdf:type}, \text{schema:Person})$ of Example 11 consists of the solution mapping $\mu = \{?x \rightarrow \text{ex:Bob}\}$ because apply$(VM', G) = G$ (cf. Definition 5). However, a version of Algorithm 3 without line 4 would create the FedQPL expression $\varphi = \text{l2g}^{VM'}(\text{req}_{fm}^{P'})$ with P' as in Example 11, and this plan would produce the empty result, sols$(\varphi) = \emptyset$, because there are no matches for P' in the data of fm. In contrast, Algorithm 3 with line 4 creates $\text{l2g}^{VM'}(\text{req}_{fm}^{P''})$ with $P'' = \big((?x, \text{rdf:type}, \text{schema:Person})\ \text{UNION}\ P'\big)$, which produces the expected result consisting of solution mapping μ.

While having line 4 in Algorithm 3 fixes the illustrated incompleteness issue in cases in which federation members unexpectedly use the global vocabulary, a similar issue exists if the global query uses terms of any of the local vocabularies even if there is a corresponding global term.

Example 12. Consider a federation $fed = (\{fm\}, g)$ with $g(fm) = \{(s, p_L, o)\}$, and a vocabulary context $cxt = (v_G, vm)$ such that $vm(fm) = \{p_L \equiv p_G\}$. Then, the expected result of evaluating the triple pattern $tp = (?s, p_L, ?o)$ over fed is the empty result (i.e., $[\![tp]\!]_{fed}^{cxt} = \emptyset$) because there is no matching triple for tp in $\mathsf{apply}(vm(fm), g(fm)) = \{(s, p_G, o)\}$. However, given the source assignment req_{fm}^{tp}, Algorithm 3 (with or without line 4) translates this source assignment into the FedQPL expression $\mathsf{l2g}^{vm(fm)}(\mathsf{req}_{fm}^{tp})$, which incorrectly produces a nonempty result consisting of solution mapping $\mu = \{?s \rightarrow s, ?o \rightarrow o\}$.

To fix the issue illustrated in the previous example, the only graph patterns that we support as global queries are the ones that do not contain any of the vocabulary terms used in the left-hand side of some mapping rule in the given vocabulary context. We call such patterns *purely global*, defined as follows.

Definition 14. Let $cxt = (v_G, vm)$ be a vocabulary context. A SPARQL graph pattern P is **purely global in** cxt if the following properties hold.

1. If P is a triple pattern (s, p, o), then $p \notin \mathbb{A}$ and $o \notin \mathbb{A}$, where

$$\mathbb{A} = \{x \mid x \equiv x' \text{ is a rule in some vocab. mapping in the image of } vm\} \cup$$
$$\{c_1, \ldots, c_n \mid c_1 \sqcup \cdots \sqcup c_n \equiv c' \text{ is in some mapping in the image of } vm\}.$$

2. If P is a BGP, then every triple pattern $tp \in P$ is purely global in cxt.
3. If P is of the form either $(P_1 \text{ AND } \ldots \text{ AND } P_n)$ or $(P_1 \text{ UNION } \ldots \text{ UNION } P_n)$, then every P_i is purely global in cxt, for $1 \leq i \leq n$.

Example 13. Considering cxt and tp of Example 12, tp is *not* purely global in cxt, and neither is any graph pattern that contains tp as a sub-pattern. In contrast, the triple pattern $(?s, p_G, ?o)$ is purely global in cxt.

Finally, even if we focus only on purely-global graph patterns, the correctness of the vocabulary-aware FedQPL expressions produced by Algorithm 3 depends on the correctness of the source assignments from which they are produced. Since every source assignment that is given to Algorithm 3 is assumed to be expressed in terms of the global vocabulary, the notion of correctness of such source assignments is not the same as the correctness of vocabulary-aware FedQPL expressions as given in Definition 12. Instead, such source assignments are considered as FedQPL expressions for the global-vocabulary view of the queried federation (cf. Definition 7), which means that their req operators are considered to access the global-vocabulary view of the RDF graphs of the federation members, and the correctness of such source assignments is then defined as follows.

Definition 15. Let *fed* be a federation, $cxt = (v_{\mathsf{G}}, vm)$ be a vocabulary context for *fed*, and $fed' = (M', g')$ be the *cxt*-based global-vocabulary view of *fed*. Moreover, let P be a SPARQL graph pattern. A source assignment for *fed'* **is correct for** P if it holds that $\mathsf{sols}(\varphi) = [\![P]\!]_{G_{\mathsf{union}}}$, where $G_{\mathsf{union}} = \bigcup_{fm \in M'} g'(fm)$.

Finally, the correctness of Algorithm 3 can be stated as follows. Given a federation *fed*, a vocabulary context *cxt* for *fed*, a SPARQL graph pattern P that is purely global in *cxt*, and a source assignment φ for the *cxt*-based global-vocabulary view of *fed*, if φ is correct for P (as per Definition 15), then the FedQPL expression obtained by performing Algorithm 3 with φ and *cxt* as input is a FedQPL expression for *fed* and *cxt* that is correct for P (as per Definition 12). This correctness follows from Definitions 8, 11, 12, 14, and 15, and the definition of Algorithm 3 (including the corresponding Definition 13 with its Algorithm 4).

6   Evaluation

In this section we evaluate how vocabulary-awareness, as supported by our approach, affects the performance of federated query processing. To this end, we first describe the implementation employed for our study, along with the experiment setup. Thereafter, we present the measurements and discuss our observations. All artifacts required to reproduce our experiments, as well as the measurements obtained from these experiments, are available online.[3]

6.1   Implementation

We implemented the approach in our query federation engine HeFQUIN.[4] While the approach is independent of any particular plan-enumeration algorithm based on which the engine may select a specific query plan to execute, for the evaluation we use the approach in combination with a simple greedy plan-enumeration algorithm. This algorithm takes a FedQPL expression as produced by Algorithm 3 as input and constructs a left-deep execution plan for the multiway join in this expression. To this end, the algorithm starts by estimating the cardinality of the result of each subplan under the join, which is done by sending ASK requests to the corresponding federation members [16]. Thereafter, the algorithm picks a first subplan based on the estimated cardinality and uses it as the starting point for building up the left-deep plan. Subsequently, the algorithm iterates over the remaining subplans that can be joined with the partial left-deep plan that has been built so far, disregarding subplans that would introduce cross products unless no other subplans are available. During each step of this iteration, the algorithm considers the initially-determined cardinality for all available subplans and employs a greedy strategy to pick the subplan with the lowest cardinality among the available options. As the actual join algorithm in the resulting plans, we simply use the symmetric hash join algorithm.

---

[3] https://github.com/LiUSemWeb/HeFQUIN-VocabMappingsExperiments.
[4] https://github.com/LiUSemWeb/HeFQUIN.

6.2   General Experiments Setup

All experiments described in this paper have been performed on a server machine with two 8-core Intel Xeon E5-2667 v3@3.20 GHz CPUs and 256 GB of RAM. The machine runs a 64-bit Debian GNU/Linux 10 server operation system. Federation members used in the experiments are SPARQL endpoints set up using docker images of Virtuoso v7.2.5.

Datasets: The datasets utilized in our evaluation are generated using the dataset generator of the Lehigh University Benchmark (LUBM) [8], which is a popular benchmark in the Semantic Web community for evaluating the performance of storage and reasoning systems for RDF data. These benchmark datasets capture a fictional scenario of universities that consist of departments with both students and faculty of different types (e.g., lecturers, assistant professors). These people engage in activities such as teaching or taking courses, may be co-authors of publications, and have degrees from universities. For our evaluation, we generated such data for ten universities and split into ten separate datasets (one per university). One notable aspect of these datasets is that they are interlinked through different types of "degree from" relationships; i.e., students and faculty of a university described in one dataset may have a

Table 1. The mapping rules that constitute the mapping from the vocabulary used in the generated datasets (and also in federation **Fed1**) to the global vocabulary.

Type	Mapping Rule
RuleType1	lubm:Course $\equiv$ global:Course
RuleType1	lubm:GraduateStudent $\equiv$ global:GraduateStudent
RuleType2	lubm:GraduateStudent $\sqsubseteq$ global:Student
RuleType2	lubm:Lecturer $\sqsubseteq$ global:Faculty
RuleType2	lubm:GraduateCourse $\sqsubseteq$ global:Course
RuleType2	lubm:UndergraduateStudent $\sqsubseteq$ global:Student
RuleType3	lubm:UndergraduateStudent $\sqcup$ lubm:GraduateStudent $\equiv$ global:Student
RuleType3	lubm:AssistantProfessor $\sqcup$ lubm:AssociateProfessor $\sqcup$ lubm:FullProfessor $\equiv$ global:Professor
RuleType4	lubm:advisor $\equiv$ global:supervisor
RuleType4	lubm:worksFor $\equiv$ global:worksAt
RuleType4	lubm:teacherOf $\equiv$ global:teaches
RuleType4	lubm:telephone $\equiv$ global:phoneNumber
RuleType4	lubm:emailAddress $\equiv$ global:email
RuleType4	lubm:researchInterest $\equiv$ global:researchTopic
RuleType4	lubm:memberOf $\equiv$ global:memberOf
RuleType4	lubm:subOrganizationOf $\equiv$ global:isPartOf
RuleType5	lubm:publicationAuthor $\sqsubseteq$ global:writtenBy
RuleType5	lubm:doctoralDegreeFrom $\sqsubseteq$ global:degreeFrom
RuleType5	lubm:mastersDegreeFrom $\sqsubseteq$ global:degreeFrom
RuleType5	lubm:undergraduateDegreeFrom $\sqsubseteq$ global:degreeFrom
RuleType5	lubm:headOf $\sqsubseteq$ global:worksAt
RuleType5	lubm:takesCourse $\sqsubseteq$ global:registersCourse

degree from a university described in another dataset. We leverage this feature in the test queries used for our evaluation (see below). Another relevant aspect of these datasets is that not all classes and properties of the LUBM schema are used explicitly in the generated datasets. For instance, while the LUBM schema contains classes such as lubm:FullProfessor, lubm:AssociateProfessor and lubm:AssistantProfessor as subclasses of lubm:Professor, the generated datasets contain only these subclasses. We leverage this aspect to establish a separation between local vocabularies and global vocabulary being used in our evaluation.

Base Vocabulary Mapping: While we consider three different federations for our evaluation (see below), for all of them we aim to use the same global vocabulary. As the basis of this global vocabulary we use the classes and properties that are not used explicitly in the generated datasets, encompassing IRIs such as global:degreeFrom and global:Professor. Additionally, we create a few supplementary IRIs (e.g., global:worksAt, global:registersCourse) to allow us to consider a wider range of different types of mapping rules. After establishing our global vocabulary, we manually constructed a mapping from the local vocabulary consisting of the class and property that are used explicitly in the generated datasets to this global vocabulary. Table 1 lists the mapping rules of this vocabulary mapping.

Next, we describe the three federations used for the evaluation. Each of them consists of ten federation members, created based on the aforementioned datasets.

Table 2. Characteristics of the queries used in the evaluation. C, P, and I refer to the types of terms, representing class IRIs, predicate IRIs, and instance IRIs, respectively.

Query	query plan translation			interm.result translation			joins are on	#triple patterns	types of joins	#solution mappings
	≡	⊑	⊔	≡	⊑	⊔				
Q1	P	P	C				I	6	s-s, o-o	356
Q2	P	P	C				I	5	s-s, o-o	382,803
Q3	P	P				C	C,I	6	s-s, o-o	158
Q4	P	C	C		P		P	6	s-s, s-o, o-o, p-p	270
Q5	C,P	C	C				I	5	s-s, s-o, o-o	229,170
Q6	P	C	C	C	C	C	I	5	s-s, s-o, o-o	274,699
Q7	C	C	C	P	C,P	C	C,I	5	s-s, s-o, o-o	233,560

Fed0: As a baseline, we set up a federation in which all federation members employ the global vocabulary. Thus, no vocabulary translation is needed for querying this federation. To create the datasets of the ten members of Fed0, we simply use an implementation of Algorithm 1 to apply the vocabulary mapping of Table 1 to each of the ten datasets produced by the LUBM dataset generator.

Fed1: For setting up this federation, we use the generated datasets as they are. Therefore, the vocabulary used in these datasets—which is the same in all ten of them—becomes the local vocabulary of the members in this federation. Consequently, when querying Fed1, the vocabulary mapping of Table 1 can be used commonly for all federation members.

Fed2: This federation is structurally the same as Fed1, but with the following simple variation of the local vocabularies. For each federation member, we change the IRIs of the vocabulary terms used in the dataset of that member by appending a member-specific suffix (ranging from 0 to 9) to each such IRI. For instance, the class IRI lubm:Course becomes lubm:Course0 for the first federation member, lubm:Course1 for the second, etc. As a result, the local vocabularies used by the ten members of Fed2 are different from one another (not structurally but in terms of their IRIs). As a consequence, the vocabulary mapping of Table 1 has to be adapted accordingly for each federation member and, hence, every federation member in Fed2 is associated with a different vocabulary mapping. For instance, the versions of the first mapping rule in Table 1 for the first two members of Fed2 are lubm:Course0 ≡ global:Course and lubm:Course1 ≡ global:Course, respectively.

Queries: After creating the federations, we designed seven benchmark queries that are expressed in terms of the global vocabulary. Thus, they can be used for all three federations. As shown in Table 2, these queries differ regarding the types of vocabulary mapping rules that are relevant to them, both in the context of the mapping-based rewriting of the initial query plans (cf. Sect. 5.2) and in the context of the translation of intermediate results (as per Definition 10).

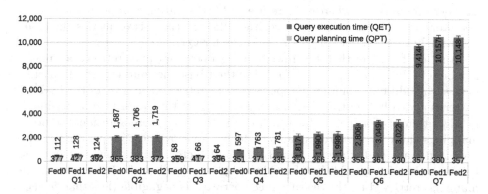

Fig. 1. Query planning time (ms) and query execution time (ms) for the test queries over different federations. **Fed0:** All federation members use the global vocabulary, no mappings needed. **Fed1:** All federation members use the same vocabulary, different from the global vocabulary. **Fed2:** Each federation member uses a different vocabulary.

Evaluation Metrics We report performance metrics based on the following definitions: i) *Query planning time* (**QPT**) is the amount of time elapsed since the input of a given source assignment until the plan for executing the query has been determined, which includes rewriting the given source assignment (if necessary, see Sect. 5.2) and selecting a join order. ii) *Query execution time* (**QET**) is the amount of time needed for executing the selected plan until completion.

6.3   Overhead of Considering Vocabulary Mappings

To identify the overhead of considering vocabulary mappings during query processing we compare the performance when executing the test queries over federations Fed1 and Fed2 using our approach versus executing them without vocabulary mappings over Fed0. For each federation, we execute the seven test queries sequentially. We run this process 11 times, with the first run as warm up. Figure 1 illustrates the average QPT and QET of the other 10 runs, with error bars representing the standard deviation of the average sum of QPT and QET.

As a first observation, we notice that the query planning times across all queries for the different federations differ only marginally. This observation suggests that the vocabulary-related query rewriting consumes no significant time.

In contrast, the query execution time increases noticeably when comparing the baseline (Fed0) to the cases in which the query plans are rewritten based on our approach (Fed1 and Fed2). This increase can be attributed to two factors.

The first, and major, factor is that the plans have been extended with l2g operators which perform extra work that is not done by the plans in the baseline case. The amount of this extra work differs for the different queries as the sizes of the intermediate results differ (some of the queries are more selective than others). For instance, there are 1,212 solution mappings to be processed by the l2g operators for Q1, whereas there are 312,248 solution mappings for the l2g operators for Q5; as a consequence, the QET of these two queries increases accordingly (+15 ms for Q1 versus +172 ms for Q5).

Another factor is that the rewritten req operators may retrieve a greater number of solution mappings compared to their baseline counterparts. In particular, such additional solution mappings may be retrieved because of the UNION patterns added by the translation process (see line 4 in Algorithm 3 and line 9 in Algorithm 4). For queries for which this is the case, these additional solution mappings cause even more extra work to be done by the l2g operators in the rewritten plans and, thereby, amplify the first factor. Among our test queries, this is the case for Q2–Q4. Yet, for Q2 and Q3, the number of additional solution mappings retrieved by the rewritten req operators is negligible (less than 5). For Q4, however, the rewritten req operators retrieve a total of 200 additional solution mappings, which contributes to an increased QET of +166 ms (+27.8%).

Overall, the increase in query execution time remains within an acceptable range, with six of the seven queries (all but Q4) experiencing an increase of less than 15% after rewriting the request operators and introducing l2g operators.

Finally, we compare the measurements for Fed1 and Fed2, which are only minimally different. This can be attributed to the fact that the datasets used in both federations are structurally the same. Although each federation member in Fed2 requires a different vocabulary mapping, these mappings are isomorphic to the vocabulary mapping used in Fed1. Consequently, the size of the intermediate results remains unchanged for each query when executed over Fed1 or over Fed2.

7 Concluding Remarks

This paper presents a formal pipeline to translate query plans for queries expressed in a global vocabulary into plans that consider the vocabulary heterogeneity of RDF federations. The translation includes the use of an operator that translates back the obtained local solutions into global ones, to be able to perform joins across federations members. The outcomes of our experimental study indicate that the integration of vocabulary mappings into query processing unsurprisingly introduces overhead, which, however, is within an acceptable range.

As part of our ongoing research, we are currently investigating various strategies to optimize query performance by applying rewriting rules to the logical query plans, with the aim of mitigating and minimizing these extra overheads.

As future work, we consider incorporating tools that can automatically generate mapping rules within our approach. In addition, we envision applying more complex mapping rules, such as those involving union and intersection. With respect to our broader long-term goals, we are interested in handling queries over federations with different types of data sources (i.e., not just RDF).

Acknowledgements. This work was funded by the National Graduate School in Computer Science, Sweden (CUGS), and by Vetenskapsrådet (the Swedish Research Council, project reg. no. 2019-05655).

References

1. Acosta, M., Hartig, O., Sequeda, J.F.: Federated RDF query processing. In: Encyclopedia of Big Data Technologies (2019)
2. Acosta, M., Vidal, M.-E., Lampo, T., Castillo, J., Ruckhaus, E.: ANAPSID: an adaptive query processing engine for SPARQL endpoints. In: Aroyo, L., et al. (eds.) ISWC 2011. LNCS, vol. 7031, pp. 18–34. Springer, Heidelberg (2011). https://doi.org/10.1007/978-3-642-25073-6_2
3. Bouquet, P., Giunchiglia, F., van Harmelen, F., Serafini, L., Stuckenschmidt, H.: C-OWL: contextualizing ontologies. In: Fensel, D., Sycara, K., Mylopoulos, J. (eds.) ISWC 2003. LNCS, vol. 2870, pp. 164–179. Springer, Heidelberg (2003). https://doi.org/10.1007/978-3-540-39718-2_11
4. Charalambidis, A., Troumpoukis, A., Konstantopoulos, S.: SemaGrow: optimizing federated SPARQL queries. In: Proceedings of the 11th SEMANTICS Conference (2015)
5. Cheng, S., Hartig, O.: FedQPL: a language for logical query plans over heterogeneous federations of RDF data sources. In: Proceedings of the 22nd International Conference on Information Integration and Web-based Applications & Services (iiWAS) (2020)
6. Collarana, D., Galkin, M., Traverso-Ribón, I., Vidal, M.E., Lange, C., Auer, S.: MINTE: semantically integrating RDF graphs. In: Proceedings of the 7th International Conference on Web Intelligence, Mining and Semantics (2017)
7. Euzenat, J., Shvaiko, P.: Ontology Matching, 2nd edn. Springer, Heidelberg (2013)
8. Guo, Y., Pan, Z., Heflin, J.: LUBM: a benchmark for OWL knowledge base systems. J. Web Semant. 3(2–3), 158–182 (2005)

9. Isele, R., Bizer, C.: Active learning of expressive linkage rules using genetic programming. J. Web Semant. **23**, 2–15 (2013)
10. Joshi, A.K.: Alignment-based querying of linked open data. In: Meersman, R., et al. (eds.) OTM 2012. LNCS, vol. 7566, pp. 807–824. Springer, Heidelberg (2012). https://doi.org/10.1007/978-3-642-33615-7_25
11. Makris, K., Bikakis, N., Gioldasis, N., Christodoulakis, S.: SPARQL-RW: transparent query access over mapped RDF data sources. In: Proceedings of the 15th International Conference on Extending Database Technology (EDBT) (2012)
12. Makris, K., Gioldasis, N., Bikakis, N., Christodoulakis, S.: Ontology mapping and SPARQL rewriting for querying federated RDF data sources. In: Meersman, R., Dillon, T., Herrero, P. (eds.) OTM 2010. LNCS, vol. 6427, pp. 1108–1117. Springer, Heidelberg (2010). https://doi.org/10.1007/978-3-642-16949-6_32
13. Pérez, J., Arenas, M., Gutierrez, C.: Semantics and complexity of SPARQL. ACM Trans. Database Syst. **34**(3), 1–45 (2009)
14. Polleres, A., Scharffe, F., Schindlauer, R.: SPARQL++ for mapping between RDF vocabularies. In: Meersman, R., Tari, Z. (eds.) OTM 2007. LNCS, vol. 4803, pp. 878–896. Springer, Heidelberg (2007). https://doi.org/10.1007/978-3-540-76848-7_59
15. Saleem, M., Potocki, A., Soru, T., Hartig, O., Ngomo, A.N.: CostFed: Cost-Based Query Optimization for SPARQL Endpoint Federation. In: Proceedings of the 14th International Conference on Semantic Systems (SEMANTICS) (2018)
16. Schwarte, A., Haase, P., Hose, K., Schenkel, R., Schmidt, M.: FedX: optimization techniques for federated query processing on linked data. In: Aroyo, L., et al. (eds.) ISWC 2011. LNCS, vol. 7031, pp. 601–616. Springer, Heidelberg (2011). https://doi.org/10.1007/978-3-642-25073-6_38
17. Vidal, M.-E., Castillo, S., Acosta, M., Montoya, G., Palma, G.: On the selection of SPARQL endpoints to efficiently execute federated SPARQL queries. In: Hameurlain, A., Küng, J., Wagner, R. (eds.) Transactions on Large-Scale Data- and Knowledge-Centered Systems XXV. LNCS, vol. 9620, pp. 109–149. Springer, Heidelberg (2016). https://doi.org/10.1007/978-3-662-49534-6_4
18. Wang, X., Tiropanis, T., Davis, H.C.: Optimising linked data queries in the presence of co-reference. In: Presutti, V., d'Amato, C., Gandon, F., d'Aquin, M., Staab, S., Tordai, A. (eds.) ESWC 2014. LNCS, vol. 8465, pp. 442–456. Springer, Cham (2014). https://doi.org/10.1007/978-3-319-07443-6_30

AIS - A Metric for Assessing the Impact of an Influencer's Twitter Activity on the Price of a Cryptocurrency

Kevin Miller[✉] and Kristof Böhmer

Faculty of Computer Science, Research Group Software Architecture, University of
Vienna, Währinger Straße 29, Vienna, Austria
{kevin.miller,kristof.boehmer}@univie.ac.at

Abstract. Individual users on social media platforms like Twitter can
significantly volatile assets, including cryptocurrencies. However, current
research has overlooked this aspect, focusing on sentiment analysis that
includes all posts from all users. Making it challenging to detect trends
caused by individuals. To address this gap, we introduce the Asset Influence Score (AIS), a percentage-based metric that assesses the likelihood
of a newly issued tweet aligning with periods of heightened trading activity. By analyzing price data and tweets concurrently, we identify correlations that enable to predict the likelihood of specific users' tweets
co-occurring with increased trading activity. Evaluating the AIS using a
publicly available prototype and Twitter data from 2020 to 2023, we find
that using the AIS as a buy signal outperforms buy-and-hold and technical trading strategies while maintaining high liquidity. Demonstrating
the applicability of AIS in improving trading decisions and identifying
key individuals on social media platforms.

Keywords: Twitter · Cryptocurrency · Prediction · Social Media
Analysis · Trading Indicator

1 Introduction

Cryptocurrencies have ushered in a new era of financial assets. The novelty and
opportunity of this asset class do not come without their fair share of price
volatility. [12] Assets like the cryptocurrency "Dogecoin" saw its price rise by
over 15000% during early 2021, despite it being abandoned by its founders and
being created as a joke. This can mostly be attributed to Elon Musk, who made
his fondness of the asset public on his personal Twitter account. Now that Musk
mostly stopped tweeting about Dogecoin, the asset has lost roughly 90% of its
value at the time of writing compared to its peak. [1,2]

The psychological phenomenon of investors following others rather than conducting their independent research is described as herd investing [5,16]. Herd
behavior can lead to extremely overvalued assets and in turn panic selling, akin
to a bubble forming and bursting, resulting in huge losses for investors that

M. Sellami et al. (Eds.): CoopIS 2023, LNCS 14353, pp. 41–58, 2024.
https://doi.org/10.1007/978-3-031-46846-9_3

made risky investment decisions due to herd mentality [5]. This effect is further amplified when spearheaded by a publicly well-known entity like Elon Musk, combined with cryptocurrency like Dogecoin which's objective fair value is difficult to determine [10].

Existing crypto-focused trading approaches are unable to identify, quantify and exploit this phenomena. Most work focuses on technical factors [6,15], tweet volume and Google search trends [3,11] or broader social media analysis, neglecting individual users behavior [7,18]. In turn the approaches that incorporate specific user behaviour are overly focused on single handpicked users, such as Elon Musk [14] or Donald Trump [8,13], lacking the general applicability to identify herd behaviour and key individuals in today's dynamic social networks.

When looking at existing work, a gap in identifying and transparently quantifying the influence of opinion leaders (fittingly described as "tastemakers" by [9]) becomes apparent. Doing so can serve as a tool for investor protection, providing insight as to who might be able to induce herd behavior in investors. Knowing who can cause market moves can also be used to create a trading advantage by making price moves caused by social influencers less unexpected.

To achieve this, we propose the Asset Influence Score (AIS), a metric that approximates the certainty (in percent) of a user's newly issued tweet coinciding with a period of abnormal (elevated trading activity - see following paragraph) price action. We combine the most relevant tweets about a cryptocurrency for each hour with the price data in OHCLV-candles (Open, High, Close, Low, Volume) for the respective hour over a long timeframe (in our case roughly 3 years) to identify users which's tweets tend to appear in a period of abnormal price action, indicating possible causation for such price moves.

To quantify price moves we propose a metric we call *Velocity* (V), which represents each candlestick's range (High to Low) amplified by the trading volume. To identify a period of abnormal price action we employ a sliding window approach [4] that computes the average V over a given timeframe. For each following candle we can compare its V to that of the sliding window average. To normalize and quantify the relation of the current candle's V to the window average, we propose the term *Magnitude* (M), which represents the factor with which the candle compares to the window average. E.g., if a candle's V is twice that of the current window, its M is 2. If a candle's M exceeds a certain threshold (we propose the term *Breakout Threshold Factor - BTF* ($\in \mathbb{Q}_{>1}$)), this candle is deemed as abnormal, indicating relevance to our model. To repeat, the AIS approximates the certainty of which a user's tweet will coincide with a candle whose magnitude exceeds the BTF (= abnormal candles).

To perform the necessary calculations, we have created a fully open-source Java-based client application[1] that performs the necessary data fetching and preparation as well as the AIS calculation for easy replicability. The user can specify parameters like the cryptocurrency, timeframe, *sliding window size* (WS) as well as the BTF, making this application universally applicable to all assets and configurations.

---

[1] https://git01lab.cs.univie.ac.at/university_research/masterarbeiten/ais.

The AIS will be evaluated by applying it to Dogecoin, a cryptocurrency which's price action has been notoriously tied to the tweets of Elon Musk. We will also evaluate the AIS on Bitcoin, which is the most established cryptocurrency to date. We will use the *AIS* as a trading indicator, entering positions based on tweets by users with a high *AIS*. We compare our results to both a buy-and-hold investor, as well as a strategy based on a technical analysis and show that the *AIS*, a model that can be run on commodity off-the-shelf hardware, is capable of generating above-market returns by minimizing losses attributable to the constant market exposure of the buy-and-hold investor.

This paper is organized as follows: Prerequisites and the proposed approach are introduced in Sect. 2. Details on the exact process of the *AIS* calculation are given in Sect. 2 and 3. The evaluation and comparison of the *AIS*-based trading algorithm with the buy-and-hold as well as the technical trading algorithm is covered in Sect. 4. In Sect. 5 we highlight comparable approaches and related work. Finally, results are discussed and concluded in Sect. 6, where future work is also outlined.

2 Prerequisites and General Approach

The *AIS* is calculated using a combination of price and Twitter data. We start by fetching hourly price data and the most popular tweets for each hour for the user-specified timeframe. For fetching price data, we use Cryptocompare[2], a free API that returns price data in OHLCV form. To quantify price moves, we propose the term *Velocity (V)*. $V \in \mathbb{Q}^+$ and captures the size of the price move (high point vs. low point) combined with the base 10 logarithm of the trading volume in US-dollars. The exact definition of the fields used in this formula can be found in Subsect. 2.2.

$$V_P = (P_h - P_l) \times \log_{10} P_v$$

We use a logarithmic approach for trading volume because it allows us incorporate it without outweighing price moves if significant trading volume occurs. Without the logarithm, a significant general increase in volume starts to dilute the weight of price moves. V plays an integral role in the *AIS* calculation process, as it represents how the market reacts to tweets in our *AIS* model. Our approach combines the *Velocity* with historic data from Twitter to identify possible correlations between twitter behavior and price activity.

For fetching tweets we use the Twitter API v2[3]. We have been granted academic access to the API, which allows us to fetch tweets from the past. We then extract relevant information like user details, text, the timestamp and the tweet's engagement metrics into dataframes. Dataframes are a data structure we propose that contains an hour of price action and the tweets that were issued within the respective hour, intended to represent an hour of market activity.

---

[2] https://min-api.cryptocompare.com/.
[3] https://developer.twitter.com/en/docs/twitter-api.

Figure 1 shows an overview of the *AIS* calculation process. In step ① the user specifies values like the name and ticker-symbol of the asset that should be analyzed, the timeframe over which the *AIS* should be calculated as well as parameters like the *BTF*, *WS (Window Size)* and the *PCC* to Bitcoin. These values and their effect on the *AIS* will be explained in greater detail in Sect. 3 and 4 respectively, but in essence, these values specify the sensitivity of the *AIS* to price changes.

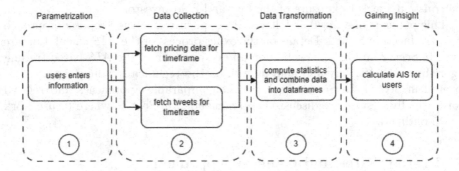

Fig. 1. An overview of the AIS calculation process

In step ② the client application fetches tweets and pricing data from the aformentioned API's. In step ③ the data is transformed into dataframes. Finally in step ④ we use the dataframes to calculate the AIS for each twitter user, which will be covered in Sect. 3. We will now go over the data and the dataframe creation from steps ② and ③ in more detail.

2.1 Tweets

Definition 1 (Tweets). *Let $T_i := \langle t_1, \cdots, t_n \rangle$, T_i being a finite bag of n tweets and $i \in \mathbb{N}$, representing the starting millisecond of a trading hour as a UNIX-timestamp.*

Let further $t_n := \{t_c, t_u, t_t, t_l, t_r\}$. $t_c \in String$ represents the content of the tweet; $t_u \in String$ represents the username of the user who issued the tweet; $t_t \in \mathbb{N}$ represents the exact UNIX-timestamp when t was issued; $t_l \in \mathbb{N}$ and $t_r \in \mathbb{N}$ represent the likes and retweets of t respectively.

Tweets were searched for both the ticker-symbol and the full name of the cryptocurrency. For Dogecoin, the query would be "Dogecoin or DOGE", which also covers the hashtags "#Dogecoin" and "#DOGE". In addition to the tweet's content we gather information about the issuing user, the exact time the tweet was issued as well as the social metrics of the tweet (likes and retweets). Only tweets written in English were considered.

Our approach uses these social metrics to calculate the *ES* (*Engagement Share* - essentially the percentage of likes and retweets a tweet garners within its time segment - covered in the subsequent chapter), which is what we use to weigh the impact of a tweet and attribute it to the *Velocity* of the price.

We fetch the first page (containing between 80–120 tweets) of the API response for every hour, sorted by Twitter's built-in relevancy algorithm. The *AIS* is based around the hypothesis that tastemakers generate high engagement on Twitter, therefore limiting the tweet data to roughly 120 tweets per hour does not pose an issue in terms of thoroughness and prediction accuracy for the most influential users.

By utilizing this approach, it is impossible to overlook significant tweets that could likely identify tastemakers, while ensuring adequate performance and reasonable size of the underlying data set by omitting users and tweets that don't generate any significant engagement. We experimented with fetching multiple pages (up to 1000 tweets per hour), but found that there was no impact on the top 100 users ranked by *AIS*. It only increased the memory requirement and data fetching time, thus degrading performance significantly.

We leverage Twitter's built in sorting algorithm, as the API sorts the tweets based on social metrics, the user's follower count and overall impressions in descending order (most engaged tweet comes first), which is exactly the approach we would employ when sorting tweets.

2.2   Price Data

Definition 2 (Price Data). *Let P_i be a set of fields $p_i := \{p_o, p_h, p_l, p_c, p_v\}$ $\in \mathbb{Q}$ and $i \in \mathbb{N}$, representing the starting millisecond of the trading hour as a UNIX-timestamp. P_i represents one hour of price activity.*

*p_o represents the **open price**, p_h represents the **high price**; p_l represents the **low price**, p_c represents the **close price** and p_v represents the **trading volume** of p_i respectively.*

In addition to tweets, we also fetch the price data in hourly OHLCV-form (Open, High, Low, Close, Volume) for the specified timeframe, both for the user-specified cryptocurrency as well as Bitcoin. The data is utilized to calculate V as well as subsequent price metrics, which will be explained in great detail in the following chapter (Sect. 3). It is an integral part of the *AIS*, as we use it to derive how the market values and interprets Twitter activity, thus allowing for the calculation of the *AIS*. The price data is fetched from Binance[4], as it is the largest and most popular exchange by trading volume.

We fetch Bitcoin's corresponding price action because most crypto assets are significantly correlated to Bitcoin, as shown in [21]. As the correlation of cryptocurrency assets changes with time, we fetch the most up to date correlation coefficient from Cryptowatch[5], a free service that provides this information. By taking that into account, we can more accurately determine whether only a specific asset experienced volatility or whether the market experienced a general

---

[4] https://www.binance.com/en.
[5] https://cryptowat.ch/correlations.

price move. The *Asset Influence Scores* can also be computed for Bitcoin. In this case, the outlined price normalization approach is skipped.

2.3 Dataframes

Definition 3 (Dataframe). *Let D_i be a Dataframe. $i \in \mathbb{N}$ represents the starting UNIX-timestamp of exactly $1\,h$ of market activity; D_i consists of the fields P_i (2), T_i (1) and S_i, therefore $D_i = \{P_i, T_i, S_i\}$.*
Let further $S_i = \{WS, \mu V\}$. Hereby, $WS \in \mathbb{N}$ represents the `size of the sliding window`, and $\mu V \in \mathbb{Q}^+$ represents the average Velocity (V) for the past $WS\ P_i$.

Dataframes are the data structure we propose to represent an hour of market activity. In addition to the aforementioned price and Twitter data, a dataframe also contains price action statistics based on *Velocity* (V), which are computed based on a sliding window. We interpret and derive V's meaning by comparing to other V in its vicinity. By utilizing a sliding window approach we can ensure that we derive outbreaks based on recent trading activity rather than overall historical trading activity.

After Musk first mentioned Dogecoin for example, the asset's baseline trading activity (and thus its hourly V) rose significantly, even without any mentions by Musk. Without a sliding window, every hour after Musk's mention would be identified as an outlier when compared with the time period before Musk's mention, whereas an appropriately sized sliding window allows us to quickly adapt to the new norm and compare V among only more recent price candles. This approach was heavily inspired by [4].

The sliding window is used to compute the mean *Velocity* μV for the past WS *(Window Size)* amount of price candles.

$$\mu V = \sum_{i=0}^{WS} \frac{V_{P_i}}{WS}$$

If a proceeding candle exceeds μV by the user-specified *Breakout Threshold Factor* (BTF), we deem this candle to be abnormal. To repeat, the AIS approximates the certainty with which a user's tweet occurs such an abnormal time segment. Each dataframe contains μV of the previous WS amount of candles. These dataframes form the necessary basis for the AIS calculation. How they are used and how the AIS is calculated will be discussed now.

3 Gaining Insight

To extract value and knowledge from the dataframes and calculate the *Asset Influence Score*, we must first define the proposed terms used in calculating the AIS. We will follow up by explaining the algorithm in detail and providing a concrete calculation example for the AIS.

3.1   Definitions

We have touched on the importance of *Velocity* (V), as it represents the measurement of the market's price activity for any given hour. As stated, we need a way to relate *Velocities* to one another. *Magnitude(M)* $(\in \mathbb{Q}^+)$ allows us to relate the Vs to each other, as is represents the **factor** by which V changes compared to the average of the sliding window.

$$M_{P_i} = \frac{V_{P_i}}{\mu V}$$

To recall, the *Breakout Threshold Factor (BTF)* defines the *Magnitude* threshold for a candle to be considered *abnormal*. The *AIS* then approximates the certainty with which a users tweet will occur within the same timeframe as a candle of which M exceeds the BTF $(= abnormal$ candles$)$.

We now have a way of discerning between standard and abnormal price movements, but we can not yet attribute these movements to any particular user. In our model, we assume that price moves can be directly related to Twitter users activities. To differentiate between users, we propose a metric called the *Engagement Share (ES)* $(\in \mathbb{Q})$. The ES is the percentage of the sum of all engagement gathered by tweets about an asset within a specific hour. We define *Engagement (E)* $(\in \mathbb{N})$ as:

$$E_t = t_l + 2t_r$$

Or in other words: *Likes* $+ 2 \times$ *Retweets*. Retweets are multiplied by two because retweeting something shows up on the retweeting user's timeline as well, generating even more reach and indicating more "commitment" to the content, if a user is willing to have it displayed on their own timeline.

We can now attribute a percentage of each hourly segment's *Engagement* E_{T_i} to each tweet. The *user's* ES is simply the $\sum ES$ of their tweets (where $t_u = user_u$) within that hourly segment. The portion of the price move attributed to a user is proportional to their ES.

$$ES_t = \frac{E_t}{\sum E_{T_i}}$$

We now have almost all necessary building blocks to move on the defining and calculating the AIS. We can compute each time segment's *Magnitude (M)*, as well as corresponding engagement metrics. Before moving on to calculating the AIS for a specific user, there is one important factor that must be incorporated - the crypto market's high correlation to Bitcoin. We cannot properly judge the price action of a cryptocurrency without looking at Bitcoin's price performance during the same period, as the top cryptocurrencies have an average Pearson Correlation Coefficient to BTC of over 0.77[6] (at the time of writing). To incorporate this aspect we propose a separate metric which expands on M - the *Magnitude attributable to External Factors (MEF)* $(\in \mathbb{Q})$. The MEF reduces a

---

[6] https://cryptowat.ch/correlations.

time segment's M by Bitcoin's M from that segment (weighted by correlation), resulting in a metric for weighing moves unrelated to Bitcoin's price action. We define the MEF as:

$$MEF_{P_i} = M_{P_i} - (M_{bitcoin_i} \times PCC)$$

We have now defined all general metrics for extracting insight from the dataframes. We use these metrics for creating *TweetMaps*, a custom structure we propose and employ for calculating the AIS for a user.

3.2 Structuring Information

During the mapping process, we iterate over each dataframe D_i (one hour at a time). We look at T_i within D_i and either create (if it's the user's first tweet) or add to an existing *TweetMap*. A TweetMap contains the Twitter user and a list of their respective tweets, that were issued during the entire timeframe which matched the search criteria specified in Sect. 2.1. We also embed the MEF of the respective hourly segment within every tweet and calculate its ES. This results in a dictionary where we can look up a specific user and find all their tweets issued on the asset (during the timeframe), the ES every tweet received during its hour of issuance, as well as the corresponding market activity during that same hour (represented by the MEF). This information is used to calculate the AIS.

3.3 Calculating the AIS

After the mapping process is finished and the TweetMaps have been created, we utilize them to start the AIS calculation on a per-user basis. All the steps described are universally applicable to all TweetMaps and therefore to all Twitter users.

In Table 1 you can see a representation of Musk's TweetMap spanning over the timeframe of January 1, 2020 until May 31, 2023. The size of the sliding window was set to 36 candles (the MEF varies depending on the WS). The tweets were sorted according to their respective MEF.

We then utilize the TweetMap to compute the average *Average Attributable Magnitude (AMM)* ($\in \mathbb{Q}$) for a user. The AAM represents the average M which we attribute to each user based on their average received ES. This metric allows us to differentiate between users that just happen to tweet during times of elevated M, and users that might have actually caused significant trading activity with their tweets. All the variables (ES_u as well as the number of tweets $|T_u|$) are user-specific.

$$AAM_u = \frac{\frac{\sum ES_u}{100}}{|T_u|} \times \frac{\sum MEF}{|T_u|}$$

If we apply this formula to Musk's TweetMap, we get an AAM for Elon Musk of 5.6971.

Table 1. Elon Musk's TweetMap from of Jan 1, 2020 until May 31, 2023

Rank	Text	ES	MEF
1	SpaceX is going to put a literal Dogecoin on the literal moo	98.46	28.14
2	Tesla will make some merch buyable with Doge & see how i	88.12	20.09
3	One word: Doge	99.70	13.93
4	Do you want Tesla to accept Doge?	92.50	10.31
5	Tesla merch can be bought with Doge, soon SpaceX merch too	92.63	9.85
6	High time I confessed I let the Doge out	96.98	7.10
7	No highs, no lows, only Doge	55.59	6.11
8	Dogecoin is the people's crypto	42.34	6.11
9	Tesla merch buyable with Dogecoin	92.61	5.91
10	Doge day afternoon	85.30	5.51
11	I will eat a happy meal on tv if @McDonalds accepts Dogecoin	95.28	5.17
12	Release the Doge!	95.63	4.37
13	I will keep supporting Dogecoin	92.77	4.34
14	If major Dogecoin holders sell most of their coins, it will	98.14	3.78
15	Bought some Dogecoin for lil X, so he can be a toddler hodle	95.15	3.36
16	Doge meme shield (legendary item)	97.48	3.32
17	Working with Doge devs to improve system transaction efficie	93.54	2.86
18	Who let the Doge out	93.72	2.52
19	Baby Doge, doo, doo, doo, doo, doo, Baby Doge, doo, doo, doo	97.72	2.25
20	If you'd like to help develop Doge, please submit ideas on G	91.24	1.42
21	How much is that Doge in the window?	92.83	1.39
22	Doge Barking at the Moon	96.84	1.16
23	Doge spelled backwards is Egod	99.03	1.00
24	SpaceX launching satellite Doge-1 to the moon next year	93.28	0.74

$$AAM_{elonmusk} = 0.907025 \times 6.2811 = 5.6971$$

The AAM is the final metric we employ to calculate the AIS. As mentioned, it represents the average MEF in relation to each user according to their ES. To recall, the MEF (*Magnitude attributable to External Factors*) is the total M adjusted for Bitcoin's M in relation to their *Pearson Correlation Coefficient*. This means that - on average - we assume that a tweet of User u will occur in a period whose MEF is equal to their AAM, or in our case, we can expect a tweet from Musk to co-occur within a period whose MEF is 5.6971. We can now move on to calculating the AIS.

AIS - Baseline: The AIS approximates the certainty with which a user's tweet will co-occur within a period whose MEF exceeds the BTF (*Breakout Threshold Factor*). This is done by dividing the AAM of user by the BTF. To address the potential for a skewed AAM and in turn a skewed AIS due to outliers, we also incorporate an *Anomaly Ratio*, which represents the ratio of tweets whose MEF

exceed the BTF (= Anomaly), compared to the total number of tweets issued by user $|T_u|$. The maximum value a user can achieve here is 100, or 100% certainty.

AIS - Penalty: From this we then deduct a *penalty*, the average difference between a tweet's MEF and the BTF (complementary values), for all tweets whose MEF did not exceed the BTF. This ensures that a user can only achieve an AIS of 100 if every single one of their tweet's MEF exceeds the BTF. Furthermore, this "punishes" users that have very low consistency in their associated MEF's, adequately adjusting the AIS if skewed to the upside by outliers. We amplify the penalty by the complementary value of the average ES to 100%, punishing users with lower ES's for failing to generate adequate engagement.

We can therefore define the AIS ($\in \mathbb{Q}$, $0 \leq x \leq 100$) as follows:

$$AIS_u = \min(\frac{AAM_u \times \frac{|Anomaly_u|}{|T_u|} \times 100}{BTF}, 100) \textbf{ (Baseline)}$$

$$-(\frac{\sum_{i \in !Anomaly} BTF - MEF_i}{|!Anomaly_u|} * (1 - \frac{\frac{\sum ES}{100}}{|T_u|}) \textbf{ (Penalty)}$$

Now we can apply the AIS calculation to our running example of Elon Musk. In our example we use a BTF of 1 and a WS of 36. Musk has issued a total of 24 tweets about Dogecoin within the timeframe between Jan 5, 2020 and May 31, 2023, 22 of which occurred within a period with a MEF above 1, 2 of which did not. This results in an *Anomaly Ratio* of 91,67% (22/24). We are left with the following calculation:

$$AIS_{musk} = \min(\frac{5,6971 \times \frac{22}{24} \times 100}{1}, 100) \textbf{ (Baseline)}$$

$$-(\frac{(1 - 1 + 1 - 0,74)}{2} * (1 - 0,907025) \textbf{ (Penalty)}$$

$$= \mathbf{99,976}$$

In other words, our model predicts a newly issued tweet of Elon Musk which matches the search term "Dogecoin OR DOGE" will co-occur within an hourly period whose V exceeds the previous 36 h's average (by a factor of 1 - which is the average; if we had set the BTF to 2 we would predict double the trading activity compared to the average) with a certainty of 99,976 %.

The AIS is naturally heavily dependent on the chosen BTF. A higher BTF requires a more substantial change in trading activity, thus raising the bar for a user to receive a high AIS. In Table 2 we demonstrate how different BTF's affect users AIS's for Dogecoin.

It becomes apparent that Musk is by far the highest ranking user for Dogecoin according to our model. When raising the BTF, other users quickly fall to single digit influence, while Musk's AIS stays pretty much unphazed. At a BTF of 10 (not shown in the table), only Musk is able to achieve an $AIS > 0$ of just 8.93,

Table 2. The AIS's for different users and different BTF's (1, 1.5, 2, 3) on May 31, 2023

BTF: 1	BTF: 1.5	BTF: 2	BTF: 3
elonmusk (99.98)	elonmusk (99.96)	elonmusk (99.92)	elonmusk (99.87)
lilyachty (60.00)	lilyachty (33.83)	frankiemuniz (15.46)	frankiemuniz (9.19)
frankiemuniz (54.22)	frankiemuniz (28.45)	KEEMSTAR (13.19)	lilyachty (4.46)
CorinnaKopf (39.99)	CorinnaKopf (21.93)	lilyachty (12.19)	KEEMSTAR (4.38)
KEEMSTAR (33.18)	KEEMSTAR (20.72)	cz_binance (7.901)	CorinnaKopf (3.52)
cz_binance (23.97)	Dexerto (13.00)	IamKrisLondon (6.71)	IamKrisLondon (3.10)
IamKrisLondon (20.60)	IamKrisLondon (12.98)	Troydan (6.63)	cz_binance (2.24)

leading us to determine that Musk is the most influential Twitter user when it comes to the suggested influence over the trading activity of Dogecoin.

To evaluate the AIS's usefulness, we will employ it as a trading indicator. Trade entries will be timed based on tweets issued by the top users ranked by the AIS and position size will be determined by their AIS.

4 Evaluation

In this section we discuss and evaluate the AIS in a trading environment. Our aim is to find the best performing configuration and compare it to simple buy-and-hold strategy as well as a trading strategy that incorporates the previous day's return and volume, price momentum and volatility. The AIS-based trading strategy was executed using our own publicly available prototypical implementation, which can be found on Github[7].

Buy-and-Hold Strategy: We compare it to a buy-and-hold strategy (also referred to as "investor"), as it a very common, hands-off investment strategy practiced by many individuals and institutions and was also used by Gjerstad et. al. [13] in a very similar evaluation setting in the context of Donald Trump and the S&P500. It relies on achieving historic market returns instead of actively managing positions. All tests will be performed on Dogecoin, as it is an asset whose price action was arguably closely tied to Twitter activity, especially that of Elon Musk. We will also showcase the AIS when applied to Bitcoin and will demonstrate, that the AIS's impact is heavily dependent on how susceptible the asset is to social media activity.

Technical Trading Strategy: The other comparison will be against the baseline strategy described by Xiao and Chen [24], who used a combination of the previous day's return and volume, price momentum and volatility as a baseline and then expanded upon said baseline to evaluate whether it could be improved by incorporating Twitter sentiment when applied to stock trading. This was the

---

[7] https://git01lab.cs.univie.ac.at/university_research/masterarbeiten/ais.

only concrete trading baseline we could find in a comparable environment. Unfortunately the authors did not describe the exact parameters they used, which is why we estimated and optimized them to the best of our ability.

We enter long or short positions when the previous day's return is positive or negative and volume as well as volatility exceed or go below their 72 h moving averages (our optimal WS) respectively. We enter every trade with 33% of the available portfolio balance (a rough estimate of the average AIS), which is also $10,000 to begin with. The exact trading script is available on Github[8] folder. It was written in Pinescript v5 and executed and backtested on Tradingview [23].

AIS-based Trading Strategy: To evaluate the AIS as a trading indicator, we iterate over the dataframes during the specified trading timeframe hour by hour, updating the TweetMaps and subsequently the AIS's for all current users, keeping a record of the top 8 users ranked by AIS. If one of the users issues a tweet, we enter a long-position (we buy Dogecoin) proportionate to that user's AIS. This means, if a user with e.g. an AIS of 15 issues a tweet, we buy Dogecoin with 15% of our available portfolio balance. If multiple users tweet during that day, we fill the positions on a first-come-first-serve basis. At the end of each day (00:00 AM), all positions, no matter the trading result, are converted back to US-dollars. If no top-user tweets, the capital sits in US-dollars, waiting to be deployed again. This comes with the added benefit of available capital for the trader - liquidity that could be used otherwise.

At any given hour, the strategy can only capture 80% of the price move. This is to emulate price moves that occurred within the hour as well as incorporate the likelihood of existing bots also utilizing tweets as buy signals.

Timeframe: We believe it is realistic to assume that an average, decently crypto-savvy investor could've started investing in Dogecoin after its first strong appearance in mainstream media at the beginning of 2021, just after it had reached 1 cent, which was on January 6, 2021. Before this date, we believe the likelihood of a rational investor with a standard risk tolerance and no insider information investing in Dogecoin to be negligible. This marks the start of our trading period. We end our evaluation on May 31, 2023, as this marks the last full month of data available at the time of performing the evaluation.

4.1   Optimizing Parameters

The AIS is heavily influenced by the user chosen parameters, those being the size of the sliding window (WS), the minimum number of issued tweets to be eligible for AIS calculation and most importantly the BTF. The parameter optimization was done semi-automatically. We used the historic data available to us to execute the trading algorithm with various parameter configurations, comparing trading performance and end-balances among the different iterations to find the best configuration.

---

[8] https://git01lab.cs.univie.ac.at/university_research/masterarbeiten/ais/-/blob/main/eval/Doge_PDR_Vol_Momentum_Vol.pine.

Breakout Threshold Factor (BTF): How the BTF influences the AIS has already been shown in Table 2. A higher BTF significantly reduces certainty of a tweet's co-occurence with the elevated $Magnitude$, therefore reducing the frequency of trades taken. The most successful BTF in terms of trading results was a BTF of 1, meaning any M above the current window's average was considered as an anomaly or elevated trading activity.

Window Size (WS): WS impacted the trading results in a bell-curve-like manner, where both very small and very large windows performed significantly worse compared to medium sized windows. We tested configurations with a WS of 6, 12, 24, 30, 36, 48, 60, 72 and 96, with the best performing WS being 72 for both Dogecoin and Bitcoin. We attribute the poor performance of smaller windows to the inability to identify proper breakouts. The smaller windows too quickly averaged out during hours of high activity, causing the algorithm to miss trades during periods of high Twitter activity. If the window is too large, it likely incorporates other high-activity periods, causing recent ones to be drowned out by previous activity. A WS of 72 seems to be a sweet spot in our evaluation scenario.

Minimum Tweets: The results for the minimum number of tweets similarly followed a bell-curve-like distribution, where both comparatively low and high numbers yielded the worst results. We tested a minimum number of 1, 2, 3, 4, 5, 6, 7 and 10 tweets. We attribute the poor performance of the low number to poor trades induced by individuals that could not be described as tastemakers, but rather lucky individuals that just happened to tweet with fortunate timing. The increase of the minimum comes at the tradeoff of the algorithm taking longer to incorporate actual tastemakers (like Musk), which explains its poor performance. The best performance was achieved with a minimum of 4 tweets.

Optimal Configuration: The best trading performance was achieved with a BTF of 1, a WS of 72 and a minimum number of tweets issued by a user of 4, for both BTC and DOGE. The full result set for all combinations can be found in CSV format on Github[9].

4.2 The AIS as a Trading Indicator

We can now backtest and plot the results of our AIS-based trading algorithm and compare them to the results of the buy-and-hold-investor as well as our technical trading strategy. As mentioned, the trading algorithm entered a long position whenever one of the top 8 AIS users issued a tweet, at 80% of that hourly candle's total price move (open - close). All positions were liquidated at the end of each day and the algorithm would be wait until further tweets occurred. The trading timeframe starts on January 6, 2021 (the date we argue a rational investor could've started investing) and ends on May 31, 2023. Both the investor and trading algorithms start with a balance of $10,000.

---

[9] https://git01lab.cs.univie.ac.at/university_research/masterarbeiten/ais/-/tree/main/eval.

The *AIS* as well as the trading algorithm were executed and tested on two separate machines with the same results.

Windows Machine: Ryzen 5 1600 (6-core CPU) and 16 GB DDR4 Memory.
MacOS Machine: M1 Macbook Air (2021) with 16 GB of Memory.

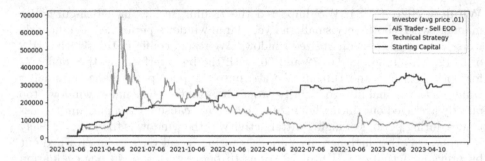

Fig. 2. Dogecoin - Comparison of *AIS* Trading Algorithm and Investor - Jan 6 2021 until May 31 2023

As shown in Fig. 2, the *AIS* algorithm was able to significantly outperform the buy-and-hold investor, while only deploying capital on 182 out of a total of 873 trading days.

In its first trading year, a period with extremely bullish price action and heavy twitter activity, it achieved a gain of 2,534% on its balance. While the buy-and-hold investor did temporarily outperform the trading algorithm, the balance after the first year amounted to $171,100, or a gain of 1,711%.

In its second trading year, a bearish period over which Dogecoin lost 60% of its value, the *AIS* algorithm managed to increase its balance by a further 16,7% to $296,030, suggesting the *AIS*'s effectiveness for Twitter-correlated assets like Dogecoin. This increase was also achieved using only long positions and no short-selling, a method that trading strategies generally employ, especially during bearish periods. The buy-and-hold investor lost 60% of their portfolio, ending the year 2022 with a balance of $68,400.

The *AIS* algorithm ended with a final balance of $301,965.93, a gain of 3,019% compared to the start, while the investor's balance stands at $72,310, a gain of 723%, on May 31, 2023. This means that the algorithm outperformed the trader by 417,6% while maintaining full liquidity 79.15% of the time. The *AIS*-based trading algorithm also displays a very strong upward trajectory, almost steadily increasing its balance during the entire trading period.

The trading strategy inspired by Xiao et. al. [24] generated a profit of 2.38% over the same period, while taking 1,798 trades. The strategy peaked at a maximum profit of 7.83% early on, but slowly lost capital afterwards. The technical strategy's performance gets dwarfed by the AIS in Fig. 2, therefore we provide a more detailed view of its performance in Fig. 3.

Fig. 3. Dogecoin - Technical Trading Strategy Performance - Jan 6 2021 until May 31 2023

The absence of exposure and only entering trades on Twitter impulses can also prove beneficial for less Twitter-correlated assets like Bitcoin. Bitcoin is arguably much less susceptible to Twitter activity due to its comparatively large market capitalization and higher trading volume as well as broader public adoption as an investment vehicle, but its price can still be susceptible to news or opinions published on Twitter. As can be seen in Fig. 4, the AIS trading algorithm was not able to capture initial highs, but still managed to nearly steadily increase its balance over the trading period by 20% to \$12,021.66 while maintaining a similar 78,4% liquidity rate, while the investor lost 12,2% over the same period with no excess liquidity.

The technical trading strategy did not execute a single trade when tested on Bitcoin, which is why it was omitted from the graph.

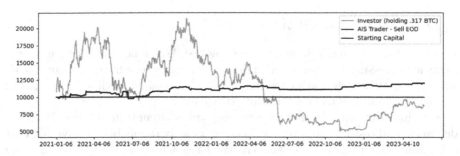

Fig. 4. Bitcoin - Comparison of AIS Trading Algorithm and Investor - Jan 6 2021 until May 31 2023

5 Related Work

Existing work fails to focus on the influence of a single user, but rather utilizes Twitter to source broad sentiment [7, 20, 22] or twitter volume [17]. Xiao et.

al. [24] incorporate sentiment analysis in addition to technical indicators (as described in our evaluation approach) to predict price direction and actually provide backtests that supplement their predictions, something that hardly any authors do.

Gjerstad et al. [13] employ a similar approach to ours by utilizing a baseline of buy-and-hold on the S&P500 and entering a temporary short position when Trump tweeted in the context of "Trade War", but their approach failed to outperform the buy-and-hold strategy. The strategy also differs from ours, as both their baseline and their trading strategy rely on holding shares of S&P500.

Oliveira et. al. [19] focus on forecasting stock market variables for the S&P500, but don't evaluate subsequent trading performance nor do they focus on individual users either.

Bollen et al. [7] used sentiment analysis on large-scale Twitter feeds and mapped the determined sentiment to the Dow Jones Industrial Average (DJIA) by using a self- organized fuzzy neural network. They were able to make a price direction with 87.6% accuracy. They did however not focus on the influence of an individual user, but rather a broad and homogenous user group. Abraham et al. [3] focused their research on tweet volume and Google trends, rather than sentiment alone. They did find significant correlation between both Google trends data as well as tweet volume and the price of Bitcoin but determined sentiment analysis to be a non-reliable indicator.

Given these limitations in existing work we saw a necessity in developing a user-agnostic, universally applicable metric to assess the suggested influence of a Twitter user over the trading activity of a cryptocurrency. Abraham et. al.'s findings of sentiment analysis not being a useful indicator in their evaluation led us to omitting this aspect for our prototypical implementation.

6   Discussion and Outlook

This paper focused on developing and testing the AIS, a novel, fully transparent metric for assessing the suggested influence twitter users have over an asset's trading activity, which was successfully evaluated against both a buy-and-hold investing, as well as a technical trading strategy.

Our challenge was to provide complete transparency in the development, calculation and testing of our metric, making it easily replicable for anybody that might want to expand on our research. We have achieved this by documenting and open-sourcing every necessary step to replicate the exact results achieved by us. We conclude that our proposed approach was successful by proving that it would've been able to outperform both a buy-and-hold investor as well as similar technical trading strategies, solely employing the AIS as a trading indicator.

We attribute the success of the AIS trading algorithm to reduced exposure during times of market downturns, effectively capturing market upside caused by Twitter activity while maintaining significant liquidity during low social media activity.

For future work we plan on incorporating the aspect of network science, specifically how users influence each other among themselves and determining the degree of influence one user has over the actions of other users. This could lead us to more efficiently discover influential users compared to our current approach.

Another aspect we plan on incorporating in future iterations is sentiment analysis. While some authors like Abraham et. al. [3] found sentiment analysis to be a non-reliable indicator, others like Bollen et. al. [7] did achieve success with it, therefore we believe this is an aspect worth exploring.

We will also explore the application of the AIS to other cryptocurrency assets and even other asset classes like stocks. Furthermore, we plan on experimenting with aspects like dynamic holding periods (the algorithm always sold at the end of the trading day), the option of short-selling during bearish market periods (the *AIS* algorithm could only enter long-positions) as well as the option to trade multiple assets simultaneously.

Finally, we only incorporated solely Twitter as a data source. For future iterations we will explore data streams from other social media networks, e.g. Facebook and LinkedIn, as well as other microblogging platforms like Mastodon or Meta's newly released Threads.

References

1. Cryptocurrency Prices, Charts And Market Capitalizations. https://coinmarketcap.com/
2. Home / Twitter (2023). https://twitter.com/home
3. Abraham, J., Higdon, D., Nelson, J., Ibarra, J.: Cryptocurrency price prediction using tweet volumes and sentiment analysis. **1**(3), 22 (2018)
4. Alostad, H., Davulcu, H.: Directional prediction of stock prices using breaking news on twitter. In: Proceedings of - IEEE/WIC/ACM Internetional Conference on Web Intelligence Agent Technology, WI-IAT, vol. 1, pp. 523–530. Institute of Electrical and Electronics Engineers Inc. (2016). https://www.scopus.com/inward/record.uri?eid=2-s2.0-85013941912&//doi=10.1109%2fWI-IAT.2015.82&partnerID=40&md5=748f91f377245996d40e1b586900c3da. journal Abbreviation: Proc. - IEEE/WIC/ACM Int. Conf. Web Intell. Intell. Agent Technol., WI-IAT
5. Bikhchandani, S., Sharma, S.: Herd behavior in financial markets. IMF Staff Papers 2001(002) (2001). https://www.elibrary.imf.org/view/journals/024/2001/002/article-A001-en.xml. iSBN: 9781451973747
6. Biswas, S., Pawar, M., Badole, S., Galande, N., Rathod, S.: Cryptocurrency price prediction using neural networks and deep learning. In: 2021 7th International Conference on Advanced Computing and Communication Systems (ICACCS), vol. 1, pp. 408–413 (2021). iSSN: 2575-7288
7. Bollen, J., Mao, H., Zeng, X.: Twitter mood predicts the stock market. J. Comput. Sci. **2**(1), 1–8 (2011)
8. Brans, H., Scholtens, B.: Under his thumb the effect of president Donald Trump's Twitter messages on the US stock market. PLoS ONE **15**(3), e0229931 (2020)
9. Cary, M.: Down with the #dogefather: evidence of a cryptocurrency responding in real time to a crypto-tastemaker. J. Theor. Appl. Electron. Commer. Res. **16**(6), 2230–2240 (2021)

10. Cheah, E.T., Fry, J.: Speculative bubbles in Bitcoin markets? An empirical investigation into the fundamental value of Bitcoin. Econ. Lett. **130**, 32–36 (2015). https://www.sciencedirect.com/science/article/pii/S0165176515000890
11. Choi, H., Varian, H.: Predicting the present with Google trends. Econ. Rec. 88(s1), 2–9 (2012). https://onlinelibrary.wiley.com///doi/abs/10.1111/j.1475-4932.2012.00809.x. number: s1 _eprint: https://onlinelibrary.wiley.com///doi/pdf/10.1111/j.1475-4932.2012.00809.x
12. Conrad, C., Custovic, A., Ghysels, E.: Long- and short-term cryptocurrency volatility components: a GARCH-MIDAS analysis. J. Risk Finan. Manage. **11**(2), 23 (2018). https://www.mdpi.com/1911-8074/11/2/23. number: 2 Publisher: Multidisciplinary Digital Publishing Institute
13. Gjerstad, P., Meyn, P., Molnar, P., Naess, T.: Do President Trump's tweets affect financial markets? Decision Support Syst. **147**, 113577 (2021)
14. Huynh, T.L.D.: When Elon Musk changes his tone, does bitcoin adjust its tune? Computational economics (2022). https://doi.org/10.1007/s10614-021-10230-6
15. Kim, G., Shin, D.H., Choi, J., Lim, S.: A deep learning-based cryptocurrency price prediction model that uses on-chain data. IEEE Access **10**, 56232–56248 (2022)
16. Lytvyniuk, K., Sharma, R., Jurek-Loughrey, A.: Predicting information diffusion in online social platforms: a twitter case study, vol. 812, p. 417 (2019). https://www.scopus.com/inward/record.uri?eid=2-s2.0-85059101499&//doi=10.1007%2f978-3-030-05411-3_33&partnerID=40&md5=e865cfcd9f26a4be31c34a65739bd3e7
17. Mao, Y., Wei, W., Wang, B.: Twitter volume spikes: analysis and application in stock trading. In: Proceedings of the 7th Workshop on Social Network Mining and Analysis, pp. 1–9. SNAKDD 2013, Association for Computing Machinery, New York, NY, USA (2013). https://dl.acm.org///doi/10.1145/2501025.2501039
18. Mohapatra, S., Ahmed, N., Alencar, P.: KryptoOracle: a real-time cryptocurrency price prediction platform using twitter sentiments. In: Baru, C., Huan, J., Khan, L., Hu, X., Ak, R., Tian, Y., Barga, R., Zaniolo, C., Lee, K., Ye, Y. (eds.) University of Waterloo, pp. 5544–5551 (2019)
19. Oliveira, N., Cortez, P., Areal, N.: Some experiments on modeling stock market behavior using investor sentiment analysis and posting volume from twitter. In: ACM International Conference Proceeding Series Association for Computing Machinery, Madrid (2013). https://www.scopus.com/inward/record.uri?eid=2-s2.0-84879739902&//doi=10.1145%2f2479787.2479811&partnerID=40&md5=962737483370786e5e6a80b61dd85346. journal Abbreviation: ACM Int. Conf. Proc. Ser
20. Pano, T., Kashef, R.: A complete VADER-based sentiment analysis of bitcoin (BTC) Tweets during the Era of COVID-19. Big Data Cogn. Comput. **4**(4), 33 (2020)
21. Stosic, D., Stosic, D., Ludermir, T.B., Stosic, T.: Collective behavior of cryptocurrency price changes. Physica A: Stat. Mech. Appl. **507**, 499–509 (2018). https://www.sciencedirect.com/science/article/pii/S0378437118305946
22. Sul, H., Dennis, A.R., Yuan, L.I.: Trading on Twitter: the financial information content of emotion in social media. In: 2014 47th Hawaii International Conference on System Sciences, pp. 806–815 (2014). iSSN: 1530–1605
23. Tradingview: Total Crypto Market Capitalization. https://www.tradingview.com/symbols/TOTAL/
24. Xiao, C., Chen, W.: Trading the Twitter Sentiment with Reinforcement Learning (2018). https://arxiv.org/abs/1801.02243. arXiv:1801.02243

Deployment and Migration in CISs

Managing the Variability of Component Implementations and Their Deployment Configurations Across Heterogeneous Deployment Technologies

Miles Stötzner[1]([✉])(iD), Uwe Breitenbücher[2](iD), Robin D. Pesl[3](iD),
and Steffen Becker[1](iD)

[1] Institute of Software Engineering, University of Stuttgart, Stuttgart, Germany
{miles.stoetzner,steffen.becker}@iste.uni-stuttgart.de
[2] Herman Hollerith Zentrum, Reutlingen University, Reutlingen, Germany
uwe.breitenbuecher@reutlingen-university.de
[3] Institute of Architecture of Application Systems, University of Stuttgart, Stuttgart,
Germany
robin.pesl@iaas.uni-stuttgart.de

Abstract. Application systems often need to be deployed in different variants if requirements that influence their implementation, hosting, and configuration differ between customers. Therefore, deployment technologies, such as Ansible or Terraform, support a certain degree of variability modeling. Besides, modern application systems typically consist of various software components deployed using multiple deployment technologies that only support their proprietary, non-interoperable variability modeling concepts. The Variable Deployment Metamodel (VDMM) manages the deployment variability across heterogeneous deployment technologies based on a single variable deployment model. However, VDMM currently only supports modeling conditional components and their relations which is sometimes too coarse-grained since it requires modeling entire components, including their implementation and deployment configuration for each different component variant. Therefore, we extend VDMM by a more fine-grained approach for managing the variability of component implementations and their deployment configurations, e.g., if a cheap version of a SaaS deployment provides only a community edition of the software and not the enterprise edition, which has additional analytical reporting functionalities built-in. We show that our extended VDMM can be used to realize variable deployments across different individual deployment technologies using a case study and our prototype OpenTOSCA Vintner.

Keywords: Deployment configuration · Deployment models ·
Variability management · Infrastructure as code · VDMM · EDMM

1 Introduction

Application systems often need to be deployed in different variants if requirements that influence their implementation, hosting, and deployment configuration differ between customers. Therefore, deployment technologies, such as Ansible or Terraform, support a certain degree of variability modeling using proprietary mechanisms that do not follow a standardized variability modeling approach. For example, Ansible and Terraform both support conditional components but use different modeling constructs: A condition can be directly assigned to a component in Ansible[1], whereas a condition can be only indirectly assigned to a component in Terraform as part of the scaling configuration by conditionally setting the instance count of the component to zero or one[2]. Since these deployment technologies have all their area of application [1], developers and operators need to understand the heterogeneous variability concepts in different technologies, which requires deep technical expertise.

Moreover, today's deployments often require the combination of multiple different deployment technologies [36]. For example, in cooperative information systems, we often need to integrate diverse systems managed by different organizations using their preferred deployment technologies. A common combination of deployment technologies is to use Terraform for provisioning virtual machines on which Ansible then installs application components. Since this virtual machine might be a conditional component, Ansible must be aware of the presence or absence of this component. Thus, the variability modeling needs to be integrated across the used deployment technologies in order to automate the entire deployment process of an application in a variable fashion. Since the common deployment technologies support only their proprietary mechanisms that are not interoperable with each other, integrated variability modeling is not possible.

Therefore, we presented the *Variable Deployment Metamodel (VDMM)* in previous work [33] that manages the deployment variability across heterogeneous deployment technologies based on a *single variable deployment model* that contains conditional elements. When the variability of a variable deployment model is resolved, a normal, fixed deployment model is derived, which conforms to the *Essential Deployment Metamodel (EDMM)* [37]. EDMM is a metamodel for declarative deployment models that can be mapped to the most popular deployment technologies, such as Ansible, Docker Compose, Terraform, and TOSCA. Furthermore, an EDMM model can be executed to deploy an application by combining different deployment technologies [36]. This solves the deficit mentioned above and, thus, provides a homogeneous method to model the presence of elements across heterogeneous deployment technologies.

However, VDMM currently only supports modeling conditional components and their relations, whereas component implementations and deployment configurations are unconditional and static. This makes the approach for many scenarios unnecessarily coarse-grained and suboptimal. For example, a cheap version of a Software-as-a-Service (SaaS) deployment provides only a community edition of the software on a small virtual machine and not the enterprise version, which has additional analytical reporting built-in and which runs in an elastic environment for enterprise customers. Furthermore, a lightweight SQLite database is used for

---

[1] Ansible: Conditionals, https://bit.ly/46KELJe.
[2] Terraform: The count Meta-Argument, https://bit.ly/44yNBaW.

the community version instead of a production-ready MySQL database for the enterprise version. Thus, the deployment configuration of the software must be configured to use the correct SQL dialect. Modeling a separate conditional component for each different combination of implementation and deployment configuration of this software quickly results in a large number of components that are error-prone to maintain. Thus, for such situations in which single components have a high variability that also depends on other conditional components, often an exponential number of conditional components is required to represent all valid deployment variants.

In this paper, we tackle this VDMM deficit and present a more fine-grained approach for managing the variability of component implementations and their deployment configurations across heterogeneous deployment technologies. Therefore, we extend VDMM by additional conditional elements through our contributions as follows. We also highlight these contributions visually in the figures.

(i) We introduce *conditional deployment artifacts* representing component implementations by extending VDMM, thus, different deployment artifacts can be deployed based on different requirements.
(ii) We introduce *conditional properties* representing deployment configurations by extending VDMM, thus, components can be differently configured based on different requirements.
(iii) We implement the *open-source prototype* OpenTOSCA Vintner based on TOSCA and the satisfiability solver MiniSat.

We show that our extended VDMM can be used to realize variable deployments across different deployment technologies based on a case study and our extended prototype OpenTOSCA Vintner [33]. In this case study, we act as a SaaS provider and manage application instances that use different deployment artifacts and are differently configured due to different customer requirements. Thereby, we make use of conditions that access the presence of elements across Ansible and Terraform, e.g., to configure the correct SQL dialect. Thus, we show that our newly introduced conditional deployment artifacts and conditional properties provide a variability modeling approach that can be applied even when integrating multiple deployment technologies, which would be challenging without our approach due to proprietary variability mechanisms.

The remainder of this work is structured as follows. Section 2 introduces a motivating scenario that is used throughout this work. In Sect. 3, we extend VDMM with conditional deployment artifacts and properties. We validate our approach by conducting a case study based on our prototype in Sect. 4. In Sect. 5, we discuss related work and conclude our work in Sect. 6.

2 Motivating Scenario

In our motivating scenario, we act as an organization that develops a web shop application and offers managed instances of this application to its customers as Software-as-a-Service (SaaS). We use this scenario throughout the entire paper to explain and validate our variability modeling approach.

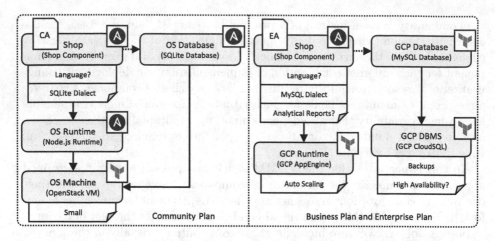

Fig. 1. The community deployment artifact of our motivating scenario deployed on the private cloud OpenStack on the left and the enterprise deployment artifact of our motivating scenario deployed on the hyperscaler Google Cloud Platform on the right.

2.1   Deployment Variants of the Motivating Scenario

The web shop application consists of a shop component that is connected to a database, as presented in Fig. 1. There exist two different Node.js implementations of the shop component: the community deployment artifact and the enterprise deployment artifact. The community deployment artifact implements the core functionality of the shop component, whereas the enterprise deployment artifact additionally implements analytical reporting functionalities. A customer can choose between different deployment variants by choosing a pricing plan that fits their requirements. These plans offer different features, such as the implementation of the shop component, auto-scaling, data backups, and analytical reporting, but also different types of databases. Besides the pricing plan, the customer can configure the display language (English, German, or Spanish) of the shop component. The following plans are available.

The *community plan* is a free plan that targets new customers who can explore the application without any costs. This plan deploys the community deployment artifact of the shop component on a virtual machine. To reduce costs and management overhead, this deployment artifact is deployed along with an SQLite database on a single small virtual machine on a private cloud powered by OpenStack, as presented on the left in Fig. 1. Since an SQLite database is used, the shop component is configured to use the SQLite dialect. This deployment does not provide any scaling capabilities, data backups, or high availability. Terraform is used to provision the virtual machine, and Ansible to install the components on this virtual machine. Thus, multiple deployment technologies are involved that must be coordinated.

The *business plan* is the first paid plan that targets small and medium businesses. In contrast to the community plan, this plan deploys the enterprise deployment artifact of the shop component on the hyperscaler Google Cloud Platform (GCP) using GCP AppEngine, which is a Platform-as-a-Service offering that provides an elastic runtime environment, as presented on the right in Fig. 1. Furthermore, the database is a MySQL database hosted on GCP CloudSQL, which has backups enabled. Since a MySQL database is used, the shop component is configured to use the MySQL dialect. However, this database is not configured to be highly available. Moreover, analytical reporting functionalities are still disabled. The customer can see only a preview but must upgrade to the *enterprise plan* to access the complete functionalities. Ansible is used to deploy the shop application, whereas the remaining components are managed by Terraform. Thus, in this deployment variant, multiple deployment technologies must be coordinated.

The *enterprise plan* is the most expensive plan and extends the business plan with access to all analytical reporting functionalities. This includes, among others, weekly sales reports along with sales forecasting. Furthermore, the database is highly available. Thus, this plan uses the same deployment artifact as the business plan but with a different configuration. As a result, this plan is well-suited for handling the production workload of enterprises.

2.2   Managing Deployment Variability of the Motivating Scenario

To automate the deployment of our motivating scenario, we use the declarative deployment modeling pattern. A *declarative deployment model* describes *what* has to be deployed in the form of a graph but not *how*. Such a graph consists of nodes and edges that represent application components, respectively relations between those components. Required deployment tasks are then automatically derived by the deployment technology. Even though we chose a simple motivating scenario, the *deployment variant space* is already huge. Managing a separate deployment model for each different possible combination quickly results in a large number of deployment models, which is error-prone and time-consuming. In fact, this results in one separate deployment model for each plan and language, thus, 9 models with a total of 120 elements.

Using a so-called *variable deployment model* [33] also leads to a large number of conditional elements, which is error-prone and time-consuming to maintain. A variable deployment model is a deployment model with conditional components and relations that have conditions assigned under which they are present after the variability has been resolved based on the requirements of a specific customer. In total, the variable deployment model of our motivating scenario contains 77 elements. For example, there is one deployment variant for the shop component for each plan and language. Thus, 9 conditional components must be modeled solely for the shop component. In addition, all the relations between the shop component and all the deployment variants of the hosting component and database must be modeled.

The current version of variable deployment models is suitable for managing the variability of deployment variants which mainly differ in the presence of components and relations. However, it is not suitable if individual components have

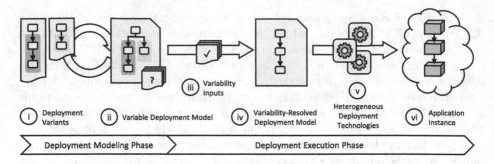

Fig. 2. Overview of the variable deployment modeling method [33].

a high variability considering their implementations and deployment configurations. In this work, we tackle this deficit and introduce conditional deployment artifacts and properties. As a result, the shop component must be only modeled once while corresponding deployment artifacts and properties have conditions assigned to specify their presence. This significantly reduces the number of elements of a variable deployment model from 77 to 28, as discussed in more detail during our validation in Sect. 4.4.

3   Extending Variable Deployment Models

In our previous work, we presented so-called *variable deployment models* [33] for modeling different deployment variants inside a single model based on conditional elements and discussed in detail how applications are modeled and deployed using this method. This concept of handling variability is known from product line engineering [26, 27] and forms a product line for deployment models. In the following, we give an overview of the method and extend the metamodel.

3.1   The Variability Deployment Modeling Method

In the following, we give an overview of the *variable deployment modeling method* [33] which consists of a *deployment modeling phase* and a *deployment execution phase*, as presented in Fig. 2.

During the first phase, a deployment expert conducts (i) a requirement analysis to identify which deployment variants of an application are required and which commonalities and differences exist. Afterward, the deployment expert creates (ii) a *variable deployment model* which is a *declarative deployment model* with conditional elements that have *variability conditions* over *variability inputs* assigned to specify their presence. Originally, this variable deployment model contains only conditional components and relations. In this work, we extend this model to also contain conditional deployment artifacts and conditional deployment configurations.

In the second phase, a human operator or a deployment system (iii) assigns values to the variability inputs based on the requirements of a specific customer.

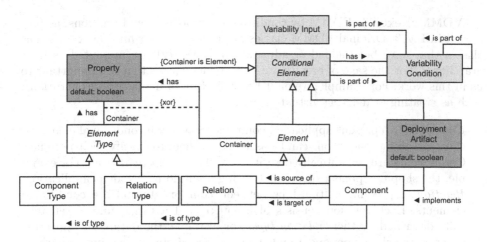

Fig. 3. Class diagram of the Variable Deployment Metamodel Version 2 (VDMMv2) (Classes originally introduced by EDMM are presented as white boxes, classes added or adjusted by VDMMv1 as light gray boxes, and classes added or adjusted by VDMMv2 as dark gray boxes).

A so-called *variability resolver* then uses these values to (iv) automatically derive the *variability-resolved deployment model*, which represents the desired deployment variant. The variability resolver is a software component that evaluates the conditions assigned to conditional elements in the variable deployment model. Thereby, all assigned conditions must hold, otherwise, the conditional element is not present in the variability-resolved deployment model, i.e., it is removed by the variability resolver. Furthermore, the variability resolver executes consistency checks to ensure that the derived deployment model is consistent, e.g., every relation must have a source and target. Such inconsistencies occur due to modeling errors and result in an inconsistent deployment model that cannot be executed. The derived deployment model is then (v) automatically deployed by combining different deployment technologies [36] and, therefore, (vi) an instance of the desired deployment variant of the application is created.

3.2 Variable Deployment Metamodel Version 1

The *Variable Deployment Metamodel Version 1 (VDMMv1)* [33] is the original VDMM and is based on the *Essential Deployment Metamodel (EDMM)* [37]. EDMM is a metamodel for declarative deployment models and is derived from an analysis of the most popular deployment technologies, including Ansible, Kubernetes, Puppet, Terraform, and TOSCA. An EDMM deployment model is represented as a graph whose nodes are application components and whose edges are relations between those components. Thereby, components and relations are configured by properties and are semantically described by a type. There exists a mapping between EDMM and the analyzed deployment technologies making EDMM the greatest common denominator of them.

VDMMv1 extends EDMM by conditional components and relations, as presented in Fig. 3. Original EDMM classes are presented as white boxes, whereas classes that have been added or adjusted by VDMMv1 are presented as light gray boxes. For the sake of brevity, we only model classes that are important to us in this work. For example, we omit the definition of management operations, such as creating or deleting virtual machines.

- *Components* represent application components and are conditional elements, thus, variability conditions can be assigned to them to specify their presence. Components are semantically described by their *component types*. For example, the shop component of our motivating scenario is a Node.js application.
- *Relations* represent relationships between components and are conditional elements. Each relation consists of a source and a target and is semantically described by their *relation type*. For example, the database connection between the shop component and the database of our motivating scenario.
- *Variability conditions* are Boolean expressions over variability inputs. They are assigned to conditional elements to specify their presence. For example, the virtual machine of our motivating scenario has a condition assigned to be only present if the community plan is selected.
- *Variability inputs* are used inside variability conditions. For example, the variability inputs for the plan and language of our motivation scenario.
- *Properties* configure components or relations. Each property consists of a property name and a property value. For example, the property that enables the analytical reporting at the shop component of our motivating scenario. We refer to components and relations as *property containers* since they *contain* their properties.
- *Deployment artifacts*[3] implement components. Each deployment artifact consists of a deployment artifact name and a deployment artifact. For example, the Node.js source code of the community deployment artifact of the shop component of our motivating scenario.

Furthermore, VDMMv1 specifies consistency checks to detect inconsistencies in the variability-resolved deployment model, as discussed in Step (iv) of our method. Such inconsistencies occur due to modeling errors. For example, a component might have two hosting relations if the assigned variability conditions do not ensure that only one hosting relation can be present. For the sake of brevity, we do not further discuss them.

3.3 Variable Deployment Metamodel Version 2

In the following, we extend VDMMv1 by conditional deployment artifacts and properties and introduce the *Variable Deployment Metamodel Version 2 (VDMMv2)*, as presented as dark gray boxes in Fig. 3.

---

[3] EDMM does not differentiate between artifacts for implementing components and artifacts for implementing management operations. This differentiation does not raise any conflicts since VDMM deployment artifacts are of type *EDMM artifact*.

- *Deployment artifacts* are extended in this work to be conditional elements, thus, variability conditions can be assigned to them to specify their presence. We do not restrict deployment artifact names to be unique within their component. Thus, it is possible to model multiple conditional deployment artifacts having the same name since some management operations expect specific names. Furthermore, deployment artifacts can be marked as the default deployment artifact that is present when there is no other deployment artifact present at the component that has the same name.
- *Properties* are extended in this work to be conditional elements, thus, variability conditions can be assigned to them to specify their presence. Similar to deployment artifacts, we do not restrict property names to be unique within their container. Thus, it is possible to model multiple conditional properties having the same property name to enable different property values based on assigned conditions, such as the language property of the shop component in our motivating scenario. Furthermore, a property can be marked as the default property that is present when there is no other property present at the component that has the same name. Note that properties that are assigned to component types and relation types are not conditional elements, as depicted by the constraint checking if the container is an element in Fig. 3.

With the newly introduced conditional elements, additional consistency checks are required to detect modeling errors regarding these new conditional elements. Therefore, we introduce the following additional consistency checks.

- Ensure that the container of each present property is present.
- Ensure that the property name of each present property is unique within its container, i.e., component or relation.
- Ensure that the component of each present deployment artifact is present.
- Ensure that the deployment artifact name of each present deployment artifact is unique within its component.

3.4 Modeling the Motivating Scenario

The variable deployment model of our motivating scenario using VDMMv2 is presented in Fig. 4. Instead of modeling 9 conditional shop components when using VDMMv1, our variable deployment model contains only a single shop component with conditional deployment artifacts and properties. Therefore, the community deployment artifact has a condition assigned to be only present when the community plan is selected. The enterprise deployment artifact is supposed to be present if either the business or enterprise plan is selected. We assign a respective condition. Also, we assign a condition that checks if the enterprise plan is selected to the analytical reports property at the shop component. Considering the language, a property for each language choice exists with a condition checking for the selected language. Similar conditions are assigned to the remaining elements (also to relations and properties whose conditions are omitted for clarity in Fig. 4). Notably, the GCP runtime managed by Terraform has a condition checking for the presence of the enterprise deployment artifact managed

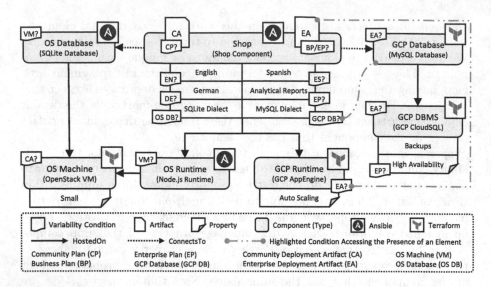

Fig. 4. Variable deployment model of our motivating scenario using VDMMv2. There are two conditions highlighted: The MySQL dialect is configured at the shop component if a MySQL database is deployed on GCP CloudSQL and the GCP AppEngine is used if the enterprise deployment artifact is present.

by Ansible. Similarly, either the SQLite or MySQL dialect is configured at the shop component, depending on which database is present. Instead of using the conditions that we chose, we could also only use conditions that check for the used plan and not, e.g., for the presence of the enterprise deployment artifact or the MySQL database. By doing so, we decouple them from the plans, which eases extensibility.

4   Prototypical Validation and Complexity Evaluation

We validate the technical feasibility of our method by implementing a prototype and by conducting a case study in which we deploy our motivating scenario. We also evaluate the complexity when modeling our motivating scenario using separate deployment models, VDMMv1, and VDMMv2. The prototype is based on the *Topology and Orchestration Specification for Cloud Applications (TOSCA)* [25], which is an open standard for the deployment and management of cloud applications in a vendor-neutral and technology-independent manner. We model the variability directly in TOSCA and not in EDMM and generate TOSCA models instead of EDMM models. However, to guarantee to be EDMM-conform, we only use modeling concepts from *TOSCA Light* [38], which is a subset of TOSCA which can be mapped directly to EDMM.

4.1   Variability4TOSCA

Variability4TOSCA [33] is a TOSCA extension for managing variability. The full specification, along with examples, is publicly available on GitHub[4]. In the following, we briefly describe the mapping of VDMMv2 to TOSCA and extend Variability4TOSCA for VDMMv2.

In TOSCA, an application is modeled as a *topology template* which consists of *node templates* and *relationship templates*. Node templates represent application components and correspond to VDMMv2 components, while relationship templates represent relationships between node templates and, thus, correspond to VDMMv2 relations. Furthermore, they are configured using *properties* corresponding to VDMMv2 properties. Node templates and relationship templates are semantically described by their *node types* and their *relationship types*, which correspond to VDMMv2 component types and VDMMv2 relation types, respectively. Node templates are implemented by *deployment artifacts*, which correspond to VDMMv2 deployment artifacts.

In our previous work [33], we extended TOSCA to Variability4TOSCA and introduced *variability conditions* and *variability inputs* in TOSCA. Variability conditions are modeled with their variability inputs inside a *variability definition* as part of the topology template and can be assigned to node templates and relationship templates to model their conditional presence. We apply this concept to further extend Variability4TOSCA by conditional deployment artifacts and properties. Also, deployment artifacts and properties can be marked as the default deployment artifact and property, respectively.

4.2   OpenTOSCA Vintner

OpenTOSCA Vintner[5] is an open-source TOSCA management and preprocessing layer written in TypeScript. For this work, we extend the already existing *Variability4TOSCA model importer* and *variability resolver* of OpenTOSCA Vintner to support conditional deployment artifacts and properties. Furthermore, we integrate the satisfiability solver MiniSat[6] to support cyclic dependencies regarding the presence of elements. MiniSat is originally written in C++ but has been compiled to JavaScript[7]. The architecture is presented in Fig. 5.

To deploy an application, the user imports the corresponding Variability4TOSCA model along with variability inputs either using the command line or the REST API. This realizes Step (iii) of our method. The Variability4TOSCA model is then transformed into an internal data structure using the *Variability4TOSCA model importer*. This internal data structure is then passed to the *variability resolver*. The variability resolver realizes Step (iv) of our method and, thus, (a) computes the presence of the conditional elements with the use of the satisfiability solver MiniSat, (b) removes absent elements, and (c) checks

---

[4] https://github.com/OpenTOSCA/opentosca-vintner.
[5] https://vintner.opentosca.org.
[6] http://minisat.se.
[7] https://github.com/meteor/logic-solver.

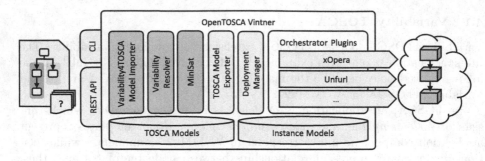

Fig. 5. System architecture of OpenTOSCA Vintner (added or adjusted components are presented as dark gray boxes).

the consistency. The *TOSCA model exporter* then exports a variability-resolved TOSCA-conform model, which is then passed to the *deployment manager*. The deployment manager realizes Steps (v) and (vi) of our method and uses orchestrator plugins for the deployment of the derived TOSCA model. Currently, we have implemented an integration for the TOSCA orchestrators Unfurl[8] and xOpera[9].

4.3 Deploying the Motivating Scenario

We continue our case study by modeling the Variability4TOSCA model of our motivating scenario and by deploying it for a customer who requires the enterprise plan. The executable Variability4TOSCA model, along with a step-by-step guide, is publicly available on GitHub. The case study shows that our TOSCA extension and the implemented prototype provide the required capabilities for the presented conditional deployment artifacts and conditional properties.

In the deployment modeling phase, we conduct a requirements analysis as described in Step (i) of our method and identify that we require one deployment variant for each plan. In addition, the display language must be configurable independently of the plan. After the requirement analysis, we follow Step (ii) of our method and create a Variability4TOSCA model, as presented in Fig. 4. Notably, our model uses only TOSCA Light [38] features, thus, when variability is resolved, a TOSCA Light model is generated that can be directly mapped to EDMM.

In the execution deployment phase, as described in Step (iii) of our method, we first analyze the requirements of our customer, who requires the enterprise plan and English as the display language. Afterward, we import the Variability4TOSCA model into OpenTOSCA Vintner along with the variability inputs using the command line. OpenTOSCA Vintner then automatically resolves the variability and generates a TOSCA-conform model, as described in Step (iv) of our method. This TOSCA-conform model, which also conforms to TOSCA Light, is then automatically passed to Unfurl, which executes the model and,

---

[8] https://github.com/onecommons/unfurl.
[9] https://github.com/xlab-si/xopera-opera.

thus, deploys the enterprise deployment artifact on GCP AppEngine using Ansible and a MySQL database using Terraform on GCP CloudSQL, as described in Step (v) and (vi) of our method. Since a MySQL database is used, the enterprise deployment artifact is configured to use the MySQL dialect.

4.4 Complexity Evaluation

With the introduction of VDMMv2, we significantly reduce the number of models and elements that need to be modeled. Considering our motivating scenario, when using a separate deployment model for each deployment variant, 9 separate deployment models (one for each plan and language combination) are required, which have in total 120 elements (36 components, 30 relations, 45 properties, and 9 artifacts) (See Footnote 4). This number can be already reduced by using a single variable deployment model using VDMMv1, resulting in a total of 77 elements (16 components, 22 relations, 30 properties, and 9 artifacts) since components and relations that are present in several deployment variants must be modeled only once. However, this number can be further reduced by using VDMMv2, resulting in a total of 28 elements (7 nodes, 7 relations, 12 properties, and 2 artifacts) since VDMMv2 introduces conditional deployment artifacts and conditional properties, thus, providing a more fine-grained variability modeling approach than VDMMv1. As a result, component variants do not need to be modeled as separate conditional components but are modeled as a single conditional component having conditional deployment artifacts and conditional properties.

Considering the generalizability of the case study, the complexity reduction also holds for other scenarios because, due to the presented more fine-grained variability approach, the same elements do not need not be modeled multiple times but only once. Note that the executable TOSCA Light models have additional properties, such as credentials for the cloud provider. We decided to omit these in our analysis for a better alignment with our figures. When taking these properties into account, the complexity reduction still holds.

5   Related Work

We discuss related work in the context of variability management of architectural models and deployment models. In general, we use established concepts to model variability applied in the domain of deployment models that can be directly executed to deploy and manage applications. Furthermore, we address the variability management across heterogeneous deployment technologies by generating EDMM models.

Software product line engineering [26,27] is a methodology to manage the variability of software. A generator derives a specific software variant based on a product configuration. This configuration contains decisions about which features are enabled and is used by the generator, e.g., to remove software modules whose presence conditions do not hold. Features and their dependencies are modeled in a feature model. We use the concept of conditional elements in our domain to manage the deployment variability. Thereby, the product configuration corresponds to variability inputs and the generator to our variability resolver. Feature modeling is part of the so-called *problem space*, whereas the generation process is part of the so-called *solution space* on which we focus.

Czarnecki and Antkiewicz [6] present a general product line engineering approach for mapping feature models to domain models using presence conditions. In this approach, an element can only be present if its container is also present. Additionally, they discuss meta-expressions that are used to compute attributes of model elements like names. They evaluate their approach using UML class and activity diagrams. We employ a similar process but tailored to deployment models and use consistency checks to ensure that required containers are present.

Moreover, Czarnecki and Antkiewicz [6] discuss patching and simplifying the derived model after resolving variability. Considering our domain, such processing could be used to complete or refine variability-resolved deployment models with missing components and configurations. For example, abstract components that represent cloud patterns, such as an elastic platform, are refined into concrete components, or new components are added to fulfill pending relations. Related work on such processing methods for TOSCA and EDMM [13–15,31] can be easily integrated into our approach.

Modeling the deployment of applications along with their configuration using product line engineering has been researched in, e.g., [16–18,20,22,24,28,32,35]. Typically, one or potentially multiple feature models are used to model different configuration aspects and their dependencies, such as resource location or resource consumption, in the problem space. In contrast, we provide a metamodel to model the variability of deployment models in the solution space. Thus, this related work complements our work since a feature selection can be used as variability inputs for our variability resolver.

Another well-researched product line engineering field is the extension of UML [5,8,9,19,29,34,39] for managing variability. Typically stereotypes are used, e.g., to model optional and alternative components, and the Object Constraint Language is used to define constraints, such as conflicts or requirements between components. Variability is also discussed in the context of UML deployment diagrams [8,9,34], which visualize the allocation of artifacts to nodes and the connections between nodes. In contrast, we operate on EDMM, which can be mapped to several deployment technologies. Furthermore, in contrast to UML deployment diagrams, deployment models can be directly executed.

Mietzner [23] addresses the problem of managing the variability of applications based on product line engineering with a focus on multi-tenancy. An application is modeled using an application model, whereas variability is modeled using an orthogonal variability model consisting of variability points and their dependencies. Similarly to our conditional properties, variability points have different alternatives with conditions assigned used to configure components. In contrast to Mietzner, we also explicitly model conditional deployment artifacts and architectural variability, whereas Mietzner focuses on the configuration of components.

Le Nhan et al. [21] present a product line for virtual machine images along with the deployment of applications. They transform a feature model into a Chef deployment model. In contrast, we focus on the metamodel for such kinds of transformations and do not only support Chef but also, e.g., Ansible and TOSCA, due to the use of EDMM. Furthermore, their approach is restricted to virtual machines, whereas we generate a deployment model for arbitrary applications.

Glaser [11] present a metamodel for extracting information out of domain models to configure TOSCA models. Thereby, they optimize the configuration of components with the goal of optimizing resource usage of the hosting environment. In contrast, they do not consider any architectural variability.

Moreover, we rely on EDMM [36] for combining heterogeneous deployment technologies. There is related work [2-4,7,10,12,30] that also generates deployment technology-specific models or artifacts out of abstract models using, e.g., model-to-model and model-to-text transformations. However, none of these focus on deployment variability management considering conditional components, relations, configurations, and deployment artifacts.

6   Conclusion

We present an integrated variability modeling approach for the deployment variability of component implementations and deployment configurations across heterogeneous deployment technologies to cope with an exponential amount of variants. Therefore, we extend VDMM by conditional deployment artifacts and properties. This significantly reduces the number of conditional components and relations that would have been required to model for each implementation and deployment configuration variant of a component. Since our metamodel is based on EDMM, our variability management is integrated across deployment technologies to which EDMM can be mapped. This includes, among others, Ansible, Docker Compose, Terraform, and TOSCA. We show the validity of our concept in a case study using our prototype OpenTOSCA Vintner and the deployment technologies Ansible and Terraform.

In future work, we plan to introduce a variability modeling approach considering the conditional use of deployment technologies. Moreover, we plan to automatically generate conditions, e.g., to remove a virtual machine that is not required anymore since it does not host any components anymore.

Acknowledgements. This publication was partially funded by the German Federal Ministry for Economic Affairs and Climate Action (BMWK) as part of the Software-Defined Car (SofDCar) project (19S21002).

References

1. Bergmayr, A., et al.: A systematic review of cloud modeling languages. ACM Comput. Surv. (CSUR) **51**(1), 1–38 (2018)
2. Bogo, M., Soldani, J., Neri, D., Brogi, A.: Component-aware orchestration of cloud-based enterprise applications, from TOSCA to Docker and Kubernetes. Softw. Pract. Experience **50**(9), 1793–1821 (2020)
3. Brabra, H., Mtibaa, A., Gaaloul, W., Benatallah, B., Gargouri, F.: Model-driven orchestration for cloud resources. In: 2019 IEEE 12th International Conference on Cloud Computing (CLOUD), pp. 422–429 (2019)
4. Chiari, M., et al.: DOML: a new modelling approach to infrastructure-as-code. In: Indulska, M., Reinhartz-Berger, I., Cetina, C., Pastor, O. (eds.) CAiSE 2023. LNCS, vol. 13901, pp. 297–313. Springer, Cham (2023). https://doi.org/10.1007/978-3-031-34560-9_18 ISBN 978-3-031-34560-9
5. Clauß, M., Jena, I.: Modeling variability with UML. In: GCSE 2001 Young Researchers Workshop, Citeseer (2001)
6. Czarnecki, K., Antkiewicz, M.: Mapping features to models: a template approach based on superimposed variants. In: Glück, R., Lowry, M. (eds.) GPCE 2005. LNCS, vol. 3676, pp. 422–437. Springer, Heidelberg (2005). https://doi.org/10.1007/11561347_28 ISBN 978-3-540-31977-1
7. Di Cosmo, R., Eiche, A., Mauro, J., Zacchiroli, S., Zavattaro, G., Zwolakowski, J.: Automatic deployment of services in the cloud with Aeolus blender. In: Barros, A., Grigori, D., Narendra, N.C., Dam, H.K. (eds.) ICSOC 2015. LNCS, vol. 9435, pp. 397–411. Springer, Heidelberg (2015). https://doi.org/10.1007/978-3-662-48616-0_28 ISBN 978-3-662-48616-0
8. Dobrica, L., Niemelä, E.: Modeling variability in the software product line architecture of distributed services. In: Proceedings of the 2007 International Conference on Software Engineering Research & Practice, SERP 2007, Las Vegas Nevada, USA, 25–28 June 2007, vol. I, pp. 269–275. CSREA Press (2007)
9. Dobrica, L., Niemelä, E.: A UML-based variability specification for product line architecture views. In: Proceedings of the Third International Conference on Software and Data Technologies - Volume 3: ICSOFT, pp. 234–239. INSTICC (2008). ISBN 978-989-8111-52-4, ISSN 2184-2833
10. Düllmann, T.F., van Hoorn, A.: Model-driven generation of microservice architectures for benchmarking performance and resilience engineering approaches. In: Proceedings of the 8th ACM/SPEC on International Conference on Performance Engineering Companion, ICPE 2017, Companion, pp. 171–172. Association for Computing Machinery, New York (2017). ISBN 9781450348997
11. Glaser, F.: Domain model optimized deployment and execution of cloud applications with TOSCA. In: Grabowski, J., Herbold, S. (eds.) SAM 2016. LNCS, vol. 9959, pp. 68–83. Springer, Cham (2016). https://doi.org/10.1007/978-3-319-46613-2_5 ISBN 978-3-319-46613-2
12. Guillén, J., Miranda, J., Murillo, J.M., Canal, C.: A service-oriented framework for developing cross cloud migratable software. J. Syst. Softw. **86**(9), 2294–2308 (2013). ISSN 0164-1212
13. Harzenetter, L., Breitenbücher, U., Falkenthal, M., Guth, J., Krieger, C., Leymann, F.: Pattern-based deployment models and their automatic execution. In: Proceedings of the 11th IEEE/ACM International Conference on Utility and Cloud Computing (UCC 2018), pp. 41–52. IEEE Computer Society (2018)

14. Harzenetter, L., Breitenbücher, U., Falkenthal, M., Guth, J., Leymann, F.: Pattern-based deployment models revisited: automated pattern-driven deployment configuration. In: Proceedings of the Twelfth International Conference on Pervasive Patterns and Applications (PATTERNS 2020), pp. 40–49. Xpert Publishing Services (2020). ISBN 978-1-61208-783-2

15. Hirmer, P., Breitenbücher, U., Binz, T., Leymann, F.: Automatic topology completion of TOSCA-based cloud applications. In: Proceedings des CloudCycle14 Workshops auf der 44. Jahrestagung der Gesellschaft für Informatik e.V. (GI). LNI, vol. 232, pp. 247–258. Gesellschaft für Informatik e.V. (GI), Bonn (2014)

16. Hochgeschwender, N., Gherardi, L., Shakhirmardanov, A., Kraetzschmar, G.K., Brugali, D., Bruyninckx, H.: A model-based approach to software deployment in robotics. In: 2013 IEEE/RSJ International Conference on Intelligent Robots and Systems, pp. 3907–3914 (2013)

17. Jamshidi, P., Pahl, C.: Orthogonal variability modeling to support multi-cloud application configuration. In: Ortiz, G., Tran, C. (eds.) ESOCC 2014. CCIS, vol. 508, pp. 249–261. Springer, Cham (2015). https://doi.org/10.1007/978-3-319-14886-1_23

18. Jansen, S., Brinkkemper, S.: Modelling deployment using feature descriptions and state models for component-based software product families. In: Dearle, A., Eisenbach, S. (eds.) CD 2005. LNCS, vol. 3798, pp. 119–133. Springer, Heidelberg (2005). https://doi.org/10.1007/11590712_10 ISBN 978-3-540-32281-8

19. Junior, E.A.O., de Souza Gimenes, I.M., Maldonado, J.C.: Systematic management of variability in UML-based software product lines. J. Univers. Comput. Sci. **16**(17), 2374–2393 (2010)

20. Kumara, I.P., Ariz, M., Baruwal Chhetri, M., Mohammadi, M., Heuvel, W.J.V.D., Tamburri, D.A.A.: FOCloud: feature model guided performance prediction and explanation for deployment configurable cloud applications. IEEE Trans. Serv. Comput. **16**, 302–314 (2022)

21. Le Nhan, T., Sunyé, G., Jézéquel, J.-M.: A model-driven approach for virtual machine image provisioning in cloud computing. In: De Paoli, F., Pimentel, E., Zavattaro, G. (eds.) ESOCC 2012. LNCS, vol. 7592, pp. 107–121. Springer, Heidelberg (2012). https://doi.org/10.1007/978-3-642-33427-6_8 ISBN 978-3-642-33427-6

22. Lee, K.C.A., Segarra, M.T., Guelec, S.: A deployment-oriented development process based on context variability modeling. In: 2014 2nd International Conference on Model-Driven Engineering and Software Development (MODELSWARD), pp. 454–459 (2014)

23. Mietzner, R.: A method and implementation to define and provision variable composite applications, and its usage in cloud computing. Ph.D. thesis, Universität Stuttgart, Fakultät Informatik, Elektrotechnik und Informationstechnik (2010)

24. Mietzner, R., Leymann, F.: A self-service portal for service-based applications. In: Proceedings of IEEE International Conference on Service-Oriented Computing and Applications (SOCA 2010). IEEE (2010)

25. OASIS: TOSCA Simple Profile in YAML Version 1.3. Organization for the Advancement of Structured Information Standards (OASIS) (2020)

26. Pohl, K., Böckle, G., van der Linden, F.: Software Product Line Engineering. Springer, Heidelberg (2005)

27. Pohl, K., Metzger, A.: Software product lines. In: Gruhn, V., Striemer, R. (eds.) The Essence of Software Engineering, pp. 185–201. Springer, Cham (2018). https://doi.org/10.1007/978-3-319-73897-0_11 ISBN 978-3-319-73897-0

28. Quinton, C., Romero, D., Duchien, L.: Automated selection and configuration of cloud environments using software product lines principles. In: 2014 IEEE 7th International Conference on Cloud Computing, pp. 144–151 (2014)
29. Razavian, M., Khosravi, R.: Modeling variability in the component and connector view of architecture using UML. In: 2008 IEEE/ACS International Conference on Computer Systems and Applications, pp. 801–809 (2008). ISSN 2161-5330
30. Sandobalin, J., Insfran, E., Abrahao, S.: An infrastructure modelling tool for cloud provisioning. In: 2017 IEEE International Conference on Services Computing (SCC), pp. 354–361 (2017)
31. Soldani, J., Breitenbücher, U., Brogi, A., Frioli, L., Leymann, F., Wurster, M.: Tailoring technology-agnostic deployment models to production-ready deployment technologies. In: Ferguson, D., Helfert, M., Pahl, C. (eds.) CLOSER 2021. CCIS, pp. 1–24. Springer, Cham (2022). https://doi.org/10.1007/978-3-031-21637-4_1 ISBN 978-3-031-21637-4
32. Sousa, G., Rudametkin, W., Duchien, L.: Automated setup of multi-cloud environments for microservices applications. In: 2016 IEEE 9th International Conference on Cloud Computing (CLOUD), pp. 327–334 (2016)
33. Stötzner, M., Becker, S., Breitenbücher, U., Kálmán, K., Leymann, F.: Modeling different deployment variants of a composite application in a single declarative deployment model. Algorithms 15(10), 382 (2022)
34. Sun, C., Rossing, R., Sinnema, M., Bulanov, P., Aiello, M.: Modeling and managing the variability of web service-based systems. J. Syst. Softw. 83(3), 502–516 (2010). ISSN 0164-1212
35. Tahri, A., Duchien, L., Pulou, J.: Using feature models for distributed deployment in extended smart home architecture. In: Weyns, D., Mirandola, R., Crnkovic, I. (eds.) ECSA 2015. LNCS, vol. 9278, pp. 285–293. Springer, Cham (2015). https://doi.org/10.1007/978-3-319-23727-5_24 ISBN 978-3-319-23727-5
36. Wurster, M., et al.: Automating the deployment of distributed applications by combining multiple deployment technologies. In: Proceedings of the 11th International Conference on Cloud Computing and Services Science (CLOSER 2021), pp. 178–189. SciTePress (2021)
37. Wurster, M., et al.: The Essential Deployment Metamodel: a systematic review of deployment automation technologies. SICS Softw.-Intensive Cyber-Phys. Syst. 35, 63–75 (2019)
38. Wurster, M., Breitenbücher, U., Harzenetter, L., Leymann, F., Soldani, J., Yussupov, V.: TOSCA Light: bridging the gap between the TOSCA specification and production-ready deployment technologies. In: Proceedings of the 10th International Conference on Cloud Computing and Services Science (CLOSER 2020), pp. 216–226. SciTePress (2020)
39. Ziadi, T., Hélouët, L., Jézéquel, J.-M.: Towards a UML profile for software product lines. In: van der Linden, F.J. (ed.) PFE 2003. LNCS, vol. 3014, pp. 129–139. Springer, Heidelberg (2004). https://doi.org/10.1007/978-3-540-24667-1_10 ISBN 978-3-540-24667-1

Adaptive Multi-agent System for Dynamic Clustering Applied to Itineraries Regularities and Traffic Prediction

Alexandre Perles[1]([✉])(iD), Ha Nhi Ngo[1,2](iD), Elsy Kaddoum[1](iD), and Valérie Camps[1](iD)

[1] IRIT, University of Toulouse, CNRS, Toulouse INP, UT3, UT2J, Toulouse, France
{alexandre.perles,ha-nhi.ngo,elsy.kaddoum,valerie.camps}@irit.fr
[2] Continental Digital Services France, Toulouse, France
ha-nhi.ngo@continental.com

Abstract. Nowadays, electronic devices such as mobile phones, sensors embedded in vehicles, and more generally digital acquisition devices continuously provide information relating the state of the surrounding environment at nearly real-time. These data provide important information required for real-time systems monitoring such as temperature regulation in smart building, traffic planning to relieve network congestion in smart cities, etc. The growing demand for analysing such data encourages researchers to adopt an approach known as "streaming analysis" which aims at processing data streams at real-time to continuously capture data evolution over time. Data stream clustering approaches already exist but require keeping in memory all the input data and have a slow adaptation to data changes. To solve these problems, we propose to agentify the clusters and allow them to fuse and evolve locally and autonomously. This work presents AMAS4DC a generic Dynamic Clustering model based on Adaptive Multi-Agent System approach. AMAS4DC processes acquired data on the fly using local similarity evaluation for cluster's creation or fusion. AMAS4DC is then instantiated on two use cases: the dynamic clustering of itineraries to detect regularities and the dynamic clustering of traffic data to predict future traffic. The conducted experiments underline the performance of AMAS4DC in terms of memory usage, processing time and clustering quality compared to well-known models for dynamic clustering.

Keywords: Dynamic clustering · Cooperative multi-agent system · Data stream analysis

1 Introduction

Data clustering aims at grouping similar data together, allowing to detect different structures, analyse these data and extract important information. Traditionally carried out offline (i.e. on all acquired data at once), requirements have

M. Sellami et al. (Eds.): CoopIS 2023, LNCS 14353, pp. 79–96, 2024.
https://doi.org/10.1007/978-3-031-46846-9_5

now evolved due to the growing quantity of collected data and the frequency of acquisition. It is now necessary to be able to take **new data into account on the fly** by adjusting learned data without having to start the process all over again. On top of this, data is likely to evolve. Thus, it is no longer just a question of placing new data in existing clusters. It is important to consider the evolution of clusters. Finally, given the growing amount of data, it is not feasible to keep all of it in memory when clusters evolve. However, deleting certain data (because of their age or poor representation, for example) can lead to the loss of information that could be useful.

This paper presents a **generic data stream clustering model** enabling a significant reduction of memory usage while maintaining a high clustering quality. It is based on an **adaptive Multi-Agent System (MAS)** approach, providing clustering techniques with the following characteristics:

- Distributing the computation, which is ideal for edge-computing and load distribution.
- Scalability, which means that the clustering is able the handle huge amount of data stream.
- Autonomous decisions performed by the agents leading to creation and modification of clusters based on rules that can be different for all agents.
- Openness, allowing the system to take into account new data arriving dynamically without restarting the process.

This article is structured as follows: Sect. 2 addresses related work on dynamic clustering methods underlining their advantages and limitations and presents the Adaptive Multi-Agent System approach. The dynamic clustering problem is formalised in Sect. 3. The AMAS4DC model is then presented in Sect. 4, before its instantiation on two use cases: searching for regularities in itineraries (Sect. 5), and traffic prediction (Sect. 6). Finally, the paper is concluded with a review of the main presented points and some perspectives.

2   Related Works

Streaming analysis includes the studies of mining techniques for data in a stream. A data stream can be defined as a sequence of potentially infinite data points arriving continuously over time and coming from geographically distributed sensors [19]. The properties of data stream make the access and the storage of all data impractical. Thus, in order to analyse the structure of data stream, the dynamic clustering technique has been widely explored [10] thanks to its ability of flexible structural changes referring to the following behaviors: (1) create new clusters when detecting novel data behaviors, (2) adjust or update the centroid of clusters when aggregating new data, (3) merge clusters when their centroids are close to each other and (4) split clusters containing dispersed data.

CluStream [1] and DenStream [5] are the most well-known clustering algorithms for data stream. Their clustering process is divided into 2 phases: **online micro-cluster creation** and **offline macro-cluster creation**. In the first phase, micro-clusters are constructed using an online similarity evaluation mechanism. The final clusters are determined in phase two by applying K-Means [2] or DBSCAN [7] algorithms on the set of micro-clusters centroids. CluStream and DenStream enable the online construction of clusters from the arrival data stream. However, the final clustering structure is still determined by the offline algorithms, which are inadequate for the continuous and infinite data stream. To fill this gap, the clustering algorithms based on Self-Organising Maps (SOM) provide the fully online data stream processing by combining SOM with Growing Neural Gas (GNG) [3,8,9] and Density-Based Clustering [13]. These methods capture data structure by finding topological structures that closely reflect the structure of the input distribution. However, these models were tested on applications with homogeneous clusters. That means, clusters have same assignment decision and same data nature/characteristic.

To enable the local decision at cluster level, a clustering system needs to distribute the assignment decision at cluster level and decentralise the control and data storage. This requirement can be satisfied by the Multi-Agent System (MAS) paradigm. The aims of MAS is to decentralise the modeling and distribute the global task at agent's levels. An agent is defined as an autonomous entity pursuing its own local goal, having partial knowledge on the system environment. Agents have to cooperate together to achieve the global goal of the system that cannot be reached individually. During their interactions, agents can autonomously organise and evolve to adapt to different situations and solve potential conflicts. Work in [11] introduces a self-organisation mechanism to form the clusters with continuous adaptive decisions. Agent's actions are evaluated, and they are validated if these actions allow to increase the overall system performance (e.g. density of cluster as used in [11]). [6] presents a multi-agent clustering system whereby each cluster is agentified. The decisions of cluster agents are based on K-Means and KNN strategies. The K-Means-based strategy aims to minimize the sum of distance from all data points to their nearest cluster. Meanwhile, the objectives of KNN-based strategy is to ensure that each data point is assigned to its closest cluster. However, the existing MAS-based clustering methods need to memorize all the historical data to evaluate agent's actions. That is why for data stream, this requirement can lead to high demand of storing capacity and costly computational capacity due to the huge amount of arrival data.

This paper presents an adaptive Multi-Agent System for data clustering called AMAS4DC. It is designed to fulfill the following requirements:

1. A limited memory usage, among all the received data, only the most representative ones have to be stored.
2. A dynamic structure of the established clusters: new clusters can be added at runtime, clusters can dynamically fuse with each other if required.

3   Problem Formalisation

In data stream clustering, data is added continuously, which is characterised as a sequence of potentially infinite, dynamically changing data over time. Thus, the data stream clustering problem can be formalised as:

> **given as input**: $DS = \{DP_{t_1}, \ldots, DP_{t_N}\}$ a data stream consisting of a sequence of N data points arriving at times $t_1, \ldots, t_N$,
> where $DP_{t_n} = (dp_{t_n}^i), (i = 1, \ldots, I)$ a data point added at time t_n represented as a vector of I characteristics.
> **provide as output**: $CR_{t_n} = \{C_1, \ldots, C_M\}$ a set of clusters C_x obtained from all the data points added until time t_n with $M \leq N$ and each C_x is a cluster represented by a representative data point called centroid.

The centroid is computed as a combination of the values V of the different input data points (i.e. generally an average) considered **similar** to this cluster. When a new data point is added, the set of clusters evolve by:

- adding a new cluster: $CR_{t_{n+1}} = \{C_1, \ldots, C_M, C_{M+1}\}$
- or modifying an existing cluster: $CR_{t_{n+1}} = \{C_1, \ldots, C_j^*, \ldots, C_M\}$ where C_j^* is the cluster that has been modified by integrating the new acquired data point.

When a data point is added, it is compared to the centroid of existing clusters. This comparison is made with a **similarity function** that determine the degree of similarity between a data point and a centroid. When comparing the new data point to existing clusters, two situations occur: (i) if one or multiple clusters have a similarity score higher than a given **fusion threshold**, then they will be fused with the new data point, to form a new cluster with an updated centroid; (ii) if no clusters have a similarity score higher than the threshold, then a new cluster is created. The similarity function and threshold depend on the studied use case.

Based on this formalisation, we propose AMAS4DC, a generic agent model, to solve the data stream clustering problem. AMAS4DC is then instantiated on two different use cases.

4   AMAS4DC: Adaptive Multi-agent System for Dynamic Clustering

As stated in Sect. 1, MAS approach can provide clustering techniques with interesting characteristics such as distribution, openness, decentralised and autonomous decisions. Based on that, we investigate an adaptive MAS approach to perform the dynamic data stream clustering as formalised in the previous section. As the main point is to enable local decision at cluster level, agents of AMAS4DC are made up of Cluster Agents (CA) created as data arrives.

The CA Behavior. CA have been designed as states machines where transitions happen depending on the exchanged messages between them. Figure 1 presents these states and the transitions from one to another. Five different states are distinguished:

- **Init**: the agent is created in an initialising state and provided with the list of already existing cluster agents. Depending on the considered application, this list can be shortened to only potentially similar clusters. CA starts by sending a *request for similarity message* to agents in this list;
- **Waiting for reply**: in this state, the agent is waiting for the similarity scores of the contacted agents;
- **Deciding**: the agent has received all the replies and is now deciding if it is possible to fuse or not with already existing cluster agents (Algorithm 1);
- **Dormant**: agents in this state are considered as representative cluster of the acquired data, they wait for similarity score requests from other agents;
- **Active**: the agent computes and sends the similarity score between its centroid and the acquired data point of the arriving CA (Algorithm 2). In case the computed similarity score is greater than or equal to the fusion threshold, the agent decides to delete itself after sending its cluster information. Indeed, in this case, the agent requesting the similarity score will fuse with it.

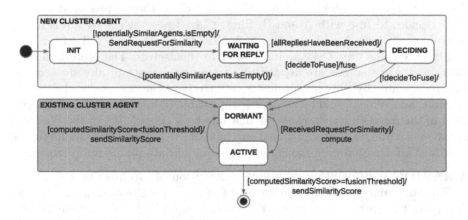

Fig. 1. Cluster Agents' states

In the deciding state, the cluster agent decides to fuse with all the cluster agents computing a similarity score above a fusion threshold τ. It is then considered as the representative cluster of these agents that decide to delete themselves. If no cluster with the similarity score above τ is detected, the new CA switches to the dormant state.

By deciding to fuse or not, the agents form a set of clusters where the centroid of each cluster is computed as a combination of initial data points and a set of Additional Values (AV) such as the number of fused data points. Those AV are used to compensate the removal of acquired data points.

Algorithm 1. CA behaviour in DECIDING state

1: **if** any received score is higher or equal to the similarity score **then**
2:      **for** $A \in$ agents where A.similarityScore $>= fusionThreshold$ **do**
3:          fuse(A, current)
4:      **end for**
5: **end if**
6: $state_{next} \leftarrow DORMANT$

Algorithm 2. CA behaviour in ACTIVE state

1: $similarityScore \leftarrow computeSimilarityScore()$
2: Send similarity score to requester CA
3: **if** $similarityScore >= fusionThreshold$ **then**
4:      Send cluster information to requester CA
5:      $state_{next} \leftarrow DEAD$ ▷ The requester CA will absorb this CA
6: **else**
7:      $state_{next} \leftarrow DORMANT$
8: **end if**

Fusing Clusters. When a CA decides to fuse with one or multiple other clusters, it starts a fusion process that works as follows: Let A and B be two existing clusters, C a new cluster and CA_A, CA_B and CA_C their representative CAs. CA_C decides to fuse with A and B. First, CA_C fuses with A by adjusting its centroid to include A and updating the AVs. Then, modified CA_C fuses with B using the same way. CA_A and CA_B delete themselves. The centroid adjustments and AVs updates are dependent on the importance of already acquired data represented by the existing clusters relatively to the new acquired data. For example, an average could be used, or it is possible to move the value of the centroid of the fused cluster towards the new one by a step of 10% of the similarity distance. Thanks to this adjustment mechanism, it is possible to maintain the wealth of information even though initial acquired data points are removed.

AMAS4DC instantiation requires the definition of two functions:

The **similarity measure** $similarity : Cluster_{new} \times Cluster_{existing} \rightarrow Float$ that takes two clusters and returns a value corresponding to the similarity score between the characteristics of both clusters. A **fusion threshold** must also be set to define above which similarity score similar clusters should be fused.

The **fusion process** $fuse : Cluster_{new} \times Cluster_{existing} \rightarrow Cluster_{updated}$ that takes a new and an existing clusters and fuses them to create another one in replacement.

Both similarity measure and fusion process are considered as cooperative mechanisms used by the CAs. The similarity measure helps CA to identify the clusters that represent similar information. The fusion process enables them to cooperate in order to delete redundant information. Thanks to this MAS structure, the system continuously adapts and evolves with data evolution.

5   Detecting Regularities in User Itineraries

Thanks to our GPS-equipped mobile devices, it is possible to follow the movements of a user during the day. Data are retrieved at a given rate and can be combined to identify users itineraries. Finding itineraries regularities provide information on a user regular movement behaviour and enables the development of new mobility services known as Mobility as a Service (MaaS) [12]. In this context, we investigate the instantiation of AMAS4DC in order to detect regularity in user's movement behavior.

5.1   AMAS4DC Instantiation

To detect regularity in user's movement behavior, user's itineraries must be recorded. An itinerary from D to A at time t is defined as follows:

$$It_t = (WD_D, DT_D, D, P_1, P_2, ..., P_x, A, M_{DP_1}, M_{P_1P_2}, ..., M_{P_xA})$$

where WD_D is the weekday of departure, DT_D is the departure time, $P_{i=1,...,N}$ are the Points of Interest (PoI) representing a change in the mode of transport $M_{ij}, i \in \{D, 1, ..., x\}, j \in \{1, ..., x, A\}$ as shown in Fig. 2.

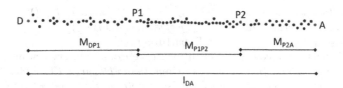

Fig. 2. Itinerary representation from a departure point D to an arrival point A passing through 2 PoIs P_1 and P_2 using three modes of transport.

The input data stream is then $DS = \{It_{t_1}, ..., It_{t_N}, ...\}$ where It_{t_n} is the detected itinerary at time t_n. The output of the clustering of all detected itineraries until t_n is expressed as a set of clusters noted $CR_{t_n} = \{C_1, ..., C_M\}$ that evolves with the detection of a new itinerary. The centroid of a cluster is the representative itinerary calculated by the combination of historical data assigned to the cluster (Algorithm 3). To capture the evolution of user's behaviour, additional values such as the interval around the departure time, the frequency of the itinerary, etc. are required. In this paper, we investigate the interval around the departure time ΔT to the clusters. ΔT is initially set to ± 15 min and adjusted by the fusion process locally to each itinerary.

Similarity Measure. For itineraries clustering, we want to consider the temporal, spatial and semantic aspect of itineraries. Thus, the *similarity* measure takes the new cluster C_{new} and an existing cluster $C_{existing}$ and computes three functions:

- $areTemporallySimilar : C_{new} \times C_{existing} \rightarrow BOOL$ checks that the weekdays WDD are the same and the departure time of C_{new} is within the interval around ΔT of $C_{existing}$.
- $areSpatiallySimilar : C_{new} \times C_{existing} \rightarrow BOOL$ checks that the number of PoIs Px is the same and that the distance between the PoIs is lower than 500 m. Note that this distance can also be adjusted at cluster level.
- $areSemanticallySimilar : C_{new} \times C_{existing} \rightarrow BOOL$ checks that the modes of transport $M_{P_x P_y}$ are exactly the same.

If these three functions returns true, then the similarity is 1, 0 otherwise. Any fusion threshold τ, such as $0 < \tau \leq 1$, is then valid. We set it to 0.5 for this study.

Algorithm 3. fuse($C_{existing}$, C_{new})

1: $existingPoIs \leftarrow C_{existing}.getPointsOfInterest()$
2: $newPoIs \leftarrow C_{new}.getPointsOfInterest()$
3: **for** i = 1 to $existingPoIs$.size() **do**
    $updatedPoI.X \leftarrow (existingPoIs[i]).getX() + newPoIs[i].getX()) / 2$
    $updatedPoI.Y \leftarrow (existingPoIs[i].getY() + newPoIs[i].getY()) / 2$
    $updatedPoIs$.add($updatedPoI$)   ▷ list of updated PoIs
4: **end for**
5: $existingClusterDepartureTime \leftarrow C_{existing}.getDepartureTime()$
6: $newClusterDepartureTime \leftarrow C_{new}.getDepartureTime()$
7: $\Delta T \leftarrow C_{existing}.getIntervalAroundDeparture()$
8: $\delta t \leftarrow \Delta T.durationInSeconds() * durationPercentage$ ▷ interval adjustment value
9: **if** | $newClusterDepartureTime - existingClusterDepartureTime$ | > 60 **then**
10:     **if** $newClusterDepartureTime.isBefore(existingClusterDepartureTime)$ **then**   ▷ shift ΔT left
11:         $\Delta T.start() \leftarrow \Delta T.start() - \delta t$
12:         $\Delta T.end() \leftarrow \Delta T.end() - \delta t$
13:     **else if** $newClusterDepartureTime.isAfter(existingClusterDepartureTime)$ **then**   ▷ shift ΔT right
14:         $\Delta T.start() \leftarrow \Delta T.start() + \delta t$
15:         $\Delta T.end() \leftarrow \Delta T.end() + \delta t$
16:     **end if**
17: **else**   ▷ reduce ΔT size (in seconds)
18:     $\Delta T.start() \leftarrow \Delta T.start() + \delta t$
19:     $\Delta T.end() \leftarrow \Delta T.end() - \delta t$
20: **end if**
21: $updatedDepartureTime \leftarrow \Delta T.start() + \Delta T / 2$
22: $C_{new} \leftarrow (updatedPoIs, updatedDepartureTime, \Delta T, modesOfTransport)$

Fusion Process. At each detected itinerary, a new CA representing it is created. The CA is provided with existing CAs representing itineraries with the same departure ad arrival points. Once the similarity scores of those CAs are received,

CA applies Algorithm 3 to fuse with similar ones. The locations of PoIs are updated by taking the average of old and new PoIs (lines 3–4). ΔT associated to the existing representative itinerary is adjusted towards the left or the right (lines 11–17) if the difference between the new cluster departure time and the existing cluster departure time is greater than 60 s or reduced (lines 18–19) otherwise. We choose 60 s to reduce the interval, as it represents the fact that the user departure time is very steady (the same time each day).

5.2 Experiments

In this section, we evaluate our approach for detecting regularities in the user's movement behaviour using a publicly available Geolife dataset [21] and we compare the obtained results with DBSCAN [7] and DENStream [5].

The Geolife dataset is a dataset of trajectories containing GPS points of 182 users collected mostly in Beijing (China) between April 2007 to August 2012. Each point in the dataset is represented as a latitude-longitude pair, and the dataset has a high sampling rate (around 1–5 s). In [14], the authors evaluated their similarity measures using this dataset as well. They defined five regions (Dormitory, Park, Starbucks, Market, Microsoft) in Beijing and considered trajectories intersecting these regions. For our experiments, in order to define the PoIs, we consider the same five regions and the trajectories intersecting these regions (Fig. 3).

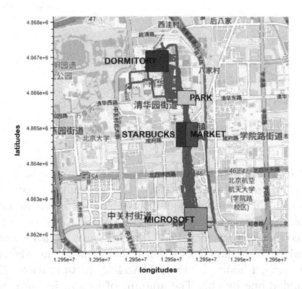

Fig. 3. Trajectories intersecting five regions as defined in [14] using the Geolife dataset

We have then combined these trajectories to create a set of 406 itineraries. For all itineraries, we assigned three modes of transport corresponding to each segment, and the trajectory's start time acted as the departure time for the corresponding itinerary.

The instantiation of AMAS4DC was implemented in Java using AMAK [17] an open source framework for developing Adaptive Multi-Agent Systems. All the experiments are conducted on a MacBook Pro 2021 with an Apple M1 Pro CPU and 32 GB of RAM. We also implemented DBSCAN and DENStream. As for now our system is not able to "forget outdated data", we have decided not to implement the "forget" part of DENStream. DBSCAN is a trivial solution and DENStream is one of the most well-known clustering algorithm [15]. Furthermore, they are able to provide a solution without setting the number of clusters beforehand, these methods are relevant to our case-study.

Memory Usage. Figure 4 presents the amount of itineraries needed in memory during the resolution for each algorithm. The horizontal axis is the percentage of the resolution progress. The vertical axis is the amount of itineraries needed in memory.

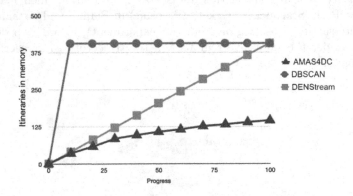

Fig. 4. Registered itineraries for each algorithm

DBSCAN (Circle line) requires all the data at startup and keep them in memory during the whole resolution. Therefore, the amount of itineraries needed in memory is constant. DENStream (Square line) is able to handle new itineraries during resolution. However, it must necessarily keep in memory all the itineraries to be able to compute average values. The amount of itineraries needed in memory is equal to the amount of itineraries given to the algorithm. Therefore, it grows linearly. Finally, for the AMAS4DC instantiation (Triangle line), itineraries are added one by one. The amount of itineraries in memory initially evolves linearly. Then, the increase is less important. At the end, less than 150 itineraries are needed in memory thanks to the fusion process.

Thanks to its self-adaptive characteristic performed by the implemented cooperative mechanisms, the proposed system is able to reduce drastically the memory usage.

Performances Comparison. To measure the effectiveness of a clustering algorithm, several measures can be used [16], in this study we focus on the silhouette coefficient [18] as it indicates if each point is associated to the adequate cluster, as well as the Calinski-Harabaz Index [4] to determine the internal coherence of the clusters. As shown in Table 1, the silhouette score is almost the same for the three methods. However, the AMAS4DC approach has a higher Calinski-Harabaz Index which indicates that clusters have a higher internal coherence than other approaches. Also, DENStream creates more clusters with only one itinerary. These results show that all three algorithms are quite efficient for clustering these itineraries. However, it can be seen that DENStream has a tendency to create more clusters with only one itinerary and that AMAS4DC creates clusters with a higher quality. This is due to how new itinerary are compared to existing clusters.

Table 1. Clustering results comparison

Algorithm	Clusters	Clusters (size = 1)	Silhouette	Calinski-Harabaz Index
DBSCAN	205	114	.97	226.27
DENStream	243	137	.98	247.04
AMAS4DC	216	118	.98	271.26

Time to Cluster a New Itinerary. Table 2 presents the time required by each algorithm to cluster a new acquired itinerary. To conduct this experiment, we launched the three algorithms on the same dataset, with the same parameters, and we measured the time the algorithms took to process a new itinerary from the data stream as well as the time it took to process all the dataset. As DBSCAN does not support data stream, we only measured the total processing time.

Table 2. Average time to process itineraries

Algorithm	Time for one itinerary (in ms.)	Time for all itineraries (in ms.)
DBSCAN	N/A	37
DENStream	0.81	481
AMAS4DC	0.40	164

DBSCAN clearly outperforms DENStream and AMAS4DC and is more efficient for a one-shot clustering. However, for dynamic clustering, adding a new itinerary requires DBSCAN to restart the whole process. For DENStream and AMAS4DC, it might take longer to process all the itineraries. However the benefit in terms of time is very important when adding a new itinerary. Noting that, AMAS4DC is in average 2 times faster than DENStream.

Discussion. AMAS4DC seems to be a good solution for itineraries stream clustering. It provides similar performance as DBSCAN and DENStream in terms of clustering quality, and is more efficient regarding memory usage and computation time. Additionally, the multi-agent architecture allows more flexibility in data points representation, comparison and fusion.

The results of this clustering is an evolving database of the most representative itineraries which can be useful for many aspects such as predicting the future itineraries of a user, determining user's preferences or even identifying relations between itineraries that could be useful for generating synthetic agendas.

6 Application for Traffic Prediction

Accurate traffic prediction plays an essential role in many Intelligent Transport Systems to bring solutions for traffic efficiency and safety improvement. Traffic prediction is a challenging task due to the high variation and unpredictability of many traffic factors including accident, weather conditions, social events, *etc.* Thus, the data-driven approaches applying traffic prediction must include the following components to capture efficiently the historical traffic evolution and enable the accurate prediction estimation: (1) spatio-temporal dependency analysis to study historical data, (2) continuous update of the learned model to adapt to new data sets, (3) strong interpretability to understand the causality between input data and the predictions and (4) dynamic and open system for large-scale applications. From this intuition, our solution for traffic prediction problem applies AMAS4DC to detect the different traffic dynamics from the perceived data stream.

6.1 AMAS4DC Instantiation

The traffic prediction problem considered in this application is described as, given:

- a set of vehicles $V = v_1; v_2; ...; v_n$, each following an itinerary I segmented into a sequence of road segments noted $I = \{rds_1, \ldots, rds_d\}$ and communicating its *mobility profile* to each crossed road segment;
- a set of road segments determined according to the road network in Open Street Map (OSM), its starting and ending points located by GPS devices;

to conceive a system able to learn and predict future traffic dynamics at the level of each road segment. AMAS4DC is deployed at each road segment to detect different traffic dynamics on it from the stream of *Mobility Profiles* communicated by the crossing vehicles. Thus, the data point DP in this application is then the **Mobility Profile (MP)** defined as the distribution of travel time at different speed ranges on the crossed road segment. Figure 5 illustrates the MP of a vehicle crossing a segment of 72 m length with maximum speed of 30 km/h using 7 speed ranges.

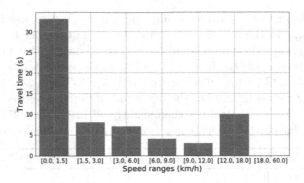

Fig. 5. Illustration of one MP

The input data stream is then $DS = \{MP_{t_1}, \ldots, MP_{t_N}, \ldots\}$ where MP_{t_n} is the mobility profile communicated from the crossing vehicle at timestamp t_n. The output of the clustering from all the data points added until time t_n is expressed as a set of clusters noted $CR_{t_n} = \{C_1, \ldots, C_M\}$. Noting that the set of clusters may change at each arrival of new MPs. The **centroid of a cluster** is the representative MP calculated by the combination of historical data assigned to the cluster. To capture the historical evolution of traffic dynamics, a list of **Range of Use (RU)** associated to this representative MP is stored as additional values. Finally, a fusion threshold α is added and defined locally according to each road segment characteristics.

Similarity Measure. The **difference between two MPs** is an array whose elements are the absolute differences in time travel of respective speed ranges of two MPs. We formulate the expression of MP difference as follows:

$$MPDiff(MP^k, MP^l) = (|MP_i^k - MP_i^l|)_{i=1,\ldots,N} \qquad (1)$$

where N is the number of speed ranges, MP_i^k and MP_i^l are the values of time travel corresponding to the ith speed range.

If all elements of $MPDiff$ are smaller than the fusion threshold α, both compared MPs are considered similar, otherwise they are different.

$$MP^k \text{ similar to } MP^l \Leftrightarrow \forall i \in \{1, \ldots, N\}: \quad MPDiff(MP^k, MP^l)_i \leq \alpha \qquad (2)$$

Fusing Similar Cluster Agents. Algorithm 4 describes the fusing process used by the cluster agent C_{new} created when a new DP is acquired. C_{new} first computes the distance between its centroid $C_{new}.centroid$ and the existing cluster agents to find the list of similar agents $SimilarClusters$ (lines 1–6). Then, C_{new} computes its most similar cluster (line 7) and selects the clusters that must be fused with it and fuse them (lines 9–23). This step is done as two similar clusters to C_{new} are not necessarily similar to each other. Thus, starting from the most similar cluster to C_{new} avoids fusing non-similar clusters together. In addition, the $C_{existing}$ in the $SimilarClusters$ can merge together if needed. That allows the clustering structure to adapt to new arrival data without depending on initial data, while keeping the historical evolution. Once the database of existing clusters is updated, C_{new} fuse with the updated $C_{closest}$ (lines 24–31). β (line 25) is an adjustment rate computed as the mean time difference between the $C_{closest}$ and C_{new}. The $C_{closest}$ centroid is then slightly adjusted (line 27) to integrate C_{new}. If no similar cluster exists, C_{new} is added to the learned database.

Algorithm 4. fuse(ExistingClusters, C_{new}, α, T_{entry}, NbSpeedRange)

1: SimilarClusters = []
2: **for** C $\in$ ExistingClusters **do**
3:     **if** C.isSimilarTo(C_{new}) **then**
4:         SimilarClusters.append(C)
5:     **end if**
6: **end for**
7: $C_{closest} \leftarrow getClosestCluster(SimilarClusters, C_{new})$
8: $J \leftarrow length(SimilarClusters)$
9: **if** J $\geq$ 2 **then**
10:     MergingClusters $\leftarrow [C_{closest}]$
11:     **for** C $\in$ SimilarClusters $\neq C_{closest}$ **do**
12:         **if** C.isSimilarTo($C_{closest}$) **then**
13:             MergingClusters.append(C)
14:         **end if**
15:     **end for**
16:     K $\leftarrow$ length(MergingClusters)
17:     **for** $i = 1 \ldots NbSpeedRange$ **do**
18:         $C_{closest}.centroid_i = \frac{\sum_{k=1}^{K} MergingClusters[k].centroid_i}{K}$
19:     **end for**
20:     **for** $k = 1 \ldots K$ **do**
21:         $C_{closest}$.listRUs.append(MergingClusters[k].listRUs)
22:     **end for**
23: **end if**
24: **if** J $\geq$ 1 **then**
25:     $\beta = \frac{\sum_{i=1}^{NbSpeedRange}(MPDiff(C_{closest}.centroid_i, C_{new}.centroid_i)}{\sum_{i=1}^{NbSpeedRange}(C_{closest}.centroid_i)}$
26:     **for** i=1 $\ldots$ NbSpeedRange **do**
27:         $C_{closest}.centroid_i = (1-\beta)*C_{closest}.centroid_i+\beta*C_{new}.centroid_i$
28:     **end for**
29:     $C_{closest}$.listRUs.append(T_{entry})
30:     $C_{new} \leftarrow C_{closest}$
31: **end if**

6.2   Experiments

Scenario. The performance of this instantiation of AMAS4DC is evaluated on generated floating car data using MovSim [20]. Vehicles follow the proposed

Intelligent Driver Model and the Adaptive Cruise Control models. We select an on-ramp scenario (Fig. 6) with road bottleneck, consisting of two main road segments with respective lengths of 1000 m and 500 m, separated at the level of an intersection with one on-ramp segment. The scenario simulates the traffic during five hours. The entering traffic flow for main road increases from 1000 vehicles/hour to 1500 vehicles/hour from t_0 to $t_0 + 300$ s and maintains a flow of 1500 vehicles/hour until the end of the simulation. The entering on-ramp flow increases from 0 to 500 vehicles/hour between $[t_0; t_0 + 300$ s$]$; decreases to 300 vehicles/hour between $[t_0 + 300$ s$; t_0 + 600$ s$]$ and maintains this flow for the rest of the simulation. This simulation is run twice. Trajectory data are collected from 10000 vehicles which cross both road segments with the frequency of speed measurement at 1 Hz.

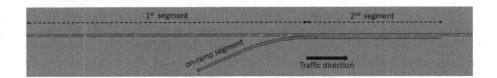

Fig. 6. Road scenario

By varying the traffic flow, we diversify traffic dynamics. As a result, the obtained MPs characterize the different driving behaviors. Figure 7a shows an example with the 1000 first MPs crossing the 1st segment of the scenario.

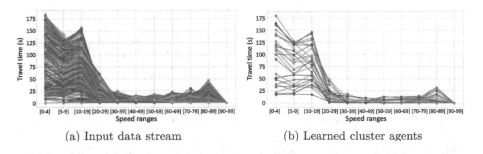

(a) Input data stream   (b) Learned cluster agents

Fig. 7. From the 1000 first MPs perceived from vehicles crossing the 1st road segment, 27 cluster agents are obtained by AMAS4DC

Parameter's Values. The fusion threshold α is based on the length of road segment: $\alpha = 10$ for the 1st road segment and $\alpha = 5$ for the 2nd since the 1st road segment is twice longer than the 2nd. The choice of different values of fusion threshold shows the benefit of the distributed learning process. Noting that the fusion thresholds are chosen to obtain a reasonable number of clusters at the studied road segments. Further experiments with different values for these thresholds is required to study the sensitivity of AMAS4DC's performance.

We compare the obtained results with CluStream using its implementation in Python[1]. The maximum numbers of micro-clusters and macro-clusters are respectively set at 50 and 10, the time horizon is equal to 10000 (corresponding to the size of used data) and the other parameters are set as defaults. Time horizon is divided into 20 frames. Each frame contains 500 MPs.

Results and Analysis. Figure 7b shows that 27 cluster agents are detected from the 1000 perceived MPs on the 1st road segment. Figure 8 summarizes the silhouette score values over 20 frames on both road segments. The means of silhouette scores of CluStream and AMAS4DC are respectively 0.22 and 0.40 (improvement of 82%) on the 1st road segment, 0.24 and 0.42 (improvement of 75%) on the 2nd. The silhouette scores of CluStream are low due to the non-adaptive property with fixed number of clusters. Even, AMAS4DC silhouette scores are higher than CluStream most of time, they present a lot of variation especially on the 2nd road segment. This variation is due to the arrival of data representing new behavior or the existence of similar existing clusters that have not been detected to merge yet. The continuous adaptation of AMAS4DC allows to deal with these issues by adapting the clustering structure and thus recovering the silhouette scores. Experimentation on larger data set will be conducted to measure the stabilisation of AMAS4DC's performance and the amount of data required to reach the stabilisation.

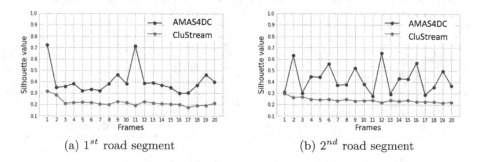

(a) 1st road segment   (b) 2nd road segment

Fig. 8. Silhouette values over 20 frames of AMAS4DC system and CluStream

7   Conclusion

Dynamic data stream clustering has multiple challenges with the growing amount of data available and their variability. This paper presents AMAS4DC an adaptive MAS model to perform dynamic data stream clustering. This model has

---

[1] Package clusopt core. https://pypi.org/project/clusopt-core/, accessed: 2021-04-16.

been instantiated on two use cases: finding itineraries regularities and traffic prediction. Obtained results underline AMAS4DC efficiency in terms of reduction of used memory, low computing time and dynamic adaptation of the clustering structure. The cooperative mechanisms used by the cluster agents to locally compare data and fuse with other cluster agents when required, increases the system flexibility and self-adaptability to evolve with data evolution.

Several perspectives are planned for this work. First, adding the forgetting mechanism to allow cluster agents representing obsolete data to delete themselves and thus maintain a low level of memory usage. Then, we plan to work on the generalisation of the different fusion strategies by proposing ready-to-use functions. Concerning the concept of additional values, these values make it possible to extend data analysis beyond the acquired data itself. An example of values we intend to study is the number of data points assigned to a cluster. This information can be integrated into the fusion process in order to consider the relative importance of the different clusters to be fused. Another perspective concerns the removal of historical information by the fusion process that can impact the wealth of information despite the good clustering results. To evaluate this, experiments using the obtained clusters for real time dynamic predictions are being conducted with encouraging results. The link between the clustering and the prediction, combined with the instantiation of AMAS4DC on other case studies will allow a complete evaluation of the genericity of the model. The results obtained will also be compared with other clustering techniques, such as Growing Neural Gas, using real and non-simulated data streams. We also aim to conduct a study on the scalability of the system using large-scale data streams. Finally, we plan to release the code as open source.

Acknowledgements. These works were carried out within the VILAGIL MaaS action with the support of the French Government as part of the Territoire d'Innovation program, an initiative of the Grand Plan d'Investissement linked to France 2030, Toulouse Métropole, and the GIS neOCampus. Also, we would like to thank Continental Digital Services France for supporting these works.

References

1. Aggarwal, C.C., Philip, S.Y., Han, J., Wang, J.: A framework for clustering evolving data streams. In: Proceedings 2003 VLDB Conference, pp. 81–92. Elsevier (2003)
2. Ahmed, M., Seraj, R., Islam, S.M.S.: The *k-means* algorithm: a comprehensive survey and performance evaluation. Electronics **9**(8), 1295 (2020)
3. Bouguelia, M.R., Belaïd, Y., Belaïd, A.: An adaptive incremental clustering method based on the growing neural gas algorithm. In: ICPRAM (2013)
4. Caliński, T., Harabasz, J.: A dendrite method for cluster analysis. Commun. Stat. Theory Methods **3**, 1–27 (1974)
5. Cao, F., Ester, M., Qian, W., Zhou, A.: Density-based clustering over an evolving data stream with noise. In: SDM (2006)

6. Chaimontree, S., Atkinson, K., Coenen, F.: A multi-agent based approach to clustering: harnessing the power of agents. In: Cao, L., Bazzan, A.L.C., Symeonidis, A.L., Gorodetsky, V.I., Weiss, G., Yu, P.S. (eds.) ADMI 2011. LNCS (LNAI), vol. 7103, pp. 16–29. Springer, Heidelberg (2012). https://doi.org/10.1007/978-3-642-27609-5_3

7. Ester, M., Kriegel, H.P., Sander, J., Xu, X.: A density-based algorithm for discovering clusters in large spatial databases with noise. In: Proceedings of the Second International Conference on Knowledge Discovery and Data Mining (1996)

8. Fritzke, B.: A growing neural gas network learns topologies. In: Proceedings of the 7th International Conference on Neural Information Processing Systems, pp. 625–632. MIT Press (1994)

9. Ghesmoune, M., Lebbah, M., Azzag, H.: Clustering over data streams based on growing neural gas. In: Cao, T., Lim, E.-P., Zhou, Z.-H., Ho, T.-B., Cheung, D., Motoda, H. (eds.) PAKDD 2015. LNCS (LNAI), vol. 9078, pp. 134–145. Springer, Cham (2015). https://doi.org/10.1007/978-3-319-18032-8_11

10. Ghesmoune, M., Lebbah, M., Azzag, H.: State-of-the-art on clustering data streams. Big Data Anal. 1, 13 (2016). https://doi.org/10.1186/s41044-016-0011-3

11. Grachev, S., Skobelev, P., Mayorov, I., Simonova, E.: Adaptive clustering through multi-agent technology: development and perspectives. Mathematics 8(10), 1664 (2020)

12. Hensher, D.A., Ho, C.Q., Mulley, C., Nelson, J.D., Smith, G., Wong, Y.Z.: Understanding Mobility as a Service (MaaS): Past, Present and Future. Elsevier, Amsterdam (2020)

13. Isaksson, C., Dunham, M.H., Hahsler, M.: SOStream: self organizing density-based clustering over data stream. In: Perner, P. (ed.) MLDM 2012. LNCS (LNAI), vol. 7376, pp. 264–278. Springer, Heidelberg (2012). https://doi.org/10.1007/978-3-642-31537-4_21

14. Lehmann, A.L., Alvares, L.O., Bogorny, V.: SMSM: a similarity measure for trajectory stops and moves. Int. J. Geogr. Inf. Sci. 33(9), 1847–1872 (2019)

15. Ngo, H.N., Kaddoum, E., Gleizes, M.P., Bonnet, J., Anaïs, G.: Life-long learning system of driving behaviors from vehicle data streams. In: 2021 IEEE International Intelligent Transportation Systems Conference (ITSC), pp. 1132–1139 (2021)

16. Palacio-Niño, J.O., Berzal, F.: Evaluation metrics for unsupervised learning algorithms. arXiv preprint arXiv:1905.05667 (2019)

17. Perles, A., Crasnier, F., Georgé, J.-P.: AMAK - a framework for developing robust and open adaptive multi-agent systems. In: Bajo, J., et al. (eds.) PAAMS 2018. CCIS, vol. 887, pp. 468–479. Springer, Cham (2018). https://doi.org/10.1007/978-3-319-94779-2_40

18. Rousseeuw, P.J.: Silhouettes: a graphical aid to the interpretation and validation of cluster analysis. J. Comput. Appl. Math. 20, 53–65 (1987)

19. Rundensteiner, E.A., Ding, L., Zhu, Y., Sutherland, T., Pielech, B.: CAPE: a constraint-aware adaptive stream processing engine. In: Chaudhry, N.A., Shaw, K., Abdelguerfi, M. (eds.) Stream Data Management. ADBS, vol. 30, pp. 83–111. Springer, Boston (2005). https://doi.org/10.1007/0-387-25229-0_5

20. Treiber, M., Kesting, A.: Traffic Flow Dynamics: Data Models and Simulation. Springer, Heidelberg (2013). https://doi.org/10.1007/978-3-642-32460-4

21. Zheng, Y., Zhang, L., Xie, X., Ma, W.Y.: Mining interesting locations and travel sequences from GPS trajectories. In: Proceedings of the 18th International Conference on World Wide Web, WWW 2009, pp. 791–800 (2009)

Double Deep Q-Network-Based Time and Energy-Efficient Mobility-Aware Workflow Migration Approach

Nour El Houda Boubaker[1]([✉]), Karim Zarour[1], Nawal Guermouche[2],
and Djamel Benmerzoug[1]

[1] LIRE Laboratory, Constantine2 - Abdelhamid Mehri University, Constantine,
Algeria
{nour.boubaker,zarour.karim, djamel.benmerzoug}@univ-constantine2.dz
[2] LAAS-CNRS, University of Toulouse, INSA, Toulouse, France
nguermou@laas.fr

Abstract. With the emergence of the Fog paradigm, the relocation of
computational capabilities to the network's edge has become imperative to support the ever-growing requirements of latency-sensitive, data-
intensive, and real-time decision-making applications. In dynamic and
mobile environments, services must adapt to accommodate the mobility of users, resulting in frequent relocations across computing nodes to
ensure seamless user experiences. However, these migrations incur additional costs and potentially degrade the Quality of Service (QoS) parameters. In this paper, we propose a mobility-aware workflow migration
approach based on Deep Reinforcement Learning (DRL). This approach
aims to minimize the system's overall delay and energy consumption by
optimizing the number of workflow task migrations, considering resource
performance and network conditions in different regions. The problem
is first formulated as a Markov Decision Process (MDP), and then a
Double Deep Q-network (DDQN) algorithm is proposed to identify the
optimal policy for workflow offloading and migration. Comprehensive
experiments have been conducted and the results demonstrate that our
approach outperforms significantly the existing approaches.

Keywords: Workflow Migration · Fog · Cloud · Deep Reinforcement
Learning · Mobility

1 Introduction

The emergence of Fog computing has filled the gap of Cloud computing and
paved the way for distributed computing architectures that bring computational
capabilities closer to the network edge [7]. This paradigm shift is driven by the
need to support the increasing demands of various services, such as Internet
of Things (IoT) applications, real-time analytics, and latency-sensitive tasks.
Fog computing enables efficient data processing, reduced network latency, and

M. Sellami et al. (Eds.): CoopIS 2023, LNCS 14353, pp. 97–115, 2024.
https://doi.org/10.1007/978-3-031-46846-9_6

improved user experience by distributing computing resources across a network of interconnected devices and Fog nodes [3].

The mobility of users poses a significant challenge in Fog computing environments [20]. As users move within the network, their devices may connect and disconnect from different Fog nodes, leading to potential service disruptions and degraded performance. To overcome these challenges and ensure uninterrupted service delivery, migration techniques are employed to dynamically transfer the execution of services from one Fog node to another, aligning with the user's mobility patterns [24]. However, frequent transfer of services may incur additional migration latency and increased energy consumption [4]. These latter can affect the responsiveness and perceived performance of the services, leading to a degradation in Quality of Service (QoS) parameters.

Furthermore, the variability of resources in Fog computing environments introduces a significant level of heterogeneity in terms of performance. This heterogeneity can be observed in both computing capabilities and network bandwidths [10]. Consequently, certain regions may encounter restrictions in resource performance or have a lower bandwidth capacity, while others may exhibit enhanced performance. This diversity in resource and network performance poses a significant challenge when considering migration scenarios, as transferring services or data from a source fog node to a destination fog node with inferior performance characteristics can potentially lead to a decline in overall system performance. Therefore, it becomes crucial to investigate strategies and mechanisms that aim to minimize the frequency of service migrations according to resources and network performance associated with each region, thereby, reducing associated costs and optimizing resource utilization within the system. Several research studies have been proposed to tackle the challenge of service migration induced by user mobility in the context of Fog and Edge Computing [14,17,25]. These studies predominantly focus on achieving a trade-off between delivering high QoS and minimizing the costs incurred during the migration process. The main objective is to ensure a seamless user experience during the transition between computing environments. However, these existing solutions have limitations when it comes to addressing the challenges that emerge when dealing with the migration of entire workflows in multi-heterogeneous resource environments where resources may have varying capabilities, capacities, and network bandwidths. Moreover, in the literature, the existing works commonly adopt always migration strategies as long as the user is mobile [9,23]. Such approaches can lead to additional migration costs, such as time latency and energy consumption. As a result, the overall QoS of systems can be significantly compromised. Consequently, the only necessary workflow migration, which involves dependent tasks, introduces additional challenges that need to be addressed effectively. Concurrently, Deep Reinforcement Learning (DRL) has emerged as a powerful decision-making algorithm, enabling agents to develop and refine policies by leveraging feedback from the environment [16]. The Reinforcement Learning (RL) agent has been widely recognized for its remarkable capabilities in acquiring knowledge, making rapid decisions, and effectively navigating in dynamic and unstable environments [4].

Therefore, DRL techniques prove to be well-suited for effectively managing the uncertainties associated with migration scenarios, where the mobility of users introduces dynamic features that require adaptive decision-making strategies. Motivated by this, this paper introduces a novel workflow migration approach based on DRL and designed for Fog-Cloud environments. The primary objective of our approach is to minimize the number of dependent tasks migrations while fulfilling user expectations regarding delay and energy consumption. The contributions of this paper are outlined as follows:

1. We propose a new and efficient Double Deep Q-network-based approach to tackle the necessary entire workflow migration problem.
2. The proposed model enables to achieve efficient migration strategy that enhances overall system performance while striking a balance between minimizing delays, optimizing energy consumption, and streamlining migration operations.
3. The proposed approach has been implemented and evaluated using different scenarios. The results demonstrate clearly the efficiency and effectiveness of the proposed work.

The remainder of this paper is structured as follows. Section 2 provides an overview of the related work. Section 3 presents the problem formulation. The proposed workflow migration algorithm is detailed in Sect. 4. Section 5 reports the experimental results. Finally, Sect. 6 concludes.

2   Related Work

DRL-based algorithms have been widely used to solve service migration problems induced by user mobility. These algorithms have proven to be highly effective in handling such scenarios, with the main objective of preventing any potential degradation in QoS. Many solutions adopt an *always migration-based strategy*, wherein services migrate continuously across Edge-Fog nodes to accommodate user movement. In [13], the authors developed OctoFog, an intelligent Fog service migration framework based on Deep Determinist Policy gradient (DDPG) for smart city applications. The proposed approach aims to efficiently migrate the services over the Fog platform with respect to reactive and proactive decision models. Wu et al. [23] have proposed a mobility-aware DRL (MDRL) offloading and migration approach in Mobile Edge Computing (MEC). The goal is to minimize the average latency of tasks. The MDRL consists of a glimpse mobility prediction model based on the seq2seq model, which provides coarse grain mobility information for MDRL training. In [8], a migration approach based Deep Q-learning is designed to move data in multi-access edge computing according to user mobility. Chen et al. [5] proposed a service migration decision algorithm based on Deep recurrent Q-learning (DRQNSM) to minimize user delay and system energy consumption. In [6], the authors proposed a multi-user service migration strategy based on MEC, in which each user randomly moves and learns a dynamic service migration strategy. Both DQN and DDQN were used to satisfy the trade-off between the users' aware delay and the system energy consumption. Gao et al. [9] considered a single-user Edge system exploiting the predefined movement of the user. The authors made use of Q-learning and DQN to minimize migration costs. Nevertheless, adopting a frequent migration strategy introduces several challenges such as the additional computational and communication overhead involved in the migration process. Additionally, the performance of the computing resources and networks may vary across different regions. This poses a challenge when frequent migration of tasks occurs, as there is a possibility that tasks are relocated to regions with lower-performing resources.

Few works specifically focus on mitigating frequent migration issues. In [18], the authors used DQN to design a service migration model in MEC to address user proximity issues. The main objective is to minimize migration costs. Using the same technique, in [19], Pang et al. developed a dynamic service migration policy according to the velocity of vehicles. The goal is to achieve a good trade-off between the QoS and migration cost. However, It is important to highlight that these solutions predominantly focused on migrating a single service on a single resource within each region, assuming homogeneous characteristics. As a result, they do not address the intricate complexities that arise when migrating workflows in multi-heterogeneous resource environments with diverse bandwidth links.

In contrast to the aforementioned works, our study aims to minimize the frequency of workflow migrations by considering the performance of resources and network conditions within each region. The primary objective is to minimize the overall delay and energy consumption while ensuring the fulfillment of dependent task requirements. Furthermore, we employ a DRL-based algorithm to effectively handle the dynamic and intricate environment caused by workflow migration.

3   System Model and Problem Formulation

In this section, we describe the problem and system model of the proposed approach.

3.1   System Model

As depicted in Fig. 1, we consider an Industrial IoT Network with a mobile user (e.g. automated guided vehicles, autonomous mobile robots) representing an Edge device and M distributed Fog resources (e.g. industrial machines). The Fog machines are characterized by limited computational capacities. The user keeps moving from one region to another (e.g. production units, warehouse). Each region is covered by an Access Point (AP). The Fog resources are connected to their according AP through a wireless link. At first, the user offloads its computation tasks to the first region. With consideration of user mobility, we need to decide at each region whether to migrate each task or not and which resources are optimal to move the tasks into. Our system operates in a time-slotted model $T = \{t_1, t_2, .., t_t\}$. The length of time slot t_t is δ_t. We also assume that user mobility between regions occurs at the beginning of each time slot and the user mobility inside each region is negligible.

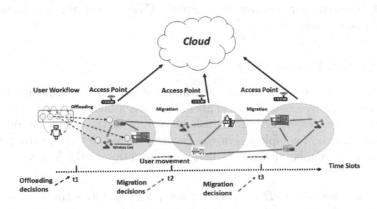

Fig. 1. Illustration of the system model

Our approach considers workflows that rely on the patterns commonly used by composition languages as BPEL (Business Process Execution Language) [12]: sequential, parallel, conditional, and loops. Each one of these structures can be mapped into a sequential model using the techniques presented in [22].

A workflow W $= <Ts, D>$ which is composed of a set of tasks Ts $\in\{\tau_1, \tau_2, .., \tau_N\}$ and a set of sequential dependencies D, where d_{ij} represents the link between tasks τ_i and τ_j. We emphasize that task τ_j can not be executed only if task τ_i is completed.

Each task τ_i has a set of requirements. In this paper, we consider the following requirements $\tau_i = <CPU_i, Ram_i, Disk_i, NI_i, TZ_i, DataOut_i, DataIn_i>$, which includes: the required computing cycle CPU_i (GHz), the required memory space Ram_i (Mb), the required disk space $Disk_i$ (Mb), the number of instructions NI_i (MI), the task size TZ_i (Mb), and the size of the output data generated by the task $DataOut_i$ (Mb). It is worth mentioning that the output data of the last task is transmitted back to the user. In addition, the attribute $DataIn_i$ represents a set of data transmitted from the user to the first task τ_1. It is required to launch the execution process of the workflow.

R is a set of resources, where $r_x \in \{$ Edge device, Fog, Cloud$\}$. Fog encompasses a wide range of entities such as industrial robots, operating machines, and servers. We model the network of the Edge device-Fog-Cloud continuum as a set of communication links L, where the link between r_x and r_z is denoted as $l_{xz} = \{Bandwidth_{xz}\}$. The bandwidth differs from one resource to another. Fog resources are characterized by their location representing the AP to which they are connected (e.g. Location $\in\{$AP1, AP2,....$\}$). Additionally, each resource in

R is defined by its maximum computational capacities, expressed through the following attributes:

rx $=$ $<CPUFrequency_x^m, ComputingCapacity_x^m, Memory_x^m, Storge_x^m, \varrho_x^c,$ $P_x^{comm}, Location_x>$ that describes respectively CPU frequency (GHz), the number of instructions per second (MIPS), memory size (MB), permanent storage size (MB), computational power consumption (Watt), transmission power consumption (Watt), and location.

3.2   Objective Function

Our primary goal is to develop an algorithm that efficiently minimizes the overall delay and energy consumption. This encompasses offloading, execution, and migration metrics, calculated from task offloading in the initial region to the final task's execution completion in the last region. We detail the computation of these criteria, namely delay and energy consumption in the following.

Delay. The total delay D comprises four parts: **(1)** the transmission time between the mobile user and resources (Ttransm), **(2)** the execution time (Tex), **(3)** the transfer time between tasks (Ttransf), and **(4)** the migration time (Tmig).

1. **Transmission time:** It represents the time taken to offload a task τ_i from the user to the resources of the first region, denoted R^1, including the Cloud. It is calculated based on the size of the task (Mb) and the bandwidth between the user and the selected resource (Mbps). Importantly, the $i+1^{th}$ task is transmitted by the mobile user only after the ith task has been successfully placed in the designated resource.

$$Ttransm_i^{xz}(t_{=1}) = \frac{TZ_i}{Bandwidth_{xz}}, \text{ where x = \{Edge-device\} and z } \in\{R^1, \text{Cloud}\} \tag{1}$$

   The total transmission time for all tasks is calculated as follows:

$$Ttransm = \sum_{i=1}^{N} Ttransm_i^{xz}(t_{=1}), \text{ where x = \{Edge-device\} and z } \in\{R^1, \text{Cloud}\} \tag{2}$$

2. **Execution time:** It represents the time taken to perform the task τ_i on the resource r_x. It is mainly calculated based on the number of instructions of the task and the CPU processing capacity of the resource (MIPS).

$$Tex_i^x(t) = \frac{NI_i}{ComputingCapacity_x^m}, \text{ where x } \in\{\text{Fog, Cloud}\} \tag{3}$$

The total execution time in all time slots can be expressed as follows:

$$Tex = \sum_{t=1}^{T}\sum_{i=1}^{N} Tex_i^x(t), \text{ where x} \in \{\text{Fog, Cloud}\} \tag{4}$$

3. **Transfer time:** It includes two parts: **(1)** the transmission of *Data In* from the user to the resource that hosts the first task, and **(2)** the transmission of *Data Out* generated from task τ_i performed by resource r_x to either resource r_z hosting the task τ_{i+1} or back to the user. It is determined by the ratio between the size of *Data In/Data Out* and the available bandwidth between r_x and r_z. It is important to note that when consecutive tasks are executed on the same resource, the transfer time becomes negligible.

$$Ttransf_i^{xz}(t)\begin{cases} \frac{DataIn}{Bandwidth_{xz}}, \text{ where x} = \{\text{Edge-device}\} \text{ and z} \in \{\text{Fog, Cloud}\} & (i=1) \\ \frac{DataOut_i}{Bandwidth_{xz}}, \text{ where x} \in \{\text{Fog, Cloud}\}, \text{ and z} \in \{\text{Edge device, Fog, Cloud}\} & (i => 1) \\ 0 & (x=z) \end{cases} \tag{5}$$

The total transfer time in all time slots is given by the following equation:

$$Ttranf = \sum_{t=1}^{T}\sum_{i=1}^{N} Ttransf_i^{xz}(t), \text{ where x, z} \in \{\text{Edge device, Fog, Cloud}\} \tag{6}$$

4. **Migration time:** It is the time taken for transmitting τ_i between resources r_x of kth region and r_z of yth region. It represents the ratio between the size of the task and the bandwidth between r_x and r_z.

$$Tmig_i^{xz}(t)\begin{cases} \frac{TZ_i}{Bandwidth_{xz}} & (x! = z) \\ 0 & (x=z) \end{cases} \tag{7}$$

The consideration of the total migration time begins from the second time slot, and its calculation is determined by the following equation:

$$Tmig = \sum_{t=2}^{T}\sum_{i=1}^{N} Tmig_i(t) \tag{8}$$

The total delay is expressed as follows:

$$T^{total} = Ttransm + Tex + Ttransf + Tmig \tag{9}$$

Energy Consumption. We consider the summation of the energy consumption of transmission, execution, transfer, and migration.

1. **Execution energy consumption:** It corresponds to the energy consumed by Fog and Cloud resources during the execution of a task. It is primarily calculated based on the computational power consumption ϱ_x^c of the resource r_x [15].

$$Engex_i^x(t) = \varrho_x^c \times Tex_i^x(t) \tag{10}$$

The total execution in all time slots can be expressed as follows:

$$Engex = \sum_{t=1}^{T} \sum_{i=1}^{N} Engex_i^x(t) \tag{11}$$

2. **Transmission energy consumption:** Transmission, transfer, and migration energy consumption denote the energy expended by Edge devices, Fog, and Cloud resources during task and data transmission in the network. This energy consumption is primarily calculated based on the power consumption associated with the data transmission P^{comm} [11].

$$Engtransm_i^{xz}(t_{=1}) = P_x^{comm} \times Ttransm_i^{xz}(t_{=1}), \text{ where x } = \{\text{Edge device}\} \tag{12}$$

The total energy consumption required to transmit all tasks can be stated as follows:

$$Engtransm = \sum_{i=1}^{N} Engtransm_i^{xz}(t_{=1}) \tag{13}$$

3. **Transfer energy consumption:**

$$Engtransf_i^{xz}(t) = P_x^{comm} \times Ttransf_i^{xz}(t), \text{ where x } = \{\text{Edge device, Fog, Cloud}\} \tag{14}$$

The total transfer time of all tasks in all time slots can be defined as follows:

$$Engtransf = \sum_{t=1}^{T} \sum_{i=1}^{N} Engtransf_i^{xz}(t) \tag{15}$$

4. **Migration energy consumption:**

$$Engmig_i(t) = P_x^{comm} \times Tmig_i^{xz}(t) \tag{16}$$

The total migration energy consumption can be expressed as follows:

$$Engmig = \sum_{t=2}^{T} \sum_{i=1}^{N} Engex_i(t) \tag{17}$$

The total energy consumption is expressed by the following equation:

$$E_{total} = Engtransm + Engex + Engtransf + Engmig \tag{18}$$

Objective Function Formulation. The optimization goal of the proposed work is to minimize the total latency and energy consumption of the system. We define the objective function as follows:

$$\min F = T_{total} + E_{total} \tag{19}$$

$$\text{st.} \begin{cases} CPU_i <= CPUFrequency_x^m & \forall i \in \{1,2,..,N\} \forall x \in \{1,2,...,M\} \textbf{(c1)} \\ Ram_i <= Memory_x^m & \forall i \in \{1,2,..,N\} \forall x \in \{1,2,...,M\} \textbf{(c2)} \\ Disk_i <= Storage_x^m & \forall i \in \{1,2,..,N\} \forall x \in \{1,2,..,M\} \textbf{(c3)} \end{cases} \tag{20}$$

The task-resource allocation constraints, represented by **c1**, **c2**, and **c3**, guarantee that the CPU, memory, and disk capacities required by the tasks are fulfilled.

4 DRL-Based Workflow Migration Strategy

The proposed DRL-based approach seeks an optimal migration policy to minimize delay and energy consumption. To accomplish this, it employs the off-policy DRL algorithm *DDQN*, known for enhanced stability, reduced bias, balanced exploration-exploitation trade-off, and efficient utilization of experience replay [21]. These attributes render DDQN a dependable choice for optimizing migration policy in dynamic and uncertain environments.

4.1 DRL Model

The problem of workflow migration under constraints of delay and energy is formulated as an MDP (S, A, R, P), where S is the state space, A is the action space, R is the reward function, and $P(s'|s, a) \in [0, 1]$ is the transition probability. Notably, the number of states in a single episode is equal to $N * T$, representing the total number of tasks and time slots, respectively. At each time slot t_t, the agent interacts with the environment, making migration decisions for each workflow task to the current region, considering factors like task dependencies, bandwidth between resources, and resource performance in the current region.

1. **State Space:** The state S_i^t is defined by the tuple $\{t_t,\ \tau_i,\ R^t,\ A_i^{t-1}\}$ where:
   - t_t identifies the current time slot.
   - τ_i represents the information related to the current task in workflow to place such as data size and computational requirements.
   - R^t is the information related to the state of resources considered in the current time slot, including the Cloud (CPU, the remaining Memory, the remaining Disk).
   - A_i^{t-1} $(t > 1)$ the action taken for the task τ_i in the previous time slot. It represents the information related to the machine host selected to perform τ_i in the previous time slot. It is important to mention that the action taken for each task in each time slot is stored by the agent in a table denoted ϕ.
2. **Action Space:** In each time slot, an action A_i^t must be chosen for each task τ_i. $A_i^t \in \{a_0, a_1\}$, where a_0 denotes no migration decision, and a_1 involves migrating the task to the current region by selecting a suitable resource with adequate computational capacity. It's worth noting that the number of valid actions for A_i^t at time slot t for τ_i is equivalent to the number of valid resources in the region, including Cloud resources. Valid actions are those that fulfill task requirements. Additionally, for the first time slot t_1, the only possible action for all tasks is $A_i^1 = a_1$, as this study assumes full offloading where all tasks are transmitted to the resources in the first region.

3. **Reward:** The reward is a function that maps state-action pairs to a real-valued reward, i.e. R: $S_i^t \times A_i^t \to R_i^t$. The value of the reward is mainly related to the current time slot. For instance, the transmission metrics (time and energy) that occur when offloading each task from the end-user to Fog resources of the first region, including Cloud, are added to the reward of each task in the first time slot. Additionally, the transfer metrics associated with the transfer of output data from τ_i to τ_j are included in the reward of state S_j^t. Furthermore, the migration metrics are taken into account starting from the second time slot. The total reward in each time slot is calculated as follows:

$$\sum_{i=1}^{N} R_i^t = \begin{cases} \sum_{i=1}^{N} -(Ttransm_i^{xy}(1) + Engtransm_i^{xy}(1) + Tex_i^x(1) + Engex_i^x(1) \\ +Ttransf_{i_{dataIn}}^{xz}(1)_{(i=1)} + Engtransf_{i_{dataIn}}^{xz}(1)_{(i=1)} + Ttransf_{i-1_{dataOut}}^{xz}(1)_{(i>1)} \\ +Engtransf_{i-1_{dataOut}}^{xz}(1)_{(i>1)} + Ttransf_{i-1_{dataOut}}^{xz}(1)_{(i=N)} \\ +Engtransf_{i_{dataOut}}^{xz}(1)_{(i=N)}) \quad (t=1) \\ \sum_{i=1}^{N} -(Tex_i(t) + Engex_i(t) + Ttransf_{i_{dataIn}}^{xz}(t)_{(i=1)} + Engtransf_{i_{dataIn}}^{xz}(t)_{(i=1)} \\ +Ttransf_{i-1_{dataOut}}^{xz}(t)_{(i>1)} + Engtransf_{i-1_{dataOut}}^{xz}(t)_{(i>1)} + Ttransf_{i_{dataOut}}^{xz}(t)_{(i=N)} \\ +Engtransf_{i_{dataOut}}^{xz}(t)_{(i=N)} + Tmig_i(t) + Engmig_i(t)) \quad (t>1) \end{cases} \tag{21}$$

The agent seeks to maximize the total rewards obtained in all time slots, and it is equal to the negative value of the objective function formulated in Sect. 4:

$$\max[\sum_{t=1}^{T} \sum_{i=1}^{N} R_i^t(S_i^t, A_i^t)] = \max(-F) \tag{22}$$

4.2 Double Deep Q-Network Based Migration

The Dynamic Service Placement DDQN involves two phases: **training** and inference. During training, the agent learns the optimal placement policy by interacting with the environment. In the inference phase, the trained Q-network guides decision-making based on the current environment state.

Figure 2 depicts the framework of the proposed DDQN-based migration strategy which consists of *environment, Main DQ-Network, Target DQ-Network, and replay memory M.*

The Main Q-Network is the agent that interacts directly with the environment by performing actions and then evaluating decisions' quality values. At first, the agent requires information related to the first state. The environment responds by indicating the first time slot and sending the information related to the first task, and the resources of the first region, including the Cloud (**1**). Next, the agent takes an action a_1^1 based on the ϵ-greedy policy (**2**). This policy consists of choosing an action randomly with a probability of ϵ or selecting the action with the highest Q-value predicted by the neural network, $a_1^1 = argmaxQ(s_1^1, a_1^1)$, with probability $1 - \epsilon$. It is noteworthy that the agent selects exclusively a valid resource that meets the requirement of the task. The environment calculates r_1^1 the reward (**3**) and moves to the next state s_2^1 to place the second task of the workflow in the first region (**4**). The agent stores the experience $\{s_1^1, a_1^1, r_1^1, s_2^1\}$

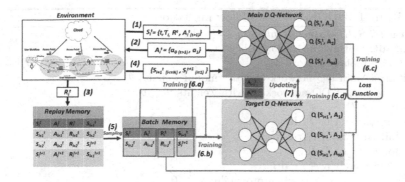

Fig. 2. DDQN-based migration Framework

in *replay memory M*. When the agent completes the tasks offloading process, it requires information related to the first task denoted s_1^2, including its previous placement decision to make a migration decision a_1^2 to the second region. The agent proceeds in this manner until decisions are made for all tasks across all regions.

Meanwhile, when the replay memory contains enough experiences, the agent randomly samples a mini-batch to create a training dataset **(5)**. The latter is used to perform the training process on the main DDQN. For each transition, the agent calculates the target Q-value using the target DQ-Network, but instead of directly selecting the action with the maximum Q-value from the main DQ-Network, it uses the main DQ-Network to estimate the action index **(6.a)**. Then, uses the target DQ-Network to obtain the Q-value for that action **(6.b)** [21]. Next, the agent calculates the loss between the predicted Q-values from the main DQ-Network and the target DQ-values **(6.c)** by the following equation:

$$Loss^{DDQN} = (R_i^t + \gamma Q'(S', argmaxQ(S', A'; \theta); \theta') - Q(S_i^t, A_i^t; \theta))^2, \quad (23)$$

where R_i^t denotes the reward obtained when action A_i^t is taken in state S_i^t. This reward reflects the immediate benefit or penalty associated with the action. On the other hand, $Q(S_i^t, A_i^t; \theta)$ represents the Q-value of action A_i^t given the state S_i^t. This Q-value is calculated using the main DQ-Network with parameters θ. It serves as an estimation of the expected cumulative reward when taking action A_i^t in state S_i^t. Furthermore, $Q'(S', argmaxQ(S', A'; \theta); \theta')$ corresponds to the target Q-value estimation. This estimation is obtained using the target DQ-Network with parameters θ'. The target Q-value is determined by taking the maximum Q-value for the next state S' and the corresponding action selected by the main DQ-Network. Thereafter, the network parameters of the Main DQ-Network θ are updated **(6.c)**. During the training, the parameters of the target DQ-Network are synchronized with the main Q-Network periodically **(7)**, typically after a certain number of steps or episodes. This synchronization process helps in stabilizing the training and improving the learning performance.

Algorithm 1. DDQN-based workflow migration

1: **Input:** $TS, R, MatrixBandwidth$
2: **Output:** Optimal migration policy
3: Initialize replay Memory M
4: Initialize Main DQ-network Q with random weights θ
5: Initialize target DQ-network Q' with weights $\theta' = \theta$
6: Initialize ϵ, P, T
7: **for** $episode = 1$ to P **do**
8:     Initialize $S = \{ t_1, \tau_1, R^1 \}$
9:     **for** $t = 1$ to T **do**
10:         **foreach** $\tau_i \in Ts$ **do**
11:             Choose a random probability $e \in [0, 1]$
12:             **if** $e < \epsilon$ **then**
13:                 Choose action A_i^t randomly
14:             **else**
15:                 Choose action $A_i^t = argmaxQ(S_i^t, A_i^t; \theta)$
16:             **end if**
17:             Execute action A_i^t, observe reward R_i^t and next state $S' \in \{S_{i+1}^t, S_i^{t+1}\}$
18:             Store transition $(S_i^t, A_i^t, R_i^t, S')$ in D
19:             Sample a random minibatch of transitions from M
20:             **if** episode terminates at $T + 1$ **then**
21:                 $y_t = R_i^t$
22:             **else**
23:                 $y_t = R_i^t + \gamma Q'(S', argmaxQ(S', A'; \theta); \theta')$
24:             **end if**
25:             Update Q-network weights by minimizing the loss:
26:             $Loss^{DDQN} = (y_j - Q(S_i^t, A_i^t; \theta))^2$
27:             Every C steps, update target network: $\theta' \leftarrow \theta$
28:             Update state: $S \leftarrow S'$
29:         **end foreach**
30:     **end for**
31:     Decrease ϵ
32: **end for**

The DDQN migration process is given in Algorithm 1. P is the total number of episodes required to train the DDQN, T is the number of time slots considered in our system, and Ts is the total set of tasks (**lines 7, 9, 10**). In **line 8**, the agent receives information about the first state. Next, it performs data acquisition to train the Main DQ-Network for each episode (**lines 11–18**). It selects an action according to ϵ greedy policy (**lines 11–16**). Initially, the parameter ϵ is initialized to an initial value. Subsequently, it undergoes a decay process, as specified in **line 31**.

According to the current action and state, the agent obtains a reward and the information of the next state (**line 17**). This transition is stored in replay memory M (**line 18**). The agent randomly samples a minibatch to update the Main DQ-network parameters using the loss function by applying the gradient descent (**lines 19–26**). After C steps, the target DQ-network parameters are synchronized by the Main DQ-network (**line 27**).

5 Experimental Evaluation and Discussion

The approach was implemented using Python 3.9 and TensorFlow to build and train Deep Neural Networks (DNNs). Experiments were conducted on a 64-bit Windows 10 system with an Intel(R) Core i7 CPU clocked at 1.20 GHz and 16 GB RAM.

5.1 Experiment Setting

In the context of a Fog-Cloud network, we examine a scenario involving three APs connected to heterogeneous Fog resources and a centralized Cloud. Each AP establishes connectivity with five nodes. These resources have diverse attributes, including capacity (CPU, RAM, Disk) and data size, with varying Fog resource bandwidth. We simplify the analysis by limiting bandwidth values from 1 to 9 Mbps [2]. Our focus is on a 10-task workflow with a 15-minute slot duration. Tables 1, 2, and 3 detail the utilized values.

Table 1. Resources parameters.

Resources	Fog	Cloud
Computing capacity (MIPS)	[100–2000]	[2100–10000]
CPU frequency (GHz)	[1–3]	
Memory size (Mb)	[200–4000]	[10.000–40000]
Disk size (Mb)	[200–5000]	[10.000–230000]
Computing power (W)	[1–5]	12
Transmission power (W)	[1–2]	5
Wireless bandwidth (Mbps)	[5–9]	UPLink/DownLink 1
End-user transmission energy consumption (per unit)	1.5W	

Table 2. Tasks parameters.

Tasks	Values
Data size (Mb)	[20–150]
Data output (Mb)	[10–90]
Data in (Mb)	90
Number of instructions (MI)	[200–18000]

Table 3. DDQN parameters.

Parameters	Values
Episodes	[4000, 5000]
Replay Memory	10000
Batch size	556
Hidden Layers	2
Learning Rate (lr)	0.0001

We examined the impact of resource performance and network variability across different regions on our solution in three scenarios. Simulation values follow Tables 1 and 2. In Scenario 1 (**S1**), we intentionally created suboptimal resource performance and bandwidth conditions in the second region. This demonstrates that the second region's resources and network are not conducive to desired outcomes. In Scenario 2 **(S2)**, we combined favorable and unfavorable conditions in each region. In Scenario 3 **(S3)**, all regions had good conditions.

5.2   Training Model Evaluation

Figure 3a, Fig. 3b, and Fig. 3c show the system reward for the DDQN-based migration training phase for the three scenarios. The total number of episodes is set between 4000 and 5000 episodes. In each episode, decisions for all tasks in all time slots are made and the total reward of the system is obtained. Initially, as the agent explores the environment and takes random actions, the total reward per episode is low and exhibits fluctuations in the three scenarios. However, as training episodes increase, the total reward gradually improves and eventually converges. It starts to converge in the first, second, and third scenarios after approximately 1000, 700, and 1500 episodes, respectively. On the other hand, Fig. 3d, Fig. 3e, and Fig. 3f illustrate the loss minimization which measures the discrepancy between the predicted Q-values and the target Q-values during the training phase for the three scenarios.

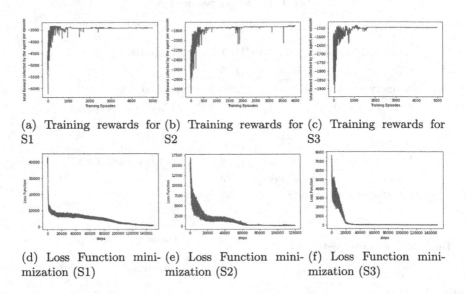

(a) Training rewards for S1

(b) Training rewards for S2

(c) Training rewards for S3

(d) Loss Function minimization (S1)

(e) Loss Function minimization (S2)

(f) Loss Function minimization (S3)

Fig. 3. The performance evaluation results in the training phase

The loss value is initially high as the network starts with random weights and cannot accurately predict the Q-values. However, as the training progresses, the loss value gradually decreases, indicating that the network is learning and improving its predictions. The convergence of the loss to 0 signifies that the DDQN algorithm has successfully trained the network to accurately estimate the Q-values and make optimal decisions based on the learned policy in the three scenarios.

5.3 Comparative Study

To evaluate the efficiency of our workflow migration approach, we compare it with the following two DDQN-based strategies:

1. **No migration:** This is a static strategy, where the agent offloads the user's tasks to the resources of the initial region and does not perform any migrations throughout the various time slots.
2. **Always migration:** The tasks follow the user mobility pattern in this strategy [1]. The agent needs to determine a new placement strategy based on the current location in each time slot. The only possible action allowed by the agent is $A_i^t = a_1$.

Figure 4a, Fig. 4b, and Fig. 4c show the performance of the proposed DDQN-based solution compared to *always migration-based* and *no migration-based* strategies during the inference phase for the three scenarios. Staring with *S1*, it can be observed in Fig. 4a that the approach we propose significantly outperforms the other two approaches in terms of both delay and energy consumption, achieving approximately 848 (s) and 2572 (w), respectively. This advantage stems from our solution's ability to identify an optimal migration policy across all time slots, considering the overall objective function. Conversely, the Always migration strategy produces inferior outcomes of 1504 (s) and 4302 (w). This can be attributed to the fact that in this strategy, the agent attempts to migrate tasks at every time slot, disregarding the potential suboptimal performance capacities and bandwidth links associated with the current resources.

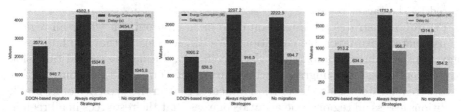

(a) Comparison of rewards for S1   (b) Comparison of rewards for S2   (c) Comparison of rewards for S3

Fig. 4. The performance evaluation results in the inference phase

Moving to *S2*, Fig. 4b clearly illustrates the superior performance of the DDQN-based strategy, achieving around 683 (s) and 1066 (w). However, the always migration and no migration strategies exhibit similar performance levels, both around 1000 (s) and 2222 (w) in this particular scenario.

In Fig. 4c, it can be observed that the no migration strategy outperforms the other strategies in terms of delay with 584 (s) in the particular context of the scenario *S3*. This outcome is attributed to the favorable circumstances arising from the computational capabilities of resources in the first region, thereby contributing to the improved delay. On the other hand, our proposed solution demonstrates significantly lower energy consumption around 913 (w).

Furthermore, we examined the migration ratio of our DDQN solution for each scenario in every time slot. This metric offers insights into the proportion of tasks migrated during a specific time slot, enabling comparisons of migration patterns and identification of variations across time slots. This ratio is defined as follows:

$$\text{Migration ratio}(t) = \frac{\text{Number of migrated tasks}(t)}{\text{Total number of tasks (N)}} \quad (24)$$

Figure 5a illustrates the migration ratio in each time slot for *S1*. In the second time slot, the migration ratio is 0, indicating no tasks were migrated. During the training phase, the agent placed tasks in the second region despite its suboptimal conditions, resulting in a lower overall reward. Therefore, the no migration strategy was applied in this time slot. However, in the third time slot, the environmental conditions improved, prompting the agent to migrate 80% of tasks and achieve a higher objective function than the no migration strategy.

Figure 5b provides a clear depiction of the migration pattern observed in *S2*, where regions 2 and 3 are associated with a mix of favorable and unfavorable conditions. It can be seen that all tasks were migrated during the second time slot. This migration pattern occurred because the agent identified resources in the second region that offered superior performance compared to those in the first region. However, in the third time slot, only 30% of the tasks were migrated. This selective migration pattern demonstrates the adaptive behavior of the agent, as it strategically chooses to migrate tasks based on the performance advantages offered by the target region.

Figure 5b illustrates the migration ratio in an environment where all regions are associated with favorable conditions. We can see clearly that the number of migrations is reduced compared to *S2*. Specifically, during the second time slot, only 50% of tasks were migrated, while during the third time slot, only 10% of tasks were migrated. This observation indicates that in the presence of favorable conditions across all regions, the agent recognizes that the resources in all regions provide satisfactory performance, which prevents unnecessary migrations.

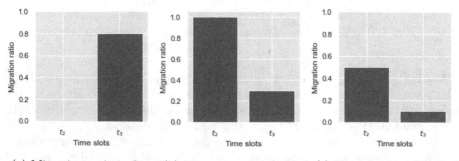

(a) Migration ratio in S1   (b) Migration ratio in S2   (c) Migration ratio in S3

Fig. 5. Comparaison of migration ratio in the different time slots

This adaptive behavior reflects the agent's ability to efficiently allocate tasks and exploit the favorable conditions available in the system.

6 Conclusion

In this study, we proposed an adaptive offloading and migration policy for Fog and Cloud Computing environments using Deep Reinforcement Learning (DRL) techniques. Our approach, based on a DDQN agent, optimizes system delay and energy consumption by making intelligent task offloading and migration decisions in dynamic environments. Experimental results across various scenarios showed the superiority of our DDQN-based approach over commonly used strategies like Always migration-based and No migration-based solutions.

The proposed work relies on a centralized DRL approach. Centralized DRL faces scalability issues, particularly, when the number of resources and regions increases. To address this issue, in our future work we plan to extend this research with decentralized policies. Additionally, we aim to conduct assessments using real-world datasets, such as the Google cluster trace[1] and the Alibaba dataset[2].

Acknowledgements. This work was supported by the ANR LabEx CIMI (grant ANR-11-LABX-0040) within the French State Programme "Investissements d'Avenir".

References

1. Bao, W., et al.: Follow me fog: toward seamless handover timing schemes in a fog computing environment. IEEE Commun. Mag. **55**(11), 72–78 (2017)
2. Bessai, K., Youcef, S., Oulamara, A., Godart, C., Nurcan, S.: Bi-criteria workflow tasks allocation and scheduling in cloud computing environments. In: 2012 IEEE Fifth International Conference on Cloud Computing, pp. 638–645 (2012)
3. Bonomi, F., Milito, R., Zhu, J., Addepalli, S.: Fog computing and its role in the Internet of Things. In: Proceedings of the First Edition of the MCC Workshop on Mobile Cloud Computing, pp. 13–16 (2012)
4. Boubaker, N.E.H., Zarour, K., Guermouche, N., Benmerzoug, D.: Fog and edge service migration approaches based on machine learning techniques: a short survey. In: Proceedings of the TACC Conference (2022)
5. Chen, W., Chen, Y., Liu, J.: Service migration for mobile edge computing based on partially observable Markov decision processes. Comput. Electr. Eng. **106**, 108552 (2023)
6. Chen, W., Chen, Y., Wu, J., Tang, Z.: A multi-user service migration scheme based on deep reinforcement learning and SDN in mobile edge computing. Phys. Commun. **47**, 101397 (2021)

---

[1] https://github.com/google/cluster-data.
[2] https://github.com/alibaba/clusterdata/tree/master/cluster-trace-gpu-v2020.

7. Dastjerdi, A.V., Gupta, H., Calheiros, R.N., Ghosh, S.K., Buyya, R.: Fog computing: principles, architectures, and applications. In: Internet of Things, pp. 61–75 (2016)
8. De Vita, F., Bruneo, D., Puliafito, A., Nardini, G., Virdis, A., Stea, G.: A deep reinforcement learning approach for data migration in multi-access edge computing. In: 2018 ITU Kaleidoscope: Machine Learning for a 5G Future (ITU K), pp. 1–8 (2018)
9. Gao, Z., Jiao, Q., Xiao, K., Wang, Q., Mo, Z., Yang, Y.: Deep reinforcement learning based service migration strategy for edge computing. In: 2019 IEEE International Conference on Service-Oriented System Engineering (SOSE), pp. 116–1165 (2019)
10. Hong, C.H., Varghese, B.: Resource management in fog/edge computing: a survey on architectures, infrastructure, and algorithms. ACM Comput. Surv. (CSUR) 52(5), 1–37 (2019)
11. Jayanetti, A., Halgamuge, S., Buyya, R.: Deep reinforcement learning for energy and time optimized scheduling of precedence-constrained tasks in edge-cloud computing environments. Future Gener. Comput. Syst. 137, 14–30 (2022)
12. Juric, M.B., Mathew, B., Sarang, P.G.: Business Process Execution Language for Web Services: An Architect and Developer's Guide to Orchestrating Web Services Using BPEL4WS. Packt Publishing Ltd. (2006)
13. Lan, D., Taherkordi, A., Eliassen, F., Chen, Z., Liu, L.: Deep reinforcement learning for intelligent migration of fog services in smart cities. In: Qiu, M. (ed.) ICA3PP 2020, Part II. LNCS, vol. 12453, pp. 230–244. Springer, Cham (2020). https://doi.org/10.1007/978-3-030-60239-0_16
14. Liu, G., Wang, J., Tian, Y., Yang, Z., Wu, Z.: Mobility-aware dynamic service placement for edge computing. EAI Endorsed Trans. Internet Things 5, e2 (2019)
15. Mehran, N., Kimovski, D., Prodan, R.: MAPO: a multi-objective model for IoT application placement in a fog environment. In: Proceedings of the 9th International Conference on the Internet of Things, pp. 1–8 (2019)
16. Mnih, V., et al.: Human-level control through deep reinforcement learning. Nature 518, 529–533 (2015)
17. Moon, S., Park, J., Lim, Y.: Task migration based on reinforcement learning in vehicular edge computing. Wirel. Commun. Mob. Comput. 2021, 1–10 (2021)
18. Park, S.W., Boukerche, A., Guan, S.: A novel deep reinforcement learning based service migration model for mobile edge computing. In: 2020 IEEE/ACM 24th International Symposium on Distributed Simulation and Real Time Applications (DS-RT), pp. 1–8 (2020)
19. Peng, Y., Liu, L., Zhou, Y., Shi, J., Li, J.: Deep reinforcement learning-based dynamic service migration in vehicular networks. In: 2019 IEEE Global Communications Conference (GLOBECOM), pp. 1–6 (2019)
20. Puliafito, C., Mingozzi, E., Anastasi, G.: Fog computing for the internet of mobile things: issues and challenges. In: 2017 IEEE International Conference on Smart Computing (SMARTCOMP), pp. 1–6 (2017)
21. Van Hasselt, H., Guez, A., Silver, D.: Deep reinforcement learning with double Q-learning. In: Proceedings of the AAAI Conference on Artificial Intelligence, vol. 30 (2016)
22. Wang, S.G., Sun, Q.B., Yang, F.C.: Web service dynamic selection by the decomposition of global QoS constraints. Ruanjian Xuebao/J. Softw. 22(7), 1426–1439 (2011)

23. Wu, C.L., Chiu, T.C., Wang, C.Y., Pang, A.C.: Mobility-aware deep reinforcement learning with glimpse mobility prediction in edge computing. In: ICC 2020–2020 IEEE International Conference on Communications (ICC), pp. 1–7 (2020)
24. Yi, S., Li, C., Li, Q.: A survey of fog computing: concepts, applications and issues. In: Proceedings of the 2015 Workshop on Mobile Big Data, pp. 37–42 (2015)
25. Zaki, A.M., Elsayed, S.A., Elgazzar, K., Hassanein, H.S.: Heuristic-based proactive service migration induced by dynamic computation load in edge computing. In: GLOBECOM 2022–2022 IEEE Global Communications Conference, pp. 5668–5673 (2022)

Security and Privacy in CISs

Decentralized and Autonomous Key Management for Open Multi-agent Systems of Embedded Agents

Arthur Baudet[1,2]([✉]) [ID], Oum-El-Kheir Aktouf[1] [ID], Annabelle Mercier[1] [ID],
and Philippe Elbaz-Vincent[2] [ID]

[1] Univ. Grenoble Alpes, Grenoble INP, LCIS, 26000 Valence, France
{arthur.baudet,oum-el-kheir.aktouf,annabelle.mercier}@lcis.grenoble-inp.fr
[2] Univ. Grenoble Alpes, CNRS, IF, 38000 Grenoble, France
{arthur.baudet,philippe.elbaz-vincent}@univ-grenoble-aples.fr

Abstract. This paper presents a public key infrastructure for open multi-agent systems of embedded agents. Open multi-agent systems of embedded agents are a set of network embedded systems cooperating in real time to achieve their goal without a central server issuing commands. In this context, agents are very prone to attacks as they can be confronted with new agents with unknown goals and as they often rely on wireless ad hoc communications. The key infrastructure we propose allows the agents to communicate without the risk of their messages being tampered with. Thus, providing foundations for more advanced security solutions such as trust management systems. In order to do that, we leverage the agent's capabilities to establish and maintain the infrastructure by providing self-organization and trust management rules. Once established, the infrastructure provides a way for the agents to assert their right to take part in the system operations with certificates and to secure their communications with asymmetric cryptography. As a result, agents can communicate securely without the risk of their identities being stolen and their communications being tampered with. They are also being able to exclude intruders. The work proposed in this paper paves the way to build more secure open decentralized systems of autonomous embedded systems. To make our solution general and adaptable to many situations, we decoupled the cryptographic and trust management details from the infrastructure itself.

Keywords: Public key infrastructure · Multi-agent systems · Embedded agent · Decentralized security

1 Introduction

The Multi-Agent Systems (MAS) paradigm proposes a decentralized approach to software and system architectures. Distributed systems such as wireless sen-

This work is supported by the French National Research Agency in the framework of the "Investissements d'avenir" program (ANR-15-IDEX-02).

sor networks, Internet-of-Things, autonomous vehicles, etc., can be deployed as a MAS with each embedded device being autonomous in its decision-making. This approach results in a network of embedded devices, each one executing one agent, autonomously communicating and collaborating to reach a common goal. We define these systems as Multi-Embedded-Agent Systems (MEAS), i.e., multi-agent systems of embedded agents. In this context, we focus our study on heterogeneous open MEAS, a class of systems that allow agents of different capabilities and origin to connect and disconnect from the system at run-time.

Recent studies [3,8] show that MEAS and similar systems are particularly vulnerable to insider attacks, attacks coming from one or more malicious agents within the system, as well as attacks on communications, as they often rely on wireless ad hoc networks. Both types of attacks can have devastating effects on the communications integrity and the availability of the system. They also show that trust management systems (TMS) are a common way of mitigating those threats. However, these TMS often take strong hypotheses on the lower layers capabilities, especially the cryptographic layer [14,17]. For example, those hypotheses may require the presence of a third party to provide a root of trust or to preload certificates in the agents, making them inapplicable in an open and decentralized context. As a consequence, a specific solution to provide agents with cryptographic keys to allow them to securely communicate is required.

In the next section, we establish the threat model and review the security concerns related to our work. We introduce our contribution in Sect. 4 and discuss its validity through model checking in Sect. 5 and simulation in Sect. 6. Finally, we conclude the paper in Sect. 7.

2   Security Considerations and Threat Model

We aim to secure the communications in multi-agent systems of embedded agents so that any unauthorized modifications can be detected (integrity checks), and that the source of each message can be verified (authenticity) while supporting accountability. As we add new behaviors and possibly increase the attack surface, we also establish the vulnerabilities induced by our approach.

Regarding other security concerns, we consider the following assumptions:

- The cryptographic primitives that are used, the hardware they run on, and their implementations are secured.
- A suitable and robust TMS is running on each agent.
- Sybil attacks are mitigated by using either the TMS or by other means.

We define a threat model with a mote-class attacker, i.e., of similar resources as the agents of the system, which has complete control over the communication medium. It would be able to eavesdrop on, to replay and to tamper with any message. Moreover, we make no assumption on the intentions or capabilities (inside the spectrum of the mote class) of other agents, their behaviors are modeled as Byzantine behaviors.

3 Related Work

This is not the first attempt to provide a distributed and decentralized PKI, but most of the previous works do not go far enough in the context of open decentralized autonomy. For example, the works presented in [18] and [13] rely on threshold cryptography or Simple Distributed Security Infrastructure to provide a decentralized Public Key Infrastructure (PKI) but they still require either out-of-band verification or preloaded certificates to provide authentication. In [5], the authors propose an enhanced Distributed PKI for industrial control systems using an agent-based framework that requires an operator to add or remove systems from the PKI, which conflicts with our openness characteristic. Both the works in [1,7] base their decentralized PKI on a distributed hash table to allow the signature, storage, and certification of certificates. While they solve the problem of consensus in managing certificates, they do not provide ways to autonomously filter out untrustworthy nodes. Lastly, the LocalPKI [12] seems to be a good candidate but requires user input.

Efforts toward designing a decentralized PKI also involves Blockchain Technology (BCT) [22,24,25]. The BCT is designed to provide a consensus on information in decentralized systems where no trust pre-exists, making it an ideal solution to deliver, store and revoke certificates, like the two previously cited works. Yet, BCT is not adapted to our problem. Regardless of the used consensus algorithm, which can be highly power-consuming in the case of the proof-of-work, the security of a blockchain partly relies on storing the history of all the exchanged information during the life of the system. This means that it will only grow and eventually reach a size too large to be stored.

Identity- and attribute-based approaches such as the ones presented in [11,21] are promising but they too strongly rely on prior knowledge about the agents, an assumption difficult to meet in open heterogeneous systems.

Our problem is also related to the field Self-Sovereign Identity [10]. But, just as the work cited above, the solution brought to achieve decentralized self-sovereign identity usually requires a third party or a ledger for validation.

Consequently, we could not find any existing infrastructure satisfying the three main requirements of the studied systems: decentralized autonomy, openness and heterogeneity. This is why we provide in our work the foundations of such a PKI through Multi-Agent Key Infrastructure (MAKI), an infrastructure designed for open MEAS. MAKI empowers TMS by enabling secure communications and enforcing exclusions. It also leverages it to deploy a resilient self-organization against insiders' attacks.

4 Multi-agent Key Infrastructure

The sole use of cryptographic signatures enables integrity and authenticity verification as well as accountability. This only requires agents to generate asymmetric keys and use them to sign all the messages they send. This mechanism alone meets the decentralized cryptographic requirements we set. However, doing so also enables abusive behaviors such as agents using multiple pairs of keys at the same time or changing their keys over time. We prevent those behaviors by linking an agent's identity to a key with certificates and by leveraging the TMS to make identity changing inefficient. Then, we empower the TMS by allowing the certificate of malicious agents to be revoked, leading to their exclusion.

Algorithm 1 Algorithm describing how the decision of becoming a CA is taken.

$T \in [0, 1)$ ▷ *The probability that an agent decides to become a CA even other trust-worthy CAs are close.*
1: Role ← None
2: CAs ← GETNEIGHBORCALIST()
3: TrustedCAs ← FILTER(CAs, TrustLevel.Moderate)
4: **if** CANBECOMECA() **and** (TrustedCAs is empty **or** RANDOM(0, 1) < T) **then**
5: └ Role ← CA
6: **return** Role

4.1 Architecture

As we are focusing on open heterogeneous MEAS, we do not expect new agents to enter with preloaded certificates nor do we want to enforce specific authentication protocols. Instead, we designed MAKI without requiring authentication. In MAKI, agents are anonymous and are only categorized as friendly or malicious based on their actions. This is possible thanks to the accountability induced by the use of cryptographic signatures but it requires a strong coupling between an agent's identity and one pair of cryptographic keys. To enforce this coupling, MAKI uses a subset of the principles of standard PKIs, such as the X.509 PKI. It only includes the role of Certificate Authority (CA), the mandatory use of certificates and signatures, and the certificate revocation.

The CAs are designated using a self-organization algorithm (see Sect. 4.2). Thus capitalizing on the autonomy of the agents. They have the responsibility to deliver certificates and revoke them when necessary. They are autonomous in their choice of delivering and revoking. To prevent abuses, we defined TMS rules (see Sect. 4.3) to sanction improperly behaving CAs.

Revocation is carried out using two mechanisms. First, the CAs will add the revoked certificates to their Certificate Revocation Lists (CRLs) and broadcast them. This method is direct and instantaneous but, depending on the network capabilities, the CRL updates may take time to reach every agent. So, to mitigate this issue, we also use short-lived certificates, which will not be renewed by CAs that are aware of the revocation.

4.2 Self-organization

The proper functioning of the self-organization depends on rules MAKI adds to the TMS. The way we avoid the pitfalls of self-signed CAs, the likeliness a malicious agent will become CA or the rewards of being cross-certified are explained in the next section.

CAs are self-elected. Agents capable of being CA (if they have enough resources) decide for themselves if they will become a CA, otherwise they remain None, the default role which does not hold any responsibility toward the PKI. Algorithm 1 describes how the choice is made. This algorithm was designed with two modular goals: (i) every agent should be close to a CA and (ii) CAs will not become a single-point-of-failure. This will lead to a uniform distribution, depending on T, the probability that an agent decides to become a CA, of CAs with one or more CAs by groups of agents. It is possible to adapt the definition of "close" to reduce the number of CAs. There will be more CAs if close means being in communication range than if it means being in three times the communication range. It is also possible to adapt the value of T to increase or lower the number of redundant CAs. If T is high, almost all agents that can be CA will be, but if T is low, only agents far from a CA will become one. Both the definition of close and the value of T should be tailored to the application, density and capabilities of the application MAKI runs on. Moreover, since we do not want to rely on third parties to establish a root of trust, CAs are all initially self-signed and can later use cross-certification to create a network of trustworthy CAs.

Choosing a CA for a None agent is similar to deciding to become a CA. Once they know the identity of their neighbors CAs, they choose one of them. We do not recommend choosing the most trustworthy each time since it can create single-point-of-failure situations if all the agents have the same CA as their most trustworthy CAs. We rather recommend using an exploration scheme such a simple weighted sum or a multi-arm bandit strategy. This way, the most trusted CAs are still selected and less trusted CAs are given the opportunity to prove themselves, creating some redundancy and increase the resilience of the system.

Adding a new agent in MAKI is straightforward. The agent will first determine if it needs to become a CA and, if not, it requests a certificate from a CA. It may then decide to select a more trustworthy CA by requesting trust information from its neighbors or keep the CA it chose. In any case, it will advertise its certificate to ensure that its neighbors learn about it.

As self-signed CAs are not susceptible to the revocation mechanisms, the only way to exclude them is to ignore them and suggest new agents to avoid them. A way to reduce this advantage is to allow cross-certification. This means that CAs could request that other CAs sign their certificates which would make them susceptible to have their certificate revoked. This has no intrinsic benefit for the cross-certified CA as it will only make it harder to obtain and maintain a valid certificate, but it is considered as a show of good faith and is rewarded in the TMS.

4.3   Trust Management

MAKI is not designed for a specific TMS. Moreover, defining a trust model for each specific use case of MEAS is out of scope. Instead, we specify here how MAKI leverages the TMS to deploy its self-organization.

We present in Table 1 a risk assessment of the interactions in MAKI and recommended trust thresholds to reach to carry them out. These trust thresholds

Table 1. Trade-offs between risk and benefit for each possible interaction between agents depending on their roles.

Interaction	Risk	Benefit	Required trust
Certificate Authority			
Delivering a certificate	Moderate. Allowing malicious agents to operate	High. Having its own legitimacy increase since one more agent is trusting it to deliver trustworthy certificates	Moderate or none[†]
Revoking a certificate	High. Decreasing the trust of agents not agreeing with the revocation. Excluding a benevolent agent	High. Helps the overall system by excluding a malicious agent	Moderate
Requesting a cross-certification	High. Having its reputation* decreased if the cross-certifier is distrusted. Giving more legitimacy to a malicious CA	Moderate. Higher trust is given to cross-certified CA	High
Accepting a cross-certification request	High. Giving more legitimacy to a malicious CA	High. Having its own legitimacy increase since a CA is trusting it	High
None			
Requesting a certification	Moderate. If the CA is not trusted, having to renew the certificate with another one. Giving more legitimacy to a malicious CA	High. Holding a valid certificate is mandatory to participate in the system	Moderate or none[‡]

*The term "reputation" is used as a way to describe the trust other agents have in one agent.
[†]CAs have no way in checking the trustability of new agents at first so the required trust is set to none for them.
[‡]New agents have no way in checking the trustability of CAs at first so the required trust is set to none for them.

are representations of the trust an agent should have in other agents to interact with them. Their values depend on the trust model. In addition to the presented interactions, we add that any agent should be able to request and share their certificates without risk nor required trust, as doing so allows checking or proving that the requirement of holding a valid certificate is met.

MAKI also leverages the TMS to mitigate the proliferation of malicious self-signed CAs by adding a cost to the role of CA. In MAKI, a CA can only be legitimate if it continuously replies to certification requests, and illegitimate CAs should be ignored. This way, even a malicious CA must contribute to the system by delivering certificates to requesting agents. This can be translated by a small increase of the trust in a CA each time it answers a certification request. Moreover, the trust put in certified agent is weighted by the trust of the CA that signed its certificate. This is done to encourage agents to choose CAs they trust but that other agents also trust. This aims at making the CAs properly behave to every agent and not only to some of them.

While we explained how to mitigate the risk of malicious agents becoming CA and thus self-signed CAs, we can also provide a way to reduce the number of self-signed CA by adding a trust reward for cross-certified CA. Cross-certified CAs will end up more selected. This will force self-signed CAs to get cross-certified and take the risk of having their certificates revoked if they behave maliciously.

```
Identity ::= SEQUENCE { name INTEGER, publicKey BIT STRING }
```

(a) ASN.1 representation of the Identity field used in MAKI certificates and CRL.

```
1 Certificate ::= SEQUENCE {          1 CertificateRevocationList ::=
2   version [0]  INTEGER,                 SEQUENCE {
3   serialNumber INTEGER,             2   version [0]            INTEGER,
4   signature    BIT STRING,          3   signature             BIT STRING,
5   issuer       Identity,            4   holder                Identity,
6   validity     SEQUENCE {           5   thisUpdate            UTCTime,
7     notBefore UTCTime,              6   certificates SEQUENCE OF
8     notAfter  UTCTime                     SEQUENCE {
9   },                                7     serialNumber  INTEGER,
10  subject      Identity,            8     issuer        Identity,
11  subjectRole  Role,               9     subject       Identity,
12  subjectInfo  SubjectInfo         10    revocationDate UTCTime,
13 }                                 11    reasonCode     ReasonCode
14 Role ::= INTEGER {                12   }
15  NONE(0),                         13 }
16  CA(1)                            14 ReasonCode ::= ENUMERATED {
17 }                                 15   idComprise(0),
                                     16   cessationOfOperation(1)
                                     17 }
```

(b) ASN.1 representation of the MAKI certificates.

(c) ASN.1 representation of the MAKI CRL.

Fig. 1. ASN.1 representation of the MAKI certificate and CRL formats.

Overall, MAKI does not reduce the security brought by the TMS since, even though they cannot be revoked, self-signed CAs can still be ignored and their bad reputation shared to new agents. This means that the number of malicious agents MAKI can handle only depends on the TMS and the complexity of the attacks executed against it. We show in Sect. 6 how, with a simple TMS, MAKI handles malicious agents once the TMS detects their malicious behaviors.

4.4   Certificate Management

Certificate and CRL representations can be found in Fig. 1. Excluding the fields we did not keep from the X.509 format [6], the main differences are the inclusion of the public key of the issuer since it is part of its identity and the additional field, subjectInfo, which is let to be defined by the system designers. Using this format, with an empty subjectInfo field, 4-byte time_t for UTCTime, 193 bytes for the public key OpenSSH format, 105 bytes for the raw signature, 1-byte integer for Version, Role and ReasonCode, and 2-byte integer for SerialNumber and Name, and no padding, the size of a certificate is 507 bytes.

Since MAKI does not rely on registration authorities to deliver and distribute certificates, the distribution of certificates falls to the agents themselves. Agents may broadcast their certificates periodically and should attach them to the first messages of each exchange. An agent can also request the certificate of another agent. These distribution methods are less efficient than having a third party gathering and sharing the certificates. But they remove any threat coming from this third party and any risk of it becoming a single-point-of-failure as well as enable better scalability and decentralization.

Concerning the CRL format, we moved the reasonCode field from the CRL Extension to the mandatory fields so that CAs can be held accountable for each revocation. To keep the CRL format as small as possible, it is only meant to hold information related to agents exclusion. Hence, from the ten possible values, we only kept the KeyCompromise (renamed IdCompromise) and CessationOfOpera- tion. Other reason codes could be added to indicate malicious behaviors specific to the application. Following the same memory size choices as in the certificate format, a CRL with $n \in \mathbb{N}$ certificates is $305 + n \times 397$ bytes. CAs should keep and distribute, gratuitously or on demand, their CRL.

5   Model Checking

5.1   Tool and Hypotheses

To validate our approach, we applied model checking with Model Checker for Multi-Agent Systems (MCMAS) [19]. MCMAS allowed us to describe our agents' behaviors directly and easily using a language designed for it: ISPL (Interpreted Systems Programming Language). Using algorithms based on ordered binary decision diagrams, MCMAS supports the verification of epistemic and temporal modalities. In particular, we used computation tree logic operators to describe the properties that interest us. However, MCMAS makes several hypotheses in its model:

A. The internal states are only known by their owner and actions are public.
B. There is no explicit ways to communicate between agents.
C. The number of agents is bound, meaning that each agent in the model is explicitly described. E.g., for 5 agents, we have to describe: Agent1, Agent2, Agent3, Agent4 and Agent5, even if their behaviors are the same.

D. The agents have no power or computational limits.

Due to hypotheses A and B, we modeled communications with agent's actions, e.g.: `request_certificate`. Hypothesis C leads to many repetitions and to the use of a templating tool and code generation to describe multi-target interactions. E.g.: with three agents, `Agent1`, `Agent2` and `Agent3`, the ISPL representation of one agent checking if the other two are waiting is:

- In `Agent1`: `Agent2.Action = wait and Agent3.Action = wait`.
- In `Agent2`: `Agent1.Action = wait and Agent3.Action = wait`.
- In `Agent3`: `Agent1.Action = wait and Agent2.Action = wait`.

Lastly, hypothesis D means that proper evaluation of the energy and memory consumption of the algorithm should be done elsewhere.

On top of the constraints due to the hypotheses, we also decided not to add security properties and trust as it would greatly increase the complexity of the models. We relied on simulations, presented in the next section, to validate these aspects.

5.2 Model

Due to the complexity of representing security and trust characteristics in ISPL, we only validated the self-organization algorithm. To do so, we divided it in three sub-behaviors: a default behavior, a self-organization behavior and re-organization behavior. These behaviors were defined such as the whole algorithm could be described as a first self-organization behavior followed by a default behavior with a re-organization behavior repeated as needed. Thus, validating these behaviors would mean validating the self-organization behavior.

5.3 Default Behavior

In an organization including at least one CA, eventually, each agent will own a valid certificate. This is the nominal behavior and it is used as a base behavior for the two others. In this model, one or more None agents will ask to a CA to deliver a certificate and the CA will do so. ISPL does not support function or structures, so, we used the `Environment` to indicate the destination and type of a message. To successfully send a message, an agent will first send it then it will check if the environment chooses it and it will retry if not. Then, the environment state will change to indicate which message is chosen to be sent. Its default behavior consists of waiting for a message and changing its state to choose a message. As choosing a message and changing its state so it can be read by the agents takes two steps, it also makes sure to allow agent to read the state before it changes again.

5.4   Self-organization Behavior

From a set of Nones, with at least one agent able to become CA, an organization with at least one CA will emerge. In this model, all agents start as None and, using the algorithm described in Algorithm 1, they will set their role. In this model, agents with the capacity of becoming CA (`ca_able`) will decide or not to become one. If not, they will wait for a CA. However, if no CA advertises while they wait, they will change their role to make sure that at least one CA is available. This behavior is the one a new agent should consider when entering the system.

5.5   Re-organization Behavior

From an organization including at least one CA, if all the CAs stop, a new organization with at least one CA will emerge. In this model, several agents start as self-signed CA and the remaining ones start with their certificate signed by one of the CAs, then, the CAs change their role and the Nones have to drop their certificates since the signer are not CAs anymore. Moreover, some agents (as the one we present the model here) can become CA and thus, do become CA to ensure that there is at least one CA in the system. At last, None agent will request a certificate to the new CA.

It is noteworthy that the self-organization behavior and re-organization behavior situations are similar: CAs emerge from a set of None agents, we differentiate them here to validate two distinct parts of the self-organization algorithm. The self-organization behavior illustrates the choice each agent has to make, including waiting for others to choose before them. The re-organization behavior illustrates the adaptation mechanism when an incident (the loss of CAs) disrupts the system.

5.6   Validity of the Models and Results

As there is no tool to check that the models we wrote are a reflection of the algorithm, we used an incremental, in the number of agents, approach and manually checked the output graphs, using the `-exportmodel` option of the MCMAS binary. The models wrote during the whole process can be found in [4].

For each of these models, the execution of MCMAS leads to an execution graph consistent with our expectations and a result of true for each of the properties we described as to be verified.

6   Simulations

In this section, we present results obtained using one implementation of MAKI in Yet Another Multi-Agent Systems Simulator (YAMASS), an in-house multi-agent simulator based on the Mesa framework [16]. These results show that revocation is achieved when an agent is deemed untrustworthy. We also used this implementation to observe the MAKI overhead, for example, of the number of exchanged messages or of the time required to obtain, and renew, a certificate. The source code and instructions to reproduce all the results presented below are given in [4].

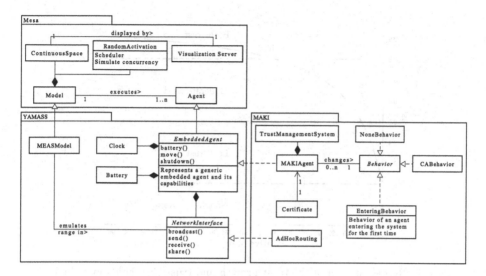

Fig. 2. Simplified UML class diagram of the simulator and MAKI

6.1 Simulator Overview

We built YAMASS to provide a straightforward way to describe embedded agents behavior with a focus on simulation setup and reproducibility. In YAMASS, agents have coordinates, a range and a battery. As such, they can only communicate with the agents in their range and have to rely on ad hoc routing to communicate with the other agents. All their characteristics are described in an input file along with the seeds used by the different pseudorandom number generators. Moreover, for total reproducibility, the agents are not attributed a thread but are executed in randomized sequence. However, this solution removes the notion of time from the simulation. A step in time includes one step per agent, in random order. During one step, an agent processes the messages it receives, sends the message it needs to send and then adapt its state accordingly. This means that, in one step, an agent can react to the messages it received and adapt its states, once, afterward.

A simplified UML class diagram of the simulator and MAKI is given in Fig. 2. It shows the main elements of a MAKI agent, its TMS, its network stack and the behavior which it selects depending on its capabilities and its neighbors. The basic block of YAMASS are also shown, an interface representing an embedded agent and its network stack as well as the time emulation through the Clock and the EMASModel making sure that agents cannot exceed their capabilities. We also indicate the components of Mesa we rely on, including the Visualization Server allowing for graphical representation when necessary and the DataCollector used to collect trust values during the simulations.

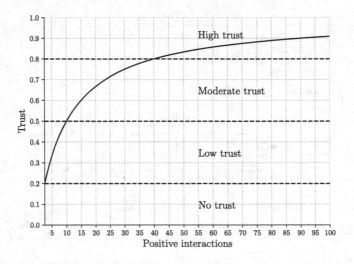

Fig. 3. Representation of the trust growth and trust thresholds in MAKI.

6.2   Setup

To use YAMASS, we first had to implement a dynamic routing algorithm. We implemented a lightweight version of [15] which provides a way to establish and maintain routes between agents in a mesh network without prior knowledge on the network topology.

Then, we also implemented a minimalistic TMS based on a trust model with a low initial trust, the common mitigation to whitewashing presented in [23]. The model was tailored to the duration of the simulation. The value of the trust is bound between 0 and 1 with a growth following the function defined in Eq. (1). The value 10 was chosen to set the slop of the curve.

$$f : x \mapsto \frac{x}{x + 10} \tag{1}$$

The *Low*, *Moderate* and *High* trust thresholds are respectively set to 0.2, 0.5 and 0.8 and the initial value is set to *Low*. In this model, a trust value below the *Low* thresholds implies that the agent is to be ignored. The graph of this trust growth function, with the thresholds, is given in Fig. 3. The trust also slightly decay over time to compel agent to keep behaving correctly over time. Its value also depends on the duration of a simulation. The TMS also includes indirect information. An agent can ask other agents how much they trust a given agent and add this information to its model. Trust from direct and indirect information is aggregated using the ratio of experience to recommendations, the more interactions an agent A_0 will have with another agent A_1, the less it will rely on recommendations to compute its trust in A_1. Moreover, every agent eavesdrops on the communications to update in real time their trust model, in particular concerning the certificate deliveries. This can be done to cross-check the cooperation of the CA for example.

We followed the NIST recommendations [2] for the choice of cryptographic primitives. Thus, we used Elliptical Curve Cryptography with the Elliptic Curve Digital Signature Algorithm (ECDSA) and 256-bit keys using the P-256 Curve. The communications of MAKI are not meant to be encrypted, only signed, as all the information is public and might be eavesdropped for verification purpose. While ECDSA is the standard, it may not be adapted to embedded systems due to its high computational cost. The "NIST Report on Lightweight Cryptography" [20] can be referred to for dealing with devices too constrained to run it.

We implemented a mock multi-agent application for the agents to cooperate and increases their trust in each other. This mock application consists of requests and replies between agents, each one increase the trust of the requester and requestee. Each step, each agent has a 0.7 chance to send a request to one of the agents it knows and the requestee will always correctly reply.

Then, we needed to define physical configurations representing different formation agents could take and ran enough simulations to make sure that no unexpected behavior would emerge and do gather execution traces to process. We used the fast Poisson disk sampling function [9] to populate the space given to the agents. This way, the agents were randomly placed while remaining near enough to communicate with each other but not close enough to form clusters. Using this method, we generate configurations of 10, 20, 30, and 40 agents. In each of the configuration, about 50% of the agents are able to become CA, independently to their position. To create diversity, we defined a "density" as the average number of neighbors, agents in communication range, an agent range (the higher the density, the more the agents will be packed) and try to obtain configurations with different densities. Then, for each configuration and each density we ran 5 simulations of 500 steps each, with a certificate duration of 100 steps. The details on the exact number of simulations are given in Table 2.

Table 2. Details on the number of simulations.

Number of agents	10	20	30	40
Density per number of agents	1–4	2–4	2–4	2–4
Configurations per density	10	10	10	10
Repetitions per configuration	5	5	5	5
Total	200	150	150	150
	650 simulations			

Lastly, we defined scenarios describing the general behavior of the agents. In the next sub-section, we focus on two scenarios:

Scenario 0. The agents cooperate and all follow the rules. This scenario corresponds to the agents nominal behavior. The results concerning the average time to obtain and renew a certificate and the general overhead, in messages exchange, of MAKI are computed from this scenario.

Scenario 1. After some time (300 steps), one randomly chosen agent will be deemed untrustworthy by ∼60% of the agents cooperating with it and those agents will request its revocation. This scenario aims at showing the efficiency of MAKI in excluding untrustworthy agents and the benefit compared to only using the TMS.

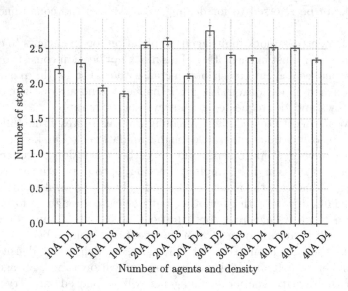

Fig. 4. Average time to obtain a certificate in systems with different numbers of agents and densities.

6.3   Results

Average Time to Obtain and Renew a Certificate (Scenario 0). While MCMAS allowed us to be confident in the self-organization algorithm validity, we also wanted to ensure its efficiency. In particular, we wanted to make sure that agents could easily and quickly obtain or renew their certificates. Especially since the CA-able agents are not always homogeneously located in the systems, which leads to situations where, even when using the self-organization algorithm we described, not all agents have a CA in their neighborhood, as it might simply

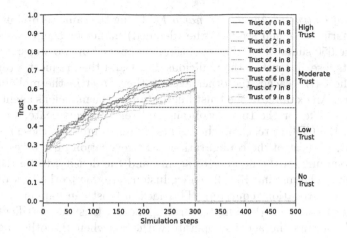

Fig. 5. Trust fluctuations in the malicious agent over time.

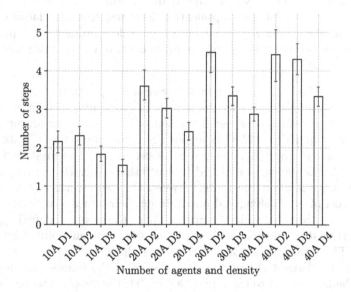

Fig. 6. Average time for the CRL to reach all the agents of the system, with different numbers of agents and densities.

not be possible. Using Scenario 0 on the 650 simulations described in Table 2 and measuring the average time between a certificate request and the advertisement of the newly received certificate, we obtained an average between 1.5 and 2.5 steps, as presented in Fig. 4. These values seem reasonable as they show that, even without a CA in the neighborhood, obtaining or renewing a certificate is almost instantaneous.

Revocation of Untrusted Agents (Scenario 1). Using the same setup but with the second scenario, we could see that the (deemed) malicious agent was excluded in 500 of the 650 simulations. The exclusions happened in two steps: (i) the first aware agents lose all trust in the malicious agent and then request a revocation; (ii) when the CRL reaches the other agents, their trust in the malicious agent drops to zero. An example of the trust fluctuation in the malicious agent is shown in Fig. 5. Just like for the time to obtain and renew a certificate, we estimate the time for the CRL to reach all the agents. Figure 6 presents these results. We can see that, in most of the configurations, the revocation only takes from 2 to 5 steps, depending on the number of agents and the density, to be received by all the agents. The missing 150 (22%) exclusions are due to the lack of trust of the CA in the revocation requesters. This lack of trust can happen as CAs can cooperate with an agent (leading to earning enough trust for certification) but not with the agents the agent cooperate with. So, when the other agents ask for revocation, the trust the CA puts in them is not high enough to take the revocation into account. However, this is mainly due to the absence of a real organization at the multi-agent application level which is only lacking because we emulate it. We expect real applications to be less prone to this problem as the cooperation between agents may be more consistent, and less random, than in our simulations.

Number of Sent Messages (Scenario 0 & Scenario 1). As the simulation only includes a mock application, we do not try to compute an overhead but we rather estimate the number of necessary sent messages. A first situation where exchanges are required in MAKI is for an agent to obtain a certificate, it must send a request and the CA must send the certificate: 1 request and 1 reply, plus the number of messages required to route them, plus the routing messages to establish and maintain the route between the two agents if it wasn't done before, the cost of establishing and maintaining the route is also shared with the application since it also requires routing. Then, the newly certified agent may share its certificate. This process is repeated each time an agent must renew a certificate. The total number of sent messages also depends on the duration of a certificate, the longest the duration is, the lesser the number of messages to send, but the harder it is to exclude an agent. This trade-off is to be considered in very constrained networks with low latency. The overall number of necessary sent messages, for one certification is:

$$N_{certification} = 2 \times RouteLength + N_{sharing}$$

with $N_{sharing}$ the number of messages sent to share the certificate. $N_{certification}$ is then to be multiplied by the number of certificates to renew and the frequency of renewal. It is to note that the lower the number of CA, the higher the number of messages to send to renew all the not self-signed certificates and the longer the average route length.

A second situation where messages are to be sent is to request a revocation and share a CRL. As for the certificate sharing, the number of sent messages depends on the implemented strategy as discussed in Sect. 4.

7 Conclusion

We introduced a decentralized public key infrastructure, coined MAKI, designed for open heterogeneous multi-agent systems of embedded agents and with a focus on autonomy of its management. This infrastructure allows agent to securely communicate and enforce the exclusion of intruders. This revocation is possible thanks to a subset of trusted certification authority agents maintained with no third parties involved.

Future works include a deployment of MAKI on embedded systems to confront our approach to real-time situations. We are also exploring a solution to provide a way for agents to reliably share their identities and the lists of excluded agents, a minimalistic blockchain-based solution is currently being studied.

References

1. Avramidis, A., Kotzanikolaou, P., Douligeris, C., Burmester, M.: Chord-PKI: a distributed trust infrastructure based on P2P networks. Comput. Netw. **56**(1), 378–398 (2012). https://doi.org/10.1016/j.comnet.2011.09.015
2. Barker, E., Dang, Q.: Recommendation for key management part 3: application-specific key management guidance (2015). https://doi.org/10.6028/NIST.SP.800-57pt3r1
3. Baudet, A., Aktouf, O.E.K., Mercier, A., Elbaz-Vincent, P.: Systematic mapping study of security in multi-embedded-agent systems. IEEE Access **9**, 154902–154913 (2021). https://doi.org/10.1109/ACCESS.2021.3128287
4. Baudet, A., Aktouf, O.E.K., Mercier, A., Elbaz-Vincent, P.: Models & Simulation code and data for reproduction of results published in CoopIS (2023). https://doi.org/10.5281/zenodo.8129629
5. Blanch-Torné, S., Cores, F., Chiral, R.M.: Agent-based PKI for distributed control system. In: 2015 World Congress on Industrial Control Systems Security (WCICSS), pp. 28–35 (2015). https://doi.org/10.1109/WCICSS.2015.7420319
6. Boeyen, S., Santesson, S., Polk, T., Housley, R., Farrell, S., Cooper, D.: Internet X.509 public key infrastructure certificate and certificate revocation list (CRL) profile. RFC 5280 (2008). https://doi.org/10.17487/RFC5280
7. Bonnaire, X., Cortés, R., Kordon, F., Marin, O.: A scalable architecture for highly reliable certification. In: 2013 12th IEEE International Conference on Trust, Security and Privacy in Computing and Communications, pp. 328–335 (2013). https://doi.org/10.1109/TrustCom.2013.44
8. Boubiche, D.E., Athmani, S., Boubiche, S., Toral-Cruz, H.: Cybersecurity issues in wireless sensor networks: current challenges and solutions. Wirel. Pers. Commun. **117**(1), 177–213 (2021). https://doi.org/10.1007/s11277-020-07213-5
9. Bridson, R.: Fast Poisson disk sampling in arbitrary dimensions. In: ACM SIGGRAPH 2007 Sketches, p. 22-es (2007). https://doi.org/10.1145/1278780.1278807
10. Čučko, Š, Turkanović, M.: Decentralized and self-sovereign identity: systematic mapping study. IEEE Access **9**, 139009–139027 (2021). https://doi.org/10.1109/ACCESS.2021.3117588
11. Cui, H., Deng, R.H.: Revocable and decentralized attribute-based encryption. Comput. J. **59**(8), 1220–1235 (2016). https://doi.org/10.1093/comjnl/bxw007

12. Dumas, J.-G., Lafourcade, P., Melemedjian, F., Orfila, J.-B., Thoniel, P.: LocalPKI: an interoperable and IoT friendly PKI. In: Obaidat, M.S., Cabello, E. (eds.) ICETE 2017. CCIS, vol. 990, pp. 224–252. Springer, Cham (2019). https://doi.org/10.1007/978-3-030-11039-0_11

13. Goffee, N.C., Kim, S.H., Smith, S., Taylor, P., Zhao, M., Marchesini, J.: Greenpass: decentralized, PKI-based authorization for wireless LANs. In: 3rd Annual PKI Research and Development Workshop, pp. 26–41 (2004)

14. Jhaveri, R.H., Patel, N.M.: Attack-pattern discovery based enhanced trust model for secure routing in mobile ad-hoc networks. Int. J. Commun Syst **30**(7), e3148 (2017). https://doi.org/10.1002/dac.3148

15. Johnson, D., Hu, Y., Maltz, D.: The dynamic source routing protocol (DSR) for mobile ad hoc networks for IPv4. RFC 4728 (2007). https://doi.org/10.17487/RFC4728

16. Kazil, J., Masad, D., Crooks, A.: Utilizing python for agent-based modeling: the mesa framework. In: Thomson, R., Bisgin, H., Dancy, C., Hyder, A., Hussain, M. (eds.) SBP-BRiMS 2020. LNCS, vol. 12268, pp. 308–317. Springer, Cham (2020). https://doi.org/10.1007/978-3-030-61255-9_30

17. Kukreja, D., Dhurandher, S.K., Reddy, B.V.R.: Power aware malicious nodes detection for securing MANETs against packet forwarding misbehavior attack. J. Ambient. Intell. Humaniz. Comput. **9**(4), 941–956 (2017). https://doi.org/10.1007/s12652-017-0496-2

18. Lesueur, F., Me, L., Tong, V.V.T.: An efficient distributed PKI for structured P2P networks. In: 2009 IEEE Ninth International Conference on Peer-to-Peer Computing, pp. 1–10 (2009). https://doi.org/10.1109/P2P.2009.5284491

19. Lomuscio, A., Qu, H., Raimondi, F.: MCMAS: an open-source model checker for the verification of multi-agent systems. Int. J. Softw. Tools Technol. Transfer **19**(1), 9–30 (2015). https://doi.org/10.1007/s10009-015-0378-x

20. McKay, K., Bassham, L., Turan, M.S., Mouha, N.: Report on lightweight cryptography (2017). https://doi.org/10.6028/NIST.IR.8114. https://tsapps.nist.gov/publication/get_pdf.cfm?pub_id=922743

21. Okamoto, T., Takashima, K.: Decentralized attribute-based encryption and signatures. IEICE Trans. Fundam. Electron. Commun. Comput. Sci. **E103.A**(1), 41–73 (2020). https://doi.org/10.1587/transfun.2019CIP0008

22. Qin, B., Huang, J., Wang, Q., Luo, X., Liang, B., Shi, W.: Cecoin: a decentralized PKI mitigating MitM attacks. Future Gener. Comput. Syst. **107**, 805–815 (2020). https://doi.org/10.1016/j.future.2017.08.025

23. Ruan, Y., Durresi, A.: A survey of trust management systems for online social communities - trust modeling, trust inference and attacks. Knowl.-Based Syst. **106**, 150–163 (2016). https://doi.org/10.1016/j.knosys.2016.05.042

24. Singla, A., Bertino, E.: Blockchain-based PKI solutions for IoT. In: 2018 IEEE 4th International Conference on Collaboration and Internet Computing (CIC), pp. 9–15 (2018). https://doi.org/10.1109/CIC.2018.00-45

25. Yakubov, A., Shbair, W.M., Wallbom, A., Sanda, D., State, R.: A blockchain-based PKI management framework. In: NOMS 2018–2018 IEEE/IFIP Network Operations and Management Symposium, pp. 1–6 (2018). https://doi.org/10.1109/NOMS.2018.8406325

An Empirical Study on Socio-technical Modeling for Interdisciplinary Privacy Requirements

Claudia Negri-Ribalta[1]([✉]), Rene Noel[2], Oscar Pastor[3], and Camille Salinesi[4]

[1] SnT, University of Luxembourg, Esch-sur-Alzette, Luxembourg
claudia.negriribalta@uni.lu
[2] Escuela de Ingenieria Civil Informatica, Universidad de Valparaiso, Valparaiso, Chile
[3] VRAIN, Universidad Politécnica de Valencia, Valencia, Spain
[4] CRI, Université Paris 1 Panthéon-Sorbonne, Paris, France

Abstract. Data protection regulations impose requirements on organizations that require interdisciplinary. Conceptual modeling of information systems, particularly goal modeling, has served to communicate with stakeholders of different backgrounds for software requirements analysis. An extension for a Socio-Technical Security (STS) modeling language was proposed to include data protection modeling concepts to help represent relevant issues of the European Union's General Data Protection Regulation. This article examines whether models designed with this extension serve as communication facilitators for privacy compliance and common ground across stakeholders.

Through a series of 8 focus groups, with 21 subjects, we observed if professionals with different backgrounds (software developers, business analysts, and privacy experts) could detect discuss about the GDPR principles and identify privacy compliance "red flags" that we seeded in a use case. Using a qualitative approach to analyze the data, all the groups discussed the majority of the GDPR principles and identified more than 80% of the seeded red flags, with privacy experts identifying the most. This research provides preliminary results on using conceptual modeling as a communicator facilitator between stakeholders to contribute to a common ground between them.

Keywords: Privacy · Modeling Language · Compliance · Requirements

1 Introduction

Data protection laws seek to protect the fundamental human right of privacy [12], and against unfair practice [13]. Indeed, the GDPR [13] in Article 5 defines

This project has received funding from the European Union's Horizon 2020 research and innovation programme under grant agreement No 956562. Part of first (and corresponding) author work was done at Paris 1 as part of her PhD. thesis.

seven guiding principles that guide the regulation: (1) Lawfulness, fairness, and transparency; (2) Purpose limitation; (3) Data minimization; (4) Accuracy; (5) Storage limitation; (6) Integrity and confidentiality; (7) Accountability; setting a series of requirements that information systems (IS) must include in the software development lifecycle (SDLC) [13].

Compliance requirements must start from the early phases of the SDLC to avoid re-developing the IS [5]. These requirements are usually not included in the first stages, particularly privacy requirements [5,6]. Furthermore, developers seem to have difficulties understanding regulatory privacy and data protection requirements [6,16]. This situation has led to a lack of "common ground" [16] - that is, establishing a shared understanding - over what data protection regulatory requirements are and how to satisfy them. Common ground is vital, as cross-functional teams that achieve it identify requirements from early phases, with fewer defects and reworkd in their IS [9].

For decades, conceptual models have enabled the communication of stakeholders with different backgrounds. Different established conceptual models have privacy extensions for goal [23], business process [1], and system modeling languages [2]. In particular, the Socio-Technical Security modeling language (STS-ml) [8] was designed to help analysts address security requirements at an early stage from a socio-technical point of view. However, empirical evidence on their facilitator role is an open challenge.

In previous work, an extension for STS-ml [8] has been proposed for data protection [24] to allow stakeholders to specify, share and negotiate data protection requirements from an interdisciplinary perspective. In this research, we identify the extension of [24] as STAGE (Socio-Technical Analysis of GDPR rEquirements). We aim to provide empirical evidence on the usage of STAGE, more specifically:

RQ1 - How do the subjects interact to identify and discuss GDPR compliance risks exposed in STAGE's model?

RQ2 - What are the GDPR principles discussed? And how?

Through the qualitative analysis of 8 different focus groups, where 21 subject experts in their area participated, our results show that conceptual modeling — even with limited knowledge of data protection — allowed subjects to discuss and identify privacy risks and compliance, even when they had different mental models [16]. Subjects also resolved conceptual inconsistencies seeded in the model regarding data protection, even without prior knowledge and experience of goal modeling. Most groups discussed and related most GDPR principles in the proposed scenario. Our results show that conceptual modeling can help interdisciplinary teams discuss regulatory requirements among stakeholders with different mental models and limited previous knowledge, helping establish common ground and identifying requirements from early phases [9].

The paper is structured as follows: in Sect. 2 we introduce the background work, followed by the research method in Sect. 3. Section 4 shares the results and their discussion. Threats to validity and future work are discussed in Sect. 5, while Sect. 6 presents the related work. Section 7 concludes and presents future work.

2 Background

2.1 The Socio-technical Security Modeling Language (STS-ml)

Socio-technical systems are those systems encompassed by stakeholders of different natures: humans, organizations, and technology [8]. Building on this paradigm, STS-ml seeks to support modeling the relationships and intentions of the different actors, with a particular emphasis on security requirements. STS-ml is a security goal and actor-oriented modeling, part of the i* paradigm [25] based on the work of [31]. Modeling languages based on i* allow actors to have goals (intentions, desired state of the world [8]) and own assets and resources [31]. Goal models also specify how actors can also interact with other actors and delegate primitives (such as goals) between them, establishing social relationships. The STS-ml follows this approach by integrating security concepts.

In the STS-ml, actors can be agents, humans, or socio-technical systems and have (multiple) roles [8]. Actors can delegate to each other to achieve their needs through *delegating* one or more *goals*, for which they need to *transmit* information in the form of *documents*. Such transmissions can have six security requirements: *non-repudiation, redundancy, non-delegation, trustworthiness, goal-availability,* and *authentication.* Actors' inner goals can be decomposed into sub-goals through *AND/OR relationships,* which are achieved through documents. Documents are composed of *information* that an actor owns. An actor who owns information and depends on other actors, *authorizes* other actors to perform certain operations on the information for one or more specific goals. The operations that an actor can authorize are *reading, modifying, transmitting,* or using the information to *produce* new information.

The STS-ml considers three views to represent the above concepts, with different objectives [8]. First, in the *social view,* the intentions and interactions of the stakeholders are modeled. It gives a system overview, with decomposition of goals and relationships between the different actors, goals, and documents. Documents are modeled, and their transmissions are specified, detailing the relevant security requirements. In the *information view,* documents are decomposed into the information they contain, as well as the actors that own the information. It allows the analyst to revise the hierarchy of the information. Finally, the *authorization view* represents the authorizations regarding information across the actors, aiming to represent the permissions and prohibitions on how to use the data, with an emphasis in *read, modify, produce, and transmit.*

2.2 GDPR Extensions for the Socio-technical Security Modeling Language

The first STS-ml GDPR extension was first proposed by [26]. This proposal addressed specific aspects of the GDPR: identification of *personal data, employment relationships* between actors, and *legal basis* for data processing. However, this extension is insufficient to address issues regarding GDPR principles [24]. Hence, [24] proposes STAGE. STAGE works on top of [26] and uses legal reasoning on the effects of not addressing the GDPR principles. STAGE proposes a way to identify *special categories of personal data, asymmetrical relationships* between actors, identify actors which provide information about *minors*, define the *data retention time* for personal data, and whether an actor *belongs to the EU*. Through this 5 semantically charged attributes, the objective is to provide more rich data protection semantics to help stakeholders to discuss compliance while keeping the language clean and simple. The metamodel for the extended STS-ml highlighting the STAGE contributions is shown in Fig. 1.

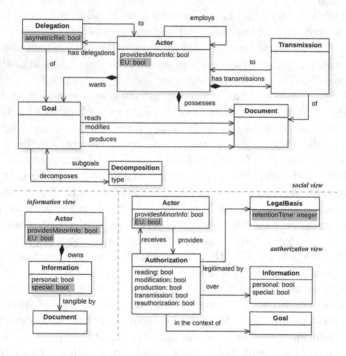

Fig. 1. Metamodel for the STS+GDPR modeling language extension, presented in [24]. This extension is called STAGE in this article.

3 Materials and Research Methods

3.1 Research Method

The main goal of the study is to explore how conceptual modeling helps professionals with different backgrounds establish common ground on data protection compliance analysis in the context of the early requirements stage of information systems development. As presented in Sect. 1, we focus on early stages of requirements engineering since it involves stakeholders from multiple areas, such as business analysts, data protection experts and software engineers [31], where the main conceptual modeling approach is goal oriented. Although different modeling frameworks have been proposed for to cover different requirement domains, we focus on the Socio-Technical Security method (STS) [8] and its extensions for GDPR compliance analysis [24, 26].

The research questions of the study are:

RQ1 - How do the subjects interact to identify and discuss GDPR compliance risks exposed in STAGE's model?

RQ2 - What are the GDPR principles discussed? And how?

We address the research questions with a mixed methods approach as defined by Creswell, particularly a *concurrent embedded strategy* [7]. This approach is recommended to achieve a broader understanding of the phenomena under observation. One of the advantages of this strategy is that qualitative and quantitative data are collected simultaneously, allowing us to use the time of the professionals participating in the study better.

The data collection method is through a series of focus groups. The focus group's source data comes from the interaction of the participants in the activity [22]. Given that STAGE aims to facilitate stakeholders' communication of different backgrounds to establish common ground over data protection requirements, a focus group is suitable to gather data on how STAGE is used for interaction [22]. Hence, for each focus group, we followed a triangulation approach, with subjects with different professional backgrounds and a moderator (that took a more or less structured approach guiding the discussion). Finally, [22] indicates that the number of focus groups necessary will depend on saturation levels, with a "rule of thumb" around four and six focus groups.

For analyzing the focus groups, we followed a deductive qualitative content analysis (CQDA) approach [11,17]. The idea of CQDA is to analyze data - verbal, written, audio, or in other forms - and classify the words into concepts or categories in a rather "flexible manner" [11,17]. The objective of content analysis is not just to "counting" words, but understanding and interpreting what is being said [17].

As content analysis deals with significant amounts of text and data, a coding process is done [11]. Consequently, codes and categories must be created for the coding process, which may be inductive or deductive, depending on the research objective [11,17]. As our research question is how STAGE can be used to discuss GDPR principles, our codes are defined on the seven GDPR principles [13]. This objective implies we followed a deductive approach, using previous theory or research [17]. Furthermore, in our coding process, we followed a manifest content analysis rather than a latent approach [11] (meaning non-verbal or underlying intentions of what was communicated).

Focus groups were recorded and transcribed with the subjects' consent. In addition, live annotation and modifications of the STAGE diagrams were produced for data gathering and transparency purposes. As previously mentioned, the codes used are based on the different GDPR principles. Figure 2 is an example of how different verbatims were coded as the first GDPR principle.

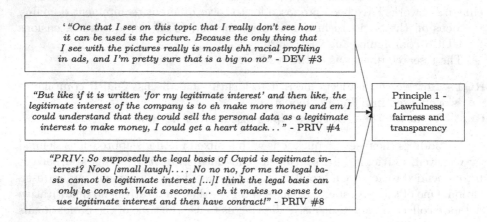

' "One that I see on this topic that I really don't see how it can be used is the picture. Because the only thing that I see with the pictures really is mostly ehh racial profiling in ads, and I'm pretty sure that is a big no no" - DEV #3

"But like if it is written 'for my legitimate interest' and then like, the legitimate interest of the company is to eh make more money and em I could understand that they could sell the personal data as a legitimate interest to make money, I could get a heart attack. . . " - PRIV #4

"PRIV: So supposedly the legal basis of Cupid is legitimate interest? Nooo [small laugh]. . . . No no no, for me the legal basis cannot be legitimate interest [...]I think the legal basis can only be consent. Wait a second. . . eh it makes no sense to use legitimate interest and then have contract!" - PRIV #8

Principle 1 - Lawfulness, fairness and transparency

Fig. 2. Example of the content analysis procedure.

On the other hand, to complement the qualitative approach, we provide descriptive statistical analysis of the results to better characterize and support the discussion of the qualitative findings. The quantitative approach is used for describing the effectiveness of each focus group in terms of the number compliance risks identified. For this, we noted down the background of the subject who identified the risk. Similarly, we measured how many of the GDPR principles were addressed during the analysis and by who, to provide further transparency of our qualitative approach.

3.2 Planning

Focus Group Details. Following Basili's template [4] the study's goal is *analyzing* IS stakeholders with different technical backgrounds, *for the purpose of* exploring how they interact and collaborate concerning the identification and discussion of GDPR compliance risks, *from the point of view of* data protection *in the context of* a meeting for reading socio-technical conceptual models of an IS.

We gathered volunteers online to form focus groups using purposive sampling. We published a survey online in different social media and selected the participants based on the characteristics we sought (expertise in development, business analysis, and data protection laws) [3]. As the objective is to analyze the interaction between subjects who have specific characteristics (context) with the usage of STAGE (artifacts), and if it can be used as an artifact to discuss privacy compliance requirements (effects), non-random sampling techniques can be used [29]. The aim is not to analyze causal mechanisms. The subjects are tagged according to their background as software developers (DEV), business analysts (BUS) and Privacy Experts (PRI), aiming for a three-people triangulation focus group.

Table 1. Red flags seeded in the focus group problem.

View	Red Flag
Social	PRF1 - Non EU: Data from EU data subjects is transferred to a (fictional) Non EU data processor (NexCloud Co.).
Social	PRF2 - Asymmetric relationship: One of the data subjects (Employee) is in an asymmetric relationship with the data controller (Cupid).
Social	MRF1 - Ambiguous goals: The data controller collects data with a second purpose that is ambiguously modeled ("better know users").
Information	PRF3 - Minor Information: The data controller is requesting information to the data subject that might be from other data subjects which are minors ("data subject's children data").
Information	MRF2 - Special Category: Some data that could be special category of personal information (Pictures) is not labelled using the STAGE construct (S-P).
Information	MRF3 - Ambiguous information modeling: information about the data subject's children is ambiguously modeled ("children information").
Authorization	PRF4 - Using other goals: The data controller is transferring data to the data processor for a purpose that is not delegated by the data subject ("better know users").
Authorization	MRF4 - Transmission not Allowed: The data controller is transmitting data to the data processor even though the transmission is not allowed.
Authorization	PRF5 - Arguable Legal Basis: The data controller is using an arguable legal basis (Legitimate Interest) to collect data that should be authorized through consent.
Authorization	PRF6 - Unlimited Retention time: the data controller requires storing data for unlimited time.
Authorization	PRF7 - Using ambiguous goal for auth: The data controller is transmitting information using an ambiguously defined goal ("better know users")

Scenario and Red Flags. The participants are exposed to a real-life inspired case presenting the intention of a software-as-a-service company (named Cupid) of adding new features to its dating app for divorced adults with children. The new features are aimed to gather more data about their user base to provide better results and a targeted marketing campaign[1]. The scenario is introduced by a textual description, and further exposed through the social, information, and authorization view models using STAGE. The models describe the scenario, but they have been designed with seeded GDPR compliance risks (identified as "Red Flags") which should be identified and resolved using the STAGE model

---

[1] The complete exercise is available here: https://doi.org/10.5281/zenodo.7729512.

(check Table 1). We aimed to assess whether the participants could reason about the model to identify compliance issues (e.g. data for unlimited time), or inconsistencies in the model (e.g. unauthorized transferring rights).

Problem Red Flags (PRF) were introduced based on each new attribute of STAGE, plus re-using data for other purposes. PRF are GDPR compliance risks associated with the domain logic correctly modeled in the three views rather than issues with the models. On the other hand, Model Red Flags (MRFs) are semantic ambiguities caused by not using or misusing STAGE constructs; either not all attributes are identified, actors have rights that are not authorized, or the goals are not well specified, among others[2]. They were not systematically seeded. Table 1 gives details on each red flag.

We presented the subjects with different models to address the research questions. The moderator told them that these models had red flags they needed to identify, from a data protection and modeling perspective. Thus, we asked them if they could see any issues. The moderator would re-guide the discussion into data protection requirements if it strayed too far from this aspect. Once the subjects discussed the compliance and modeling issues and agreed on these, we added annotations for each agreement in the STAGE diagrams and marked it as established common ground.

Focus Groups Stages. The overall design of the focus group considered five stages:

Stage 1 — Subjects Selection: We gathered the participants based on an online form, as already discussed, for focus groups of 45 min. Given that we were missing people with privacy backgrounds, we contacted some experts that we knew from the domain. The focus groups were done between a business analyst, a developer, and a privacy expert, for triangulation.

Stage 2 — Initial Survey and Method Training: We sent via e-mail an initial survey form to collect informed consent and demographics that may affect conceptual model understandability. We also provided a handout on the STS-ml language, presenting the three views. The handout covers a subset of the original STS-ml language constructs and all the STAGE constructs[3].

Stage 3 — Focus Group Execution: The main task of the focus group is to analyze an STAGE model to identify the red flags. The case describes a scenario where *Cupid*, a fictional dating app company focused on divorced people, wants to better characterize its users to implement targeted advertisement, as in described Sect. 3.2.

The execution of the focus group starts by presenting a short text describing the problem context, which does not reveal the potential issues, e.g., it does not detail that the data processor is non-eu. Then, the social, information, and authorization views are presented sequentially. The views were seeded with two types of red flags: Problem Red Flags (PRF) and Model Red Flags (MRF), which

---

[2] Due to space issues, the models are available onlinehttps://doi.org/10.5281/zenodo.7729512.

[3] On an anecdotal note, some subjects said at the end of the activity that they had not read the handout and were a little lost at the beginning of the activity.

are explained in detail in Table 1 and in Sect. 3.2. The results of the identification of the MRF and PRF are presented in Table 4 and the percentage of how many red flags and how they were identified in Table 3. The materials of the focus group are available online[4].

Stage 4 — Final Survey: After the task, subjects were asked to fill out a survey on their perception of the usefulness, utility, and intention to use the method, according to the understandability framework of [10] and the questionnaire of [21].

To answer the research questions, we examined the video recordings and transcription of each focus group, the modifications done to the models, and the data about which participants identified the red flags and the GDPR principles during the sessions. Regarding the identification of red flags, we recorded who identified which red flag when a participant:

- Individually identified a red flag, marked as an "I";
- Collaboratively identified a red flag (i.e., the red flag was identified in an interaction between two or more participants) marked as an "IA";
- Agreed to a red flag identified by another participant marked as an "A"; and
- Did not agree to a red flag identified by another participant as a "D".

The record is presented in Table 4. Based on the record, we defined the metrics, detailed in Table 3. Figure 3 is an example on how we recorded a red flag as collaboratively identified (IA), individual identified (I), and agreed (A) for PRF and MRF.

- Group Effectiveness (GE): the percentage of identified red flags of the total number of seeded red flags.
- Group Collaboration (GC): the percentage of red flags identified jointly by two or more participants from the total number of seeded red flags.
- Contribution (C): The percentage of red flags identified by a participant from the total identified by the group, whether they were agreed upon or not by the rest.
- Agreement (A): The percentage of red flags to which the participant agrees were identified by another participant (s) from the group's identified red flags.
- Disagreement (D): The percentage of red flags identified by a participant to which the rest does not agree from the total of red flags identified by the group.

3.3 Conducting

The focus groups were conducted through the Zoom platform between October 2022 and February 2023. We organized 8 focus groups — achieving high levels of saturation [22] — where none of the subjects was familiar with the dating app scenario — meaning, none of them had or was working in a company with

---

[4] https://doi.org/10.5281/zenodo.7729512.

"**DEV:** Two things, the first, is eh on the information that the customer gives Cupid... the T is not marked there. But then I understand that they give it with the authorized goal, with is the potential dating partner met, they then just use it for something else.... (... PRI presented connected issues) **DEV:** That it is... it is like it is violating the agreement because as I say, I give you data for this and then you use it for what you want. And I didn't authorize you for what you are doing with the data originally. **Moderator:** A little bit of what PRI#4 was saying about the authorization? **PRI:** Ah yes, I didn't see that what DEV#4 was saying, it makes sense... [...] well what do you do with those profiles?"

Fig. 3. Quote translated from Spanish on Group #4 agreement and identification on PRF4 and MRF4 . PRF7 was only identified by DEV#4 but not agreed upon by the others.

such a business model. Each focus group lasted 45 - 70 min, depending on the subject's interest[5].

We gathered a total number of 21 participants, which is a similar number of participants as other studies [20,27]. Participants' ages ranged from 28 to 46, all of them professionals with at least four years of experience in information system projects, as business analyst (BUS), developers (DEV) or privacy experts (PRI). Their experience working with GDPR ranged from zero to more than ten years. Participants were classified according to their professional background into three categories. Eight participants were classified as DEV, though their current professional roles were varied (software architects, software development researchers, and actual developers). Seven participants were classified as PRI, having current professional roles such as Data Protection Officers (DPO) and/or privacy researchers. Six participants were classified as BUS accordingly to their current professional roles.

In groups 1 and 5, the BUS did not attend the activity. In group 7, the PRI did not attend. In group 2, the BUS participated in the surveys but did not speak during the activity, although requested, so we do not include the its results. In group 8, the DEV would only wonder why we did not use UML and did not discuss data protection.

To control if the subjects knew about modeling languages and data protection, we asked for these issues. Table 2 shows how nine subjects knew about modeling, four answering UML. Regarding data protection, we asked to identify the definition of personal data through multiple questions and list out the principles of the GDPR. All PRI subjects identified the principles, but the other subjects did not. Everybody gave the correct answer regarding personal data, except two BUS.

During the focus groups, we modified live the different model views by writing the identified red flags to ensure the agreement and shared understanding of all the participants. Hence, one of the authors acted as moderator, which took a

---

[5] Some subjects contacted us even after the focus groups to continue discussing STAGE.

structured approach and guided the discussion into data protection requirements, and wrote down in red in the models the agreed-upon red flags, desired modifications, and interesting questions brought up by the subjects. These modifications are published online[6].

4   Results and Discussion

Question/Answer	Yes	No	I don't know
Do you know modeling? Which?	9	8	3
Are you familiar with goal modeling?	2	13	5
Are you familiar with STS-ml?	1	12	7

Table 2. Modeling knowledge answers

The focus group results are summarized in Table 4. At a high level, we have identified that STAGE allowed the different subjects to identify most of the privacy risks in the model, discuss the GDPR principles, and agree on them. Furthermore, the subjects were able to reason about these topics, even with little domain or modeling knowledge.

4.1   RQ1 - How Do the Subjects Interact to Identify and Discuss GDPR Compliance Risks Exposed in STAGE's Model?

Qualitative Analysis. To answer RQ1, we performed a content analysis of the focus group. We defined "interactions" as the statements made by the participants aiming to achieve common ground on what are the red flags. We found three ways of interactions which we named as "identification" (statements made by a subject to explicit a red flag, without further interaction of other participants), "identification and agreement", made by two or more subjects that collaboratively identified a red flag, and "agreement", statements, made by participants that just agreed to a red flag identified by another participant without providing further comments. The results are summarized in Table 3, based on what was presented in Sect. 3. The data is presented and discussed according to the subjects' backgrounds: Privacy experts (PRI), software developers (DEV), and business analysts (BUS). Based on these results, next we comment on group effectiveness, group collaboration, problem and model red flags, and on interdisciplinary aspects of the results.

Group Effectiveness. As an overview, all groups found at least 50% of the implanted red flags, and six of them at least 80% of the red flags, as seen in Tables 3 and 4. Although the sample size is not statistically significant, as this is an exploratory study [24], specific trends can be noticed and analyzed without statistically significant samples [29], as discussed in Sect. 3. Thus, these preliminary results suggest that STAGE was effective in helping subjects identify and discussing GDPR compliance risks and requirements.

In all groups, PRI subjects identified most of the PRF, except in group 4, where the DEV identified most red flags, and group 7, where the PRI subject did

---

[6] https://doi.org/10.5281/zenodo.7729512.

not arrive, as seen in table 4[7]. In group 7, where the PRI subject was missing, the group struggled to find some red flags and even questioned if certain elements were part of the GDPR. However, they asked the moderator questions about data protection. This questions appears as both BUS and DEV of group 7 do not possess much knowledge of the GDPR, as screened in the domain knowledge questionnaire.

Group	GE	GC	Role	C	A	D
1	82%	22%	DEV	30%	40%	10%
			PRI	50%	20%	10%
			BUS	-	-	-
2	55%	17%	DEV	17%	50%	0%
			PRI	67%	33%	17%
			BUS	-	-	-
3	100%	45%	DEV	9%	55%	0%
			PRI	18%	36%	0%
			BUS	27%	55%	0%
4	100%	18%	DEV	55%	27%	18%
			PRI	18%	45%	0%
			BUS	9%	55%	9%
5	91%	30%	DEV	20%	50%	10%
			PRI	50%	0%	0%
			BUS	-	-	-
6	100%	73%	DEV	9%	9%	0 %
			PRI	9%	0 %	9%
			BUS	18%	0%	9%
7	64%	14%	DEV	43%	0%	29%
			PRI	-	-	-
			BUS	29%	0%	29%
8	100%	55%	DEV	0%	0%	0%
			PRI	45%	0%	0%
			BUS	0%	0%	27%

Table 3. Results for red flag identification metrics per group and subject background, as defined in Sect. 3.2.

Given that, in most cases, the PRI subject identified most of the PRF and led the discussion, we believe this situation supports the idea that PRI subjects could understand and reason about privacy risks using STAGE's model. None of the PRI and BUS subjects had prior knowledge about conceptual modeling, but PRI subjects outperformed DEV subjects in identifying the problem red flags. In fact, for the PRI subject of group 8, the difference between agent and role was evident. In group 4, there was an exception: the DEV participant outperformed PRI and BUS. This could be explained because the DEV has previous knowledge in conceptual modeling, which has been identified in previous works on business process modeling as positively affecting model understandability [10].

Group Collaboration. On another topic, Table 3 shows that groups—specifically groups 2, 6, and 8—that have high group collaboration (GC as seen in Sect. 3.2) have also identified 100% of the red flags (GE, group efficiency, revise Table 3). In particular, this refers were efficient in collaboration when identifying red flags, having GC indicators of 45% or higher. This indicates that STAGE seems to help with group collaboration and communication on GDPR requirements discussion.

However, other groups that do not have high GC (such as group 4) also recognized 100% of the red flags. Even so, as previously explained, group 4 DEV had an exceptionally high understanding of modeling, which could help explain why this group, with such a low level of GC, could recognize all the red flags. In addition, group 5 had a GC of 30% and identified 91% of the red flags. Future

---

[7] DEV of group 4 contributed significantly more than others, as it has a sound knowledge of goal modeling and could be treated as an atypical case.

Table 4. Table representing the identified red flags in the model, the GDPR principles discussed and the understandabilities scores. */†: resp. did not attend/participate IA = Identified and agree, A = Agreed, I = identified, as presented in Sect. 3.2. Understandability scores explained in Sect. 2

Focus group	Individual	Identification Problem Red Flag F1 F2 F3 F4 F5 F6 F7	Identification Model Red Flag F1 F2 F3	F4	Discussion of GDPR principles 1 2 3 4 5 6 7	PEU	PU	IU
1	PRI	IA IA IA A IA IA	I IA	A	✓✓ ✓ ✓	15	30	7
	DEV	A A IA IA A IA I	A	IA	✓ ✓ ✓✓	14	33	5
	BUS*	- - - - - - -	- - -	-	- - - - - - -	-	-	-
2	PRI	A IA IA IA	IA I		✓✓✓ ✓ ✓	23	32	7
	DEV	IA A A A	IA		✓✓✓ ✓✓ ✓	21	31	9
	BUS†	- - - - - - -	- - -	-	- - - - - - -	-	-	-
3	PRI	IA IA A A IA IA IA	A IA A	IA	✓✓✓ ✓✓ ✓	21	31	9
	DEV	IA IA A A A IA A	A A A	IA	✓✓✓✓✓✓ ✓	24	25	7
	BUS	IA A IA IA A A IA	IA A IA	A	✓✓ ✓ ✓	25	34	7
4	PRI	IA A IA A IA A	A	A	✓✓✓✓ ✓ ✓	21	24	7
	DEV	A IA A IA A IA I	IA I	IA	✓✓✓ ✓✓ ✓	23	32	9
	BUS	A A IA A A A	I A	IA	✓ ✓ ✓	23	35	8
5	PRI	IA IA IA IA IA IA IA IA			✓✓✓ ✓ ✓	19	27	6
	DEV	A IA A A IA IA A IA A	I		✓ ✓ ✓✓ ✓	23	33	9
	BUS*	- - - - - - -	- - -	-	- - - - - - -	-	-	-
6	PRI	IA IA IA IA IA IA	I IA		✓✓✓ ✓✓ ✓	15	28	6
	DEV	IA IA IA IA IA IA	A I		✓✓ ✓ ✓	22	31	5
	BUS	A IA IA IA IA IA IA A	IA	I	✓✓✓ ✓✓	n/a	n/a	n/a
7	PRI*	- - - - - -	- - -	-	- - - - - - -	-	-	-
	DEV	IA A IA	I A	I	✓ ✓	n/a	n/a	n/a
	BUS	A IA I IA	IA		✓✓ ✓✓	18	24	6
8	PRI	I IA IA IA I IA IA IA IA I	IA		✓✓✓ ✓✓ ✓	n/a	n/a	n/a
	DEV					13	27	5
	BUS	A IA IA A IA IA A IA IA	IA		✓✓✓ ✓✓ ✓	15	18	2
Avrg.	PRI					20	30,29	7
	DEV					19	28,67	7
	BUS					20,25	27,75	5,75

research could compare statistically how the different groups behave over these indicators.

Problem and Model Red Flags. In most cases, all the subjects agreed to the red flags identified by others, as seen in Table 3. Since PRI identified most of the problem red flags (PRF), DEV and BUS agreed. Indeed, once the PRF were identified and explained by a PRI, the rest of the participants would add more details and arguments as to why such a element was a risk. A possible explanation could be due to a "maturation", this is, subjects improve their performance during the study because they learned something [29]. This guides us to think that using STAGE could also help BUSs and DEVs learn about privacy when reviewing models with a PRI.

> *"PRI: Is all that data necessary to do the marketing profile? [Group laughs]*
> **Moderator:** *What do you think?*
> **PRI:** *honestly, no [laughs] [...] The sexual orientation data might be complicated for marketing and I don't really know why they need it for targeting for people. Pf... I don't know, maybe they need it for toys? [...]*
> **DEV:** *One that I see on this topic that I really don't see how it can be used is the picture. Because the only thing that I see with the pictures really is mostly ehh racial profiling in ads, and I'm pretty sure that is a big no no ... but yeah I find this very flimsy"*

Fig. 4. Verbatim focus group 3, coded as discussing the GDPR principles of data minimization and lawfulness, fairness and transparency

Alternatively, model red flags (MRF) were less consistently identified by the subjects. Only group 3 could identify and agree upon all the MRFs. Groups 5, 6, and 8 also identified all the MRFs; however, the other participants agreed only with some. The MRF generally sparked less discussion between the subjects when reviewing the recordings and model modifications. Most subjects would agree upon identified MRF and would not generate discussion. The exception to this situation is group 8, which, although it did not identify all MRFs, did have a rich debate over the ones identified.

Interdisciplinary Aspects. The results in Table 3 show that, except for group 5, groups with the three disciplines were highly effective in identifying the red flags. Groups 2 and 7 identified only 55% and 64% of the red flags, respectively. Although a PRI was present in group 2— playing the role of domain expert — with a DEV, most of their remarks were on presentation elements of the model (such as colors) than the data protection requirements. Even though the moderator tried guiding them into more data protection topics, they focused on design elements. While in group 7, they asked and requested the moderator to act as a privacy expert, given their data protection misconceptions and struggled to identify MRF. Both of these situations highlight the importance of the inter-disciplinary approach for discussing GDPR compliance and the importance of having a triangulation in STAGE for its successfulness.

As a result, looking at the group results and our analysis, we see that the groups with three subjects (DEV, PRI, and BUS) were the only ones that identified all the seeded red flags and had proper discussions about them. It seems the groups achieved synergy in identifying red flags when discussing STAGE models. Moreover, groups 3, 6, and 8 had the higher proportion of red flags identified by collaboration as shown in Table 3; i.e., the group identified the red flags and not by a single subject. Although the number of participants and focus groups offer exploratory and preliminary results, it does show a trend that might be interesting to look at in the future.

To summarize the answer to RQ1, subjects use the STAGE's models as prompts to discuss data protection requirements. Subjects would identify a compliance risk to the group depending on their background. Afterward, the other subjects would either (1) agree/disagree on the identification and complement with information depending on their expertise; (2) agree/disagree without adding extra information; (3) not interact at all. Most of the interactions we saw fall under the first category, which is a promising result.

4.2   RQ2 - What Are the GDPR Principles Discussed? and How?

Qualitative Analysis. As previously exemplified in Fig. 2, we analyzed each participant's interventions to identify whether they were talking about a GDPR principle. The results are shown in the column "Discussion of GDPR principles" in table 4.

GDPR Principles. Most GDPR principles were discussed in all focus groups, with all groups discussing at least six principles. Only "accuracy" was not systematically discussed, as seen in table 4, with one DEV and PRI sharing their preoccupation in groups 3 and 4. This principle might not have appeared so frequently in the discussion because there is no clear primitive in [24, 26] about it, except for "Retention Time".

All focus groups and participants (except one) showed interactions that were coded under principles 1, 3, and 7. Principle 1, lawfulness, fairness, and transparency, is one of the important values behind the GDPR [13]. Therefore, it is not surprising that most subjects discussed this topic. This principle is closely related to PRF2, PRF4-5, PRF7 and MRF1. Usually, the topic would appear when discussing the asymmetrical relationship between the employee/employer, the re-purposing of personal data and the legal basis for data processing. To illustrate, PRF2 was identified mainly by PRIs, but when highlighted, some DEVs would raise the concern that fairness and asymmetry were not part of data protection principles. We saw this situation, for example, in groups 1, 2, and 5. In group 1, the DEV thought that an "asymmetrical" relationship referred to the actors' geographical location; in groups 2 and 5, the DEV did not know this was a requirement. What happened next was that PRIs would explain the GDPR and the logic behind the asymmetrical relationship. DEVs would either nod or acknowledge that they did not know that and agree it is a red flag (Fig. 5).

Principle 1 also appear between PRIs, when discussing the legal basis of "legitimate interest". For example, verbatim of PRI#4 in the authorization view *"legitimate interest is nowadays abused for everything and not everything is legitimate interest. I think it is too much, um unfair, to use..."*. Alternatively, verbatim PRI#3 *"It is complicated to use that legal basis, every time, everywhere..."*. Or the verbatim of PRI of groups 4 and 5 (Fig. 2) show how principle 1 appeared in the discussions. This principle would also appear in the discussion during the authorization and social views regarding the re-purposing of data and the lack of transparency from the company. Fairness was also discussed regarding using minors' information for marketing.

The subjects would also discuss principle 3, data minimization. This discussion happened on the information and authorization view. Several subjects would

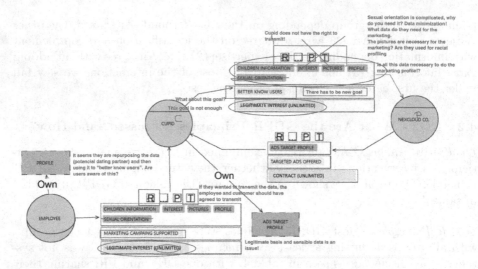

Fig. 5. Original model, with annotations in red of the modifications of Group 3. Other model modification are available online, at https://doi.org/10.5281/zenodo.7729512. (Color figure online)

question the amount and type of data used for marketing. They even highlighted that the information "interest" could be special categories of data. Data minimization was also discussed in the authorization view, as subjects could relate the amount of information used to a specific goal, illustrated in Fig. 4. Finally, most subjects would talk about accountability. Accountability is the GDPR principle that sums up all the other values, as it implies holding organization accountable for their practices [24]. To summarize the answer to RQ2, we could say that STAGE allowed the subjects to discuss the GDPR principles, even without proper knowledge. The principle of accuracy is lacking in the discussions, which could be addressed in future work.

4.3   Overall Discussion

Overall, the STAGE extension was conceived the GDPR and its regulator(s) have interpreted as vital. This design decision is reflected by the fact that PRIs could understand the models, as they are the domain experts. This could explain why it seems that for PRIs it was not complex to contribute to the discussion, even without knowledge of modeling. Although it may seem "intuitive" or "common knowledge" that PRIs should always find the PRF regardless of the communication medium, this research provides empirical evidence for this assumption. This observation provides evidence on the importance of interdisciplinary reasoning when creating artifacts for multiple stakeholders. Indeed, privacy experts could identify and discuss MRF, implying that STAGE was understandable enough that they could reason about conceptual modeling. Therefore, even if they did not know modeling, they could deduce information from the different views, identify most red flags and participate.

Another focus group finding shows that subjects could extract information from the models and discuss compliance without fully understanding the model's complexity. Seven out of eight groups identified at least 80% of the red flags (as seen in Table 3) hinting that an intuitive and understandable artifact could facilitate communication and establish common ground. Furthermore, given the interdisciplinary reasoning behind STAGE, groups composed of PRI, BUS, and DEV seem to outperform in finding red flags, having richer discussions on GDPR compliance requirements. These observations allow us to deduce that conceptual models can help interdisciplinary teams discuss and analyze regulatory requirements with different mental models.

5   Threats to Validity Analysis

Concerning threats to internal validity we think that one threat is about subject selection: the participants were recruited purposive, though they were randomly grouped. Furthermore, there was no control over the subjects' years of experience. The study's objective is not to produce statistical nor conclusive results but to validate a proposal through analogical inference [28]; this situation can be tolerated but acknowledged nonetheless.

Regarding the construct validity, whether the study is representative of the theory constructs, we think that the activity and the measurements are consistent with our focus on the collaboration of the subjects around STAGE models from the perspective of cognitive contribution to problem-solving. However, other variables could help study collaboration, such as participants' nonverbal and paraverbal cues. Using different cases would be helpful to discard the effect of the problem on the results. However, it would require more groups to get to the comparative results per role we presented in the article. Finally, it is impossible to generalize the study's conclusions about external and conclusion validity. However, this does not diminish the value of the empirical insights towards the evolution of the proposal.

6   Related Work

Many initiatives have extended the capabilities of existing modeling languages to address privacy and data protection requirements. In [23], proposed Secure Tropos, a modeling language based on Tropos, to address security requirements in the early requirements stage. The extension allowed users to tag dependencies and entities and added the threat concept. [14] have proposed an automated approach to deal with NL requirements that can detect ambiguities and interpret them. [18] presents Nòmos 3, a continuation of Nòmos2 modeling language, which is "a modeling language for law". Nòmos3 seeks to model roles and responsibilities and analyze compliance through the modeling [18]. Legal GRL [15] is a method proposed to systematically extract legal requirements from regulations.

Using the Hohfelding model to extract these requirements, then requirements can be modeled with Legal GRL, which is goal-oriented with deontic modalities language. In [2], present a UML profile for privacy-aware data lifecycle models. The UML profile proposes stereotypes for an eight-step data life cycle and activities and events affecting the data.

Other proposals have sought to include GDPR requirements in their modeling frameworks. In [1], propose a set of business process modeling patterns to model GDPR constraints. The article presents BPMN models representing the behaviors needed to address data breaches, data use consent, right of portability, and rights to access, withdraw, rectify, and be forgotten. In [19], the authors extend use and misuse cases models by introducing templates for specifying misuse cases and mitigation actions. In [30], LINDUUN GO— based on LIND-DUN, a privacy threat modeling framework — extension is proposed, which is a lightweight and gamified approach, which also includes a GDPR data subjects rights, but the GDPR principles [30].

Nevertheless, even with all these frameworks, artifacts, tools, and proposals for dealing with regulatory requirements ambiguity and analysis, it still needs to tackle the challenge of specific knowledge in law and software engineering [5]. Lately, [5] have proposed the creation of a new type of quality requirement, namely Legal Accountability. This new requirement would measure legal traceability, completeness, validity, auditability, and continuity [5]. Furthermore, [5] indicates that regulatory requirements are still not properly included in the design, and technical and legal divisions compete. Hence, tools and methods for cooperation are required [5]. STAGE seeks to address this identified gap by helping establish "common ground" between interdisciplinary teams, an essential element for software development [9] and helping with interdisciplinary approaches [5].

7   Conclusions and Future Work

Through focus groups, we aimed to validate the usage of STAGE extension of the STS-ml [24], as an artifact to analyze and discuss privacy compliance between stakeholders with different privacy backgrounds. Our preliminary data show that STAGE allowed the stakeholders to identify privacy risks, discuss the GDPR principles, and act as a communication tool. These preliminary results are promising, as data protection requirements are not usually included in the early stage of the software development lifecycle. STAGE could prompt discussion between interdisciplinary teams, helping IS comply with data protection regulations, such as the GDPR.

Although they had little to no knowledge of modeling, privacy experts identified most of the privacy risks and contributed to the discussion. Developers could also identify privacy risks and, when in disagreement with privacy experts relating to privacy requirements - such as asymmetric relationships - could resolve their doubts and agree on the technicalities of this conflicting requirement. Furthermore, even despite the models' complexity, the stakeholders together were able to extract information from the models to check compliance. These results provide preliminary and exploratory evidence on the role of STAGE models as a facilitator for stakeholders with different backgrounds to analyze privacy compliance in the organization. These results provide preliminary and exploratory evidence on the role of STAGE models as a facilitator for stakeholders with different backgrounds to analyze privacy compliance in the organization. Moreover, the results provide new insights into how stakeholders with different backgrounds interact with and discuss around conceptual models. Future research will focus on the experimental validation of the proposal with a larger sample and statistical analysis of the results.

References

1. Agostinelli, S., Maggi, F.M., Marrella, A., Sapio, F.: Achieving GDPR compliance of BPMN process models. In: Cappiello, C., Ruiz, M. (eds.) Information Systems Engineering in Responsible Information Systems, CAiSE 2019. Lecture Notes in Business Information Processing, vol. 350, pp. 10–22. Springer, Cham (2019). https://doi.org/10.1007/978-3-030-21297-1_2
2. Alshammari, M., Simpson, A.: A UML profile for privacy-aware data lifecycle models. In: Katsikas, S.K., et al. (eds.) CyberICPS/SECPRE -2017. LNCS, vol. 10683, pp. 189–209. Springer, Cham (2018). https://doi.org/10.1007/978-3-319-72817-9_13
3. Babbie, E.R.: The Practice of Social Research. Cengage Learning, Boston (2020)
4. Basili, V.R., Rombach, H.D.: The tame project: towards improvement-oriented software environments. IEEE Trans. Softw. Eng. 14(6) (1988)
5. Breaux, T., Norton, T.: Legal accountability as software quality: a US data processing perspective. In: 2022 IEEE 30th International Requirements Engineering Conference (RE). IEEE (2022)
6. Breaux, T.D., Antón, A.I.: A systematic method for acquiring regulatory requirements: a frame-based approach. RHAS-6), Delhi, India (2007)
7. Creswell, J.W., Creswell, J.D.: Research Design: Qualitative, Quantitative, and Mixed Methods Approaches. Sage Publications, Thousand Oaks (2017)
8. Dalpiaz, F., Paja, E., Giorgini, P.: Security Requirements Engineering: Designing Secure Socio-technical Systems. Massachusetts, Cambridge (2016)
9. Damian, D., Chisan, J.: An empirical study of the complex relationships between requirements engineering processes and other processes that lead to payoffs in productivity, quality, and risk management. IEEE Trans. Software Eng. 32, 433–453 (2006). https://doi.org/10.1109/TSE.2006.61
10. Dikici, A., Turetken, O., Demirors, O.: Factors influencing the understandability of process models: a systematic literature review. Inf. Softw. Technol. 93, 112–129 (2018)
11. Elo, S., Kyngäs, H.: The qualitative content analysis. J. Adv. Nurs. 62, 107–15 (2008). https://doi.org/10.1111/j.1365-2648.2007.04569.x
12. European Union: Charter of Fundamental Rights (2000). Article 8
13. European Union: Regulation (EU) 2016/678 of the European Parliament and of the Council - General Data Protection Regulation (2016)
14. Ezzini, S., Abualhaija, S., Arora, C., Sabetzadeh, M., Briand, L.C.: Using domain-specific corpora for improved handling of ambiguity in requirements. In: 2021 IEEE/ACM 43rd International Conference on Software Engineering (ICSE), pp. 1485–1497. IEEE (2021)

15. Ghanavati, S., Amyot, D., Rifaut, A.: Legal goal-oriented requirement language (legal GRL) for modeling regulations. In: Proceedings of the 6th International Workshop on Modeling in Software Engineering, pp. 1–6 (2014)
16. Hadar, I., et al.: Privacy by designers: software developers' privacy mindset. In: Proceedings of the 40th International Conference on Software Engineering, Gothenburg, Sweden. ICSE 2018, Association for Computing Machinery, New York, NY, USA (2018)
17. Hsieh, H.F., Shannon, S.E.: Three approaches to qualitative content analysis. Qual. Health Res. **15**(9), 1277–1288 (2005)
18. Ingolfo, S., Jureta, I., Siena, A., Perini, A., Susi, A.: Nòmos 3: legal compliance of roles and requirements. In: Yu, E., Dobbie, G., Jarke, M., Purao, S. (eds.) ER 2014. LNCS, vol. 8824, pp. 275–288. Springer, Cham (2014). https://doi.org/10.1007/978-3-319-12206-9_22
19. Mai, P.X., Goknil, A., Shar, L.K., Pastore, F., Briand, L.C., Shaame, S.: Modeling security and privacy requirements: a use case-driven approach. Inf. Softw. Technol. **100**, 165–182 (2018)
20. Mendling, J., Recker, J., Reijers, H.A., Leopold, H.: An empirical review of the connection between model viewer characteristics and the comprehension of conceptual process models. Inf. Syst. Front. **21**, 1111–1135 (2019)
21. Moody, D.L.: The method evaluation model: a theoretical model for validating information systems design methods. In: Proceedings of the European Conference on Information Systems 2003, pp. 1–17. AIS Electronic Library (2003)
22. Morgan, D.L.: Focus groups. Ann. Rev. Sociol. **22**(1), 129–152 (1996)
23. Mouratidis, H., Giorgini, P.: Secure tropos: a security-oriented extension of the tropos methodology. Int. J. Softw. Eng. Knowl. Eng. **17**(02), 285–309 (2007)
24. Negri-Ribalta, C., Noel, R., Herbaut, N., Pastor, O., Salinesi, C.: Socio-technical modelling for GDPR principles: an extension for the STS-ml. In: 2022 IEEE 30th International Requirements Engineering Conference Workshops (REW) (2022)
25. Paja, E., Dalpiaz, F., Poggianella, M., Roberti, P., Giorgini, P.: STS-tool: socio-technical security requirements through social commitments. In: 2012 20th IEEE International Requirements Engineering Conference (RE). IEEE (2012)
26. Robol, M., Salnitri, M., Giorgini, P.: Toward GDPR-compliant socio-technical systems: modeling language and reasoning framework. In: Poels, G., Gailly, F., Serral Asensio, E., Snoeck, M. (eds.) PoEM 2017. LNBIP, vol. 305, pp. 236–250. Springer, Cham (2017). https://doi.org/10.1007/978-3-319-70241-4_16
27. Stitzlein, C., Sanderson, P., Indulska, M.: Understanding healthcare processes. Proc. Human Factors Ergonom. Soc. Ann. Meet. **57**, 240–244 (2013). https://doi.org/10.1177/1541931213571053
28. Wieringa, R.: Empirical research methods for technology validation: scaling up to practice. J. Syst. Softw. **95**, 19–31 (2014)
29. Wieringa, R.J.: Design Science Methodology for Information Systems and Software Engineering. Springer, Berlin, Heidelberg (2014)
30. Wuyts, K., Sion, L., Joosen, W.: LINDDUN GO: a lightweight approach to privacy threat modeling. IEEE (2020)
31. Yu, E.: Modeling strategic relationships for process reengineering. Soc. Model. Requirements Eng. **11**(2011), 66–87 (2011)

Enhancing Workflow Security in Multi-cloud Environments Through Monitoring and Adaptation upon Cloud Service and Network Security Violations

Nafiseh Soveizi$^{(\boxtimes)}$ (iD) and Dimka Karastoyanova (iD)

Information Systems Group, University of Groningen, Groningen, The Netherlands
{n.soveizi,d.karastoyanova}@rug.nl

Abstract. Cloud computing has emerged as a crucial solution for handling data- and compute-intensive workflows, offering scalability to address dynamic demands. However, ensuring the secure execution of workflows in the untrusted multi-cloud environment poses significant challenges, given the sensitive nature of the involved data and tasks. The lack of comprehensive approaches for detecting attacks during workflow execution, coupled with inadequate measures for reacting to security and privacy breaches has been identified in the literature. To close this gap, in this work, we propose an approach that focuses on monitoring cloud services and networks to detect security violations during workflow executions. Upon detection, our approach selects the optimal adaptation action to minimize the impact on the workflow. To mitigate the uncertain cost associated with such adaptations and their potential impact on other tasks in the workflow, we employ adaptive learning to determine the most suitable adaptation action. Our approach is evaluated based on the performance of the detection procedure and the impact of the selected adaptations on the workflows.

Keywords: Security-aware workflows · Cloud-based workflows · Workflow Adaptation · Cloud Service Monitoring · Violation detection · Adaptation Recommendation

1 Introduction

Cloud computing has emerged as a vital solution for organizations dealing with data- and compute-intensive workflows, offering unparalleled scalability and flexibility to meet dynamic demands. By providing a platform for outsourcing workflow execution and storage, the cloud has revolutionized the way organizations operate and cooperate. However, despite all the advantages of cloud-based workflows, cloud security is a major area of concern [1,2], limiting its adoption for workflows involving sensitive data and tasks.

The distributed nature of workflows allows for dynamic binding to cloud services, which can lead to increased security risks and vulnerability to malicious

M. Sellami et al. (Eds.): CoopIS 2023, LNCS 14353, pp. 157–175, 2024.
https://doi.org/10.1007/978-3-031-46846-9_9

attacks, as these services may encounter security issues that were unknown during the modelling or even during the binding phase. Additional security-related challenges are introduced by the transmission of sensitive data among cloud components, such as Data Centers (DCs), over potentially untrusted network channels. Therefore, it is crucial to closely monitor the behavior of cloud services and network infrastructure in order to detect and react to any potential violations. Towards this goal, in this paper, we propose an approach that focuses on monitoring, detecting, and reacting to security violations during workflow execution, focusing on cloud services and network violations through the analysis of network traffic data and log files received from cloud providers.

The subsequent step of reacting to the detected security violations boils down to selecting the appropriate adaptation action to minimize the impact of these detected violations. This task is complex due to the presence of *uncertain overhead costs associated with each adaptation action*, which cannot be accurately determined during the workflow modeling, scheduling, or even when reacting to detected violations. These uncertainties vary across different workflow types. For example, analyzing past instances of reworking tasks in a particular workflow reveals that certain task types tend to have more uncertain delays when reworked compared to others. Similarly, examining the consequences of skipping tasks in previous workflow instances highlights the potential negative effects on other tasks, even leading to failures.

These uncertain costs within the workflow are closely connected to several key factors: 1) *The current state of the workflow* has a significant influence on the potential risks and uncertain costs. For instance, if the workflow is already experiencing delays due to the dynamic nature of cloud performance [3] or has encountered multiple violations, the costs of reworking or resequencing tasks can be higher due to the requirement of additional resources or potential disruptions to ongoing tasks. 2) *The previously accrued violations and their respective adaptations* play a crucial role in determining the uncertain costs. Each violation and its adaptation can have a cascading effect on the entire workflow, impacting subsequent tasks and introducing further uncertainties. Considerations such as dependencies and compatibility issues need to be taken into account when deciding on the next adaptation action. 3) *Workflow complexity* which includes the number of possible tasks, branching paths, and potential variants [4], also contributes to the uncertain costs. Tasks often involve conditional instructions that lead to multiple program branches and loops. The variations in these branches or loops result in diverse task computations, varying execution times, and different outcomes based on different data inputs [5]. Hence, the larger the number of possible tasks, branching paths, and potential variants, the greater the uncertainties associated with different inputs, making the estimation of uncertain costs more challenging.

Therefore, there is a need for a method that effectively addresses these uncertainties associated with each adaptation action, particularly when such uncertainties cannot be determined at the time of adaptation action selection. To address this need, our approach is based on learning from past adaptations of workflows to predict the most suitable adaptation action. We consider the uncertain cost of each action and its potential impact on other tasks, taking a holistic perspective that considers the entire workflow at runtime. This approach mitigates risks, supports decision-making, and enhances the system's ability to proactively respond to security violations.

Our approach is based on the *SecFlow* [6] architecture that enables adaptation on two levels – tenant level and middleware level – to ensure a balance between security and efficiency. Our solution separates workflow instances of different tenants, thus meeting their specific functional and non-functional requirements within isolated environments. This model incorporates a logically centralized middleware, which facilitates informed decision-making for all tenants and simplifies the cloud infrastructure, thereby hiding complexity from its tenants while minimizing the amount of information possessed by the middleware regarding individual tenants.

The rest of this paper is organized as follows: Sect. 2 provides an overview of the existing monitoring and adaptation mechanisms for security violations in cloud-based workflows. In Sect. 3, we present the architecture upon which our proposed method is built. Section 4 describes our proposed adaptive approach for monitoring and adapting cloud services and networks to mitigate security violations. Section 5 presents the evaluation of the proposed approach. Finally, Sect. 6 concludes the paper and outlines potential future research directions.

2   Related Works

In this section, we give a brief overview of the existing WfMS featuring monitoring and/or adaptation mechanisms for security violations in multi-cloud environments. We base this overview on a recent systematic review of the state of the art in security and privacy of cloud-based workflows that considers both business and scientific workflows [7].

We conducted a comparison of existing research in the field, as summarized in Table 1. The majority of these studies primarily focus on scientific workflows, with some utilizing cloud-side monitoring, which raises concerns regarding its full trustworthiness. On the other hand, works that solely rely on engine-side monitoring tend to narrow their focus on task failures [13] or specific types of violations [9,14]. In addition, only two papers encompass all three essential security objectives: Confidentiality, Integrity, and Availability (CIA) [8,12]. One significant limitation observed across these works is the absence of a structured solution for adaptation, as they often address only one type of reaction to detected violations. As a result, none of the existing approaches comprehensively tackle all potential attacks that could compromise the CIA of outsourced workflow tasks in multi-cloud environments. Furthermore, the available adaptation actions do not sufficiently mitigate the risks associated with various types of violations. For a more in-depth analysis of these studies, please refer to the original sources or consult the survey in [7].

Table 1. Comparison of existing cloud-based WfMSs regarding their abilities to monitor and react to security violations.

Paper	Workflow Type	Monitoring Module	Considered Security Objectives	Considered Attacks	Adaptation Options
[8], 2020	Business	Cloud-side Monitoring	CIA	VM-based, Network attacks	Static Trust Calculation
[9], 2020 [10], 2021	Scientific	Engine-side Monitoring	I	VM-based attacks	Redundancy
[11], 2020	Scientific	Cloud-side Monitoring	A	Clouds fail	Rescheduling the uncompleted tasks
[12], 2018	Scientific	Cloud-side Monitoring	CIA	VM-based attacks	Rescheduling the affected tasks
[13], 2021	Scientific	Engine-side Monitoring	A	Hardware and Software faults	Re-work
[14], 2021	Scientific	Engine-side Monitoring	A	Unavailability of VMs	Re-work

3   System Overview

This section presents a brief overview of our security-aware Workflow Management System (WfMS), called *SecFlow* [6][1] It is specifically designed to provide comprehensive protection for workflows throughout their entire lifecycle, safeguarding them against a wide range of security violations and ensuring defense against all potential attackers. Figure 1 depicts the proposed architecture, highlighting key components such as the Tenant's Kernel, the Middleware, and the multi-cloud environment.

In our architecture, we assume that tenants' resources are securely isolated from each other, possibly residing on the same cloud node. The middleware, which acts as a logically centralized component, can be hosted by a trusted third party. To ensure comprehensive monitoring of all potential malicious actors, tenants actively monitor users, while the Middleware oversees Clouds, networks, and tenants, utilizing learned behavioral patterns. In the scope of this paper, we primarily concentrate on identifying and responding to security breaches in cloud services and network infrastructure. In the following, we describe these procedures within the context of the *SecFlow* architecture.

In *SecFlow*, the security-aware management of workflows comprises two main phases: the pre-submission phase (steps 1–4 in Fig. 1) occurring before task submission to cloud environments, and the monitoring and adaptation phase (steps 5–11 in Fig. 1) for detecting and addressing security violations in cloud services and networks.

During the pre-submission phase, tenants utilize the **Workflow Modeller** module to design their workflows under consideration of security requirements

---

[1] Preprint available at the ArXiv: https://arxiv.org/abs/2307.05137.

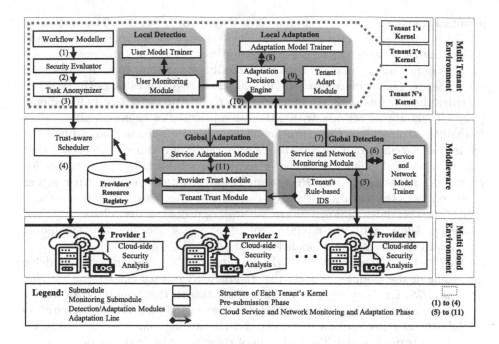

Fig. 1. The architecture of SecFlow

(step 1). These workflows are then analyzed using the **Security Evaluator** module to specify potential adaptation actions for each task and incorporate them into the workflow model (step 2). This step is important because certain tasks might have specific eligibility criteria for some actions. For instance, while some tasks may be eligible for skipping, authentication tasks are deemed indispensable for maintaining workflow security. Subsequently, sensitive information is removed from the tasks (step 3) using client-side obfuscation techniques and conflict detection methods. Finally, the **Trust-aware Scheduler** module schedules the workflows, considering tenant requirements and integrating trustworthiness information (step 4).

In the monitoring and adaptation phase, the **Service and Network Monitoring** module continuously analyzes network traffic and cloud logs to detect malicious activities (step 5), comparing it with expected behavior from the **Service and Network Model Trainer** module (step 6). Detected anomalies trigger alerts to the Adaptation Decision Engine from the corresponding tenant (step 7). The **Adaptation Decision Engine** selects a suitable adaptation option for the detected attack, employing two distinct strategies. The first strategy prioritizes actions that minimize system impact, considering factors like price, time, value, and mitigation score. The second strategy utilizes an adaptive model (step 8) trained by the *Adaptation Model Trainer* module, which takes into account system reactions, current workflow state, and dependencies.

Finally, adaptations are implemented at two levels: tenant- and middleware-level. At the tenant level, the **Tenant Adapt Module** executes tenant-specific adaptation actions (step 9), including Skip, Switch, or Insert [15]. The purpose of this level is to ensure tenant privacy and shield them from the complexities of the underlying cloud infrastructure. At the middleware level, adaptations focus on changes in providers and cloud services, including Reconfiguration, Rework, and Redundancy. The *Service Adaptation Module* re-executes tasks (Rework) or executes them redundantly (Redundancy) to meet evolving tenant requirements (step 10), modifying services within the same provider or exploring alternatives from different providers. Configuration adaptation (Reconfiguration) adjusts the settings of specific cloud services to enhance decision-making. The middleware acts as a central point for receiving feedback, establishing trust factors for providers and services. The *Provider Trust Module* updates trust scores based on detected violations (step 11), updating the trust repository accordingly. These updates improve future scheduling decisions, overall security, and efficiency. Additionally, the module may adjust the service and network model to enhance the monitoring of malicious provider behavior.

Due to the extensive scope of the architecture, this paper does not delve into some of the modules, namely the *Tenant's Rule-based Intrusion Detection System (IDS)* for detecting tenant-originated attacks, the *Tenant Trust Module* for reacting to malicious behavior from tenants, and the *Tenant's Detection module (Local Detection)* for detecting and monitoring malicious user behavior using a pre-trained model. The inclusion of these modules in this paper is meant to provide a complete overview of the entire architecture, however no further discussion will be dedicated to them.

4   Monitoring and Adaptation of Security Violations

In this section, we introduce our proposed monitoring and adaptation system, specifically designed to identify security violations occurring during the execution of workflows in both network and cloud services.

To establish a clear understanding of the key concepts involved, we begin this section by introducing important definitions (Sect. 4.1). These definitions serve as the foundation for subsequent formulas and explanations, ensuring comprehension of the proposed solution. In the subsequent sections, we describe the proposed solution for security violation detection and decision-making regarding the best adaptation action.

4.1   Definitions

Definition 1 (Workflow): A workflow, denoted as w, consists of a set of abstract service tasks that are assigned to concrete cloud services for execution during the deployment phase. It is represented as a tuple (ST, D, E_c, E_d) where ST is a set of abstract Service Tasks (t), D denotes intermediate Data exchanged between workflow tasks, E_c is a set of control Edges that determine the task execution order based on specified conditions $(Conds)$ that must be satisfied $(E_c \subset ST \times ST \times Conds(D))$, E_d is a set of data Edges that specify the flow of data between the tasks $E_d \subset ST \times ST \times D$.

Definition 2 (Task): A task t in w represents an abstract service task that does not refer to any specific concrete cloud service. It is defined as a tuple (C, I, A, V, AA), where C, I, and A represent the Confidentiality, Integrity, and Availability requirements of task t, respectively. Additionally, V indicates the Value of the task within the overall workflow, reflecting its contribution to the whole workflow value. This parameter is introduced to assess various adaptation actions for the task. For example, if the value assigned to a task is negligible, skipping it will not significantly impact the final result of the workflow. Moreover, AA indicates a set of feasible Adaptation Actions for task t, which can include a combination of actions from both Tenant Adaptation Actions (TAA) and Middleware Adaptation Actions (MAA). Mathematically, this set can be represented as $AA = \{aa \mid aa \in TAA_t \cup MAA_t\}$.

Definition 3 (Tenant Adaptation Action): Tenant Adaptation Actions (TAA_t) refers to the actions that can be taken at the tenant level to minimize the damage caused by a violation in task t. Each of these actions denoted as Taa_t $(Taa_t \in TAA_t)$ is defined as a tuple (P, T, MI, V) that represents the Price, Time, Mitigation Impact, and Value of the adaptation action for task t in the workflow. These parameters are determined during the workflow modeling phase by considering the specific characteristics and requirements of each action, based on the parameters of task t (refer to Table 2).

Definition 4 (Middleware Adaptation Action): Middleware Adaptation Actions (MAA_t) represents the actions that can be employed at the middleware level to minimize the damage caused by a violation in task t. Each of these actions denoted as Maa_t $(Maa_t \in MAA_t)$ is defined as a tuple (P, T, MI, V) that indicates the Price, Time, Mitigation Impact, and Value of the adaptation action based on task t parameters in the workflow. The parameters P and T cannot be predefined during the modeling phase due to the dynamic nature of middleware-level adaptation, which depends on the current workflow state and availability of cloud services. Instead, these parameters are dynamically determined at runtime when an attack is detected, using a backup service $(BackupSrc)$ for re-executing the violated tasks (refer to Table 2).

Definition 5 (Attack): An attack a refers to a security violation that can potentially occur during the execution of a workflow w at task t, compromising the security of the task that utilizes service s. It is defined as a tuple $(C, I, A, AT, MA_H, MA_M, MA_L)$, where C, I, and A represent the impacts of the attack a on Confidentiality, Integrity, and Availability, respectively. AT denotes the Attack Type of a. Additionally, MA_H, MA_M, and MA_L categorize available Mitigation Actions that can reduce the impact of the attack. These levels correspond to High, Medium, and Low severity, indicating appropriate actions to mitigate the attack's impact with a specific severity (refer to Table 3).

Definition 6 (Multi-cloud Environment): A multi-cloud environment consists of a set of cloud services provided by different providers $p_1, \ldots, p_m$. It can be represented as $MC = \bigcup_{p_i \in \{p_1, \ldots, p_m\}} \bigcup_{s \in p_{i_{\text{services}}}} (s)$. In this definition, a service s is defined as a tuple (P, T, C, I, A, AFR). Here, P and T represent the Price and average response Time of the service, respectively. The levels of Confidentiality, Integrity, and Availability offered by the service are denoted by C, I, and A respectively. Additionally, AFR represents the Attack Frequency Rate of service s for different types of attacks. It is calculated as follows $AFR = \bigcup_{AT \in \text{all AttackTypes}} AFR(AT)$, where $AFR(AT)$ reflects the likelihood of each attack type AT occurring within the service s based on historical data specific to the service.

Definition 7 (Scheduling Plan): Scheduling Plan (SP) is the process of assigning cloud services to specific tasks within a workflow. It involves the binding of a concrete service s to each abstract service task t. It can be expressed as $SP(w) = \bigcup_{t \in w_{ST}, s \in MC} Sched(t \to s)$.

4.2   Service and Network Monitoring

The service and network monitoring module plays a crucial role in the real-time detection of service and network attacks using data obtained from various sources, including the real-time service information file and network traffic data. An overview of the monitoring procedure can be found in Algorithm 1.

The algorithm employs the trained attack detection model ($\mathcal{M}_{AttackDetection}$) to analyze real-time data and identify potential attacks (line 2). The attack detection model is trained using Algorithm 2, elaborated in Sect. 4.2.1 Upon detection of attack a_k in service task t_i, the algorithm employs Algorithm 3 from Sect. 4.2.2 to determine the severity of the attack (line 3). Furthermore, considering rework and redundancy as the potential options for middleware-level adaptation actions (MAA_{t_i}), the algorithm aims to find an appropriate backup service, referred to as $BackupSrc_{t_i}$, for t_i (line 4). It computes the parameters P, T, MI, and V associated with this backup service, taking into consideration the currently available cloud service offerings. Following this, the algorithm proceeds to the adaptation decision module of the relevant tenant ($relatedTenant$) to determine the most suitable adaptation action in response to the detected attack (line 5). This process will be further explained in Algorithm 4 in Sect. 4.3.

Algorithm 1. Service Monitoring Algorithm

Require: $\mathcal{N}$: Real-time Data, $severity$: Attack Severity Model
Ensure: Monitoring and Detecting Attacks in Real-time Data
1: **while** system is operational **do**
2:     **if** a_k is detected on $\mathcal{N}$ based on $\mathcal{M}_{AttackDetection}$ (Algorithm 2) **then**
3:         $l_{a_k} \leftarrow severity_{AT_{a_k}}(a_k)$ (based on Algorithm 3)
4:         $BackupSrc_{t_i} \leftarrow$ findBackupServiceParameters(t_i)
5:         $relatedTenant$.AdaptationDecisionEngine($a_k, l_{a_k}, BackupSrc_{t_i}$)(Algorithm 4)
6:     **end if**
7: **end while**

4.2.1   Attack Detection Trainer

This section focuses on training a robust model to effectively detect attacks using Random Forest and Linear Regression machine learning algorithms. Algorithm 2 provides an overview of the training process. Two datasets are utilized: Network Traffic Data (NTD) and Cloud Log File (CLF). The NTD dataset contains historical records of network traffic data, exchanged between the middleware and cloud services, enabling the identification of potential network attacks. The CLF dataset consists of the cloud log file, providing resource utilization information such as RAM, CPU, and Bandwidth, for various services, and aiding in the detection of attacks targeting the services.

Algorithm 2. Attack Detection Trainer Algorithm

Require: $\mathcal{DS}$: NTD , CLF
Ensure: $\mathcal{M}_{AttackDetection}$: Trained Model for Attack Detection
1: **for all** $\mathcal{D}$ in $\mathcal{DS}$ **do**
2:     $\mathcal{D}train, \mathcal{D}test \leftarrow \text{Split}(\mathcal{D})$ into training and testing sets
3:     $\mathcal{M}_{AttackDetection} \leftarrow \text{Train(RandomForest}(\mathcal{D}train), \text{LinearRegression}(\mathcal{D}train))$
4:     $Accuracy_{\mathcal{M}_{AttackDetection}} \leftarrow \text{TestAlgorithm}(\mathcal{M}_{AttackDetection}, \mathcal{D}test)$
5: **end for**

4.2.2 Attack Severity Trainer

This section introduces an approach to learning the attack severity model for multiple attack types, as depicted in Algorithm 3. It employs K-means clustering and chi-square feature selection techniques to assign a severity level to each attack. By considering the distinctive features of each attack type, the algorithm accurately scores their severity. The Chi-Square Feature Selection is applied to identify the most informative features for each attack type. This ensures that the severity scoring incorporates the specific characteristics and patterns associated with different types of attacks. By considering different features for each attack type, the algorithm significantly enhances the accuracy and granularity of the severity assignment.

Algorithm 3. Attack Severity Learning Algorithm

Require: $\mathcal{DS}$: NTD , CLF , $AttackTypes$: List of Attack Types
Ensure: $severity$: Attack Severity Model for all attack types in the $AttackTypes$
1: **for all** $\mathcal{D}$ in $\mathcal{DS}$ **do**
2:     **for all** AttackType AT in $AttackTypes$ **do**
3:         $\mathcal{DS}_{AT} \leftarrow \text{Filter}(\mathcal{DS})$ based on AT
4:         $\mathcal{F}' \leftarrow \text{Chi-SquareFeatureSelection}(\mathcal{DS}_{AT})$
5:         Initialize K-means clustering with K clusters using $\mathcal{DS}_{AT}$ and features $\mathcal{F}'$
6:         Train K-means on $\mathcal{DS}_{AT}$
7:         **for all** clusters c in K-means **do**
8:             $severity_{AT_{\mathcal{D}}}[c] \leftarrow$ Calculate the mean attack severity in cluster c
9:         **end for**
10:     **end for**
11: **end for**

4.3   Adaptation Decision

In this section, we present the Adaptation Decision procedure, which plays a crucial role in dynamically identifying the most suitable adaptation actions to mitigate the impact of attacks on the workflow. The procedure is described in Algorithm 4.

Algorithm 4. Adaptation Action Selection Algorithm

Require: l_{a_k}: severity level of the detected attack, $BackupSrc_{t_i}$: the backup service.
Ensure: Selecting the suitable Adaptation Actions for the detected attack
1: $attackScore \leftarrow ComputeAttackScore(a_k, t_i, s_j, l_{a_k})$ based on Equation 1
2: **if** $attackScore > Tenant.AdaptTriggerThresh$ **then**
3:    **if** Lowest-Cost Strategy **then**
4:       $finalAA \leftarrow MA_{l_{(a_k)}} \cap AA_{t_i}$
5:       **for all** Adaptation Action aa in $finalAA$ **do**
6:          $AC[aa] \leftarrow$ ComputeAdaptationCost(aa, t_i) based on Equation 2
7:       **end for**
8:       Sort AC in Ascending order
9:       $Selectedaa \leftarrow aa$ corresponds to the first item in AC
10:    **end if**
11:    **if** Adaptive Strategy **then**
12:       $Selectedaa \leftarrow$ Predicted aa based on $\mathcal{M}_{ActionSelection}$ (Algorithm 5)
13:    **end if**
14:    **if** $Selectedaa \in$ tenant-level adaptation actions **then**
15:       TenantAdaptation$(Selectedaa)$
16:    **else**
17:       MiddlewareAdaptation$(Selectedaa)$
18:    **end if**
19: **end if**

The Adaptation Action Selection algorithm starts by calculating the attack score (line 1), which measures the impact of the detected attack in the current task, taking into account the severity of the attack as well as the security requirements of the task. This computation is based on Eq. 1 described in Sect. 4.3.1. If the attack score exceeds the pre-defined Adaptation Trigger Threshold ($Tenant.AdaptTriggerThresh$) (line 2), the algorithm proceeds with the adaptation action selection process (lines 3–13).

Two distinct strategies are employed to select the optimal adaptation action: the Lowest-Cost Strategy (lines 3–10) and the Adaptive Strategy (lines 11–13).

The Lowest-Cost Strategy starts by identifying a set of potential adaptation actions, denoted as $finalAA$. This set is determined by intersecting the mitigation actions suitable for the severity of the detected attack ($MA_{l_{(a_k)}}$) and the feasible adaptation actions for the current task (AA_{t_i}). The potential actions are then evaluated based on factors such as price, time, mitigation score, and value, computed using Eq. 2 described in Sect. 4.3.2. The actions are subsequently sorted based on their computed costs, and the one with the lowest cost is selected as the optimal choice for mitigating the attack.

Furthermore, to address the uncertain costs associated with each adaptation action in the workflow, we propose an Adaptive Strategy. This strategy uses a trained model described in Sect. 4.3.3, utilizing historical system reactions and adaptations to violations. This model predicts the optimal adaptation action by considering the current state of the workflow, the previously accrued violations, their corresponding adaptations, and the overall workflow complexity. By employing this approach, we effectively account for the dynamic and uncertain costs associated with each action, which cannot be statically determined during the adaptation action selection process. In other words, our approach extends beyond the specific task where the attack is detected, encompassing the entire workflow. Through a holistic view, we incorporate any violations occurring in other tasks that may impact the selection of the most suitable adaptation action for the current task. This assessment enables us to make informed decisions regarding the appropriate adaptation action, taking into account the broader scenario and its implications.

After the selection of the adaptation action(s), the algorithm determines whether they belong to the tenant-level actions or the middleware-level actions. If the action(s) falls under the tenant-level category (line 14), the Tenant Adaptation module is invoked to initiate the necessary adaptations at the tenant level (line 15). Conversely, if the action(s) are categorized as middleware-level adaptations, the Middleware Adaptation module is called upon to implement the required changes (line 17).

4.3.1   Attack Score

The Attack Score serves as a crucial metric for evaluating the impact of a detected attack on the current task and plays a vital role in guiding the selection of appropriate adaptation actions to effectively mitigate its impact on the workflow. The Attack Score is calculated using the following equation:

$$AttackScore(a_k, t_i, s_j, l_{a_k}) = (1 - \prod_{obj \in \{CIA\}} (1 - obj_{t_i} \cdot obj_{a_k})) \cdot AFR_{s_j}(AT_{a_k}) \cdot l_{a_k}$$

(1)

In this equation, obj_{t_i} represents the security requirement of the current task t_i in the workflow for each security objective (CIA, including confidentiality, integrity, and availability). obj_{a_k} denotes the security impact of the detected attack a_k on each security objective. $AFR_{s_j}(AT_{a_k})$ represents the Attack Frequency Rate (AFR) in the cloud service s_j for the type of detected attack AT_{a_k}. Lastly, l_{a_k} corresponds to the severity of the detected attack a_k learned by the Algorithm 3.

4.3.2   Adaptation Cost

We define the Adaptation Cost as a metric to evaluate and score potential adaptation actions, with the goal of mitigating the detected attack. It plays a critical role in the Adaptation Decision Engine, enabling evaluation and comparison of the available actions based on the tenant's preferences. The Adaptation Cost takes into account various parameters, such as price, time, mitigation score, and value. It calculates these parameters for each adaptation action and computes the final adaptation cost, considering the weights assigned by the tenant. The Adaptation Cost is calculated using the following equation:

$$AdaptationCost(aa) = W_{Price} \cdot P_{normalized}(aa) + W_{Time} \cdot T_{normalized}(aa) -$$
$$W_{Security} \cdot MS_{normalized}(aa) - W_{Value} \cdot V_{normalized}(aa)$$
$$(2)$$

In Eq. 2, the terms W_{Price}, W_{Time}, $W_{Security}$, and W_{Value} represent the weights assigned by the tenant to price, time, security, and value, respectively, for the given workflow. On the other hand, $P_{normalized}(aa)$, $T_{normalized}(aa)$, $MS_{normalized}(aa)$, and $V_{normalized}(aa)$ denote the normalized price, time, mitigation score, and value, respectively, for the adaptation action aa. The time, price, and value are directly assigned based on the adaptation type (refer to Table 2), while the mitigation score is calculated using Eq. 3. This equation considers the security requirements of task t_i (represented by obj_{t_i}), the impact of the detected attack a_k on the CIA aspects (represented by obj_{a_k}), and the mitigation impact of the adaptation action on each aspect (represented by $obj_{MI_{aa}}$).

$$MitigationScore(aa, t_i, a_k) = \sum_{obj \in C, I, A} (1 - obj_{t_i} \cdot obj_{a_k}) \cdot obj_{MI_{aa}} \qquad (3)$$

4.3.3   Adaptation Model Trainer

In this section, we present our approach for selecting the best adaptation actions using Reinforcement Learning (RL) [16]. This approach aims to address the uncertain costs associated with each action, which may impact the entire workflow. These uncertain overhead costs cannot be determined statically at the time of action selection, and it becomes necessary to learn their patterns for each specific workflow. So, we use RL to take a holistic view of the workflow and make informed decisions, considering the unpredictable impact of each adaptation action on other tasks within the workflow. This is particularly important due to the presence of data and control dependencies between tasks in the workflow, as well as the violations that have occurred up to the current state of the workflow and the corresponding adaptations made.

RL is a machine learning approach that deals with decision-making in dynamic environments. We utilize RL within our approach, employing a Markov Decision Process (MDP) to model the decision-making problem. MDP provides a formal framework for representing and solving such problems by defining states, actions, transition probabilities, and rewards. To find optimal policies by learning from previous decision-making experiences, we employ Q-learning [17], a model-free reinforcement learning algorithm.

In the following, we will describe the key elements of the Q-learning problem and present the algorithm for selecting the best adaptation action.

Markov Decision Process: A Markov decision process MDP is defined as a 4-tuple MDP=(*State*, *Action*, *Probability*, *Reward*), with the following definitions:

– *State*: Represents the set of all possible states. Each state is defined by a 2-tuple $st = (St_T, St_W)$, where St_T denotes the current state of task t_i, including the detected attack, and its severity, St_W signifies the present state of the workflow capturing information about the previously occurred violation, their respective adaptations, as well as the time, price, mitigation score, and value of the workflow up to the current point.
– *Action*: Denotes the set of available actions at a given state. The action set $A(st)$ represents the collection of actions (a) that can be taken at state st, expressed as $A(st) \subseteq MA_{l_{(a_k)}} \cap AA_{t_i}$ (same as line 4 in Algorithm 4).
– *Probability*: Describes the probability of transitioning from one state to another when performing a particular action. It is represented by the probability distribution $P(st'|st, a)$.
– *Reward*: Represents the measure of adaptation action selection efficiency. If action a is selected, the reward function is defined as:

$$R(st) = \sum W_i \frac{att_i - att_i^{\min}}{att_i^{\max} - att_i^{\min}} \tag{4}$$

In Equation (4), att_i represents the observed values for price, time, value, and mitigation score for the entire workflow, while $att_i^{\max}$ and $att_i^{\min}$ represent the maximum and minimum values of att_i across all adaptation actions. W_i is the weighting factor of att_i, where W_i is positive for mitigation score and value and negative for price and time.

The mean Q-value of action a on state st following policy π is denoted as $Q_\pi(st, a)$. The optimal Q-value function is defined as:

$$Q(st, a) = \sum_{st'} \gamma(st'|st, a) \left[R(st'|st, a) + \gamma \max_{a'} Q(st', a') \right] \tag{5}$$

Here, γ represents the discount factor, $R(st'|st, a)$ is the reward received when transitioning from state st to st' by performing action a, and $\max_{a'} Q^*(st', a')$ calculates the maximum Q-value for the next state st'. This optimal value function is nested within the Bellman optimality equation.

Algorithm 5. Action Selection Trainer Algorithm

Require: st: The current state
Ensure: Trained Model for Selecting the proper Adaptation Action
1: **for** each episode **do**
2:     $st \leftarrow st_0$
3:     **for** $st \notin St_r$ **do**
4:         Choose $a \in A(st)$ based on ϵ-greedy policy
5:         Perform a, observe reward r and new state s'
6:         $Q(st,a) \leftarrow Q(st,a) + \alpha\left[r + \gamma \max_{a'} Q(st',a') - Q(st,a)\right]$
7:         $st \leftarrow s'$
8:     **end for**
9: **end for**

---

5   Evaluation

We implemented $SecFlow^2$ by extending the jBPM (Java Business Process Management) [18] engine and integrating it with the Cloudsim Plus [19] simulation tool. jBPM offers a pluggable architecture that allows for easy replacement of different module implementations. Additionally, the integration of the simulation framework Cloudsim Plus has allowed us to accurately model the complexities of a multi-cloud environment.

5.1   Experimental Setting

To evaluate our approach, we utilized three distinct categories of process models: Small (3–10 tasks), Medium (10–50 tasks), and Large (50–100 tasks). Our scenario assumed the availability of 5 cloud providers, each offering 3 different services for the service tasks. The specifications of these services fell within the following ranges: Response time [1, 50], Cost [0.1, 10], and confidentiality, integrity, and availability [0, 1]. The response times are selected randomly such that the fastest service is roughly three times faster than the slowest one, and accordingly, it is roughly three times more expensive.

Table 2 provides an overview of the relative properties associated with each adaptation type, where T, P, and V are the original task's response time, price, and value. Additionally, MI denotes the mitigation impact of each action on CIA.

Table 2. The Properties of Different Adaptation Types

AdaptType	T	P	V	MI(C,I,A)
Insert	$T_{newTask}$	$P_{newTask}$	$V_{newTask}$	$(0.7, 0.9, 0.9)$
Switch	T_{Switch}	P	V_{Switch}	$(0.7, 0.6, 0.8)$
Skip	0	0	0	$(0.5, 0.4, 0.6)$
Rework	$T_{BackupSrc}$	$P_{BackupSrc}$	V	$(0.5, 0.9, 0.7)$
Redundancy	$Max(T_{BackupSrc}, T)$	$P + P_{BackupSrc}$	$V + V_{Redundancy}$	$(0.5, 0.8, 0.9)$
Reconfiguration	$T + T_{reconfig}$	$P + P_{reconfig}$	$V + V_{Reconfig}$	$(0.6, 0.7, 0.5)$

---

^{2} Our code is available at https://github.com/nafisesoezy/SecFlow.

In this paper, we specifically focus on four prevalent types of attacks in cloud services and networks, namely Denial of Service (DoS), probe attacks, Remote-to-Local (R2L), and User-to-Root (U2R). The specifications of these attacks are provided in Table 3. The table presents the Impact on CIA, which indicates the effect of each attack type on CIA security objectives [20]. It also includes Mitigation Actions, which specify the adaptation actions that effectively mitigate each attack type, classified by attack severity levels (Low, Medium, High).

5.2 Main Results

In this section, we present the main results of our experiment, focusing on the evaluation of the detection module and the subsequent discussion on the adaptation process.

Table 3. Attack Specifications

AT	Impact on (C,I,A)	Mitigation Actions		
		(Low,	Medium,	High)
DoS	(0.56,0.56,0.56)	Switch, Rework	Insert, Rework	Insert, Rework, Redundancy, ReConfiguration
Probe	(0.22,0.22,0)	Skip	Skip, ReConfiguration	Skip, ReConfiguration
U2R	(0.56,0.22,0.22)	Insert, Rework	Insert, Rework	Insert, Rework, Redundancy, ReConfiguration
R2L	0.56,0.56,0.22)	Rework	Insert, Rework	Insert, Rework, ReConfiguration

5.2.1 Detection Method Evaluation

We begin by evaluating the performance of our detection method (refer to Algorithm 2) using two datasets[3]: network traffic data (NTD) and cloud log files (CLF). Given the absence of comprehensive existing log files for executing workflows within cloud services, we use synthetic data as follows. To construct the NTD dataset, we simulate various attacks on network traffic data using the KDD dataset [21] and subsequently integrate it with workflow tasks and cloud service specifications. In a similar way, the CLF dataset is created by simulating attacks within cloud services from different providers, thereby capturing CPU, Bandwidth, and RAM utilization data. Subsequently, the service model trainer module utilizes the Random Forest and Linear Regression algorithms independently to train a model capable of detecting attacks. To evaluate the effectiveness of our detection procedure using these two algorithms, we employ a set of metrics including F1-score, Accuracy, and False Alarm Rate (FAR). Figure 2 and Table 4 present the performance comparison between the Random Forest and Linear Regression algorithms for both NTD and CLF datasets. The evaluation demonstrates that the choice between the two methods depends on the specific

---

[3] https://github.com/tamaratataru/Bachelors_Project.

type of attack being considered. Furthermore, in terms of accuracy, the Random Forest model consistently outperforms Linear Regression across both datasets.

Table 4. Detection Accuracy and False Alarm Rate (FAR) for Various Attack Types

DataSet	Accuracy (%)	DoSFAR (%)	ProbeFAR (%)	R2LFAR (%)	U2RFAR (%)
RandomForest-NTD	99.97	0.00	0.03	0.03	0.03
LinearRegression-NTD	99.73	0.00	0.01	0.00	0.00
RandomForest-CLF	90.15	1.56	3.45	6.51	3.45
LinearRegression-CLF	72.07	5.01	3.78	8.53	5.83

5.2.2 Adaptation Method Evaluation

In this section, we compare the performance of two adaptation strategies: the Lowest-Cost Strategy and the Adaptive Strategy. We consider uncertain overhead costs introduced by adaptation actions under specific conditions.

For the Lowest-Cost Strategy, we calculate the average price, time, and value across 1000 executions of three process categories (small, medium, and large) at an attack rate of 0.3. On the other hand, the Adaptive Strategy is evaluated by calculating the average price, time, and value across every 100 executions over 1000 execution rounds of the three process categories at an attack rate of 0.3.

The results, presented in Fig. 3, show superiority of the Adaptive Strategy for the majority of cases. By intelligently learning the conditions that lead to uncertain costs from adaptation actions in the workflow, it selects the most suitable adaptation action while considering these uncertainties. This selection effectively minimizes the overall execution time and price, while simultaneously maximizing the value and mitigation score. We also observe that finding the optimal set of adaptation actions by the Adaptive Strategy takes longer for the large class workflow compared to the medium and small class workflows due to the larger solution space involved.

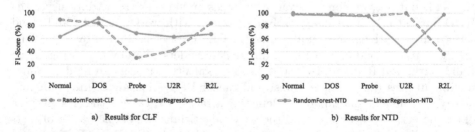

Fig. 2. F1-Score Performance of Detection Method for Various Attack Types on CLF and NTD Datasets

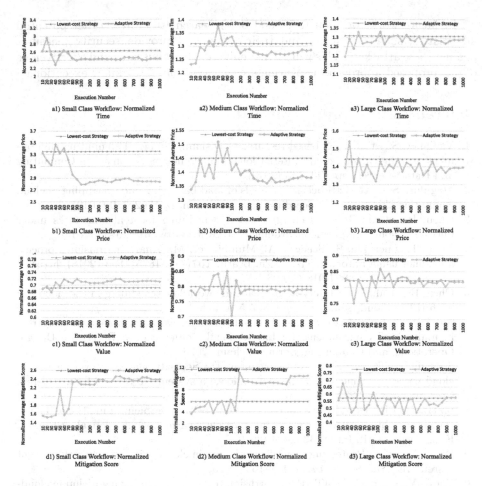

Fig. 3. Lowest-Cost vs. Adaptive Strategy Considering Uncertain Overhead Costs

6 Conclusion

In this paper, we have addressed critical research gaps in monitoring, detecting, and responding to security violations in cloud-based workflow execution. Our approach focuses on monitoring and detecting security violations, specifically targeting cloud services and network violations. We have presented two strategies for selecting the best action to minimize the impact of such violations. The first strategy selects the most cost-effective adaptation action, while the second leverages adaptive learning from past reactions.

To conclude, this paper has established an approach for detecting and subsequently adapting workflows in response to security violations using the introduced strategies. Our approach, implemented as an extension of JBPM and Cloudsim Plus, demonstrated its ability to monitor, detect, and adapt to security violations through simulation results.

In future work, we plan to extend our research to address other potential adversaries, such as tenants and their users, and provide security measures against these attackers. This will further enhance the robustness and effectiveness of our proposed approach in ensuring secure cloud-based workflow execution.

References

1. Varshney, S., et al.: QoS based resource provisioning in cloud computing environment: a technical survey. In: International Conference on Advances in Computing and Data Sciences, pp. 711–723 (2019)
2. Maguluri, S.T., et al.: Stochastic models of load balancing and scheduling in cloud computing clusters. In: Proceedings IEEE Infocom, pp. 702–710 (2012)
3. Chen, H., et al.: Towards energy-efficient scheduling for real-time tasks under uncertain cloud computing environment. J. Syst. Softw. **99**, 20–35 (2015)
4. Nolle, T., Luettgen, S., Seeliger, A., Mühlhäuser, M.: Analyzing business process anomalies using autoencoders. Mach. Learn. **107**(11), 1875–1893 (2018). https://doi.org/10.1007/s10994-018-5702-8
5. Chen, H., et al.: Uncertainty-aware real-time workflow scheduling in the cloud. In: 2016 IEEE Cloud Conference, pp. 577–584. IEEE
6. Soveizi, N., et al.: SecFlow: adaptive security-aware workflow management system in multi-cloud environment. In: International Conference on Enterprise Design, Operations, and Computing. Springer, cham (2023)
7. Soveizi, N., Turkmen, F., Karastoyanova, D.: Security and privacy concerns in cloud-based scientific and business workflows: a systematic review. Future Gener. Comput. Syst. (2023)
8. Shirvani, M.H.: Bi-objective web service composition problem in multi-cloud environment: a bi-objective time-varying particle swarm optimisation algorithm. J. Exp. Theor. Artif. Intell. **33**, 1–24 (2020)
9. Wang, Y., et al.: Protecting scientific workflows in clouds with an intrusion tolerant system. IET Inf. Secur. **14**(2), 157–165 (2020)
10. Wang, Y., et al.: INHIBITOR: an intrusion tolerant scheduling algorithm in cloud-based scientific workflow system. Futur. Gener. Comput. Syst. **114**, 272–284 (2021)
11. Wen, Z., et al.: Dynamically partitioning workflow over federated clouds for optimising the monetary cost and handling run-time failures. IEEE Trans. Cloud Comput. **8**(4), 1093–1107 (2020)
12. Abazari, F., et al.: MOWS: multi-objective workflow scheduling in cloud computing based on heuristic algorithm. Simul. Modell. Pract. Theory **93**(2018), 119–132 (2019)
13. Ahmad, Z., Nazir, B., Umer, A.: A fault-tolerant workflow management system with quality-of-service-aware scheduling for scientific workflows in cloud computing. Int. J. Commun. Syst. **34**(1), e4649 (2021)
14. Alaei, M., et al.: An adaptive fault detector strategy for scientific workflow scheduling based on improved differential evolution algorithm in cloud. Appl. Soft Comput. **99**, 106895 (2021)
15. Nolle, T., Seeliger, A., Mühlhäuser, M.: BINet: multivariate business process anomaly detection using deep learning. In: Weske, M., Montali, M., Weber, I., vom Brocke, J. (eds.) BPM 2018. LNCS, vol. 11080, pp. 271–287. Springer, Cham (2018). https://doi.org/10.1007/978-3-319-98648-7_16

16. Kaelbling, L.P., et al.: Reinforcement learning: a survey. J. Artif. Intell. Res. **4**, 237–285 (1996)
17. Watkins, C.J.C.H., Dayan, P.: Q-learning. Mach. Learn. **8**, 279–292 (1992)
18. jBPM: Business Process Management Suite. https://www.jbpm.org/
19. CloudSim Plus Contributors. CloudSim Plus. GitHub repository. https://github.com/manoelcampos/cloudsim-plus
20. Yang, H., et al.: Network security situation assessment with network attack behavior classification. Int. J. Intell. Syst. **37**(10), 6909–6927 (2022)
21. KDD Cup. In: The UCI KDD Archive (1999). http://kdd.ics.uci.edu/databases/kddcup99/kddcup99.html

Process Modeling

Beyond Rule-Based Named Entity Recognition and Relation Extraction for Process Model Generation from Natural Language Text

Julian Neuberger$^{(\boxtimes)}$, Lars Ackermann, and Stefan Jablonski

University of Bayreuth, Bayreuth, Germany
{julian.neuberger,lars.ackermann,stefan.jablonski}@uni-bayreuth.de

Abstract. Process-aware information systems offer extensive advantages to companies, facilitating planning, operations, and optimization of day-to-day business activities. However, the time-consuming but required step of designing formal business process models often hampers the potential of these systems. To overcome this challenge, automated generation of business process models from natural language text has emerged as a promising approach to expedite this step. Generally two crucial subtasks have to be solved: extracting process-relevant information from natural language and creating the actual model. Approaches towards the first subtask are rule based methods, highly optimized for specific domains, but hard to adapt to related applications. To solve this issue, we present an extension to an existing pipeline, to make it entirely data driven. We demonstrate the competitiveness of our improved pipeline, which not only eliminates the substantial overhead associated with feature engineering and rule definition, but also enables adaptation to different datasets, entity and relation types, and new domains. Additionally, the largest available dataset (PET) for the first subtask, contains no information about linguistic references between mentions of entities in the process description. Yet, the resolution of these mentions into a single visual element is essential for high quality process models. We propose an extension to the PET dataset that incorporates information about linguistic references and a corresponding method for resolving them. Finally, we provide a detailed analysis of the inherent challenges in the dataset at hand.

Keywords: Process-aware Information Systems · Process Extraction · Named Entity Recognition · Relation Extraction · Co-Reference Resolution

1 Introduction

Automated generation of formal business process models from natural language process descriptions has become increasingly popular [1,2,7,10,19]. This is motivated, for instance, with the comparatively high time expenditure for manually

© The Author(s), under exclusive license to Springer Nature Switzerland AG 2024
M. Sellami et al. (Eds.): CoopIS 2023, LNCS 14353, pp. 179–197, 2024.
https://doi.org/10.1007/978-3-031-46846-9_10

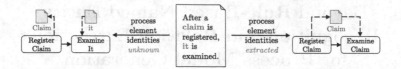

Fig. 1. Example for differences between information extraction phase with and without resolving process element identities. Resolving process element identity from their mentions (right) allows generation of correct data flow, without (left) data flow is disjointed.

designing said process models. Up to 60% of the total duration in process management projects is spent on the design of process models [10]. Techniques for automated process model generation from natural language text aim to reduce this effort, but have to solve several sub-tasks for this, categorized into two distinct phases: *(i) The information extraction phase* and *(ii) the process model generation phase.* During the information extraction phase, techniques recognize process elements (e.g., activities, actors, data objects), extract relations (e.g., sequence-flow relations between activities), and resolve references (e.g., mentions of the same data object). Building on this information, the process model generation phase creates a concrete process model [10,13,19]. The current state of the art for the information extracting phase exhibits two core issues, which we will briefly discuss in the following.

Core Issue 1. Existing approaches are largely rule-based, i.e., approaches use manually crafted rules rooted in domain knowledge [2,10,21]. Rule-based systems usually show remarkable precision and recall for the datasets they are created for. However, they *a)* require significant amounts of labor to capture linguistic subtleties, *b)* require deep technical knowledge, as well as knowledge of the target domain, and *c)* are hard to adapt to even minor changes in the underlying data, which leads to unacceptable expansion in the number of required rules [26]. Using machine learning, these drawbacks can be resolved, especially deep learning methods have been shown to greatly reduce the amount of effort and domain knowledge required [15]. However, deep learning methods usually need considerable amounts of data for stable training [14], something the field of business process modeling research currently can not provide [12]. Using less expressive machine learning models constitute a middle ground to this dilemma, as they can be trained stably with orders of magnitude less data.

Core Issue 2. Existing approaches are scoped too narrowly [18]. This includes systems, that do not capture enough information for the generation of complete process models, as well as systems that impose unrealistic assumptions concerning the structure of input text. For high-quality process models, resolving references between mentions of the same process element is crucial. Consider, for instance, the example depicted in Fig. 1. For a human reader it is obvious, that both "*a claim*" and "*it*" refer to the same instance of a *claim*. To automatically extract a process model encoding this knowledge the system needs to resolve the two mentions "*a claim*" and "*it*" to a single entity. Without this step, at least two problems manifest in the extracted process models: *(i)* Two distinct data objects for *claim* would be created and, thus, the model is not able to correctly express that both the registration and the examination activities process the same data, and *(ii)* one of the created data objects is labeled *it*, because it is unknown that *it* is a reference to *a claim*. Though the *claim* example is solely focusing on the data perspective, entity resolution is also necessary for organizational process elements like, for instance, actors. Here, it is necessary to be able to create process models that contain a single actor type for the two mentions of the *claim officer*, which is expressed as a single swimlane in BPMN, for instance. This issue is rooted in a lack of data. Most notably, the currently largest dataset for the information extraction phase (PET [7]) does not include information about linguistic references between mentions of process elements. In summary, it can be said that entity resolution is what makes it possible in the first place to correctly express relations to data and to actors. Following from these two core issues we state three main research questions.

RQ1. Are deep learning methods able to extract process information with precision and recall comparable to rule-based methods given the same dataset?

RQ2. If deep learning methods prove inadequate for small datasets, such as PET, can classical machine learning models (e.g., gradient boosting techniques) compete with rule-based methods in terms of precision and recall?

RQ3. Can a pre-trained co-reference resolution approach outperform naïve word matching, and can therefore be used as a baseline for resolving linguistic references between process element mentions?

Our work proposes an improved pipeline which tackles both of these issues, which we describe in detail in Sect. 4. We propose a relation extraction approach based on established machine learning methods, while adopting the approach to extracting process elements, as it is based on machine learning already. Future work could investigate other methods and compare them, but this is out of scope for this paper. Additionally, we extend PET with information about the identity of process element mentions, and provide a baseline approach for resolving process element identities from process element mentions. We compare our pipeline to the current state of the art of information extraction on PET and show that we outperform it in five out of six relation types, with an absolute increase of 6% in F_1 scores.

The remainder of this paper is structured as follows: In Sect. 2 we formalize the task of process model extraction. In Sect. 3 we discuss differences to work related to this paper. Our thorough investigation of the PET dataset and the extraction approaches in Sect. 6 is based on a rigorous experiment setup introduced in Sect. 5. Short summaries of the answers to our research questions are provided in Sect. 7. Both the source code for our experiments and the extended dataset are publicly available[1], therefore laying the foundation for further focused research.

---

[1] see https://github.com/JulianNeuberger/pet-baselines

2   Task Description

Natural language processing (*NLP*) is a discipline that aims to exploit natural language input data and spans a wide variety of subfields. One of these subfields is Information Extraction from human-readable texts. In the following, we describe the extraction of process elements and of relations between them as instances of three sub-problems of information extraction, which are *Named Entity Recognition* (NER), *Relation Extraction* (RE), and *Entity Resolution* (ER). We then detail the three subproblems with respect to the extended PET dataset as described in Sect. 5.1. Each task assumes that the input text has already been pre-processed, i.e., *tokenized*. Refer to Fig. 2 for visual examples of input and output of the steps described below.

Named Entity Recognition (NER). NER is the task of extracting spans of tokens corresponding to exactly one element from a set of entities [15]. While NER traditionally only considered extraction of proper nouns, the definition now depends on the domain [23]. For the process domain named entities are process relevant facts, such as actors (e.g., *the CEO* vs. *Max*) or activities (e.g., *approve* vs. *the approval*). The PET dataset defines a set of seven process relevant facts, providing a general schema for process model generation from natural language text [6]. Formally the NER task is extracting a set of triples M from a given list of tokens T, so that for each triple $m = (i_s, i_e, t_e) \in M$, the indices i_s and i_e denote start and end tokens of the span in T respectively, and t_e refers to the entity type. Throughout this paper, we will refer to the triple m a *mention* of an *entity*. An extracted mention is considered correct, iff its triple has an exact match in the list of ground truth triples given by the dataset.

Entity Resolution (ER). During ER techniques extract a set of unique entities from a given set of mentions M. This step can be seen as resolving references between mentions of the same process element, which is crucial information for generating useful business process models further down-stream, as shown in Fig. 1. Formally the ER task is defined as finding a set of non-empty *mention clusters* E, so that each mention $m \in M$ is assigned to exactly one cluster $e \in E$. These clusters are called *entities*. To disambiguate between the use of entity as in NER, and entity as used in ER, we will call the result of NER *mentions* from now on, and the result of ER *entities*. An entity prediction is considered correct, iff the set of contained mentions is exactly the same as the ground truth defined by the dataset. Entity resolution itself is a super-set of the tasks *Anaphora Resolution*, i.e., back-referencing pronouns, *Coreference Resolution*, i.e., use of synonyms, and *Cataphora Resolution*, i.e., forward-referencing pronouns [24]. While there are subtle differences and overlap between these sub-fields, this work focuses on coreference resolution. The addition of cataphora and anaphora resolution is potentially useful, but is out of scope for our planned baseline. Thus, we refer to coreference resolution, whenever we mention the ER task in later sections. The PET dataset only contains two entity types, where entity identity is relevant: *Actors*, describing a natural person, department, organization, or artificial agent, and *Activity Data*, which are objects or data used by an *Activity* [6]. Further details can be found in Sect. 5.1.

Relation Extraction (RE). RE is the task of identifying a set of semantic relations R between pairs of entities. Current literature distinguishes between global and mention level RE [16]. Global RE is the task of extracting a list of entity pairs forming a certain relation from a text, without any additional information. On the other hand, mention level RE methods are given a pair of entity mentions and the sentence containing them, and have to predict the relation between the two. The PET dataset contains relation information on mention level, which allows our approach to learn on local level. There are six relation types defined in the PET dataset, such as *Flow*, which captures the execution order between behavioural elements [6]. Each relation is formally defined by a triple $r = (m_h, m_t, t_r)$, where m_h is the head entity mention or source of the relation, m_t the tail entity mention or target, and t_r the type of the semantic relation. This definition implies relations are directed, that is $(m_h, m_t, t_r) \neq (m_t, m_h, t_r)$ for $m_h \neq m_t$. A predicted relation tuple $r \in R$ is considered correct, iff its triple has an exact match in the list of ground truth triples given by the dataset.

3   Related Work

[7] presents the currently largest collection of natural language business processes descriptions with annotations for process relevant facts. They also propose a pipeline for extracting said process relevant facts. The paper at hand is founded on their work and is therefore closely related, as we use, extend, and analyze both data and pipeline. We adopt the approach to NER, and compare our proposed RE approach to their method. They are missing a more in-depth description of their data, especially regarding qualities important for prediction performance, including but not limited to: correlation between a relation's type and its argument types, or the amount of variation in language of their data. Furthermore, the implementation of their pipeline is not publicly available, impeding further research and development.

There are several approaches related to the baselines we present and analyze in this work. An annotation approach based on rule-based pattern matching across the dependency tree representation of a textual process description is presented in [21], which is then used to generate an event log. This allows the extraction of a formal process model via established process mining techniques. While it achieves state-of-the-art results, it uses a tagging schema different from the one used in PET, which makes it unfeasible for use in a direct comparison. [10] presents a pipeline able to extract formal process models in Business Process Model and Notation (BPMN), and therefore is locked into this process notation language. The same limitation holds for the approach presented in [2], which extracts process models utilizing the Declare language. PET follows a different tagging scheme and, thus, a direct comparison is not possible. In [18] a neural method for entity and relation classification is proposed, but assumes that relevant text fragments are already extracted. This is a significantly easier task, since separating relevant process information from redundant, superfluous, and incidental information, appearing in natural language, is a hard task in itself. [3]

presents an efficient deep learning method using formal meaning representations as an intermediary feature. Since they only solve NER, we can not compare their approach with our proposals.

Due to the strong relation between process extraction and the combined NLP task of NER, ER, and RE, there are several approaches potentially able to solve the process extraction task [8,9,11,22]. [4] studies several approaches built for joint NER, ER, and RE on small documents. Applying them to the BPM domain entails fragmenting the larger documents of PET properly, as well as dealing with long distance relations, which is out of scope for this paper. However, we chose Jerex [9], since [8] and [11] predict mentions as their textual representation (*surface forms*) only, meaning the span of text containing them might be ambiguous, and therefore token indices not resolvable. This violates our definition of mentions (Sect. 2) and hampers the evaluation of the predictions.

Using pre-trained large language models seems promising for the task at hand, as shown in [5], which uses in-context learning with GPT3 to extract process relevant facts. These are limited to a small subset of the information extracted in [7] and the paper at hand, though. Furthermore their evaluation only uses a portion of the PET-dataset, i.e., 9 out of a total of 45 documents, without repeated runs, e.g., k-fold cross validation. A direct comparison is therefore impossible.

4   Process Information Extraction Approach

In the following we present a short overview of the implementation for the three pipeline steps for *NER*, *ER*, and *RE*. The entire pipeline as we propose it is depicted in Fig. 2. We will refer to this pipeline implementation as *Ours* from now on. We do not detail preprocessing steps, nor the actual generation of a business process model, as both are out of scope for this paper. Our approach extracts the text and location of mentions of process elements (NER), resolves those mentions to unique sets of entities (ER), and extracts the (entity) arguments and type of relations (RE). The types of extracted entities and relations are identical with [7], refer to [6] for an in-depth description.

The NER step is identical to the implementation from [7]. The approach is based on Conditional Random Fields (*CRF*), a powerful technique for tagging a sequence of observations, here tokens in a text [25]. Given a sequence of tokens tagged in this way, we then resolve mentions, where each mention contains a set of token indices and the predicted process element type. We did not change or optimize this step, as the main focus of this paper is extracting process relevant facts with machine learning methods, and CRF methods are known to be a strong choice for tagging.

We implemented two modules for **the ER step**, namely a *naive ER method*, and a method based on *pre-trained end-to-end neural coreference resolution*, as described in [13] and implemented in spaCy[2]. The naive ER method, which

---

[2] See https://explosion.ai/blog/coref for more details.

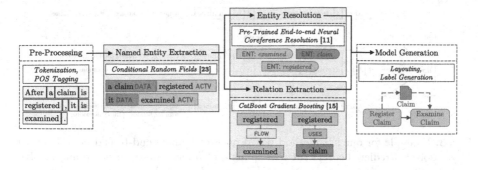

Fig. 2. Outline of our proposed extended extraction pipeline.

we will call *naive ER* for short, iteratively selects the best matching mentions with identical NER tags. The match of two mentions is calculated based on the percentage of *overlapping*, i.e., the fraction of shared tokens over the total number of tokens. Ranking mention pairs by this score, the naive ER method merges mentions into clusters. If one of the selected mentions already is part of a cluster, the other mention is added to that cluster as well. If both selected mentions are part of a cluster, the clusters are merged. This is repeated until there are only matches left, which overlap less than some threshold o. We ran an optimization to select this overlap optimally and chose $o = 0.5$ The pre-trained end-to-end neural coreference resolution module, which we will call *neural ER* from now on, predicts co-referent spans of text, i.e., spans of text referring to each other. It does so without any domain knowledge, i.e., knowledge about mentions of process elements extracted in prior steps. We then align these predictions with mentions. Here we discard predictions, if **(1)** the corresponding span of text is not a mention at all, **(2)** the corresponding span of text does not overlap with a mention's text by a certain percentage α_m, **(3)** the mention corresponding with the predicted span of text was not tagged with the majority tag of other mentions of this entity, or **(4)** not at least a certain portion α_c of predicted text spans was previously accepted. We optimize these parameters using a grid search approach, choosing $\alpha_c = 0.5$ and $\alpha_m = 0.5$. A simple example of this process is shown in Fig. 3

Finally the **RE step** extracts relations between mentions using CatBoost, a gradient boosting technique for classification using numerical, as well as categorical data [17]. We call this module *BoostRelEx* for short in following sections. For each combination of head and tail mention of a relation we build features containing tags, distance in tokens and in sentences between them, and a number c of neighboring mention tags as context. This feature set is then presented to the model, which predicts a class for it. Classes are the set of relation tags and an additional *nothing* tag to enable the model to predict that there is no relation between two mentions. During training we present each of the mention combinations containing a relation to the model exactly once per iteration, as well as a given number of negative examples. These negative examples only consist of

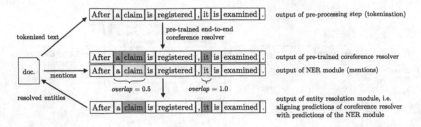

Fig. 3. Example for our ER method based on a pretrained end-to-end neural coreference resolver. Predicted coreferent text spans *a claim* and *it* are accepted and resolved to an entity containing the mentions *claim* and *it*, since both text spans overlap at least 50% with the mention's texts.

mention combinations, where corresponding entities do not have a relation. This concept, called negative sampling, is important, as there are many more mention combinations without a relation between them (44,708), as there are ones with one (1,916). Without negative sampling the precision of our relation extraction module would be extremely low, visualized in Fig. 4. For each positive sample we select r_n randomly drawn negative ones. Increasing r_n has a positive impact on the accuracy with which the model predicts the existence of relations between given pairs of mentions, which is called the *precision P*. Since the model learns it has to reject some mention combinations, it also inevitably rejects correct combinations. Following directly from this, the model misses more combinations of mentions, where a relation actually would have existed, thus resulting in a lower *recall R*. The harmonic mean between the two scores R and P gives us a good idea of the model's performance. We discuss this metric in more detail in Sect. 5.3. We train the *BoostRelEx* module for $i = 1000$ iterations, which is the most computationally intensive step in the whole pipeline, taking about 25 min on an Intel i9-9900K CPU @ 3.60 GHz, using a negative sampling rate of $r_n = 40$ and context size of $c = 2$. A sampling rate $r_n \geq 40$ improves the result quality significantly.

5   Experiment Setup

In the following we describe the extension of the original PET dataset accompanied with dataset statistics (Sect. 5.1). To enable empirical evaluation Sect. 5.3 introduces performance measures that are most adequate for the task and the concrete dataset.

5.1   Dataset

The PET dataset is presented in detail in [7], in the following we will only discuss aspects of this dataset directly related to our extension and analysis. PET contains a total of 45 documents, with seven entity types, and six relation types. To facilitate the entity resolution task described in Sect. 2, we assign each

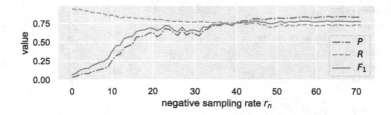

Fig. 4. Values of metrics P, R, and F_1 for different negative sampling rates r_n.

mention of a process element to a cluster[3]. Thus, each cluster refers to exactly one instance of a process element (e.g., a particular actor) that is mentioned in several places in the text. In Fig. 1 the same claim is mentioned twice, i.e., **the claim** is registered and then **it** is examined. This resulted in a total of 163 clusters with two or more mentions, of which 75 are *Activity Data* mention clusters, and 88 *Actor* mention clusters. All other entity types and the remaining *Activity Data* and *Actor* mentions belong to clusters with only a single mention.

We define the *intra-entity distance* as the maximum of each mention's minimal distance to each other mention in the entity. This gives us the largest span an extraction method has to reason over to detect two mentions as part of the same entity. Averaged over all entities this measure is 31.93 tokens for *Activity Data* elements and 54.84 tokens for *Actors*. Distances between referent mentions are significantly longer for *Actors*, indicating that they possibly are harder to extract. Our experiments seem to support this notion, as shown in Fig. 6c) and d), but further analysis may be required to come to a conclusive rationale.

Intuitively, resolving references between mentions of an entity, is easier, when the texts of those mentions are very similar. Consider, for example, two entities, both made up of two mentions each. One entity has the mentions *"a claim"* and *"the claim"*, while the other has the mentions *"the claimant"* and *"a applicant"*. Resolving the first entity should be much easier, since its mentions share common text. Thus, calculating the lexical diversity of entities of a given type lets us predict how hard it is to extract them without errors. The *type-token ratio* (TTR) can be used to measure the lexical diversity of a given input text [20]. It is calculated as the ratio between unique tokens and total number of tokens. High ratios imply very diverse phrases, while low ratios indicate very uniform text. We select all entities, which contain at least two mentions, and calculate the TTR for each of them. Take for example the entity consisting of the three mentions *"a claim"*, *"the claim"*, and *"it"*. Its TTR would therefore result in $TTR = \frac{4}{5} = 0.8$. We then calculate the mean of these TTR values, split by entity type. On average, *Activity Data* mention clusters exhibit higher type-token ratios compared to *Actors*, as visualized in Fig. 5b. This result is leading us to assume *Actors* should be easier to resolve. Our experiments support this notion, as can be seen in Fig. 6c).

---

[3] All clusters are defined by two experts, with the help of a third for cases, where their initial annotations differed.

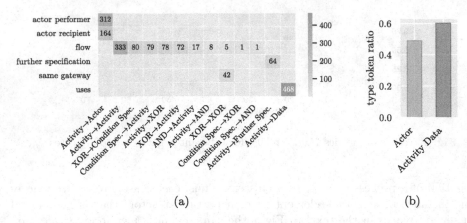

(a)   (b)

Fig. 5. Statistics of the original dataset. 5a shows the number of relations aggregated by argument types denoted with *head* → *tail*. Only combinations where at least one relation exists are shown. 5b shows the mean type-token ratio for mention clusters with at least two mentions.

Figure 5a shows the distribution of relation types depending on the types of their arguments. For relations of type *Actor Performer*, *Actor Recipient*, *Same Gateway*, and *Flows*, knowing the types of their arguments is no discriminating feature. For these cases, a data driven approach, such as the one we propose in this paper, is very useful, as complex rules are inferred from data automatically, saving a lot of manual effort. In contrast, there are also relation types, where their type can directly be inferred from their argument's types, e.g., all relations that have an *Activity* as head argument, and an *Activity Data* element as tail, are of type *Uses*. This is hardly surprising when factoring in domain knowledge, as in *PET Activity Data* is only used with *Activities*. Predicting relations of those types is therefore more a matter of detecting them (*recall*), rather than correctly classifying them (*precision*).

5.2   Compared Approaches

We compare our proposed pipeline to the baseline presented in [7], extended with our ER module. The pipeline looks very similar to ours visualized in Fig. 2, but instead of the *BoostRelEx* module, it uses a rule-based relation extractor, which we will denote *RuleRelEx*. These rules are defined in [7], but have no public implementation, to our knowledge our code is the first executable version available to the community. There are a total of six rules, which are applied to documents in order. This means that rule 1 takes precedence over, e.g., rule 3, which relies on this fact, as it needs information about previously extracted *Flow* relations. We will denote this pipeline with *Bellan + ER* from now on.

Answering RQ1 requires a deep learning approach, which is able to extract mentions, entities, and relations. *Jerex* [9] is suitable for this task, as it is a jointly trained end-to-end deep learning approach, and promises to reduce the effect of error propagation. Jerex takes raw, untokenized text as input, tokenizes it, and produces predictions for mentions, entities, and relations between them. It is state of the art for the *DocRed* dataset [27], which is a large benchmark dataset for the extraction of mentions, entities, and relations from documents – a task description very similar to the one we gave in Sect. 2. Furthermore, Jerex is able to extract the exact location of mentions inside the input text, unlike competing approaches, which only extract the text of mentions[4]. While this drawback may not be as relevant in applications where only the text of a process element is interesting, for the task of business process generation, i.e., the task of generating human-readable, rich labels for activities in a BPMN process model needs the text surrounding a predicted *Activity* [10].

5.3   Evaluation

For performance evaluations of existing baselines, as well as our contributions, we adopted the evaluation strategy from [7]. This means we run a 5-fold cross validation for the entire pipeline and average individual module scores, folds are chosen randomly. This leads to 5 repeated runs, each with 80% of documents used for training, and the remaining 20% for testing. Errors made by modules during prediction are propagated further down the pipeline, potentially even amplifying in severity, as down-stream modules produce errors themselves as a result. To evaluate a given module's performance in isolation, we inject ground-truth data instead of predictions as inputs. This leads to a total of five different scenarios, for which results are discussed in detail in Sect. 6. These scenarios are **(S1)** *entity resolution* using predictions from the *Mention Extraction* module, and **(S2)** using ground-truth mentions. Furthermore, *relation extraction* **(S3)** using entities predicted by the pipeline thus far, **(S4)** using entities predicted during *entity resolution* using ground-truth mentions, and finally **(S5)** using ground-truth entities.

In each case we use the F_1 score as a metric, as it reflects the task of finding as many of the expected mentions, entities, and relations as possible (*recall R*), without sacrificing *precision P* in type or existence prediction. F_1 is then calculated as the harmonic mean of P and R, i.e., $F_1 = \frac{2 \cdot P \cdot R}{P+R}$. As there is more than one class within each prediction task, F_1, P, and R have to be aggregated. Throughout Sect. 6 we use the micro averaging strategy, which calculates P and R regardless of a given prediction's class. This strategy favours classes with many examples, as high scores in those may overshadow bad scores in classes with few examples. Should this be of concern, the macro averaging strategy can be used, where P, R, and F_1 are calculated for each class separately and averaged afterwards. We argue that it is most useful to find as many process elements as possible regardless of their type, i.e., it is better to find 90% of all *Activities* and only 10% of all *AND Gateways*, instead of 50% of all elements, as there are 501 *Activities* and only 8 *AND Gateways* in PET [7]. As such the micro F_1 score is better suited to the task. Following the task description in Sect. 2, we use

---

[4] See for example the discussion https://github.com/Babelscape/rebel/issues/57.

the following matching strategies. We count a *mention* as correctly predicted, iff it contains exactly the same tokens, as the corresponding ground-truth label, and has the same tag. We count an *entity* as correctly predicted, iff it contains exactly the same mentions, as the ground-truth label. Finally, we count a *relation* as correctly predicted, iff both its arguments, and its tag match the ground-truth label. Therefore, e.g., a single missing *"the"* in the mention *"the claim"* would render this mention prediction incorrect, as well as all entities and relations that refer to it. This effect is called *error propagation* and is the reason why we opted for several scenarios that evaluate modules in isolation, or with some degree of ground-truth input, such as in (**S4**). It may be, that users are fine with slightly less precise predictions, especially if they only miss inconsequential tokens, such as determiners. Surveying how users rank the importance of different levels of precision is out of scope of this paper and part of future work.

6 Results

The following section reports results for the experiments defined in the previous Sect. 5. Based on these results, it answers the research questions posed in Sect. 1. In Sect. 6.1 we provide results for the ER step and compare the naive approach to the one based on pretrained end-to-end neural coreference resolution, both for the modules in isolation (scenario (**1**)) and based on predictions of the NER module (scenario (**2**)). Section 6.2 presents the results for experiments with the RE step in the end-to-end pipeline setting (scenario (**3**)), and in isolation (scenario (**5**)). Finally, we discuss factors affecting the quality of RE results in Sect. 6.3, such as error propagation (scenarios (**4**) to (**6**)).

6.1 Entity Resolution Performance

We calculate the F_1 scores for all mention clusters with at least two mentions, since resolving single mention clusters is trivial. Figure 6d) visualizes the difference between the two approaches. Overall, the naive version reaches $F_1 = 0.26$, while our proposed pretrained method outperforms it significantly and reaches $F_1 = 0.52$. This stark difference is rooted in the fact, that we use exact matching, where a single missing or superfluous mention in a cluster renders the entire prediction incorrect. By design, the naive approach is unable to resolve anaphoras and cataphoras, i.e., back-referencing and forward-referencing pronouns. This means that every entity containing at least one anaphora, or cataphora, will be predicted incorrectly. Using the results from the NER step reduces performance greatly, similar as in the RE step. Based on the results from our experiments we conclude that a naive ER method is not feasible, and significant gains in performance can be achieved by using neural methods. It would be interesting, if fine-tuning the pretrained model would result in improved accuracy. Additionally, using information about mentions extracted in the NER step could be integrated into ER, instead of using a task-agnostic model, as we do currently. These considerations are currently out of scope, as the work on ER in

Table 1. a: Overall performance for Jerex, the PET baseline, and our proposed enhanced pipeline. b: Performance of our proposed machine learnt and the rule-based baseline relation extraction modules in isolation.

	P	R	F_1
Jerex[9]	0.20	0.27	0.22
Bellan[7] + ER	0.32	0.29	0.30
Ours	**0.34**	0.29	**0.31**

(a)

	P	R	F_1
Baseline[7] + ER	0.79	0.66	0.72
Ours	**0.83**	**0.82**	**0.82**

(b)

this paper is aimed at bridging the gap between the current state of the art in machine-learning focused data for extracting business process models from natural language text (PET), and the needs of down stream methods. The discussion in this section leads us to answering RQ3: The pretrained coreference resolution approach we presented is able to outperform naive text matching significantly, and is a useful baseline for resolving entities from mentions in the setting of business process model generation from natural language text.

6.2   Relation Extraction Performance

Our proposed *BoostRelEx* step clearly beats *RuleRelEx* from [7] by $F_1 = 0.10$, $P = 0.04$, and $R = 0.16$ in our experiments. This is visualized in Fig. 6 (Table 1b lists exact numbers). *BoostRelEx* profits greatly from correct predictions during the *NER step*, as is evidenced by greatly reduced performance when running our proposed pipeline end to end, as well as *Bellan + ER*. While our pipeline is still able to beat *Bellan + ER* in our experiments, the margin is narrowed substantially, with a difference of $F_1 = 0.01$, $R = 0.02$, and equivalent recall. One reason for this drastic performance loss, is the exact matching strategy we employ. A missing, superfluous, or misclassified mention will produce errors during the RE step, as a relation is only considered correct, if all involved mentions are correct (cf. Sect. 5.3). Considering the strong effect error propagation has on *BoostRelEx*, using a jointly trained end-to-end model seems natural. In Sect. 5.2 we presented *Jerex* as a promising candidate. Yet, following from our experiments, *Jerex* is not able to compete, and performs significantly worse, with a difference of $F_1 = 0.11$, $P = 0.14$, and $R = 0.02$, compared to our pipeline. We suspect that this is rooted in PET's small size, as well as the huge number of trainable parameters of Jerex. We therefore have to answer RQ1 with *No*.

Figure 7 breaks down the F_1 score by relation type. Following these results we conclude that the dataset PET is not yet suitable to train deep learning models in a supervised manner. The amount of data currently available makes stable training impossible. To alleviate the issue of low data, further research into the use of pretrained models, such as LLMs is warranted. These models make use of large quantities of unlabeled data to learn the structure and makeup of natural language. They are then either employed in a zero-shot setting (never explicitly trained for the task), few-shot setting (fine-tuned on small quantities

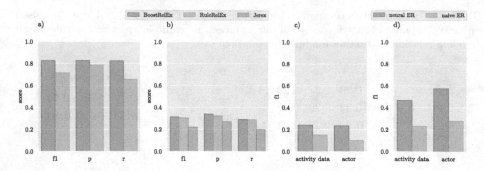

Fig. 6. a) shows the comparison between *BoostRelEx* and *RuleRelEx*. b) shows the performance of end-to-end runs of our proposed pipeline *Ours*, and *Bellan + ER*. c) compares the performance of the *naive ER* and *neural ER* using the result of the NER step. d) shows the same comparison as c), but based on ground truth mentions.

of task specific data), or composited into new models (used for extracting useful features from natural language text).

A significant portion of the improvements we present in this work, come from the better extraction of *Actor Recipient* and *Actor Performer*, as well as the *Uses* relations. *BoostRelEx* is clearly outperformed by *RuleRelEx* when extracting the *Same Gateway* relation type. A possible reason for this is how *RuleRelEx* uses information about already extracted *Flow* relations (cf. Sect. 5.2), which is impossible for our machine learnt approach, as it extracts all relations at once. Defining an order of extraction for relation types would defeat the purpose of using our method in the first place: It would be tightly coupled to the dataset and could not be applied easily to others. The overall performance is not affected very much by this, as there are only a handful of examples for the *Same Gateway* relation. Still, further research into useful features for extracting *Same Gateways* is needed, as well as possible training techniques that allow learning more complex rules. Promising features are, e.g., synonyms and hypernyms for key phrases of mentions. Training the model in multiple passes could be useful in predicting relations featuring mutual exclusivity, such as *Same Gateways*.

6.3 Performance Analysis

Gradually reducing the quality of inputs to the *BoostRelEx* and *RuleRelEx* steps results in gradually worse performance, a clear indication of error propagation (cf. Sect. 5.3). Using ground-truth mentions from the dataset, but entities predicted by the *neural ER* step, results in a drop in F_1 scores of about 0.20 for *BoostRelEx* and 0.12 for *RuleRelEx*. Introducing errors even further upstream, by using the *NER* module, i.e., running the complete pipeline end-to-end results in a drop in F_1 of 0.51 for *BoostRelEx* and 0.42 for *RuleRelEx*. Figure 7 visualizes this performance degradation for each relation type individually. Further studies regarding less strict evaluation is warranted, as described in Sect. 5.3, to get a less conservative assessment of prediction quality.

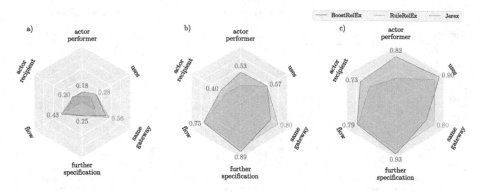

Fig. 7. a) Results for relation extraction by relation type for scenario (**4**), the complete pipeline, b) scenario (**5**), relation extraction using entities resolved from perfect mentions, c) scenario (**6**), relation extraction from perfect entities.

Additionally, we found that the distance between a relation's arguments is also negatively correlated with correctness. Longer distance between the head and tail entity of a relation increases the likelihood of misclassifying it, or not detecting it at all. We calculate the distance of a relations arguments as the minimal distance between the two entity's mentions. Examples for this effect are shown in Fig. 8. We created datasets from all predictions of each approach, with tuples of the form $(distance, o)$, where $o = 1$ denotes a correct prediction, and $o = 0$ an incorrect prediction. We then fitted a logistic regression model to these datasets using the *statsmodels*[5] python package. A logistic regression model tries to predict an outcome (response variable) via some input variable (predictor variable). It uses the logistic regression, which is given by $y = \frac{1}{1+e^{-(\beta_0+\beta_1 x)}}$, and chooses β_0 and β_1 in such a way, that the model predicts the observed outcome $y = o$ given an input x as best as possible. We can then use the resulting curve to discuss how well an approach is able to predict certain relation types.

The *Flow* relation can be solved very well for short distances by both *Boost-RelEx* and *RuleRelEx*. A very narrow confidence interval indicates a very good fit, leading us to believe, that relations with argument distances upwards of 33 tokens are misclassified by both methods with a significant probability. If this fact is detrimental to the quality of generated business process models is interesting, but out of scope for this paper. The *Same Gateway* relation shows frequent misclassification by the *BoostRelEx* method, something that was already evident in Fig. 7. *BoostRelEx* seems to be very sensitive to the distance between arguments for this relation, more often misclassifying, or outright not recognizing examples, as soon as the distance in tokens exceeds 15 tokens. *RuleRelEx* is significantly more robust in this regard, and able to correctly identify *Same Gateway* relations more often than not, until the distance between their argu-

---

[5] See https://www.statsmodels.org/stable/generated/statsmodels.discrete.discrete_m odel.Logit.html.

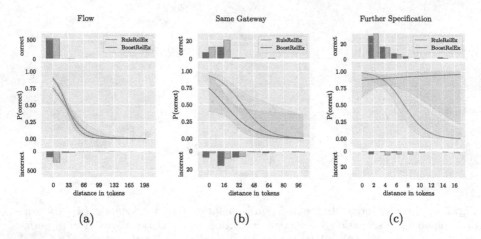

Fig. 8. Logistic regression fits for correlation between correctness of a prediction and the distance in tokens between its arguments. Bars show the number of correct (top) and incorrect (bottom) predictions. The main plot shows the fitted logistic regression and the 95% confidence intervals as a transparent channel.

ments exceeds 32 tokens. The fit produces very wide confidence intervals for both approaches, something that could be fixed with more examples for this relation, given a larger dataset. Relations of type *Further Specification* can be extracted by *BoostRelEx* with very high precision and recall. This is already shown in Fig. 7, where the F_1 score for *Further Specification* is given as 0.93. The logistic regression fit estimates that there is no correlation between argument distance and correctness. Yet, a very wide confidence interval for distances upwards of 10 tokens leaves open the possibility that there is a correlation given more examples. While *RuleRelEx* predicts more *Further Specification* relations erroneously than *BoostRelEx*, it is able to classify the majority (distances 0 – 6 tokens) correctly. This leads to similar performance overall, as shown in Fig. 7.

In summary, our machine learning based RE method outperforms the rule based RE method, in the best case, and is equivalent in the worst case, we can answer RQ2 with *Yes*. Our in-depth evaluation shows, that *BoostRelEx* robustly extracts long relations, beaten only by *RuleRelEx* on the *Same Gateway* relation, which matters not as much overall, given the small number of examples for this relation.

7   Conclusion and Future Work

In this paper we extend the task of business process information extraction by ER. We enrich PET with entity identity information and propose an extraction approach based on pretrained end-to-end neural coreference resolution. Motivated by benefits regarding rapid adaption to new data, domains, or tag sets, we propose a novel gradient boost based approach for the relation extraction task. We show that our proposed method is able to produce equivalent or better results in the end-to-end setting, and significantly outperform the baseline given higher quality inputs. We show that PET is not yet extensive enough for training a state-of-the-art deep learning approach from the NLP domain, Jerex, even though this approach achieves state-of-the-art results on other, bigger benchmark datasets of a related task. Finally, we discuss traits of the PET dataset that are detrimental to prediction quality, e.g., high linguistic variance, and distance between relation arguments. Our experiments attest to the phenomenon of error propagation, i.e., errors made in early steps are amplified in later ones. Thus, we plan to incorporate joint models for extracting mentions, relations, and for resolving process entities, since they are trained to solve these three tasks simultaneously, and mitigate the error propagation effect. While Jerex did not produce high quality predictions, it, and similar approaches, are predetermined for application in the task of business process generation from natural language text. Therefore, further research into applying deep learning in the low data domain of BPM is needed. We plan to improve performance of the entity resolution module, e.g., by incorporating mention information. Additionally, fine-tuning the pretrained neural coreference resolver on in-domain data is a potential way to improve performance further. Best practises recommend the use of micro F_1 scores for judging the quality of predictions in the business process information extraction task. While certainly a useful metric, we suspect it may not capture the needs of down stream tasks and users entirely. We plan to investigate alternative metrics, and their correlation with human expectation. Finally, creating a business process model from the information extracted with our pipeline was out of scope for this paper. More work regarding methods towards solving activity label generation, layouting, and completeness checks is needed.

References

1. Van der Aa, H., Carmona Vargas, J., Leopold, H., Mendling, J., Padró, L.: Challenges and opportunities of applying natural language processing in business process management. In: COLING (2018)
2. van der Aa, H., Di Ciccio, C., Leopold, H., Reijers, H.A.: Extracting declarative process models from natural language. In: Giorgini, P., Weber, B. (eds.) CAiSE 2019. LNCS, vol. 11483, pp. 365–382. Springer, Cham (2019). https://doi.org/10.1007/978-3-030-21290-2_23
3. Ackermann, L., Neuberger, J., Jablonski, S.: Data-driven annotation of textual process descriptions based on formal meaning representations. In: La Rosa, M., Sadiq, S., Teniente, E. (eds.) CAiSE 2021. LNCS, vol. 12751, pp. 75–90. Springer, Cham (2021). https://doi.org/10.1007/978-3-030-79382-1_5
4. Ackermann, L., Neuberger, J., Käppel, M., Jablonski, S.: Bridging research fields: an empirical study on joint, neural relation extraction techniques. In: Indulska, M., Reinhartz-Berger, I., Cetina, C., Pastor, O. (eds.) CAiSE 2023. LNCS, vol. 13901, pp. 471–486. Springer, Cham (2023). https://doi.org/10.1007/978-3-031-34560-9_28

5. Bellan, P., Dragoni, M., Ghidini, C.: Extracting business process entities and relations from text using pre-trained language models and in-context learning. In: Almeida, J.P.A., Karastoyanova, D., Guizzardi, G., Montali, M., Maggi, F.M., Fonseca, C.M. (eds.) EDOC 2022. LNCS, vol. 13585, pp. 182–199. Springer, Cham (2022). https://doi.org/10.1007/978-3-031-17604-3_11

6. Bellan, P., Dragoni, M., Ghidini, C., van der Aa, H., Ponzetto, S.: Guidelines for process model annotation in text (2022)

7. Bellan, P., Ghidini, C., Dragoni, M., Ponzetto, S.P., van der Aa, H.: Process extraction from natural language text: the pet dataset and annotation guidelines. In: Proceedings of the Sixth Workshop on NL4AI (2022)

8. Cabot, P.L.H., Navigli, R.: Rebel: relation extraction by end-to-end language generation. In: EMNLP (2021)

9. Eberts, M., Ulges, A.: An end-to-end model for entity-level relation extraction using multi-instance learning. In: ACL (2021)

10. Friedrich, F., Mendling, J., Puhlmann, F.: Process model generation from natural language text. In: Mouratidis, H., Rolland, C. (eds.) CAiSE 2011. LNCS, vol. 6741, pp. 482–496. Springer, Heidelberg (2011). https://doi.org/10.1007/978-3-642-21640-4_36

11. Giorgi, J., Bader, G., Wang, B.: A sequence-to-sequence approach for document-level relation extraction. In: Workshop on Biomedical Language Processing (2022)

12. Käppel, M., Schönig, S., Jablonski, S.: Leveraging small sample learning for business process management. Inf. Softw. Technol. (2021)

13. Lee, K., He, L., Lewis, M., Zettlemoyer, L.: End-to-end neural coreference resolution. In: EMNLP (2017)

14. Li, H.: Deep learning for natural language processing: advantages and challenges. Natl. Sci. Rev. 5, 24–26 (2018)

15. Li, J., Sun, A., Han, J., Li, C.: A survey on deep learning for named entity recognition. IEEE Trans. Knowl. Data Eng. 34, 50–70 (2020)

16. Pawar, S., Palshikar, G.K., Bhattacharyya, P.: Relation extraction: a survey. arXiv preprint arXiv:1712.05191 (2017)

17. Prokhorenkova, L., Gusev, G., Vorobev, A., Dorogush, A.V., Gulin, A.: CatBoost: unbiased boosting with categorical features. In: NeurIPS (2018)

18. Qian, C., et al.: An approach for process model extraction by multi-grained text classification. In: Dustdar, S., Yu, E., Salinesi, C., Rieu, D., Pant, V. (eds.) CAiSE 2020. LNCS, vol. 12127, pp. 268–282. Springer, Cham (2020). https://doi.org/10.1007/978-3-030-49435-3_17

19. Quishpi, L., Carmona, J., Padró, L.: Extracting annotations from textual descriptions of processes. In: Fahland, D., Ghidini, C., Becker, J., Dumas, M. (eds.) BPM 2020. LNCS, vol. 12168, pp. 184–201. Springer, Cham (2020). https://doi.org/10.1007/978-3-030-58666-9_11

20. Richards, B.: Type/token ratios: what do they really tell us? J. Child Lang. 14, 201–209 (1987)

21. Sànchez-Ferreres, J., Burattin, A., Carmona, J., Montali, M., Padró, L., Quishpi, L.: Unleashing textual descriptions of business processes. Softw. Syst. Model. 20(6), 2131–2153 (2021). https://doi.org/10.1007/s10270-021-00886-x

22. Sanh, V., Wolf, T., Ruder, S.: A hierarchical multi-task approach for learning embeddings from semantic tasks. In: Proceedings of the AAAI Conference on Artificial Intelligence (2019)

23. Sharnagat, R.: Named entity recognition: a literature survey. Center For Indian Language Technology (2014)

24. Sukthanker, R., Poria, S., Cambria, E., Thirunavukarasu, R.: Anaphora and coreference resolution: a review. Inf. Fusion 59, 139–162 (2020)
25. Wallach, H.M.: Conditional random fields: an introduction. Technical reports (CIS) (2004)
26. Waltl, B., Bonczek, G., Matthes, F.: Rule-based information extraction: advantages, limitations, and perspectives. Jusletter IT (02 2018) 4 (2018)
27. Yao, Y., et al.: DocRED: a large-scale document-level relation extraction dataset. arXiv preprint arXiv:1906.06127 (2019)

LABPMN: Location-Aware Business Process Modeling and Notation

Leo Poss[(✉)], Lukas Dietz, and Stefan Schönig

University of Regensburg, Regensburg, Germany
leo.poss@ur.de
https://go.ur.de/iot

Abstract. The combination of IoT and BPM enables new possibilities
for the use of contextual information during the modeling and execution
of process models. Nevertheless, many approaches for the use of location
data only exist as concepts, and most existing extensions for BPMN do
not fully use the potential gained through IoT.

In this paper, we introduce a novel BPMN Extension for location
awareness that is, conceptually well-defined and adheres to the BPMN
meta-model, and can be used both graphically, and during the execution
of a process. We introduce two new main elements: The possibility of
dynamically assigning or allocating actors to one or a number of tasks,
and different location-based events to be able to react to location changes
of active and passive resources during process execution.

Keywords: Location-awareness · Distributed processes · BPMN
extension

1 Introduction

The Internet of Things (IoT) has the potential to revolutionize the way businesses operate by providing contextual information, including location data,
throughout the entire lifecycle of business processes [7,14,20]. This can lead
to significant improvements in effectiveness and efficiency in value creation, as
well as the automation of non-value-adding tasks. By leveraging the power of
IoT devices, businesses can gain a competitive advantage by streamlining their
operations [22,28] and aiding with everyday processes by removing non-value-
adding steps and supporting actors during the execution of value-adding process
steps [8].

In [20], we presented a non-exhaustive list of patterns for the utilization of
location data from IoT devices in Business Process Management (BPM) based
on real-world processes from three crafts businesses and established approaches
from the literature. All main parts of business processes can benefit from the

This work is funded by the "Bayrische Forschungsstiftung (BFS)" within the project
IoT-basiertes Daten- und Prozessmanagement im Handwerk (TRADEmark).

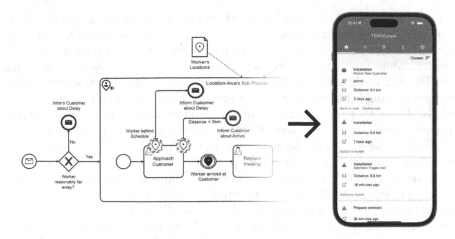

Fig. 1. LABPMN-based real-world process executed with mobile device interface

inclusion of location data, e.g., starting processes, making decisions based on location data, automatically allocating an actor to the currently closest task, monitoring the execution of a task, automatically terminating tasks or supporting in documentary and non-value-adding work. Despite including an executable and functional version for each pattern, location data is not treated as a first-class citizen in business process modeling [10], resulting in the underlying logic required for the integration of location data being obscured outside the process model itself. This contradicts the fundamental model character, which aims to serve as both a visual representation of all critical information and a foundation for supported execution using a BPMS, i.e., abstracting from the real world and conveying visual information while remaining executable [4]. The use of location information differs fundamentally from using other data coming from IoT devices, as the inherent spatial constraints within mobile distributed processes surface different problems and opportunities [13].

Using Business Process Modeling and Notation (BPMN) as the de facto standard for modeling processes enables us to extend the meta-model by introducing domain-specific concepts and appending additional information to existing standard modeling elements [23]. Trying to narrow the existing gap between the visual representation and the practical use of location within business processes leads to the following research question: *How can we comprehensively use location information for a graphical, executable notation for location-aware process modeling and execution?*

In the following sections, we address this gap by extending BPMN with location-aware elements for previously presented patterns for the use of location within BPM, providing both a visual representation for the modeling phase and an implementation for the actual execution of process models using location as a first-class citizen. Extending the BPMN meta-model can provide a foundation for further exploration of the use of location data and, more generally, context data stemming from IoT devices in BPM. While the integration into BPM has the potential to significantly improve business processes and their handling, to fully realize this potential, it is necessary to both, visually represent the functionality, while providing possibilities for execution and by supporting actual everyday use. Until now, many applications used for value creation were static and directly coupled to small parts of value creation, but the union of IoT data and BPM can lead to dynamically adapting applications supporting different involved actors and process steps. Figure 1 shows a currently running enhanced business process at a crafts business that motivated the BPMN extension and the mobile application in use showing open tasks as well as the current distance to the tasks' location. The approach has been implemented and applied to a real-life scenario and will be presented in Sect. 5. A short video explaining the main concepts can be found at https://youtu.be/PHE6b4pQUWE.

Starting with Sect. 2, we will explain the theoretical background of business process management, the Internet of Things, and the use of contextual data, as well as a short overview of related works. The following Sect. 3 introduces the extension for incorporating location in BPMN, by adhering to the steps provided in [23], including both, the conceptual as well as the graphical extension. Section 4 explains the actual implementation used for the exemplary real-world example provided in Sect. 5. This publication ends in Sect. 6 with the current status and future research topics based on our experience.

2   Theoretical Background and Related Work

The subsequent segment contains an introduction to BPMN and its mechanism of extension, succeeded by a brief contextual backdrop on subjects such as context, location, and the Internet of Things. This is followed by an overview of existing research efforts.

2.1   Extension Mechanism of BPMN

Business processes are a series of actions taken to achieve a specific business outcome [7]. They can be represented by one or more business process models, which consist of activity models and instructions for how the processes should be executed. These models serve as a blueprint for real-world scenarios and cases, providing a structured representation [25].

Various modeling languages exist for this purpose, with BPMN [17] being the widely accepted current standard. BPMN includes different standardized elements, that facilitate both human and machine readability while allowing the machine-supported execution of business processes. On the other hand, BPMN also enables the extension of the meta-model to introduce new functionality, that is not part of the standards' core functionality.

Over the years, the extension mechanism introduced in BPMN in 2011 [2,27] has facilitated the development of numerous specialized extensions tailored to various application domains, enhancing the functionality and adaptability of

BPMN to meet the specific requirements of diverse real-world scenarios (cf. [5,27]). The reuse and enhancement of standard BPMN elements offer advantages like standardization and widespread tool support. The extension mechanism of BPMN is tightly coupled to the Meta Object Facility (MOF) meta-model [18], separating the meta-model, process model, and process instances, which introduces enhanced flexibility in the form of interchangeable model properties and parts – extending single elements of the BPMN meta-model does not strictly require the modification of standard BPMN elements. [23] complement the BPMN extension interface outlined by the OMG [17] by offering methodological guidance on how to extend BPMN elements, which we will adapt to develop and introduce our new elements within this paper.

2.2   IoT, Context and Location Data

Combining BPM and the Internet of Things (IoT) enables new possibilities for enhancing and enriching business processes using contextual information like the location of active resources like actors and passive resources (e.g., tools needed for a task). The Internet of Things describes a world where every object can connect to a network with its own identity. This enables the use of sensors for business process execution, leading to improved data-driven decision-making and optimized processes [9] on the one hand and a more comprehensive view of business processes on the other [22].

The context of a process describes the involved entities' conditions and circumstances [1]. It can be used during the execution of business processes to enhance and support their realization [22]. One part of the process context is the location of different involved entities, it can be divided into two categories: First, descriptive locations, which are referenced by descriptions like names or numbers, related to either natural geographic objects or human-made geographical objects, which are well defined, and second spatial locations, which refer to an explicit numerical representation of a position in a coordinate system. Location data can further be classified as primary or secondary context [16]: Information about the location of an entity (location data) is part of the primary context, as the location of an entity can directly be sensed by sensors. Other information derived from spatial data, e.g., the distance between two entities, belongs to the secondary context [20].

Three important capabilities of location awareness in business process management are outlined in [28], including knowledge of the current status of the process in a specific location or knowledge of the location of a particular resource within a business process, awareness of relevant location-based information in real-time, and finally, the business process' ability to adapt based on location-based information.

2.3   Related Work

The subsequent section presents a review of related literature augmenting BPMN with IoT data, particularly focusing on location data (referred to as IoT-,

Table 1. Related work concept matrix following Webster and Watson [24]

Name	Goal	Location integration	Illustrative example	Location	Executable	Annotation	Data Object	Event	Gateway	Task	Drawbacks
IoT											
[3] —	Event extension for IoT	Location Event (Differentiation between cause and impact of event)	Temperature controlling process based on location of a person	E	○	○	○	●	○	○	*Not executable, focus on location events, could be modeled using conditional events*
[11] BPMN4CPS	Enable the modeling of CPS processes	Location information as part of sensor data	Ambulance drone case study	I	●	○	○	○	○	○	*Implicit representation, separation of processes, no standard conformity*
[19] I4PML	Create a comprehensive BPMN extension for IoT	Location information as part of sensor data	Predictive Maintenance for conveyor belts	I	○	○	○	●	○	○	*Implicit representation, not executable, "semi-formal" process model*
[9] —	Enable the modeling, execution, and monitoring of IoT-aware processes	Location information as part of sensor data	Smart home, production process	I	○	●	○	●	○	○	*Implicit representation, artifacts normally for "additional information" [17]*
[12] BPMN-CARX	integrate process automation, IIoT context, and AR	Location information in task context	Maintenance process	I	○	○	○	○	○	●	*Implicit representation, no description of actual BPMN extension.*
Independent of Domain											
[6] —	Constrain the location of task execution	Introduction of location constraints	Commissioning of items	E	○	○	○	○	○	○	*Not executable, separate location model necessary, relies on deprecated BPMN version, does not actively influence process execution*
[15] —	Include mobility aspect in BPMN events	Location Event (position achieved, position update, conditional position event)	Ordering support service	E	○	○	○	●	○	○	*Not executable, focus on location events, could be modeled using conditional events*
[21] sBPMN	Take special concerns into account in BPMN	Location as context and important decision variable	Crops planting on several fields	E	○	○	○	○	●	○	*Separate location model necessary, assumption: only modeled processes influence the environment, notation not adjusted, few spatial functions*
Mobile Devices											
[8] Context4BPMN	Enable modeling of influence of mobile context information on business processes	Location as part of the context	Work safety inspection process	I	○	●	○	○	○	○	*Implicit representation, not executable, no decision logic, explicit model of context needed*
Ubiquitous Computing											
[26] uBPMN	Address BPMN's deficiency in representing ubiquitous business processes	Location information as part of sensor data	Distributed sales process for specific customer	I	○	○	●	○	○	○	*Implicit representation, not executable, any data can be collected*

Notation: E: Explicit, I: Implicit; ● Element is extended or considered, ○: Element is not considered

Context-, and Location-Awareness in BPM). Following the methodology proposed by [24], an initial step was performed by searching significant contributions using the specified search string: *"BPMN AND (extension* OR extend* OR enhanc* OR expan* OR adapt*) AND (location* OR spatial OR geographic OR IoT OR 'Internet of Things' OR context*)"*. The retrieved results were then manually evaluated for relevance, employing a set of exclusion criteria established in [27].

Throughout the literature review, several similar works were identified, including those by [2,27], and [5]. It is noteworthy that these works consist primarily of systematic reviews of the literature that refer to BPMN extensions in a broader sense. However, none of them address location-aware extensions specifically. Moreover, the systematic literature reviews mentioned above were conducted in 2014, 2019, and 2020, respectively, thereby not encompassing possible most recent publications.

The retrieved publications which will be explained in short in Table 1: Following the name of the introduced extension (if applicable), the goal and the main domain targeted by the extension are presented, followed by the way of inclusion of location information (either explicitly mentioned or implicitly as part of generic sensor data), followed by affected BPMN elements and drawbacks of each of the approaches.

Based on these publications, three different mechanisms for the incorporation of location information in BPMN could be identified: The first extends existing constructs, such as gateways and conditional sequence flows, to incorporate location information [21], enabling location-dependent decision-making and dynamic routing. The second mechanism introduces new constructs designed for handling location information in BPMN models. [6] for example proposes the concept of location constraints, which specify spatial constraints for tasks, and [15] suggests using location events to trigger process activities based on changes in the physical location. The third mechanism involves using a separate model linked to the main process model for depicting location information [21], allowing for an explicit representation of location-related data and its association with process elements. However, both, an implicit representation and the use of a separate model have disadvantages, as it lacks explicit indicators for location-aware elements, requiring additional explanation, documentation, and models. It may also result in unnecessarily large and complex process models, as affected elements are not explicitly adjusted for location-specific concerns. But, by explicitly incorporating location information into business process models, our following extension enhances the expressiveness and effectiveness of BPMN in capturing real-world scenarios where location plays a crucial role.

3   Extending BPMN for Location-Awareness

The diverse patterns outlined in [20] can be seamlessly illustrated and operationalized through the proposed extension. The core patterns are already delineated in Table 2, encompassing the start of processes, decision-making, automated actor allocation, task execution monitoring, event dispatching, and task

Table 2. Patterns for the use of location in business processes [20] and their extension elements

Pattern	Extension Element
Automatic start of process instances	Location Start Event
Decision-making based on location data	Standard BPMN Gateway
Location-based allocation *and* assignment	Annotation for Task/Subprocess/Call Activity
Location-based monitoring of tasks *and* event dispatching	Location-Aware non-interrupting boundary event
Location-based automatic completion of tasks	Throwing Location Event
Location-based automation of tasks	Location Data Object and standard User Task

termination. Moreover, the extension serves to facilitate documentary and non-value-adding tasks. A comprehensive exposition of each pattern can be found in [20].

Based on the motivated goals and the identified drawbacks of existing methods, the following requirements and goals arise, that will be fulfilled by our extension for the use of location data during the execution of business processes.

R1 BPMN 2.0 conformity: The extension must adhere to the BPMN 2.0 standard to fully support existing BPMN tools BPMN 2.0 conformity increases the acceptance of our extension within the BPMN community, as all properties and concepts of standard BPMN also apply to the extension.

R2 Explicit representation of location concerns: Location-related events and actions must be explicitly represented in business process models. This enhances the comprehensibility of process models, improves their reflection of reality, and facilitates the appropriate implementation of location concerns.

R3 Influence the process execution based on location information: This requirement is self-explaining and can be derived from conceptual modeling extensions introduced in Sect. 2.3: Both, the functional (process flow and actual execution of a single task), as well as the organizational perspective (candidate groups and task allocations) must be influenced by external data.

R4 Ability to react to internal and external changes in location: This requirement necessitates that the BPMS is aware of the location of each relevant element of a business process, as listed as one of the capabilities in [28]. It is also noteworthy that external changes in location have to be considered, including all location changes that do not explicitly result from the execution of the processes modeled in the BPMS.

[23] explain the key actions of building an extension for the BPMN meta-model with the following steps: (*i*) Definition of a Conceptual Domain Model of

the Extension (CDME) in Unified Modelling Language (UML), (*ii*) Transformation of the CDME to a BPMN plus Extensions (BPMN+X) model describing the extension, (*iii*) Definition of an XML Schema Extension Definition Model based on the BPMN+X model, (*iv*) Transformation of the XML Schema Extension Definition Model into an XML Schema Extension Definition Document.

The following sections will adhere to that schema by first describing the definition of the CDME as well as the BPMN+X model for each of the three extension elements, and, combining all parts for the XML Schema Extension Definition Model and Document, completing the conceptual BPMN extension.

3.1 Definition of CDME and BPMN+X Model

The first step for conceptualizing the BPMN extension is the development of the CDME and the BPMN+X model for each of the provided extension elements (Location Data, Location-Based Task Assignment/Allocation and different categories of Location Event).

Location Data. As already defined in our previous paper, location data can be seen as part of IoT-Data next to other data values like environment, descriptive or sensor data [20]. This location data is inherently the basic building block of all patterns, thus having to be transferred to the BPMN meta-model, which already includes different data concepts like **Data Objects**, **Properties**, **Data Inputs** and **Outputs** as well as **Messages** (see [17, p. 96]). Each process participant and other objects like used tools are seen as **Resources** within BPMN, which can be further characterized by **ResourceParameters** specified by **ItemDefinitions**, which can include their current location.

The place of fulfillment for a specific task (task location) on the other hand can be represented using the already existing **Property** concept in BPMN (see [17, p. 210]), acting as a container for data associated with certain flow elements that inherit from **ItemAwareElement**. Each **ItemAwareElement** has an **ItemDefinition** that contains the variable's value as well as other information and might refer to a **DataState** element containing the state of the data. This enables us to simply extend the already defined **DataObject** with our new **LocationObject** to elegantly introduce the foundation needed for the other concepts (see Fig. 2a). The next step is to transform newly introduced concepts following the rules presented in [23], which will lead to Fig. 2b.

Location-Based Task Assignment/Allocation. As presented in [20] as well as in [22], tasks can be allocated to actors during run time based on their current location. To implement such behavior, the executing system must be aware of the place of fulfillment of the activity as well as the locations of process participants and must implement a location-based operator. Closely coupled to that is the act of assigning a group of eligible actors, mostly during process modeling, and because both terms are not used coherently in literature, we will use the

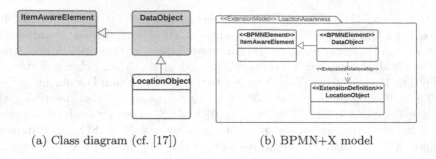

(a) Class diagram (cf. [17])   (b) BPMN+X model

Fig. 2. Class diagram and BPMN+X model of location object

assignment as having a list of possible actors for a task or subprocess ([0; n] elements) whereas allocation will be used for the 1:1-connection between an actor and a task or subprocess, independently of the lifecycle phase.

The *Conceptual Domain Model of the Extension* (CDME) for the allocation and assignment of actors based on their location is shown in Fig. 3. Base BPMN concepts are shown in gray, whereas new elements of the extension at hand are colored in white. Associated with the base class `ResourceRole`, we introduce the new class `LocationBasedAssignment`, which is responsible for the assignment of resources to an activity (i.e., the abstract superclass for tasks, subprocesses, and call activities within BPMN).

The new class needs to have access to the locations of the process participants as well as the location of the activity at hand. On one hand, the location of the activity is stored as a `Property` whereas the location of a `Resource` is stored as a `ResourceParameter`. The operator needed to compare both locations is modeled abstractly as a `LocationOperator`, which is inherited by two operators, namely `RangeOperator` and `DistanceOperator`. The first is either *greaterThan* or *lessThan* returning zero or more eligible actors for the task, whereas the latter returns exactly one process participant that is either *closest* or *farthest* from the activity's location. We also defined two different types of distances to get used within the extension, namely `linearDistance` and `travelDistance` which can also be selected for each of the extension elements.

Similar to the standard BPMN element of `ServiceTask`s, the already provided `Operation` classes from the standard are used to execute the needed logic. In combination with the already existing `ResourceAssignmentExpression`, the relevant resources can be restricted to a specific group of resources.

The next step again is to transform the CDME to a valid BPMN+X model (see Fig. 4): All existing BPMN concepts like `Activity`, `Property`, `Operation` and `ResourceAssignmentExpression` can be created as BPMNElements, whereas newly introduced elements are all explicitly marked as `ExtensionElements` or `ExtensionEnums`. Applying the rules presented in [23], we can transform both, generalizations as well as associations based on the concept of the class (BPMN vs. extension), its originality (original vs. new) and the concept of the property's type (BPMN concept, extension concept or simple data type).

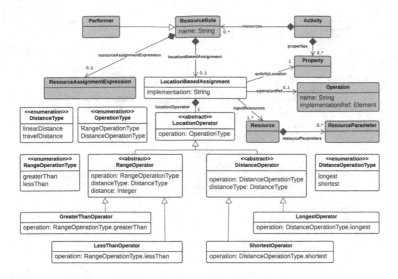

Fig. 3. CDME of location-based allocation/assignment

Table 3. Location event types and derived required inputs

Event Type	Required Inputs
entersGeofence/ leavesGeofence	[$location_{t-1}$, $location_t$, polygon, implementation]
distanceGreaterThan/ distanceLessThan	[location1, location2, distanceThreshold, distanceType, implementation]
locationUpdate	[$location_{t-1}$, $location_t$, distanceThreshold, distanceType, implementation]

Location Event Extension. The following section will explain the steps taken to introduce location-based events into BPMN. While [15] distinguished between three different types, we only introduce one explicit type of location event that is sufficient to represent any kind of location-related event.

The extension element enables the modeler to properly react to events like arriving at a location or a change in the location of a resource. By directly inheriting from the standard BPMN class EventDefinition, we can reuse existing concepts and automatically extend all types of events (namely: Throwing, Catching, Start, Intermediate, and End events, as well as Boundary events).

The events themselves need different parameters distinguishing between five different types seen in Table 3: One commonly found event definition based on the location of an actor could be if they or any mobile resource entered or left a specific area (*entering* and *leaving a geofence*). For that, we need two locations with different timestamps that represent a location change. Combining spatial and temporal context we can then check if a resource started outside a polygon and ends up inside the polygon (corresponds to entering the geofence) or vice versa. The plain location event introduced in [15] (*location update event*) also needs two different locations, as well as a minimum distance to trigger and the distance type. The last two identified event types (*distance greater than* and *distance less than*) both need two locations to be able to calculate or query a

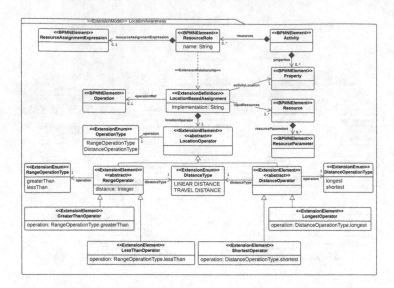

Fig. 4. BPMN+X model of location-based allocation/assignment

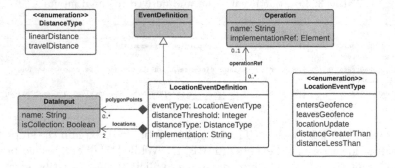

Fig. 5. CDME of location-based event

distance metric between them, the threshold to compare the metric against as well as the distance type that should be used for the comparison. Each of the needed locations is modeled as a Location Data Object introduced earlier in this section. The needed implementation is dependent on the modeler and represents the Operation executed with the parameters. Translating the CDME to the BPMN+X model happens analogously to the allocation and assignment extension by applying given rules and converting the concepts step-by-step (Figs. 5 and 6).

3.2 XML Schema Extension

The next step for providing a completely BPMN 2.0 conform extension is to extend the XML schema building the base of the BPMN meta-model (see Fig. 7).

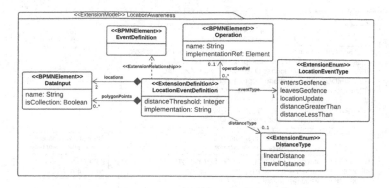

Fig. 6. BPMN+X model of location-based event

The schema `LocationAwareness` contains three `GroupDefinition` elements, one for each location-based element, we introduce (`LocationBasedAssignment`, `LocationEventDefinition` and `LocationObject`). The `LocationObject` itself contains no more information, whereas the Assignment contains all needed Resources as well as exactly one of the provided and already presented operators – explicitly differentiated into all options here, because both introduced operator classes are abstract, and to the best of the author's knowledge XML does not provide any constructs to represent abstract elements. Each of the operators is then specified individually, containing all conceptually and formally needed parameters and their specifications for the decision to be made. The last GroupDefinition contains the element declarations for the `LocationEventDefinition`, including the type of the event as well as the needed parameters already explained above.

Because the resulting schema is specified in plain XML, the extension can be imported into different BPMN models to make use of the location-aware BPMN elements, independently of the actual realization of the BPMN meta-model.

3.3 Graphical Extension of Notation

As explained in the introduction and during the presentation of the related work, the modeling of business processes aims at two goals at the same time: supporting the execution of processes using computer systems but also helping process participants understand how a process works. For that reason, we also introduce a graphical representation for all new elements, according to the key elements and basic rules for the extension of elements described within the BPMN standard [17] (see Fig. 8).

4 Implementation for Modelling and Execution

The implementation of the modeling aspect of the extension is based on the open-source implementation bpmn.js[1], which provides the modeling tools needed

---
[1] https://bpmn.io/toolkit/bpmn-js/.

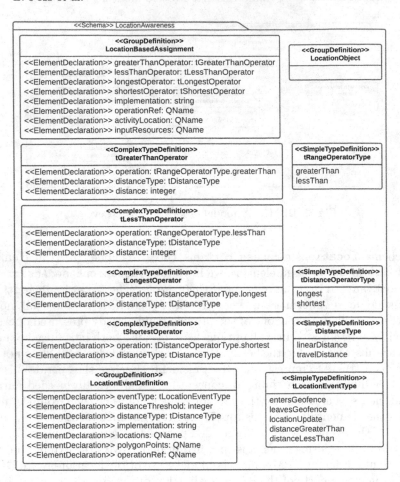

Fig. 7. XML schema

for our BPMS of choice, Camunda[2], that is responsible for executing the process model, providing the needed logic. Even though Camunda is widely spread and can mostly be easily extended for implementing new features, it still comes with several restrictions for an actual implementation of extensions: Some standard concepts like `ResourceRoles` are not used, but instead own attributes like `camunda:assignee,` or the use of expressions instead of `ResourceParameters` which implied removing unused properties and adjusting for implementation-specific needs amongst others. Nevertheless, the implementation includes all parts of the conceptual extension presented above. Including the needed functionality as well as the visual representation within the process model.

For the allocation/assignment, we extended the properties panel within the modeler to reflect the additionally needed attributes for the allocation task (see

---

[2] https://camunda.com.

(a) Graphical extension for Location-Aware Data Objects

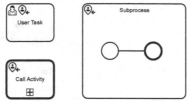

(b) Graphical extension for Location-Aware Assignment/Allocation of Tasks

| Start Event | Intermediate Catching Event (interrupting) | Intermediate Catching Event (non-interrupting) | Intermediate Throwing Event | End Event |

(c) Graphical extension for the different types of Location-Aware events

Fig. 8. Graphical representation of all elements added to the BPMN meta model

Fig. 9a). The result of the location-based allocation, either a single user in the case of the Distance operator or a list of users in the case of the Range operator, gets stored in the provided variable name and can then be used as either a slimmed-down list of candidate users or directly as the assignee for any given task or subprocess, implicitly constraining and guarding the lifetime of the allocation/assignment.

On the other hand, for implementing location-aware events we had to fall back to extending Conditional and Message Events instead of the parent class **Event** itself, to receive an executable and usable process model (see Fig. 8c and Figure 9b). The five different event types can be further get classified into two distinct categories: catching events and throwing events, where the first includes the start event, as well as both catching events (interrupting and non-interrupting), whereas the throwing event and the end event are both throwing events, pushing data that then can be used somewhere else in the process model. This enabled us to also extend the properties panel with the needed parameters for the task itself, as well as providing both, the visual representation and the functionality itself.

Compared to the assignment task and events, the actual extension of Data Objects is rather simple as they can directly be inherited to new types of objects (here: `LocationObject`). But again, both bpmn.js and Camunda differ from the BPMN specification as they do not display `bpmn:DataObjects` but rather only their references (`bpmn:DataObjectReference`), meaning the extension is visual, not directly implying a specific datatype.

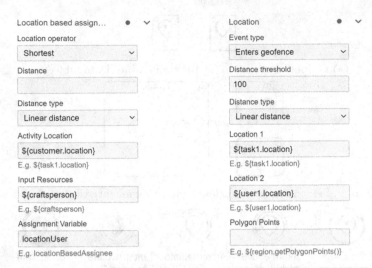

(a) Added variables in the properties panel for task allocation/assignment

(b) Implemented parameters for event extension in properties panel

Fig. 9. Extension of process modeling to include needed variables and parameters

5 Exemplary Real-World Application

Based on a slimmed-down and simplified version of an actual process from our research project from a crafts business, we will show the currently running applied BPMN extension (see Figure 10). We already presented a version of the process in [20], where we first introduced the patterns for the use of location data during the execution of business processes. Now, as mentioned above, we are using the presented extension to reintroduce the visual aspect of the model while also proving its usability based on the real-world process.

The business process at hand describes an everyday process lived in a crafts business. The process starts with an incoming order, immediately a worker gets assigned to the task, drives to the customer, works there, and returns. After the creation of an invoice, the job, and the process instance is finished.

All user tasks within the expanded subprocess are assigned to a user or group of users based on the newly introduced location-based assignment. The location-based assignment is dependent on the location of the customer, the locations of the workers, and a location operator – in this case, the "nearest" operator. The respective locations are visualized by the two location objects, which increases the process transparency. It is also immediately evident when and for how long one actor takes over all parts of the process instance based on their location.

The two non-interrupting location boundary events facilitate monitoring of the *Approach Customer* task's progress and enable notification of the customer regarding the worker's arrival based on their current position. The location intermediate throw event communicates the current worker's position to other active

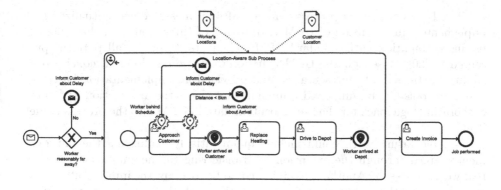

Fig. 10. Simplified real-world process using LABPMN

process instances, which can respond accordingly if necessary. Furthermore, the gained and collected information can be used to support the creation of an invoice by providing additional information about the task's execution (like an automatic way of distinguishing between time spent traveling and time spent working at the customer). The subprocess ends with a location end event, where the thrown location can also be caught by other processes e.g. to trigger a *Replenishment Process* for the worker's vehicle.

As clearly visible, all different parts of the extension are used to improve the execution of the process. Compared to our earlier approach, the visibility and the actual use of IoT-origin location data are enhanced and simplified, leading to a clearer process understanding and a more accurate representation of reality, while also supporting the actors carrying out the tasks.

When directly comparing this process model to our previous one (c.f. [20]), the inclusion of location data is evident within the model. Whereas previously, various decisions were made inconspicuously in the background, the model now displays both the assignment and the utilization of location data itself (`LocationDataObjects`). The use of throwing and catching events facilitates the interaction between different process instances as well as different processes.

6   Conclusion and Future Work

As demonstrated in the related works, the use of contextual information, especially the location of entities, within business processes is not a completely new approach, and several different attempts were made and presented over the last few years. Nevertheless, the use of IoT as an enabler for directly incorporating location data in BPM, as we presented in this paper, cuts down drawbacks of earlier approaches that were mostly only visual or executable but quite complex in their form, whereas we presented a novel approach for using location data in both, visualization and execution of business processes increasing the transparency and narrowing the gap between BPM and the actors actually executing the tasks therein.

Based on a simplified process from a crafts business, we conceptualized and implemented an extension of BPMN consisting of three elements, that enabled us, in combination with standard BPMN elements, to depict all patterns presented in [20]. Based on the BPMN meta-model, we developed a concise possibility for the visual representation and provided an implementation based on standard tools like bpmn.js and Camunda that closes the abstraction gap, reincorporating logic back for the use of location data in BPM into the process model itself.

Possible future work could include quantitatively evaluating the improvements gained through the extension by transferring the new notation to other real-world processes. Another possibility could be to adapt the implementation to directly extend the execution engine of the BPMS, which would lead to even more lock-in and probably pushes the extension further away from its current BPMN meta-model conformity. Most promising looks the focused extension towards different types of contextual information, further improving the support in executing manual and user tasks in business processes.

References

1. Abowd, G.D., Dey, A.K., Brown, P.J., Davies, N., Smith, M., Steggles, P.: Towards a better understanding of context and context-awareness. In: Gellersen, H.-W. (ed.) HUC 1999. LNCS, vol. 1707, pp. 304–307. Springer, Heidelberg (1999). https://doi.org/10.1007/3-540-48157-5_29
2. Braun, R., Esswein, W.: Classification of domain-specific BPMN extensions. In: Frank, U., Loucopoulos, P., Pastor, Ó., Petrounias, I. (eds.) PoEM 2014. LNBIP, vol. 197, pp. 42–57. Springer, Heidelberg (2014). https://doi.org/10.1007/978-3-662-45501-2_4
3. Chiu, H.H., Wang, M.S.: Extending event elements of business process model for internet of things. In: CIT/IUCC/DASC/PICom 2015, pp. 783–788. IEEE, October 2015
4. Colburn, T., Shute, G.: Abstraction in computer science. Minds Mach. **17**(2), 169–184 (2007)
5. Compagnucci, I., Corradini, F., Fornari, F., Polini, A., Re, B., Tiezzi, F.: Modelling notations for IoT-aware business processes: a systematic literature review. In: Del Río Ortega, A., Leopold, H., Santoro, F.M. (eds.) BPM 2020. LNBIP, vol. 397, pp. 108–121. Springer, Cham (2020). https://doi.org/10.1007/978-3-030-66498-5_9
6. Decker, M., Che, H., Oberweis, A., et al.: Modeling mobile workflows with BPMN. In: 2010 Ninth International Conference on Mobile Business and 2010 Ninth Global Mobility Roundtable (ICMB-GMR). IEEE (2010)
7. Dumas, M., Rosa, M.L., Mendling, J., et al.: Fundamentals of Business Process Management. Springer, Berlin, Heidelberg (2018). https://doi.org/10.1007/978-3-662-56509-4
8. Dörndorfer, J., Seel, C.: A framework to model and implement mobile context-aware business applications. In: Modellierung 2018, pp. 23–38. Gesellschaft für Informatik e.V., Bonn (2018)
9. Gallik, F., Kirikkayis, Y., Reichert, M.: Modeling, executing and monitoring IoT-aware processes with BPM technology. In: 2022 International Conference on Service Science (ICSS). IEEE, May 2022

10. De Giacomo, G., Oriol, X., Estañol, M., Teniente, E.: Linking data and BPMN processes to achieve executable models. In: Dubois, E., Pohl, K. (eds.) CAiSE 2017. LNCS, vol. 10253, pp. 612–628. Springer, Cham (2017). https://doi.org/10.1007/978-3-319-59536-8_38
11. Graja, I., Kallel, S., Guermouche, N., et al.: BPMN4cps: a BPMN extension for modeling cyber-physical systems. In: 2016 IEEE 25th International Conference on Enabling Technologies: Infrastructure for Collaborative Enterprises (WETICE). IEEE, June 2016
12. Grambow, G., Hieber, D., Oberhauser, R., Pogolski, C.: A context and augmented reality BPMN and BPMS extension for industrial internet of things processes. In: Marrella, A., Weber, B. (eds.) BPM 2021. LNBIP, vol. 436, pp. 379–390. Springer, Cham (2022). https://doi.org/10.1007/978-3-030-94343-1_29
13. Gruhn, V., Book, M.: Mobile business processes. In: Böhme, T., Heyer, G., Unger, H. (eds.) IICS 2003. LNCS, vol. 2877, pp. 114–133. Springer, Heidelberg (2003). https://doi.org/10.1007/978-3-540-39884-4_10
14. Janiesch, C., Koschmider, A., Mecella, M., et al.: The internet of things meets business process management: a manifesto. IEEE Syst. Man Cybern. Mag. **6**(4), 34–44 (2020)
15. Kozel, T.: Bpmn mobilisation. In: Proceedings of ECS'10/ECCTD'10/ECCOM'10/ECCS'10, pp. 307–310. World Scientific and Engineering Academy and Society (WSEAS), Stevens Point, Wisconsin, USA (2010)
16. Küpper, A.: Location-Based Services - Fundamentals and Operation. John Wiley & Sons Ltd., Hoboken, August 2005
17. OMG: Business Process Model and Notation (BPMN), Version 2.0.2, January 2011. https://www.omg.org/spec/BPMN/2.0.2/
18. OMG: Meta Object Facility (MOF) Core Specification, Version 2.5.1, January 2019. https://www.omg.org/spec/MOF/2.5.1
19. Petrasch, R., Hentschke, R.: Process modeling for industry 4.0 applications: towards an industry 4.0 process modeling language and method. In: 2016 13th International Joint Conference on Computer Science and Software Engineering (JCSSE). IEEE, July 2016
20. Poss, L., Schönig, S.: A generic approach towards location-aware business process execution. In: van der Aa, H., Bork, D., Proper, H.A., Schmidt, R. (eds.) Enterprise, Business-Process and Information Systems Modeling. BPMDS EMMSAD 2023 2023. LNBIP, vol. 479, pp. 103–118. Springer, Cham (2023). https://doi.org/10.1007/978-3-031-34241-7_8
21. Saddem-Yagoubi, R., Poizat, P., Houhou, S.: Business processes meet spatial concerns: the sBPMN verification framework. In: Huisman, M., Păsăreanu, C., Zhan, N. (eds.) FM 2021. LNCS, vol. 13047, pp. 218–234. Springer, Cham (2021). https://doi.org/10.1007/978-3-030-90870-6_12
22. Schönig, S., Zeising, M., Jablonski, S.: Towards location-aware declarative business process management. In: Abramowicz, W., Kokkinaki, A. (eds.) BIS 2014. LNBIP, vol. 183, pp. 40–51. Springer, Cham (2014). https://doi.org/10.1007/978-3-319-11460-6_4
23. Stroppi, L.J.R., Chiotti, O., Villarreal, P.D.: Extending BPMN 2.0: method and tool support. In: Dijkman, R., Hofstetter, J., Koehler, J. (eds.) BPMN 2011. LNBIP, vol. 95, pp. 59–73. Springer, Heidelberg (2011). https://doi.org/10.1007/978-3-642-25160-3_5
24. Webster, J., Watson, R.T.: Analyzing the past to prepare for the future: writing a literature review. MIS Q. **26**(2), xiii–xxiii (2002)

25. Weske, M.: Business Process Management. Springer, Berlin, Heidelberg (2007). https://doi.org/10.1007/978-3-540-73522-9
26. Yousfi, A., Bauer, C., Saidi, R., et al.: uBPMN: a BPMN extension for modeling ubiquitous business processes. Inform. Softw. Tech. **74**, 55–68 (2016)
27. Zarour, K., Benmerzoug, D., Guermouche, N., et al.: A systematic literature review on BPMN extensions. Bus. Process. Manag. J. **26**(6), 1473–1503 (2019)
28. Zhu, X., Recker, J., Zhu, G., et al.: Exploring location-dependency in process modeling. Bus. Process Manag. J. **20**(6), 794–815 (2014). https://doi.org/10.1108/BPMJ-06-2013-0066

On the Semantic Transparency of Declarative Process Models: The Case of Constraints

Dung My Thi Trinh[1], Amine Abbad-Andaloussi[2], and Hugo A. López[1]([✉])(iD)

[1] DTU Compute, Technical University of Denmark, Kongens Lyngby, Denmark
`hulo@dtu.dk`
[2] University of St Gallen, St. Gallen, Switzerland

Abstract. Process modeling notations are essential for analyzing, designing, improving, and digitalizing business processes in organizations. In particular, for knowledge-intensive processes, notations that allow flexible orchestration of activities are crucial for supporting discretionary work. Declarative Process Modeling notations allow describing the interplay between the process activities with constraints that need to be met, without specifying how to meet them. Despite being well-suited for modeling flexible processes, declarative notations are not as widely adopted as imperative notations where the process is usually depicted using a flow-based approach. This paper focuses on investigating the semantic transparency of declarative notations, specifically how the visual representation of constraints aligns with the underlying formal concepts used in Declarative Process Models (DPMs). The study concentrates on Dynamic Condition Response (DCR) Graphs, a representative notation of DPMs extensively used in industry and academia. The research employs semi-structured interviews with experts in DCR Graphs, as well as an analysis of semantic transparency based on theoretical models of understandability. The findings indicate that generally colors contribute to the understanding of relations in DPMs, while the shapes used to describe constraints do not accurately convey their semantics. Based on these results, the study proposes an alternative representation of constraints, paving the road for an enhanced representation of DPMs.

Keywords: Knowledge-Intensive Processes · DCR Graphs · Visualization · Human-Computer Interaction · Human-centric Information Systems

1 Introduction

Process models are graphical representations of processes, typically used to understand, analyze, and improve the underlying control flow [10]. In the literature, these models have been organized using the imperative-declarative paradigm spectrum [13]. Imperative process models represent the process control flow explicitly. Hence, they are adequate for rigid processes with a small number of variants. Conversely, Declarative Process Models (DPMs) represent the process control flow implicitly, i.e., they specify the constraints governing the execution of the process activities and allow any execution not violating these constraints to occur [13]. Thereby, they are more adequate for modeling flexible processes [13]. However, their constraint-based approach challenges their understandability, especially when users are required to interpret the process constraints to infer the allowed process executions [13,34].

The usage of DPMs in digital transformation initiatives involves both the education of domain specialists who are novices in modeling, as well as the crafting of DPMs by experts in modeling, who lack domain knowledge. As such, the representation of DPMs must consider the perception of users, so their semantics are better interpreted. Despite being present in the literature for more than 15 years [32], surprisingly little research has focused on the understandability of DPMs. The empirical work by Figl et al. [15] hints that the visual representation of constraints in DPMs may be semantically perverse, meaning that this representation provides the contrary intuition than what the underlying concepts are intended for. The work by López and Simon coincides with this hypothesis following an analysis of DPMs under two understandability frameworks [25]. However, these works hint at the problem but do not propose solutions to improve the understandability of DPMs.

In this study, we investigate the representation of constraints in DPMs and propose an alternative representation to provide better semantic transparency to constraints and potentially support the understandability of DPMs. We use the Dynamic Condition Response (DCR) Graphs [20] notation as a proxy for declarative languages. Our choice of this notation is not accidental. Although other notations are strongly represented in academia (e.g. Declare [32], CMMN [28]), they lack industrial adoption. Conversely, DCR has an ecosystem of users including developers, consultants, and teachers from all over the world. In addition, the notation is extensively used to support the digital transformation of the public sector in Denmark [19]. Furthermore, the official documentation [40] and relevant literature (e.g., [12,20]) on DCR Graphs seem to provide little insights about the design rationales behind the current representation of constraints [25] (i.e., *relations* in the DCR terminology), which further motivates our investigation and proposal for a new representation of DCR relations.

We define the following research questions: ***RQ1. What concrete strengths and weaknesses are associated with the perception of the relations in DCR Graphs?*** and ***RQ2. How to design a new representation of DCR relations with enhanced semantic transparency?*** To address RQ1, we conduct a series of interviews with experts in declarative process modeling in both academia and industry. Then, we analyze their verbal utterances in the light of two existing frameworks i.e., the Physics of Notations [30] and the Semiology of Graphics [11]. With regards to RQ2, we propose a new representation of constraints considering experts' insights from the interviews as well as the guidelines derived from the existing frameworks [11,30].

The outcome of this work is meant to provide an alternative representation of constraints in DPMs based on experts' insights and existing theoretical models of understandability. Upon empirical validation, this representation can be adapted in existing modeling tools (e.g., DCR modeling portal[1]) and used to support the teaching of DCR Graphs as well as facilitating the communication between different process stakeholders. Moreover, we believe that the elicitation method and the insights provided may be generalizable to other DPM notations. In particular, the DPM notation Declare shares with DCR two of the five relations studied (e.g. condition and response), and our new notation could be applicable to their notation.

The rest of this paper is structured as follows. Section 2 explains the DCR notation and relevant theoretical models for understandability. Section 3 explains our research method. Sections 4 and 5 present the findings of our study. Section 6 presents our new proposal for DCR relations. Section 7 discusses the threats to validity. Section 8 provides an overview of the related work. Finally, Sect. 9 summarizes the paper and paves the road for future work.

2 Background

This section presents the key DCR concepts (cf. Sect. 2.1) and the relevant theoretical models of understandability (cf. Sect. 2.2).

2.1 DCR Graphs

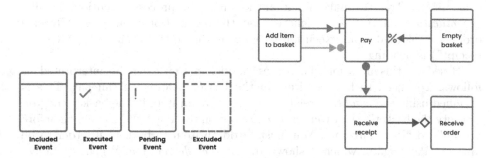

Fig. 1. Events and markings.

Fig. 2. An example of a DCR graph depicting a simple online shopping process.

A DCR Graph is a directed graph that consists of nodes that represent *events* and edges that represent *relations* between events. A more formal definition is available at [20]. An *Event* is the occurrence of an *activity* within a process [39]. It is visualized by a rectangle (see Fig. 1). The state of an event is represented by *markings*. As shown in the leftmost event in Fig. 1, the most common state of an event is *included*, not executed, and not pending. An *executed event* is visualized by a green check mark (the second event in Fig. 1). This marking

---

[1] See https://www.dcrgraphs.net.

indicates that the event has been executed. A *pending* event is visualized by a blue exclamation mark (the third event in Fig. 1). This marking indicates that the event must eventually be executed before the process ends, and is therefore required (i.e., pending). An *excluded event* is visualized by a dashed outline (the fourth event in Fig. 1). This marking indicates that the event cannot be executed. All events that are not excluded are *included* by default. The marking of events can be changed during the process execution using *relations*.

Relations are constraints that can be applied to the events. There are five basic relations in DCR (i.e., condition, response, exclude, include, and milestone). In the following, we explain these relations using the DCR Graph describing a simple online shopping process in Fig. 2.

We use the terms "source event" and "destination event" to describe two events connected with a relation running from the source event to the destination event. The *condition* relation ($\rightarrow\bullet$) specifies that the source event (e.g., "Add item to basket") needs to be executed at least once before executing the destination event (e.g., "Pay"). The *response* relation ($\bullet\rightarrow$) specifies that when the source event is executed (e.g., "Pay"), the destination event (e.g., "Receive receipt") must eventually be executed before ending the process. In this case, the destination event becomes *pending*. The *exclude* relation ($\rightarrow\%$) allows the source event (e.g., "Empty basket") to disable the included marking of the destination event (e.g., "Pay"), which makes it not anymore relevant in the current process execution. Conversely, the *include* relation ($\rightarrow+$) allows the source event (e.g., "Add item to basket") to enable the included marking of the destination event (e.g., "Pay") to make it relevant again in the process execution. Finally, the *milestone* relation ($\rightarrow\diamond$) denotes that the destination event (e.g., "Receive order") is blocked from execution as long as the source event (e.g., "Receive receipt") is pending.

Based on this notation the process model in Fig. 2 can be interpreted as follows. You need to have an item in the basket before you can pay. This is specified using the *condition* relation. If you have an item in the basket and you "Empty the basket", then you *exclude* the option to "Pay" and you are therefore not able to "Pay" anymore. You must "Add an item to basket" in order to be able to "Pay" again, which is shown by the *include* relation. When the "Pay" event has been executed, you will receive a receipt eventually and thus the event "Receive receipt" becomes pending. This is shown by the *response* relation. As long as the event "Receive receipt" is pending, you are not able to "Receive the order". This is shown by the *milestone* relation.

2.2   Theoretical Models of Understandability

To enhance the understandability of the current visual representation of relations, two theoretical models (i.e., Semiology of Graphics [11] and the Physics of Notations [30]) are used. Both theoretical models consist of several aspects of graphical representations. Of the two theoretical models, only aspects relevant to DCR relations are described and discussed in this paper. We refer the reader to [11] and [30] for a broader explanation of these two theoretical models and their empirical support.

Semiology of graphics is a theory on information visualization [11]. For this work, it is used to analyze and construct effective graphical representations. The Semiology of Graphics introduces a set of *visual variables*.

Visual variables refer to the visual characteristics of a representation. They are divided into two categories: *Planar variables* and *Retinal variables*. Planar variables denote the position of a graphical representation, e.g., determined in a 2-dimensional space. Retinal variables refer to the visual aspects of the representation itself [21,36] and include shape, size, color, brightness, orientation, and texture. For DCR relations only shape and color are information-carrying variables, thus we will only these variables relevant in our study.

The perceptive attitude of a visual variable refers to how a person perceives a visual variable. The Semiology of Graphics [11] introduces four perceptive attitudes: *associative* perceptive attitude, *selective* perceptive attitude, *ordered* perceptive attitude, and *quantitative* perceptive attitude. For the aforementioned visual variables (i.e., shape and color) of DCR relations, only the *associative* and *selective* perceptive attitudes are relevant.

An *associative* perceptive attitude refers to how the reader can immediately group similar representations. The *shape* visual variable is associative. When looking at Fig. 3, one should be able to group the different shapes (circle, square, and triangle). A *selective* perceptive attitude refers to how the reader can distinguish representations that belong to the same visual category and disregard all others. This allows the reader to only perceive the desired category. The *color* visual variable is both associative and selective. When looking at Fig. 4, one should be able to group the different colors (red, blue, and green). In addition, one should be able to focus on a single color only (e.g., the blue color) and disregard the others (i.e., red and green colors).

Fig. 3. Shape: Associative   **Fig. 4.** Color: Associative and selective

Besides the importance of the perceptive attitudes of the representation of relations, these relations must also be directly perceived and easily learned. These two criteria are important for semantic transparency which is a principle in the Physics of Notations.

222   D. M. T. Trinh et al.

Physics of Notations (PoN) is a theory providing a set of principles for designing cognitively effective visual notations [30]. There are 9 principles in total (listed here in no particular order): (1) Semantic Transparency, (2) Semiotic Clarity, (3) Perceptual Discriminability, (4) Manageable Complexity, (5) Cognitive Integration, (6) Visual Expressiveness, (7) Dual Coding, (8) Graphic Economy, and (9) Cognitive Fit. We will discuss the most relevant principles in our setting.

Semantic Transparency is a principle that refers to the use of a visual representation to convey meaning in an intuitive manner [30]. This means that the meaning of the visual representation should either be perceived directly or learned easily. For example, it can be directly perceived and easily learned that the meaning of a "stickman" symbol is a person, which is typically the intention. Semantic transparency is perceived on a spectrum (cf. Fig. 5). Thus, the stickman as a visual representation can be placed on the right side of the spectrum as eliciting *semantic immediacy*. However, if the stickman as a visual representation suggests a meaning different from the intended one of a person, then it is to be placed on the left side of the spectrum to elicit *semantic perversity*.

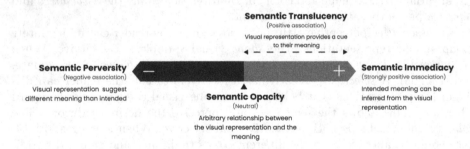

Fig. 5. Semantic transparency as a spectrum (Redesign of Fig. 19 in [30])

The literature recommends different approaches to foster the association between visual representations and the underlying concepts [30]. Notably, *icons* can provide a graphical representation that perceptually reflects the desired concepts. Moreover, the use of icons enhances the speed of recognition and therefore decreases the time it takes to understand and comprehend a representation of a concept. Besides, *semantically transparent relationships* can be used to visualize the relationship between different concepts effectively through several arrangements of visual elements (cf. Fig. 6).

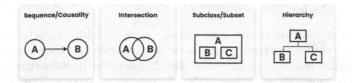

Fig. 6. Semantically transparent relationships (Redesign of Fig. 21 in [30])

Perceptual Discriminability is a principle that refers to different graphical representations being clearly distinguishable from each other, which makes them easier and faster to recognize [30]. The concept of *visual distance* [30] is used to describe how different (i.e., distant) two visual representations are. The following are some approaches to increase visual distance:

- *The primacy of Shape*: Shape should be used as a primary visual variable since it represents how humans identify objects in the real world.
- *Perceptual Popout*: Having at least one unique visual variable to make the graphical representation stand out from its surroundings.
- *Textual Differentiation*: Text should not be used as the only different variable, since it has zero visual distance.

Visual Expressiveness is a principle that refers to the number of used visual variables in a notation [30]. One can differentiate *information-carrying variables* and *free variables*. Information-carrying variables are visual variables that are formally used to encode information in a graphical notation, whereas free variables are not formally used for that purpose [30]. The visual expressiveness principle suggests that one should maximize the number of information-carrying variables and therefore minimize the number of free variables since this will create more effective and clear visualizations [30]. This principle motivates the use of colors, as it is a cognitively effective visual variable, since the human visual system is able to quickly and accurately distinguish between different colors [30].

Based on the aforementioned theoretical models of understandability, we are studying the extent to which the current visual representation of relations in DCR Graphs align with these theories.

3 Research Method

A qualitative study in the form of semi-structured interviews with experts in DCR Graphs was conducted to identify the strengths and weaknesses of the current visual representation of DCR relations. The following sections summarize the design of our interview study (cf. Sect. 3.1), experiment procedure (cf. Sect. 3.2), and data analysis approach (cf. Sect. 3.3).

3.1 Study Design

Participants: Using purposive (judgement) sampling [6], 8 participants were recruited into the study. There were 7 male participants and 1 female participant of ages ranging from 25 to 52 years old. Among the participants, 63% were Scandinavian and 37% were from other European countries. The participants had experience with DCR Graphs ranging from 5 months to over 10 years. As such, all participants were familiar with DPMs and DCR Graphs and were therefore all considered to be experts in DCR Graphs. 75% were experts in academia and 25% were experts in the industry. The academic degrees of the participants ranged from bachelor's degrees to doctoral degrees.

Materials: The interviews were conducted either in person or via online meetings. The verbal utterances of the participants were recorded with their consent. As support, a camera was used to record both video and audio and as reserve, pen and paper were used to note important points during the interview.

A set of questions and requests were formulated for the interview sessions. The set consisted of questions and requests that addressed the participants' background (e.g., *In which field have you studied?*), expertise (e.g., *Are you teaching about process models or otherwise sharing your knowledge about process models?*), the visual representation of DCR relations (e.g., *Please explain the condition relation assuming that you were to explain it to a person from the general public.*), and current challenges of DCR relations (e.g., *In your current position, what are the most salient features you use to describe relations in DCR?*). A number of questions were designed to elicit concrete strengths and weaknesses of relations in terms of their semantic transparency. For example, the participants were asked to explain the concept of a relation to novices and afterward asked *what other symbol(s) could represent this concept?* Since the participants might have had different levels of expertise, experience, and knowledge about DCR Graphs, some questions were customized to the individual participants. The full set of questions is available in Appendix 03 [41].

3.2 Experiment Procedure

The participants were interviewed individually. All of them have signed and filled out a consent form (cf. Appendix 01 in [41]) and a demographics information document (cf. Appendix 02 in [41]) prior to the interview. The individual interview sessions had an average duration of 50 min.

Each interview session was conducted using the prepared set of questions (cf. Sect. 3.1) that addressed the participants' background, expertise, the visual representation of DCR relations, and current challenges of DCR relations (cf. Appendix 03 in [41]).

3.3 Data Analysis

The participants' responses were transcribed using *Riverside.fm AI Transcription* and Microsoft Word. They were then checked and corrected manually to ensure accuracy and guarantee the anonymity of the participants (cf. rules in Appendix 04 [41]). Then, qualitative coding [8] was used to infer meaningful insights from the data (cf. Appendix 07 [41]). This coding process was conducted in three main steps following the guidelines in [8].

1. Extracting statements on the visual representation of DCR relations: This step consisted of an initial coding phase [8], browsing the transcripts and identifying the statements where participants discussed the visual representation of DCR relations. The statements were exacted and enriched with additional information (i.e., participant, context, timestamp) as illustrated in Table 1.

Table 1. Example of step 1 in the coding process. Details in Appendix 05 [41]

Participant	Visual representation of DCR relations	Context	Timestamp
Participant 5	*I can't state... In black and white, I always have a problem with condition and response. I always forget which side is the dot on. When we got the colors, it's easy.*	When asked about the relations in general.	[00:14:48]

2. Fragmenting statements into units: This step consists of splitting the statements in Step 1 into smaller units describing aspects of the visual representation of the DCR relations. Each unit is referred to as an *item* with the form:

$$[\text{For } X\ Y][opt.context]\,text,$$

where $X \in \{current, potential\}$: *current* refers to items that describe the current design and *potential* refers to items that may be applied to a potential design. $Y \in \{general, condition, response, include, exclude, milestone, multiple\}$:   *general* refers to the overall relations of DCR, *condition, response, include, exclude, milestone* refers to the five basic relations, and *multiple* refers to items that include more than one relation. *[opt.context]* denotes an optional coding, for additional context. *text* describes statements from Step 1 divided into units (Table 2).

Table 2. Example of step 2 in the coding process. Details in Appendix 06 [41]

Participant	Statement fragments
Participant 5	[For current multiple] *In black and white, I always have a problem with condition and response. I always forget which side is the dot on.*
Participant 5	[For current multiple][For condition and response] *When we got the colors, it's easy.*

3. Identifying strengths and weaknesses in terms of visual variables
This step consisted of applying focused coding [8] to categorize each item from Step 2 as either *current* notation or *potential* notation, and further either as

Table 3. Example of step 3 in the coding process.

P#	Type	Current				Potential			
		Strengths		Weaknesses		S...		W...	
		Color	Shape	Color	Shape	C...	S...	C...	S...
P5	Multiple	[For condition and response] *When we got the colors, it's easy*			*In black and white, I always have a problem with condition and response. I always forget which side is the dot on*				

strength or *weakness* and finally either as *color* or *shape*. This step is illustrated in Table 3, while its full outcome is available available in Appendix 07 [41].

Finally insights were systematically extracted from the categorized items based on the following criteria:

- Similar statements are merged. For example, the two statements *"what was helping me the most was the color distinction"* and *"the colors for me are important. This is what my brain uses to distinct each arrow."* are merged to become: **As an information-carrying visual variable, colors are better than shapes to differentiate between the relations**.
- Concrete suggestions of symbols are reduced to a general concept. For example, the two statements *"a gate you have to first unlock and then you can decide if you walk through it or don't."* and *"for a condition maybe a wall. [...] a wall or door you have to... remove before you can continue."* are reduced to become: **The visual representation should reflect the concept of blocking and unblocking something**.
- Statements that are not contradicting but describe the same relation are merged. For example, the two statements for the *include* relation *"stick with the plus for inclusion"* and *"I would say green to be like green we open a road. [...] we can go this way"* are merged to become: **The color and the shape reflect the concept of include**.

– If two statements are contradicting, then the statement that is mentioned by most participants is kept. For example, when asked about the most salient features used to describe relations the two statements *"Definitely the color"* and *"I think shape is first for me"* were mentioned. However, similar answers to the first statement were mentioned seven times while a similar answer to the second statement was only mentioned once. These statements are therefore reduced to become: ***As an information-carrying visual variable, colors are better than shapes to differentiate between the relations***.

The outcome of this step led to the results reported in Table 4.

4   Findings of the Interview Study

This section addresses RQ1 (cf. Sect. 1). Table 4 summarizes our findings on the strengths and weaknesses of the representation of relations in DCR.

Overall the participants suggest keeping both *shape* and *color* as visual variables. Generally, color is perceived as a better variable to differentiate between the relations. However, the arrows used in the relations impede the understanding of DCR Graphs as they become confused with flowcharts.

For some specific relations, i.e., *include* and *exclude*, the participants were satisfied with their shapes and colors as they clearly reflected their semantics. In others (e.g. *condition* and *response*), the shapes and colors were not perceived as informative or semantic transparent. The *milestone* relation, in turn, was easy to remember for the participants, however, its representation was not transparent. Thus, some participants preferred to choose a shape that is similar to the *condition* relation while indicating the pending marking (i.e., the exclamation mark) in the relation.

Table 4. Insights regarding expert perception DCR graphs and its relations (cf. Sect. 2.1). (S) refers to strengths, (W) refers to weaknesses.

Theme	Deducted insights
General	• (S) Shape and color should still be used. • (S) As an information-carrying visual variable, colors are better than shapes to differentiate between the relations. • (S) The relations should indicate the direction of the effect of a source event on a destination event. • (W) The representation of effects should avoid common representations used to denote flow-based relationships between events. • (S) The shape of the relations should reflect their corresponding semantics. • (W) The current symbols at the head or tail of the arrows are disliked. • (W) There should be no physical space between events and the relations connecting the events.
Condition	• (W) The color and the shape do not reflect the semantics of the *condition* relation. • (S) The visual representation should reflect the concept of blocking and unblocking something. • (W) The shape is hard to differentiate from the *response* relation.
Response	• (W) The color and the shape do not reflect the semantics of the *response* relation. • (S) The visual representation should reflect the concept of alerting and reminding that something must be done. • (W) The shape is hard to differentiate from the *condition* relation.
Include	• (S) The color and the shape reflect the semantics of the *include* relation.
Exclude	• (S) The color and the shape reflect the semantics of the *exclude* relation. • (W) The symbol for the *exclude* relation should be a minus instead of a percentage sign.
Milestone	• (S) The shape of the *milestone* relation is easy to remember. • (W) The visual representation does not reflect the semantics of the *milestone* relation. • (S) The visual representation should reflect a concept similar to the one underlying the *condition* relation but with the pending part. • (S) The pending part should be indicated in the visual representation.

5 Discussion

The results from the expert interviews highlighted several strengths and weaknesses of the current design of the visual representations of the five basic DCR relations. In terms of semantic transparency, participants expressed that some of the representations of relations reflect their semantics while other representations do not. The participants generally favored the use of colors (cf. Table 4). They considered that while not all the colors used reflect the concept of the relations, it is still easy to remember the colors and thus differentiate the relations. This aligns with the principle of visual expressiveness in Physics of Notation [30] (cf. Sect. 2.2), which specifies that color is a very cognitively effective visual variable [30]. Therefore, the participants would prefer not to change the colors of the DCR relations, but instead change the shapes to align with the colors. By keeping the color as a visual variable, each of the five basic relations has a unique color and the principle of perceptual discriminability in the Physics of Notation [30] is therefore satisfied.

Condition and Response Relations. The participants experienced difficulty when differentiating the shapes of the *condition* and *response* relations. Considering the perceptive attitudes from the Semiology of Graphics [11] (cf. Sect. 2.2), the shapes should lead to an associative perceptive attitude. The removal of the colors from the *condition* and *response* relations is illustrated in Fig. 7.

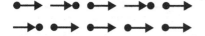   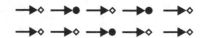

Fig. 7. Colors removed from the *condition* and *response* relation.

Fig. 8. Colors removed from the *condition* and *milestone* relation.

Initially, it can be seen in Fig. 7 that the perceptive attitude is not as associative as in Fig. 8, where the shapes of two other relations (i.e., *condition* and *milestone*) are shown. This could partially explain why the participants could not easily differentiate the *condition* and *response* relations.

Use of Arrows. As a general matter, participants showed disfavor toward the use of arrows in relations. They considered that arrows are associated with sequences and thereby flowcharts, which they believed could be confusing for novices. The principle of semantic transparency in the Physics of Notation addresses the relationships "Sequence/Causality", which is visualized by an arrow between two elements (cf. Fig. 6). Considering the participants' insights, this suggests that the arrows indicate sequence more than causality (i.e., reflecting the cause–effect relationship implied by DCR relations). One possible reason could be associated with the arrowheads (i.e., >) implying sequence more than causality.

6 A Proposal for a Semantic Transparent Representation of Relations

Based on the findings of the interviews (c.f. Section 4) and the theoretical models of understandability (c.f. Section 2.2), we propose an alternative visual representation of the five basic relations of DCR graphs.

Table 5. The five current basic visual representations of relations and the corresponding proposed visual representations of relations

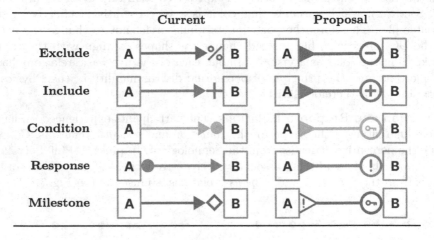

Exclude Relation. The participants had generally no difficulties understanding the *exclude* relation. However, as reported in Table 4, some participants suggested that a minus symbol ("-") could replace the percentage symbol ("%") to better align with the semantics of the *exclude* relation. This suggestion is reasonable since the "-" symbol is typically used to describe "taking something out from something else (i.e., subtraction)", while the "%" is more commonly used as a percentage sign which does not reflect the semantics of the *exclude* relation.

Our proposal for the *exclude* relation is shown in Table 5. Firstly the "%" symbol is replaced with a "-" as a traditional symbol for "minus". To easily isolate "-" from the body of the arrow, the "-" can be placed inside a simple shape, such as a circle, a square, or a triangle. While most of the participants described the semantics of the *exclude* relation as "This should be removed/subtracted", one participant explained it as "Exclude, don't go". Therefore, by placing the "-" inside a circle, the "-" inside the circle can be associated with a "no entry" sign. Concerning semantic transparency, although the "-" inside a circle can be perceived as just a "minus" or as a "no entry" sign, there is no violation of the principle of semantic transparency, since both associations are valid explanations for the semantics of the *exclude* relation. Furthermore, the color of a "no entry" sign is typically red, thus the "-" inside a circle can be considered to align with the red color. From Fig. 6, the use of arrows could be misinterpreted as illustrating sequential graphs instead of causal graphs. This can be solved by removing the arrowheads. However, without arrowheads or other directional indicators for the effect of one event on another, a relation can be read in both directions in terms of causality, which is not the intention. Therefore, to indicate direction without the association with arrows used for flowcharts, the arrowhead can be placed where they have no shaft. Since the association of the arrows with a flowchart applies to all relations, the arrowhead of each proposed relation is therefore moved.

Include Relation. Similar to the *exclude* relation, the participants generally had no difficulties understanding the *include* relation. They understood the plus symbol ("+") to indicate the semantics of the *include* relation as intended. In addition to the replacement of the arrowhead and also the use of a circle to enclose the relevant symbol at the end of the relation, the final proposal for the *include* relation can be seen in Table 5. In terms of its color, green is commonly associated with something positive [25] which aligns with the use of a "+" symbol.

Condition Relation. From the expert interviews, the weakness of the *condition* relation was both the color and the shape, as neither reflects the semantics of the *condition* relation. Participants described the semantics of the *condition* relation to be a relation that blocks and unblocks something. Specific metaphors that were mentioned include a gate, a padlock, and a door. A commonality between these metaphors is that they all imply that something can be blocked or unblocked by a lock. The closest relation to a lock is the padlock. The direction of the relation resulted in using a key to indicate the locking and unlocking motion. The final proposal for the *condition* relation can be seen in Table 5. In terms of its color, the yellow color fits well since it is the typical color for keys (e.g., gold, bronze). Thus, the shape and the chosen key color are adequate for the *condition* relation.

Response Relation. From the expert interviews, the weakness of the *response* relation related to both the color and the shape, which both do not reflect the semantics of the *response* relation. The participants described the semantics of the *response* as alerting or reminding about something that must be done. In DCR, the concept of remembering to do something is referred to as pending. As previously mentioned (cf. Sect. 2.1), a pending state is marked with a blue exclamation mark (!). The "!" is typically used to show emphasis. This can be related to the participants' statements about alerting. Thus, using the "!" produces a *response* as in Table 5. The color of the "!" used as a marking is the same color as the current *response* relation. Although this does not strongly reflect the semantics of the *response* relation, it can be compromised for the design of a shape that better reflects the semantics.

Milestone Relation. The expert interviews showed that the weakness of the *milestone* relation was less related to the visual aspect but more related to its semantics (cf. Table 4). A participant suggested that they wanted to visualize the part that is pending. For example, if ($A \rightarrow \diamond B$), then there should be an indication that shows that A is the pending part. The conceptual definition of the *milestone* relation is: "If A is pending (by a *response* relation), then B cannot be executed)". This can be considered in terms of two parts: "A is pending" and "B cannot be executed". For the first part, A is pending by a *response* relation, which means that the "!" can be reused. For the second part, B can only be executed if A is executed, which is like the *condition* relation. Therefore, the *response* and *condition* relations can be merged to form the *milestone* relation as shown in Table 5. In terms of the color, the purple color does not strongly reflect the semantics of the *milestone* relation. However, this can be compromised for the design of a shape that better reflects the semantics.

7   Threats to Validity

This work has a set of limitations. First, the sample size was rather limited and might not provide generalizable insights. Nevertheless, the interviews lasted for long periods and were rich in insights. Secondly, qualitative coding was conducted to analyze the collected verbal utterances. Although this procedure was conducted systematically, an external coder could have been invited to enable more transparency, consistency, and validity of the data. To mitigate this limitation, the coding was discussed between the co-authors in several meetings to ensure the consistency, and validity of the obtained insights. Moreover, although the proposed representations of DCR relations are based on experts' insights (cf. Sect. 4) and existing theoretical frameworks of understandability (cf. Sect. 2.2), empirical validation is still required to provide empirical evidence supporting our new proposal. This validation is planned as part of future work (cf. Sect. 9). Another important limitation could be associated with the generalization of our results to other declarative process modeling languages. Herein, we argue that many of the concepts covered by the DCR relations are also present in other declarative languages such as Declare [32].

8   Related Work

The comprehension of process models has been subject to extensive research in the literature (cf. overview in [14]). This research delves into various aspects associated with the representation of process models and process data (e.g., [2–4,7,15,17,33]), users' background and expertise (e.g., [29,35]), the tasks in which the models are used (e.g., [27,38]) and the tools supporting these tasks (e.g., [1, 26,37]). Many of these aspects have been shown to have a significant impact on the comprehension of process models [14].

Our work relates to the ongoing research investigating the representation of process models in the light of existing theoretical models of understandability (e.g., Semiology of Graphics [11] and Physics of Notations [30]). In this vein, imperative process models have received more attention than their declarative counterparts [5,25]. Genon et al. [16] have, for instance, investigated the cognitive effectiveness of Business Process Modeling Notation (BPMN) models. Similarly,

Duarte et al. [9] conducted a semiotic analysis of BPMN models. A more detailed overview of studies investigating the visual representation of imperative process models can be found in the literature review of Koschmider et al. in [22].

Nevertheless, with the growing use of declarative languages to model flexible processes, a new stream of research has emerged to study the visual representation of DPMs. For instance, Hasner et al. [18] proposed a new framework for modeling processes declaratively based on the Physics of Notations [30]. Figl et al. [15] investigated whether DPMs in Declare [32] can mitigate the cognitive bias related to business rules. In recent work, López and Simon investigated the extent to which DPMs in DCR align with the principles of the Physics of Notations [30] and the SEQUAL framework [23,24].

9 Conclusion

This study investigated experts' perception of the visual representation of the DCR relations based on semi-structured interviews and guidelines from existing theoretical frameworks of understandably. By combining expert feedback and frameworks for the understandability of notations, we proposed a new representation of DCR relations. We believe this study helps in building a body of knowledge regarding the representation of DPMs with a direct impact on user perceptions and the understandability of models, providing design guidelines for notation and architects of DPM solutions, for instance, in the creation of cognitively efficient editors of declarative process models

As future work, we are planning to validate our proposal empirically. Herein, eye-tracking could be used to investigate and compare users' cognitive, behavioral, and affective states when dealing with the old representation of DCR relations and the new one. Additionally, one can extend this study to other declarative process modeling languages such as Declare [32] and the Case Management Model and Notation (CMMN) [31]. It would be also relevant and interesting to investigate how people from other cultures and backgrounds would perceive the visual representation of DPMs. Last but not least, other principles of the existing theoretical frameworks of understandability can be explored and used to further improve the representation of DPMs.

References

1. Abbad Andaloussi, A., Buch-Lorentsen, J., López, H.A., Slaats, T., Weber, B.: Exploring the modeling of declarative processes using a hybrid approach. In: Laender, A.H.F., Pernici, B., Lim, E.-P., de Oliveira, J.P.M. (eds.) ER 2019. LNCS, vol. 11788, pp. 162–170. Springer, Cham (2019). https://doi.org/10.1007/978-3-030-33223-5_14
2. Abbad Andaloussi, A., Davis, C.J., Burattin, A., López, H.A., Slaats, T., Weber, B.: Understanding quality in declarative process modeling through the mental models of experts. In: Fahland, D., Ghidini, C., Becker, J., Dumas, M. (eds.) BPM 2020. LNCS, vol. 12168, pp. 417–434. Springer, Cham (2020). https://doi.org/10.1007/978-3-030-58666-9_24

3. Abbad Andaloussi, A., Zerbato, F., Burattin, A., Slaats, T., Hildebrandt, T.T., Weber, B.: Exploring how users engage with hybrid process artifacts based on declarative process models: a behavioral analysis based on eye-tracking and think-aloud. Softw. Syst. Model. **20**, 1437–1464 (2021)
4. Andaloussi, A.A., Burattin, A., Slaats, T., Kindler, E., Weber, B.: On the declarative paradigm in hybrid business process representations: a conceptual framework and a systematic literature study. Inf. Syst. **91**, 101505 (2020)
5. Andaloussi, A.A., Burattin, A., Slaats, T., Kindler, E., Weber, B.: Complexity in declarative process models: metrics and multi-modal assessment of cognitive load. Expert Syst. Appl. 120924 (2023)
6. Ayhan, H.Ö.: Non-probability sampling survey methods. Int. Encycl. Stat. Sci. **2**(14), 979–982 (2011)
7. Bera, P., Soffer, P., Parsons, J.: Using eye tracking to expose cognitive processes in understanding conceptual models. MIS Q. **43**(4), 1105–1126 (2019)
8. Charmaz, K.: Constructing grounded theory (introducing qualitative methods series). Constr. grounded theory (2014)
9. Duarte, E.B., Duarte, R.B., da Silveira, D.S.: A semiotic analysis of the representativeness of BPMN graphic elements. In: Shishkov, B. (ed.) Business Modeling and Software Design. BMSD 2023. LNBIP, vol. 483, pp. 225–234. Springer, Cham (2023). https://doi.org/10.1007/978-3-031-36757-1_14
10. Dumas, M., Van der Aalst, W.M., Ter Hofstede, A.H.: Process-Aware Information Systems: Bridging People and Software Through Process Technology. John Wiley & Sons, Hoboken (2005)
11. El Ahmar, Y.: Enhancing the Cognitive Effectiveness of UML Diagrams: Application of the Semiology of Graphics. Ph.D. thesis, Université de Lille (2018)
12. Eshuis, R., Debois, S., Slaats, T., Hildebrandt, T.: Deriving consistent GSM schemas from DCR graphs. In: Sheng, Q.Z., Stroulia, E., Tata, S., Bhiri, S. (eds.) ICSOC 2016. LNCS, vol. 9936, pp. 467–482. Springer, Cham (2016). https://doi.org/10.1007/978-3-319-46295-0_29
13. Fahland, D., et al.: Declarative versus imperative process modeling languages: the issue of understandability. In: Halpin, T., et al. (eds.) BPMDS/EMMSAD -2009. LNBIP, vol. 29, pp. 353–366. Springer, Heidelberg (2009). https://doi.org/10.1007/978-3-642-01862-6_29
14. Figl, K.: Comprehension of procedural visual business process models. Bus. Inf. Syst. Eng. **59**(1), 41–67 (2017)
15. Figl, K., Di Ciccio, C., Reijers, H.A.: Do declarative process models help to reduce cognitive biases related to business rules? In: Dobbie, G., Frank, U., Kappel, G., Liddle, S.W., Mayr, H.C. (eds.) ER 2020. LNCS, vol. 12400, pp. 119–133. Springer, Cham (2020). https://doi.org/10.1007/978-3-030-62522-1_9
16. Genon, N., Heymans, P., Amyot, D.: Analysing the cognitive effectiveness of the BPMN 2.0 visual notation. In: Malloy, B., Staab, S., van den Brand, M. (eds.) SLE 2010. LNCS, vol. 6563, pp. 377–396. Springer, Heidelberg (2011). https://doi.org/10.1007/978-3-642-19440-5_25
17. Gulden, J.: Visually comparing process dynamics with rhythm-eye views. In: Dumas, M., Fantinato, M. (eds.) BPM 2016. LNBIP, vol. 281, pp. 474–485. Springer, Cham (2017). https://doi.org/10.1007/978-3-319-58457-7_35
18. Hanser, M., Di Ciccio, C., Mendling, J., et al.: A new notational framework for declarative process modeling. Softwaretechnik-Trends **36**(2), 53–56 (2016)
19. Hildebrandt, T.T., et al.: Ecoknow: engineering effective, co-created and compliant adaptive case management systems for knowledge workers. In: Proceedings of the International Conference on Software and System Processes, pp. 155–164 (2020)

20. Hildebrandt, T.T., Mukkamala, R.R.: Declarative event-based workflow as distributed dynamic condition response graphs. arXiv preprint arXiv:1110.4161 (2011)
21. Kaur, P., Owonibi, M., Koenig-Ries, B.: Towards visualization recommendation-a semi-automated domain-specific learning approach. In: GvD, pp. 30–35 (2015)
22. Koschmider, A., Drescher, A., Lehner, J.: A survey-based analysis of principles to evaluate visual notations of process modeling languages. Technical report, Karlsruhe Institute of Technology (2018). https://doi.org/10.5445/IR/1000079942
23. Krogstie, J., Krogstie, J.: Quality of Business Process Models. Springer, Cham (2016). https://doi.org/10.1007/978-3-319-42512-2_2
24. Lindland, O.I., Sindre, G., Solvberg, A.: Understanding quality in conceptual modeling. IEEE Softw. 11(2), 42–49 (1994)
25. López, H.A., Simon, V.D.: How to(re) design declarative process notations? A view from the lens of cognitive effectiveness frameworks. In: 15th IFIP Working Conference on the Practice of Enterprise Modeling (2022)
26. Lübke, D., Ahrens, M., Schneider, K.: Influence of diagram layout and scrolling on understandability of BPMN processes: an eye tracking experiment with BPMN diagrams. Inf. Technol. Manag. 22(2), 99–131 (2021). https://doi.org/10.1007/s10799-021-00327-7
27. Mandelburger, M.M., Mendling, J.: Cognitive diagram understanding and task performance in systems analysis and design. MIS Q. 45(4), 2101–2157 (2021)
28. Marin, M.A.: Introduction to the case management model and notation (CMMN). arXiv preprint arXiv:1608.05011 (2016)
29. Mendling, J., Strembeck, M.: Influence factors of understanding business process models. In: Abramowicz, W., Fensel, D. (eds.) BIS 2008. LNBIP, vol. 7, pp. 142–153. Springer, Heidelberg (2008). https://doi.org/10.1007/978-3-540-79396-0_13
30. Moody, D.: The "physics" of notations: toward a scientific basis for constructing visual notations in software engineering. IEEE Trans. Softw. Eng. 35(6), 756–779 (2009)
31. Object Management Group: CMMN standard. https://www.omg.org/cmmn/. Accessed 14 July 2023
32. Pesic, M.: Constraint-based workflow management systems: shifting control to users. Ph.D. thesis, Eindhoven University of Technology (2008)
33. Petrusel, R., Mendling, J.: Eye-tracking the factors of process model comprehension tasks. In: Salinesi, C., Norrie, M.C., Pastor, Ó. (eds.) CAiSE 2013. LNCS, vol. 7908, pp. 224–239. Springer, Heidelberg (2013). https://doi.org/10.1007/978-3-642-38709-8_15
34. Pichler, P., Weber, B., Zugal, S., Pinggera, J., Mendling, J., Reijers, H.A.: Imperative versus declarative process modeling languages: an empirical investigation. In: Daniel, F., Barkaoui, K., Dustdar, S. (eds.) BPM 2011. LNBIP, vol. 99, pp. 383–394. Springer, Heidelberg (2012). https://doi.org/10.1007/978-3-642-28108-2_37
35. Reijers, H.A., Mendling, J.: A study into the factors that influence the understandability of business process models. IEEE Trans. Syst. Man Cybern. 41(3), 449–462 (2010)
36. Roth, R.E.: Visual variables. International Encyclopedia of Geography: People, the Earth, Environment and Technology, pp. 1–11 (2017)
37. Sanchez-Ferreres, J., et al.: Supporting the process of learning and teaching process models. IEEE Trans. Learn. Technol. 13(3), 552–566 (2020)
38. Schreiber, C., Abbad-Andaloussi, A., Weber, B.: On the cognitive effects of abstraction and fragmentation in modularized process models. In: Business Process Man-

agement: 21st International Conference, BPM 2023, (Accepted for publication) (2023)

39. Schützenmeier, N., Käppel, M., Ackermann, L., Jablonski, S., Petter, S.: Automaton-based comparison of declare process models. Softw. Syst. Model. 1–19 (2022)

40. Solutions, D.: Using data in business rules - guards (2021). https://documentation. dcr.design/documentation/using-data-in-business-rules-guards/. Accessed 29 Apr 2023

41. Trinh, D.M.T., Abbad-Andaloussi, A., López, H.A.: Online appendix (2023). https://andaloussi.org/COOPIS2023/. Accessed 14 July 2023

Process Analytics

Discovering Guard Stage Milestone Models Through Hierarchical Clustering

Leyla Moctar M'Baba[1,2](✉)[iD], Mohamed Sellami[1][iD], Nour Assy[3][iD],
Walid Gaaloul[1][iD], and Mohamedade Farouk Nanne[2][iD]

[1] Télécom SudParis, SAMOVAR, Institut Polytechnique de Paris, Paris, France
`leyla.moctar_mbaba@telecom-sudparis.eu`
[2] University of Nouakchott Al Aasriya, Nouakchott, Mauritania
[3] Bonitasoft, Boulogne-Billancourt, France

Abstract. Processes executed on enterprise Information Systems (IS), such as ERP and CMS, are artifact-centric. The execution of these processes is driven by the creation and evolution of business entities called artifacts. Several artifact-centric modeling languages were proposed to capture the specificity of these processes. One of the most used artifact-centric modeling languages is the Guard Stage Milestone (GSM) language. It represents an artifact-centric process as an information model and a lifecycle. The lifecycle groups activities in stages with data conditions as guards. The hierarchy between the stages is based on common conditions. However, existing works do not discover this hierarchy nor the data conditions, as they considered them to be already available. They also do not discover GSM models directly from event logs. They discover Petri nets and translate them into GSM models. To fill this gap, we propose in this paper a discovery approach based on hierarchical clustering. We use invariants detection to discover data conditions and information gain of common conditions to cluster stages. The approach does not rely on domain knowledge nor translation mechanisms. It was implemented and evaluated using a blockchain case study.

Keywords: Guard-Stage-Milestone · Artifact-Centric Processes · Process mining · Artifact-Centric Event Logs

1 Introduction

In recent times, there has been a growing interest in artifact-centric systems, leading to the development of artifact-centric process mining techniques. These techniques include artifact-centric process discovery, conformance checking, and enhancement. Artifact-centric process discovery techniques aim to uncover the lifecycles of involved artifacts and their interactions [5]. Most current artifact-centric discovery approaches use event data stored in a relational database containing information about data creation, modification, and deletion [5]. Alternatively, they utilize the Object-Centric Event Log (OCEL) standard format [6]. Some approaches can also be applied to the traditional activity-centric event log format called eXtensible Event Log (XES)[1] with additional processing and filtering steps. Additionally, these techniques discover flat procedural models, focusing on the order of execution, while neglecting the influence of data on execution and interactions between artifacts. These models are typically represented using directly-follows graphs [2] or Petri nets [18]. Some approaches propose translating Petri nets into the Guard-Stage-Milestone (GSM) language [16,18], which is a well-known declarative approach for modeling artifact-centric processes. This work also concentrates on discovering GSM models. Data conditions and hierarchical abstractions are essential to artifact-centric languages like GSM [8]. In fact, GSM relies on data conditions to model authorized behaviors and parallelism within and between the lifecycles of artifacts. GSM also supports hierarchy between groups of activities which allows the representation of different levels of abstraction of the business operations. The discovery of data conditions was not described in existing approaches where GSM models discovery is based on translation mechanisms from Petri nets [16,18]. These conditions were considered as provided by domain experts or extracted using existing tools (e.g. decision miner). These approaches also omit the discovery of the hierarchical structure of a lifecycle as supported by GSM and do not consider interactions between artifacts.

Furthermore, the input of existing approaches cannot be directly used to discover GSM models. In case of OCEL logs, the data changes depicting the evolution of objects are not stored which hinders the discovery of GSM data conditions. As for classic XES logs, a processing is required to generate a log for each artifact which may cause convergence and divergence problems [1]. The discovery of the relational model from these logs requires using databases and or domain knowledge. To solve these issues we previously introduced ACEL (Artifact-Centric Event Log) [12], an extension of OCEL which is specific for artifact-centric event data. An ACEL log supports multiple case notions and contains information about artifacts, their evolution (lifecycle) and their relations.

To address the aforementioned limitations, we propose a discovery technique that takes as input an ACEL log and gives as output a GSM model. Taking ACEL as input avoids classic convergence and divergence problems and alleviates the pain of processing, translating and fetching additional external knowledge. The novelty of our proposed technique compared to existing ones is i) its ability to discover stages' data conditions (i.e. guards) by analyzing the data changes of objects' evolution stored in ACEL logs; ii) discovering nested stages based on the idea of hierarchically clustering stages according to the Information Gain [19] obtained by grouping their data conditions and iii) discovering interactions between different artifacts as well as between instances of the same artifact type using data conditions. The approach has been evaluated in terms of feasibility using an ACEL log generated from a blockchain application. We used blockchain logs because they are an immutable trustworthy source of data for process mining. Process mining shows the business process perspective of smart contracts and it has been demonstrated for activity-centric processes [7]. However, to the best of our knowledge, no work used blockchain logs to discover artifact-centric processes.

---

[1] https://xes-standard.org/.

The paper is organized as follows. Section 2, provides some background on GSM and ACEL. The approach is briefly presented in Sect. 3 along with a running example. The approach is detailed in Sect. 4 and 5. Section 6 presents the implementation and evaluation through a case study and a discussion. Section 7 reviews the related work. Finally, Sect. 8 concludes the paper.

2 Preliminaries

In this section we provide an overview of the GSM model and the artifact-centric event log format (ACEL) we consider in this work.

2.1 The Guard-Stage-Milestone Model

Artifact-centric processes revolve around the progression of business entities known as artifacts as they undergo various business operations. Each artifact possesses an information model and a lifecycle. The information model stores data in the form of attributes that capture information about the artifact throughout its existence. On the other hand, the lifecycle represents a "micro process" model that outlines the sequence of operations or tasks that can be performed on the artifact to transition it from one state to another. In addition, artifacts have the ability to interact with one another and establish relations. These relations are represented by nested foreign key attributes, allowing for the establishment of connections between artifacts. GSM is a declarative approach to specifying artifact lifecycles [9]. It represents (i) the lifecycle of an artifact in terms of guards, stages, and milestones, and (ii) the information model in terms of data and state attributes. Stages are groups of tasks (activities) which modify an artifact in order to achieve a certain business goal. A stage with only one task is called an atomic stage. A stage can have multiple guards and milestones. Guards consist of sentries which are comprised of triggering external or internal events and/or conditions on data. Internal events and data conditions may refer to the modeled artifact or other artifacts. External events can come from external services or human actions. Milestones correspond to business-relevant operational objectives and are achieved (or invalidated) based on a sentry. A stage becomes active/open when the sentry of one of its guards becomes true and inactive/closed when the sentry of one of its milestones becomes true. Stages can be nested, i.e., a stage can contain several stages [8]. Figure 1 illustrates a sample GSM model for a blockchain-based application (Sect. 3.1 details this running example).

2.2 The Artifact-Centric Event Log Format

Artifact-Centric Event Log (ACEL) [12] is an enhanced version of the Object-Centric Event Log (OCEL) standard [6] designed for storing event data in artifact-centric business processes. ACEL extends OCEL by supporting the storage of object relations and attribute changes of both objects and relations. In

ACEL, each event contains information about the execution of a business process activity, including the objects and relations modified by that activity. Moreover, ACEL captures attribute-level changes, meaning that the new value of an attribute reflects the specific alteration made. Objects in ACEL represent relevant business entities or artifacts, while relations represent the connections between artifacts, including one-to-one, one-to-many, and many-to-many relationships. Within an ACEL log, events, objects, and relations are uniquely identified and can possess multiple attributes. Certain attributes are mandatory, such as the lifecycle attribute for objects, which indicates their state, and the source and target attributes for relations, which identify the objects involved in the relation. Each object or relation in ACEL is associated with a specific object or relation type, and multiple objects or relations can be associated with a single event [12]. Table 1 provides an excerpt of a sample ACEL log.

3 Approach Overview

3.1 Running Example

Cryptokitties[2] is an Ethereum Dapp[3] where cats are auctioned for sale or breeding purposes. The sale auction procedure can be considered as a GSM stage. A cat is auctioned for sale when its owner triggers the opening of the CreateAuction stage, which creates a new auction in the Created state. Other users can buy the auctioned cat by making bids. When a satisfying bid is made, the CompleteAuction stage is opened which triggers the transfer of the cat to the new owner and the auction becomes in the Successful state. The user who initiated the auction can also cancel it by triggering the CancelAuction stage which puts the auction in the Cancelled state. A user can also obtain a new cat by breeding one of his cats with another cat. After Breeding, the mother and the father are expecting, i.e., the mother is in the Pregnant state and the father is in the FutureFather state. After a prefixed amount of time, called cooldown period, the user can trigger the opening of the Birth stage and the mother gives birth to a new cat which is in the Born state. After the Birth, the mother and the father become in the BecameMother and BecameFather states, respectively.

Figure 1 shows an excerpt of the representation of a cat's and an auction's lifecycles in GSM. Both artifacts, i.e., cat and auction, have data attributes constituting their information model, e.g., tokenId, cooldownPeriod and startingPrice. These attributes also indicate relations between artifacts by referring to other artifacts or other instances of the same artifact, e.g., SiringWithId and KittyId. Artifacts are also characterized by status attributes indicating a stage's or a milestone's status, e.g., Pregnant and Successful, is achieved. Figure 1 also illustrates the possible nesting of stages, it shows two nested stages, Procreation and SaleAuction. The Procreation stage has one guard whose sentry is one data condition (k.'cooldown'≤currentTime) and one

---

[2] https://www.cryptokitties.co/.
[3] A Dapp is a decentralized application running on a blockchain platform.

milestone (BecameMother) whose sentry is an internal event about the cat's milestone (k.'Pregnant'.achieved()). When its guard is true, the Procreation stage is opened and its sub-stages, Breeding and Birth, can be activated when their respective guards are true. For example the sentry of Birth's guard is composed of one external event (k.'giveBirth'.onEvent()), to be sent by a user, and a data condition (k.'Pregnant'). The previous data condition is an internal event but expressed as a data condition because sentries can have only one event. In our previous paper [12], we proposed an approach to generate ACEL logs for blockchain applications. We used it to generate a log for our running example, as shown in Table 1.

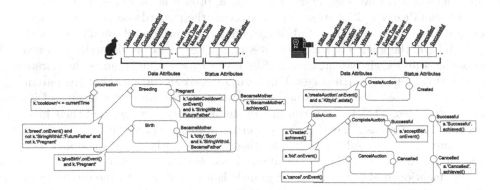

Fig. 1. GSM process model associated with the Cryptokitties example

Table 1. Sample of Cryptokitties ACEL log

EventId	Activity	Timestamp	Attribute		Objects	Relations
			Name	Value		
e1	Breeding	23/10/2021 04:11:51	Resource	0x22D1A..	1960326	r1

ObjectChanges			RelationChanges		
ObjectId	Attribute	NewValue	RelationId	Target	ChangeStatus
1960326	lifecycle	Pregnant	r1	1688830	addedTarget
1960326	CooldownPeriod	11115513			
1688830	lifecycle	FutureFather			
1688830	CooldownPeriod	11115513			

(a) Events

ObjectId	Type	genes
1960326	kitty	5321000..
1688830	kitty	62855942..

(b) Objects

RelationId	Type	Source
r1	siringWith	1960326

(c) Relations

3.2   Discovering GSM Models from ACEL Logs

Discovering a GSM model, similar to Fig. 1, consists of discovering *(i)* the information model of each involved artifact, *(ii)* its different stages and their hierarchical structure, *(iii)* the guard(s) and milestone(s) of each stage, and *(iv)* the interaction between the different artifacts.

Discovering a GSM information model from an ACEL log is simply an extraction process because ACEL stores the artifact relational model. The extraction consists of collecting the attribute names for each artifact. Then, following the relations, foreign keys are added to the information model. Therefore, the required steps can be reduced to discovering stages' guards, their interactions and hierarchy. An overview of our proposed approach is illustrated in Fig. 2.

We can discover GSM stages by discovering their guards because two stages cannot have the same guards. Sub-stages have their own guards, and in addition they inherit the guards of their parent stage. This creates a hierarchy between sub-stages and their parent, e.g., in Fig. 1 the Procreation stage is the parent of the Breeding and Birth stages. Furthermore, we can consider that the parent stage is a cluster of sub-stages and each sub-stage can also be a cluster of its own sub-stages. Therefore, we can model the discovery of stages and their hierarchical structure as a hierarchical clustering problem where similarity is based on common guards. Additionally, the clusters have to be loosely coupled, i.e., the guards of one stage should not allow the activation of another stage.

As mentioned above, discovering guards is a prerequisite to the discovery of stages and their hierarchy. A guard consists of a sentry which contains an event, internal or external, e.g., (k.'Pregnant'.achieved()) and (k.'giveBirth'.onEvent()) in Fig. 1, and data conditions, e.g., (k.'cooldown' $\leq$ currentTime). Since ACEL logs do not contain external events, we only consider internal events for the discovery of guard sentries. Furthermore, the internal events we consider are about achieving milestones, the latter are stored in ACEL as values of the object attribute lifecycle. Therefore, we can discover them by discovering data conditions and since in GSM, internal events can be expressed through data conditions, e.g., in Fig. 1 (k.'Pregnant'), we represent them as such. Thus, the discovery of guard sentries (internal event and data conditions) becomes a problem of discovering data conditions on artifact attributes and their milestones. Milestones of a stage can be some or all milestones of its sub-stages but they can also be new milestones. In the case of an atomic stage we consider that its milestones are those of its task (activity) and the milestones of its parent stage can be independent of the task's milestones. Task independent milestones are not supported by ACEL. In ACEL, an activity (task) is linked to one lifecycle (milestone) change, since it is not GSM specific. Stage specific milestones can be introduced through an optional custom object attribute [12]. However, since we rely on classic ACEL logs we will not introduce stage specific milestones and we will define the milestones of an atomic stage as the milestones of its task.

In GSM, interactions between artifacts can be represented by internal events about achieved milestones of other artifacts. We discover these events through data conditions, as mentioned above.

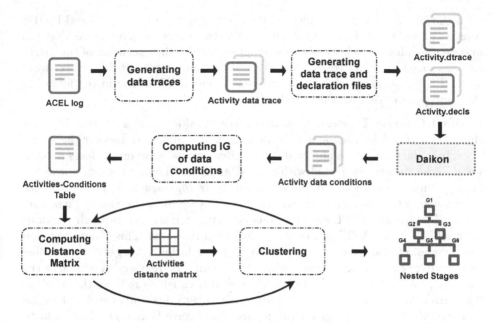

Fig. 2. Overview of the GSM models discovery approach

The following sections detail these different steps: **discover guards and interactions** as data conditions (Sect. 4) and clustering activities to **discover nested stages** (Sect. 5).

4   Discovering Guards and Interactions

As stated in Sect. 3.2, for an ACEL log, discovering guards and interactions amounts to discovering data conditions. Data conditions are properties verified by observed attribute values before the execution of an activity. They are similar to invariants that hold at a certain point in a program [4]. Techniques used to dynamically detect program likely invariants can be applied to data conditions in a process as demonstrated in [10]. We adapted the latter approach to our context as detailed in the following subsections. We first generate data traces to store the values of attributes before an activity. Then we rely on invariant detection to discover the data conditions that hold in these traces.

4.1   Generating Data Traces

In the context of program likely invariants detection, a data trace contains the values of variables at points of interest in a program. In the case of a business process (BP), a data trace contains the values of variables before or after the execution of an activity. Systems like Daikon [4] generate data traces for a program given its source code. For a BP on the other hand, these traces are extracted from the BP event logs. The method for extracting data traces followed by [10] consists of replaying the events of a process instance against a reference model to update the value of each variable and stopping before the execution of the target activity to get one data trace. We propose a method to extract data traces from an ACEL log without relying on a reference model. We define in the following the concepts we used to generate data traces.

Artifact-Centric Process Instances. We consider that a process instance should be defined for each artifact's lifecycle as our aim is to discover the stages of each artifact. Since we aim to discover interactions between artifacts as well, we consider events associated with related artifacts. Thus, we propose the following simple definition: *"A process instance is the sequence of events linked to one artifact instance and its related instances up until the end of their relations"*. Identifying ACEL events of related artifact instances through relations is possible because ACEL stores the evolution of relations. This is done through the changeStatus attribute, associated to the relation's target, whose value 'deletedTarget' indicates the end of a relation. The relation's end marks the end of an interaction between two artifact instances which reduces the possibility of irrelevant data conditions. For example, after a breeding event, a relation breedingWith links a pregnant cat pk and the future father fk. After a birth event this relation is deleted. fk is not allowed to breed again while it is in a breedingWith relation. Thus it is affected by the events of pk, i.e., it is waiting for a birth event to occur for pk. After the end of the relation, fk is no longer affected by the events of pk. For instance, if after the end of the breedingWith relation a breeding event occurs for pk with a third cat this has no consequence for fk. We also consider the case where objects do not "die" and the log contains several iterations of the lifecycle for one artifact instance. Previous approaches reviewed in [5] consider the cases where artifact instances go through their lifecycle only once (i.e.,created→updated... →terminated). We take into consideration the cases where artifact instances can revisit parts of their lifecycle several times or indefinitely, e.g., a cat never dies and can go through breeding endlessly.

Artifact-Centric Activity Specific Traces. Given the previous definition of an artifact-centric process instance and the possibility of revisiting artifacts' lifecycle states, we define an activity specific trace as: *"a sequence of events, from a process instance, delimited by two events related to the activity"*. The events of the activity are of course not included in the activity specific trace since we aim to discover data conditions preceding it.

Data Trace Generation. To generate a data trace from an activity specific trace, we apply a reverse traversal of the events to get data values instead of replaying the events. Starting from the last event we get the first value we encounter for each attribute of each artifact instance. We rename the attributes to improve readability, to quantify the artifact interactions, and shed light on eventual new types of interactions, as detailed in the following.

In GSM, related artifacts are referenced in the information model of the main artifact through a foreign key attribute. However, the name of this attribute might not provide information about the artifact's type. Thereby, we prefix it (in the data trace) by the latter's artifact type. For example in Fig. 1, the k.siringWithId attribute references another cat and to make this explicit we prefix it with its type (i.e., k.kitty.siringWithId). However, in ACEL an artifact does have such foreign key attribute since the relations are stored and thus the notion of foreign key is unnecessary. Therefore we extend the previous prefix with the type of the relation (k.breedingWith.kitty.siring-WithId) to provide business relevant semantics and enhance the readability of the discovered model. This also allows us to indicate the cardinality of interactions[4] and define a new type of interaction which were not considered in previous works, to the best of our knowledge. Indeed, previous works considered only interactions between different artifacts, while we consider interactions between instances of the same artifact which we call reflexive interactions. To illustrate interaction cardinalities and reflexive interactions, we refer again to the Cryptokitties example and specifically to the Birth stage. The birth of a cat relates him to a father and a mother cat. In this case, the born cat is the main artifact and it interacts twice (cardinality) with instances of the same type (reflexive interaction).

4.2 Discovering Data Conditions

For the discovery of data conditions from data traces we use the same implementation of dynamic detection of likely invariants as [10], named Daikon. Along with data traces, Daikon [4] requires declaration files specifying the corresponding program points and variables in a data trace. In these declaration files, we also specify the comparability[5] property of the variables. This property assists Daikon in discovering relevant invariants, i.e., invariants involving only comparable variables, and in our case relevant data conditions. We can infer correlations between variables from the ACEL, e.g., which variables appear frequently together in the ObjectChanges list Table 1a. However this statistical analysis is out of the scope of this paper, we consider that the comparability is provided. Specifically, to discover data conditions using Daikon, we merge the activity specific data traces generated in Sect. 4.1 for each artifact instance in one Daikon data trace file. We then generate for it a declaration file. We use these two files as input to generate invariants for the activity data trace.

The steps, described in Sect. 4.1 and 4.2, to generate data traces and discover data conditions are illustrated in Algorithm 1.

5 Discovering Nested Stages

To discover nested stages we use common data conditions with the same information gain. Information gain ($\mathcal{IG}$) measures how well a feature helps predict

---

[4] Cardinality of interaction is the number of artifact instances of the same type interacting with the main artifact.

[5] A signed integer that indicates to Daikon comparable variables. Two variables with the same value for comparability are considered comparable.

248   L. M. M'Baba et al.

Algorithm 1: Data Conditions discovery

    Data: acelLog $< E, O, R >$, E set of events, O set of objects and R set of relations.
        $OT \leftarrow \emptyset$, set of object types and $A \leftarrow \emptyset$, set of activities.
    Result: DT, a function which associates to each object and activity a set of data traces

1 **Let** *TA be a function whose domain is OT $\forall ot \in OT$,*
    $\exists (a_1, ..., a_n) \in A^n, TA(ot) \leftarrow (a_1, ..., a_n)$.

2 **Let** *OI be a function whose domain is $OT \times A$ $\forall ot, a \in OT, A$,*
    $\exists (o_1, ..., o_n) \in O^n, OI(ot, a) \leftarrow (o_1, ..., o_n)$.

3 **Let** *T be a function whose domain is $OT \times A \times O$ $\forall ot, a, o \in OT, A, O$,*
    $\exists n, m \in \mathbb{N}, T(ot, a, o) \leftarrow (E^n)^m$.

4 **ForEach** *e of E*
5    $a \leftarrow activityName(e)$;
6   **ForEach** *o of objectList(E)*
7       $ot \leftarrow type(o)$;
8   **ForEach** *act of TA(ot)*
9   **If** $a = act$
10   Close last set of T(ot, a, o) ;
11   **else**
12   **If** *last set of T(ot, a, o) closed*
13   Open new set in T(ot, a, o);
14   Add e to last set of T(ot, a, o);
15   **end**
16 **ForEach** *ot of OT*
17   **ForEach** *a of TA(ot)*
18   **ForEach** *o of OI(ot, a)*
19   **ForEach** *set of Reverse(T(ot, a, o))*
20   Open new set in $DT(ot, a)$;
21   **ForEach** *e of Reverse(set)*
22   **ForEach** *ob in objectChangeList(e)*
23   **ForEach** *att in objectAttributes(ob)*
24   **If** $ob = o$
25   **If** *name(att) = 'lifecycle'*
26   Add (ot.'milestone', value(att)) to last set in $DT(ot, a)$;
27   **else**
28   Add (ot.name(att), value(att)) to last set in $DT(ot, a)$;
29   **end**
30   **else**
31   **If** *ob in relation with o and relation not ended*
32   **If** *name(att) = 'lifecycle'*
33   Add (ot.relationName(o,ob).type(ob).'milestone', value(att)) to last set in $DT(ot, a)$;
34   **else**
35   Add (ot.relationName(o,ob).type(ob)name(att), value(att)) to last set in $DT(ot, a)$;
36   **end**
37   **end**
38   Close last set in $DT(ot, a)$;
39 **return** DT

a label. It is based on the entropy which is, in the context of classification in machine learning, the measure of the diversification of the labels in a data set. The lowest entropy is equal to zero and correspond to a pure data set, i.e., all elements have the same label. The highest entropy is equal to one and corresponds to a data set with equal subsets for each label. $\mathcal{IG}$ is inversely proportional to the entropy, i.e., an entropy equal to zero corresponds to an $\mathcal{IG}$ equal to one.

We consider that stages having a common parent will be discriminated equally by this parent's guard from other stages of the artifact's lifecycle. This means that the guard will have the same $\mathcal{IG}$ each time it discriminates one activity of the sub-stages from other stages in the artifact. This is true because we can consider the parent stage as a label and the data condition as a feature. For example in Fig. 1, if we label all activities as `partOfProcreation` or `notPartOfProcreation`, the data condition (k. 'cooldown' $\leq$ currentTime) that best splits the population, i.e., the activities, will be the guard of the `Procreation` stage.

Furthermore, sub-stages share the guard of their parent stage. Thus, discovering nested stages amounts to grouping stages with the same $\mathcal{IG}$ for their common data conditions. These common conditions represent the guard of the parent which can be merged with other stages when their guards overlap. The discovery of nested stages is therefore a hierarchical clustering where similarity is based on common data conditions with the same $\mathcal{IG}$. In the following, we propose a similarity function that we consider for clustering activities (Sect. 5.2) and an approach for hierarchically clustering the stages (Sect. 5.3).

5.1 Limitations of Branching Conditions for Discovering GSM Stages

The authors of [10] use $\mathcal{IG}$ to discover conditions that discriminate between two tasks in a branching point. This is not our case because GSM supports parallelism between stages and activities of a same stage. They also use $\mathcal{IG}$ to simplify the conditions, i.e., they only keep the condition or conjunction of conditions with the highest $\mathcal{IG}$. For example, in the `Breeding` stage (Fig. 1), $if\ IG(!k.\ 'Pregnant') == IG(!k.\ 'Pregnant'\ \&\&\ (k.\ 'cooldown' \leq$ currentTime)), the condition (!k. 'Pregnant'&& k. 'cooldown' $\leq$ current Time) will be discarded according to [10]. Such simplification makes the discovery of the `procreation` stage impossible. Therefore, we do not discard any condition since conditions with the lowest $\mathcal{IG}$ might represent guards for parent stages. Nevertheless, the use of $\mathcal{IG}$ for branching conditions in [10] inspired our approach to detect stages.

5.2 Similarity Between Activities

Similarity is measured through distance, two points of a cluster are similar when they are the closest. We consider that two activities are close when they share common data conditions with the same $\mathcal{IG}$. The closest activities will have the same data conditions with the same $\mathcal{IG}$ and their distance is equal to zero. The furthest apart share no common data conditions or their common data conditions do not have the same $\mathcal{IG}$ and their distance is equal to one. In the following, we define a similarity function to compute the distance between two activities based on their data conditions and their $\mathcal{IG}$.

Definition 1 ($\mathcal{IG}$ of an Activity Condition). *Let $\mathcal{A}$ be the set of an artifact's activities, C the set of these activities' data conditions, $\mathcal{DT}$ the set of all data traces, and $adt\colon \mathcal{A} \longrightarrow \mathcal{DT}$ a mapping associating activities $\in \mathcal{A}$ to their data traces $\in \mathcal{DT}$. The information gain of an activity's condition is defined as:*

$$\forall a \in \mathcal{A}, \forall c \in C, \mathcal{IG}_a(c) = \mathcal{IG}(adt(a), adt(\mathcal{A} \setminus a), c)$$

Definition 2 (Similarity Function). *Let $a, b \in \mathcal{A}, C_a, C_b \subset C, CC_{ab} = \{c | c \in C_a \wedge c \in C_b \wedge \mathcal{IG}_a(c) = \mathcal{IG}_b(c)\}$ the set of common data conditions with the same $\mathcal{IG}$ between two artifact's data conditions a and b. $\forall c_k \in CC_{ab}, k \in \{1 \ldots n\}, n = |CC_{ab}|, \mathcal{IG}(c_k) = \mathcal{IG}_a(c_k) = \mathcal{IG}_b(c_k)$. The distance between a and b is given by:*

$$dist(a, b) = \begin{cases} 1 & |CCab| = 0 \\ 1 - \dfrac{1}{1 + \dfrac{\log \dfrac{|Ca| + |Cb|}{2 \times |CCab|}}{\sum\limits_{k=1}^{n} IG(c_k)}} & |CCab| \neq 0 \end{cases}$$

5.3   Hierarchical Clustering to Discover Nested Stages

We rely on a hierarchical agglomerative clustering [13] with a distance matrix computed using the similarity function *dist* and a different linkage criterion to determine similarity between clusters. As a linkage criterion in our context, we consider that all points, i.e., activities, of one cluster must have the same distance with all the points of the other cluster. We optimize this criterion by measuring the distance between two random activities, one of each cluster, based on the data conditions shared by all activities of each cluster. The merging condition we consider is that the similarity between two clusters is different from one. Indeed, because activity with no data condition in common, or different $\mathcal{IG}$ for their common data condition, cannot be in the same stage.

The clustering starts with the computation of a distance matrix between all activities of an artifact. Then (first iteration), the two closest activities are merged. After this merge, the distance matrix between the rest of the activities and this new cluster is computed using the common data conditions shared by its activities. Next (second iteration), the next two closest activities, or one activity with the previous cluster if their distance is the shortest, are merged. The clustering continues with the re-computation of the distance matrix before each iteration and then merging of clusters until only one cluster or when the distance between all clusters is equal to one (stopping condition). The result is a hierarchical structure indicating the nesting of the stages.

6 Evaluation

In the following we present the implementation and the evaluation of the approach through a case study.

6.1 Implementation

We implemented the approach as several python modules, accessible via https:// gitlab.com/disco5/Gsm/-/tree/main/discovery. The first module takes as input an ACEL log and generates a data trace file for each activity of each artifact. The second module converts this data trace file into the daikon .dtrace format and generates a declaration file in the daikon .decls format for each data trace. It then runs Daikon with the previous files to discover data conditions for each activity. The third module takes as input the data trace and the discovered data conditions of all activities of an artifact and computes for each activity the $\mathcal{IG}$ of data conditions, including their conjunctions. It outputs a table with as header all data conditions and a line for each activity with the $\mathcal{IG}$ of its data conditions. The previous table is the input of the fourth module in charge of the clustering, which first uses the table to run the clustering algorithm and discover the nested stages, then assigns to each stage its guard.

6.2 Case Study

As a case study we chose the blockchain application Cryptokitties and extracted its corresponding ACEL from Ethereum using [12]. The model discovered using our approach is accessible via https://gitlab.com/disco5/Gsm. For the cat artifact, the discovered lifecycle is briefly presented in Table 2 and illustrated in Fig. 3. The lifecycle presents two atomic stages $S1$ and $S2$ containing the activities Birth and Breeding, respectively. The data conditions (K.milestone = Pregnant) and (K.breedingWith.Kitty.milestone = FutureFather) of the Birth stage are a result of the closing of the Breeding stage which indicates that the latter always precedes the Birth stage. The condition ('K.breedingWith.Kitty'.milestone) is an internal event indicating a reflexive interaction with cardinality one, i.e., a cat instance has a relation 'breedingWith' with the main cat instance. For the auction artifact, a sample of the discovered lifecycle is presented in Table 3 and illustrated by Fig. 4. The lifecycle presents one stage $S1$ containing the two atomic stages with the activities CompleteAuction and CancelAuction. The data condition (A.milestone = Created) indicates that an auction needs to be created to be completed or cancel and guards both from occurring to the same auction. Indeed, as indicated in Fig. 1, once an auction is created, it can only be completed or cancelled.

Table 2. Sample of a discovered cat lifecycle.

Stages	Guards
S1 (Birth)	(K.cooldownPeriod < Timestamp and K.milestone == Pregnant and K.breedingWith.Kitty.milestone == FutureFather)
S2 (Breeding)	(K.milestone == Transferred or K.milestone == Sold or K.milestone == BecameMother)

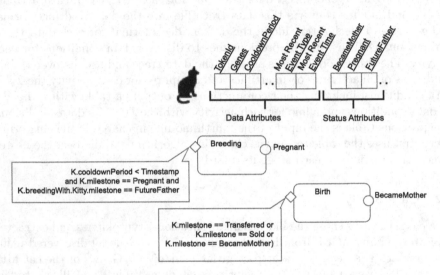

Fig. 3. Discovered GSM model: cat lifecycle

Table 3. Sample of a discovered Auction lifecycle.

Stages	Guards
S1 (CompStaglesleteAuction, CancelAuction)	(A.milestone == Created)

6.3   Evaluation and Discussion

We evaluate in this section our approach in terms of its ability to discover data conditions and interactions as well as the performance of the clustering algorithm.

Guards and Interactions Discovery Evaluation. To evaluate our approach, we refer to the GSM model of Cryptokitties derived from the whitepaper[6] of the application and illustrated in Fig. 1. For the Birth stage, we denote two data conditions (k.'Pregnant' and K.cooldownPeriod < Timestamp) and one external

---

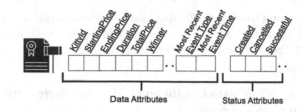

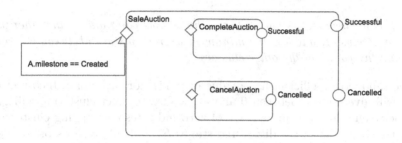

Fig. 4. Discovered GSM model: auction lifecycle

event (k.'giveBirth'.onEvent()). Using our approach, the data conditions were discovered in addition to one more condition (K.breedingWith.Kitty.milestone = FutureFather). This additional condition is the opposite of the condition (not k.'siringWithId'.'FutureFather') of the Breeding stage, thus its discovery is accurate since it differentiates between the two stages. External events were not considered as explained in Sect. 3.2. Regarding the interactions, in Fig. 1 no interactions are shown for the Birth stage but our approach detected a reflexive interaction represented by the attribute K.breedingWith.Kitty.milestone. This shows that the Father's lifecycle affects that of the Mother.

However, the Procreation stage was not discovered since the condition (K.cooldownPeriod < Timestamp) was only discovered for the Birth activity. This is due to the fact that in the extracted log, the attribute 'cooldown' only appears in events related to Breeding and not to Birth. When we examined the source code of Cryptokitties we found that it checked and updated the value of 'cooldown' for both Birth and Breeding activities, but only logged it for Breeding related events. Therefore, a more precise logging mechanism would have allowed us to discover the Procreation stage.

This deduction is valuable for the redesign phase of the DApp and offers appropriate data for conformance checking techniques. Indeed, if the logging was accurate DApp developers would have noticed the need to add more guards before the execution of certain activities.

Furthermore, our approach accurately discovered the SaleAuction stage, as it appears in Fig. 1, with two atomic stages CompleteAuction and CancelAuction. The guards of the atomic stages were not discover as they are solely composed of external events which are out of the scope of this paper.

Nested Stages Discovery Evaluation. We evaluated our hierarchical clustering based approach using the silhouette coefficient (Definition 3), a metric for evaluating the performance of clustering algorithms in terms of clusters' cohesion and separation [15].

Definition 3 (Silhouette Coefficient). *The silhouette coefficient of one sample point in a cluster is given by:*

$$S = \frac{b - a}{max(a, b)}$$

where, a is the average distance between the sample point and all the other points in the same cluster; and b is the minimum average distance between the sample point and the points of the other clusters.

The silhouette coefficient has a value in $[-1, 1]$ for each point. Incorrect clustering will give a score between 0 and -1, while a correct clustering will give a score between 0 and +1 and a score of zero indicates overlapping clusters. The silhouette coefficient of the discovered stages $S1$ and $S2$ gives a score of 1 since each cluster contains only one point and the distance between the two points is 1 because they have no condition in common. Therefore, our algorithm produced dense well separated clusters.

Discussion. The accuracy of the discovered lifecycles is due to our definition of artifact-centric process instance (Sect. 4.1) and also to our use of ACEL logs. Normally convergence and divergence problems arise when events of related artifacts objects are duplicated in an artifact-centric process instance [5]. This did not happen in our case since we only collect data from related events without considering their related activities in the stage discovery. However, in the case of reflexive interactions this problems could still arise. For example the Birth event is linked to three instances of the cat artifact and can be duplicated for all of them. However, since ACEL supports transition relations, i.e., an event can affect an instance without being part of its trace, the event relating to the Birth activity is linked to the mother only and affects the father and the new born cat. One of the limitations of our GSM models discovery approach is the fact that it does not discover stage specific milestones, and hence milestone sentries (post data conditions). It also allows for discovering only one guard per stage.

7   Related Work

Several approaches in the literature have explored the discovery of artifact-centric processes. Most of them focus on the discovery of artifact types, their relations and the lifecycle of each artifact. They use classic discovery techniques to discover the artifact lifecycles [5]. The resulting lifecycles are represented as procedural processes not suited for the declarative nature of GSM. These approaches do not consider data conditions in their discovery and only few of them consider interactions between lifecycles [3,11,17]. Interactions between artifacts are essential to determine behavioral dependencies in an artifact-centric process. Furthermore, to the best of our knowledge, no work considers blockchain logs as a source to discover artifact-centric processes. To the best of our knowledge, only one work attempted to discover GSM models from event logs [18] and they also used classic discovery techniques with a translation step. They discover a petri-net for each lifecycle and then translate it to a GSM model by considering that each transition is a stage. They do not take into account the interactions between different artifacts and consider the data conditions of the petri-net as provided. They also do not discover the hierarchy between stages, i.e., they only consider atomic stages. The different levels of abstraction of operations are thus not discovered. The approach of [17] discovers unbounded synchronization conditions between artifacts in GSM models. These conditions are the number of related artifact instances that need to reach a certain milestone before the stage of the main artifact can be opened. They represent these conditions as part of the data conditions of a guard. However, they do not discover other data conditions nor consider reflexive interactions. In [14], the authors propose to group activities as stages through graph cuts. However they do not discover stages' nesting and rely only on directly follows relations, not data conditions, when discovering stages. This is not applicable with GSM models because two stages can be active at the same time and all their activities will have strong directly follows relations.

8   Conclusion and Future Work

In this paper we presented a technique to discover GSM models from ACEL logs using hierarchical clustering where similarity is determined by common data conditions with the same information gain. We implemented and tested it on Cryptokitties, a blockchain application. The results show that the technique discovers stages according to the data recorded in the log. It also discovers interactions between artifacts, including reflexive interactions. Future work will be focused on addressing limitations discussed in Sect. ??. We will explore the use of post conditions in the discovery of nested stages. We will also work on discovering several guards per stage using disjunctive data conditions. Furthermore, we will investigate the refining of the clustering by setting a threshold to IG when computing the distance. We are also planning a larger study to further evaluate our approach using more case studies with more complex processes and richer larger logs. We will also apply our approach to data source other than blockchain.

References

1. Aalst, W.M.P.: Object-centric process mining: dealing with divergence and convergence in event data. In: Ölveczky, P.C., Salaün, G. (eds.) SEFM 2019. LNCS, vol. 11724, pp. 3–25. Springer, Cham (2019). https://doi.org/10.1007/978-3-030-30446-1_1

2. Berti, A., van der Aalst, W.M.P.: Extracting multiple viewpoint models from relational databases. CoRR abs/2001.02562 (2020)
3. van Eck, M.L., Sidorova, N., van der Aalst, W.M.P.: Guided interaction exploration in artifact-centric process models. In: IEEE CBI, Thessaloniki, Greece, 24–27 July, pp. 109–118. IEEE Computer Society (2017)
4. Ernst, M.D., Perkins, J.H., Guo, P.J., McCamant, S., et al.: The daikon system for dynamic detection of likely invariants. Sci. Comput. Program. **69**, 35–45 (2007)
5. Fahland, D.: Artifact-centric process mining. In: Encyclopedia of Big Data Technologies (2019)
6. Ghahfarokhi, A.F., Park, G., Berti, A., van der Aalst, W.M.P.: OCEL: a standard for object-centric event logs. In: Bellatreche, L., et al. (eds.) ADBIS 2021. CCIS, vol. 1450, pp. 169–175. Springer, Cham (2021). https://doi.org/10.1007/978-3-030-85082-1_16
7. Hobeck, R., Klinkmüller, C., Bandara, H.M.N.D., Weber, I., van der Aalst, W.M.P.: Process mining on blockchain data: a case study of augur. In: Polyvyanyy, A., Wynn, M.T., Van Looy, A., Reichert, M. (eds.) BPM 2021. LNCS, vol. 12875, pp. 306–323. Springer, Cham (2021). https://doi.org/10.1007/978-3-030-85469-0_20
8. Hull, R., et al.: Introducing the guard-stage-milestone approach for specifying business entity lifecycles. In: Bravetti, M., Bultan, T. (eds.) WS-FM 2010. LNCS, vol. 6551, pp. 1–24. Springer, Heidelberg (2011). https://doi.org/10.1007/978-3-642-19589-1_1
9. Hull, R., Damaggio, E., Masellis, R.D., Fournier, F., et al.: Business artifacts with guard-stage-milestone lifecycles: managing artifact interactions with conditions and events. In: 5th ACM on DEBS, New York, NY, USA, 11–15 July, pp. 51–62 (2011)
10. de Leoni, M., Dumas, M., García-Bañuelos, L.: Discovering branching conditions from business process execution logs. In: Cortellessa, V., Varró, D. (eds.) FASE 2013. LNCS, vol. 7793, pp. 114–129. Springer, Heidelberg (2013). https://doi.org/10.1007/978-3-642-37057-1_9
11. Lu, X., Nagelkerke, M., van de Wiel, D., Fahland, D.: Discovering interacting artifacts from ERP systems. IEEE Trans. Serv. Comput. **8**, 861–873 (2015)
12. Moctar M'Baba, L., Assy, N., Sellami, M., Gaaloul, W., Nanne, M.F.: Extracting artifact-centric event logs from blockchain applications. In: IEEE ICSC, SCC, Barcelona, Spain, 10–16 July, pp. 274–283. IEEE (2022)
13. Murtagh, F.: A survey of recent advances in hierarchical clustering algorithms. Comput. J. **26**, 354–359 (1983)
14. Nguyen, H., Dumas, M., ter Hofstede, A.H.M., Rosa, M.L., et al.: Stage-based discovery of business process models from event logs. Inf. Syst. **84**, 214–237 (2019)
15. Palacio-Niño, J., Berzal, F.: Evaluation metrics for unsupervised learning algorithms. CoRR abs/1905.05667 (2019)
16. Popova, V., Dumas, M.: From Petri nets to guard-stage-milestone models. In: La Rosa, M., Soffer, P. (eds.) BPM 2012. LNBIP, vol. 132, pp. 340–351. Springer, Heidelberg (2013). https://doi.org/10.1007/978-3-642-36285-9_38
17. Popova, V., Dumas, M.: Discovering unbounded synchronization conditions in artifact-centric process models. In: Lohmann, N., Song, M., Wohed, P. (eds.) BPM 2013. LNBIP, vol. 171, pp. 28–40. Springer, Cham (2014). https://doi.org/10.1007/978-3-319-06257-0_3
18. Popova, V., Fahland, D., Dumas, M.: Artifact lifecycle discovery. CoRR abs/1303.2554 (2013)
19. Quinlan, J.R.: Induction of decision trees. Mach. Learn. **1**, 81–106 (1986)

Discovery of Workflow Patterns - A Comparison of Process Discovery Algorithms

Kerstin Andree[1]($\boxtimes$), Mai Hoang[2], Felix Dannenberg[2], Ingo Weber[1], and Luise Pufahl[1] (ORCID)

[1] Technical University of Munich, School of Computation, Information and Technology, Heilbronn, Germany
{Kerstin.Andree,Ingo.Weber,Luise.Pufahl}@tum.de
[2] Technische Universität Berlin, Berlin, Germany
felixd@win.tu-berlin.de

Abstract. Process mining provides a set of techniques and algorithms to analyze, support, and improve business processes based on process execution data. Process discovery aims at deducing a representative process model of real-world execution. So far, process discovery algorithms have been mainly compared regarding their output quality but not yet with regard to their functional capabilities. The well-established workflow control flow patterns imperatively describe process behavior, originally used to compare modeling languages, but to date, not to compare discovery algorithms. In this work, we analyze a representative set of process discovery algorithms with regard to their coverage of 23 control flow patterns. For this purpose, we implemented each workflow pattern as an executable colored Petri net, simulated it, and ran various discovery algorithms on the obtained event log. A comparison of the results shows that the discovery algorithms mainly cover basic control flow patterns and iterative structures, while multi-instance, state-base, and cancellation patterns are only partially covered.

Keywords: Process Mining · Discovery Algorithms · Workflow Patterns

1 Introduction

Process mining is a data-driven approach that aims to extract insights and knowledge from event logs, enabling organizations to understand, analyze, and improve their business processes [26, Ch. 2]. One of its main operations is process discovery [26, Ch. 6], which offers insights into the real-world execution of business processes, e.g., the analysis of how students perform their studies [17]. Thus, several process discovery algorithms [7] have been introduced to automatically identify and create process models based on process execution data in the form of event logs. They provide a representation of how business processes are

M. Sellami et al. (Eds.): CoopIS 2023, LNCS 14353, pp. 257–274, 2024.
https://doi.org/10.1007/978-3-031-46846-9_14

executed within an organization that can be used for analysis, simulation, and compliance checking [26, Ch. 6].

So far, process discovery techniques have been compared regarding their output quality, including accuracy, complexity, and soundness of the resulting process models [7, 10]. However, a structured comparison regarding their functional capabilities, i.e., logic and semantics of business process models, is missing. Originally, the workflow patterns [4] were developed as a conceptual basis to assess the relative strengths and weaknesses of process modeling approaches and business process execution tools in five dimensions: control flow, data, resources, exception handling, and imperfection. Based on the control flow patterns [22], we set up an experimental study to compare and analyze the functional capabilities of a set of process discovery algorithms. This best reflects the focus of process discovery, namely to discover activities and their control flow relations. For each pattern, we modeled one colored Petri Net [18] in CPN Tools [1]. Simulating the model generates an event log, which serves as an input for the set of selected process discovery algorithms. The algorithms' output is then compared with the event log and original workflow model. With this study, we make the following contributions:

- An experimental comparison of discovery algorithms with regards to their functional capabilities;
- 23 implemented workflow patterns and their event logs;
- The state-of-the-art coverage of workflow patterns; and
- A discussion of future research options and improvement avenues for discovery algorithms.

In the remainder of this paper, we will first introduce related work in Sect. 2. The methodology of the coverage analysis is explained in Sect. 3 and its results are presented in Sect. 4. Section 5 discusses the results in the context of the current approaches for discovery algorithm improvement and addresses the limitations of this work. Finally, Sect. 6 concludes.

2   Related Work

The comparison of discovery algorithms is essential as it supports selecting and evaluating discovery techniques to gain valuable insights into process data. Thus, literature already compares different process discovery algorithms [7, 13]. Augusto et al. [7] present a benchmark of 35 existing process discovery algorithms. They focus on the four quality attributes generalization, precision, complexity, replay fitness, and soundness. They also compare basic semantic constructs, such as XOR, OR, AND, and loops. In contrast, van Dongen et al. [13] provide a comparison based on completeness, support of control-flow constructs, abstraction, and tendency to over- and underfitting. However, both approaches do not consider all control-flow patterns.

In 1998, Agrawal et al. [5] presented one of the first approaches and ideas to mine process models from workflow logs. Their research highlights the importance of applying process mining techniques in the context of workflow patterns in order to get better access to the workflow system. Based on this motivation, the Workflow Miner was developed [5,14,15] that can discover workflow patterns using algorithmic and statistical analysis techniques. However, this miner has only been analyzed for the basic control-flow patterns such as Sequence, Parallel Split, and Exclusive Choice.

Furthermore, the importance of workflow patterns is addressed by Cardoso [11]. He introduces a new approach to workflow analysis and evaluation of workflow models by presenting metrics and mechanisms that define the complexity of control-flow patterns to get an indication of the overall system complexity.

Related work shows that workflow patterns are an important tool to better understand and discover processes. However, discovery algorithms have not yet been compared on the basis of the complete set of control flow patterns, which is why this type of coverage analysis is the subject of this paper.

3   Research Method

We perform an experimental coverage analysis to compare the process discovery algorithms based on the workflow patterns. Each pattern is modeled and simulated so that we can then execute the selected discovery techniques on it. This section describes the research method of this work: First, the selection of workflow patterns and discovery algorithms is explained and justified. Then, our experimental setup is explained in detail.

3.1   Selection of Workflow Patterns

The workflow control flow patterns were defined to specify fundamental business process behavior [4] imperatively. Originally, 20 control flow patterns were formally described as a colored Petri net (CPN) [18], but the set was extended by Russell et al. [22] to 42 patterns in 2006. This paper's main focus is the original 20 workflow control flow patterns and the Structured Loop, the Recursion, and the Explicit Termination from the extended set. In total, we selected 23 control-flow patterns for our analysis. They are listed in Table 2. The patterns are grouped into seven categories, briefly revisited in this section. A detailed description of the patterns is provided in [4,22].

Basic Control-Flow Patterns are considered the most essential ones being observed in various business processes: Sequence, Parallel Split, Synchronization, Exclusive Choice, and Simple Merge. We include all of them in the analysis.

Advanced Branching and Synchronization Patterns represent more complex branching and merging behavior, including the patterns Multi-Choice and Structured Synchronizing Merge (OR split/join), which can often be observed in real-world processes as well. Many of these patterns are already challenging to discover. For example, distinguishing a Structured Discriminator from the Simple Merge is quite challenging from a simple event log. Both merge multiple incoming branches into a subsequent branch once an incoming branch completes. The minor difference is that activities before a discriminator can happen without triggering it again. In contrast, completing activities before a `Simple Merge` always triggers the subsequent branch. Thus, we omit the majority of the extended patterns from [22] in our analysis but include: `Multi-Choice`, `Multi-Merge`, `Structured Synchronizing Merge`, and the `Structured Discriminator`.

Iteration Patterns include patterns on loops and repeating behavior. As loops are supported by several process discovery algorithms [7], we include the `Structured Loop` and `Recursion`.

Termination Patterns deal with the completion of workflow instances. A standard assumption of process discovery algorithms is that instances end after the last event is present in each log trace. Hence, `Implicit Termination` is inherently supported. Furthermore, we also include the `Explicit Termination` pattern due to its relevance for business analysts. Especially for business processes, including parallel threads, this pattern allows for an abrupt termination in case of reaching a specific process state.

Multiple Instance Patterns covers the occurrence of multiple activity instances. Distinguishing multi-instance from iterative behavior is challenging, which is why we decided to include the four basic multi-instance patterns without considering the extended patterns such as `Static Partial Join for Multiple Instances`.

State-based Patterns consider the state of a process instance, which is often defined based on its associated data, such as the case data or the output data of previous tasks. Thus, discovery algorithms need to consider data from the cases and events. In this work, we focus on the basic state-based patterns, e.g., `Deferred Choice` and `Milestone`, and omit extended ones such as the `Critical Section` pattern. Finally, we select the patterns `Cancel Task` and `Cancel Case` from the group of *Cancellation Patterns*.

3.2   Selection of Process Discovery Algorithms

The benchmark paper of Augusto et al. [7] provides a comprehensive overview of existing process discovery algorithms based on structured literature analysis. For this work, we selected seven out of the presented 35 algorithms, namely the α-Miner [16], Inductive Miner [20], Evolutionary Tree Miner (ETM) [10], Fodina Miner [9], Split Miner [28], Hybrid Integer Linear Programming (HILP) Miner [30], and the BPMN Miner [12]. Details on the selected miners can be found in the referenced research works. The selection offers a wide range of different approaches and covers several modeling languages such as Petri nets, process trees, causal nets, and BPMN each being transferrable to Petri nets to warrant comparability to the implemented workflow patterns. Additionally, these discovery algorithms are supported by the process mining framework ProM, its plugins, or Java applications and are thus publicly accessible.

We want to highlight here that `Simple Merge` and the `Multi-Merge` are often similarly represented by an XOR gateway in process models. However, a relevant difference exists between them: whereas the `Simple Merge` assumes that only one incoming path of multiple ones can be activated, the `Multi-Merge` can also be triggered by multiple incoming paths resulting in multiple process threads running independently. In most process modeling notations, particularly Petri Nets and BPMN, this implies that, in the general case, proper termination cannot be guaranteed following a `Multi-Merge` because it becomes unclear how many tokens result from it. Hence, soundness is generally not given, and, thus, a `Multi-Merge` cannot be discovered by algorithms that guarantee sound outputs.

3.3 Approach

The goal of this work is an analysis of state-of-the-art discovery algorithms regarding their coverage of workflow patterns. For this purpose, (1) each selected workflow pattern was implemented as an executable colored Petri net (CPN) to (2) generate an event log by simulation (cf. Fig. 1). Based on this generated data, (3) different discovery algorithms were executed, and their outputs were compared with the modeled workflow patterns to evaluate the coverage.

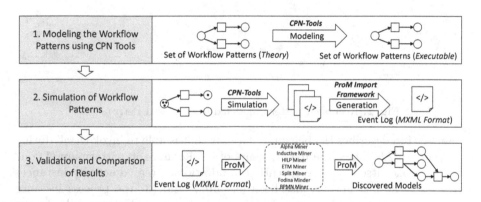

Fig. 1. Approach

To implement the workflow patterns as CPNs and to generate an event log, we use *CPN Tools*[1] (v.4.0.1), a publicly available software tool for editing, simulating, and analyzing (colored) Petri nets. We use *ProM Import Framework*[2] (v.7.0) to merge and convert the simulated event log data of a workflow pattern into the MXML format to be used as an input for process mining tools (e.g., ProM). For process discovery, we use the framework *ProM*[3] (v.6.12). Each of the selected discovery algorithms presented above is supported by ProM so that we

---

[1] https://cpntools.org/.
[2] http://www.promtools.org/promimport/.
[3] https://promtools.org/prom-6-12/.

can use the framework to run different discovery techniques. This section explains each of these steps. All of the implemented Petri nets, the simulated event logs, and the outputs of each discovery algorithm are published via figshare[4].

Modeling. To generate event log data in order to run several discovery algorithms, we implemented each control-flow pattern as a colored Petri net (CPN) using CPN Tools [1]. Thus, we can distinguish different cases, and each workflow pattern is represented by exactly one executable CPN, resulting in 23 uniquely identifiable CPN models. In the following, we exemplify the modeling of the patterns on the `Recursion` shown in Fig. 2. Afterward, we describe the necessary elements of the CPN model to simulate and log the pattern execution.

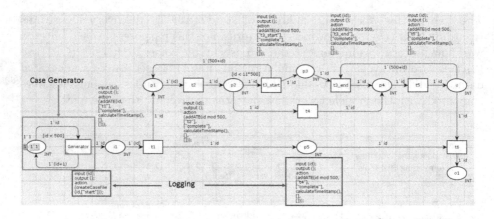

Fig. 2. Recursion pattern modeled as a colored Petri net

`Recursion` describes the behavior of a task that is able to invoke itself during its execution [22]. Thus, the requirements of the `Recursion` pattern are (1) one activity invokes itself, (2) the execution of additional created activity instances starts after the last activity has been executed, and (3) the process instance terminates only after all activity instances are terminated successfully. In the CPN shown in Fig. 2, transition *t3* can invoke itself. As soon as *t4* and *t5* are executed once, the process instance starts to continue with all created instances of *t3*. To ensure proper termination, each child of *t3* has its own id so that *t6* is only enabled when the initial instance of *t3* has terminated. Note that *t6* is not part of the execution sequence we want to log.

In general, we strictly followed the described behavior of the patterns given by [22]. For some patterns, we enriched the behavior to include several cases of the pattern. For instance, we included a skipping and a redoing option to implement the `Cancel Task` pattern to have different variants of the canceling behavior. However, we restricted the cancellation of a task before its execution to at most once to avoid loop behavior.

---

[4] https://figshare.com/s/40a65e1fdab01c58e3d1.

Additionally, we modeled the external behavior needed for the `Deferred Choice` pattern as a separate transition that is only enabled when the process waits for an external event. This transition then generates a random integer between 1 and 10. Depending on the number (even or odd), one of two transitions is enabled, representing external events. We changed the labeling accordingly to differentiate between activity and event transitions.

Simulation. When simulating process models, multiple instances of the model are executed, and their activities are logged as traces in the event log. To ensure representative event log data for each pattern, we run 500 process instances per CPN. An ID generator within each CPN increments the case ID and generates tokens accordingly (see Fig. 2). CPN Tools are used for logging the execution of each process instance. As the logging output of CPN Tools is incompatible with ProM, we apply the approach of Alves de Medeiros and Günther [6] to create S-MXML logs by enriching the CPN nets with ML functions on the transitions that represent process activities of the workflow pattern (cf. blue boxes in Fig. 2). The ProM Import Framework bundles the output log files into a single MXML file containing 500 cases for each workflow pattern. Note that not all transitions of the CPN are logged, only the ones that are process activities. For example, transition *t6* in the CPN shown in Fig. 2 is not logged as it is a helper transition and ensures process termination without being part of it.

Validation. The simulated event logs are used as input for each selected discovery algorithm. We use ProM 6.12 to run the algorithms because of its large pool of process discovery algorithms and compatibility with external plugins.

A general setup and configuration of input parameters are needed to run discovery algorithms. Except for the Split Miner and the BPMN Miner, which are standalone Java applications, and the Fodina Miner, which must be included manually into ProM, all other algorithms can be found and executed via the process mining tool. Table 1 shows an overview of the used plugins for the selected algorithms and the configurations, respectively.

The discovered process models are compared as Petri nets to ensure better comparability with the modeled workflow patterns. However, not all algorithms discover a Petri net. For example, the Split Miner and BPMN Miner output BPMN process models, the ETM Process Trees outputs a Process Tree, and the Fodina Miner outputs a Causal Net. Therefore, the converters in ProM are used accordingly.

For each pattern and algorithm, we evaluate whether there is full coverage, i.e., the pattern has been completely discovered, partial coverage, i.e., the pattern is only covered under certain conditions or no coverage. Figure 3 shows two discovered process models of the `Recursion` pattern. We observe that the process model shown in Fig. 3a represents the pattern partially because the information about how many instances of *t3* are needed to continue in execution is not transferred to the last gateway. The Fodina Miner, however, is not able to detect the pattern. The requirement that the execution of additional created activity

Table 1. Overview of the used process discovery plugins

Algorithm	Plugin	In ProM	Configuration
α	*Alpha Miner*	yes	α++ Miner
HILP	*ILP-Based Process Discovery*	yes	Basic algorithm
Inductive	*Mine Petri Net with Inductive Miner*	yes	Inductive Miner - infrequent, noise threshold 0.2
ETM	*Mine Configured Process Tree with ETMc*	yes	Default settings kept, number of generations set to 100
	Convert Process Tree to Petri net (by Leemans)	yes	
Fodina	*Mine Causal net with Fodina*	yes	external dependencies required [8]
	Convert Causal Net to Reduced Petri Net	yes	
Split	*Split Miner [2]*	no	parallelism threshold = 0.1, percentile for frequency threshold = 0.4, boolean flag = false
	Convert BPMN diagram to Petri net	yes	default settings
BPMN	*BPMN Miner [25]*	no	Heuristic Miner (hm), pull-up rule flag p, force structuring flag f
	Convert BPMN diagram to Petri net	yes	default settings

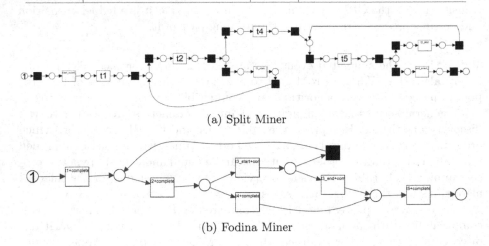

(a) Split Miner

(b) Fodina Miner

Fig. 3. Outputs of two discovery algorithms for Recursion pattern

instances starts after the last activity has been executed is not true for the output process model. Moreover, completing several instances of *t3* is impossible.

4   Results

This section presents the coverage analysis results summarized in Table 2. The table gives an overview of the coverage of 23 control-flow patterns by seven discovery algorithms. We denote the successful coverage of a workflow pattern by a checkmark (✓). A cross (×) indicates a failed coverage, whereas a circle (○) indicates the case that the algorithm only partially discovered the pattern.

As shown in Table 2, all discovery algorithms have successfully discovered all the basic control-flow patterns except the Simple Merge. Advanced branching and synchronization patterns are only partially covered by the Inductive Miner, the ETM Miner, the Split Miner, and the BPMN Miner.

Table 2. Results of workflow patterns coverage by discovery algorithms

Discovery Algorithm	α++	HILP[a]	Inductive	ETM[b]	Fodina	Split	BPMN
Output	PN[c]	PN[c]	PN[c]	PT[d]	CN[e]	BPMN	BPMN
Year of Release	2004	2017	2013	2014	2017	2017	2016
Basic Control-Flow							
Sequence	✓	✓	✓	✓	✓	✓	✓
Parallel Split	✓	✓	✓	✓	✓	✓	✓
Synchronization	✓	✓	✓	✓	✓	✓	✓
Exclusive Choice	✓	✓	✓	✓	✓	✓	✓
Simple Merge	○	✓	✓	✓	○	○	○
Advanced Branching + Sync.							
Multi-Merge	○	×	×	×	○	○	○
Multi-Choice	×	×	✓	✓	×	✓	✓
Structured Sync. Merge	×	×	✓	×	×	×	✓
Structured Discriminator	×	×	×	×	×	×	×
Iteration							
Arbitrary Cycles	×	✓	×	×	✓	✓	✓
Structured Loop	○	✓	✓	×	✓	✓	✓
Recursion	×	○	×	×	×	○	○
Termination							
Implicit Termination	✓	✓	✓	✓	○	○	✓
Explicit Termination	×	×	×	×	✓	×	×
Multiple Instances							
without Synchronization	×	×	×	×	×	×	×
with a Priori Design-Time	○	○	○	✓	○	○	×
with a Priori Run-Time	×	×	○	○	○	○	○
without a Priori Run-Time	✓	✓	✓	✓	✓	✓	✓
State-Based Patterns							
Deferred Choice	○	○	○	○	×	○	○
Interleaved Parallel Routing	×	×	×	×	×	×	✓
Milestone (deadline)	×	×	×	×	×	×	✓
Cancellation							
Cancel Task	×	×	×	×	✓	×	✓
Cancel Case	×	✓	×	×	×	○	✓

[a] Hybrid Integer Linear Programming
[b] Evolutionary Tree Miner
[c] Petri Net
[d] Process Tree
[e] Causal Nets

We observe a strong coverage for iterative patterns. Implicit Termination is covered by almost all discovery algorithms whereas Explicit Termination is only covered by the Fodina Miner. A low coverage also applies to multiple instances, state-based, and cancellation patterns. Complex workflow patterns such as Cancel Task are only covered by the Split Miner and the Fodina Miner. In the following, we present the results for each process discovery algorithm.

4.1   α-Miner

The α-Miner is one of the first process model discovery algorithms and, therefore, a pioneer in this area of research. Based on the observed directly-follows relations in an event log, it detects basic ordering relations, i.e., the alpha relations, between the events, such as parallelism and exclusiveness. This behavior can also be discovered in our coverage analysis. The algorithm covers all basic control-flow patterns. However, because the α-Miner cannot identify sound workflow nets, it cannot differentiate between a Simple Merge (only one out of multiple incoming paths can be triggered) and a Multi-Merge (multiple incoming paths can be triggered). Advanced branching and synchronization patterns were not discovered correctly since no ordering relations for these were defined for the algorithm to detect them.

Furthermore, we observe that the algorithm did not perform well on the Recursion pattern, the state-based, the multiple instance patterns (except for the Multiple Instance Without a Priori Run-Time Knowledge pattern), and the cancellation patterns. Multiple Instances with a priori Design-Time Knowledge is partially covered. The algorithm discovers the multiple instance activity but neglects the number of instances defined at design time. The discovered Petri net allows for an arbitrary number of instances at run-time. We explain these results with the fact that these patterns depend on the processing of further information of the event logs in addition to the directly-follows relations, and, thus, the α-algorithm cannot detect any of these patterns.

Deferred Choice is only partially covered by the α-Miner. The pattern contains a decision from an external source that could not be identified. Instead, simple exclusive choice behavior is discovered. Arbitrary Cycles is not discovered correctly. The α++ Miner cannot identify the multiple entry points of the arbitrary loop and fails in detecting the correct execution sequences. In contrast, the Structured Loop is partially discovered. The entry and exit points of the structured loop are correctly identified, but the conditional entry, as stated in the workflow pattern, is not represented in the discovered model.

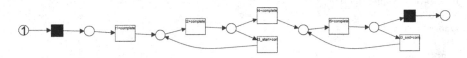

Fig. 4. Discovered process model by the HILP Miner of the Recursion pattern

4.2   Hybrid Integer Linear Programming (HILP) Miner

Similar to the α-Miner, the HILP-Miner [30] produces relaxed sound Petri nets from event logs as input. An optimization technique is used to set the places for a process model. The results show that the HILP-Miner is able to identify all basic control-flow patterns. However, `Multi-Merge` is not covered since relaxed soundness implies proper termination. Other advanced branching and synchronization patterns are also not covered. We explain this observation because the HILP-Miner focuses on optimizing the distinction between exclusive and parallel behavior. Moreover, the discovery technique does not cover all multiple instances or state-based patterns. Similar to the α-Miner, only the `Multiple Instance Without a Priori Run-Time Knowledge` pattern is fully discovered, whereas the `Multiple Instances with a Priori Design-Time Knowledge` pattern was only partially discovered because of missing information regarding the number of instances. Regarding more complex patterns, the `Cancel Case` pattern is covered. The discovered model for `Recursion` correctly represents the workflow pattern but does not specify conditions for XOR splits, as shown in Fig. 4. Having the discovered model as a basis, it is unclear when and how many invoked activity instances are executed. Therefore, we indicate the discovery as partial.

From the state-based patterns, the HILP Miner only partially discovers the `Deferred Choice` pattern. Similar to the alpha Miner, the algorithm could not identify that the decision was made externally. Nevertheless, the HILP-Miner can detect `Structured Loops` and `Arbitraty Cycles`.

4.3   Inductive Miner

The Inductive Miner [20] focuses on the soundness, fitness, and rediscoverability of the discovered process models. It outputs a Petri net.

All basic control-flow patterns and the `Structured Loop` pattern are covered. The algorithm works with a divide-and-conquer approach with the directly-follows relation used for partitioning. Exclusive choice, sequence, concurrent, and looping relation are fundamental to this approach, which is why the algorithm performs well for this group of patterns. However, `Arbitrary Cycles` could not be identified because of the nature of block-structured process models. Cycles with multiple entry points cannot be localized.

Advanced branching and synchronization patterns are partly discovered. There is no dedicated split for the `Multi-Choice` and `Structured Synchronizing Merge` patterns, but process trees themselves display these patterns with a conjunction of XOR and AND splits and joins.

The `Multi-Merge` pattern is not discovered. This is due to the fact that the resulting process model would not be sound anymore, which is not allowed by the algorithm. `Structured Discriminator` could also not be detected because it falls under infrequent behavior.

Similar to the HILP and α-Miner, the Inductive Miner can also detect the `Multiple Instance Without a Priori Run-Time Knowledge` pattern and is able to partially identify the two multiple instances patterns `with a priori Design-Time Knowledge` and `with a priori Run-Time`, but fails in discovering state-based and cancellation patterns. The `Deferred Choice` is partially covered.

4.4 Evolutionary Tree Miner (ETM)

The ETM algorithm [10] outputs process trees. This discovery method focuses on emphasizing certain quality dimensions while using process trees ensures the soundness of the resulting models.

The algorithm's coverage is similar to the Inductive Miner. All basic control-flow patterns and the Multi-Choice pattern could be identified. However, in contrast to the inductive miner, the Structured Synchronizing Merge and the Strucutured Loop patterns were not discovered by the algorithm. In comparison to the other algorithms, it cannot discover any of the iteration patterns.

The Evolutionary Tree Miner is able to (partially) detect three of the multiple instance patterns but has almost no coverage of the state-based, recursion, or cancellation patterns. Compared to other algorithms, the ETM is able to correctly identify the number of instances for the Multiple Instances with a Priori Design-Time Knowledge. Instead of a loop, the algorithm detects the correct number of instances that are put in sequence. However, it fails in detecting the number of instances for the Multiple Instances with a Priori Run-Time Knowledge pattern. The Deferred Choice pattern is partially covered for the same reason as explained for the previous algorithms. Cancellation patterns are not covered because the discovered Petri nets still allow to execute transitions, although the case was canceled.

Moreover, the ETM does not consider any additional information in the event logs and only tries to build process trees with each activity and does not, e.g., consider multiple instances of activities.

4.5 Fodina Miner

The Fodina Miner [8] first converts event logs to task logs, with additional information used to mine duplicates of activities. It discovers relationships using a dependency graph, starting with length-one and length-two loops and ending with split and join semantics. It has a dedicated step for long-distance dependencies, unlike other discovery algorithms. The output is causal nets.

As shown in Table 2, the results reflect the algorithm's functionalities. The Miner is able to identify all basic control-flow patterns, Arbitrary Loop, and Structured Loop. Since the soundness of the output model is not guaranteed, the algorithm cannot differentiate between Simple Merge and Multi-Merge. All other advanced branching and synchronization patterns are not covered. Nonetheless, iteration patterns except the Recursion pattern are discovered.

Surprisingly, the Fodina Miner cannot discover Implicit Termination. Although there are no duplicates of tasks $t2$ and $t4$ in the simulated event log, the algorithm identifies that these tasks are executed twice for each case (Fig. 5). Similar behavior can be observed for the Cancel Case pattern; looping behavior is identified, which is not recorded in the event log. Regarding state-based patterns, Fodina cannot identify any of them but performs well on the multiple instances patterns, with the two patterns dealing with a priori knowledge being partially covered. The discovered model does not indicate the number of instances, allowing more activity instances to be instantiated than initially defined.

Fig. 5. Discovered process model by the Fodina Miner for Implicit Termination pattern

4.6 Split Miner

The Split Miner [2] discovers uses also directly-follows relations, similar to the α-Miner, the Inductive Miner, and the Fodina Miner. After some filtering, different discovery steps will be applied to the directly-follows graph, leading to a BPMN model. It is able to identify all basic control-flow patterns. The discovery of the Simple Merge pattern, however, is only covered for acyclic processes because of soundness. For cyclic processes, the algorithm fails in differentiating between Simple Merge and Multi-Merge. Furthermore, the Split Miner is able to detect the Multi-Choice but fails in identifying the Structured Synchronizing Merge pattern and the Structured Discriminator.

Looping behavior such as the Arbitrary Cycles and Structured Loop patterns are covered by the discovery technique, whereas the Recursion pattern is only partially covered due to missing gateway conditions. Regarding multiple instances patterns, the Split Miner does not cover the pattern Multiple Instances without Synchronization. The asynchronous and independent behavior of the multiple activity instances to other parallel branches is not captured in the model. Patterns dealing with a priori knowledge are partially covered because the information on the number of instances was not discovered. The general behavior, however, is correct, which is why the algorithm performs well on the pattern dealing without a priori run-time knowledge.

Moreover, the Split Miner partially covers the Deferred Choice pattern and the Cancel Case pattern. The Deferred Choice pattern cannot be identified completely because external events are not distinguished from lifecycle events of activities. The quality of the Cancel Case depends on the observation frequency of canceling at different activities in a log. For example, the Cancel Case would have been correctly identified (cf. Fig. 6, blue markings indicate correct cancellation behavior) but due to low occurrences of cancellation after *t3*, the Split Miner abstracts from the process data and does not include the cancellation option after *t3* in the output model as marked in red.

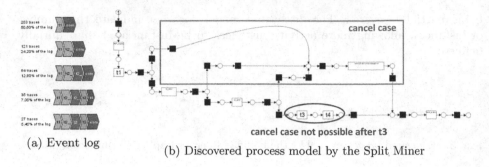

(a) Event log

(b) Discovered process model by the Split Miner

Fig. 6. Event log and discovered model of the Cancel Case pattern

4.7 BPMN Miner

The BPMN Miner [25] does not provide a flat process model, and therefore, it can detect many more patterns than most other discovery algorithms. Functionality-wise, the BPMN Miner starts by extracting a hierarchy from the event logs based on instance identifiers. Afterward, each subprocess will be processed independently with different algorithms to identify different event types. To detect advanced patterns, the event logs must include specific information in a certain *key* format and the information on the event types. Thus, the BPMN miner introduces stronger assumptions about the input log than the other miners.

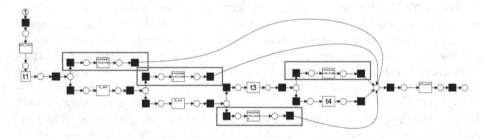

Fig. 7. Discovered process model by the BPMN Miner of the Cancel Case pattern

All of the basic control flow patterns and the `Multi-Choice` and `Structured Synchronizing Merge` from the advanced branching and synchronization patterns were discovered. The `Structured Discriminator` is not discovered since the focus of the BPMN Miner is on multiple instances and boundary events, and this pattern would need specific handling. However, general looping behavior is covered by the algorithm. The `Arbitrary Cycles` and `Structured Loop` patterns were discovered by the BPMN Miner. Considering the more complex patterns, which the classical process mining techniques could not discover, the BPMN Miner can detect one of the multiple instances patterns, namely `Multiple Instances without a priori Run-Time Knowledge`. The patterns

Multiple Instances without Synchronization and with a priori Design-Time Knowledge are not detected. The BPMN Miner fails to identify the multiple instance activity, so the discovered model does not allow for multiple instance behavior. In particular, with regard to cancellation patterns, this discovery technique is different to all other discovery algorithms because it can identify both patterns Cancel Case and Cancel Task. Figure 7 shows the discovered process model for the Cancel Case pattern with the blue boxes showing the correct cancellation points after each activity and during the execution of t2.

5   Discussion

Our analysis of which existing discovery algorithms currently cover workflow patterns shows that only a limited number of workflow patterns are supported by most algorithms. This section discusses the results and compares them to research works developed to support certain workflow patterns.

Almost all discovery algorithms detected the Simple Merge. Nevertheless, it is not ensured this pattern is always identified. Depending on the event log and algorithms' functionality, the Multi-Merge pattern could be detected instead (unless proper termination/soundness is guaranteed for the output models). The challenge for a business analyst might be distinguishing these two in the resulting process model, especially when they do not expect the presence of Multi-Merge.

Analyzing workflow patterns, where case attributes or external factors determine business process routing, is an important and understudied area. Sarno et al. [23] introduce process model modifications for multi-choice behavior to ensure decision mining for the Multi-Choice pattern in Petri nets. An extension of the discovery of Recursion and hierarchical behavior was done by Leemans et al. [19]. They compared process mining techniques and dynamic and statistical analysis techniques and showed the failure of these methods in identifying Recursion and hierarchy. The approach extended the process tree representation with a new tree operator to support both behaviors.

Mining multi instantiation is difficult for traditional process mining approaches because most (except for the BPMN miner) produce flat process models. However, to detect multiple instance patterns and the Interleaved Parallel Routing pattern, sub-structures between events have to be detected. Thus, besides the state-based patterns, the group of multiple instance patterns has the lowest coverage. Weber et al. [27] propose a method to discover multi-instance sub-processes, also with the help of additional annotations in event logs. Recent developed hierarchical process discovery techniques [21,24] support the automatic detection of generic sub-process structures.

Some control-flow patterns, like the Structured Discriminator, might not be present in most real-life business processes. Therefore, it is reasonable to not focus on full coverage of control-flow patterns but on a useful subset of patterns that should be identified in future research. For some algorithms, e.g., the Split Miner [2], it is already mentioned that it intentionally omitted the OR-split and -join to generate a simpler process model for the business analyst. Another strategy is to let the business analyst decide which patterns should be detected. Based on these two observations, we believe that either enriched event logs with additional information on sub-process structures, activities, and events or automatic techniques, e.g., with the help of natural language processing, can help to overcome current limitations in identifying advanced control-flow patterns.

Because existing discovery algorithms do not distinguish between activities and external events[5] in the output process model, they cannot distinguish a `Exclusive Choice` from a `Deferred Choice`. Conceptually speaking, activities in a process take time to perform the corresponding work, while process events instantly happen in the environment and are either produced or received by a process [29]. In existing algorithms, the events stored in a log are assumed to be life cycle transitions of activities [3]. Thus, process events are not actively detected and distinguished from activity life cycle transitions.

Finally, we want to discuss some threads to the validity of our work. First, we only compared a limited number of process discovery algorithms, omitting the full range of techniques available. However, we aimed to include a representative set of diverse techniques with existing implementations. Additionally, simulating workflow patterns cannot fully replace real event logs from comprehensive workflow management systems. Our implemented patterns intentionally exhibit certain behaviors more frequently than in reality, such as case cancellations. For comparability reasons, we convert all discovered process models to Petri nets, implying a loss of information since reducing BPMN constructs or causal nets, for example, to silent transitions means losing relevant process behavior. Nonetheless, this paper introduces an approach for comparing discovery algorithms using workflow patterns and provides a collection of implemented colored Petri nets for 23 control-flow patterns and event logs. These resources can serve as input for further research in process discovery.

6   Conclusion

This paper analyzes the coverage of existing discovery algorithms regarding the control-flow patterns. In conclusion, most discovery techniques cover the basic control-flow patterns well. Advanced control flow patterns are only partially covered. The `Multi-Choice` pattern, for example, was discovered by four out of seven selected process discovery algorithms. In contrast, the `structured Discriminator` remains undiscovered. While iteration patterns and `Implicit Termination` are well covered, `Explicit Termination` and advanced patterns are almost not covered at all. In our discussion, we argue that existing algorithms also have the potential to extend their coverage by adding further heuristics or ordering relations that are detected by the algorithms. Furthermore, hierarchical discovery techniques, as developed recently, can also help to detect additional patterns. The analysis in this work can stimulate the future development of discovery algorithms, possibly targeted at clearer or broader coverage of patterns. Furthermore, the comparison can be extended to more existing discovery

---

[5] Note the distinction here between process events and log events.

algorithms and more workflow patterns, including those concerning data and resources. For 23 workflow patterns, we provide executable colored Petri nets and the corresponding event logs, which can be used for further analysis.

References

1. CPN tools - a tool for editing, simulating, and analyzing colored petri nets. https://cpntools.org/
2. Augusto, R.A., Conforti, M.D., Rosa, M.L.: Research lab split miner. https://apromore.com/research-lab/
3. van der Aalst, W.M.P.: Process Mining - Discovery, Conformance and Enhancement of Business Processes. Springer, Heidelberg (2011). https://doi.org/10.1007/978-3-642-19345-3
4. van der Aalst, W.M.P., ter Hofstede, A.H.M., Kiepuszewski, B., Barros, A.P.: Workflow patterns. Distrib. Parallel Databases 14(1), 5–51 (2003)
5. Agrawal, R., Gunopulos, D., Leymann, F.: Mining process models from workflow logs. In: Schek, H., Saltor, F., Ramos, I., Alonso, G. (eds.) EDBT 1998. LNCS, vol. 1377, pp. 469–483. Springer, Cham (1998). https://doi.org/10.1007/BFb0101003
6. Alves De Medeiros, A., Günther, C.: Process mining: using CPN tools to create test logs for mining algorithms, pp. 177–190. DAIMI, University of Aarhus (2005). 6th Workshop and Tutorial on Practical Use of Coloured Petri Nets and the CPN Tools (CPN 2005), Aarhus, Denmark, CPN 2005
7. Augusto, A., et al.: Automated discovery of process models from event logs: review and benchmark. IEEE Trans. Knowl. Data Eng. 31(4), 686–705 (2019)
8. vanden Broucke, S.K., De Weerdt, J.: Fodina: robust and flexible process discovery. http://www.processmining.be/fodina/
9. vanden Broucke, S.K.L.M., Weerdt, J.D.: Fodina: a robust and flexible heuristic process discovery technique. Decis. Support Syst. 100, 109–118 (2017)
10. Buijs, J.C.A.M., van Dongen, B.F., van der Aalst, W.M.P.: Quality dimensions in process discovery: the importance of fitness, precision, generalization and simplicity. Int. J. Cooperative Inf. Syst. 23(1), 1440001 (2014)
11. Cardoso, J.: Business process quality metrics: log-based complexity of workflow patterns. In: Meersman, R., Tari, Z. (eds.) OTM 2007. LNCS, vol. 4803, pp. 427–434. Springer, Heidelberg (2007). https://doi.org/10.1007/978-3-540-76848-7_30
12. Conforti, R., Dumas, M., García-Bañuelos, L., Rosa, M.L.: BPMN miner: automated discovery of BPMN process models with hierarchical structure. Inf. Syst. 56, 284–303 (2016)
13. van Dongen, B.F., de Medeiros, A.K.A., Wen, L.: Process mining: overview and outlook of petri net discovery algorithms. Trans. Petri Nets Other Model. Concurr. 2, 225–242 (2009)
14. Gaaloul, W., Baïna, K., Godart, C.: Towards mining structural workflow patterns. In: Andersen, K.V., Debenham, J., Wagner, R. (eds.) DEXA 2005. LNCS, vol. 3588, pp. 24–33. Springer, Heidelberg (2005). https://doi.org/10.1007/11546924_3
15. Gaaloul, W., Baïna, K., Godart, C.: A bottom-up workflow mining approach for workflow applications analysis. In: Lee, J., Shim, J., Lee, S., Bussler, C., Shim, S. (eds.) DEECS 2006. LNCS, vol. 4055, pp. 182–197. Springer, Heidelberg (2006). https://doi.org/10.1007/11780397_15

16. Günther, C.W., van der Aalst, W.M.P.: Fuzzy mining – adaptive process simplification based on multi-perspective metrics. In: Alonso, G., Dadam, P., Rosemann, M. (eds.) BPM 2007. LNCS, vol. 4714, pp. 328–343. Springer, Heidelberg (2007). https://doi.org/10.1007/978-3-540-75183-0_24
17. Hobeck, R., Pufahl, L., Weber, I.: Process mining on curriculum-based study data: a case study at a German university. In: Montali, M., Senderovich, A., Weidlich, M. (eds.) ICPM 2022. LNBIP, vol. 468, pp. 577–589. Springer, Cham (2022). https://doi.org/10.1007/978-3-031-27815-0_42
18. Jensen, K., Kristensen, L.M.: Colored petri nets: a graphical language for formal modeling and validation of concurrent systems. CACM 58(6), 61–70 (2015)
19. Leemans, M., van der Aalst, W.M.P., van den Brand, M.G.J.: Recursion aware modeling and discovery for hierarchical software event log analysis. In: Oliveto, R., Penta, M.D., Shepherd, D.C. (eds.) SANER 2018, Campobasso, Italy, 20–23 March 2018, pp. 185–196. IEEE Computer Society (2018)
20. Leemans, S.J.J., Fahland, D., van der Aalst, W.M.P.: Discovering block-structured process models from event logs containing infrequent behaviour. In: Lohmann, N., Song, M., Wohed, P. (eds.) BPM 2013. LNBIP, vol. 171, pp. 66–78. Springer, Cham (2014). https://doi.org/10.1007/978-3-319-06257-0_6
21. Leemans, S.J.J., Goel, K., van Zelst, S.J.: Using multi-level information in hierarchical process mining: balancing behavioural quality and model complexity. In: van Dongen, B.F., Montali, M., Wynn, M.T. (eds.) ICPM 2020, Padua, Italy, 4–9 October 2020, pp. 137–144. IEEE (2020)
22. Russell, N., Ter Hofstede, A.H., Van Der Aalst, W.M., Mulyar, N.: Workflow control-flow patterns: a revised view. BPM Center Report BPM-06-22, BPMcenter.org (2006)
23. Sarno, R., Sari, P.L.I., Ginardi, H., Sunaryono, D., Mukhlash, I.: Decision mining for multi choice workflow patterns. In: 2013 International Conference on Computer, Control, Informatics and Its Applications, IC3INA 2013, Jakarta, Indonesia, 19–21 November 2013, pp. 337–342. IEEE (2013)
24. Schuster, D., van Zelst, S.J., van der Aalst, W.M.P.: Incremental discovery of hierarchical process models. In: Dalpiaz, F., Zdravkovic, J., Loucopoulos, P. (eds.) RCIS 2020. LNBIP, vol. 385, pp. 417–433. Springer, Cham (2020). https://doi.org/10.1007/978-3-030-50316-1_25
25. S.E.R.G. at University of Tartu: the BPM Discipline at Queensland University of Technology: Bpmn miner 2.0 - a tool for automated discovery of structured BPMN models from event logs. https://sep.cs.ut.ee/Main/BPMNMiner/
26. Van Der Aalst, W.: Process Mining: Data Science in Action, vol. 2. Springer, Heidelberg (2016). https://doi.org/10.1007/978-3-662-49851-4
27. Weber, I., Farshchi, M., Mendling, J., Schneider, J.: Mining processes with multi-instantiation. In: Wainwright, R.L., Corchado, J.M., Bechini, A., Hong, J. (eds.) Proceedings of the 30th Annual ACM Symposium on Applied Computing, Salamanca, Spain, 13–17 April 2015, pp. 1231–1237. ACM (2015)
28. Weijters, A.J.M.M., Ribeiro, J.T.S.: Flexible heuristics miner (FHM). In: Proceedings of the IEEE Symposium on Computational Intelligence and Data Mining, CIDM, 11–15 April 2011, Paris, France, pp. 310–317. IEEE (2011)
29. Weske, M.: Business Process Management - Concepts, Languages, Architectures, 3rd edn. Springer, Heidelberg (2019). https://doi.org/10.1007/978-3-662-59432-2
30. van Zelst, S.J., van Dongen, B.F., van der Aalst, W.M.P., Verbeek, H.M.W.: Discovering workflow nets using integer linear programming. Computing 100(5), 529–556 (2018)

From Process Mining Insights to Process Improvement: All Talk and No Action?

Vinicius Stein Dani[1]([envelope]), Henrik Leopold[2], Jan Martijn E. M. van der Werf[1], Iris Beerepoot[1], and Hajo A. Reijers[1]

[1] Utrecht University, Princetonplein 5, 3584 CC Utrecht, The Netherlands
{v.steindani,j.m.e.m.vanderwerf,i.m.beerepoot,h.a.reijers}@uu.nl
[2] Kühne Logistics University, Großer Grasbrook 17, 20457 Hamburg, Germany
henrik.leopold@the-klu.org

Abstract. Organizations from various domains use process mining to better understand, analyze, and improve their business processes. While the overall value of process mining has been shown in several contexts, little is known about the specific actions that are taken to move from process mining insights to process improvement. In this work, we address this research gap by conducting a systematic literature review. Specifically, we investigate which types of actions have been taken in existing studies and to which insights these actions are linked. Our findings show that there exists a large variety of actions. Many of these actions do not only relate to changes to the investigated process but also to the associated information systems, the process documentation, the communication between staff members, and personnel training. Understanding the diversity of the actions triggered by process mining insights is important to instigate future research on the different aspects of translating process mining insights into process improvement. The insights-to-action realm presented in this work can inform and inspire new process mining initiatives and prepare for the effort required after acquiring process mining insights.

Keywords: Process mining · Insights to action · Process improvement · Systematic literature review

1 Introduction

Process mining techniques allow organizations to obtain insights that help them improve their processes [55]. The core idea of process mining is to exploit so-called *event logs*. These event logs are extracted from different IT systems that are used throughout the organization and, therefore, reveal how processes are actually executed [2]. Process mining has been successfully applied in various domains, including healthcare [45], auditing [28], and supply chain management [30].

Despite the success and popularity of process mining in practice, there is a limited understanding of how process mining insights eventually lead to process improvements. Specifically, it is unclear which *actions* organizations can consider based on the insights they have obtained through process mining. Existing process mining methodologies (e.g. [17]) provide structured guidance on how to use process mining to obtain relevant insights. However, they do not provide details on how to translate these insights into process improvements. We argue that understanding this *realm of actions* is a valuable aspect to complement existing process mining methodologies. By understanding which actions toward process improvement can be taken and how they are connected to the obtained insights, organizations can more easily identify the best path toward process improvement.

Against this background, we use this work to address the following research question: *"What are the actions organizations can take towards process improvement and how are they connected to process mining insights?"*. To answer our research question, we conduct a systematic literature review. Based on the identified literature, we first investigate the different actions that are recommended or performed by process mining projects. Second, we investigate which insights lead to specific actions. Finally, we derive an overview of the actions triggered by process mining insights. Our contribution, therefore, is a systematic overview of actions, insights, and their connection. What is more, we identify the *intervention space*, i.e., the aspects of the organization that are affected by the actions, since process improvements actions may not only concern the process itself.

The remainder of this paper is structured as follows. In Sect. 2, we present the background and highlight the research gap. In Sect. 3, we describe our research method. In Sect. 4, we report our findings. In Sect. 5, we provide a reflection on our findings and, finally, Sect. 6 concludes the paper.

2   Background

In this section, we introduce the background for our work and highlight the research gap. First, we briefly explain what process mining is and what it offers to organizations. Second, we elaborate on process mining methodologies, i.e. works that specify which steps organizations need to take to successfully apply process mining. Third, we discuss the relationship between process mining and process improvement and argue that there is a missing link between the two.

Process Mining. Process mining is a family of techniques that facilitate the analysis of business processes based on so-called event logs [1,55]. These event logs are extracted from different types of information systems that support the process execution and are usually captured using the dedicated and standardized format XES [61]. It is important to highlight that event logs are not available per se and that the extraction of event logs from information systems may require considerable manual effort [57]. Once an event log is available, different types of analyses can be performed. The three most prominent process mining use cases in practice include process discovery, conformance checking, and enhancement [1]. The goal of process discovery is to generate a process model from the given event log that appropriately captures the as-is process. In conformance checking, a normative process model (capturing the desired process) is compared against the event log to detect deviations. Enhancement relates to a variety of use cases where a process model (e.g., discovered by means of process discovery) is enriched with additional information such as execution time, resources, or costs. Among others, this facilitates predictions related to the remaining execution time or the chances of successful process completion.

Process Mining Methodologies. Different process mining methodologies have been developed [1,9,15] with the goal of supporting process mining initiatives in practice. They typically outline specific steps, such as defining scope, collecting data, applying process discovery or conformance-checking techniques, analyzing results, and improving processes. Although these methodologies generally follow a similar high-level flow, they often do not provide specific guidance on how to translate process mining insights into process improvements [17] nor do they outline the different actions that *could* be used to follow up on the obtained insights.

The authors of the Process Diagnostics Methodology [9] recognize the importance of the recommendation phase (i.e., results transfer) of a process mining project. However, they make clear that it is the organization's responsibility to interpret and take action based on the acquired process mining insights. Although the authors of PM^2 [15] recognize the importance of the process improvement phase, they argue that this is usually part of a separate project. The authors of L* [1] propose improvement actions (e.g., redesigning, intervening) to follow up on the acquired insights. However, they do not provide much details about these actions.

Process Mining for Process Improvement. A key driver behind the application of process mining for many organizations is the desire to improve their business processes. However, successfully using process mining for process improvement comes with several challenges. Recognizing this, several studies investigate how process mining is implemented and, among others, identify key success factors [41] and key challenges for the adoption of process mining [32,42].

Other studies also more explicitly focus on the link between process mining and process improvement. For example, Eggers et al. [16] investigate how process mining can support improving process awareness in organizations. They identify seven mechanisms related to achieving increased process awareness pertaining to, for example, the inter-individual process level (i.e., when stakeholders share awareness of their sub-process within one department) or the inter-functional process level (i.e., when stakeholders share awareness of the end-to-end process across different departments). Lashkevich et al. [35] develop an analysis template to support identifying improvement opportunities based on process mining insights systematically. In their paper, they provide an example of a template relating to bottleneck analysis.

What is currently still missing is a comprehensive understanding of the actions that can be used to follow up on process mining insights. We believe that making these actions explicit can help organizations to understand the different options they can consider and, in this way, complement existing process mining methodologies.

3   Research Method

To answer our research question, we conducted a systematic literature review according to [33, 48], which involves four main stages: 1) literature review protocol definition, 2) study selection and data extraction processes execution, 3) data analysis, and 4) reporting. To ensure reproducibility, we involved several authors in these four stages. Three of the authors were involved in defining the literature review protocol. The search string and exclusion criteria were applied via the search engines by one of the authors, as defined in the review protocol. The inclusion criteria were defined and applied by two authors independently. Finally, two authors conducted the data extraction while discussing with the other authors the derivation of codes and themes reported in Sect. 4. We resolved disagreements through discussions among the authors. Below, we discuss the first three stages of our literature review. In Sect. 4, we report our findings.

3.1   Literature Review Protocol Definition

In this stage, we defined the research question and the study selection and data extraction processes. We were particularly interested in identifying which actions are performed after process mining insights have been acquired.

Based on our research question, we defined the following search string: "(process mining) AND ('case study' OR 'case studies') AND (application OR apply OR applied)", to focus on process mining application and not in, for example, the implementation of a new process discovery technique. Then, inspired by other literature review studies in the process mining field [55, 65], we defined the following set of search engines to apply our search string on: ACM Digital Libray, IEEE Xplore, Science Direct, Scopus, and Web of Science. We did consider including Springer Link in the set of search engines. Still, based on a pilot run of our study selection process, we identified that it would only add duplicates to the papers retrieved by the other search engines.

We defined exclusion and inclusion criteria to support our study selection process composed of four main stages: 1) application of search string into search engines, 2) application of exclusion criteria, 3) removal of duplicates, and 4) application of inclusion criteria. A study selection process of a systematic literature review determines how the exclusion and inclusion criteria will be applied to derive the final set of papers to be fully read [33]. The following exclusion criteria were defined: a) the paper is not written in English, b) the paper is not a conference paper, journal, or book chapter, c) the paper is not from computer science, decision sciences, business, management and accounting, healthcare, or social sciences. We further defined the following inclusion criteria: a) the paper is about the application of process mining or the use of process mining in a case study and b) the paper discusses what happens with process mining insights after they have been acquired.

The studies conforming to both inclusion criteria were kept and then further analyzed in the study selection and data extraction stage (cf. Sect. 3.2). The exclusion criteria supported us in filtering out papers directly from the search engines and the inclusion criteria supported us in deciding which papers were to be fully read, via a three-step application of the inclusion criteria, further detailed in the next section.

3.2 Study Selection and Data Extraction

Figure 1 presents our study selection process and shows the number of papers obtained from the execution of each stage. We applied the search string to the search engines, applied the exclusion criteria to the resulting papers, and removed duplicates. Then, we applied the inclusion criteria via a three-stage screening of the remainder papers: first, we screened the papers' titles and keywords (and their abstracts, when it was not yet clear if the paper should be excluded); second, we screened the abstracts of the remaining papers (and, in some cases, the conclusions); third and, finally, we screened the conclusions (and, in some cases, the methodology or the full text) to then reach to the final set of 57 selected papers to be fully read.

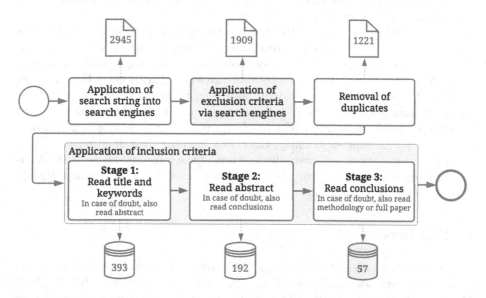

Fig. 1. Study selection process with number of papers yielded per stage.

For the data extraction process, we imported the complete list of 57 selected papers into an evidence table where we kept track of the following features extracted from each paper: reported insight, quote (from which the action was coded), coded action (i.e., what happened -or was recommended- triggered by the reported insight), action sphere (i.e., the coded action was either performed or recommended).

3.3 Data Analysis

We conducted an inductive content analysis with open coding, inspired by [53], to make sense of the extracted data from the selected papers resulting from our study selection process. The generated codes were grouped into different higher-level categories. The themes naturally emerged from the categories. In Sect. 4, we present the themes, categories, subcategories, and codes derived from the selected papers of our literature study.

While performing the coding of the quotes extracted from each of the 57 selected papers, the codes naturally assumed the format *verb + object*, which then enabled us to categorize our findings in terms of "actions" (verbs) and "intervention space" (composed by objects target of the actions). An example of a code that emerged from our open coding is "update documentation" where we have the *verb* "update" and the *object* "documentation". Because of the high amount of different verbs related to the same objects (e.g., information system, process case, etc.) of the intervention space, we identified a clear pattern pointing out the important role the objects target of the actions themselves play in understanding the realm of actions related to translating process mining insights into process improvement.

In total, 156 quotes related to what happened with process mining insights after they had been acquired were extracted from the 57 papers fully read. Because each quote may derive one or more codes, summing up all supporting quotes for each category leads to a total of 226 supporting quotes. For example, we derived the codes "justify conduct" and "clarify conduct" out of the following quote from [40]: "*The use of both manual and online document approval by the director needs to be justified and clarified whether it will be a permanent practice (...)*". As another example, the codes "identify data quality issues" and "adjust data quality issues" were derived out of the following quote: "*The business improvement team will use the conformance checking results to identify and rectify potential (...) data quality issues*" [39].

4   Findings

In this section, we present the findings of our paper. In Sect. 4.1, we first provide a high-level overview. In Sects. 4.2 through 4.4, we then take a detailed look into three themes we identified and discuss the specific actions for each theme. Finally, in Sect. 4.5, we discuss the most recurrent insights and the actions they trigger.

4.1 Overview

Studies reporting on what organizations do after they have acquired insights through process mining refer to both actions performed and recommended (i.e., actions to be performed). In this paper, to develop an overview of the realm of actions that can be triggered by process mining insights, we consider both kinds of reported actions simply as "action". The rationale behind this decision is that the recommendations are made by experienced professionals in the field and, therefore, can be considered as feasible. As a result, we identified three main themes of actions: i) supporting process understanding and documentation; ii) improving the involved information system supporting the investigated process; and iii) improving the investigated process. Each theme refers to one or more *intervention spaces*, such as *analysis* or *documentation*.

Figure 2 summarizes our results visually. It shows the main themes (dark gray), the intervention spaces (light gray), and the objects (white background) that are related to the intervention space. The numbers attached to the intervention spaces and the objects reveal the total number of supporting quotes from the analyzed papers. While these numbers should not be interpreted as a relevance factor, they do indicate how frequently a certain intervention space or object is the subject of an action after a process mining analysis.

In the next sections, we discuss each theme in more detail and provide a snapshot with respect to the identified actions.

4.2 Supporting Process Understanding and Documentation

This theme contains actions related to three intervention spaces: analysis, documentation, and communication and training. Next, we discuss each intervention space in detail.

Analysis. This intervention space contains actions related to different flavors of investigation that can be triggered by process mining insights. Several studies report on conducting or specifying follow-up investigations [5,25,29]. As an example, consider the domain expert checking if the identified relationships among members of collaboration groups match the designed procedures [29]. Other studies report on simulating or testing recommended proposed changes [8,25,43,51]. Other kinds of follow-up investigation are related to investigating or discussing root-causes of the insights [3,11,64]. For example, in [11], the authors investigated the causes of a high ticket resolution time variance. Studies also report on investigating causality or correlation [5,49,52]. In [52], the authors investigated the causal relation between two different activities of interest, while in [5], the authors investigated (alongside experts) the correlation between the involvement of specific organizational units and the process performance achievement. Studies also reported on clarifying or justifying conduct related to unexpected behavior in process cases [40,52], reviewing performance indicator [64], deriving background arguments to support decision making [22,44] and deriving improvement initiatives [4,14,40].

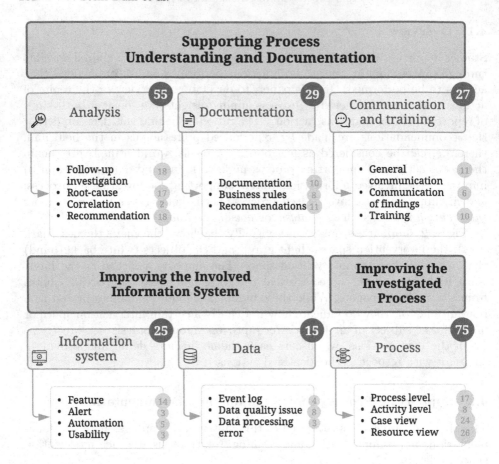

Fig. 2. Themes and intervention spaces of actions triggered by process mining insights as reported in the literature.

Documentation. This intervention space contains actions directed at the documentation itself, business rules within a documentation, and reports (i.e., a specific type of documentation that will be used to report on process mining findings). Actions related to the documentation itself include: creating, reviewing, updating, and improving a documentation [6,39,47] or using specific techniques to organize information (e.g., ontologies) to add up to a documentation [6]. In [39], the authors mention that the directly-follows graphs were used to document processes with outdated or missing documentation. Regarding business rules and documentation, there are papers that refer to isolating, adapting, or reviewing business rules [11,22,28]. For example, in [28], the authors mention the need to review business rules in the sense of checking if they are being enforced. In addition, other papers refer to adjusting service level agreements [50,56] based on process mining insights. Finally, regarding reporting, papers refer to writing, sharing, and presenting a report with the acquired insights [38,46,49], as well as formulating recommendations to be added to the report [25].

Communication and Training. This intervention space contains actions concerned with communication, information sharing, and training. Actions regarding communication include challenging conventional beliefs, increasing awareness about the process, or creating an ad-hoc custom visualization for communicating findings [22,36,46]. Regarding information sharing, reported actions are related to providing feedback on performance measurements [3,27]. For example, in [3], the authors provide feedback regarding specific detected loops in the process under investigation. Other papers report on discussing the likelihood of partial findings [46,52], informing the manager about specific findings [3], or improving information sharing [5,52,64] to, for example, improve coordination between collaborating stakeholders [64]. Training may be used to reinforce internal controls or good practices [62,63]. Other studies report on conducting training for staff members [20,47,63] leading to, for example, quality improvement, or reducing the need to perform a specific corrective activity [47]. Also, the discussion of potential training issues [39] was reported as an action triggered by process mining insights.

4.3 Improving Involved Information System

This theme contains the actions related to two intervention spaces: information system and data. Next, we discuss each intervention space in detail.

Information System. This intervention space contains actions directed at the information system(s) of the organization. They include creating, introducing, or testing a new feature [12,22,24,40], testing or improving test scripts of a feature [52], or simply using existing features [5]. For example, in [40], the authors used process mining in the context of the adoption of a new Enterprise Resource Planning system. Based on the insights, they identified the need to reinforce testing new features to ensure they behave as expected. Other papers report on adjusting feature settings [11,34,37], creating alerts [23,28], improving system usability [52,60], identifying automation opportunities [7,21], and adopting or implementing automation [18,50,63]. For example, in [21], the authors report on identifying automation opportunities by calculating the ratio between cases in which an activity was executed by a user and the total number of instances of the activity under investigation.

Data. This intervention space contains actions directed at the event log. They include filtering or re-collecting the event log [4,24,54], as well as identifying or rectifying data quality issues [39,54,59,63]. In [63], the authors reported deriving recommendations for improving data quality issues of the event log based on the argument that the input data quality interferes with the quality of a process mining project. They recommended, for example, the verb-object naming style for activities and keeping track of both start and end timestamps of activities, as these are helpful for process analysis. Other papers report identifying, reviewing, or rectifying data processing errors [39,64]. For example, in [39], the authors discuss that the business improvement team would use conformance checking-related insights to identify and rectify data processing errors and data quality issues. Note that the actions related to identifying or reviewing could also fit into the intervention space "Analysis". However, because the papers explicitly discuss these actions being directed at the event log itself, we included them in the "Data" intervention space.

4.4 Improving the Investigated Process

This theme represents the intervention space that contains actions toward the process. These actions can be more generic, such as redesigning, simplifying, changing, or standardizing the process [14,19,24,40]. However, the actions can also be more specific toward a particular aspect of the process, such as isolating or checking potential deviation in cases [28,29]. The actions can also refer to analyzing process cases [18,27,39] such as in [18], where the authors report on analyzing process cases containing high time-consuming tasks [18] or, as in [29], where the authors report on analyzing process cases from a resource perspective.

Some papers refer to actions directed at activities, such as parallelizing, removing, increasing the frequency of, or limiting, preventing or postponing the execution of an activity [5,10,13]. For example, in [13], the authors report preventing customers from going through a specific activity multiple times. Several papers refer to actions toward resources, such as waiting for, involving more actively, increasing, replacing, reallocating, aggregating, manually inspecting, increasing the visibility of, protecting, or restricting access to a resource [11,23,58]. In [58], the authors observed that the pattern separation of duty should be applied to restrict access to certain parts of the information systems only to specific employees. In [11], the authors reported that the stakeholders are considering increasing the number of developers to resolve a ticket resolution time issue. Other papers refer to actions toward specific detected patterns in the process (either desired, i.e. good practice, or undesired), such as adopting or removing specific patterns [14], defining or improving good practices [6,64]. Other papers report on identifying or understanding specific patterns, or identifying the following –or possible exploitation– of good practices [27,47]. Although these papers reporting on identifying or understanding specific patterns or good practices could fit the intervention space "Analysis", we kept them under the "Process" intervention space because of the explicit relation to the intervention to the process.

4.5 Most Frequently Reported Insights and Actions

The most recurrent insights reported in the literature are related to:

1. *Low data quality*: Low data quality may refer to both the data from the databases as well as the event log itself. For example, in [54], the authors reported on missing fields in records and incorrect event sequences in the

event log. In [26], the authors reported on identifying incomplete traces. As such data quality issues may compromise the validity of the obtained insights, they need to be addressed before any further action can be taken.

2. *High wait time*: High wait time is a common concern in different contexts. For example, in [60], the authors noticed that it was taking more time for a process participant to take over a specific task than to work on that task. In [31], the authors report on identifying the delivery of goods taking longer than the defined service standard.

3. *High amount of rework*: Rework is another frequent concern. For example, the authors of [63] identified rework caused by manually misclassified documents. In [52], the authors identified that a specific system feature-related data had not been cached, requiring the user to unnecessarily repeat the execution of another related task within the system.

4. *Discovered process model*: The discovered process model is used for a variety of purposes. If, however, the discovered process model does not allow the analyst to obtain the required insights, this might be addressed before any further action can be taken. For example, the authors of [59] obtained spaghetti-like process models, which did not allow them to conduct a proper analysis of the process. In [19], the authors discussed the suitability of the discovered process model to support the definition of a standard process.

5. *Non-compliant behavior*: Besides performance-related insights, non-compliant behavior, i.e. conformance violations, represent a very common trigger for actions. For example, in [40], the authors identified actions performed by process participants that were not conforming to the expected behavior. In [62], the authors reported on an inward cargo handling where they identified many instances of the process that did not properly complete according to a normative process model.

Other insights refer to, for example, high or low demand on a specific resource (e.g., process participant), high execution time of specific activity, low automation rate, lack of domain knowledge, among others.

Figure 3 presents the top five most frequently reported insights and actions in the literature, respectively, in terms of the number of supporting quotes from the selected papers, as described in Sect. 3.3. For the reader to distinguish with ease the connections between insights and the process-related artefacts of the intervention space, we chose to repeat both action verbs and objects as triggered for each reportedly acquired process mining insight. Two aspects stand out from Fig. 3. First, the intervention space is quite large, highlighting that process mining insights not only trigger interventions to the process under investigation, but also to process-related artefacts. Second, there are many-to-many relations between acquired process mining insights and triggered actions, as well as between insights and process-related artefacts, objects of the intervention space. Have in mind that because there is a wider variety of actions than insights reported and the same amount of supporting quotes connecting insights and actions, the amount of supporting quotes for the most recurrent reported action is lower than for the most recurrent reported insight.

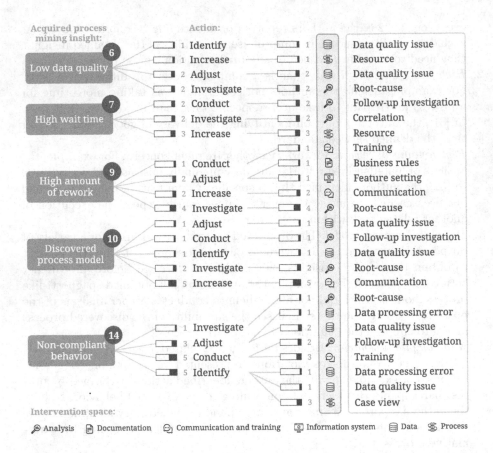

Fig. 3. Most frequently reported process mining insights and triggered actions.

5   Discussion

From our findings, it is clear that translating process mining insights into process improvement requires cooperation and coordination as different levels of knowledge and expertise are needed to support understanding and documenting the process, improving the involved information system supporting the investigated process, and improving the investigated process. We can reason that there is a need to properly operationalize the integration between technical and organizational workers to intervene in the process itself and in the underlying information system(s) while understanding and documenting the process, both coordinately and supported by domain and data knowledge.

While we do not claim to provide a comprehensive list of actions triggered by process mining insights, we provide an initial step toward understanding the diversity of the insight-to-action realm. We acknowledge that further research is needed to investigate the representativeness of the actions herein shown and a deeper understanding of each action, precisely detailing what they entail. Only then we'll be able to move towards ultimately recommending assertively follow-up actions from acquired process mining insights and triggering (semi-) automated actions not only related to prediction-based alert systems but also towards undertaking specific changes to the process or process-related artefacts.

Having this said, there are several important findings we were able to derive in this paper. Below, we discuss the three main points.

Actions are Concerned with Much More than the Process Itself. Intuitively, one would expect that process improvement is mostly about the process itself, especially when the basis for improvement are insights obtained through process mining. Our findings show that the investigated process is indeed subject to several actions, such as parallelizing or removing activities. We, however, could also show that there are several intervention spaces besides the process itself. Among others, we identified that actions are taken towards understanding or improving other process-related artefacts, such as documentation, communication, training, and supporting information systems. These findings highlight that process improvement requires a holistic view, including several facets, such as the IT infrastructure and the human resources that are involved in the process execution.

The Relationship Between Insights and Actions is Highly Complex. Our analysis revealed that there is a many-to-many relation between insights and actions. This means that one insight can trigger several actions and that one action can be triggered by several insights. While this is not totally unexpected, it helps to better understand the relationship between insights and actions. What is more, researchers and practitioners conducting a new process mining initiative can plan ahead for actions they may need to perform based on the insight they have obtained. In addition, they can also acquire a broader vision of potential insights to consider obtaining. Assume the actions they may need to perform are related to another insight that was not previously considered to be obtained. In this case, this not previously considered to be obtained insight could be added to the pool of insights to be acquired.

Gap Between Recommended and Taken Actions. During our analysis, we observed a gap between recommended and taken actions. For several insights, e.g., high wait time and high rework rate, we identified recommended but not any taken actions. This observation shows that certain actions seem to be either associated with too much effort or they are not considered for other reasons. While we cannot provide specific insights into why this gap exists, it is important to note that it is there. We believe that this represents an important direction for future work: understanding which actions are (not) performed to improve processes and why.

6   Conclusion

In this paper, we used a structured literature review to investigate which types of actions organizations have taken in the context of process mining initiatives and to which insights these actions are linked. We found that there exists a large variety of actions and that many of these actions do not only relate to changes to the investigated process but also to the associated information systems, the process documentation, the communication between staff members, and personnel training.

With these findings, our study provides an important step towards enhancing the implementation phase (as reported by Emamjome et al. [17]) of existing process mining methodologies. Specifically, the derived overview of actions triggered by process mining insights can serve as a catalog for practitioners that aim to translate process mining insights into actual process improvement. We believe that such a catalog can be particularly useful for novice process mining consultants and managers as it provides guidance on which actions they might consider given particular insights. Such catalog may also support practitioners sketching initial *plans of action* for their projects, supported by evidence from real-life case studies.

From an academic point of view, our results complement existing process mining methodologies, such as [1,9,15]. By including our findings, it is possible to devise a methodological framework for process mining that does not stop with obtaining insights but with realizing process improvements. Having this said, there are several aspects that require further investigation. First, it is interesting to conduct a deep investigation of what each action entails. For example, what are the different departments and personnel involved and what were the challenges faced while implementing a specific action. Second, it would be useful to conduct case studies with successful and unsuccessful process mining projects to highlight commonalities and differences between these projects and further understand which actions ultimately lead to a successful translation of process mining insights into process improvement.

In future work, we will conduct a survey with experts and a multiple case study to complement the intervention space taxonomy presented in this study. We will further investigate the relations between recommended and performed actions to move towards well-informed recommendations supported by performed actions. Finally, we will derive a catalog of the many-to-many relations between insights and the affected process or process-related artefacts.

Acknowledgements. Part of this research was funded by NWO (Netherlands Organisation for Scientific Research) project number 16672.

References

1. van der Aalst, W.: Process Mining: Discovery, Conformance and Enhancement of Business Processes. Springer, Heidelberg (2011). https://doi.org/10.1007/978-3-642-19345-3
2. van der Aalst, W.: Process Mining: Data Science in Action. Springer, Heidelberg (2016). https://doi.org/10.1007/978-3-662-49851-4
3. van der Aalst, W., et al.: Business process mining: an industrial application. Information Systems, pp. 713–732 (2007)

4. Agostinelli, S., Covino, F., D'Agnese, G., Crea, C.D., Leotta, F., Marrella, A.: Supporting governance in healthcare through process mining: a case study. IEEE Access **8**, 186012–186025 (2020)
5. Aksu, Ü., Reijers, H.A.: How business process benchmarks enable organizations to improve performance. In: International Enterprise Distributed Object Computing Conference (EDOC). IEEE (2020)
6. Alvarez, C., et al.: Discovering role interaction models in the emergency room using process mining. J. Biomedi. Inform. **78**, 60–77 (2018)
7. Bahaweres, R.B., Amna, H., Nurnaningsih, D.: Improving purchase to pay process efficiency with RPA using fuzzy miner algorithm in process mining. In: International Conference on Decision Aid Sciences and Applications. IEEE (2022)
8. van Beest, N., Maruster, L.: A process mining approach to redesign business processes - a case study in gas industry. In: International Symposium on Symbolic and Numeric Algorithms for Scientific Computing (SYNASC). IEEE (2007)
9. Bozkaya, M., Gabriels, J., van der Werf, J.M.: Process diagnostics: a method based on process mining. In: International Conference on Information, Process, and Knowledge Management (eKNOW), pp. 22–27 (2009)
10. Bozorgi, Z.D., Teinemaa, I., Dumas, M., Rosa, M.L., Polyvyanyy, A.: Process mining meets causal machine learning: discovering causal rules from event logs. In: International Conference on Process Mining (ICPM). IEEE (2020)
11. Cela, O., Front, A., Rieu, D.: CEFOP: a method for the continual evolution of organisational processes. In: International Conference on Research Challenges in Information Science (RCIS). IEEE (2017)
12. Cho, M., Song, M., Comuzzi, M., Yoo, S.: Evaluating the effect of best practices for business process redesign: an evidence-based approach based on process mining techniques. Decision Support Systems, pp. 92–103 (2017)
13. Dees, M., de Leoni, M., van der Aalst, W., Reijers, H.: What if process predictions are not followed by good recommendations? In: BPM Industry Forum, pp. 61–72 (2019)
14. Delias, P., Nguyen, G.T.: Prototyping a business process improvement plan. An evidence-based approach. Inf. Syst. **101**, 101812 (2021)
15. van Eck, M.L., Lu, X., Leemans, S.J.J., van der Aalst, W.M.P.: PM^2: a process mining project methodology. In: Zdravkovic, J., Kirikova, M., Johannesson, P. (eds.) CAiSE 2015. LNCS, vol. 9097, pp. 297–313. Springer, Cham (2015). https://doi.org/10.1007/978-3-319-19069-3_19
16. Eggers, J., Hein, A., Böhm, M., Krcmar, H.: No longer out of sight, no longer out of mind? How organizations engage with process mining-induced transparency to achieve increased process awareness. Business & Information Systems Engineering, pp. 491–510 (2021)
17. Emamjome, F., Andrews, R., ter Hofstede, A.H.M.: A case study lens on process mining in practice. In: Panetto, H., Debruyne, C., Hepp, M., Lewis, D., Ardagna, C.A., Meersman, R. (eds.) OTM 2019. LNCS, vol. 11877, pp. 127–145. Springer, Cham (2019). https://doi.org/10.1007/978-3-030-33246-4_8
18. Esiefarienrhe, B.M., Omolewa, I.D.: Application of process mining to medical billing using L* life cycle model. In: International Conference on Electrical, Computer and Energy Technologies (ICECET). IEEE (2021)
19. Fleig, C., Augenstein, D., Mädche, A.: Process mining for business process standardization in ERP implementation projects - an SAP S/4 HANA case study from manufacturing. In: International Conference on Business Process Management (BPM). Karlsruhe (2018)

20. Gerke, K., Petruch, K., Tamm, G.: Optimization of service delivery through continual process improvement: a case study. In: INFORMATIK Business Process and Service Science, pp. 94–107. Gesellschaft für Informatik e.V. (2010)

21. Geyer-Klingeberg, J., Nakladal, J., Baldauf, F., Veit, F.: Process mining and robotic process automation: a perfect match. In: International Conference on Business Process Management (BPM) (2018)

22. Goel, K., Leemans, S.J.J., Wynn, M.T., ter Hofstede, A.H.M., Barnes, J.: Improving PhD student journeys: insights from an Australian higher education institution. In: BPM Industry Forum, pp. 27–38. CEUR-WS.org (2021)

23. Gupta, M., Serebrenik, A., Jalote, P.: Improving software maintenance using process mining and predictive analytics. In: International Conference on Software Maintenance and Evolution (ICSME). IEEE (2017)

24. Huang, C., Cai, H., Li, Y., Du, J., Bu, F., Jiang, L.: A process mining based service composition approach for mobile information systems. Mob. Info. Syst. **2017**, 1–13 (2017)

25. van Hulzen, G., Martin, N., Depaire, B., Souverijns, G.: Supporting capacity management decisions in healthcare using data-driven process simulation. J. Biomed. Inform. **129**, 104060 (2022)

26. Ingvaldsen, J.E., Gulla, J.A.: Industrial application of semantic process mining. Enterp. Inf. Syst. **6**, 139–163 (2012)

27. Jans, M., Alles, M., Vasarhelyi, M.: The case for process mining in auditing: sources of value added and areas of application. Int. J. Account. Inf. Syst. **14**, 1–20 (2013)

28. Jans, M., Hosseinpour, M.: How active learning and process mining can act as continuous auditing catalyst. Int. J. Account. Inf. Syst. **32**, 44–58 (2019)

29. Jans, M., van der Werf, J.M., Lybaert, N., Vanhoof, K.: A business process mining application for internal transaction fraud mitigation. Expert Syst. Appl. **38**, 13351–13359 (2011)

30. Jokonowo, B., Claes, J., Sarno, R., Rochimah, S.: Process mining in supply chains: a systematic literature review. Int. J. Electr. Comput. Eng. **8**(6), 4626–4636 (2018)

31. Kedem-Yemini, S., Mamon, N.S., Mashiah, G.: An analysis of cargo release services with process mining: a case study in a logistics company. In: International Conference on Industrial Engineering and Operations Management (IEOM) (2018)

32. Kipping, G., et al.: How to leverage process mining in organizations - towards process mining capabilities. In: Di Ciccio, C., Dijkman, R., del Río Ortega, A., Rinderle-Ma, S. (eds.) BPM 2022. LNCS, vol. 13420, pp. 40–46. Springer, Cham (2022). https://doi.org/10.1007/978-3-031-16103-2_5

33. Kitchenham, B., Charters, S.: Guidelines for performing systematic literature reviews in software engineering. Technical report, EBSE (2007)

34. Kudo, M., Nogayama, T., Ishida, A., Abe, M.: Business process analysis and real-world application scenarios. In: International Conference on Signal-Image Technology and Internet-Based Systems (SITIS). IEEE (2013)

35. Lashkevich, K., Milani, F., Danylyshyn, N.: Analysis templates for identifying improvement opportunities with process mining. In: European Conference on Information Systems (ECIS) (2023)

36. Lee, C., Choy, K., Ho, G., Lam, C.: A slippery genetic algorithm-based process mining system for achieving better quality assurance in the garment industry. Expert Syst. Appl. **46**, 236–248 (2016)

37. Lee, C., Ho, G., Choy, K., Pang, G.: A RFID-based recursive process mining system for quality assurance in the garment industry. Int. J. Prod. Res. **52**, 4216–4238 (2013)

38. Leemans, M., van der Aalst, W.M.P., van den Brand, M.G.J., Schiffelers, R.R.H., Lensink, L.: Software process analysis methodology – a methodology based on lessons learned in embracing legacy software. In: International Conference on Software Maintenance and Evolution (ICSME). IEEE (2018)
39. Leemans, S.J., Poppe, E., Wynn, M.T.: Directly follows-based process mining: exploration and a case study. In: International Conference on Process Mining (ICPM). IEEE (2019)
40. Mahendrawathi, E., Zayin, S.O., Pamungkas, F.J.: ERP post implementation review with process mining: a case of procurement process. Procedia Comput. Sci. **124**, 216–223 (2017)
41. Mamudu, A., Bandara, W., Wynn, M., Leemans, S.: A process mining success factors model. In: Di Ciccio, C., Dijkman, R., del Río Ortega, A., Rinderle-Ma, S. (eds.) BPM 2022. LNCS, vol. 13420, pp. 143–160. Springer, Cham (2022). https://doi.org/10.1007/978-3-031-16103-2_12
42. Martin, N., et al.: Opportunities and challenges for process mining in organisations - results of a Delphi study. Bus. Inf. Syst. Eng. **63**, 511 (2022)
43. Mărușter, L., van Beest, N.R.T.P.: Redesigning business processes: a methodology based on simulation and process mining techniques. Knowl. Inf. Syst. **21**, 267–297 (2009)
44. Meincheim, A., dos Santos Garcia, C., Nievola, J.C., Scalabrin, E.E.: Combining process mining with trace clustering: manufacturing shop floor process - an applied case. In: International Conference on Tools with Artificial Intelligence. IEEE (2017)
45. Munoz-Gama, J., et al.: Process mining for healthcare: characteristics and challenges. J. Biomed. Inform. **127**, 103994 (2022)
46. Partington, A., Wynn, M., Suriadi, S., Ouyang, C., Karnon, J.: Process mining for clinical processes. Trans. Manag. Inf. Syst. **5**, 1–18 (2015)
47. Peters, E.M., Dedene, G., Poelmans, J.: Understanding service quality and customer churn by process discovery for a multi-national banking contact center. In: International Conference on Data Mining Workshops. IEEE (2013)
48. Petersen, K., Feldt, R., Mujtaba, S., Mattsson, M.: Systematic mapping studies in software engineering. In: International Conference on Evaluation & Assessment in Software Engineering (2008)
49. Polyvyanyy, A., Pika, A., Wynn, M.T., ter Hofstede, A.H.: A systematic approach for discovering causal dependencies between observations and incidents in the health and safety domain. Saf. Sci. **118**, 345–354 (2019)
50. Ramires, F., Sampaio, P.: Process mining and lean six sigma: a novel approach to analyze the supply chain quality of a hospital. Int. J. Lean Six Sigma **13**, 594–621 (2021)
51. Rismanchian, F., Kassani, S.H., Shavarani, S.M., Lee, Y.H.: A data-driven approach to support the understanding and improvement of patients' journeys: a case study using electronic health records of an emergency department. Value Health **26**, 18–27 (2023)
52. Rubin, V.A., Mitsyuk, A.A., Lomazova, I.A., van der Aalst, W.M.P.: Process mining can be applied to software too! In: International Symposium on Empirical Software Engineering and Measurement (ESEM). ACM (2014)
53. Saldana, J.: The Coding Manual for Qualitative Researchers. SAGE (2015)
54. Samalikova, J., Kusters, R., Trienekens, J., Weijters, T., Siemons, P.: Toward objective software process information: experiences from a case study. Softw. Qual. J. **19**, 101–120 (2010)
55. dos Santos Garcia, C., et al.: Process mining techniques and applications - a systematic mapping study. Expert Syst. Appl. **133**, 260–295 (2019)

56. Smit, K., and J.M.: Process mining in the rail industry: a qualitative analysis of success factors and remaining challenges. In: Humanizing Technology for a Sustainable Society (HTSS). University of Maribor Press (2019)

57. Stein Dani, V., et al.: Towards understanding the role of the human in event log extraction. In: Marrella, A., Weber, B. (eds.) BPM 2021. LNBIP, vol. 436, pp. 86–98. Springer, Cham (2022). https://doi.org/10.1007/978-3-030-94343-1_7

58. Tawakkal, I., Kurniati, A.P., Wisudiawan, G.A.A.: Implementing heuristic miner for information system audit based on DSS01 COBIT5. In: International Conference on Computer, Control, Informatics and its Applications. IEEE (2016)

59. Toth, K., Machalik, K., Fogarassy, G., Vathy-Fogarassy, A.: Applicability of process mining in the exploration of healthcare sequences. In: NC. IEEE (2017)

60. Trinkenreich, B., Santos, G., Confort, V., Santoro, F.: Toward using business process intelligence to support incident management metrics selection and service improvement. In: International Conferences on Software Engineering and Knowledge Engineering (SEKE). KSI (2015)

61. Verbeek, H.M.W., Buijs, J.C.A.M., van Dongen, B.F., van der Aalst, W.M.P.: XES, XESame, and ProM 6. In: Soffer, P., Proper, E. (eds.) CAiSE Forum 2010. LNBIP, vol. 72, pp. 60–75. Springer, Heidelberg (2011). https://doi.org/10.1007/978-3-642-17722-4_5

62. Wang, Y., Caron, F., Vanthienen, J., Huang, L., Guo, Y.: Acquiring logistics process intelligence: methodology and an application for a Chinese bulk port. Expert Syst. Appl. **41**, 195–209 (2014)

63. Weerdt, J.D., Schupp, A., Vanderloock, A., Baesens, B.: Process mining for the multi-faceted analysis of business processes - a case study in a financial services organization. Comput. Ind. **64**, 57–67 (2013)

64. Zerbino, P., Aloini, D., Dulmin, R., Mininno, V.: Towards analytics-enabled efficiency improvements in maritime transportation: a case study in a mediterranean port. Sustainability **11**, 4473 (2019)

65. Zerbino, P., Stefanini, A., Aloini, D.: Process science in action: a literature review on process mining in business management. Technol. Forecast. Soc. Change **172**, 121021 (2021)

Rectify Sensor Data in IoT: A Case Study on Enabling Process Mining for Logistic Process in an Air Cargo Terminal

Chiao-Yun Li[1,2]([✉]), Aparna Joshi[1], Nicholas T. L. Tam[3],
Sean Shing Fung Lau[3], Jinhui Huang[3][iD], Tejaswini Shinde[1],
and Wil M. P. van der Aalst[1,2]

[1] RWTH Aachen University, Aachen, Germany
{chiaoyun.li,wvdaalst}@pads.rwth-aachen.de,
{aparna.joshi,tejaswini.shinde}@rwth-aachen.de
[2] Fraunhofer FIT, Birlinghoven Castle, Sankt Augustin, Germany
[3] Hong Kong Industrial Artificial Intelligence and Robotics Centre Limited,
Shatin, NT, Hong Kong
{nicholastam,seanlau,gavinhuang}@hkflair.org

Abstract. The Internet of Things (IoT) has empowered enterprises to optimize process efficiency and productivity by analyzing sensor data. This can be achieved with process mining, a technology that enables organizations to extract valuable insights from data recorded during process execution, referred to as *event data* in a process mining context. In our case study, we aim to apply process mining to sensor data collected within a logistic process at an air cargo terminal, specifically from device-to-device communication. By representing the sensor data as event data, we rectify them to accurately capture the movement of package distribution in the logistic process. However, due to the communication dynamics, challenges arise from the presence of irrelevant data that does not impact the process instance's status. Moreover, issues such as faulty sensor readings and ambiguous data interpretation further compound these challenges. To overcome the obstacles, we collaborate with domain experts to develop rules that take into account the context of each event in a trace, enabling us to effectively capture package distribution within the system. We present the results of our process mining analysis, which have been validated by domain experts. This case study contributes to the understanding and utilization of sensor data for process mining in IoT environments, with a specific focus on data collected from device-to-device communication.

Keywords: Process mining · IoT · Sensor data · Logistic process · Data rectification · Device-to-device communication

This work was supported by the InnoHK funding launched by Innovation and Technology Commission, Hong Kong SAR. Additionally, we would like to thank Eric Poon, Bill Sio, and Sebastiaan van Zelst for their support.

M. Sellami et al. (Eds.): CoopIS 2023, LNCS 14353, pp. 293–310, 2024.
https://doi.org/10.1007/978-3-031-46846-9_16

1   Introduction

The Internet of Things (IoT), a network of interconnected devices exchanging data through embedded sensors via the internet, has unlocked new possibilities for modern enterprises to digitize and automate their business processes [28]. Sensors integrated into devices collect valuable data about various aspects of a process such as machine conditions, order location, or individual health metrics. By analyzing these data, companies can derive actionable insights to improve efficiency and productivity in their processes [27].

Process mining is a data-driven technology that empowers organizations to extract fact-based insights using *event data* generated and recorded in information systems during process execution [1]. For example, *process discovery* unveils the behavior of *activities* in a process [4,7,22], i.e., well-defined process steps, while *conformance checking* compares the observed behavior against predefined expectations [5,14,18]. By leveraging process mining on event data, organizations gain valuable insights for enhancing the execution and design of their processes.

Process mining typically assumes event data organized based on process instances (i.e., *cases*), with each event representing a status change within a case. In our case study of a logistic process in an air cargo terminal, our goal is to apply process mining to sensor data and extract insights on package distribution performance within the system. However, the sensor data collected primarily facilitates device-to-device communication to determine device availability for distribution. When applying process mining to event data transformed from the sensor data, we may include events not directly relevant to package distribution, i.e., an event that does not signify a status change of package distribution within the system. Such misalignment between the sensor data and the event data hinders the application of process mining.

Figure 1 exemplifies the challenges, necessitating the rectification of sensor data for process mining. The figure portrays the distribution of a package. The process begins with a package residing on device A, which communicates with device B to facilitate the package transfer. Following device A's readiness signal, the package is forwarded to device B. Subsequently, device B communicates with device C in an attempt to transfer the package; yet the latter declines to receive it. Consequently, the distribution proceeds to device D. Throughout the process, the sensor data contributes extraneous data unrelated to the package's movement within the system. One example is the presence of data originating from device C, which the package never traversed. This example demonstrates how the specific sensor data contribute to the analysis of package distribution, which is the focus of this case study. In contrast, other data serve the communication purpose between the devices and are considered extraneous noise that impedes the application of process mining. Such misalignment arises from the inherent divergence in their respective purposes. The sensor data utilized in our case study is primarily intended to support and enable device-to-device communication, which stands as one of the fundamental objectives of sensors within an IoT environment. Hence, to effectively apply process mining, it is crucial to rectify and align the sensor data with the behavior of interest.

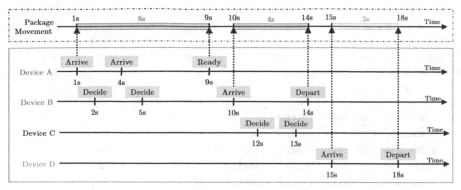

(a) Misalignment between the sensor data and the event data indicating the package movement in the system. The lower timelines depict data samples collected by sensors on the devices for a package distribution at a given point in time, labeled with the signals that indicate the corresponding device's availability. The upper timeline displays the actual package movement. Dashed arrows highlight the data samples that *actually* signify the package movement.

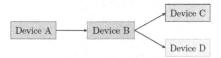

(b) Relationship of devices in the system, with arrows indicating the possible direction of package distribution on the devices.

Fig. 1. An example of sensor data from device-to-device communication for package distribution. Consistent coloring represents information related to the corresponding devices.

This paper illustrates the rectification applied to the collected sensor data in our case study. Through careful analysis, we identified and examined the challenges arising from the misalignment between the communication among the devices and *actual* distribution of packages. Practical challenges, such as legacy systems and the ambiguity in interpreting sensor data (e.g., the departure of a package from a device may be signified by various signals like readiness or departed, as exemplified in Fig. 1), further contribute to the complexity of the rectification. We overcome these challenges and rectify the sensor data to align them with the package distribution within the terminal. This collaborative effort involves leveraging domain expertise to ensure the reliability of the decisions made in the solutions. The effectiveness of our approach is demonstrated through an analysis of the behavior of package distribution using the rectified event data with process mining techniques, leading to valuable and validated insights.

The remainder of the paper is structured as follows. In Sect. 2, we introduce the available sensor data and provide an example of rectification. Section 3 illustrates the challenges and the approach developed. In Sect. 4, we apply process mining on the repaired sensor data and demonstrate the outcomes. Section 5 presents related work in the field, while Sect. 6 summarizes the lessons learned from our case study.

Table 1. Every row represents a data sample from a sensor installed on a device (`DID`) to exchange its status (`Sig`) in relation to a package (`PID`) placed in a tray (`TID`) to be distributed at a specific point in time (`Timestamp`). The device's location is identified by its associated floor and zone, and the device type (`Type`), such as a conveyor belt or lift shaft, is also provided.

TID	PID	Sig	DID	Timestamp	Floor	Type	Zone	
FFD541256	2365884459	Initiate	KJDQ4414	12:05:23	9	LB	J	...
FFD541256	2365884459	Ready	KJDQ4414	12:05:24	9	LB	J	...
FFD541256	2365884459	Ready	KJDQ4414	12:14:30	9	LB	J	...
FFD541256	2365884459	Decide	BRMI1121	12:15:35	0	RS	J	...
FFD541256	2365884459	Arrive	BRMI1121	12:16:31	0	RS	J	...
FFD541256	2365884459	Depart	BRMI1121	12:17:25	0	RS	J	...
FFD541256	2365884459	Arrive	UGOI9833	12:17:26	2	CB	J	...
FFD541256	2365884459	Arrive	NXVR3307	12:17:35	2	CB	J	...

2   Overview

In this section, we present a sample of sensor data provided and an example illustrating the rectification.[1]

Representation of Sensor Data as Event Data. Table 1 presents an excerpt of the sensor data collected. Each row corresponds to a data sample generated by a sensor for communication between the devices. For example, the first row specifies that the package 2365884459 is in the tray FFD541256 on device KJDQ4414 with type LB, which *initiates* the package distribution in zone J (written as ZJ) on floor 9 (written as F9) at 12:05:23.

We consider a data sample an event. A case consists of events describing package distribution, identified by the package identifier PID. Except for TID, which is a case attribute, other fields are assigned as event attributes. A *trace* is a sequence of events in a case ordered based on their timestamps as visualized in Fig. 2, and an *event log* is the collection of traces.

Fig. 2. A visualization of a fragment of the trace based on Table 1, where every chevron represents an event annotated with the corresponding attributes, i.e., timestamp and signal, and is colored based on its *activity*, i.e., device identifier.

---

[1] Due to confidentiality, the data are manipulated and anonymized, while preserving the relative relationships between data samples to illustrate the observed behavior in the paper.

Rectification of Event Data for Package Movement. Our objective is to align event data with the package movement throughout its distribution. We aim to determine the specific device on which the package resides and the corresponding timeframe. Figure 3 presents an excerpt of the rectification. The package 2365884459 was on KJDQ4414 from 12:05:23 to 12:14:30, which is inferred by the first and last events among the continuous events of KJDQ4414. Next, the package arrived and departed BRMI1121 at 12:16:31 and 12:17:25, respectively, as indicated by the events of the arrival and departure of the package on BRMI1121. Then, the package arrived UGOI9833 at 12:17:26; without another event for the package on UGOI9833, we assume that the departure occurred at the same time as it arrived at the next device, i.e., 12:17:35. In this example, we demonstrate some rectification performed, involving renaming the signals, filtering out communication overhead, and creating an artificial event.

We present a sample of the provided sensor data and illustrate the rectification conducted through an example. By showcasing the raw sensor data and its corresponding repair, this section highlights the necessity of rectifying sensor data within the context of this case study.

3 Event Data Rectification

We recognized several challenges in aligning the event data with the package movement. To address the challenges, we drew on domain knowledge and developed a rectification process to repair the event data. In this section, we present the challenges, detail the devised rectification process, showcase its application to the sensor data, and discuss the limitations of our approach.

3.1 Challenges

We analyzed the event data and discovered some challenges specific to sensors and the system. In the IoT environment, device-to-device communication facilitates information exchange. However, this communication dynamic also introduces a challenge where some events derived from the transformed event data

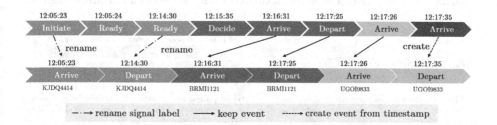

Fig. 3. Rectifying event data based on the sensor data presented in Table 1. The top figure depicts the trace fragment in Fig. 2. The bottom one illustrates the rectified trace fragment that aligns with the package movement in the system. Different arrow types are used to distinguish the implemented solutions.

are not directly related to the physical movement of a package. For instance, the events labeled with Decide in Fig. 1 and Table 1 are specifically transmitted to assess the suitability of the respective device for package reception. Another example is depicted by the second Arrive from device A in Fig. 1, which is regarded as timeout noise resulting from an unexpectedly extended duration of stay on the device.

Furthermore, we discovered an improbable situation depicted in Fig. 4a, where a package appeared to be simultaneously present on two devices, as indicated by its arrival at CJYB3150 before its departure from OVTI3564. Collaborating with domain experts, subsequent investigation revealed that this unrealistic behavior was due to faulty sensors – CJYB3150 detects the arrival of the package before OVTI3564 signifies its departure. To address this issue, we implemented a solution by interchanging the timestamps, as illustrated in Fig. 4b.

Finally, the devices in our case study exhibit varying communication patterns, where not all devices are capable of sending all types of messages. This diversity in programming logic among the devices results in different combinations of signals being transmitted, as illustrated in Fig. 2. Additionally, when a package distribution encounters obstacles and a device along its path is not ready for package dispatch or reception, further communication is required. However, the communication pattern may not be universally applicable to other devices in the system. As a result, the interpretation of a signal extends beyond its literal meaning and relies on the contextual information associated with the corresponding event. For instance, in Fig. 3, the second Ready is aligned to the departure from KJDQ4414 since no events are labeled as Depart from KJDQ4414 before the package arrives on BRMI1121.

The challenges encountered in our case study have implications that extend beyond our specific scenario and are relevant to various IoT settings involving sensor data and physical object movement. First, the presence of extraneous data resulting from device-to-device communication dynamics can introduce noise in process mining. For instance, an online order or a package delivery experiences repeated notifications of *waiting* or delayed status for several days, despite the absence of any meaningful progress or updates from the business perspective. Second, the presence of faulty sensors is not limited to our case study. In different contexts, such as logistics or manufacturing, faulty sensors can produce mislead-

(a) Event data with sensor fault, where a package arrives on the next device before departing the previous device.

(b) Repaired event data with sensor fault, where the timestamps of the implausible arrival and departure are swapped.

Fig. 4. Repairing event data with sensor fault. We highlight the corrective measures implemented on the observed behavior in Figure (a), resulting in the behavior depicted in Figure (b).

Fig. 5. Schematic diagram of the rectification process. First, we process the event data based on explicit rules. Next, we filter the events solely for communication messages and noises. Then, we merge and relabel events for the stay of a package on a device. The rectified event data signifies the package movements in reality.

ing readings, causing a discrepancy between the perceived status of a case and its actual condition. Finally, the existence of different programming logic among sensors introduces additional challenges in process mining. This challenge is not limited to legacy systems, as demonstrated in our case study, but also extends to IoT environments encompassing devices from different manufacturers. These challenges emphasize the importance of rectifying sensor data in IoT environments to ensure the reliability of the insights obtained through process mining.

3.2   Rectification Process

We develop a rectification process based on three principles identified during the analysis. This section outlines the process and we further illustrate the principles.

Overview. With the aim of reducing ambiguities, we developed a rectification process outlined in Fig. 5. The process consists of three phases. First, we process the event data using explicit business rules to handle the data quality issues arising from the data extraction process. Second, we address ambiguities and filter out noise, which includes events that are not directly associated with the physical movement of a package, as well as events that exhibit improbable behavior resulting from sensor malfunctions. Finally, we merge the consecutive events from the same device and relabel the events for the arrival and departure of a package on each device.

Principles. We demonstrate the principles that we applied for the rectification of the event data in the process.

1. **Signal category.** There are eight different signals. We categorize them based on their literal meaning, which is described in Table 2. The first category, *physical movement*, includes signals that primarily indicate the physical movement of a package. Next, the category of *communication* consists of signals that often show the status of a device. Lastly, the category of *package distribution* comprises signals that indicate the distribution of a package, e.g., a package distribution is canceled with an event labeled with `Cancel`.
2. **Certainty based on signals.** Due to the challenges identified, the categories defined are insufficient to determine the actual arrival or departure of a package on a device Hence, in collaboration with domain experts, we establish a

Table 2. Categories of signals based on their literal meaning and domain knowledge.

Category	Description	Signal Values (`Sig`)
Physical Movement	*Mostly* indicating the physical movement of a package	`Arrive, Depart`
Communication	*Often* for exchanging the status of the device	`Decide, Ready, Initiate`
Package Distribution	*Always* updating the distribution of a package	`Cancel, Insert, Change`

ranking of the *certainty*, i.e., whether an event indicates the *actual* movement of a package, based on its signal, taking into account the context of the event in a trace. This ranking is separately defined for the arrival and departure of a package, allowing us to demonstrate the relative certainty associated with each event in relation to its context.

- *Certainty for arrival:* `Arrive, Initiate, Decide, Ready`
- *Certainty for departure:* `Depart, Ready, Decide, Initiate`

Note that an `Arrive` only signifies the arrival of a package on a device, and a `Depart` indicates the departure; hence, they are not considered in the complementary ranking.

3. **Interpretation based on the context.** In addition to the literal meaning of the signals, whether an event indicates actual package movement depends on the context of the event. For instance, in the case of the second `Ready` from `KJDQ4414` in Fig. 3, it is considered as indicating actual movement because there are no events labeled as `Depart` from `KJDQ4414`.

Due to the large number of devices involved, it is impractical to identify and resolve all the ambiguities with the assistance of domain experts. Moreover, as the system was constructed long ago and some of the original domain experts are no longer associated with the organization, the available domain knowledge for addressing these ambiguities is limited. Reprogramming all the sensors solely for the purpose of process mining is not a viable option due to time and budget constraints. Hence, we define these principles to guide the rectification of various solutions in each phase of the process, incorporating limited domain knowledge and effectively addressing the ambiguities.

3.3   Application of Principles

In this section, we present examples that demonstrate the application of the principles in each phase of the rectification process. The implementation of the solutions follows a rule-based and automated approach, which has been developed through rigorous testing and iterative refinement. We carefully define the rules through extensive analysis of the event data, along with discussions and validation with domain experts. Our objective is to minimize the potential for false corrections during the automated rectification process. This iterative app-roach allowed us to continually enhance the effectiveness and accuracy of the automated solutions, ensuring the reliability of the results.

For simplicity, we adopt the same expression to represent a trace fragment, without displaying the timestamp or device identifier. First, we address the data quality issues arising from the collection and extraction of sensor data.

Example 1: Identify incomplete cases. The presence of `Arrive` is assigned with significantly higher importance compared to other signals. A package is consid-ered more likely to actually reach a device when an `Arrive` is sent from the device. By prioritizing `Arrive`, we address the completeness of cases by consid-ering those without an `Arrive` event as incomplete.

Example 2: Reorder events with identical timestamps. We observed a peculiar behavior in which a package appears to be rapidly shuttled back and forth between two pieces of devices within an unreasonably short duration (less than a second). This behavior is impossible within the normal operation of the system. The anomaly may stem from the arrival of data samples at the data lake in an order that does not correspond to the package movement. We address it by reordering such events based on their context as shown in Fig. 6.

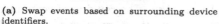

(a) Swap events based on surrounding device identifiers.

(b) Reorder events while preserving the order for the other events.

Fig. 6. Reorder events of identical timestamps based on the context. Events sharing the same timestamp are grouped and highlighted, with additional emphasis on the correction focus.

Next, we resolve the ambiguities arising from the challenges discussed in Sect. 3.1 and filter out noises. The following examples illustrate the solution implemented to address four types of noise caused by ineffective cancellations, timeouts, communication, and sensor faults.

Example 3: Detect effective cancellations. Cancellation of package distribution occurs due to business reasons. The cancellation can be reversed by an `Insert`. When a cancellation is retracted, we consider the associated events as noise. However, the relationship between a `Cancel` and an `Insert` is undefined. To establish their relation, we determine their proximity in a trace. Retraction is considered effective within a *distance* of 2 in the trace as depicted in Fig. 7.

Fig. 7. Detection of retraction of cancellation, noise (the second `Insert`), and effective cancellation (the last `Cancel` since there is no subsequent `Insert`).

Example 4: Remove timeout noise. Events labeled with the same signal from the same device are classified as timeout noise and are eliminated based on the defined ranking. For instance, in the case of `Arrive`, the timeout noise refers to those that are not the first occurrence among consecutive events from the same device. The timeout noise for `Depart` is defined symmetrically. Figure 8 highlights the events as timeout noise under other different conditions.

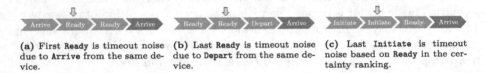

(a) First `Ready` is timeout noise due to `Arrive` from the same device.

(b) Last `Ready` is timeout noise due to `Depart` from the same device.

(c) Last `Initiate` is timeout noise based on `Ready` in the certainty ranking.

Fig. 8. Identification of timeout noise across various scenarios. We identify timeout noise based on the context and the defined certainty ranking, which are highlighted with arrows.

Example 5: Filter communication noises. According to the ranking of certainty, we identify communication noise based on context. If an event is surrounded by other events with signals that rank higher according to the defined ranking, we classify it as communication overhead and exclude it from the event data. The examples in Fig. 9 demonstrate the mechanism and the identification of communication noise across various scenarios.

(a) Both `Decide` and `Ready` are considered as communication overhead due to the existence of both `Arrive` and `Depart`.

(b) `Decide` is regarded as communication overhead while `Ready` is not due to the presence of `Arrive` and the absence of `Depart`.

Fig. 9. Recognition of communication noise based on category and certainty ranking. We point out the communication overhead with arrows.

Example 6: Swap timestamps for faulty sensors. Based on the high confidence placed on `Arrive` for the actual arrival, we identify noise caused by malfunctioning sensors and address it by swapping the timestamps, as explained in Fig. 4.

This phase of the process heavily relies on the context to identify and eliminate noise. As the context evolves, we iteratively apply the solutions to reduce the communication overhead. This process continues until no further events can be removed. Once the communication overhead is eliminated, in the next phase, we relabel and create artificial events to align them with the package movement and ensure the consistency of event format per device.

Example 7: Relabel events. Suppose only two events of a device remain that exhibit a clear logical order in a trace; relabeling is not required or is straightforward. In situations where only one `Arrive` is sent, we create an artificial event to represent the departure, using the timestamp of the next device's arrival in the package distribution. If only a `Depart` exists, the implementation follows a symmetrical approach. Figure 3 demonstrates the scenarios described. Note that these decisions are based on context and category. If only communication signals exist, we assume the package never reaches the device and consequently remove the associated events. For example, in Fig. 1, the events from device C are appropriately eliminated during this step due to the absence of signals in the category of physical movement.

Building upon the principles, we have effectively devised solutions to tackle the challenges discussed in Sect. 3.1. These solutions have been seamlessly integrated into our project partner's information system, enabling the computation of proprietary key performance indicators.

3.4   Limitations

While the developed methodology effectively addresses complex challenges within our case study, it is crucial to delve into potential limitations. This section provides a discussion that contributes to understanding both the potential and the boundaries of the proposed approach.

As we examine the context of an event for data rectification, the need for a comprehensive event context introduces challenges in real-time scenarios. Furthermore, the rankings on signal labels are defined on the basis of domain expertise to establish rules for conditions identified within the system. While the integration of domain knowledge could limit seamless generalization across various scenarios, our methodology can be aligned with domains characterized by attributes like queue-based operations, common in logistics, and the device-to-device communication typical of the IoT environments. In such cases, our approach can be applied by defining system-specific rules. Moreover, our methodology entails iterative rectification. This iterative process carries an inherent risk — a cascade effect that could inadvertently jeopardize the integrity of the original data. Identifying and mitigating these cascade effects becomes crucial. Nonetheless, our observations have not unveiled such effects.

The elucidated limitations warrant acknowledgement. By addressing these constraints, we provide a balanced perspective on our methodology and empower one to formulate rules for real-world applications.

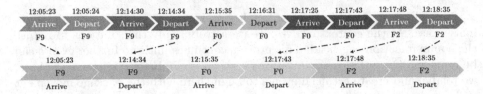

Fig. 10. Abstracting event data based on `floor` attribute. The top trace showcases a fragment of rectified trace and the bottom one is the corresponding abstracted fragment based on *floor*.

4   Process Mining

The rectified event data consists of approximately 5,000 unique device identifiers and 20,000 distinct variants. Given the complexity of the event data, validating every path with the physical situation in the terminal is not feasible. Meanwhile, the classical discovery and conformance-checking algorithms fall short in terms of scalability. Hence, we abstract the event data based on the device attributes to uncover process models and validate the insights obtained from process mining outcomes instead. The models are discovered through inductive mining techniques and further enhanced with domain knowledge [15,16], which are colored with the relative frequency of the distribution and annotated with labels for readability. The abstraction is performed as in Fig. 10, where we *merge* and rename the events based on `floor`. Abstraction based on other attributes is performed in a similar manner.

Figures 11 and 12 present the models discovered based on the location information, where the numbers indicate the relative path frequency. Figure 11 reveals that most of the package distributions are initiated on F9 but can end up on different floors, mainly exiting on F0. Except for F0, most floors are rarely revisited. It is also worth noting that not all the data samples from the sensors on lift shaft (LS) are received when packages are distributed across floors, indicating missing sensor readings. Figure 12 demonstrates the distribution based on zones in F0. Two stages are identified. In the first stage, no dominant paths across zones are identified; meanwhile, some zones are closely related based on their values, which reflects the geographical naming conventions. In the second stage, the distributions leave the F0 from zones U, K and R.

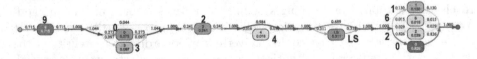

Fig. 11. Package distribution based on floors. Since lift shafts (LS) are used for distributing packages across floors, we do not classify them to floors.

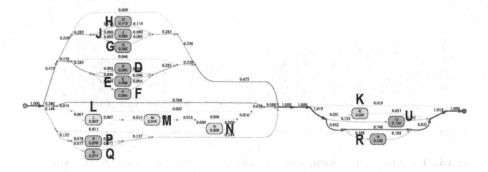

Fig. 12. Package distribution based on zones on F0.

Figure 13 presents another aspect of package distribution. Similarly, we see the combination of device types that are often applied together. Moreover, it shows a sequential pattern across the three stages of distribution: the beginning, during, and end on F0. Besides packages arriving from the lift shafts (LS), some packages are stacked in storage-type devices, i.e., hand-operated lift (HL) and lifting boom (LB), before being distributed throughout the floor.

We evaluate the fitness [2] and the precision [21] of the models based on the event data before and after rectification. At the floor level, the fitness is approximately 0.7 for both datasets, while the precision is 0.97 and 0.93 for the pre- and post-rectification datasets, respectively. We assume that the models in Fig. 12 and 13 represent behavior on all floors and compare them against the package distribution on other floors. Figure 14 presents the results. The metrics do not differ much at the floor and zone levels. However, regarding device type, the fitness increases for most floors, while the change in precision varies depending on the floor. In most cases, F-Score is enhanced. Moreover, the metrics for F9 exhibit lower fitness values due to the limited device types on the floor, which primarily serves as the entry floor for package distribution.

5   Related Work

In this section, we explore existing work regarding challenges surrounding sensor data in IoT and the application of process mining with IoT sensor data. In addition, we examine preprocessing techniques in process mining and discuss

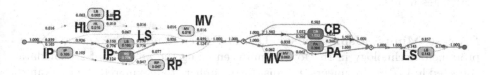

Fig. 13. Discovering package distribution on F0 at the level of device type.

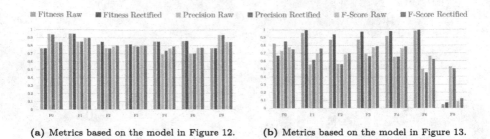

(a) Metrics based on the model in Figure 12.   (b) Metrics based on the model in Figure 13.

Fig. 14. The fitness, precision, and F-score of the models based on F0, which are compared against two datasets per floor: *raw* (before rectification) and *rectified*. The metrics are color-coded consistently, with the hue differentiating datasets.

their applicability to our case study. Through this review, we clarify the specific research gap our case study aims to address.

Sensor Data in IoT. Sensor data in the context of the IoT present unique challenges in terms of quality and reliability. Extensive research has been conducted to address these challenges. Teh et al. conducted a systematic review focusing on the quality-related issues of sensor data, categorizing eight types of sensor data errors and discussing existing solutions for error detection and correction [26]. Similarly, Gaddam et al. provided a comprehensive review that specifically examined the detection of sensor faults in the IoT [12]. Additionally, Mansouri et al. identified and discussed various IoT data quality issues based on existing research [19]. These issues align with the challenges encountered in our case study, including the misalignment arising from faulty sensors, inconsistencies due to different sensor programming logic, redundancy owing to device-to-device communication, and ambiguity in data interpretation. However, while these existing techniques aim to tackle general data quality issues in IoT, they may not directly address the specific challenges encountered in our case study, which focuses on analyzing and extracting insights from package distribution within the system. Our approach rectifies sensor data by considering the real-world behavior of package distribution and addresses the ambiguity in data interpretation through the context of an event in a case. The customized approach bridges the gap between the data used for process mining and the specific data quality considerations of our case study. These findings highlight the relevance and potential applicability of our work in addressing the broader challenges in IoT.

Process Mining Using Sensor Data. Process mining has emerged as a prominent technology in the IoT domain, enabling the analysis of sensor data collected in IoT environments. For instance, Dreher et al. explored the feasibility and application of process mining in manufacturing-related processes [10]. Considering the similarities between logistic processes and manufacturing processes, where the efficient flow of goods and services is a crucial objective, the research gap identified in manufacturing-related processes is also relevant to our case study. Specifically, the paper acknowledges the research gap we aim to address in this case study, stating that "implementing process mining in manufacturing faces a significant disconnect between the physical flow of materials and the digital information flow" [10]. Janssen proposed a technique to discretize sensor data into event data suitable for process mining by correlating events, discovering activities, and abstracting events [13]. The work focuses on elevating the sensor data to the business level. Similarly, van Eck et al. conducted a study where they abstracted sensor data by mapping temperature and acceleration measurements from a smart baby bottle to human activities and identifying process instances through activity grouping [11]. By applying process mining to the transformed data, their work demonstrated the value of process mining in facilitating the design process of smart products. Our case study shares the same objective, aiming to identify significant events or sensor data that represent meaningful status changes within a case, facilitating analysis at the business level. However, our study specifically addresses the challenges posed by device-to-device communication and focuses on resolving the ambiguity in data interpretation based on contextual information.

Preprocessing Event Data in Process Mining. Preprocessing event data has long been a recognized challenge, leading to various techniques proposed. Our approach to refining event order through timestamp manipulation and removing communication overhead falls into the category of the transformation techniques discussed in a review [20]. Nevertheless, these techniques are insufficient for our case study due to distinct challenges and conditions.

The timestamp attribute signifies event order, a fundamental concept in process mining. Various techniques have been proposed for manipulating timestamps for process mining purposes. The authors proposed using domain expertise interactively to rectify event order [9]. van der Aalst and Santos visualized events with time and allowed for grouping and generating partially ordered events based on domain knowledge [3]. Tax et al. refined event labels using a distribution model based on time attributes [25]. However, our case study introduces a data quality challenge rooted in IoT sensor malfunctions, setting it apart from these time granularity-focused timestamp manipulations in process mining.

Conventional interpretation often considers noise as outliers, typically identified based on the frequency or probability of event label occurrences [8,23,24]. Furthermore, some techniques require a reference process model for their application [6,17], which is absent in our circumstances. Instead, our case study presents a unique challenge deviating from typical causes of outliers. The scale of our system yields a scarcity of data points collected from each device, rendering frequency-based approaches ineffective. Adding complexity, the applied domain knowledge or constraints stems from real-world operational behaviors, such as the restriction against a package simultaneously existing on two devices, rather than deducing solely from event data.

Our case study addresses the specific challenges that arise from device-to-device communication in the context of process mining. While existing techniques for addressing sensor data issues in IoT environments and preprocessing event data in process mining may not be directly transferable to our case study, we have developed customized rules tailored to the challenges observed in the real-world package distribution scenario. This approach benefits from iterative discussions and presentations with stakeholders and domain experts, ensuring the effectiveness and reliability of our approach. Moreover, existing research in process mining predominantly focuses on identifying key concepts such as activities and cases from sensor data capturing continuous measurements. In contrast, our case study fills an important gap by proposing an approach to address the integration of sensor data from device-to-device communication within the process mining framework and provides a novel methodology that harnesses relative certainty based on behavioral constraints.

6   Lessons Learned and Opportunities

Sensor data presents unique challenges in applying process mining to extract business-level insights. In addition to the high volume of data points typically found in sensor data, we identified various inherent challenges, including sensor malfunctions, missing readings, and communication overhead, in the case study. Furthermore, the limited availability of domain knowledge in a legacy system adds to the complexity, with ambiguities arising in the interpretation of sensor data. Meanwhile, conducting a simulation on a large system is expensive. To tackle these challenges, we developed a rectification process based on the principles identified and discussed throughout our analysis. The solutions were implemented specifically tailored to the identified conditions, to effectively repair sensor data and align them with the package movement. We demonstrate the effectiveness of the solutions with the validated process mining outcomes based on the rectified event data. For future work, although the implemented solutions have been customized to achieve optimal quality, there is an opportunity to apply them to a broader range of IoT use cases. By utilizing the certainty ranking and conducting repeated checks on the contextual information of events, a general solution is to be developed to *match* event pairs for every package distribution on a device to enhance the applicability and effectiveness of our approach.

References

1. van der Aalst, W.M.P.: Process Mining - Data Science in Action, 2nd edn. Springer, Cham (2016). https://doi.org/10.1007/978-3-662-49851-4
2. van der Aalst, W.M.P., Adriansyah, A., van Dongen, B.F.: Replaying history on process models for conformance checking and performance analysis. WIREs Data Mining Knowl. Discov. **2**(2), 182–192 (2012)
3. van der Aalst, W.M.P., Santos, L.: May i take your order? - on the interplay between time and order in process mining. In: Marrella, A., Weber, B. (eds.) BPM 2021. LNBIP, vol. 436, pp. 99–110. Springer, Cham (2022). https://doi.org/10.1007/978-3-030-94343-1_8

4. Bänziger, R.B., Basukoski, A., Chaussalet, T.J.: Discovering business processes in CRM systems by leveraging unstructured text data. In: 20th IEEE International Conference on High Performance Computing and Communications; 16th IEEE International Conference on Smart City; 4th IEEE International Conference on Data Science and Systems, HPCC/SmartCity/DSS 2018, Exeter, United Kingdom, 28–30 June 2018, pp. 1571–1577. IEEE (2018)
5. Bauer, M., van der Aa, H., Weidlich, M.: Sampling and approximation techniques for efficient process conformance checking. Inf. Syst. **104**, 101666 (2022)
6. Cheng, H., Kumar, A.: Process mining on noisy logs - can log sanitization help to improve performance? Decis. Support Syst. **79**, 138–149 (2015)
7. Chiudinelli, L., et al.: Mining post-surgical care processes in breast cancer patients. Artif. Intell. Medicine **105**, 101855 (2020)
8. Conforti, R., Rosa, M.L., ter Hofstede, A.H.M.: Filtering out infrequent behavior from business process event logs. IEEE Trans. Knowl. Data Eng. **29**(2), 300–314 (2017)
9. Dixit, P.M., et al.: Detection and interactive repair of event ordering imperfection in process logs. In: Krogstie, J., Reijers, H.A. (eds.) CAiSE 2018. LNCS, vol. 10816, pp. 274–290. Springer, Cham (2018). https://doi.org/10.1007/978-3-319-91563-0_17
10. Dreher, S., Reimann, P., Gröger, C.: Application fields and research gaps of process mining in manufacturing companies. In: Reussner, R.H., Koziolek, A., Heinrich, R. (eds.) 50. Jahrestagung der Gesellschaft für Informatik, INFORMATIK 2020 - Back to the Future, Karlsruhe, Germany, 28 September–2 October 2020. LNI, vol. P-307, pp. 621–634. GI (2020)
11. van Eck, M.L., Sidorova, N., van der Aalst, W.M.P.: Enabling process mining on sensor data from smart products. In: Tenth IEEE International Conference on Research Challenges in Information Science, RCIS 2016, Grenoble, France, 1–3 June 2016, pp. 1–12. IEEE (2016)
12. Gaddam, A., Wilkin, T., Angelova, M., Gaddam, J.: Detecting sensor faults, anomalies and outliers in the internet of things: a survey on the challenges and solutions. Electronics **9**(3), 511 (2020)
13. Janssen, D., Mannhardt, F., Koschmider, A., van Zelst, S.J.: Process model discovery from sensor event data. In: Leemans, S., Leopold, H. (eds.) ICPM 2020. LNBIP, vol. 406, pp. 69–81. Springer, Cham (2021). https://doi.org/10.1007/978-3-030-72693-5_6
14. Leemans, S.J.J., van der Aalst, W.M.P., Brockhoff, T., Polyvyanyy, A.: Stochastic process mining: earth movers' stochastic conformance. Inf. Syst. **102**, 101724 (2021)
15. Leemans, S.J.J., Fahland, D., van der Aalst, W.M.P.: Using life cycle information in process discovery. In: Reichert, M., Reijers, H.A. (eds.) BPM 2015. LNBIP, vol. 256, pp. 204–217. Springer, Cham (2016). https://doi.org/10.1007/978-3-319-42887-1_17
16. Leemans, S.J.J., Fahland, D., van der Aalst, W.M.P.: Scalable process discovery and conformance checking. Softw. Syst. Model. **17**(2), 599–631 (2018)
17. de Leoni, M., Maggi, F.M., van der Aalst, W.M.P.: An alignment-based framework to check the conformance of declarative process models and to preprocess event-log data. Inf. Syst. **47**, 258–277 (2015)
18. de Leoni, M., Munoz-Gama, J., Carmona, J., van der Aalst, W.M.P.: Decomposing alignment-based conformance checking of data-aware process models. In: Meersman, R., et al. (eds.) OTM 2014. LNCS, vol. 8841, pp. 3–20. Springer, Heidelberg (2014). https://doi.org/10.1007/978-3-662-45563-0_1

19. Mansouri, T., Moghadam, M.R.S., Monshizadeh, F., Zareravasan, A.: IoT data quality issues and potential solutions: a literature review. Comput. J. **66**(3), 615–625 (2023)
20. Marin-Castro, H.M., Tello-Leal, E.: Event log preprocessing for process mining: a review. Appl. Sci. **11**(22), 10556 (2021)
21. Muñoz-Gama, J., Carmona, J.: A fresh look at precision in process conformance. In: Hull, R., Mendling, J., Tai, S. (eds.) BPM 2010. LNCS, vol. 6336, pp. 211–226. Springer, Heidelberg (2010). https://doi.org/10.1007/978-3-642-15618-2_16
22. Pan, Y., Zhang, L.: Automated process discovery from event logs in BIM construction projects. Autom. Constr. **127**, 103713 (2021)
23. Sani, M.F., van Zelst, S.J., van der Aalst, W.M.P.: Improving process discovery results by filtering outliers using conditional behavioural probabilities. In: Teniente, E., Weidlich, M. (eds.) BPM 2017. LNBIP, vol. 308, pp. 216–229. Springer, Cham (2018). https://doi.org/10.1007/978-3-319-74030-0_16
24. Fani Sani, M., van Zelst, S.J., van der Aalst, W.M.P.: Applying sequence mining for outlier detection in process mining. In: Panetto, H., Debruyne, C., Proper, H.A., Ardagna, C.A., Roman, D., Meersman, R. (eds.) OTM 2018. LNCS, vol. 11230, pp. 98–116. Springer, Cham (2018). https://doi.org/10.1007/978-3-030-02671-4_6
25. Tax, N., Alasgarov, E., Sidorova, N., Haakma, R., van der Aalst, W.M.P.: Generating time-based label refinements to discover more precise process models. J. Ambient Intell. Smart Environ. **11**(2), 165–182 (2019)
26. Teh, H.Y., Kempa-Liehr, A.W., Wang, K.I.-K.: Sensor data quality: a systematic review. J. Big Data **7**(1), 1–49 (2020). https://doi.org/10.1186/s40537-020-0285-1
27. Valencia-Parra, Á., Ramos-Gutiérrez, B., Varela-Vaca, A.J., López, M.T.G., Bernal, A.G.: Enabling process mining in aircraft manufactures: extracting event logs and discovering processes from complex data. In: vom Brocke, J., Mendling, J., Rosemann, M. (eds.) Proceedings of the Industry Forum at BPM 2019 co-located with 17th International Conference on Business Process Management (BPM 2019), Vienna, Austria, 1–6 September 2019. CEUR Workshop Proceedings, vol. 2428, pp. 166–177. CEUR-WS.org (2019)
28. Wójcicki, K., Biegańska, M., Paliwoda, B., Górna, J.: Internet of things in industry: research profiling, application, challenges and opportunities-a review. Energies **15**(5), 1806 (2022)

Using Process Mining for Face Validity Assessment in Agent-Based Simulation Models: An Exploratory Case Study

Rob Bemthuis[1,2]($\boxtimes$), Ruben Govers[1], and Sanja Lazarova-Molnar[2]

[1] University of Twente, Drienerlolaan 5, 7522 NB Enschede, The Netherlands
r.h.bemthuis@utwente.nl, r.r.govers@student.utwente.nl
[2] Karlsruhe Institute of Technology, Kaiserstraße 89, 76133 Karlsruhe, Germany
rob.bemthuis@partner.kit.edu, sanja.lazarova-molnar@kit.edu

Abstract. In the field of simulation, the key objective of a system designer is to develop a model that performs a specific task and accurately represents real-world systems or processes. A valid simulation model allows for a better understanding of the system's behavior and improved decision-making in the real world. Face validity is a subjective measure that assesses the extent to which a simulation model and its outcomes appear reasonable to an expert based on a superficial examination of the simulator's realism. Process mining techniques, which are novel data-driven methods for obtaining real-life insights into processes based on event logs, show promise when combined with effective visualization techniques. These techniques can augment the face validity assessment of simulation models in reflecting real-life behavior and play a key role in supporting humans conducting such assessments. In this paper, we present an approach that utilizes process mining techniques to assess the face validity of agent-based simulation models. To illustrate our approach, we use the Schelling model of segregation. We demonstrate how graphical representation, immersive assessment, and sensitivity analysis can be used to assess face validity based on event logs produced by the simulation model. Our study shows that process mining in combination with visualization can strongly support humans in assessing face validity of agent-based simulation models.

Keywords: Face validity · Agent-based simulation · Agent-based modeling · Process mining · Schelling model

1 Introduction

Simulations provide a powerful tool for researchers and practitioners to model and analyze complex systems and processes [24]. The primary objective for designers of simulation models is to develop models that accurately represent the real-world systems or processes of interest, while also being capable of performing specific tasks and gaining insights into the real-world process or system [33].

With the increasing availability of data, simulation models can now be developed with greater sophistication, allowing for a deeper understanding of the behavior of the system and improved decision-making in real-world scenarios [18,23,29].

When constructing simulation models, one of the initial techniques employed to enhance validity is performing a face validity assessment [20]. Face validity is a subjective measure that evaluates the degree to which a simulation model and its outcomes appear plausible to an expert, based on the realism of the simulator [10,27]. This involves having individuals, often experts, assess the realism of the model and/or its behavior [28]. Face validity can help identify potential issues or limitations in the simulation model, and can be determined through a combination of expert judgment, comparison with empirical evidence, and critical evaluation of the model's design and assumptions. Despite its potential utility during the early stages of simulation model development, face validity has been subject to criticism from the scientific community [25]. For example, a review of face validity assessment [15] identified concerns regarding inconsistency and inadequate guidance during the expert evaluation phase.

Process mining has emerged as a promising tool for conducting data-driven validation checks of simulation models. This technique involves analyzing event logs to discover, monitor, and improve processes within a system [1]. By applying process mining techniques to simulation output and using appropriate data processing and visualization methods, practitioners can identify patterns and anomalies in a model's behavior. This allows for a comparison with the real system underlying the model, and for the identification of discrepancies or errors in assumptions or parameters [3]. For instance, streaming process mining can be employed for real-time analysis of event data [8], providing continuous feedback on simulation processes. As a result, the correctness of the model implementation can be verified and the simulation model's capability to perform its intended tasks can be ensured through validation, increasing its utility for decision-making in various fields. Despite its potential, research on evaluating the effectiveness of process mining techniques in conducting face validity assessments is limited.

In this article, we explore the application of process mining techniques to assess the face validity of agent-based simulation models. Process mining has demonstrated its utility in the domain of agent-based simulation modeling, including model verification and performance analysis [5,9,35]. These techniques can also be used to analyze various properties, including agent behavior [14,37]. However, available studies do not cover agent-based simulations that are characterized by for example numerous interactions, heterogeneous populations, and complex topologies. Additionally, the evolving nature of agent behavior and their available knowledge are often overlooked [4,6], raising concerns about model validity. Leveraging process mining techniques to support face validity assessments can enhance the validity of agent-based simulation models.

This paper aims to demonstrate and evaluate the application of process mining techniques for assessing face validity of agent-based simulation models. We apply process mining techniques to extract insights from the event logs generated by the simulation model. Subsequently, we perform a face validity assessment using the insights obtained from process mining. To illustrate our approach, we employ a well-researched agent-based simulation model, namely the Schelling model of segregation, and demonstrate how a face validity assessment can be conducted using process mining techniques. Through this assessment, we aim to determine if insights obtained through process mining tools can be used to assess whether an agent-based model appears reasonable in the context of face validity.

The remainder of the paper is structured as follows. Section 2 provides a literature review of existing methods that use process mining to analyze or evaluate agent-based simulation models. Section 3 outlines the research design used for the study. The experimental results are discussed in Sect. 4. Finally, Sect. 5 provides conclusions and recommendations for future research.

2   Literature Review

Several studies have explored the use of process mining to extract knowledge from agent-based simulation models. In [9], the authors integrate process mining with multi-agent models, using Petri-net semantics to monitor and debug multi-agent systems during the development phase. They analyze agent interactions within simulated organizations and present a plug-in for recording interaction logs. The article uses agent interaction protocol diagrams as a descriptive form that combines organizational and control-flow information, which can be mapped to executable Petri nets. This enables mining results to be used for validating and verifying actual behavior during the design phase [9]. In [12], the authors develop a hierarchical Markov model to capture high and low-level behavior in business processes using an event log and process description. They aim to understand agent behavior from both control-flow and organizational perspectives and compare the results with those from existing process mining techniques using an agent-based simulation platform. In [19], the authors enhance MAREA, a multi-agent simulator, to enable process mining analysis. They formalize its architecture and show how a multi-agent system can record event logs for later process mining analysis. The authors extract event logs from simulations, implement a model of a trading company, and perform process structure verification and social network analysis with process mining [19]. The work discussed in [4] proposes an agent-based simulation framework that can discover and analyze emergent behavior arising in cyber-physical systems. They show a form of agents' self-learning capabilities by incorporating knowledge obtained from process models into the agent decisions. In [6], the authors propose an approach to extract agents' underlying models from log data generated from their behaviors, utilizing process mining. The authors demonstrate this approach using the Schelling model of segregation, showing how agent models can be extracted utilizing process mining techniques. In this paper, we adopt their approach in our research design (see Sect. 3). The work of [36] introduces an agent-based simulation environment for process discovery and conformance checking and describe how to handle the XES format to import data into the NetLogo platform.

The efficacy of using process mining techniques to assess the outcomes of agent-based simulation models remains under-studied, resulting in limited research in this domain. Although there is existing literature on the use of process mining for performance analysis of agent behavior in agent-based simulation systems (e.g., waiting times, anomalies, etc.), the applicability of process mining techniques for conducting face validation for agent-based simulation models is a topic that has received limited attention in the research community. A knowledge gap in the process mining discipline is the lack of guidelines for balancing quality dimensions, such as fitness and precision, when assessing the face validity of agent-based simulation models. Nevertheless, there have been initial attempts to compare different agent-process mining configurations, including multiple process mining discovery algorithms [5], agent rule settings [4,5], and variation in the number of events [2]. However, these investigations are still preliminary and have explored only a limited set of variations. Furthermore, they are not specifically focused on face validation. In [3], the authors present an approach for assessing the face validity of agent-based simulation models through process mining. However, their focus is on outlier behaviors, and their six-step approach is not described in detail, but rather outlines what should be done. Although their approach is illustrated through its application to the Schelling model of segregation, it lacks detailed descriptions of how each step can be implemented. To address this gap in the literature, we aim to demonstrate and evaluate the applicability of readily available process mining techniques for determining the face validity of a well-established agent-based simulation model.

Overall, the combination of process mining and agent-based simulation has promising potential for gaining insights into complex systems, enhancing simulation model verification and validation, and improving agent decision-making. Our proposed analysis framework is novel in that it employs a data-driven approach to extract performance metrics, taking into account both the features of an agent-based simulation model and the outcomes of process mining techniques. Ultimately, this approach can aid in developing better simulation models, achieve a deeper understanding of the underlying mechanisms of agent-based simulations, and making more informed decisions through the application of process mining techniques.

3   Research Design

Figure 1 outlines the research design, which consists of several phases. This illustration is adapted from the approach proposed by [6]. In the following part, we provide a detailed account of the execution of each phase.

3.1   Problem Context

For our study, we have selected the Schelling model of segregation as our case study and use it as an illustrative example throughout our explanation of the research design used for conducting a face validation assessment.

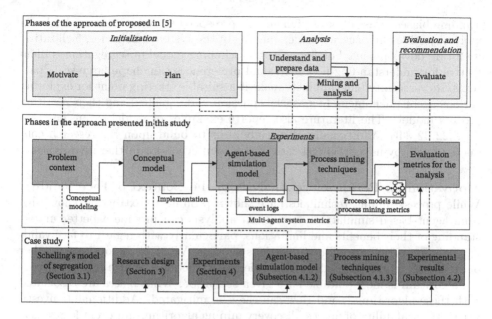

Fig. 1. Research design.

Introduction to the Case Study. The Schelling model of segregation is a widely recognized and influential social simulation model [34] that has been applied in various fields of research, including sociology [11]. This model illustrates how individual preferences can result in large-scale social patterns, even without explicit discrimination or prejudice [30]. The Schelling model of segregation was developed by economist Thomas Schelling to explain how segregation can occur even when individuals do not have a strong preference for living among people of their own race or ethnicity [31]. The Schelling model has served as a basis for developing other simulation models that explore social phenomena, such as the spread of infectious diseases [17] and the formation of social networks [16].

In this model, a grid representing a housing market is randomly populated with individuals who are characterized by a "tolerance threshold". This threshold represents the proportion of neighbors of the same race or ethnicity required for an individual to feel satisfied with their living situation. As the simulation progresses, dissatisfied individuals move to new locations on the grid in search of neighborhoods that meet their tolerance thresholds. This process can result in highly segregated neighborhoods as individuals with similar characteristics cluster together, attracting more individuals with those same characteristics. Clustering can occur when individual preferences are moderate rather than extreme.

Performance analysis in terms of extracting agent rules and patterns, and evaluating task or function performance (e.g., time, costs, quality, etc.) from the Schelling model of segregation through process mining can be valuable, as it can provide insights into underlying mechanisms and identify previously unknown patterns or relationships, improving our understanding of complex systems, and avoiding biases or assumptions inherent in pre-specified rules. This can lead to a more objective and accurate understanding of the system's behavior, facilitating its future development. Furthermore, the Schelling model of segregation is illustrative for understanding how individual preferences can shape large-scale patterns. Its versatility and simplicity make it a suitable starting point for exploring various agent phenomena (e.g., social cohesion and equality) and their resulting process models. The literature also reports examples of model extensions (see e.g., [22,32,34]). Additionally, this study aims to build upon the research conducted by [6] by using their case study as a foundation for further investigation.

Motivation for Performance Analysis in the Context of Face Validity. While process mining techniques have shown promise in extracting knowledge from agent-based simulation systems, an analysis can provide a better understanding of their benefits and limitations, particularly with regard to face validity. It is important to address questions such as: What is the optimal number of event logs required for effective knowledge extraction?, Which process discovery algorithm is most suitable for a given scenario?, What biases are associated with these algorithms?, and How can they be mitigated? Additionally, investigating the scalability of process discovery mining algorithms for event logs generated by agent-based simulation models and quantifying the computational time required for knowledge extraction using these techniques is relevant. Answering these questions can provide context, such as scalability, timeliness, and quality of results, for determining the face validity of agent-based simulation models through process mining techniques.

Addressing the questions raised in this paper can help develop a deeper understanding of process mining's potential as a tool for face validity, and inform the design of innovative algorithmic process mining solutions specifically tailored for agent-based modeling and simulation. In [37], the authors called for efforts to design process mining techniques specifically for agent-based simulation systems. A systematic analysis can be a step towards achieving this goal.

To assess face validity, we incorporate features such as heterogeneous agents, network typologies, and agent rule behavior into Schelling's model by varying the parameters of the underlying agent model. These features help to make the model more realistic and representative of real-life settings. This approach can enhance our understanding of emergent phenomena in agent-based modeling and simulation. Heterogeneous agents represent a more realistic view of the world, where individuals have different characteristics, capabilities, and behaviors. Network typologies are important because agents often interact within a larger environment or network, and the structure of the network can have a significant impact on the behavior of the system. Finally, considering agent behavior is key because it allows us to model the decision-making logic of individual agents.

3.2   Conceptual Model

Figure 2 presents an overview of the conceptual model that underlies our simulation. The model consists of four main components: input parameters (Step 1 in the figure), model implementation (Steps 2.a, 2.b, and 2.c), and output evaluation metrics (Steps 3.a and 3.b). Below, we provide a brief description of these components. A more detailed account can be found in the experiment section (Sect. 4).

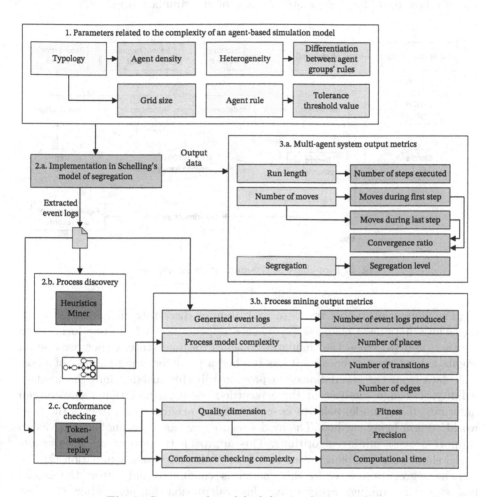

Fig. 2. Conceptual model of the simulation study.

Input Parameters. To evaluate the face validity of the model, we systematically vary its input parameters, assuming that these variations will affect the emergent behaviors that result from agent interactions. To produce a range of results, we select three types of parameters: typology, heterogeneity, and agent behavior rules. By varying these parameters, we anticipate observing changes in the frequency and nature of interactions between agents and their environment, which can help to determine the model's face validity.

Model Implementation. For the implementation of our simulation model, we based our design on the approach proposed by [6]. Additionally, we have used an existing simulation implementation developed by [13] for verification purposes. However, we have made modifications to suit our specific research needs. Figure 3 shows a flowchart that represents the logic of our simulation model.

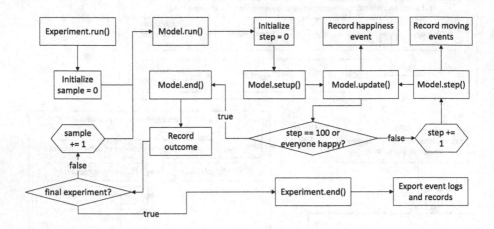

Fig. 3. Flowchart of the simulation model setup.

The simulation model tracks several updates discretely, including (1) when an agent's happiness changes, (2) when an agent moves from one location to another, and (3) when the simulation reaches its final state, either because all agents are satisfied or because it has reached a predetermined number of steps. The data from the simulations can provide valuable insights into the model's validity. Through analysis of these recorded events, simulation modelers can determine if the model behaves as expected and accurately represents the real-world system being studied. The model records events in chronological order to support process mining algorithms. This approach is appropriate since agent-based simulation can be regarded as a type of discrete-event simulation [21].

The segregation level in this model is calculated only after the model has stopped running. Specifically, this calculation happens after the last `Model.update()` call, which follows the last `Model.Step()` call. If the model runs for fewer than 100 steps, it means all agents are happy and the model has reached maximal segregation.

Evaluation Metrics. We use evaluation metrics related to the multi-agent system and process mining techniques to assess our system's validity. These metrics are depicted in Fig. 2. The process mining metrics include measurements based on both process discovery and conformance checking. We chose these metrics for their simplicity, allowing for a rapid assessment of the model's plausibility. We chose a straightforward approach instead of using more complex analytical metrics. As our research is an initial step in this field, this ensures that our findings are easily accessible and understandable.

4 Experiments

We conducted a series of experiments by adjusting the selected parameters to different levels. In the following part, we provide details about the experimental setup and present the experimental results.

4.1 Experimental Setup

Here, we outline the setup for our agent-based simulation model and the process mining techniques, followed by a brief description of their implementation.

Agent-Based Simulation Model. For the analysis, we varied one parameter at a time while keeping all others constant. This allows us to isolate the effect of a parameter on the system's behavior and identify its level of influence. The following parameters were set to fixed values: density = 0.70, grid size = 20, ruleset type (homogeneous/heterogeneous) = homogeneous, tolerance threshold = 0.55, maximum number of steps = 100, and number of agent groups = 4. "Ruleset type" means either all agent groups have the same tolerance threshold (homogeneous population) or all but one group have the same threshold (heterogeneous population). Each parameter setting was executed once, and all runs employed the same random seed values. Single-run assessments can provide valuable insights and guide early model development, as is common for face validity assessments. However, it is important to acknowledge the inherent variability in stochastic simulations when interpreting the results.

Process Mining Techniques. As a process mining discovery algorithm, we used the Heuristics Miner. This algorithm uses the Directly-Follows Graph to handle noise and identify common constructs (e.g. dependencies between two activities) [38]. Its output is a Heuristics Net, which includes the activities and their relationships, and can be converted to a Petri net. The resulting model has three elements: places (states or conditions for a trace, shown as circles), transitions (actions that move the trace between states, shown as rectangles), and edges (flow of work between places and transitions, shown as arrows).

Event logs are stored in the XES format, using the agentID as the case identifier. Activity names include move_location, change_happy_X_Y, and change_unhappy_X_Y, where X represents the total number of direct neighbors and Y represents the number of direct neighbors from the same group as the case agent. Upon application of a process discovery algorithm, activity names can be transformed into transitions. For the timestamp, we used a similar approach as described by [6]. We assigned a sequential counter to each step in the model's execution, based on the chronological order of its occurrence.

To perform conformance checking, we utilized the token-based replay method. This approach is widely employed to verify whether a trace conforms to a given (process) model, indicating that transitions can be executed without any tokens missing during the process. Token-based replay involves comparing a trace and a Petri net model from the initial position to detect the executed transitions and any tokens that may have been added or removed during the process instance [26]. In case the final marking is mandatory, a fitting trace should reach the final marking without any tokens missing or remaining.

Implementation. We implemented the experiments using Python 3.6.9 and utilized the AgentPy 0.1.5 [13] and PM4PY 2.7.2 [7] libraries. The computational resources used in our experiments consisted of a 6-core Intel(R) Core(TM) i7-8750H CPU, which runs at a maximum of 3.29 GHz, and 16 GB of RAM. No multi-threading was used.

4.2 Experimental Results

There are various techniques for conducting face validity assessments for agent-based simulation models [20]. Due to space constraints and to avoid overwhelming the reader with excessive data (e.g., particularly for process models that typically contain numerous nodes and edges), we selectively report key results. Our intention is not to conduct a thorough statistical analysis of the outcome, but rather to present intuitive methods for supporting face validity assessment through the use of process mining techniques. Below, we present a graphical representation, immersive assessment, and sensitivity analysis technique.

Graphical Representations. Figure 4 shows a generated process model that can be used to evaluate the overall system flow, including general flows that match real ones. For example, we observe that many traces of agents who became happy (green box in Fig. 4) go to the end node (see the blue arrow) and do not move anymore, while many unhappy agents (red box) generally move to a different location. Based on this simple observation, the model's face validity can be deemed plausible.

Immersive Assessment. A human expert can view the simulation model's execution through the eyes of the agent and evaluate its actions. For instance, one of the traces, partially depicted in Fig. 5, of an agent includes: unhappy_2_1, move_location, happy_1_1, unhappy_4_1, and move_location. This suggests that an agent moves when it is unhappy, but can also become unhappy again when new neighbors arrive who cause the agent to move once more. This is consistent with Schelling's model and supports the face validity assessment.

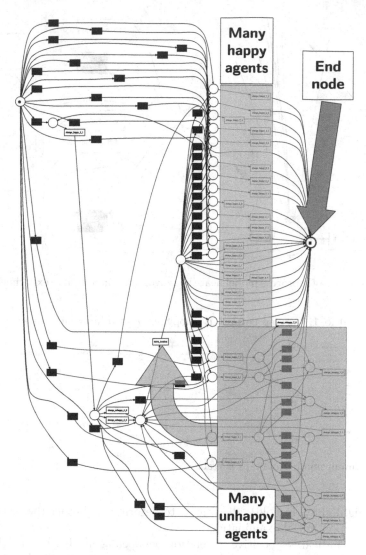

Fig. 4. High-level view of a process model from an experiment with a consistent tolerance threshold of 0.10 applied to all agents. (Note: This illustration is intended for general understanding and not for detailed examination.)

Sensitivity Analysis. As shown in Fig. 2, we used various parameters related to the complexity of our agent-based simulation model. In this paper, we only vary the agent density, which represents the percentage of grids occupied by agents, due to space restrictions. Table 1 shows the resulting output metrics. To assess face validity, we consulted an expert in the field for a preliminary evaluation of general trends and extreme values in the process mining-related output

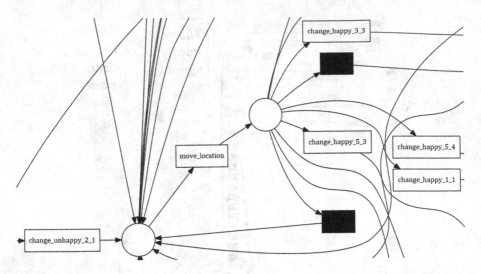

Fig. 5. A snippet of a process model near the move_location activity (experiment T13).

Table 1. Varying network typology, expressed in agent density.

#	Varying parameter	Multi-agent system output metrics					Process mining output metrics						
	Agent density (%)	Number of runs until the threshold is reached	Number of moves			Segregation level	Number of event logs produced	Number of places	Number of transitions	Number of edges	Fitness (%)	Precision (%)	Computational time (MM:SS.ss)
			First run	Last run	Ratio								
T1	0.10	100*	36	10	0.28	0.77	**1966**	**14**	**38**	**76**	**100.00**	40.83	**00:09.36**
T2	0.20	100*	80	10	0.13	0.87	3837	21	67	134	97.50	**20.84**	00:16.11
T3	0.30	100*	90	1	0.01	0.99	5118	29	94	188	96.67	42.49	00:34.56
T4	0.40	100*	146	1	0.01	0.98	6301	33	121	242	96.25	39.07	00:25.87.
T5	0.50	100*	184	1	0.03	0.70	16730	44	172	344	90.50	36.22	01:29.87
T6	0.60	100*	211	2	0.01	0.93	14912	51	227	454	82.50	43.88	04:13.67
T7	0.70	100*	257	26	0.10	0.89	19208	56	245	490	**73.93**	42.67	06:10.48
T8	0.80	100*	295	93	0.32	0.41	29014	57	**256**	**512**	78.75	44.80	08:10.22
T9	0.90	100*	334	319	0.96	0.26	35663	**63**	233	466	85.83	**47.70**	**14:28.97**
T10	0.97	100*	362	257	0.71	0.28	**39724**	49	146	292	96.39	43.89	12:03.88
T11	0.98	100*	375	355	0.95	0.28	**39724**	54	147	294	98.98	38.40	12:30.71
T12	0.99	100*	384	371	0.97	0.28	**39724**	44	123	246	98.99	36.07	08:57.56

*: the maximum number of steps is reached

metrics (highlighted in bold), allowing us to determine whether the results were reasonable upon initial examination.

The data indicates a positive correlation between agent density and the number of event logs, except for experiment T6. Experiments T10-T12 had the highest agent densities and similar number of event logs, suggesting consistent agent moves. However, the ratio of moves varied, indicating fluctuations during each run. Despite this, end segregation levels were identical, possibly due to reaching an equilibrium or cyclic state (e.g., an agent can repeatedly transition between unhappy and happy).

Agent density affects the complexity of the process model. At low densities, the model is less complex, while at high densities, it increases slightly. The greatest number of behaviors is captured at 60–80% density, despite the fact that the number of event logs is not as high as in, e.g., experiments T9-T12.

Fitness and agent density have a non-linear relationship. Fitness decreases as density increases from 0.10 to 0.70 but then increases again from 0.70 to 0.99. This could be due to the system's complexity, making it difficult for the process mining algorithm to accurately reproduce behavior, resulting in decreased fitness. Further increases in density may result in more predictable behavior, increasing fitness. Further analysis is needed to determine the exact cause.

4.3   Discussion

In this section, we will provide an analysis, interpretation, and discuss the implications of the experimental results. Our experiments show that changing the parameters of the agent-based simulation model leads to different emergent behaviors and outcomes, as shown by process mining techniques. This suggests the model is sensitive to changes in input parameters, which is important for face validity. However, we also observed that the results obtained from parameter combinations can result in process mining outcomes that need more examination to match with real-life scenarios.

Face validity is important in agent-based simulation [20], especially when interpreting experiment results, but caution should be exercised. In agent-based modeling, analysts usually do not limit themselves to only examining inputs, such as initial conditions and model specifications, to explain results. Nor do they consider the results to be solely the final state, without taking into account the history or paths taken to reach that state. Unless one is modeling a one-shot game or similar scenario, applying process mining in the manner presented in this study may not be sufficient. Analysts often plot results temporally and use other techniques to evaluate simulations that evolve over time. The variables examined are not limited to those that are measurable in experiments but may also include latent variables or other key model variables, whose physical significance may be unclear, in order to observe how they unfold over time and explain models and results.

While process mining allows for the identification of individual agent behavior in multi-agent systems, examining collective emergent behavior on various levels is also important. To address this, we propose future investigations into both individual and group levels, possibly using hierarchical or relationship-based methods. For example, object-centric process mining can enhance the analysis of an agent-based system by focusing on individual objects or entities. This, in turn, can help to identify emergent behaviors at the group or population level, particularly among populations with specific characteristics (e.g., outliers).

5   Conclusion

This paper presented a study on the application of process mining techniques for assessing the face validity of agent-based simulation models. We proposed an approach that leverages process mining as a tool for conducting face validity assessments and illustrated its effectiveness using the Schelling model of segregation. Our approach demonstrated the potential of process mining techniques to augment the face validity assessment process, thereby contributing to the development of valid agent-based simulation models. Through a proof-of-concept implementation, we showed how a human expert can assess a simulation model and its outcomes using process mining. This knowledge can ultimately aid in the development of valid agent-based simulations, providing accurate representations of real-life systems.

Future research directions include exploring the applicability of process mining to other types of agent-based simulation models, and developing more automated methods for face validity assessment of agent-based simulation models through process mining. One avenue to explore is the integration of statistical methods, such as Latin hypercube sampling or orthogonal sampling, to generate a sample set of agent model parameters, and then selectively and systematically assess the resulting simulation model and its outcomes by a human expert through process mining. Another direction includes deploying mixed methods using multiple approaches to conduct validation analysis. Furthermore, while the utilization of process mining techniques represents a valuable approach in augmenting the face validity of agent-based simulation models, further elucidation regarding their differentiation from conventional approaches may be advantageous. This could include a more detailed explication of the application of process mining techniques in the evaluation of temporally evolving simulations and their distinction from alternative methodologies employed. By addressing this concern, we could offer a more comprehensive understanding of the unique contributions afforded by process mining techniques.

Acknowledgements. We acknowledge the Helmholtz Information & Data Science Academy (HIDA) for providing financial support enabling a short-term research stay at Karlsruhe Institute of Technology (KIT), Germany.

References

1. van der Aalst, W.M.P.: Process Mining: Discovery, Conformance and Enhancement of Business Processes. Springer, Heidelberg (2011). https://doi.org/10.1007/978-3-642-19345-3
2. Belhadi, A., Djenouri, Y., Diaz, V.G., Houssein, E.H., Lin, J.C.W.: Hybrid intelligent framework for automated medical learning. Expert. Syst. **39**(6), e12737 (2022). https://doi.org/10.1111/exsy.12737
3. Bemthuis, R., Lazarova-Molnar, S.: An approach for face validity assessment of agent-based simulation models through outlier detection with process mining. In: Enterprise Design, Operations, and Computing (in press)
4. Bemthuis, R., Mes, M., Iacob, M.E., Havinga, P.: Using agent-based simulation for emergent behavior detection in cyber-physical systems. In: 2020 Winter Simulation Conference (WSC), pp. 230–241. IEEE (2020). https://doi.org/10.1109/WSC48552.2020.9383956
5. Bemthuis, R.H., Koot, M., Mes, M.R., Bukhsh, F.A., Iacob, M.E., Meratnia, N.: An agent-based process mining architecture for emergent behavior analysis. In:

2019 IEEE 23rd International Enterprise Distributed Object Computing Workshop (EDOCW), pp. 54–64. IEEE (2019). https://doi.org/10.1109/EDOCW.2019.00022

6. Bemthuis, R.H., Lazarova-Molnar, S.: Discovering agent models using process mining: initial approach and a case study. In: 2022 IEEE International Conference on Parallel & Distributed Processing with Applications, Big Data & Cloud Computing, Sustainable Computing & Communications, Social Computing & Networking (ISPA/BDCloud/SocialCom/SustainCom), pp. 163–172 (2022). https://doi.org/10.1109/ISPA-BDCloud-SocialCom-SustainCom57177.2022.00028

7. Berti, A., van Zelst, S.J., van der Aalst, W.M.P.: Process mining for python (PM4Py): bridging the gap between process-and data science. arXiv preprint arXiv:1905.06169 (2019)

8. Burattin, A.: Streaming process mining. In: van der Aalst, W.M.P., Carmona, J. (eds.) Process Mining Handbook. LNBIP, vol. 448, pp. 349–372. Springer, Cham (2022). https://doi.org/10.1007/978-3-031-08848-3_11

9. Cabac, L., Knaak, N., Moldt, D., Rölke, H.: Analysis of multi-agent interactions with process mining techniques. In: Fischer, K., Timm, I.J., André, E., Zhong, N. (eds.) MATES 2006. LNCS (LNAI), vol. 4196, pp. 12–23. Springer, Heidelberg (2006). https://doi.org/10.1007/11872283_2

10. Carter, F., et al.: Consensus guidelines for validation of virtual reality surgical simulators. Surv. Methodol. **19**, 1523–1532 (2005). https://doi.org/10.1007/s00464-005-0384-2

11. Clark, W.A., Fossett, M.: Understanding the social context of the Schelling segregation model. Proc. Natl. Acad. Sci. **105**(11), 4109–4114 (2008). https://doi.org/10.1073/pnas.0708155105

12. Ferreira, D.R., Szimanski, F., Ralha, C.G.: Mining the low-level behaviour of agents in high-level business processes. Int. J. Bus. Process Integr. Manag. 8 **6**(2), 146–166 (2013). https://doi.org/10.1504/IJBPIM.2013.054678

13. Foramitti, J.: AgentPy: a package for agent-based modeling in Python. J. Open Source Softw. **6**(62), 3065 (2021). https://doi.org/10.21105/joss.03065

14. Halaška, M., Šperka, R.: Advantages of application of process mining and agent-based systems in business domain. In: Jezic, G., Chen-Burger, Y.-H.J., Howlett, R.J., Jain, L.C., Vlacic, L., Šperka, R. (eds.) KES-AMSTA-18 2018. SIST, vol. 96, pp. 177–186. Springer, Cham (2019). https://doi.org/10.1007/978-3-319-92031-3_17

15. Hardesty, D.M., Bearden, W.O.: The use of expert judges in scale development: implications for improving face validity of measures of unobservable constructs. J. Bus. Res. **57**(2), 98–107 (2004). https://doi.org/10.1016/S0148-2963(01)00295-8

16. Henry, A.D., Prałat, P., Zhang, C.Q.: Emergence of segregation in evolving social networks. Proc. Natl. Acad. Sci. **108**(21), 8605–8610 (2011). https://doi.org/10.1073/pnas.1014486108

17. Hill, A.L., Rand, D.G., Nowak, M.A., Christakis, N.A.: Infectious disease modeling of social contagion in networks. PLoS Comput. Biol. **6**(11), e1000968 (2010). https://doi.org/10.1371/journal.pcbi.1000968

18. Hüllen, G., Zhai, J., Kim, S.H., Sinha, A., Realff, M.J., Boukouvala, F.: Managing uncertainty in data-driven simulation-based optimization. Comput. Chem. Eng. **136**, 106519 (2020). https://doi.org/10.1016/j.compchemeng.2019.106519

19. Ito, S., Vymětal, D., Šperka, R., Halaška, M.: Process mining of a multi-agent business simulator. Comput. Math. Organ. Theory **24**(4), 500–531 (2018). https://doi.org/10.1007/s10588-018-9268-6

20. Klügl, F.: A validation methodology for agent-based simulations. In: Proceedings of the 2008 ACM Symposium on Applied Computing, pp. 39–43 (2008). https://doi.org/10.1145/1363686.1363696
21. Law, A.M., Kelton, W.D., Kelton, W.D.: Simulation Modeling and Analysis, vol. 3. McGraw-Hill, New York (2007)
22. Liu, Z., Li, X., Khojandi, A., Lazarova-Molnar, S.: On the extension of Schelling's segregation model. In: 2019 Winter Simulation Conference (WSC), pp. 285–296. IEEE (2019). https://doi.org/10.1109/WSC40007.2019.9004848
23. Mourtzis, D.: Simulation in the design and operation of manufacturing systems: state of the art and new trends. Int. J. Prod. Res. **58**(7), 1927–1949 (2020). https://doi.org/10.1080/00207543.2019.1636321
24. Negahban, A., Smith, J.S.: Simulation for manufacturing system design and operation: literature review and analysis. J. Manuf. Syst. **33**(2), 241–261 (2014). https://doi.org/10.1016/j.jmsy.2013.12.007
25. Royal, K.: "Face validity" is not a legitimate type of validity evidence! Am. J. Surg. **212**(5), 1026–1027 (2016). https://doi.org/10.1016/j.amjsurg.2016.02.018
26. Rozinat, A., van der Aalst, W.M.P.: Conformance checking of processes based on monitoring real behavior. Inf. Syst. **33**(1), 64–95 (2008). https://doi.org/10.1016/j.is.2007.07.001
27. Sargent, R.G.: Validation and verification of simulation models. In: Proceedings of the 24th Conference on Winter Simulation, pp. 104–114 (1992)
28. Sargent, R.G.: Verification and validation of simulation models. In: Proceedings of the 2010 Winter Simulation Conference, pp. 166–183. IEEE (2010). https://doi.org/10.1109/WSC.2010.5679166
29. Sargent, R.G.: Verification and validation of simulation models: an advanced tutorial. In: 2020 Winter Simulation Conference (WSC), pp. 16–29 (2020)
30. Schelling, T.C.: Models of segregation. Am. Econ. Rev. **59**(2), 488–493 (1969)
31. Schelling, T.C.: Dynamic models of segregation. J. Math. Sociol. **1**(2), 143–186 (1971)
32. Sert, E., Bar-Yam, Y., Morales, A.J.: Segregation dynamics with reinforcement learning and agent based modeling. Sci. Rep. **10**(1), 11771 (2020). https://doi.org/10.1038/s41598-020-68447-8
33. Shannon, R.: Introduction to the art and science of simulation. In: 1998 Winter Simulation Conference. Proceedings (Cat. No.98CH36274), vol. 1, pp. 7–14 (1998). https://doi.org/10.1109/WSC.1998.744892
34. Singh, A., Vainchtein, D., Weiss, H.: Schelling's segregation model: parameters, scaling, and aggregation. Demogr. Res. **21**, 341–366 (2009). https://doi.org/10.4054/DemRes.2009.21.12
35. Šperka, R., Spišák, M., Slaninová, K., Martinovič, J., Dráždilová, P.: Control loop model of virtual company in BPM simulation. In: Snášel, V., Abraham, A., Corchado, E. (eds.) Soft Computing Models in Industrial and Environmental Applications. AIS, pp. 515–524. Springer, Cham (2013). https://doi.org/10.1007/978-3-642-32922-7_53
36. Sulis, E., Taveter, K.: Beyond process simulation. In: Sulis, E., Taveter, K. (eds.) Agent-Based Business Process Simulation, pp. 175–182. Springer, Cham (2022). https://doi.org/10.1007/978-3-030-98816-6_9
37. Tour, A., Polyvyanyy, A., Kalenkova, A.: Agent system mining: vision, benefits, and challenges. IEEE Access **9**, 99480–99494 (2021). https://doi.org/10.1109/ACCESS.2021.3095464
38. Weijters, A.J.M.M., van der Aalst, W.M.P., de Medeiros, A.K.A.: Process mining with the HeuristicsMiner algorithm (2006)

Human Aspects and Social Interaction
in CISs

Towards Scaling External Feedback for Early-Stage Researchers: A Survey Study

Yuchao Jiang[1]([✉]), Marcos Báez[2], and Boualem Benatallah[1,3]

[1] University of New South Wales, Sydney, Australia
yuchao.jiang@unsw.edu.au
[2] Bielefeld University of Applied Sciences, Bielefeld, Germany
marcos.baez@fh-bielefeld.de
[3] Dublin City University, Dublin, Ireland
boualem.benatallah@dcu.ie

Abstract. Feedback on research artefacts from people beyond local research groups, such as researchers in online research communities, has the potential to bring in additional support for early-stage researchers and complementary viewpoints to research projects. While current literature has focused primarily on early-stage research seeking or getting support for research skills development in general, less is known about, more specifically, empirical understanding of how early-stage researchers exchange feedback with external researchers. In this paper, we focus on understanding the critical types of external feedback that early-stage researchers desire and the prevalent challenges they face with exchanging feedback with external helpers. We report on a large-scale survey conducted with early-stage researchers of diverse backgrounds. Our findings lay the empirical foundation for informing the designing of socio-technical systems for research feedback exchange.

Keywords: Early-stage researcher · feedback · survey

1 Introduction

Feedback on research activities is a critical element for improving research skills, such as feedback on research planning [23] and feedback on research papers [19]. The feedback is especially essential for Early-Stage Researchers (ESRs), who are typically PhD students [22]. However, most ESRs get limited feedback from a small circle of advisors, reviewers and peers [23]. This is a growing challenge as the number of research students is increasing, while dedicated on-demand feedback is hardly scalable – advisors have limited time and resources to provide timely and personalized feedback to multiple ESRs [5,23].

Emergent literature and practices are starting to see the potentials of socio-technical affordances for exchanging feedback among people beyond local networks [19,23]. Socio-technical systems are affording feedback exchange for academic skills development [15], professional development [8,16], creative design [5] and creative writing [2,7].

With socio-technical affordances, research students can engage in authentic research projects with online mentorship and get feedback during the projects [19,23]. For example, agile research studios (ARSs) scale mentorship on both research planning and getting help on their research projects [23]. With ARSs, each advisor can mentor about twenty students within a traditional laboratory. As another example, Crowd Research [19] operates at a much larger scale and with more diverse participants focusing on providing open access to research experiences from seeding initial ideas to writing the final research paper. The majority of the participants were from universities lacking research training support. These efforts are attractive because they enable more people to get access to research experience and enable an advisor to coordinate students at a larger scale and with more diversity. They also provide access to distributed external feedback and expertise that were not traditionally available. However, they still rely on principal investigators and advisors scaling their efforts.

Thus, it is clear from literature (e.g., [1,15,19,23]) that ESRs wish to have external feedback on their research projects, and socio-technical systems hold the potential to afford the feedback exchange process. However, quantitative empirical understandings of ESRs' desire for external feedback on various types of research artefacts is under-explored. Meanwhile, ESRs may face challenges when seeking or adopting external support [1]. For example, many ESRs concern the potentially vague or overly concise answers to inquiries, which may lead to misinterpretation. However, quantitative empirical researches on the challenges of seeking and adopting external feedback on research projects are lacking.

In this study, we build on literature about opportunities and challenges about seeking support on research skills development [1] and extend the literature with quantitative empirical understandings of how ESRs get external feedback. More specifically, we aim to identify, among all the challenges faced by ESRs with getting external support, the challenges that future systems on exchanging research feedback need to prioritize to solve. We also aim to prioritize the types of external feedback that future systems to focus on. These priorities may allow practitioners and researchers to reflect on, as well as design systems or conduct research studies with more evident objectives. Hence, we aim to answer the research questions:

RQ1: What types of external feedback ESRs most desire and why?
RQ2: What challenges about exchanging feedback with external researchers need to prioritize to solve?

To answer the questions, we performed an online survey study with ESRs of diverse fields of study, geographic locations and opportunities in terms of accessing research support. The goal was to obtain the most varied perspectives. The survey inquired ESRs about how useful they perceive various types of external feedback, how frequently they wish to have each type of external feedback, and their perceptions on the challenges of external feedback on their research projects.

This study revealed that the majority of ESRs perceive external feedback on research methods and paper drafts as being both very useful and frequently desired. Most ESRs faced challenges with adopting external feedback, including concerns regarding the qualifications of helpers, quality of the feedback and timeliness. We also found that ESRs' background, including disciplines and access to local support, influence their desire for external feedback and the challenges they face with external feedback. Thus, the design of socio-technical affordances for research feedback exchange should consider the target users in prioritising needs and implementing collaboration models. Based on the findings in this study and related literature, we discuss how our results lead to design implications for scaling feedback on research artefacts. The findings lay the empirical foundation for informing future research and designing socio-technical systems for research feedback exchange.

2   Background and Related Work

We begin with an overview of how researchers are interacting within online communities. The emerging interactions in the communities bring numerous challenges.

2.1   Researchers' Interaction with Online Communities

Previous literature studied what researchers desire from online communities. Some researchers use ResearchGate and Academia.edu for social networking purposes, such as building communities and following research news [21]. Jeng et al. [9] studied how researchers exchange information and resources with ResearchGate Q&A and found that researchers providing answers to questions and share resources (e.g., references and links). Some researchers also communicate with the general public using platforms such as Reddit [11]. Other examples include ResearchBlogging.org for scholarly blogging, Publons for open reviewing scientific papers [17], and Mendeley for creating profiles with publications, research interests, awards, and grants [9,21]. Our previous work studied how ESRs leverage socio-technical affordances for external support [1]. We found that ESRs inquire online for other researchers' experience with research exploring process, explanations on concepts or theories, and brief introductions to research tools. Despite many studies showing that online communities and socio-technical affordances are enabling researchers to communicate with external researchers and general public, none of these studies focused on understanding ESRs exchanging feedback on research artefacts within online research communities. In this study, we further explore what are the prevalent types of external feedback that ESRs desire, as well as how ESRs' perceptions vary across disciplines and other demographic information.

2.2 Challenges Faced by Researchers When Seeking External Support

Studies have shown that researchers face challenges and barriers with seeking and adopting support and inputs from external communities. For example, although researchers can gather contributions from millions of volunteers with the availability of citizen science platforms (e.g., Zooniverse, eBird), many researchers still hesitate to adopt the platforms for generating, processing or analyzing research data [13]. We also previously reported on an in-depth interview of how early-stage researchers faced challenges and concerns when seeking support from online research communities [1]. We discuss below some of the salient challenges reported in the literature during seeking support, interacting with external helpers and adopting support.

Seeking Support: Researchers may hesitate to seek for external support for cultural, personal and project factors. For example, some researchers faced ethical issues that sensitive research data cannot be shared [13]. Van [21] found that some researchers are afraid that some online platforms would use the researchers' information in ways that they are not comfortable with. Some researchers, especially early-stage researchers, were afraid to expose weakness or pose as incompetent with an online profile [1].

Interacting with External Helpers: When interacting with external helpers for support, researchers also faced communication challenges. Examples include explaining their research projects and their need for support to external helpers; and getting instant replies that is productive.

Adopting Support: When adopting external help, many researchers concerns of the qualification of the helpers and quality of feedback or inputs from the helpers. For example, many researchers hesitate to adopt citizen science platforms for generating, processing or analyzing research data [13]. Reasons include the involvement of unqualified crowds in tasks requiring subject matter knowledge, quality control in crowdsourcing and unintended consequences of poor quality-control methods (e.g., intellectual property and privacy risks; malicious attacks) [6]. These issues may impact the validity and quality of research findings [13].

While the prior work helps us identify the challenges that researchers face with external support, we do not have a good understanding of how prevalent are the challenges for ESRs. We also do not adequately understand how the challenges are differently faced by ESRs of various backgrounds. This study helps to further understand the challenges that warrant further investigation and derive design requirements for feedback exchange system design.

3   Method

The goal of the study is to increase the quantitative empirical knowledge on ESRs' desires and challenges with seeking and adopting external feedback on research artefacts, with the purpose of identifying promising paths for future research and designs that scales feedback exchange on research artefacts. To help realize this goal, we build on prior work which identified the how ESRs seek support online and the challenges they faced while seeking support with socio-technical systems. We designed and conducted a survey to prioritize the and the challenges to solve.

Participants. We conducted online surveys with ESRs of diverse fields of study, geographic locations and opportunities in terms of accessing research support. The goal was to obtain the most varied perspectives. Respondent recruitment was open to ESRs who were PhD students or recently completed PhD study. We focused on ESRs with recent research activities, as they would more accurately recall specific details about their experience with seeking feedback [14,18]. The survey was distributed through various channels including mailing lists, snowball sampling, online discussion groups and social media platforms. Participation was voluntary. We distributed the same survey with different anonymous links for each channel to record which channel a respondent came from, in case of the potential noise in the responses. For any type of communication with respondents, we send individual emails or messages to protect their privacy and identity information.

Survey Design. Our survey[1] followed several iterations of design and was based on literature on online feedback exchange(e.g., [2,4,7]) and our previous work [1,10]. In the survey, we first inquired about the researchers' demographics. Then, we inquired respondents about whether they wished to have external research feedback. Those who reported wishing to have external research feedback (either sometimes, often or always) were further inquired about what types of external feedback they desired and what are the most salient challenges seeking the feedback. More specifically, we inquired them how often they wished to have external feedback on a set of research activities, as well as how useful they perceive the feedback (N1-N5). For each type of external feedback, we asked respondents two questions: (i) *how often they wished to get the type of external feedback* (selecting from "never, rarely, sometimes, often and always"), and (ii) *how useful they perceive each type of external feedback* (selecting from "not at all, slightly, moderately, very and extremely"). We also asked whether they need other types of feedback that we did not consider.

---

[1] The full survey is available at https://bit.ly/3bOkwzX.

We also aimed to understand the challenges that ESRs faced with external feedback on their research. Informed by the challenges with exchanging support with external helpers Sect. 2.2, we list the potential challenges with exchanging feedback on research artefacts with external helpers as in Table 1. We asked the respondents Likert-style questions on each of the challenges: how much they agree with the challenges, selecting from strongly disagree, somewhat disagree, neutral, somewhat agree and strongly agree. We further inquired open questions about any additional challenges they faced.

Respondents who never or rarely desired external research feedback skipped the questions about seeking external feedback. We inquired them about their experience and perceptions about providing feedback to other researchers as helpers. More specifically, we asked them their perception on their capability to

Table 1. Potential Challenges Faced by ESRs with External Feedback on Their Research

Requesting Feedback	C1	I feel suspicious of online helpers' intentions to give feedback
	C2	I am afraid to expose weakness or pose as incompetent with a (public available) profile
	C3	I may feel disappointed and frustrated when getting no responses after asking for feedback and thus drawing me back from asking for further feedback
	C4	I am afraid that sharing pieces of my research online before publishing might introduce confidentiality/privacy/IP conflict problems, or compromise my research
Interacting with external helpers	C5	I might not get an instant reply while discussing on my research artifacts. Thus the conversation on the feedback is not productive and fruitful
	C6	The mostly text-based interaction in online communities pose limitations in properly explaining my inquiries and understanding helpers' feedback
Adopting Feedback	C7	The ambiguity of the helpers' authority and qualification to answer my inquiry
	C8	Quality of feedback not up to the standard for scientific use (e.g., no references given)
	C9	Online help failing to provide precise and complete answers to your research inquiries (e.g., no rationale)
	C10	Feedback not timely for my deadlines

offer feedback on other' research, the frequency that they offer feedback to other, and what motivated them to give feedback and prevented them from providing feedback to others.

By the end of the survey, we asked respondents to share their positive and negative experience with external research feedback. We describe our analysis approach and the limitations as we present results to each research question.

4 Results

We collected 120 responses from ESRs of diverse demographic information[2] in terms of gender (female 49.2%, male 46%, NA 4.1%), geographic location (Oceania 49.2%, Europe 21.3%, Asia 13.9%, Latin America 8.2%, Africa 6.6%, Canada and USA 0.8%) and research experience (years since starting PhD, 1- 5+ years). In terms of field of study, they were generally grouped into Science, Technology, Engineering and Mathematics (STEM) (58%) and Humanities, Arts and Social Science (HASS) & Interdisciplinary (42%). 94 respondents(78%) reported wishing to have external feedback either sometimes, often or always, while the rest 26(22%) reported never or rarely needed external research feedback. In the following sections, we present the results from our analysis of the survey responses to answer our research questions.

4.1 ESRs' Most Desired Types of External Feedback

Our first research question (**RQ1**) inquires about what types of external feedback are essential to ESRs. For each type of feedback that we listed (N1-N5), respondents who reported wishing external feedback indicated how often they want to have the input and how useful they perceive the feedback from external helpers. We also asked respondents for their comments on the types of feedback and asked them to add other types of feedback they wish to have.

To identify the most important types of external feedback in overall, we draw an impact matrix with (*Frequency*) and (*Usefulness*) of each type of external feedback (N1-N5). The *Frequency* is demonstrated by the percentage of respondents who sometimes, often or always wished to have external feedback on their research (%). The *Usefulness* is demonstrated by the percentage of respondents who perceived external feedback on their research to be moderately, very or extremely useful (%). The resulting matrix, as captured in Fig. 1, highlights external feedback on *research methods* (N4) and *paper drafts* (N5) as being both very useful and frequently desired in overall.

Frequency of Desire for External Feedback. The results indicate that there is a frequent desire for external feedback on the five artefacts (N1-N5). Respondents reported desiring external feedback support (sometimes, often or always) especially for research methods (N4, 86% of respondents) and paper drafts and

---

[2] Full demographic information at https://bit.ly/2MVgPP8.

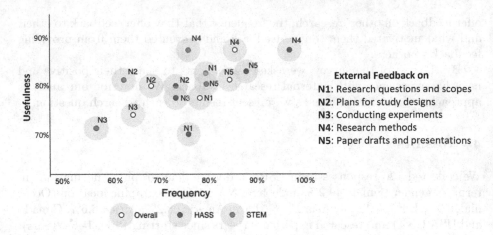

Fig. 1. The impact matrix.

presentations (N5, 84%). These artefacts are followed by research questions (N1, 68%), plans for studies (N2, 68%) and, lastly, support for conducting experiments (N3, 66%).

Breaking down the analysis by field of study we can see some differences (Fig. 2). Overall, we observed a higher number of responses expressing needing external feedback among HASS (80%) compared to STEM (73%) ESRs. In terms of specific artefacts, HASS students follow the general trend, reporting a higher need for external support on research methods (N4, 95%) and paper drafts and presentations (N5, 87%). For STEM students, instead, expressed higher need for external support on research questions and scope of their research (N1, 81%) along with paper drafts and presentations (N5, 81%). This suggests that the need for support, as well as the preference might change according to the field of study and community.

We also wanted to get insights on whether the availability of resources also influenced the desire of different types of external feedback. For this, we took the self-reported wish for external feedback, indicated at the start of the survey, as a proxy for the feedback available to the ESR.[3] Those who expressed wishing external feedback often and always were considered as being in higher demand for feedback (potentially low support available), while those who only wished for feedback sometimes as being in lower demand (potentially higher support available). We found that those who occasionally require external feedback mainly wanted feedback on N5 (80%) and N4 (78%), which are more about feedback on research methods and papers. This group of ESRs may find external feedback to be useful for some alternative viewpoints or validation on their research activities. For example, four respondents mentioned that they wish to get external feedback on whether they considered all important related work in their papers.

---

[3] We did not considered geographical location due to the distribution of responses, and for not being a reliable indicator of the individual circumstances of the ESRs.

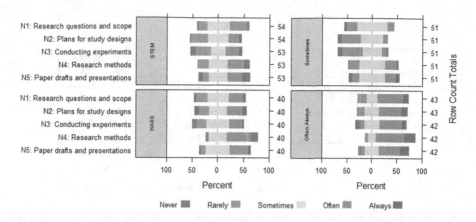

Fig. 2. Divergence analysis of frequency of desire for feedback by type of artefact, field of study and need for support.

As one respondent explained that "*I hope I can get some advice about related work on a research topic, so that I may not omit possible related works*". Another ESR asked his peers to "*read short extracts of my work to see if it makes sense to them*". On the other hand, those who wanted external feedback more often expressed their desire for external feedback on all aspects through out a research life-cycle. Indeed, besides the higher need for feedback on research methods (N4, 95%), all other types of feedback were on a narrow range (83%-88%).

We also investigated if there were any relationship between the level of desire for external feedback and the ESRs' gender and research experience. We found that, among those who desired external feedback often or always, 21 were female ESRs and 18 were male ESRs, which demonstrates relatively balanced gender distribution. As for the relationship between years of research experience and desires for external feedback, we found that ESRs desire external feedback regardless of the research experience they have.

What the above suggests is that the need for external feedback can be influenced by the discipline and available resources. The design of socio-technical affordances for research feedback exchange should consider the target users in prioritising needs and implementing collaboration models.

Perceived Usefulness of External Feedback. In addition to the frequency of desiring external feedback, we also studied ESRs' perceived usefulness of external feedback. The resulting Likert-scale analysis as in Fig. 3 revealed that the differences in perceived usefulness follows the same trends as observed before. People who only occasionally need support find it less useful and those in more need find it more useful. Furthermore, as shown in Fig. 1, comparing with HASS respondents, STEM respondents reported experiencing the need for external feedback relatively less often, but considering the feedback as more useful. Meanwhile, nine respondents reinforced, in their open-ended text responses, the usefulness

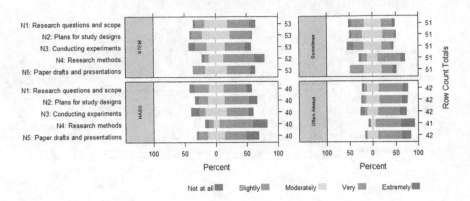

Fig. 3. Divergence analysis of perceived usefulness for external feedback by type of artefact, field of study and need for support.

of insights on the overall research scope (N1) from industry practitioners and researchers not in the same research domain as the ESRs. They wished to get feedback on how their research can contribute to other related research fields and related industry practices, as well as how they can build on knowledge from other research domains and industry practices. For example, respondents mentioned that they wish to get feedback on how to "*position better my research to current challenges in the industry*"and "*What other domain knowledge may improve my work?*". We note that ESRs' perceptions of usefulness may be biased by previous experiences and challenges faced when requesting and adoption external feedback. We investigate the challenges they faced before about external feedback in the next section.

Additional Artefacts. Some respondents shared other types of feedback that they wish to get from external helpers, which are not directly related to a research project but is important to them as a researcher. Examples of such activities that ESRs wish external feedback on include "*grant and scholarship application*", "*relationship management with research stakeholders*" and "*research networking opportunities*".

4.2   The Challenges ESRs Face When Seeking External Feedback

Although the vast majority of respondents expressed that they wish to have options to connect with more people with expertise in the research area besides supervisors, our study revealed that they also face many challenges to seek, communicate on, and adopt the feedback. In this section, we discuss the findings to **RQ2** to explore the prevalent challenges faced by ESRs in overall, and explore how the challenges ESRs face vary across disciplines and their overall need for external feedback. We also discuss the additional challenges raised by survey respondents.

How Prevalent the Challenges Are for ESRs in Overall. To understand how prevalent are the challenges, for each challenge, we analyzed the percentage of survey respondents agreeing with the challenge. The results are shown in Table 2. Beyond indicating their agreement to the challenges, 29 respondents provided further comments either elaborating on those challenges or describing other challenges they experienced. In the following, we provide representative respondent quotes, which is shown in italics. In the presentation of the challenges, we rely heavily on the ESRs' own words to bring credibility to our findings.

We found that, for respondents in overall, the challenges (C1-C10) are widespread and faced by the majority of the respondents. However, challenges about adoption are mostly agreed by respondents that over 80% survey respondents had challenges with adopting external feedback. Among challenges with adoption, the ambiguity of the helpers' authority (C7) is the most imposing challenge. As explained by some respondents in their open-ended text comments, qualified external helpers that ESRs wish to seek feedback from need to be expert in the research field or have successfully helped ESRs before: "*Whether I will seek help from others (especially for online forums) depends mainly on their authority and qualifications, or the number of people they have successfully helped (suggestions are accepted) before*".

The second most prevalent challenge is about concerns around confidentiality and intellectual property (C4), which is the most salient challenge in requesting external feedback. An interesting theme emerged in respondents' comments is that they concern less about disclosing ideas before publication when they are more experienced researchers: "*I (3rd Year PhD) have less concern about my niche and 'originality' now then in Yr 1. Hence more open to the idea of going to an online community for help.*"

Following is the concern of getting no responses, which echos previous research on feedback exchange in creative design communities that designers also hesitate to ask for feedback due to afraid of no response [5]. On the other hand, less of an obstacle, overall, is fear of exposing oneself online (C2) or suspicious about helpers intentions (C1). Interaction issues are present (C5, C6), though with less prominence as in requesting and adopting external feedback.

Differences in Challenges Faced by ESRs of Various Backgrounds. Besides analyzing the overall agreement with the challenges among all respondents, we also compare the prevalent of the challenges faced by ESRs sometimes desire external feedback and those who often or always desires external feedback; and compare the prevalent of the challenges faced by STEM ESRs and HASS ESRs. The results are shown in Table 2. We highlight some of the differences below.

Regarding overall need for external feedback, we found that respondents who occasionally desires external feedback faced challenges mainly with *adopting* the feedback. They concern about the timely and quality of external feedback, as well as how qualified are the helpers. Respondents who often or always want external feedback, instead, faced challenges distributing between requesting and

Table 2. Challenges Faced by ESRs with External Feedback on Their Research

		All (%)	Some -times (%)	Often-Always (%)	STEM (%)	HASS (%)
Requesting	C1	56	41	73	46	66
	C2	55	47	63	44	67
	C3	67	55	78	76	55
	C4	84	76	92	85	82
Interacting	C5	65	56	73	71	55
	C6	64	63	65	62	67
Adopting	C7	87	86	87	84	90
	C8	82	82	82	85	78
	C9	80	83	78	82	78
	C10	82	86	78	87	76

adopting feedback. The most salient challenge they faced was concerning about getting their work stolen.

Regarding disciplines, we found that challenges with adoption is still the main barrier no matter the discipline groups. C10 is also the highest pain-point different between HASS and STEM respondents. The most salient challenge for STEM respondents is the timeliness of getting external feedback (C10). One respondent suggested *"introducing a deadline"* so that *"you know you get your feedback in time or also you know that the feedback you provide to others is still helpful"*. However, for HASS respondents, it is less of an obstacle not getting instant reply (C10) or even not receiving responses (C3). On the other hand, the most salient challenge for HASS respondents is the ambiguity of the helpers' authority (C7). We also found that either exposing weakness online (C2) or suspicious of external helpers' intentions (C1) is less of an obstacle for STEM respondents.

Additional Challenges. Two other challenges emerged in the open-ended text responses. First, Some respondents raised the challenge with interpreting diverse viewpoints or balancing with difficulty the viewpoints in external feedback: *"There will be a lot of chances that the supervisors and others have quite a different world view and the PhD researcher will be like facing two different opposing forces"*. Meanwhile, receiving feedback from a different viewpoint is appreciated by many other respondents as a valuable learning opportunities: *"It's help to get a different angle of observation because my supervisor, colleagues and me, we can have the same opinion or the opinion can be biased so it will be preferable to ask people outside the team for feedback."* Then, another challenge raised was about formulating requests for external feedback. Some respondents found it challenging to explain their research artefacts, such as a research plan, to the external helpers who are not familiar with the research project: *"One reason not to ask for help could be the effort it takes to prepare my questions in an understandable way. I would have to provide sufficient background which* *might take a lot of time (depending on how close the helper is to my topic and how specific my question is)*".

4.3 ESRs' Perception Toward Providing External Feedback

We are also interested in ESRs' perception as helpers. In our survey, 26 respondents shared their experience and perceptions towards providing feedback as external helpers. 19 of the respondents (73%) thought that they were either moderately, very, or extremely capable of providing feedback to others or less-experienced researchers. However, 9 indicated that they sometimes provide feedback to others and 2 respondents often provide feedback to others. This gap implies that, in overall, ESRs help less than they are in principle able to do.

Barriers to Providing Feedback to External Researchers. The respondents shared the barriers that prevented them from offering feedback on others' research more often. We grouped the barriers into three types, which are lack of feedback exchange opportunities, lack of time to contribute feedback and lack of support on providing feedback. First, some respondents mentioned that they did not see much opportunity to offer feedback on others' research. Two respondents explained that they were "*not being asked for such a feedback often*" or had "*not so much contact to other(s)*". Second, some respondents mentioned that prefer to spend time and effort on working on their own research project while not much time available to support each other in a research community: "*I work, study, and am trying to publish...there really is no time left for me to be part of this kind of community*". Third, some respondents were not confident enough to offer feedback on others' research. This barrier can be either lack of confidence in others' research fields, e.g., "*I don't know enough about their fields to really help*" or lack of confidence in offering feedback, e.g., "*not so experienced with giving feedback*".

Motivations to Providing Feedback to External Researchers. Some respondents shared their motivations to provide feedback as an external helper, which we grouped into three types. First, some respondents wished to learn from other researchers. As explained by one respondent, he/she give feedback to others' research "*to help myself learn more and get response to my observation and finally enrich research*". Second, some respondents wished to build a better research community. One respondent explained that "*research is meant to help push the boundary of science and to ultimately benefit the society. I contribute if and when I have ideas that can help improve the quality of others' research*". Another respondent added that "*we are a community of learners, and I feel we have a duty to help each other out*". Third, many respondents provide feedback as a "*part of journal/conference peer review*" process.

Note that we did not aim to have a comprehensive understanding of all types of barriers and motivations. Other types of barriers and challenges may exist and need further investigation.

5 Discussion

In summary, we identified the most salient challenges that ESRs faced when exchanging feedback on research artefacts with external online research communities. The quantitative understanding of the challenges validate and extend the literature about challenges in obtaining external support for research skills. In addition, the findings about challenges also adds insights about the feedback providers' points of view. We discuss design requirements for future systems that aim at feedback exchange for research artefacts at scale.

5.1 Prioritized Desires for External Feedback

First of all, we found that, even for ESRs who already have access to resources within institutional frameworks, 78% of the respondents reported wishing to have external feedback in addition to the feedback from their supervisory teams. This finding reinforced and extend the argument about the need to provide open access to research training [19, 20, 23].

As we mentioned before, some research initiatives and systems have explored scaling research skills training opportunities, such as agile research studios (ARS) [23] and Crowd Research [19]. However, both ARS and Crowd Research still rely on advisors or principal investigators to lead the research projects. Furthermore, both of the systems focus on providing research projects and support throughout a full life-cycle of the projects. Thus, these systems are less attractive to those who already enrolled in a research program in research institutes and have supervisory teams. We found that research students who have support from research groups mainly desire alternative and complementary feedback from external helpers. Furthermore, the external feedback on research papers is perceived as important and useful for the majority of ESRs (more than 80%). Future research may prioritize to design systems that focus on providing external feedback on research papers.

In addition to feedback from experts in same research domains, some ESRs also wish to have feedback from industry practitioners and researchers from different but related research domains. They wish to have feedback on how their research can contribute to other research domains and industry practices, as well as how their research can build on other research domains and industry practices. This finding echos an aim of interdisciplinary research that brings researchers together to contribute their own disciplinary knowledge to a collective research project to produce greater insight into the subject and not to exclude certain bodies of knowledge [3]. Meanwhile, none of the respondents that expressed this wish self-identified as working on interdisciplinary projects. Future research can explore how to facilitate an online community that allow researchers to build the network and get access to external feedback.

5.2 Design Implications for Systems that Scale Feedback Exchange on Research Artefacts

In this paper, we explored and prioritized the challenges that ESRs faced with exchanging feedback on research artefacts with external online research communities. Based on the findings and related literature (e..g., [9], we derived design implications for systems on scaling feedback exchange on research artefacts.

Support Researchers to Collaboratively Contribute Feedback. Through studying how ESRs perceive providing feedback to external researchers, we identified a gap between their self-identified ability to provide feedback and their actual efforts taken to provide feedback. Most ESRs are not providing feedback to external researchers. One of the reasons that our respondents provided was the lack of time to help others, since providing comprehensive feedback takes time and effort. Instead of each research providing formal comprehensive reviews, future systems may support a community of researchers to collaboratively contribute feedback. For example, crowdsourcing techniques have shown to be useful in distributing the effort of providing support and feedback to a community of helpers [2,7,10].

Guide and Support Reviewers to Provide Feedback on Research Artefacts. As found in the study, another reason for researchers hesitating to provide feedback to other researchers is because they are not confident enough about their knowledge and experience in providing feedback. Future research may explore how to guide inexperienced reviewers to provide feedback on research papers and learn skills about reviewing research papers.

Help Feedback Requesters to Interpret and Reflect on the Feedback. As found in the study, the challenges of adopting external feedback are the most prevalent and faced by the majority of respondents. The top prioritized challenges are about identifying useful feedback and feedback that they can trust. Some respondents also added the challenge about balancing the viewpoints in feedback. In addition, we found in [1] that ESRs wish to have an overall understanding of the potentially large amount of feedback. Future systems can help ESRs interpret the feedback by summarizing all the feedback. Other potential ways to help identify useful feedback and reflect on feedback include collecting ratings on the feedback and discussing with experts on the feedback.

Support and Guide ESRs to Request External Feedback. In this study, we found that although the majority of respondents wish to get external feedback on their research artefacts, more than 50% of the respondents also hesitated to seek external feedback. First, the most salient challenge for STEM respondents is the timeliness of getting external feedback. Future systems may support feedback seekers to include a feedback deadline when they request feedback. Then, respondents who have less local support on research skills training are concerned most about confidentiality and intellectual property issues. Future systems may support feedback seekers to seek feedback from selected groups or individuals of helpers that the requesters trust.

5.3 Limitations

We mentioned some of the limitations during presenting the findings. First, ESRs' perceptions of usefulness may be biased by previous experiences and challenges faced when requesting and adoption external feedback. Second, as for ESRs' perceptions on providing feedback to external researchers, we identified some of the motivations and barriers to help. However, we did not aim to have a comprehensive understanding of all types of barriers and motivations. Other types of barriers and challenges may exist and need further investigation. As for the generalizability of the results, we conducted this study with 120 ESRs from diverse backgrounds, with various geographical locations, academic disciplines, years of doing research and balanced gender distribution. However, we only collected responses from ESRs who understood English. ESRs from less developed areas and with less access to research training might be benefit even more from external feedback than those privileged few at select universities [12,19]. Furthermore, those ESRs may face other challenges when seeking external feedback and need other types of feedback that were not included in the findings of this study.

6   Conclusion and Future Work

This work contributes to the quantitative understanding of crowdsourcing support for research skills training. In particular, the results highlight the potential and need for tools to exchange feedback on research drafts within online research communities. Furthermore, the study showed that the desire for external feedback could be influenced by the discipline and available resources. The design of socio-technical affordances for research feedback exchange should consider the target users in prioritising needs and implementing collaboration models. Besides, the results also provide clear directions and priorities for further studies on scaling research training with crowdsourced support.

References

1. Anonymous: The opportunities and challenges of using socio-technical systems to learn research skills from external communities (2021, unpublished)
2. Campbell, J., Aragon, C., Davis, K., Evans, S., Evans, A., Randall, D.: Thousands of positive reviews: distributed mentoring in online fan communities. In: Proceedings of the 19th ACM Conference on Computer-Supported Cooperative Work & Social Computing, CSCW 2016, pp. 691–704. ACM, New York (2016)

3. Castán Broto, V., Gislason, M., Ehlers, M.H.: Practising interdisciplinarity in the interplay between disciplines: experiences of established researchers. Environ. Sci. Policy **12**(7), 922–933 (2009)
4. Chen, Y., Lee, S.W., Xie, Y., Yang, Y., Lasecki, W.S., Oney, S.: Codeon: on-demand software development assistance. In: Proceedings of the 2017 CHI Conference on Human Factors in Computing Systems, CHI 2017, pp. 6220–6231. ACM, New York (2017)
5. Cheng, R., Zeng, Z., Liu, M., Dow, S.: Critique me: exploring how creators publicly request feedback in an online critique community. Proc. ACM Hum.-Comput. Interact. **4**(CSCW2), 1–24 (2020)
6. Daniel, F., Kucherbaev, P., Cappiello, C., Benatallah, B., Allahbakhsh, M.: Quality control in crowdsourcing: a survey of quality attributes, assessment techniques, and assurance actions. ACM Comput. Surv. **51**(1), 7:1–7:40 (2018)
7. Evans, S., et al.: More than peer production: fanfiction communities as sites of distributed mentoring. In: Proceedings of the 2017 ACM Conference on Computer Supported Cooperative Work and Social Computing, CSCW 2017, pp. 259–272. ACM, New York (2017)
8. Hui, J.S., Easterday, M.W., Gerber, E.M.: Distributed apprenticeship in online communities. Hum.-Comput. Interact. **34**(4), 328–378 (2019)
9. Jeng, W., DesAutels, S., He, D., Li, L.: Information exchange on an academic social networking site: a multidiscipline comparison on researchgate Q&A. J. Am. Soc. Inf. Sci. **68**(3), 638–652 (2017)
10. Jiang, Y., Schlagwein, D., Benatallah, B.: A review on crowdsourcing for education: state of the art of literature and practice. In: Proceedings of the 22nd Pacific Asia Conference on Information Systems, PACIS 2018, p. 180. AISeL, Japan (2018)
11. Jones, R., Colusso, L., Reinecke, K., Hsieh, G.: R/science: challenges and opportunities in online science communication. In: Proceedings of the 2019 CHI Conference on Human Factors in Computing Systems, CHI 2019, pp. 1–14. ACM (2019). https://doi.org/10.1145/3290605.3300383
12. Kizilcec, R.F., Halawa, S.: Attrition and achievement gaps in online learning. In: Proceedings of the Second (2015) ACM Conference on Learning @ Scale, L@S 2015, pp. 57–66. Association for Computing Machinery, New York (2015)
13. Law, E., Gajos, K.Z., Wiggins, A., Gray, M.L., Williams, A.: Crowdsourcing as a tool for research: implications of uncertainty. In: Proceedings of the 2017 ACM Conference on Computer Supported Cooperative Work and Social Computing, CSCW 2017, pp. 1544–1561. ACM, New York (2017)
14. Marlow, J., Dabbish, L.: From rookie to all-star: professional development in a graphic design social networking site. In: Proceedings of the 17th ACM Conference on Computer Supported Cooperative Work & Social Computing, CSCW 2014, pp. 922–933. Association for Computing Machinery, New York (2014). https://doi.org/10.1145/2531602.2531651
15. Motahar, T., Jasim, M., Ahmed, S.I., Mahyar, N.: Exploring how international graduate students in the us seek support. In: Extended Abstracts of the 2020 CHI Conference on Human Factors in Computing Systems, pp. 1–8 (2020)
16. Storey, M.A., Zagalsky, A., Figueira Filho, F., Singer, L., German, D.M.: How social and communication channels shape and challenge a participatory culture in software development. IEEE Trans. Softw. Eng. **43**(2), 185–204 (2017)
17. Sugimoto, C.R., Work, S., Lariviere, V., Haustein, S.: Scholarly use of social media and altmetrics: a review of the literature. J. Am. Soc. Inf. Sci. **68**(9), 2037–2062 (2017)

18. Torrey, C., McDonald, D.W., Schilit, B.N., Bly, S.: How-to pages: informal systems of expertise sharing. In: Bannon, L.J., Wagner, I., Gutwin, C., Harper, R.H.R., Schmidt, K. (eds.) ECSCW 2007, pp. 391–410. Springer, London, London (2007). https://doi.org/10.1007/978-1-84800-031-5_21

19. Vaish, R., et al.: Crowd research: open and scalable university laboratories. In: Proceedings of the 30th Annual ACM Symposium on User Interface Software and Technology, UIST 2017, pp. 829–843. Association for Computing Machinery, New York (2017)

20. Vaish, R., Goyal, S., Saberi, A., Goel, S.: Creating crowdsourced research talks at scale. In: Proceedings of the 2018 World Wide Web Conference, pp. 1–11 (2018)

21. Van Noorden, R.: Online collaboration: scientists and the social network. Nat. News 512(7513), 126 (2014)

22. Wang, T., Li, L.Y.: 'Tell me what to do' vs. 'guide me through it': feedback experiences of international doctoral students. Active Learn. High. Educ. 12(2), 101–112 (2011)

23. Zhang, H., Easterday, M.W., Gerber, E.M., Lewis, D.R., Maliakal, L.: Agile research studios: orchestrating communities of practice to advance research training. In: Companion of the 2017 ACM Conference on Computer Supported Cooperative Work and Social Computing, CSCW 2017, Companion, pp. 45–48. ACM, New York (2017)

Social Network Mining from Natural Language Text and Event Logs for Compliance Deviation Detection

Henryk Mustroph[1]([✉]), Karolin Winter[2], and Stefanie Rinderle-Ma[1]

[1] Technical University of Munich, TUM School of Computation, Information and Technology, Garching, Germany
{henryk.mustroph,stefanie.rinderle-ma}@tum.de
[2] Department of Industrial Engineering and Innovation Sciences, Eindhoven University of Technology, Eindhoven, The Netherlands
k.m.winter@tue.nl

Abstract. Social network mining aims at discovering and visualizing information exchange of resources and relations of resources among each other. For this, most existing approaches consider event logs as input data and therefore only depict how work was performed (as-is) and neglect information on how work should be performed (to-be), i.e., whether or not the actual execution is in compliance with the execution specified by the company or law. To bridge this gap, the presented approach considers event logs and natural language texts as input outlining rules on how resources are supposed to work together and which information may be exchanged between them. For pre-processing the natural language texts the large language model GPT-4 is utilized and its output is fed into a customized organizational mining component which delivers the to-be organizational perspective. In addition, we integrate well-known process discovery techniques from event logs to gather the as-is perspective. A comparison in the form of a graphical representation of both, the to-be and as-is perspectives, enables users to detect deviating behavior. The approach is evaluated based on a set of well-established process descriptions as well as synthetic and real-world event logs.

Keywords: Social Network Mining · Organizational Mining · Natural Language Processing · Compliance Checking

1 Introduction

"The discovery of organizational knowledge, such as organizational structures and social networks, enables managers to understand organizational structures and improve business processes" [24]. Hence, organizational mining, i.e., the discovery and analysis of the organizational perspective of a process, has been investigated by various approaches [3,4,9,11,13,14,17,19,23,25–27]. Especially, in cooperative environments, the understanding of the communication and interaction between resources is of utmost importance [22].

Organizational mining has mostly taken event logs as input for detecting resources and their relations, resulting in knowledge of how the actual process execution was carried out (as-is behavior). Textual information on organizational structures such as handbooks or regulatory documents has been neglected as a valuable source of information. Such documents typically prescribe the *to-be* behavior, for example, which resources are authorized to perform which tasks or which resources are supposed to work together. Taking into account both, regulatory documents and process event logs, it can be analyzed if the observed resource behavior complies with or deviates from the prescribed behavior. The results can be used for detecting compliance violations, improving the quality of organizational mining, and enhancing the process model. Quality of models and model enhancement can be realized as knowledge from two data sources is combined. The importance of checking compliance of process executions with organizational models has been confirmed in literature [26]. In previous work we presented approaches for compliance verification between textual sources and event logs [5,16]: temporal and resource compliance patterns such as *activity A must be performed by resource R* stated in natural language text are checked against event logs. In this work, we follow up on these ideas and elaborate on a novel approach to mine resource interaction and communication from textual information and event logs in parallel enabling compliance deviation detection.

To this end, literature on organizational mining from event logs is gathered and categorized in order to identify directions for organizational mining from text. Afterwards, this is contrasted with approaches that extract organizational aspects from textual sources. Unlike existing approaches for knowledge graph extraction from natural language text, this work outputs a social network that captures the communication and information exchange among resources in an organization, focusing on the to-be scenario of resource interactions. Thereby, compared to existing approaches that are mostly rule-based, this approach incorporates a Large Language Model (LLM) for pre-processing. The output of the LLM is transformed into several knowledge graphs representing the social network which serves as ground truth data for compliance deviation detection. Afterwards, for each trace in the event log a graph is generated that is checked for deviations against the graphs of the text. For this, existing social network mining approaches are taken as the starting point for developing a customized solution that allows for comparing the resulting graph (as-is model) with the graph generated based on the textual input (to-be model). In the last step, compliance deviation detection is enabled by comparing the to-be and as-is graphs. This provides an insightful output on which trace is acceptable and which one contains deviations. The approach is outlined in Sect. 3 and evaluated in Sect. 4. The paper concludes in Sect. 5.

2   Literature Review and Scope of this Work

A literature review is conducted to determine if the objectives of existing techniques for organizational mining from event logs remain valid and feasible when considering natural language texts as input (cf. Sect. 2.1). We identify social network mining as the most promising research direction as it requires the least additional knowledge and assumptions. Secondly, we explore related work explicitly focusing on extracting social networks and resource interactions from natural language texts (cf. Sect. 2.2). For the literature search various libraries including dblp, ACM digital library, Scopus, IEEExplore, and SpringerLink, targeting documents with titles containing keywords such as "(Organizational Mining)", "(Social Network) AND (Business Process)", "(Organizational Structure) AND (NLP OR Natural Language Processing)", and "(Knowledge Graph) AND (NLP OR Natural Language Processing)" were used as well as forward and backward searches to ensure comprehensive coverage of the relevant literature[1]. The presented search strings were deliberately chosen to find a list as complete as possible of all existing papers in the social network and organizational structure mining domains related to business process management, while still remaining within a manageable range of total results.

2.1 Organizational Mining from Event Logs

Based on [27] and most recent work [26], the following categories of organizational mining are identified and investigated regarding the feasibility of discovery when utilizing text data as input, instead of relying on event log data.

Social Network Mining. Social network mining (SNM) determines the information exchange and relationships among various resources. In our context, a resource can be both human or non-human and the resource structure contains users having roles that are part of organizational units, e.g., departments being defined in an organization. In [1] first the control-flow of a process is identified, then the organizational structure is expressed and lastly, a model based on the transfer of tasks through different resources being a social network of resource relationships is generated. The model can be used to further analyze the roles of resources and the identification of resource groups [1]. [9] also uses SNM for business processes to discover who is working with whom. The authors in [13,17] employ SNM by deriving an activity matrix that indicates which resources perform specific activities. Based on the handover of work, an organizational network is constructed. SNM can also be utilized for conformance and compliance checking when trying to detect anomalies in processes as demonstrated in [11]. Additionally, [21] employ SNM to generate knowledge and identify problematic communication behaviors in agile development processes. The feasibility of conducting SNM using textual data appears promising, primarily due to the availability of control-flow relations and information about the performers of specific activities, commonly found in process descriptions. By utilizing this information, it is possible to construct a directed graph in which the nodes represent resources and the edges represent the activities and information exchange between resources, thereby capturing the interaction flow. This

---

[1] The detailed results are available at https://www.cs.cit.tum.de/bpm/data/.

ground truth data can then be used to evaluate the conformity of communication structures in event logs.

Organizational Structure Discovery. This category is also called *Organizational Model Mining*. The aim is to create, e.g., an organizational hierarchical model similar to an "organigram" or to determine groups of resources by, e.g., identifying different organizational clusters of resources as described in detail in [24]. In [23,25], event log data is analyzed to construct a graphical tree format-like representation of the organizational structure. The graphical representation created from organizational structure discovery differs from the graph structure employed in SNM. In this case, the edges in the graph do not possess weights or directions, and the focus is not on modelling a network. Instead, a graph in tree format is constructed, comprising multiple tree structures associated with different activities, indicating the resources capable of performing each task and the authorities or resources' ability to perform various tasks. In the best case this results in an "organigram". Furthermore, resources can be grouped into different clusters based on similarities like the execution of the same activities or the contribution of the same amount of work to the current process from a temporal perspective. This can be combined with graphical representations and modelling approaches as described in [26]. Performing organizational structure discovery solely from text data is difficult and requires multiple additional data sources or assumptions. On the one hand, the communication structure and the flow of activities are crucial. The former could be captured through SNM. On the other hand, obtaining either the company's organizational structure would include expert knowledge of the general organizational structure within a particular domain or characteristics of graphs from the social network must be elaborated to establish an "organigram" from a social network. These requirements must be thoroughly examined to successfully build the desired model.

Resource Allocation and Mining. This category combines multiple categories found in the literature. *Resource Allocation* explores the resource activity pairs in an event log and seeks to enhance process execution efficiency by real-locating these pairs. *Role Mining* identifies which roles are allocated to which activities and aims to distribute activities among different roles. *Rule Mining* is described as allocating rules for efficient resource-task distribution and statistics for building expert teams which is similar to *Resource Allocation* and *Role Mining*. Lastly, *Behavioral Profile Mining* extracts individual resource behavior from event log data which provides statistics of resource activities and is therefore also similar to *Resource Allocation* and *Role Mining*. Those categories were merged into one category because of their similar types of output and purpose. In particular, all of them have the purpose of extracting statistical information based on execution data stored in the event logs in order to provide insights into resource-activity allocation to improve resource-task distributions and process efficiency. In [19], the presented approach utilizes event log data to perform several statistical evaluations of resource activity executions, role dependencies, and resource allocations. The data can be used to gain insights and improve process efficiency in future executions by appropriately distributing resource activities.

In [14] decision trees are built based on the resource information of event logs helping in allocating the best suitable resource to several tasks. This type of organizational mining is very difficult to apply to textual data. All resource allocation and rule mining tasks require a lot of execution data and create either statistics of resource executions such as the number of distinct activities done by a resource or train machine learning models such as decision trees with attributes of resources, i.e., the category or activity that has been executed or the roles, to classify the most suitable resource for an activity in future process executions. Since textual data only provides knowledge on the optimal resource allocation and the *to-be* model but not the *as-is* model, we lack information for creating statistics or machine learning models for optimal resource allocation.

Conclusion. From the lines of research discussed above, SNM requires the least assumptions and additional knowledge as input, i.e., a process description. Hence, we will employ SNM in the following. In addition to generating a social network graph (SNG) from textual input, we also mine event logs enabling the comparison between the *to-be* and *as-is* models.

2.2   Social Network Mining from Natural Language Text

In [3], email text data is utilized as input to generate an interaction graph as well as a hierarchy structure graph. In the former, each node represents a sender or receiver of an email and the nodes are connected with each other through directed, unweighted edges. The latter, the hierarchy structure graph, consists of a root node that is connected to intermediate nodes, and these intermediate nodes are further connected to leaf nodes. The edges in this graph are directed and point towards the bottom of the nodes, indicating the hierarchical relationship between senders and receivers of emails. These knowledge graphs fall within the scope of organizational mining, specifically in the subcategories of SNM and organizational structure mining. They provide insights into the communication patterns and hierarchical relationships within email traffic in an organization, thereby enhancing transparency in organizational processes. [3] focuses on communication through emails capturing the *as-is* scenario. In this paper, the purpose is to create communication networks representing the *to-be* scenario to check the compliance of information exchange in a process captured in the event logs.

In general, knowledge graphs create a network of entities, which are not limited to human resources as typically employed in SNM within the field of organizational mining. Previous papers have explored the utilization of NLP techniques to extract entities from unstructured text documents, e.g., [10,20]. An approach focusing on organizational aspects is [6]. NLP techniques were employed to extract organizational structure entities, i.e., the rank or organization of a resource from text data obtained from the Security Force Monitor, an institution that collects information on security forces worldwide. The authors utilized entity recognition whereas tokens within the text were classified into organizational structure categories. After that, the entities in a text were grouped into a graph based on similarity measures and relation extraction techniques embedding the resource into the full organizational structure and defining for each resource the rank, role, department, i.e., *person x* with *rank y* in *organization z*. This approach enabled meaningful insights into the composition and hierarchy of security forces globally. However, no social network displaying the relationships among the resources was constructed.

Approaches discovering process models from natural language text, e.g., [12] target the organizational structure implicitly, e.g., through visualizing actors through lanes in BPMN. In [7], a Large Language Model is used to extract activities and actors from natural language text. In contrast, our work aims at explicitly visualizing the social network and comparing it to the observed social network from an event log to reveal deviations from the *to-be* behavior.

This paper differs from our most recent work on compliance verification between process descriptions and event logs [16], as the focus is not on compliance requirements such as *activity A must be performed by resource R*, but rather on how resources interact with each other and whether this interaction violates any compliance rules or constraints and conforms with the *to-be* behavior.

Conclusion. Unlike existing organizational aspects extraction approaches from natural language text, this paper aims to capture the communication and information exchange among resources in an organization, focusing on the *to-be* scenario of resource interactions. The resulting social network will serve as ground truth data for compliance checking with the *as-is* model from event logs.

3   Social Network Graph Construction and Compliance Deviation Detection

The approach, cf. Fig. 1, requires explicit control-flow relations descriptions in the natural language text since otherwise interactions among resources are not traceable. Four types of control-flow relations are distinguished: sequential, conditional, parallel, and loop. Sequential flow is considered during social network graph (SNG) construction from text and event logs. The conditional case requires handling only for texts because if an activity, executed within a condition, terminates the process, multiple different resource interaction networks exist. The parallel case only requires particular handling for event logs. Loops are not considered explicitly for SNG construction as it is expected that they only multiply existing resource interactions without adding new resource interactions. Section 3.1 details on SNG construction from text and we denote the set of resulting SNGs as *SNG-T*. Analogously, the set of SNGs generated from event logs is denoted as *SNG-EL* and its construction is outlined in Sect. 3.2. Section 3.3 describes how to detect compliance deviations and how to visualize the results.

3.1   Social Network Graph Construction from Text

This step of the approach is divided into a pre-processing part using a LLM to transform the unstructured text data into a structured format, and the *SNG-T* set construction through Algorithm 1. Depending on whether we observe a

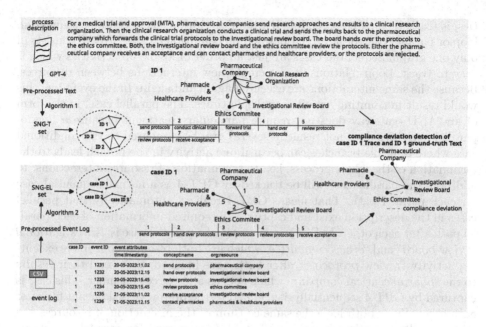

Fig. 1. Overview of SNG Construction and Compliance Deviation Detection Approach

decision or not in the text, the set *SNG-T* either contains one or multiple graphs which are considered as ground truth for detecting compliance deviations in Sect. 3.3.

Text Pre-processing. For pre-processing, OpenAI's GPT-4 model [18] is used. The output generated by GPT-4 is stored in a persistent file, allowing users to review the results generated by GTP-4 and to make modifications if necessary. A prompt, available at the corresponding repository at https://www.cs.cit.tum. de/bpm/software/, was designed to extract the source and sink activity, the resource performer and the resource consumer. While designing this prompt we recognized that GPT-4 delivers better results when using the term actor instead of resource. The source activity always serves as the starting point of the interaction and connects the resource performer with the resource consumer. The sink activity indicates the next activity that establishes an interaction between resources. In Fig. 1 an example of a source activity is *"send research approaches and results"*. It connects the resource performer *"pharmaceutical company"* with the resource consumer *"clinical research organization"*. The corresponding sink activity is *"conduct clinical trial"* which also acts as a connection to the following resource pairs. Moreover, information indicating whether the sink activity terminates the process, and the type of control-flow, i.e., whether the source and sink activities are part of a condition or not is extracted. It is important to detect control-flow relations as this will determine whether the *SNG-T* set consists of one or multiple graphs. The control-flow, represented as a sequence of activities, is tracked using an ascending ID. If a description solely contains sequential, loop or parallel control-flow relations and no conditional case, *SNG-T* consists of only one graph. Sequential cases are just an order of follow-up activities which is easy to track. Loop relations do not create new interactions between resources, because the same interactions are executed again and again. In the event log, this would result in counting activities multiple times. The parallel case, in the form of an "AND"-gateway does not require particular treatment because a flow of parallel activities does not result in several graphs compared to the conditional case where multiple branches can occur if one activity in the branch leads to the termination of the whole process, i.e., to termination of resource interactions. In addition, the parallel case will be tracked by GPT-4 as a normal sequential case for each parallel path. That means GPT-4 realizes automatically that parallel cases in the description exist and captures all required information of each parallel path after each other. In Fig. 1 an example of a parallel case is: "*investigational review board*" and "*ethics committee*" which are both resource consumers executing activity "*review protocols*"; after both have finished, they send their results to the "*pharmaceutical company*" which acts as a resource consumer. This case is captured by GPT-4 sequentially, i.e., added to the pre-processed output file after each other. Since both have the same consumer, the interaction of resources can still be built correctly and no special check is necessary for parallel executions of activities by different resources. The conditional case requires additional measures to be resolved, since activities in a conditional branch can terminate the process, i.e., a completely new and different resource interaction model will exist. This situation is illustrated in the running example in Fig. 1. The last two activities "*receive an acceptance and contact*", and "*reject protocols*" are connected through an "XOR"-gateway implying that the resource consumers "*pharmacies and healthcare providers*" are only part of the SNG if "*receive an acceptance and contact*" is executed. In the case of "*reject protocols*", a different, but also valid communication graph exists. An example pre-process output from text looks as follows: *{"actors": [{"actor_id": 1, "actor_name": "Pharmaceutical Company"}, ...], "activities": [{"activity_id": 1, "activity_name": "Send Research Approaches and Results"}, ...], "control_flow": [{"control_flow_id": 1, "activity_from": 1, "activity_to": 2, "actor_performer": 1, "actor_receiver": 2, "terminating_activity": false, "flow_type": "sequential"}, ...]}*

SNG-T Construction. Algorithm 1 outlines the *SNG-T* construction for which only the sequential control-flow and the conditional control-flow are relevant. The output from the pre-processing component is considered as input and the result consists of one or multiple *SNG-T* graphs. The edges of a graph correspond to activities and the nodes to resources. The algorithm starts by creating an empty list for *SNG-T* graphs and a counter that is necessary to check if the process terminated after an activity in a conditional statement after the last activity of the process (**Step 1**). Subsequently, the list of resources, activities and the control-flow list is derived from the pre-processed text file (**Step 2**). Furthermore, an empty list of edges is created storing information such as the resource performer, resource consumer, and source activity, which serves as the label for the edge connecting the performer and consumer (**Step 3**). A list of nodes is stored with all unique resources (**Step 4**). The main part of the algorithm starts to determine the edges and the different *SNG-T* graphs. The control-flow list is iterated through a for-loop, till all values are checked. Information, such as the source activity, resource performer, and the resource consumer is cached in a local variable respectively (**Step 5**) and added to the list of edges, only if the resource performer and the resource consumer are no null values (**Step 6**). Suppose a sink activity is identified as a terminating activity and the counter value minus one is equal to the length of the control-flow list. In that case, the edge list is closed, and the node list is checked for any uninvolved resources, which are subsequently removed from the resource list (**Step 7**). Uninvolved in this case means a resource added to the node list in the beginning does not appear in the edge list since the terminating activity stops adding edges and therefore resource interaction. The resulting lists of nodes and edges are added to the list of *SNG-T* elements (**Step 8**) since a new unique element was found that can be used to check the compliance deviations of the event log captured resource interactions. The edge representing the terminating activity is removed from the list of edges, to further process with the not terminating activities and the list of nodes is again filled with all resources in the subsequent iteration(**Step 9 & 10**). Suppose the sink activity is not a terminating activity and the control counter value minus one is equal to the length of the control-flow list. In that case, all activities have been gone through and the node list is also checked for resources that are not in the edge list and removed if found (**Step 11**). The lists of nodes and edges are added to the graph list as a new graph object (**Step 12**).

Algorithm 1. *SNG-T* Construction from LLM-based Pre-Processed Text

---

Require: Pre-processed text file (based on specified prompt)
Ensure: Create a *list of SNG-T elements*
  Step 1: Create an empty *list of SNG-T elements* and *counter* ← 0
  Step 2: Get the list of *resources*, *activities* and *control_flow* from the pre-processed text file
  Step 3: Create a new empty list *edges*
  Step 4: Fill the empty list of *nodes* with all distinct resources
  for entry **in** *control_flow* **do**
    Step 5: Get from entry
    activity_from, resource_performer, resource_consumer,
    terminating_activity
    if *resource_performer* and *resource_consumer* != null **then**
      Step 6: Add to *edges*:
      (resource_performer, resource_consumer, *from_activity*)
    end if
    if *terminating_activity* == True **and**
      counter != *length(control_flow_list)* - 1 **then**
      Step 7: Remove all resources in *nodes* that are not on *edges*
      Step 8: Add tuple: *(nodes, edges)* to *list of SNG-T elements*
      Step 9: Remove from *edges* terminating activity edge
      Step 10: Fill the list of nodes with all distinct *resources*
    end if
    if *terminating_activity* == True **and**
      counter == *length(control_flow_list)* - 1 **then**
      Step 11: Remove all resources in *nodes* that are not in *edges*
      Step 12: Add tuple: *(nodes, edges)* to *list of SNG-T elements*
    end if
    counter = counter + 1
  end for

3.2 Social Network Graph Construction from Event Log

Analogously to the previous step, this one is again divided into pre-processing the event log and *SNG-EL* construction based on the pre-processed event log. The resulting *SNG-EL* serves, together with *SNG-T*, as input for compliance deviation detection in Sect. 3.3. First, we thoroughly assessed implementations provided by the PM4Py toolkit[2] for suitability in our setting. It provides social network mining methods such as *handover of work* and *working together*. Those calculate statistics over all the traces or activities which appear in the log and return a mean resource interaction. Since we want to detect compliance deviations, all distinct traces need to be searched for deviations instead of using average or accumulated statistics of all traces. In addition, restrictive assumptions are imposed, like either the follow-up activity performer is always the previous consumer or event attributes are required indicating the mapping between input and output activities. Therefore, we take up the challenge of generating *SNG-EL* graphs without those strict assumptions on the event log.

Event Log Pre-processing. The event log data is parsed, and transformed into an event log object and all unique traces within the event log are identified. A distinct trace refers to a unique sequence of resource-activity pairs present in the log. If a trace occurs multiple times, only the corresponding case ID is recorded in a list associated with a similar unique trace. Like before, the event log's pre-processed file is persistently stored and contains information on resource performers, activities, and resource consumers. However, the pre-processed file for the log has a slightly different structure. It stores a flow of activities for each distinct trace, along with additional trace structures such as a unique ID, and all case IDs for each trace that share the same order of resource-activity pairs and are thus classified as similar traces to the stored one. Furthermore, unlike the text's pre-processed file, the event log's pre-processed file does not store multiple different lists for resources, activities, and control flow. Although this information is generally redundant, it has been observed that GPT-4 produces better results when there is a distinction between these components, while the control-flow list combines the IDs of activities and resources. The file generated after event log pre-processing offers several advantages, e.g., it can be easily modified, enhanced, and expanded, allowing for corrections to be made before conducting compliance deviation detection. An example pre-process output from an event log looks as follows: *{"pairs": [{"id": 1, "case_ids": ["1", ...], "network_trace": [{"Resource Performer": "Pharmaceutical Company", "Resource Consumer": "Investigational Review Board", "Activity": "send protocols"}, ...], ...}, ...]}*

SNG-EL Construction. The pre-processed file contains the necessary information for each distinct trace and is utilized to construct *SNG-EL* graphs that have the same structure as those in the *SNG-T* set. This ensures comparability during compliance deviation detection. Algorithm 2 details how to come up with several elements that detect sequential and parallel cases in each trace.

---

[2] https://pm4py.fit.fraunhofer.de, last access: 2023–07–06.

Algorithm 2. *SNG-EL* Construction from Pre-Processed Event Log

---

Require: Pre-processed Event Log (own defined output structure)
Ensure: Create a *list of SNG-EL elements*
    Step 1: Create an empty *list of SNG-EL elements* and *edges*
    Step 2: Get the *trace_ info_ list* containing data of each distinct trace in the pre-processed event log file
    Step 3: Create a Petri net of the event log, using a process mining algorithm
    Step 4: Create a list *and_ gateway_ activities* that stores from the Petri net the *start_ activity* before the parallel gateway, the *first_ activities_ after_gateway*, all *activities_in_ each_path*, and the *end_ activity_ after_ gateway*
    for entry in *trace_ info_ list* **do**
        Step 5: Fill the empty list of *nodes* with all distinct resources of entry
        for (*resource performer, resource consumer, activity*) in entry **do**
            if *activity* is a *start_ activity* in *and_ gateway_ activities* **then**
                Step 6: Create a list of *resource consumers*, from resources (performers) of the *first_ activities_ after_ gateway*
                for *consumer* in *resource consumers* **do**
                    for (*resource performer, resource consumer, activity*) in entry **do**
                        if *consumer* == *resource consumer* **then**
                            Step 7: Add (*resource performer, resource consumer, activity*) to *edges*
                        end if
                    end for
                end for
            else
                Step 8: Add (*resource performer, resource consumer, activity*) to *edges*
            end if
        end for
        Step 9: Add *trace id, corresponding case ids* and the (*nodes, edges*) to the *list of SNG-EL elements*
    end for

First, an empty *SNG-EL* graph and edge list are created (**Step 1**). After that, the pre-processed file is parsed to cache for each trace, the resource and activity data (**Step 2**). A Petri net is constructed using a process discovery algorithm (**Step 3**). In this case, we use the alpha miner [2], but also other process discovery techniques can be employed. The Petri net is used to detect information about activities before, in, and after an "AND"-gateway. The activity before the gateway, the first activities of each branch after the gateway, the activities of each "AND"-path and the activity after the closing tag are cached (**Step 4**). Each distinct trace creates a *SNG-EL* graph. Thereby, a list of unique valid nodes is created (**Step 5**). A node is unique if no duplicate exists and valid if it is not a null, undefined or empty value. To create an edge it is first checked if the activity is the start activity before an "AND"-gateway starts. If this is the case, a list of resource consumers is created (**Step 6**) which are basically the resource performers of all follow-up activities that will be performed in the parallel branches. Then, a list of edges is created with a resource performer, resource consumer and activity for each consumer in the gathered list (**Step 7**). Otherwise, the activity is an activity in a sequential path and the resource performer, resource consumer and the activity are added to the list of edges (**Step 8**). Generally, the information of the resource consumer is stored for each activity in each trace in the pre-processed log and is, analogously to most existing work, the performer of the next activity. Lastly, after each activity in the entry is checked, the trace ID, all corresponding case IDs and the graph object consisting of the list of nodes and edges are added to the list of *SNG-EL* graphs (**Step 9**).

3.3 Compliance Deviation Detection and Visualization

Compliance Deviation Detection. Both, *SNG-T* and *SNG-EL* can contain multiple graphs with those from *SNG-T* being considered as ground-truth. For compliance deviation detection we need to identify which graph from *SNG-EL* should be compared to which ground-truth graph from *SNG-T*. To determine this pair, all graphs from *SNG-EL* are contrasted with all graphs from *SNG-T*. Thereby, their amount of edges and nodes are compared. The graph pair with the relatively highest score, i.e., the most similar number of edges and nodes, is considered a match. Compliance deviation detection then involves analyzing all edges in the graph from *SNG-EL* and identifying any absent edges in the matched ground-truth graph from *SNG-T*. For example, in Fig. 1, in the *SNG-T* graph there is no edge between *"Investigational Review Board"* and *"Pharmacie & Healthcare Providers"* but it is present in the *SNG-EL* graph. Such disparities indicate compliance deviations. The output of this analysis can be used to improve the communication structure or highlight deviations in the process. In an optimal case the graph from *SNG-EL* and the ground-truth graph from *SNG-T* consist of the same nodes. If the graph from *SNG-EL* contains fewer nodes than the one from *SNG-T*, all nodes and edges from and to the nodes are removed from the ground-truth graph to only check the resource interaction of given granularity and data. Conversely, if the *SNG-EL* graph contains more edges or nodes than the ground-truth graph from *SNG-T*, it may be due to a high-level description lacking detail or the process being described across multiple textual descriptions. Such cases do not necessarily indicate a compliance violation.

Visualization. Two visualizations were developed. First, a directed graph representing information exchange between resources. This visualization component can be utilized for graphs in *SNG-T* as well as *SNG-EL*. Prior to visualization creation, the nodes undergo weighting and sizing based on the results obtained from the page-rank algorithm [8], which determines the importance of a node within a process and the volume of traffic passing through that resource. Second, compliance deviations are represented in a graph through red edges, indicating discrepancies previously detected in the communication patterns of resources.

4 Evaluation

The approach has been implemented as a prototype in Python 3 and can be accessed at https://www.cs.cit.tum.de/bpm/software/. All input, and intermediate files, like JSON files from GPT-4 prompt execution as well as the prompt itself, pre-processed event logs, and output files are also available. The evaluation features synthetic and real-world datasets. As synthetic data, the *Bicycle Manufacturing* (BM) and *Schedule Meetings* (SM) datasets as introduced in [16] were considered. Those exist of process descriptions from the PET dataset [7] and corresponding events logs which were generated using the Cloud Process Execution Engine (CPEE) [15]. Moreover, the running example (RE) as introduced in Sect. 3 is included for which event logs were generated as well. In addition to those three synthetic datasets, the Business Process Intelligence Challenge 2020 (BPIC2020) dataset is used consisting of event logs with resources in verbal form, e.g., *budget owner* and a detailed textual process description. All steps of the approach as outlined in Sect. 3 are evaluated. In particular, Sect. 4.1 presents the evaluation results for text pre-processing and *SNG-T* construction while Sect. 4.2 evaluates *SNG-EL* construction compared to existing social network mining approaches provided by the PM4Py toolkit. The compliance deviation detection and visualization are evaluated in Sect. 4.3.

4.1 Results Social Network Graph Construction from Text

To evaluate the different processes for each text file, a corresponding gold standard is manually created for the pre-processing and *SNG-T* construction step.

Text Pre-processing. The evaluation of the GPT-4 output encompasses both quantitative and qualitative measures. Quantitatively, the comparison includes extracted network information from the pre-processed text, such as the control-flow and order of resources and activities. Qualitatively, the evaluation examines the assigned labels for the resources and activities. The latter is crucial due to the variation in interpreting resource communication based on textual activities, making it challenging to establish a definitive standard.

Table 1 presents the quantitative evaluation results with precision and recall being calculated to assess the accuracy of the text pre-processing. True positives are identified as correct instances of resource interaction, communication presence meaning the exact prediction of the resource performer and resource consumer, while true negatives represent correct predictions of resource interaction absence. False positives occur when an

Table 1. Precision and Recall for Text Pre-Processing

	BM	SM	RE	BPIC20
Precision	1	1	1	0.57
Recall	1	1	0.86	0.67

resource interaction is absent but should be present, and false negatives occur when a resource interaction is present but should be absent. Additionally, three assumptions are considered when evaluating the resource interaction and the matched resource performers and consumers. Resource interactions in the gold standard are not counted as present if the resource is the performer and consumer or if one resource is null, or if the resource interaction can be also be seen as an optional interaction. The results for the PET dataset, specifically for BM, SM, and RE, are promising, demonstrating an overall precision and quality of social network extraction of 1. For the BPIC20 dataset, the results are also satisfactory, considering the inherent difficulty in extracting resource interaction information. For instance, the description mentions situations where *"the budget owner and the supervisor are sometimes the same"* and the *"director is not always present"*. From a qualitative perspective, in terms of activity and resource labelling and summary by the model, the results are consistently good across all datasets. In the BM dataset, variations such as *"member of the sales department" and "sales department"* are effectively merged into a single resource. Activities in the BPIC20 as *"submit and send"* are merged and only create one resource interaction instead of multiple ones.

SNG-T Construction. It is important to note that the results for this part of the approach strongly rely on the preceding outputs of GPT-4. Precision and recall are calculated by averaging the values across all different graph objects created by Algorithm 1. For instance, for the BM, and BPIC20 datasets, the *SNG-T* set contains two ground-truth graphs.

The overall results, presented in Table 2, are once again promising. Algorithm 1 successfully creates the expected number of graph objects for each dataset, such as two for BM, and BPIC20, and one for SM, and RE confirming the effectiveness of the introduced conditional split of graph objects. While the labelling of activities is less significant in this evaluation, the focus lies on the creation of edges

Table 2. Precision and Recall for *SNG-T* Construction

	BM	SM	RE	BPIC20
Precision	1	1	0.93	0.5
Recall	1	1	0.86	0.585

between resources. False negatives are detected when the labelled activity in the graph object appears nonsensical. For example, in a graph object of the BPIC20 the resources *"x"* and *"y"* are matched based on the activities *"accept request"* and *"reject request"*, one of these two edges created in this scenario would be considered as a false negative edge presence.

4.2   SNG-EL Construction Compared to Existing Solutions

To assess the *SNG-EL* construction, the resulting social network graphs are compared with those generated using the established *handover of work* and *working together* implementations for analyzing collaborative patterns in process log available in the PM4Py toolkit. The *handover of work* approach involves creating an undirected graph that captures the frequency with which another follows one resource within the process log. This graph provides insights into potential handovers of work between resources during the execution of activities. The *working together* metric focuses on quantifying the instances in which different resources collaborate to complete activities within a trace. This results in a directed graph in which nodes are assigned weights based on their frequency of occurrence in various process instances. Table 3 presents the results, i.e., the amount of constructed graphs in *SNG-EL* for each dataset, how many graphs in *SNG-EL* contain the same nodes as in the handover of work graph (HoW) in relation to all constructed graphs which are in *SNG-EL*, how many graphs in

SNG-EL visualize the same graph as the working together (WT) graph in relation to all existing graphs stored in *SNG-EL* and how many graphs visualizes a different graph with respect to nodes and edges, as the WT graph in relation to all existing graphs in *SNG-EL*.

For the BM dataset, five distinct *SNG-EL* graphs were constructed. The sales department node was connected with the engineering department node and the storehouse node in the HoW graph. Similarly, the WT graph featured several directed edges representing collaborative interactions, including reflexive edges. Notably, four out of these five *SNG-EL* graphs resulted in identical graphs to the WT graph. One of the *SNG-EL* graphs depicted a solitary node representing the sales department. This node was connected to itself through a reflexive edge, signifying

Table 3. *SNG-EL* comparison with *working together* and *handover of work*

	BM	SM	RE
Amount Graphs	5	4	3
Same as HoW	0.8	1	0.67
Same as WT	0.8	1	0
Different to WT	0.2	0	1

the exclusive involvement of this department throughout the entire process. This singular representation was a consequence of a unique process instance wherein the sales department received an order but promptly rejected it which is not reflected in a WT or HoW graph. All four resulting graphs in *SNG-EL* of the SM event log contain the same nodes as in HoW and all illustrate the same graph as the WT graph. Two-thirds of the graphs *SNG-EL* set of the RE event log contain the same nodes as in the HoW graph but no graph corresponds to the WT graph. This circumstance highlights the distinctiveness of our approach, as it not only captures typical collaborative dynamics but also accommodates exceptional cases that existing methods might overlook. Evaluating the BPIC20 dataset was challenging. It consists of multiple large event logs which are rarely connected with each other. Therefore, the working together graph and Petri net, which is mandatory to check parallel cases, are too complex and a quantitative comparison becomes infeasible.

4.3   Compliance Deviation Detection and Visualization

We evaluate whether the matching between graphs from *SNG-T* and *SNG-EL* is correct, and whether compliance deviations were correctly identified. Since user studies on the usefulness of the visualizations are beyond the scope of the paper those are only evaluated in the sense of whether results are depicted correctly. For BM, two different *SNG-T* graphs were created, and the event log contained five distinct traces. All *SNG-EL* graphs were correctly matched with a corresponding *SNG-T* graph, including matches between *SNG-EL* graph 1 and *SNG-T* graph 1, and *SNG-EL* graphs 1, 3, 4, and 5 with *SNG-T* graph 2. The detected violations in the BM event log were also all correctly identified. For the SM dataset, *SNG-T* contains one graph and *SNG-EL* four graphs. All *SNG-EL* graphs were correctly matched with their corresponding *SNG-T* graph, as there was only one possible match. The approach accurately detected compliance deviations in all cases. In RE, which consisted of three *SNG-EL* graphs and one *SNG-T* graph, all matches were correct, and all deviating edges were identified. The deviations included direct interactions between the *"pharmaceutical company"* and the *"ethics committee"*, as well as the *"return of review protocols"* from the *"ethics committee"* to the *"investigational review board"*. Figure 2 shows the compliance deviations of the running example's first trace, i.e., the *"ethics committee" sends the reviews to the "investigational review board"* being a compliance deviation as the interaction was not captured in the *SNG-T* graph. This suggests either unwanted communication or the transmission of data that should not have been sent. The *SNG-EL* construction for BPIC20 delivered too complex results, so the compliance deviation detection could not be evaluated.

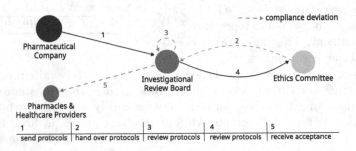

Fig. 2. Example Output Depicting Compliance Deviation for Running Example

5   Discussion and Conclusion

This work presents social network graph construction from natural language text and event logs for compliance deviation detection. First, resource interactions based on natural language texts like process descriptions using an LLM are identified and multiple *SNG-T* graphs are constructed serving as reference models for compliance deviation detection. Furthermore, the approach includes a novel algorithm that identifies more precisely the consumer of a task by taking parallel control-flow into account. The result is a set of *SNG-EL* graphs. Based on *SNG-T* and *SNG-EL*, resource interactions are identified and visualized.

The *SNG-T* construction from natural language text demonstrates promising outcomes in terms of identifying nodes and edges, facilitating the identification of interactions and communication between resources in a process. Nevertheless, some limitations have been identified. The use of large language models like GPT-4 poses challenges (cf. [16]) in terms of reliability, and transparency, particularly when labelling edges with activity names, which may differ from human-assigned labels. Additionally, the *SNG-T* construction algorithm for text requires improvement to appropriately handle the splitting of graph objects in the presence of nested conditions. The algorithm to construct *SNG-EL* elements currently neglects cases where multiple activities exist within each parallel activities path. Furthermore, the compliance deviation component assumes that matching *SNG-EL* and *SNG-T* elements entails the same resource and activity labels in the text and the event log, ideally considering word similarities.

Future work will involve implementing a pre-processing component independent of GPT-4 for extracting requirements from natural language text and comparing its results with the GPT-4-based solution. Moreover, leveraging social network models, additional mathematical assumptions, statistical calculations, and expert knowledge can be employed to generate an "organigram" for more accurate resource-activity compliance deviation detection as discussed in [16].

Acknowledgements. This work has been partly funded by the Deutsche Forschungsgemeinschaft (DFG, German Research Foundation) – project number 514769482.

References

1. van der Aalst, W.M.P., Song, M.: Mining social networks: uncovering interaction patterns in business processes. In: Business Process Management, pp. 244–260 (2004). https://doi.org/10.1007/978-3-540-25970-1_16
2. van der Aalst, W.M.P., Weijters, T., Maruster, L.: Workflow mining: discovering process models from event logs. IEEE Trans. Knowl. Data Eng. **16**(9), 1128–1142 (2004). https://doi.org/10.1109/TKDE.2004.47
3. Abdelkafi, M., Mbarek, N., Bouzguenda, L.: Mining organizational structures from email logs: an NLP based approach. In: Knowledge-Based and Intelligent Information & Engineering Systems, pp. 348–356 (2021). https://doi.org/10.1016/j.procs.2021.08.036
4. Appice, A.: Towards mining the organizational structure of a dynamic event scenario. J. Intell. Inf. Syst. **50**(1), 165–193 (2017). https://doi.org/10.1007/s10844-017-0451-x
5. Barrientos, M., Winter, K., Mangler, J., Rinderle-Ma, S.: Verification of quantitative temporal compliance requirements in process descriptions over event logs. In: Advanced Information Systems Engineering, pp. 417–433 (2023). https://doi.org/10.1007/978-3-031-34560-9_25
6. Bauer, D., Longley, T., Ma, Y., Wilson, T.: NLP in human rights research - extracting knowledge graphs about police and army units and their commanders. CoRR (2022). https://arxiv.org/abs/2201.05230
7. Bellan, P., Dragoni, M., Ghidini, C.: Extracting business process entities and relations from text using pre-trained language models and in-context learning. In: Enterprise Design, Operations, and Computing, pp. 182–199 (2022). https://doi.org/10.1007/978-3-031-17604-3_11
8. Brin, S., Page, L.: The anatomy of a large-scale hypertextual web search engine. Comput. Netw. ISDN Syst. **30**(1), 107–117 (1998). https://doi.org/10.1016/S0169-7552(98)00110-X
9. Busch, P., Fettke, P.: Business process management under the microscope: the potential of social network analysis. In: Hawaii International Conference on System Sciences (2011). https://doi.org/10.1109/HICSS.2011.93

10. Dessì, D., Osborne, F., Reforgiato Recupero, D., Buscaldi, D., Motta, E.: Generating knowledge graphs by employing natural language processing and machine learning techniques within the scholarly domain. Future Gener. Comput. Syst. **116**, 253–264 (2021). https://doi.org/10.1016/j.future.2020.10.026
11. Ebrahim, M., Golpayegani, S.A.H.: Anomaly detection in business processes logs using social network analysis. J. Comput. Virol. Hacking Tech. **18**(2), 127–139 (2022). https://doi.org/10.1007/s11416-021-00398-8
12. Friedrich, F., Mendling, J., Puhlmann, F.: Process model generation from natural language text. In: Mouratidis, H., Rolland, C. (eds.) CAiSE 2011. LNCS, vol. 6741, pp. 482–496. Springer, Heidelberg (2011). https://doi.org/10.1007/978-3-642-21640-4_36
13. Gao, A., Yang, Y., Zeng, M., Zhang, J., Wang, Y.: Organizational structure mining based on workflow logs. In: Business Intelligence: Artificial Intelligence in Business, Industry and Engineering, pp. 455–459 (2009). https://doi.org/10.1109/BIFE.2009.109
14. Ly, L.T., Rinderle, S., Dadam, P., Reichert, M.: Mining staff assignment rules from event-based data. In: Business Process Management Workshops, vol. 3812, pp. 177–190 (2005). https://doi.org/10.1007/11678564_16
15. Mangler, J., Rinderle-Ma, S.: Cloud process execution engine: architecture and interfaces (2022). https://doi.org/10.48550/ARXIV.2208.12214
16. Mustroph, H., Barrientos, M., Winter, K., Rinderle-Ma, S.: Verifying resource compliance requirements from natural language text over event logs. In: Business Process Management (2023). https://doi.org/10.1007/978-3-031-41620-0_15
17. Ni, Z., Wang, S., Li, H.: Mining organizational structure from workflow logs. In: Proceeding of the International Conference on e-Education, Entertainment and e-Management, pp. 222–225 (2011). https://doi.org/10.1109/ICeEEM.2011.6137791
18. OpenAI: GPT-4 Technical report. CoRR abs/2303.08774 (2023). https://doi.org/10.48550/arXiv.2303.08774
19. Pika, A., Leyer, M., Wynn, M.T., Fidge, C.J., ter Hofstede, A.H.M., van der Aalst, W.M.P.: Mining resource profiles from event logs. ACM Trans. Manag. Inf. Syst. **8**(1), 1:1–1:30 (2017). https://doi.org/10.1145/3041218
20. Qin, S., Xu, C., Zhang, F., Jiang, T., Ge, W., Li, J.: Research on application of Chinese natural language processing in constructing knowledge graph of chronic diseases. In: 2021 International Conference on Communications, Information System and Computer Engineering (CISCE), pp. 271–274 (2021). https://doi.org/10.1109/CISCE52179.2021.9445976
21. Raitubu, N., Sungkono, K.R., Sarno, R., Wahyuni, C.S.: Detection of bottleneck and social network in business process of agile development. In: 2019 International Seminar on Application for Technology of Information and Communication (iSemantic), pp. 208–213 (2019). https://doi.org/10.1109/ISEMANTIC.2019.8884341
22. Reijers, H.A., Song, M., Jeong, B.: Analysis of a collaborative workflow process with distributed actors. Inf. Syst. Front. **11**(3), 307–322 (2009). https://doi.org/10.1007/s10796-008-9092-5
23. Sellami, R., Gaaloul, W., Moalla, S.: An ontology for workflow organizational model mining. In: Workshop on Enabling Technologies: Infrastructure for Collaborative Enterprises, pp. 199–204 (2012). https://doi.org/10.1109/WETICE.2012.29
24. Song, M., van der Aalst, W.M.P.: Towards comprehensive support for organizational mining. Decis. Support Syst. **46**(1), 300–317 (2008). https://doi.org/10.1016/j.dss.2008.07.002

25. Tao, J., Deokar, A.V.: An organizational mining approach based on behavioral process patterns. In: Americas Conference on Information Systems. Association for Information Systems (2014). http://aisel.aisnet.org/amcis2014/EndUserIS/GeneralPresentations/11
26. Yang, J., Ouyang, C., van der Aalst, W.M.P., ter Hofstede, A.H.M., Yu, Y.: OrdinoR: a framework for discovering, evaluating, and analyzing organizational models using event logs. Decis. Support Syst. **158**, 113771 (2022). https://doi.org/10.1016/j.dss.2022.113771
27. Zhao, W., Zhao, X.: Process mining from the organizational perspective. Adv. Intell. Syst. Comput. **277**, 701–708 (2014). https://doi.org/10.1007/978-3-642-54924-3_66

Learning Hierarchical Robot Skills Represented by Behavior Trees from Natural Language

Kaiyi Wang[1,2], Yongjia Zhao[1,2(✉)], Shuling Dai[1,2], Minghao Yang[3],
Yichen He[4], and Ning Zhang[1,2]

[1] State Key Laboratory of Virtual Reality Technology and Systems,
Beihang University, Beijing, China
`zhaoyongjia@buaa.edu.cn`
[2] Jiangxi Research Institute, Beihang University, Jiangxi, China
[3] Institute of Automation, Chinese Academy of Sciences, Beijing, China
[4] Institute of Intelligent Information Processing, Beihang University, Beijing, China

Abstract. Learning from natural language is a programming-free and user friendly teaching method that allows users without programming knowledge or demonstration capabilities to instruct robots, which has great value in industry and daily life. The manipulation skills of robots are often hierarchical skills composed of low-level primitive skills, so they can be conveniently represented by behavior trees (BTs). Based on this idea, we propose NL2BT, a framework for generating behavior trees from natural language and controlling robots to complete hierarchical tasks in real time. The framework consists of two language processing stages, an initial behavior tree library composed of primitive skill subtrees, and a BT-Generation algorithm. To validate the effectiveness of NL2BT, we use it to build a Chinese natural language system for instructing robots in performing 3C assembly tasks, which is a significant application of Industry 4.0. We also discuss the positive impact of real-time teaching, visual student models, and the synonymous skill module in the framework. In addition to the demonstrated application, NL2BT can be easily migrated to other languages and hierarchical task learning scenarios.

Keywords: Embodied Interaction · Learning from Language · Natural Language Programming · Behavior Tree Generation

1 Introduction

In daily life and industrial production, programmers compose primitive skills (pre-programmed lowest-level skills) of robots into hierarchical skills to achieve various complex robot tasks. However, this can be difficult for users who do not have programming knowledge. Inspired by human social education, interactive task learning (ITL) [15] has been proposed to enable users to teach tasks to robots conveniently. The interaction can be accomplished through demonstration or natural language, but the former is problematic for people with motor

M. Sellami et al. (Eds.): CoopIS 2023, LNCS 14353, pp. 366–383, 2024.
https://doi.org/10.1007/978-3-031-46846-9_20

disabilities or those who need to teach fine skills. Therefore, in this paper, we focus on teaching robots skills from natural language.

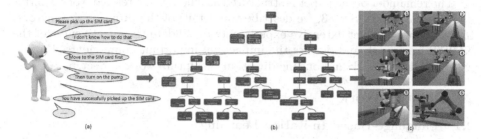

Fig. 1. An example of learning hierarchical skills represented by behavior trees from natural language. (a) The user decomposes high-level skills into low-level primitive skills through dialogue. (b) The learned hierarchical skills are represented and executed through behavior trees. (c) The robot completes manipulation tasks based on the behavior trees. The example given here is transferring a SIM card from the material box to the platform, then to the phone, and finally inserting it into the slot.

An application of learning from language is for assembly robots in Industry 4.0, such as the 3C (computer, communication, and consumer electronics) assembly robots. With the dramatically increasing demand for 3C products, it is an inevitable trend to use robots to assemble them automatically and intelligently. Many skilled workers have little knowledge of robot programming, but they are proficient in the assembly process, so it is a promising way for them to teach assembly tasks using language. The agents are regarded as students with primitive skills, and with step-by-step instructions from human teachers, they can organize primitive skills into hierarchical high-level manipulation skills.

The existing language-based teaching methods for robot manipulation tasks can be divided into two categories: one is based on end-to-end models, and the other is based on interactive task learning. The former focuses on how to perform a task better, without establishing a hierarchical composition structure of the task, which leads to large training loads and low interpretability. Our idea is the latter, which teaches robot tasks through one-shot learning. Despite the impressive results achieved by existing ITL works, there is still a lack of a universal and portable method for representing and generating hierarchical manipulation skills. To address the above issues, we propose NL2BT, a framework for learning behavior trees (BTs) from language and using them to control robots to perform hierarchical skills (see Fig. 1). The main contributions are as follows:

1. An NL2BT framework which enables robots to learn hierarchical skills represented by behavior trees from natural language. It allows users without programming knowledge or demonstration abilities to instruct robots.
2. A generic primitive skill subtree structure that includes execution condition, skip condition and action to ensure efficient execution and logical correctness.
3. A BT-Generation algorithm that generates BTs from semantic information and uses "Blackboard" to achieve parameter mapping for hierarchical skills.

4. A system for learning 3C assembly tasks from Chinese language that validates the framework.

The remainder of the paper is structured as follows: The related work is introduced in Sect. 2. In Sect. 3, we describe the details of the proposed framework. In Sect. 4, we conduct extensive experiments to validate the effectiveness of the NL2BT framework and discuss the impacts of important components. Finally, we conclude the work and outline directions for future work in Sect. 5.

2   Related Work

2.1   Language-Based Imitation Learning

In recent years, many works focus on language-based imitation learning for robot manipulation skills. Stepputtis et al. [25] propose a model for language-based control of articulated robotic arms, Mees et al. [21] provide a public benchmark for instruction following robots, and Google Robotics also proposes the Language Table [20]. They all combine language, vision, and motor to train end-to-end models for robot control, and achieve inspiring results. This shows us a promising future for language-driven robots. However, the end-to-end model is more suitable for learning primitive skills. If used for hierarchical skills, it can result in large data collection and labeling workloads, large training costs, poor interpretability, low reliability, and user customization failure. In contrast, ITL can solve these problems and is more suitable for learning hierarchical skills.

2.2   Interactive Task Learning

ITL is an emerging research topic and its ideas can be seen in many works. She et al. [24] propose a framework for robots to learn high-level actions through dialogue. They adopt combinatory categorial grammar for language processing, and propose a three-layer action representation to execute robot movements. Chai et al. [3] use the tree structure to represent the grounded task. Petit and Demiris [23] use instructions to teach a robot to perform hierarchical hand actions. They extract semantic information according to predefined templates, learn protoactions by mapping semantic information and joint values, and use them to compose high-level actions. ITL can also be applied to software agents. SUGILITE [16,17] combines instructions with demonstrations to build a conversational assistant on Android. They use a grammar-based executable semantic parser [18] for language understanding and perform tasks with scripts generated by recorded actions. Although these works have achieved impressive results, they have not proposed a general representation and generation method for hierarchical skills that can be widely used and easily ported in ITL systems. Besides, pre-trained language models can be utilized to achieve more robust language understandings. We also notice the existing works that use large language models (LLM) to implement robot tasks, such as ChatGPT for Robotics [26] and SayCan [1]. However, unlike their works, we focus on enabling humans to serve as teachers, so that the robot's behavior fully follows step-by-step instructions without relying on the reasoning of the agent itself, thereby ensuring interpretability.

2.3   Behavior Trees in Robot Manipulation

Finite state machines (FSMs) [8], And-Or graphs [19], semantic graphs [28], and behavior trees [7] are used to represent tasks in robotic manipulation. Among them, BTs have received increasing attention [5]. They are similar to FSMs, but offer advantages in terms of readability, modularity, and real-time performance, making them superior to FSMs for practical applications [6]. Colledanchise and Natale [5] provide a case example of using behavior trees to implement robotic tasks, illustrating the effectiveness of BTs in the representation and execution of robot manipulation skills. French et al. [11] propose an algorithm to learn BTs from demonstrations and validate it with a household cleaning task. However, learning from demonstration can be problematic for users with motor impairment or who need to teach fine tasks. Cao et al. [2] use LLM to generate behavior trees, but do not represent them as executable forms such as XML files or code, so they cannot be directly used to perform actual robot tasks.

3   Approach

3.1   System Overview

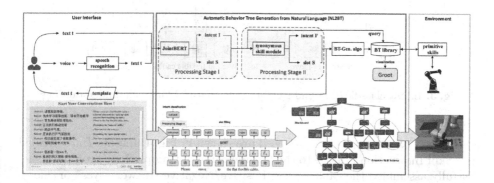

Fig. 2. Architecture of the NL2BT framework and the system built based on it.

As shown in Fig. 2, we propose an NL2BT framework and build a system for learning 3C assembly tasks from Chinese natural language based on it. The user interface (UI) allows users to provide natural language inputs and get agent's replies. Both voice and text inputs are allowed and the iFLYTEK Open Platform [13] is used for speech recognition. The agent's reply is generated based on processed semantic information (I', S) and predefined reply templates. In the framework, the text t goes through two processing stages. In the first stage, a JointBERT model [4] is used to obtain the preliminary intent I and slots S. In the second stage, the existing BT library is queried to check if the skill is already learned or has a possible synonymous skill in the library to obtain the final intent

I'. Then (I', S) is used as input of BT-Generation algorithm to generate behavior trees, and the updated BTs can be visualized and executed in real time. Finally, the nodes of the running behavior tree communicate with the robot to perform the skills. In addition to the demonstrated application, NL2BT can be easily migrated to other languages and scenarios (details are given in Sect. 5). Next, we will introduce the implementation of the framework.

3.2   Natural Language Processing

As shown in Fig. 3, JointBERT [4] is leveraged for language processing. We collect 8015 utterances used in the 3C assembly tasks and annotate their intents and slots in BIO format. We use a multilingual BERT [9] model as the pretrained model and fine-tune it with the labeled data.

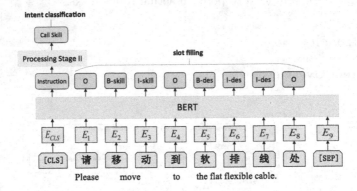

Fig. 3. Intent classification and slot filling for natural language understanding.

The classes of slot S and intent I used are shown in Fig. 4. Intents I are divided into Skill Instruction ("move to the flexible cable"), Completion ("you have successfully assembled the cable"), and Positive/Negative Answer ("yes" or "no"). The slot categories extract important semantic information such as skill names, target objects, destinations, and directions from the utterances.

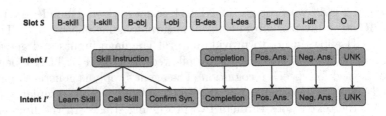

Fig. 4. Classes of slots and intents used in our system.

With the fine-tuned JointBERT model in Processing Stage I, a preliminary intent and slots are given. However, a secondary processing stage is still required before generating behavior trees. When a user inputs a skill instruction, the agent queries the BT library. If it is a learned skill existing in the library, it can be directly executed, so the intent I' is subdivided into "Call Skill"; otherwise, the agent should request instructions from humans, which means "Learn Skill".

In addition, due to the diversity of language expressions, different skill names may correspond to the same skill composition, which we call "synonymous skills". For example, "pick up a box" and "grab a box" may have the same decomposed primitive skills. To avoid redundant and repetitive teaching, when the agent receives an unlearned skill name, it compares it with all skill names in the BT library. If a synonymous skill is found, the intent I' is set to "Confirm Synonym", and the agent will ask the user to confirm whether it is a real synonymous skill. To find synonymous skills, a synonymous skill module is designed. A common idea to capture the similarity between words is to calculate the cosine similarity between their word embeddings. In [27], they provide a Chinese *Synonyms* toolkit based on Word2Vec [22] similarity. However, in addition to the words themselves, we believe that contextual information can also be helpful in synonym judgment, so we use BERT to obtain word embeddings. According to [14], phrase-level information is captured mostly in the lower layers of BERT and gets diluted in the higher layers. Besides, the lower layers capture surface features, which is helpful for judging synonymous skills, especially in Chinese, because the skill names containing the same characters are likely to have similar meanings.

The specific method for judging synonymous skills is shown in Fig. 5. The input is an instruction t_1 containing an unlearned skill name and a constructed comparison instruction t_2. The construction method of t_2 is to replace the unlearned skill in t_1 with each skill name in the BT library (candidate skill). R_A and R_B are word embeddings of the unlearned skill name and candidate skill name respectively. The cosine similarity between them is calculated as follows.

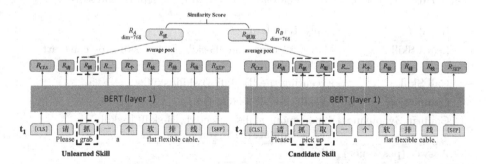

Fig. 5. Method for finding synonymous skills. t_1 is the input instruction, t_2 is a constructed instruction that replaces the unlearned skill with candidate skills from the BT library.

$$similarity\ score = \theta < R_A, R_B >= \frac{(R_A \cdot R_B)}{\|R_A\|\|R_B\|} \tag{1}$$

We construct 200 pairs of data to test the synonymous skill module. As shown in Fig. 6, the best F1 scores using BERT are all higher than that using Word2Vec. Moreover, when using the first layer of BERT, high F1 scores can be obtained over a large threshold range, indicating that the cosine similarity difference between synonymous and non-synonymous skills is large, so the results are more reliable. According to the result, the first layer of BERT and a threshold of 0.465 are selected for the synonymous skill module in our system.

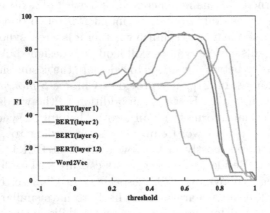

Fig. 6. F1 scores for synonymous skill judgment of each model.

After the above two processing stages, the slots S and intent I' are obtained for the agent's reply (templates are shown in Table 1) and BT generation.

Table 1. The agent reply templates based on the intent I' and slots S.

Intent I'	Reply Template
Learn Skill	I haven't learned the [B-skill] [I-skill] skill, you can start teaching me now
Call Skill	Executing the [B-skill] [I-skill] skill.
Completion	[B-skill] [I-skill] is learned.
Confirm Synonym	Synonymous skills detected: [B-skill] [I-skill] and {candidate}. Do you mean ...?
Answer (pos & neg)	OK, ...
UNK	Sorry, I don't understand.

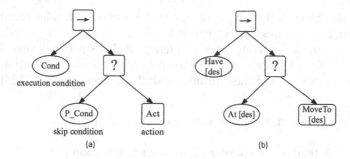

Fig. 7. (a)Structure of primitive skill subtrees. (b)An example of the primitive skill.

3.3 Primitive Skill Subtree

Complex hierarchical skills are composed of primitive skills. In our 3C assembly tasks, the primitive skills include two types of MoveTo (MoveTo$_1$ [destination] and MoveTo$_2$ [direction]), OpenPump, and ClosePump, where MoveTo$_1$ includes a rotation process to align with the object. To compose behavior trees efficiently, we propose a generic structure of primitive skill subtrees. Four standard BT nodes used in it are shown in Table 2.

Table 2. Standard node types used in the primitive skill subtree.

Node Type	Symbol	Description
Sequence	→	Route ticks to its children from left to right until anyone returns Failure.
Fallback	?	Route ticks to its children from left to right until anyone returns Success.
Condition	Cond	Check a proposition when it receives ticks.
Action	Act	Execute a command when it receives ticks.

Figure 7(a) shows the generic structure of the primitive skill subtree, which serves as the leaf nodes of the generated behavior trees. Each primitive skill has its action, execution condition, and skip condition. The execution condition refers to the condition that must be met to execute the action. As for the skip condition, when it is met, the following action node will be skipped. An example of the primitive skill "MoveTo$_1$ [des]" is given in Fig. 7(b). When ticks are sent to its Sequence node, it checks whether the destination [des] exists in the environment. If not, the Sequence node stops sending ticks to the Fallback node and the move action cannot be executed. Otherwise, it continues to check whether the robot end effector is already at [des]. If not, the end effector moves to [des], otherwise, the move action does not need to be executed. The primitive skill subtree structure ensures correct execution logic, avoids system failures with execution conditions, and improves efficiency with skip conditions. Primitive skills used in 3C assembly tasks are shown in Table 3 and the initial behavior tree library is composed of these primitive skill subtrees stored in XML format.

Table 3. Primitive skills used in 3C assembly tasks.

Action	Parameter	Execution Cond.	Skip Cond.
MoveTo$_1$	destination	Have [des]	At [des]
MoveTo$_2$	direction	/	/
OpenPump	/	Pump Ready	AlreadyOpen
ClosePump	/	Pump Ready	AlreadyClose

3.4   Behavior Tree Generation

The slots S and intent I' are obtained in Sect. 3.2, and an initial BT library with primitive skill subtrees is built in Sect. 3.3. Then hierarchical skills represented by behavior trees can be generated based on them. Despite the 7 intents I' given in Fig. 4, only the intents of Learn Skill, Call Skill, and Completion will be used to generate the behavior trees. We illustrate this in detail in Fig. 8. A BT-Generation algorithm (Algorithm 1) is proposed to generate executable behavior trees from processed semantic information.

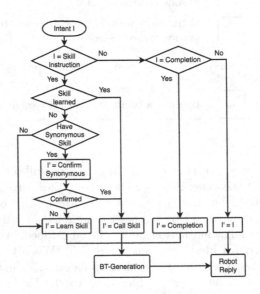

Fig. 8. Illustration of the Processing Stage II.

Algorithm 1. BT-Generation.

Require: *tree, intent, skill, params*
Ensure: *tree*
 1: **function** MAIN(*tree, intent, skill, params*)
 2:     *Stack*.init()
 3:     *root* ← *tree*.getroot()
 4:     *main_seq* ← *root*.find('MainBT').find('Sequence')
 5:     **while** input **do**
 6:         GENERATETREE(*intent, skill, params, root, main_seq*)
 7:     **end while**
 8: **end function**
 9:
10: **function** GENERATETREE(*intent, skill, params, root, main_seq*)
11:     **if** *intent* = teach_new_skill **then**
12:         *new_tree* ← *root*.AddSub("BT", "ID= *skill*")
13:         *seq_node* ← *new_tree*.AddSub("Sequence")
14:         **for** *param* ∈ *params* **do**
15:             *seq_node*.AddSub("SetBlackboard",
16:                 "key = *param*", "value = {*param*.type}")
17:         **end for**
18:         **if** *Stack*.is_empty() **then**
19:             *grand_seq* ← *main_seq*
20:         **else**
21:             *grand_seq* ← *Stack*.peek()
22:         **end if**
23:         ADDELEMENT(*grand_seq, params*)
24:         Stack.*push*(*seq_node*)
25:     **else if** *intent* = call_existing_skill **then**
26:         **if** *Stack*.is_empty() **then**
27:             *seq_node* ← *main_seq*
28:         **else**
29:             *seq_node* ← *Stack*.peek()
30:         **end if**
31:         ADDELEMENT(*seq_node, params*)
32:     **else if** *intent* = complete_teaching **then**
33:         Stack.*pop*()
34:     **end if**
35:     *tree*.write()
36: **end function**
37:
38: **function** ADDELEMENT(*seq_n, params*)
39:     **for** *p* ∈ *params* **do**
40:         **if** *p* not in *seq_n*.findall('SetBlackboard').key **then**
41:             *seq_n*.AddSub("SetBlackboard", "key = *p*", "value = *p*")
42:         **end if**
43:     **end for**
44:     *seq_n*.AddSub('SubTree', 'ID = *skill_name*', *params*)
45: **end function**

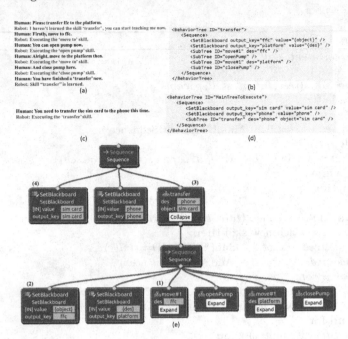

Fig. 9. A case study of parameter generalization. (a) Dialogue for teaching a "transfer" skill; (b) A "transfer" subtree generated from the first teaching in XML format; (c) Dialogue for calling the existing "transfer" skill; (d) BT for performing the "transfer" skill; (e) BT visualization, where (1)–(4) explains the parameter passing in Eq. (2).

Algorithm 1 illustrates how to update the BT library based on different intents. "AddSub" is a factory function used to create a child element of a certain element. Its first parameter is a tag, indicating the type of data being created, and the remaining parameters are attributes represented as key-value pairs. It is worth noting that, as shown in lines 15 and 41, we add "Blackboard", which implements port remapping between the subtree and the main tree, with different "key"s and "value"s to record input *params*. In this way, the learned skills allow parameter generalization. The "transfer" skill is taken as an example to illustrate this feature. In Fig. 9(a), a user teaches the robot a "transfer" skill, the object of which is a flat flexible cable (FFC), and the destination is a platform. The "transfer" subtree generated from the dialogue is shown in Fig. 9(b), where "ffc" and "platform" are stored as Blackboard keys instead of constant parameters. Their values are the variables that $\{object\}$ and $\{des\}$ denote when the skill is called later. When the "transfer" skill is used again, as shown in Fig. 9(c), its object and destination change into a SIM card and a phone. These two parameters are recorded as the values of "object" and "des", see Fig. 9(d). As can be seen from Fig. 9(e), the parameter of the first primitive skill subtree *move*#1 is "des = ffc" from the first teaching, but the argument for execution is

$$des \overset{(1)}{=} ffc \overset{(2)}{=} \{object\} \overset{(3)}{=} sim\ card \overset{(4)}{=} sim\ card\ (its\ location) \qquad (2)$$

In this way, "transfer the SIM card to the phone" is decomposed into "move to the SIM card", "open the pump", "move to the phone", and "close the pump". In other words, when the agent learns how to "transfer A to B", it no longer needs step-by-step instructions for "transfer C to D". The BT-Generation algorithm implements the generalization of parameters.

To summarize NL2BT, the agent processes the natural language input in two stages and then updates the behavior trees in XML format in real time. After each update, BTs are visualized using Groot [10] to ensure that the human teachers can view the tree structures and running status, which we call the "student model", as shown in Fig. 10.

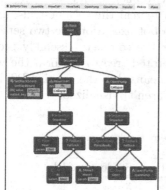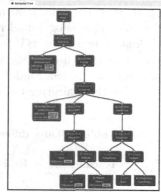

Fig. 10. Using Groot for visual student models in NL2BT. Users can view the existing BT library (left) and the running main tree (right). Colors of the main tree nodes indicate the execution status, orange for Running, green for Success, red for Failure. (Color figure online)

4   Experiment and Result

To validate NL2BT, we build a system for learning 3C assembly tasks from Chinese natural language based on it. We recruit 10 volunteers and introduce them to the functions, usage, and some considerations of the system. Volunteers use our system to teach 3 different 3C assembly tasks to the robotic arm in the virtual environment. Each volunteer teaches in the order of front camera assembly task (Task 1), FFC assembly task (Task 2), and SIM card assembly task (Task 3), which gradually increase in complexity. In Task 1, the robotic arm simply sucks the front camera from the material box and places it in the front camera slot of the phone. In Task 2, the robotic arm first sucks the FFC from the box and releases it to the platform, and then transfers it from the platform to the assmebly position of the phone. In Task 3, the robotic arm also transfers the SIM card to the platform first, then to the SIM card slot of the phone, and it also needs to push the card into the slot with the pushing board attached to the manipulator end. Two experiments are conducted. In the first experiment (see Sect. 4.1), we set up three different teaching modes to analyse the effects of real-time teaching and visual student models. In addition, we also validate the usefulness of the synonymous skill module in the second experiment (see Sect. 4.2) and conduct subjective surveys on all volunteers (see Sect. 4.3).

4.1   Impact of Real-Time Teaching and Visual Student Model

Five volunteers are asked to teach assembly tasks using three different teaching modes shown in Table 4. In the same teaching mode, the skills taught in the previous tasks can be used in the subsequent tasks. Real-time teaching means that the user can always observe the assembly environments, and each language instruction controls actions of the robotic arm in real time. None-real-time teaching means that the language dialogue and robot execution are two separate steps, in which users first generate the BT for the complete assembly process using natural language and then use the generated tree to perform the whole task. Teaching with (without) student model means that the existing BT library and the running status of the main tree are (aren't) visualized.

Table 4. Three different teaching modes.

Teaching Mode	Real-time	Student model
Mode 1	✗	✗
Mode 2	✓	✗
Mode 3	✓	✓

The teaching time of 3 different modes is shown in Fig. 11. In order to reduce the impact of users' familiarity, the teaching order of three modes is random for each user. The result shows that the teaching time of Mode 1 is the shortest, because there are fewer context switches between conversations and skill executions. Besides, users take more time to observe the world environment and robot states while real-time teaching. We also find that when the student model is provided in Mode 3, the teaching time is reduced compared with Mode 2, because the user can obtain the current execution status not only from the environment, but also the visualized running BT. In this way, the efficiency of real-time observation is improved. In addition, although Task 3 is more complicated, the average teaching time of it using Mode 2 and 3 is shorter than that of Task 2, because of the use of learned hierarchical skills. We also find that in complicated tasks with more actions, such as Task 2 and 3, the standard deviation of teaching time is large, and users who are good at teaching and using hierarchical skills complete the teaching much more efficiently.

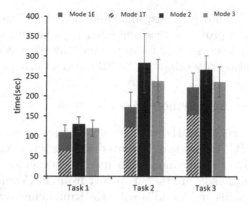

Fig. 11. Average teaching time of 3 teaching modes. Mode 1E refers to the execution time in Mode 1, and Mode 1T refers to the time of human-robot language interaction.

Success rates and numbers of generated hierarchical skills using different teaching modes are shown in Table 5. High success rates demonstrate the effectiveness of NL2BT. Real-time teaching (Modes 2 and 3) has significantly higher success rates, as users can make timely adjustments based on the environment and robot states to ensure successful execution of tasks. Besides, when teaching in real time and being able to visualize the behavior tree library (Mode 3), users prefer to teach and use more hierarchical skills.

Table 5. Success rates and numbers of hierarchical skills of different teaching modes. hier. is short for hierarchical skills.

User	Mode 1		Mode 2		Mode 3	
	success	hier.	success	hier.	success	hier.
1	3/3	5	3/3	4	3/3	5
2	1/3	4	3/3	4	3/3	6
3	2/3	4	3/3	5	3/3	5
4	2/3	4	3/3	5	3/3	5
5	2/3	3	2/3	6	3/3	6
total	66.7%	20	93.3%	24	100%	27

In summary, NL2BT is a feasible and effective framework for learning from natural language. Non-real-time teaching without student models takes less time, but the success rate is lower and fewer hierarchical skills are taught, indicating poor teaching effectiveness. In contrast, real-time teaching takes longer time, but greatly improves the success rate by enabling users to make timely adjustments in a dynamic environment. Furthermore, the student model informs users of learned skills and running status, allowing them focus more on the agent's unlearned skills and improve the teaching efficiency. Therefore, real-time teaching and student model are essential for improving the effectiveness and efficiency of learning hierarchical skills using the NL2BT framework.

4.2   Impact of the Synonymous Skill Module

In Sect. 4.1, to better explore the impact of real-time teaching and the visual student model, the BT library is only shared among the same user in the same teaching mode, and the synonymous skill module is excluded. Table 5 shows a total of 71 hierarchical skills are taught. Apart from 45 (5 volunteers * 3 modes * 3 tasks) top-level skills and 10 skills with the same names as others, there are 16 hierarchical skills with only four different composition structures, indicating that many synonymous skills are taught. In this experiment, we add these four skill subtrees to the initial BT library and invite 5 new volunteers to teach 3 tasks using the Mode 3, with and without the synonymous skill module. The average teaching time and the number of stored subtrees are shown in Table 6.

Table 6. Average teaching time and number of stored trees. w/o Syn. denotes teaching without synonymous skill module, and w/ Syn. denotes teaching with it.

	Task	w/o Syn.	w/ Syn.	decreased by
Average Teaching Time	1	111.96	82.66	26.17 %
	2	238.37	202.89	14.88%
	3	300.92	209.24	30.47%
Number of Stored Subtrees	1	11	8	27.27%
	2	14	9	35.71%
	3	16	10	37.5%

Table 6 illustrates that the synonymous skill module helps reduce the teaching time and the number of stored subtrees. In other words, it improves teaching efficiency and maintains a BT library with less storage and memory usage.

4.3   Subjective Feedback

We request that all volunteers evaluate the system's usability and usefulness using a 7-point Likert scale [12] (ranging from "strongly disagree" to "strongly agree") based on the statements 1–5 listed in Table 7. Additionally, volunteers participating in Sect. 4.2 are asked to rate an extra statement (statement 6).

We also conduct interviews with volunteers to gather their opinions on real-time teaching, visual student models, and the synonymous skill module. In general, all agree that these features contribute positively to the framework. To be specific, real-time teaching increases users' confidence in using the system.

Table 7. Average scores on system's usability and usefulness on a 7-point scale.

Num	Statement	Score
1	I learn to use this system very quickly	6.6
2	The interaction process is simple and easy to understand	6.2
3	All functions in this system are well organized and integrated	5.9
4	I feel confident using the system	6.1
5	Visual behavior tree library is helpful during my teaching process	6.7
6	I find teaching with the synonymous skill module is more efficient	6.4

Additionally, when users couldn't recall the exact name of a skill that they have taught, they could provide a vague name and rely on the synonymous skill module to suggest candidate skill names. This reduces the need for frequent querying of the BT library and minimizes context switching. One of the participants also mentions that the synonymous skill module and the visual BT library complement each other well. Without the module, the library acts as a teaching manual, requiring users to use the exact skill names to teach efficiently. However, with the module, the BT library becomes a convenient aid for users to determine whether the candidate skills given are true synonymous skills they need. This is helpful for efficient teaching, particularly when numerous skill subtrees are stored in the BT library in the future.

5   Conclusion and Future Work

In this paper, we present NL2BT, a framework for generating behavior trees automatically from natural language and using them to control robots to perform hierarchical tasks. The framework consists of two language processing stages, an initial BT library with primitive skill subtrees, and a BT-Generation algorithm. We develop a Chinese-language system using NL2BT and validate it with 3C assembly tasks in the virtual environment. We also analyse the positive impact of real-time teaching, visual student models, and the synonymous skill module. They improve the success rate and teaching efficiency, reduce memory usage, and receive better user feedback.

While we develop the system for Chinese users, the NL2BT framework can be easily migrated to task learning systems in any language that can be processed by BERT. Furthermore, the framework can be adapted to other scenarios where hierarchical skills are taught using natural language. The system developers only need to fine-tune the language model with their text dataset, find the best hyperparameters (the layer and threshold) for the synonymous skill module, and modify the primitive skills for their own tasks. Therefore, the NL2BT framework has broad application and development prospects.

This paper presents a generic and portable framework for learning hierarchical skills represented by behavior trees from natural language. Future work will focus on improving and perfecting each part of the framework. For example, natural language generation models can be used to obtain more flexible agent replies, and the best learning methods for primitive skills will be explored. Additionally, the current framework only allows for one intent and skill per input instruction. In future work, we will extend it to support multiple intents and skills using large language models.

Acknowledgments. This research was supported by the National Key Research & Development Program of China (No.2018AAA0102902). We would also like to thank the Institute for Artificial Intelligence, Tsinghua University, for providing equipment and data support.

References

1. Ahn, M., et al.: Do as i can, not as i say: grounding language in robotic affordances. arXiv preprint arXiv:2204.01691 (2022)
2. Cao, Y., Lee, C.: Robot behavior-tree-based task generation with large language models. arXiv preprint arXiv:2302.12927 (2023)
3. Chai, J.Y., Gao, Q., She, L., Yang, S., Saba-Sadiya, S., Xu, G.: Language to action: towards interactive task learning with physical agents. In: IJCAI, pp. 2–9 (2018)
4. Chen, Q., Zhuo, Z., Wang, W.: Bert for joint intent classification and slot filling. arXiv preprint arXiv:1902.10909 (2019)
5. Colledanchise, M., Natale, L.: On the implementation of behavior trees in robotics. IEEE Rob. Autom. Lett. **6**(3), 5929–5936 (2021)
6. Colledanchise, M., Ögren, P.: How behavior trees modularize hybrid control systems and generalize sequential behavior compositions, the subsumption architecture, and decision trees. IEEE Trans. Rob. **33**(2), 372–389 (2016)
7. Colledanchise, M., Ögren, P.: Behavior Trees in Robotics and AI: An Introduction. CRC Press, Boca Raton (2018)
8. De Rossi, G., et al.: Cognitive robotic architecture for semi-autonomous execution of manipulation tasks in a surgical environment. In: 2019 IEEE/RSJ International Conference on Intelligent Robots and Systems (IROS), pp. 7827–7833. IEEE (2019)
9. Devlin, J., Chang, M.W., Lee, K., Toutanova, K.: Bert: Pre-training of deep bidirectional transformers for language understanding. arXiv preprint arXiv:1810.04805 (2018)
10. Faconti, D.: Groot (2018). https://github.com/BehaviorTree/Groot
11. French, K., Wu, S., Pan, T., Zhou, Z., Jenkins, O.C.: Learning behavior trees from demonstration. In: 2019 International Conference on Robotics and Automation (ICRA), pp. 7791–7797. IEEE (2019)
12. Hinkin, T.R.: A brief tutorial on the development of measures for use in survey questionnaires. Organ. Res. Methods **1**(1), 104–121 (1998)
13. IFLYTEK: Iflytek open platform (2021). https://www.xfyun.cn
14. Jawahar, G., Sagot, B., Seddah, D.: What does BERT learn about the structure of language? In: ACL 2019–57th Annual Meeting of the Association for Computational Linguistics (2019)
15. Laird, J.E., et al.: Interactive task learning. IEEE Intell. Syst. **32**(4), 6–21 (2017)
16. Li, T.J.J., Azaria, A., Myers, B.A.: SUGILITE: creating multimodal smartphone automation by demonstration. In: Proceedings of the 2017 CHI Conference on Human Factors in Computing Systems, pp. 6038–6049 (2017)

17. Li, T.J.J., Mitchell, T., Myers, B.: Interactive task learning from GUI-grounded natural language instructions and demonstrations. In: Proceedings of the 58th Annual Meeting of the Association for Computational Linguistics: System Demonstrations, pp. 215–223 (2020)
18. Liang, P.: Learning executable semantic parsers for natural language understanding. Commun. ACM **59**(9), 68–76 (2016)
19. Liu, C., et al.: Jointly learning grounded task structures from language instruction and visual demonstration. In: Proceedings of the 2016 Conference on Empirical Methods in Natural Language Processing, pp. 1482–1492 (2016)
20. Lynch, C., et al.: Interactive language: talking to robots in real time. arXiv preprint arXiv:2210.06407 (2022)
21. Mees, O., Hermann, L., Rosete-Beas, E., Burgard, W.: Calvin: a benchmark for language-conditioned policy learning for long-horizon robot manipulation tasks. IEEE Rob. Autom. Lett. **7**(3), 7327–7334 (2022)
22. Mikolov, T., Sutskever, I., Chen, K., Corrado, G.S., Dean, J.: Distributed representations of words and phrases and their compositionality. In: Advances in Neural Information Processing Systems, vol. 26 (2013)
23. Petit, M., Demiris, Y.: Hierarchical action learning by instruction through interactive grounding of body parts and proto-actions. In: 2016 IEEE International Conference on Robotics and Automation (ICRA), pp. 3375–3382. IEEE (2016)
24. She, L., Yang, S., Cheng, Y., Jia, Y., Chai, J., Xi, N.: Back to the blocks world: learning new actions through situated human-robot dialogue. In: Proceedings of the 15th Annual Meeting of the Special Interest Group on Discourse and Dialogue (SIGDIAL), pp. 89–97 (2014)
25. Stepputtis, S., Campbell, J., Phielipp, M., Lee, S., Baral, C., Ben Amor, H.: Language-conditioned imitation learning for robot manipulation tasks. Adv. Neural. Inf. Process. Syst. **33**, 13139–13150 (2020)
26. Vemprala, S., Bonatti, R., Bucker, A., Kapoor, A.: Chatgpt for robotics: design principles and model abilities. Microsoft Auton. Syst. Robot. Res **2**, 20 (2023)
27. Wang, H., Hu, Y.: Synonyms (2017). https://github.com/chatopera/Synonyms
28. Welschehold, T., Abdo, N., Dornhege, C., Burgard, W.: Combined task and action learning from human demonstrations for mobile manipulation applications. In: 2019 IEEE/RSJ International Conference on Intelligent Robots and Systems (IROS), pp. 4317–4324. IEEE (2019)

Relating Context and Self Awareness in the Internet of Things

David Arnaiz[1,2](✉) [ID], Marc Vila[1,2](✉) [ID], Eduard Alarcón[1,3] [ID],
Francesc Moll[1] [ID], Maria-Ribera Sancho[1,4] [ID], and Ernest Teniente[1] [ID]

[1] Universitat Politècnica de Catalunya, Barcelona, Spain
{david.arnaiz,marc.vila.gomez,eduard.alarcon,francesc.moll,
maria.ribera.sancho,ernest.teniente}@upc.edu
[2] Worldsensing, Barcelona, Spain
[3] NaNoNetworking Center in Catalonia, Barcelona, Spain
[4] Barcelona Supercomputing Center, Barcelona, Spain

Abstract. Context- and self- awareness are two terms that have been living with us for many years. In principle, both state a similar meaning even though the literature points out a very different path. One is inspired by location-related mechanisms in mobile environments, whereas the other is inspired by biology. In the area of the Internet of Things, the term context-awareness has seen a higher adoption in the field of Cloud Computing, while the term self-awareness is more widely used in the area of Wireless Sensor Networks. This paper evaluates the entire IoT Cloud-to-Thing Continuum in an attempt to reconcile both terms. We contextualize and discuss the literature around context and self-awareness, and we propose a conceptual architecture that handles both concepts, with the aim of having a better understanding of how to develop a software environment that integrates both concepts. To show the real-life applicability of our proposed architecture, it is introduced in a realistic setting such as wildfire monitoring, including a conceptual overview of how the proposed architecture could be implemented in this domain. Additionally, our evaluation of a river flooding scenario concluded that the proposed architecture significantly reduced flood detection delay by over 47% compared to the naive method and over 20% compared to standalone self-awareness and context-awareness methods.

Keywords: Context-Awareness · Self-Awareness · Wireless Sensor Networks · Internet of Things · Edge-Cloud Collaboration · Cloud-to-Thing

1 Introduction

The Internet of Things (IoT) represents a new paradigm on how data is collected, shared, analyzed, stored, and used. Over the years, the IoT has seen significant adaptation and continues to grow to this day. In 2021, the number of IoT devices grew to 12.2 billion and is expected to grow to 14.4 billion by the end of 2022 [5].

M. Sellami et al. (Eds.): CoopIS 2023, LNCS 14353, pp. 384–402, 2024.
https://doi.org/10.1007/978-3-031-46846-9_21

IoT aims to interrelate smart devices, called *Things*. In this domain, a *Thing* can be some physical entity such as sensors or actuators, or even digital entities such as software components. These devices have the ability to communicate information with other entities, devices, or systems through the Internet.

One of the key enabling technologies for IoT is Wireless Sensor Networks (WSN). WSNs are made up of multiple low-cost, typically resource-constrained sensor nodes that collect environmental measurements and forward these measurements to a centralized node, called a sink node, using a wireless communication protocol. These sink nodes act as a gateway between the low-power wireless interface used by the nodes and the Internet.

Once data is received in the Cloud servers, it is then aggregated to provide insights into the monitored environment. The large number of sensors that constitute a WSN, their limited resource availability, their heterogeneous nature, and their high environmental dependency significantly complicates the management of these networks. To fully extract its full potential, the complete IoT ecosystem needs to be self-managing and able to react to changes in its operating conditions with minimal or no intervention from its operator. To achieve this, IoT networks, Things, and Fog/Cloud infrastructures must continuously monitor their own state and their operation environment, to determine the most appropriate configuration for the circumstances at hand and implement it.

The challenge of creating self-managing IoT networks has attracted significant attention in the research community. In the context of Cloud Computing, this is being addressed through the implementation of context-aware systems. Meanwhile, at the sensor node level, this challenge is being addressed using the principles of Self-awareness. This raises the challenge of where to run the decision-making for the adaptive behavior. Both techniques, Cloud and Edge, have different benefits and limitations, and whether to implement the adaptive behavior at the sensor node level or at the Cloud level depends on the specific application requirements. In this context, computing on the Edge can provide lower latency, greater privacy, and reduced bandwidth requirements, but at the expense of power consumption, whereas computing on the Cloud can provide greater scalability, more computing power, and easier maintenance, with the added benefit that power is rarely a constraint.

The contributions in this paper are twofold. First, we evaluate the two popular methods to implement adaptive behaviors in the IoT: context-awareness and self-awareness. Second, we define a reference architecture of a context- and self- aware IoT network, taking into account the different needs across the IoT Cloud-to-Thing Continuum; we demonstrate the suggested architecture's practical use by showing it in a realistic wildfire monitoring scenario; and then, we evaluate the advantages of our proposed architecture in a river flooding detection scenario, comparing the achieved performance of our proposal with other methods only exhibiting context- or self- awareness.

The remainder of this paper is structured as follows. Section 2 introduces the concepts of context- and self- awareness in the literature. In Sect. 3 we review the related work and the relevant efforts to introduce these topics in the IoT. Then, in Sect. 4 we propose a reference architecture that makes use of both concepts explained in this paper. In Sect. 5, we evaluate the proposed architecture using real-world data from river monitoring in Canada. Finally, in Sect. 6 we conclude the paper by outlining the conclusions and future work.

2   Context- and Self- awareness in the Literature

2.1   Context-Awareness

The term *Context-Aware* or *Context-Aware Computing* was coined in 1994 by Schilit et al. [29] as "The ability of a mobile user's applications to discover and react to changes in the environment they are situated in." Some months later, Schilit et al. [28] provided another definition: "Mobile applications that are aware of the context in which they are run." In both definitions, it can be acknowledged that the use case was meant for mobile applications. Still, a significant part, which is being aware or reacting to situations, is also mentioned. Furthermore, they also clarify that "context encompasses more than just the user's location." and propose dividing the context into three categories: *Computing Context* as network connectivity, communication cost and bandwidth, and nearby physical resources. *User Context* as the user profile, location, nearby people, or social situations. *Physical Context* as temperature, light and noise levels, and traffic conditions. In 1997, Brown et al. [8] defined context-aware mechanisms as applications that change their behavior according to the user's context. In 1998, Pascoe [23] proposed a taxonomy of generic context-aware capabilities, including contextual sensing, adaptation, and resource discovery. In 2000, Chen and Kotz [9] presented a survey on Context-Aware Mobile Computing that included several definitions of the context-aware concept, applications, and approaches to sense and model contexts. It is in 2007, in Baldauf et al. [7], that a more up-to-date overview of Context-Aware Computing can be found. They claim that "context-aware systems are able to adapt their operations to the current context without explicit user intervention, aiming at increasing usability and effectiveness by taking environmental context into account." They also present architectural designs and approaches on how to acquire contextual information in a system. To our knowledge, the last and most precise survey in this area was presented in 2014, where Perera et al. [25] concluded that the accepted context-awareness definition is the one provided by Abowd et al. [2]: "A system is context-aware if it uses context to provide relevant information and/or services to the user, where relevancy depends on the user's task."

2.2   Self-awareness

The notion of *Self-Awareness* originates from biology. Where Morin [20] defined Self-Awareness as "the capacity to become the object of one's own attention [...] The organism becomes aware that it is awake and actually experiencing specific mental events, emitting behaviors, and possessing unique characteristics." The roots of Self-Awareness in the context of computing systems can be traced back to *Autonomic Computing*, an IBM initiative introduced in a manifesto from 2001 to address the increasing complexity of IT infrastructure [16].

Autonomic Computing is inspired by the autonomic nervous system, the responsible for autonomously controlling bodily functions, such as breathing or pupil dilation, without any conscious effort. Following this principle, an Autonomic computing system manages itself based on operator-defined goals. Rather than providing a formal definition of the term in their manifesto, IBM defined autonomic computing by providing a list of desirable properties that a system should display in order to be considered autonomic. During the following years, different authors used different properties to define autonomic computing, creating multiple definitions for the term [17].

Self-Awareness, the ability to monitor and model its own state, was initially introduced as a property of an Autonomic system [30]. Later, in 2009 Agarwal et al. [3] introduced the notion of Self-Aware Computing using a similar definition to that of Autonomic Computing. From this point on, other publications use the terms autonomic computing and self-aware computing indistinguishably [15]. In 2015, Kounev et al. [18] formulated a new definition of self-awareness, aligning the different understandings of the term at the time: "Self-aware computing systems are computing systems that 1) *learn* models capturing knowledge about themselves and their environment (such as their structure, design, state, possible actions, and run-time behavior) on an ongoing basis and 2) *reason* using the models (e.g. predict, analyze, consider, plan) enabling them to act based on their knowledge and reasoning (e.g. explore, explain, report, suggest, self-adapt, or impact their environment) in accordance with higher-level goals, which may also be subject to change." While there is no clear consensus for any given definition, the broad nature of this definition makes it the most widely acknowledged by researchers.

Even if context- and self- awareness have different origins and formal definitions, and have been applied to different fields, they still have some similarities. Considering that, the definition of *context* also includes information about the system *itself*, then the understanding self-awareness is contained within the definition of context-awareness. Whilst, the definition of self-awareness emphasizes and restricts its definition to focus on the properties which are considered advantageous to make the system able to self-manage.

3 Related Work

Both, context- and self- awareness have been utilized to implement self-adaptive behaviors in IoT networks. Context-awareness focuses on centralized decision-making in the Fog/Cloud infrastructure, whereas Self-awareness proposes that Edge devices should manage themselves.

Adaptive control methods in IoT can be implemented in a centralized way, where the IoT application running in the Fog/Cloud server is responsible for defining the monitoring requirements for the network and defining the adaptive actions for the Edge devices, which are then responsible for following such policies. In Mudassar et al. [21], authors propose a centralized adaptive IoT surveillance system. Where the server identifies areas of interest in the low-quality frames collected by the wireless cameras that compose the network, and sends this context information to the cameras. For the next collected frame, the cameras will transmit these regions of interest in higher quality so the objects can be more accurately tracked and identified.

Alternatively, the control can be implemented in a distributed way where the IoT application defines the monitoring goals for the network, and the Edge devices decide the adaptive actions required to comply with the defined goals. Adaptive decision-making may follow a top-down approach, where decisions are propagated from the higher tiers of the network. A top-down distributed adaptive data collection method for tree-based networks is presented in Zhuang et al. [33]. In their self-aware data collection method, the Cloud application defines the maximum allowed data distortion for the network and passes this requirement for the next layer of sensors in the tree topology. These sensors autonomously allocate the distortion budget between them, based on their experienced congestion level, and propagate this process to the next tree layer until all the nodes have their distortion target allocated. Similarly, distributed decision-making may follow a bottom-up approach. In Forooghifar et al. [11], authors propose a Self-Aware epilepsy monitoring system with multiple hierarchical and progressively more complex classifiers. The monitoring system evaluates the expected confidence of the classification with each classification model, starting from the simpler model executed in the Edge device to the more complex Cloud-based classifier.

Other authors explore as well the Cloud and Edge collaboration, e.g. self and context awareness. In Wan et al. [32], authors propose a context-aware system in vehicular networks where they state that the analysis for parking information can be executed on the Cloud, but as well it can be handled in Fog or Edge tiers. Hence, creating a system that is context-and-self-aware because they claim that several attributes can be used and taken advantage of when they are handled on-site, even though some of them have to be uploaded to the Cloud for more complex processing. A similar approach is taken in Ortiz et al. [22], where they propose an architecture along the Cloud-to-Thing Continuum tiers that adapts to the needs and processing capabilities of each tier and permits interoperability, data processing and includes two-way communications between the three tiers, improving collaborative decisions in real-time. They state that processing data at the edge means being able to make faster decisions at the edge when information from other layers is not relevant for the decision-making process, therefore being able to act more quickly when the scenario conditions require it. In addition to avoiding overloading the networks, and removing unnecessary delay communications. Galar et al. [12], propose a context-aware mechanism for the maintenance of industrial equipment. They model the degradation of components and forecast when the next maintenance is needed. Acquiring context information from physical and virtual sensors; Storing context and interpreting information using models; Utilizing context information as triggers or additional information. In CA4IOT [24], authors propose an architecture that improves context-aware capabilities in IoT systems, understanding and maintaining context information (what, when, who, how, why) about sensors. Finally, Garcia-de-Prado et al. [26] introduce a context-aware service-oriented architecture for collaborative IoT, encompassing decision-making processes. They propose two distinct location-based types of processing nodes: cloud nodes and fog nodes. This helps avoiding additional resource consumption to edge devices or delays, and then, cloud nodes focus on performing higher computational tasks which can be useful for several fog nodes. In both cases, their proposal makes use of an event rules system that obtains the information from the domain and the context, then it is transformed, evaluated, and acted upon.

Reviewing the practical use cases for context- and self- aware systems, the different nature between both concepts is clearly shown, not only in how they are used but also in where they are being implemented. In resource-constrained sensor nodes, self-awareness provides the means through which the sensor nodes can autonomously and efficiently manage their limited resources to achieve their operational goals, adapting to the operating conditions. On the other hand, in a Cloud environment, where the resources are more abundant, Context-Awareness provides the mechanisms through which contextual information is collected and used. Contextual information may be used to help with semantic interpretation of data, provide alarms, or adapt the system itself or a different system, based on the operating conditions gathered.

4   Context- and Self- Awareness Architecture for the IoT

There is no single and universal architecture for managing an IoT infrastructure. However, the most common approach is to classify the smart entities on the network into edge device (or Thing) layer, fog layer, or cloud layer, based on their distance to the entity that originated the data.

4.1   IoT Infrastructure

In the IoT, most of the data processing and management is carried out at the Cloud layer, thanks to its flexibility, computational power, and budget advantages. However, there are ongoing trends focused on moving some of this computation closer to the Edge, claiming increased responsiveness, increased privacy, and reduced bandwidth usage, along with other advantages [10]. Despite the attention given to data offloading, the problem of where to perform the decision-making has been widely overlooked. This problem is particularly relevant when managing the Edge devices since they have limited resources and their operation is strongly coupled with the physical environment, thus, it is paramount that their resources are used frugally based on the operating conditions. As the adaptive behaviors of Edge devices become increasingly complex, the problem of where to close the adaptive loop gains relevance. The decision-making can be centralized if the adaptive control is implemented in the server, or distributed if each Edge device manages itself.

Edge devices are limited in terms of energy, computational power, and memory. In most cases, most of the energy budget of the Edge devices is used by their wireless interface [14]. Consequently, the energy cost and bandwidth limitation of the wireless interface limits how often the Edge devices can communicate with the higher layers, introducing communication delays. In applications where the decision-making is not computationally expensive, distributed control can save energy and increase responsiveness by performing the decision-making locally; otherwise, offloading tasks to the Fog or Cloud server becomes more advantageous. In these cases, the added cost of processing the data locally may not outweigh the energy or time savings of not transmitting the data to the Fog or Cloud. Another key difference between the distributed and centralized control approaches is their data availability. Edge devices only have access to their local data, while the Fog and Cloud can aggregate data from multiple sources, generating more precise models, which enable them to make more informed decisions.

In essence, both control approaches have two different timescales. Distributed control is optimal to guide fast adaptive actions, that do not require complex processing; while centralized control is optimal to guide precise adaptive actions that do not need to be updated as frequently. Our proposed adaptive control method exploits the different timescales from both approaches to keep the advantages of both methods.

4.2   Architecture

We show in Fig. 1 the architecture we propose to link context- and Self- awareness, based on three main elements: Entity, Thing/Edge Device, Fog/Cloud.

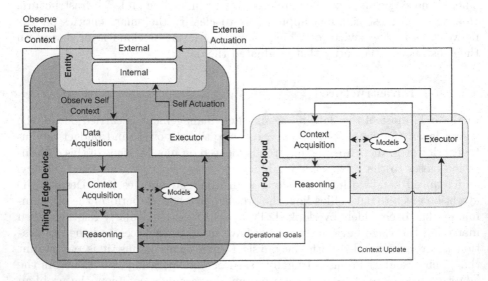

Fig. 1. Relating context- and self- awareness in one architecture for Internet of Things

Entity. These are the elements to be monitored and acted upon. They can be real-world elements, such as a wall (physical) or rain (meteorological), or logical as the processor usage of a node or the communication status of data messages. In our proposal, the entities are divided between those *external* referring to the world at large and those *internal* referring to the Things themselves, including the different subsystems that make up Things.

Thing/Edge Device. We consider devices in the IoT as Things or Edge devices, the endpoint for observing or acting on the world entities' status. These devices interact with the world using their sensors or actuators and with the rest of the network through their wireless interface, generally using wireless communication technologies, mainly LPWAN [19] or cellular, i.e. LoRa, SigFox, NB-IoT, 5G, 4G/LTE, or 2G. These devices perform four basic functions, each implemented by its own component:

1. *Data Acquisition*: Performs measurements from its connected sensors, such as an accelerometer, temperature, or a gauge; and internal sensors, such as processor heartbeat counters or radio usage. This component provides an abstraction layer between the sensors that provide the measurements and the rest of the device's components.
2. *Context Acquisition*: Collects the raw measurements gathered at the Data Acquisition and performs some processing on the data. Additionally, it uses this data to update its local models about its own state and that of its environment, sending the relevant information to the Reasoning component.
3. *Reasoning*: Uses the information observed by the Context Acquisition component; the updated models; and the Operational Goals given by the Cloud to decide which are the best actions to take, i.e., setting a specific sampling rate, or enabling additional sensors.
4. *Executor*: Is the main responsible for implementing the adaptive actions and making the actual configuration changes on the device itself. In addition, a device may be equipped with external actuators capable of directly acting upon the environment, e.g., heating or cooling element, gas valve, or door lock. In these cases, the adaptive actions may also include acting on the environment.

The Context Acquisition and Reasoning components share access to a common knowledge base, the Models, which can be updated by both[1]. The Edge device maintains models of its internal subsystems, modeling the state, availability, possible control actions, and its effect on the device itself or its environment. The device is also capable of monitoring its surrounding environment using the data collected by its connected sensors to implement simple adaptive behaviors.

Fog/Cloud. Information can be processed and reacted upon at the Edge, or transmitted to the Fog or the Cloud for reasons such as obtaining context from

---

[1] Illustrated by dashed lines in Fig. 1 to emphasize the different interactions' nature.

external entities, leveraging greater computational power for context reasoning, or energy considerations.

2. *Context Acquisition*: Receives information collected by devices in the sensor node cluster connected to the server: environmental, contextual, or about the nodes themselves. Also, the server may have information from other sources, i.e., satellite or drone data, or even third-party, i.e., weather forecasting APIs. This information is used to update the models on the nodes connected to the network and the monitored environment, ready to be enhanced with further information from different sensors.
3. *Reasoning*: This component uses the information collected by the Context Acquisition and the application requirements to decide the adaptive actions and allocate resources. It has an output, the *Operational Goals*, which contains the high-level adaptive objectives sent to the nodes to guide their behavior (i.e., target battery life or minimum accuracy data accuracy) or containing relevant information (i.e., environment state, information from other nodes). If the application requires it, the server can also send low-level commands to the devices, to directly manage their operation.
4. *Executor*: The server can also take action in the environment. For instance, it can send alarm notifications to the network operator through email or provide visual indications in the web application.

Similarly to Edge devices, the Context Acquisition and Reasoning components at the Fog and Cloud tiers share a common knowledge base. The server models all *things* connected to its network, including their available resources, state, goals, and capabilities. Periodically, *things* on the network will transmit information about themselves to update these models. The limited resource availability for the *things* limits how often they relay their state to the server, and thus, the server model will not be as up-to-date as their local model. In addition, the server also maintains a model of the monitored environment as it has abundant computing resources and access to information from multiple sources. Therefore, the environment model maintained by the server is considered the most accurate representation available in the network.

4.3   Wildfire Monitoring Conceptual Use Case

In this section, we demonstrate the practical application of the awareness model proposed, showcasing it in a Wireless Sensor Network (WSN)-based early wildfire warning monitoring scenario [13]. Early detection of wildfires is critical to minimize their expansion, thus helping to maintain forests and wildlife.

A typical early warning wildfire monitoring system is composed of wireless sensor nodes with temperature, smoke, and gas measuring capabilities, which collect the monitoring data; and a server application that aggregates and processes this data to generate the early warning alarms [13]. On a different note, Sarwar et al. [27], propose a lightweight fire warning system capable of detecting and determining the likelihood of a fire, that is executed locally by the sensor nodes. By processing the data locally, these sensors reduce their transmission power consumption, and thus, can increase how often they perform a monitoring cycle, albeit with lower accuracy than the server's model. In contrast, Arif et al. [6] evaluate the use of Machine Learning algorithms for wildfire monitoring. A central server may collect and aggregate information from multiple sources, such as sensor nodes, satellite images, weather data and forecasting, drone data, or historical data, to obtain a more accurate fire detection model.

Our architecture helps to combine the advantages of distributed and centralized fire monitoring by dynamically managing the trade-off between energy consumption and monitoring accuracy based on the current system needs. The monitoring accuracy in wildfire monitoring depends on the fire detection algorithm delay and precision. To combine the advantages of the centralized and distributed monitoring approaches, we use a hybrid approach. Nodes will periodically take measurements and process them using a lightweight local fire detection model, maintaining the responsiveness of the distributed approach. For every predefined number of periods, the node transmits sensor data to the server, where it is processed by the more accurate model, maintaining the precision of the centralized approach. The lightweight fire detection model executed by the nodes computes the predicted probability and confidence of a fire being present. If the fire probability is above the *probability threshold* or if the confidence level is below the *confidence threshold*, the sensor data is transmitted to the server to be processed using a more accurate analysis.

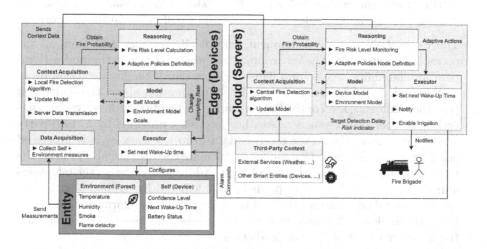

Fig. 2. Wildfire Monitoring using our architecture

A self-aware node proposal for wildfire monitoring is presented in Fig. 2. The node only monitors one *self* parameter (i.e., the confidence level of its local fire detection algorithm), one *context* parameter (i.e., the fire presence probability), and is able to adjust one parameter (i.e., its sampling period). Finally, the node has one goal, which is maintaining an average fire detection delay.

1. The *Data Acquisition* component collects the raw measurements from the sensors (i.e., temperature, humidity, smoke, and flame detector), the internal information from the node, and the confidence level of the fire presence probability estimation.
2. The *Context Acquisition* component processes the raw environmental measurements using the lightweight fire detection algorithm, calculating the probability of predicted fire presence and the confidence level. It also monitors the time since the last data transmission to the server and evaluates if the data needs to be transmitted, considering the current fire probability and confidence level values.
3. The *Reasoning* component calculates the current fire risk level, using the predicted probability of fire, the confidence level, and a risk indicator that the server periodically updates. If the risk level is higher than average, the node reacts by increasing its sampling rate, gathering measurements more frequently, and compensating it by decreasing it during periods of lower risk, so as to achieve its average fire detection delay as stated in its goals. For example, if we consider the monitoring period to be one hour, the node would allocate more resources during the hottest hours of the day, when the fire is more likely to occur, and compensates for the extra energy consumption during the night, when fires are less likely to start.
4. The *Executor* component obtains the adjusted sampling rate provided by the *Reasoning* component and adjusts the next wake-up alarm accordingly.

Furthermore, the centralized server that takes into account context-aware mechanisms for wildfire monitoring is connected to all nodes in the network.

1. The *Context Acquisition* component periodically receives data from all the nodes in the network. The environmental measurements of the nodes (temperature, humidity, smoke, and flame detector data), the fire detection probabilities calculated by the nodes, and the information about the node itself (i.e., the confidence level of the fire prediction). In addition, the server also has access to other sources such as weather forecasts, provided by a third-party service. Whenever the server receives data from the sensors, it is processed using its precise fire detection model to calculate the fire probability in all the monitored areas and predict its evolution. Additionally, the server maintains a model of the fire probability predictions calculated by the nodes with their respective confidence level metric. The server uses this information to calculate the confidence threshold required that each node must have to maintain the accuracy target of the fire prediction.
2. The *Reasoning* component uses the probability data calculated by the *Context Acquisition* component to monitor the areas where the probability has changed. In these, the new information is used to define a new fire detection delay target for the specific device. The Reasoning component also uses its fire probability forecast to calculate a *risk indicator* metric, which is sent to the nodes to improve their local predictions. In the event that a fire is detected, the server raises an alarm, during which the server defines the adaptive actions for the *Executor* to perform.

3. The *Executor* component should notify the local firefighter unit, enable the irrigation systems, and transmit the low-level commands to the sensor nodes as requested by the *Reasoning* module.

5 Comparative Analysis on Context- and Self- Aware Reasoning

To further validate the awareness model presented in this paper, we showcase a simulation test case in the context of a flood monitoring system [31], evaluating the effect of the proposed awareness model in a WSN-based flood monitoring system. Similarly to wildfire monitoring, early warning of flood events can help people in flood-prone prepare and evacuate, reducing the negative effects.

The *Calgary City Council* in Alberta (Canada), publishes river basin monitoring data from multiple monitoring wireless stations, where each station measures the flow and the depth level of the water[2], collecting one sample every 5 min. We use the *Nose Creek Above Airdrie* station, illustrated in Fig. 3, as it provides water depth level peaks, which we can use to generate alarms. However, during the monitoring period, no floods have been reported, therefore in our simulation, we defined a threshold value for the water level to simulate flood risk alarms and flooding events.

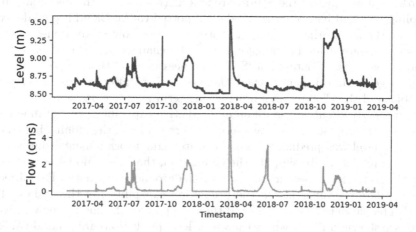

Fig. 3. Initial data exploration, water and flow levels of the river

We define the threshold value of 8.8 m to generate the flooding alarms, referred to as *threshold - ON*; and it remains active until the water level drops below 8.77 m, which is referred to as *threshold - OFF*. Figure 4 shows the temporal series of the monitored water level, the threshold - ON value is shown as a red horizontal line, and the threshold - OFF value is shown as a green horizontal line. The beginning of the flooding events is marked by a continuous vertical

---

[2] *River Level and Flows* dataset by *Alberta Environment and Parks* [4].

blue line, and the end of the events is marked by a vertical blue dashed line. Note that there are some flooding events that are only one sample long, in the simulation we removed these events as they are artifacts in the data.

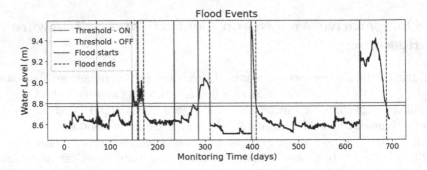

Fig. 4. Water level measurements with threshold values and flooding events

Our evaluation goal is to test the flood detection delay between when the actual flooding event starts or ends and when the tested monitoring method can detect it. Four different methods are compared in our evaluation: the naive monitoring method, where the sampling rate of the sensor node is kept constant regardless of any factor; the Self-awareness method, where the decisions on the sampling rate and how often is the data reported to the Cloud are made exclusively by the monitoring station; in contrast, in the Context-awareness method, the decisions are made in the Cloud, and the changes are relayed back to the station; Lastly, the Context-and-Self-awareness method that employs the approach suggested in this paper, where the monitoring station makes fast imprecise decisions and the Cloud makes precise long-term adaptive decisions.

To properly simulate the different predictive capabilities of the monitoring stations and the Cloud server, two models were made. In the monitoring station, the water level was predicted from the water flow measurement using a linear regression model [1]. To simplify the simulation, the Cloud model uses the data from the water level measurements, i.e., the ground truth data. The objective is to simulate the difference in the prediction capabilities of the node and the Cloud. The measured water level and the level predicted using the flow measurements are shown in Fig. 5, where the water level predictions are generally aligned with the actual water level. However, there are a few large differences; between days 450 and 550, the node predicts a flood event when there are actually no floods taking place; in addition, between days 600 and 700, there is a flooding event, which is not correctly predicted by the monitoring station. This provides a realistic environment in which to test the different capabilities of the evaluated monitoring methods.

A key parameter of the evaluated methods is the total energy consumption of the monitoring station through the simulation. To keep the comparisons between the monitored methods evaluated fair, their energy usage should be equal. Therefore, it must be ensured that improvements in detection times are

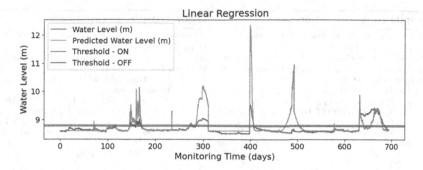

Fig. 5. Water level measurement and predicted water level

caused by more efficient energy allocation, and not by an increase in the energy consumption of the monitoring station. This is particularly relevant when comparing the Self-awareness and the Context-awareness methods, where the energy consumption of transmitting the data to the Cloud and receiving the instruction may justify making the adaptive decision locally even with a less accurate model. For our simulation, we used the measured consumption profile of a commercial node manufactured by Worldsensing[3] and shown in Table 1[4].

Table 1. Consumption profile used for the evaluation

Mode	Current	Duration (s)	Charge (mAh)
Idle	73.3 μA	N/A	N/A
Sampling and Processing	6.52 mA	1.73 s	3.13 μAh
Data Transmission	9.48 mA	7.64 s	20.1294 μAh
Data Reception	9.48 mA	7.64 s	20.1294 μAh

The different methods evaluate two different levels of flooding risk: *high* if the level exceeds the *threshold off*; otherwise, it is classified as low risk.

The Self-awareness-based monitoring algorithm is shown in Algorithm 1, where the node does not transmit every sample to the Cloud since it has its local water level prediction. Instead, the sensor node maintains a low sampling period to measure more often and only reports now and then. When its local predictor identifies that the risk level has increased to *high*, the sensor node increases its sampling rate to detect any possible event sooner. When an event is detected, then transmits the information to the Cloud to raise the alarm.

---

[3] Node datasheet: https://www.worldsensing.com/product/tilt90-x-2/.

[4] The water level prediction model–lightweight linear regression algorithm–employed in the sensor node has some energy overhead, but it is expected to have minimal impact on the sensor node's overall energy consumption. Hence, this has not been factored into the simulation nor Table 1.

Algorithm 1. Self-awareness

Parameters: *thresholdOn, thresholdOff*

```
1:  inEvent ← False
2:  tpCnt ← 0      ▷ Counter for the transmissions
3:  SP ← 0                    ▷ Sampling Period in Min.
4:  while running do
5:      f ←MeasureFlow()
6:      p ←PredictDepth(f)
7:      if p ≤ thresholdOff then        ▷ Low risk
8:          SP_n ← 5 * 12                  ▷ 1 Hour
9:          TP ← 5 * 18                  ▷ 1.5 Hours
10:     else                            ▷ High risk
11:         SP_n ← 5 * 2                   ▷ 10 Min
12:         TP ← 5 * 4                     ▷ 20 Min
13:     newEvent = DetectNewEvent(p)
14:     if (inEvent ≠ newEvent) then
15:         TransmitData(f)
16:         tpCnt ← 0
17:         inEvent ← newEvent
18:     else if tpCnt ≥ TP then         ▷ Transmit
19:         TransmitData(f)
20:         tpCnt ← 0
21:     else                  ▷ Skip transmission
22:         tpCnt ← tpCnt + SP
23:     SP ← SP_n
24:     WaitForNewData(SP)
```

Algorithm 2. Context-aware

Parameters: *thresholdOn, thresholdOff*

```
1:  procedure RUNNODE
2:      SP ← 0          ▷ Sampling Period in Min.
3:      while running do
4:          f ←MeasureFlow()
5:          TransmitData(f)
6:          if CommandReceived(f) = True then
7:              if ReceiveRisk() = Low then
8:                  SP ← 5 * 12              ▷ 1 Hour
9:              else          ▷ Server defined alarm
10:                 SP ← 5 * 7               ▷ 35 Min
11:         WaitForNewData(SP)
12:
13: procedure RUNSERVER
14:     riskLevel ← Low
15:     while running do
16:         f ←WaitForNodeData()
17:         p ←PredictDepthServer(f)
18:         if p ≤ thresholdOff then
19:             riskLevelNew ← Low
20:         else
21:             riskLevelNew ← High
22:         if riskLevelNew ≠ riskLevel then
23:             TransmitNewState(riskLevelNew)
24:             riskLevel ← riskLevelNew
```

The Context-awareness-based method, which algorithm is represented in Algorithm 2, depends exclusively on the server to perform the adaptations. Every time the sensor node performs a measurement, it is transmitted to the server for further analysis. If the server detects that the flood risk level has changed, it sends the new configuration to the sensor node. Performing the predictions in the Cloud allows using more accurate models, and thus, more accurate adaptations. Nevertheless, to keep the same energy consumption as the Self-awareness method, the sampling periods in the Context-awareness method had to be increased to compensate for the energy overhead of having to transmit every sample and receive the adaptation commands.

The Context-and-Self-awareness-based monitoring method combines both approaches. By default, it will leave the node to perform its own adaptive actions using its local predictor. This allows to keep the monitoring rate high, as it reduces the transmission energy. When the server receives a measurement from the sensor node, it compares the value predicted by the node's predictor, and the value predicted using the more accurate Cloud predictor. If the prediction from the sensor node is correct, it will continue to operate as with the Self-awareness method. Otherwise, if the node's prediction misidentifies the risk of flooding, the server will take control of the sensor node effectively behaving as the Context-awareness method. In essence, this method maintains the high sampling rate of the Self-awareness method by using the local prediction; and maintains the risk prediction accuracy of the Context-awareness method by taking control over the node as soon as its local model fails.

Using the consumption profile from Table 1, we calculated the power consumption of the node during the simulation. We manually adjusted the parameters for the different monitoring methods to achieve similar power consumption across all methods. The charge used by each method along with the average detection delay in minutes and the relative improvement in the flood detection delay is shown in Table 2.

Table 2. Flood event detection results

Monitoring Method	Average Detection Delay	Relative Improvement	Used Charge
Naive	45.5 mins	0.0%	1738.44 mAh
Self-Awareness	31.5 mins	30.77%	1693.72 mAh
Context-Awareness	36.0 mins	20.88%	1656.66 mAh
Self-Context-Awareness	24.0 mins	47.25%	1694.28 mAh

The results show that the Self-Awareness and Context-Awareness methods achieve similar average detection delays. In both cases, the detection delay is reduced concerning the Naive method. The Self-Context-Awareness method outperforms all other evaluated methods. These results confirm that the interaction between the Self-Awareness and Context-Awareness methods provides a better result than what is achieved by the methods independently.

The source code and resources, so that the reader is able to execute; modify some aspects; or replicate our evaluation, are available online at https://github. com/worldsensing/self-context-awareness-flood-detection.

6 Conclusions and Future Work

IoT networks consist of heterogeneous, resource-constrained devices that operate closely tied to the physical world and thus strongly depend on environmental conditions. To fully extract their potential, these networks need to be self-managed, and able to react to changes in their operating conditions with minimal or no operator intervention. Self-management of these networks has been addressed through the use of context and self- awareness, each with different backgrounds and application domains.

In this paper, we propose a unification between context- and self- awareness, resulting in a conceptual architecture for entity monitoring using IoT devices. We review the existing literature from both adaptive mechanisms, identifying their differences, similarities, weaknesses, strengths, and how they can complement each other. Our proposal is showcased in a wildfire detection scenario, exemplifying its applicability in a real-life monitoring scenario. In the context of a flood monitoring system, our proposed mechanism outperformed the equivalent only Context- and only Self- awareness methods, reducing the flood detection times between 24 to 33% using the same equivalent amount of energy.

This work represents a first step toward the development of aware IoT networks, where context-aware mechanisms will coordinate with self-aware mechanisms to autonomously manage networks. Additionally, it showcases the potential benefits of this coordination in the hope of guiding future research in this direction. Further work is needed to define a more complex interaction between the two awareness mechanisms showcased here, and explore surrounding topics such as the efficient transmission of the context information and operational goals between the Edge devices and the Cloud. The presented work is a theoretical framework, and further work is needed to implement and deploy this architecture in a real IoT deployment, to validate its advantages.

Acknowledgments. This work is partially funded by the Industrial Doctorates DI-2019 from Generalitat de Catalunya (2019 DI 075 to David Arnaiz and 2019 DI 001 to Marc Vila). The SUDOQU project (PID2021-127181OB-I00) from MCIN/AEI. FEDER "Una manera de hacer Europa". And the 2021-SGR-01252 project from Generalitat de Catalunya. Thanks to Xavier Vilajosana for his advice in this work. With the support of inLab FIB at UPC.

References

1. Aalen, O.O.: A linear regression model for the analysis of life times. Stat. Med. **8**(8), 907–925 (1989)
2. Abowd, G.D., Dey, A.K., Brown, P.J., Davies, N., Smith, M., Steggles, P.: Towards a better understanding of context and context-awareness. In: Gellersen, H.-W. (ed.) HUC 1999. LNCS, vol. 1707, pp. 304–307. Springer, Heidelberg (1999). https://doi.org/10.1007/3-540-48157-5_29
3. Agarwal, A., Miller, J., et al.: Self-aware computing. Technical report, Massachusetts Institute of Technology Cambridge (2009)
4. Alberta Environment and Parks - Calgary Open Data, Canada: River Level and Flows (2022). https://data.calgary.ca/Environment/River-Levels-and-Flows/5fdg-ifgr. Accessed 24 Jan 2023
5. Analytics, I.: Number of connected IoT devices growing 18% to 14.4 billion globally (2022). https://iot-analytics.com/number-connected-iot-devices/
6. Arif, M., Alghamdi, K.K., et al.: Role of machine learning algorithms in forest fire management: a literature review. J. Rob. Autom. **5**(1), 212–226 (2021)
7. Baldauf, M., Dustdar, S., Rosenberg, F.: A survey on context-aware systems. Int. J. Ad Hoc Ubiquitous Comput. **2**(4), 263–277 (2007)
8. Brown, P., Bovey, J., Chen, X.: Context-aware applications: from the laboratory to the marketplace. IEEE Pers. Commun. **4**(5), 58–64 (1997)
9. Chen, G., Kotz, D.: A survey of context-aware mobile computing research. Technical report, Dartmouth College, United States (2000)
10. Dustdar, S., Avasalcai, C., Murturi, I.: Edge and fog computing: vision and research challenges. In: IEEE International Conference on Service-Oriented System Engineering, SOSE, pp. 96–105 (2019)

11. Forooghifar, F., Aminifar, A., et al.: Self-aware anomaly-detection for epilepsy monitoring on low-power wearable electrocardiographic devices. In: IEEE 3rd International Conference on Artificial Intelligence Circuits and Systems, AICAS, pp. 1–4 (2021)

12. Galar, D., Thaduri, A., et al.: Context awareness for maintenance decision making: a diagnosis and prognosis approach. Measurement **67**, 137–150 (2015)

13. Guo, L., Wang, W., et al.: Research and implementation of forest fire early warning system based on UWB wireless sensor networks. In: 2nd International Conference Communication Systems, Networks and Applications, pp. 176–179. ICCSNA (2010)

14. Hafshejani, E., TaheriNejad, N., et al.: Self-aware data processing for power saving in resource-constrained IoT cyber-physical systems. IEEE Sens. J. **22**(4), 3648–3659 (2021)

15. Hoffmann, H., Holt, J., et al.: Self-aware computing in the angstrom processor. In: Proceedings of the 49th Annual Design Automation Conference, pp. 259–264 (2012)

16. Horn, P.: Autonomic computing: IBM's perspective on the state of information technology. Technical report, IBM Research (2001)

17. Jantsch, A., Dutt, N., Rahmani, A.: Self-awareness in systems on chip-a survey. IEEE Design Test **34**(6), 8–26 (2017)

18. Kounev, S., Zhu, X., et al.: Model-driven algorithms and architectures for self-aware computing systems (dagstuhl seminar 15041). Dagstuhl Rep. **5**(1), 164–196 (2015)

19. Martinez, B., Cano, C., Vilajosana, X.: Debunking wireless sensor networks myths. arXiv preprint arXiv:2008.01427 (2020)

20. Morin, A.: Levels of consciousness and self-awareness: a comparison and integration of various neurocognitive views. Conscious. Cogn. **15**(2), 358–371 (2006)

21. Mudassar, B.A., Ko, J.H., Mukhopadhyay, S.: Edge-cloud collaborative processing for intelligent internet of things: a case study on smart surveillance. In: 55th Annual Design Automation Conference, DAC, pp. 1–6 (2018)

22. Ortiz, G., Zouai, M., et al.: Atmosphere: context and situational-aware collaborative IoT architecture for edge-fog-cloud computing. Comput. Stand. Interfaces **79**, 103550 (2022)

23. Pascoe, J.: Adding generic contextual capabilities to wearable computers. In: 2nd IEEE International Symposium on Wearable Computers, ISWC, pp. 92–99 (1998)

24. Perera, C., Zaslavsky, A., et al.: CA4IOT: context awareness for internet of things. In: IEEE International Conference on Green Computing and Communications, GreenCom, pp. 775–782 (2012)

25. Perera, C., Zaslavsky, A., et al.: Context aware computing for the internet of things: a survey. IEEE Commun. Surv. Tutor. **16**(1), 414–454 (2014)

26. de Prado, A.G., Ortiz, G., Boubeta-Puig, J.: COLLECT: COLLaborativE ConText-aware service oriented architecture for intelligent decision-making in the Internet of Things. Expert Syst. Appl. **85**, 231–248 (2017)

27. Sarwar, B., Bajwa, I., et al.: An intelligent fire warning application using IoT and an adaptive neuro-fuzzy inference system. Sensors **19**(14), 3150 (2019)

28. Schilit, B., Adams, N., Want, R.: Context-aware computing applications. In: 1st Workshop on Mobile Computing Systems and Applications, pp. 85–90. HotMobile (1994)

29. Schilit, B., Theimer, M.: Disseminating active map information to mobile hosts. IEEE Netw. **8**(5), 22–32 (1994)

402   D. Arnaiz et al.

30. Sterritt, R., Bustard, D.: Towards an autonomic computing environment. In: 14th International Workshop Database and Expert Systems Applications, DEXA, pp. 694–698 (2003)
31. Sunkpho, J., Ootamakorn, C.: Real-time flood monitoring and warning system. Songklanakarin J. Sci. Technol. **33**(2) (2011)
32. Wan, J., Zhang, D., et al.: Context-aware vehicular cyber-physical systems with cloud support: architecture, challenges, and solutions. IEEE Commun. Mag. **52**(8), 106–113 (2014)
33. Zhuang, Y., Yu, L., et al.: Data collection with accuracy-aware congestion control in sensor networks. IEEE Trans. Mob. Comput. **18**(5), 1068–1082 (2018)

Work in Progress (WIP) Papers

BAnDIT: Business Process Anomaly Detection in Transactions

Nico Rudolf[1]($\boxtimes$), Kristof Böhmer[1], and Maria Leitner[1,2]

[1] Faculty of Computer Science, Research Group Workflow Systems and Technology, University of Vienna, Währinger Straße 29, Vienna, Austria
`nico.rudolfdgf@gmail.com, kristof.boehmer@univie.ac.at`
[2] Faculty of Informatics and Data Science, Chair of Artificial Intelligence in IT Security, University of Regensburg, Regensburg, Germany
`maria.leitner@ur.de`

Abstract. Business process anomaly detection enables the prevention of misuse and failures. Existing approaches focus on detecting anomalies in control, temporal, and resource behavior of individual instances, neglecting the communication of multiple instances in choreographies. Consequently, anomaly detection capabilities are limited. This study presents a novel neural network-based approach to detect anomalies in distributed business processes. Unlike existing methods, our solution considers message data exchanged during process transactions. Allowing the generation of detection profiles incorporating the relationship between multiple instances, related services, and exchanged data to detect point and contextual anomalies during process runtime. To validate the proposed solution, it is demonstrated with a prototype implementation and validated with a use case from the ecommerce domain. Future work aims to further improve the deep learning approach, to enhance detection performance.

Keywords: Anomaly detection · Business processes · Service-oriented systems · Deep learning · Security

1 Introduction

Process anomaly detection is a crucial methodology that enables the identification of anomalous behavior within business processes. Anomalies can signify various issues such as fraud, misuse, and errors with the potential to result in process failure. In today's process-driven organizations, where the reliability and robustness of business process executions form the backbone of their operations, the need for effective anomaly detection becomes apparent [12,21]. Existing approaches to anomaly detection often analyze each process instance's control, temporal, and resource behavior independently [3,11,19], neglecting the communication between multiple instances. This limitation restricts their applicability in use cases, where processes collaborate and communicate extensively.

Consider, for example, a straightforward online shopping scenario, like buying shoes, involving collaboration across delivery, procurement, warehouse, and accounting processes (cf. Fig. 1). Malicious actions can be concealed by orchestrating attacks over multiple process instances. For instance, an attacker could alter the communicated article count to the delivery process, while leaving the accounting process unchanged, allowing receipt of more articles than paid for. Conventional anomaly detection methods concentrating on individual instances or control flow would miss such attacks, leaving process communication vulnerabilities unnoticed. The approach for solving this issue, lies in analyzing communication and data flow in multi-instance choreographies. Examining inter-process transactions and their data exchanges uncovers this behavior.

Due to communication's dynamic nature in distributed systems, concept drift in process choreography is frequent. These deviations shouldn't be treated as anomalies but as an evolving norm. This paper addresses these challenges via an innovative deep learning anomaly detection approach. It analyzes message flow and content to spot point and contextual anomalies during live process executions. Point anomalies signify unexpected behavior within a single process event, such as an unfamiliar article request. Contextual anomalies, stem from manipulated context misaligning with the subsequent process choreography, like an attacker altering delivery item counts.

The approach combines two neural networks for unsupervised anomaly detection. With these, a two-step approach offers two settings: one involving a classifier network for message transformation and the other utilizing an autoencoder network. The proposed solution is evaluated concerning its applicability and performance in an experimental setting. For evaluation, we used two data sets and describe the synthetic one from micro-service online shop system simulation. The rest of the paper is structured as follows: Sect. 2 revisits preliminary background on service-oriented business processes. Section 3 describes the two-step profile-based anomaly detection approach. Section 4 valides the approach with a use case from the e-commerce domain. Section 5 summarizes relevant related works and Sect. 6 concludes the paper.

2   Preliminary

Many scenarios where processes are collaborating and communicating in a choreography are given by service-oriented systems. Each service s provides a certain set of operations $\mathbb{O}_s$. An operation o fulfills a specific task in the system and is available to other services in the system via an endpoint u. In the example of an online shop system (cf. Fig. 1), there could be one service responsible for managing the inventory of the shop. One operation this service may provide is requesting the availability of products. Formally this behavior is defined as:

Definition 1. *(Service, Operation, Endpoint) Let $\mathbb{S}$ be the finite set of services within a system. A service may provide one or multiple operations. Let $\mathbb{O}$ be the finite set of all possible operations, then $\mathbb{O}_s$ are all operations for the service $s \in \mathbb{S}$. Let $\mathbb{U}$ be the finite set of all endpoints, then $\mathbb{U}_s$ is the set of all endpoints for service $s \in \mathbb{S}$. There exists a bijective function $\alpha : \mathbb{U} \to \mathbb{O}$, mapping each endpoint to a specific operation, such that $o = \alpha(u)$ (cf. [22]).*

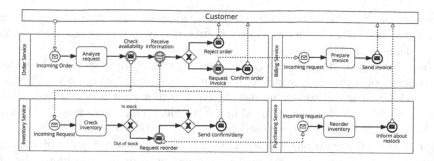

Fig. 1. Illustration of an online shop system designed as a service-oriented system.

Each operation transfers information in the form of a message m. If we look at the example of an online shop, a message for the operation that is requesting the availability of products could contain products, their quantity and other relevant information. Formally, message m is defined as:

Definition 2. *(Message) Let $\mathbb{T}$ be the finite set of all possible terms included in a message, then a message is defined as a tuple of terms, like $m_o = (t_0, t_1, ..., t_n), n \in \mathbb{N}$ and $m_o \in \mathbb{M}$ with $\mathbb{M}$ as the set of all possible messages. The message of an operation can be empty, then $m_o = \emptyset$. For a message there exists a surjective function, mapping to an operation such that $\beta : \mathbb{M} \to \mathbb{O}$.*

Some of the steps in the process instances illustrated in Fig. 1 require transactions (i.e. communication) with other services. This particular type of process step triggers an invocation of an operation o of another service in the system. We define this class of process steps to be **message events** e, as together with the invocation of an operation, they are transmitting a message to another service. The formal definition of a message event goes as follows:

Definition 3. *(Message Event) Let $\mathbb{E}$ be the finite set of all possible message events. A message event e corresponds to the invocation of an operation $o \in \mathbb{O}$. As there exists a bijective function $\alpha : \mathbb{U} \to \mathbb{O}$ each message event can be characterized by an endpoint $u \in \mathbb{U}$. Defined by the function β a message event also has a message $m \in \mathbb{M}$ corresponding to a particular message event. As a shorthand, the messages of a particular message event is denoted as $m(e)$.*

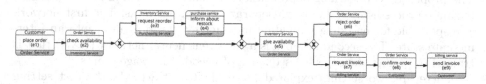

Fig. 2. Resulting process choreography of the online shop system.

Focusing solely on message events, the online shop example generates a process choreography, cf. Fig. 2. These message events are collected into a *message event log L*, defined similarly to [1].

In order to provide more fine-grained monitoring of the system, we introduce the concept of a profile *p*, which is responsible for monitoring only a specified part of the system, i.e. area of interest. When it comes to drawing the boundaries regarding which services are included in the profile, technologies from distributed tracing can be utilized as proposed in [17]. A pattern *r* can be used on the endpoints of all operations $\mathbb{U}_s$ provided by a particular service. All message events with an endpoint matching the defined pattern are considered by the profile, others are ignored. This leads to the following formal definition:

Definition 4. *(Profile, Compound, Pattern) A profile p is defined to monitor an area of interest within that system. That is a certain compound of services K such that $K \subseteq \mathbb{S}$. Let $\mathbb{R}$ be the set of specified regular expression patterns, then the compound of services for the pattern r is K_r such that two different services $s_1 \in K_r$ and $s_2 \in K_r$ both provide only operations with an endpoint matching that pattern $\delta(\mathbb{U}_{s_1}, r) = \delta(\mathbb{U}_{s_2}, r)$, with δ being a function evaluating the pattern over an endpoint.*

Based on historic process cases a model will be trained to abstract a compounds normal behavior. Given a novel process execution with the head of a trace $hd^k(\hat{c})$ to message event at step k, the model will generate the next probable message event $\hat{c}(k+1)$. In case the predicted message event deviates significantly from the observation of $\hat{c}(k+1)$ the event will be detected as an anomaly.

Types of anomalies can be grouped into two major categories: (1) Sequence anomalies and (2) content anomalies. Note, that these types are not directly corresponding to the distinction between contextual and point anomalies. Content anomalies can be contextual as well as point anomalies, whereas sequence anomalies are always contextual. Sequence anomalies involve skipping, adding and swapping message events. Content anomalies modify message content by skipping, adding or swapping terms.

3   Two-Step Profile-Based Anomaly Detection

3.1   Two-Step Deep Learning Approach

The proposed deep-learning approach for anomaly detection in service-oriented business processes consists of two separate neural networks. The first network is responsible for encoding individual message events in a trace, into an intermediate state. The second network is a recurrent neural network (RNN) that is trained to predict the expected sequence of encoded message events.

There are two settings explored for evaluating traces. In the first setting (encoder-setting), an autoencoder network is used for encoding individual message events. This network is called *message event encoder*. It projects message events into a lower-dimensional latent space. The encoder network processes the input message event and encodes it into a fixed-length vector, which is then passed to the decoder. The decoder generates the output based on this fixed-length vector. The autoencoder is trained to minimize the reconstruction loss, which measures the difference between the input and predicted vectors. After training, only the encoder network is used to encode a message event for every step in the sequence into a latent space vector. The sequence RNN takes the encoded message events until a particular step in the sequence, to predict the next probable message events latent space vector. Using this prediction, the distance to the observed message event can be computed by the loss function.

In the second setting (classifier-setting), the message event encoder is replaced by the *message event classifier*. This classifier network maps message events to a specific type. The input and output sequences are of potentially different lengths. The sequence RNN predicts the next probable message event given a starting sequence. Similar to the encoder-setting, the model is trained to minimize the distance between the predicted and observed message events.

Each of the settings focuses on a particular aspect of the evaluation of process executions. The classifier-setting gives more attention to the control flow of the process execution, while the encoder-setting focuses on the content of exchanged messages. That is, because the reconstruct from latent space can be compared to an observed message event, to spot specific deviations in the message content.

The challenge of emerging concept drift in the monitored system can be addressed by retraining the model iteratively, to gradually adapt to changes in the process over time. This can be done by training the pre-trained network with new data, that reflects the new normal behavior of the process.

The autoencoder is built as a sequence-to-sequence network [24]. All networks use gated recurrent units (GRUs) as recurrent units. These show similar performance to its close alternative the LSTM, while being relatively more efficient [7]. The decoder network of the message event encoder involves the use of an attention mechanism, allowing the network to focus on different parts of the sequence [2]. Models are optimized using negative log-likelihood (NLL) as a loss function for classification problems and cosine embedding loss for latent space comparison.

3.2   Profile Development

The trained neural networks model the system's normal behavior, creating a profile for the process choreography of the involved instances. Focusing on specific interaction parts allows finer monitoring of the whole system. Applying profiles to individual actors is particularly used in fraud and intrusion detection, which involves multiple participants [6]. This concept is uncommon in anomaly detection for business processes [11,14,19,21].

Looking at the example of an attacker altering the number of ordered items, the critical section of the entire system can be limited to the ordering and billing service. Therefore, billing and accounting service build a separate compound of services $K_{b,a}$. For this, a pattern $r_{b,a}$ has to be defined such that only relevant operations match that pattern, resulting in $K_{b,a} = (s_{billing}, s_{accounting})$. For monitoring, this results in a reduced process choreography, only involving message events emitted from the operations included by pattern $r_{b,a}$, hence reducing the complexity of process traces.

When training the neural network model for the service compound $K_{b,a}$, the reduced set of message events also results in a reduction of dimensionality for the input of the model. That is, as we can expect the set of all possible terms in a message $\mathbb{T}_{b,a}$ to be a proper subset of $\mathbb{T}$ like $\mathbb{T}_{b,a} \subsetneq \mathbb{T}$. Likewise, the number of possible types of message events can be expected to be smaller for the reduced compound of services $K_{b,a}$ like $k_{b,a} < k$, which influences the input and output dimension of the message event classifier.

3.3   Threshold Heuristic and Decision Boundary

Distinguishing between normal and anomalous message events and process executions relies on a decision boundary typically established using an anomaly score. As in [18], this score can be the reconstruction loss, measuring the prediction-observation distance. In the encoder-setting, a threshold heuristic sets this boundary. Introducing a dynamic threshold T involves using a flexible function for precise value assignment. Such adaptability is crucial due to varying anomaly score distributions across data sets, influenced by factors like message length or content diversity. This approach alignes with [11, 18, 19].

For anomaly score values we can assume a skewed normal distribution, as normal samples can be expected to occur more frequently [6]. Most anomaly scores will thus be relatively low, starting at zero as a lower boundary. Samples differing more than a chosen multiplicative of the standard deviation from the mean are then considered anomalous. A common factor is choosing three times the standard deviation [6]. Hence, the threshold can be computed as $T = \mu + 3\sigma$.

In the classifier-setting, or for point anomaly detection, where sequences are formed using probability distributions at each step, an alternative decision boundary approach is utilized. This involves examining the top n outputs of the probability distribution for each step, accumulating their probabilities to surpass a threshold $p_T \in [0; 1]$, specifically $p_T > \sum_{i=0}^{n} p_i$. These outputs are then treated as candidates. If the observed output isn't among the candidates, an anomaly is signaled. Through experimentation, a threshold of 0.9 yielded the best results after evaluating various parameter values. This dynamic candidate sampling method aligns with [9].

4   Evaluation

The evaluation combines a) real-life logs from the financial domain; b) artificial logs from a publicly available distributed online shop implementation[1] and c) artificially injected anomalies. Enabling to assess detection performance even though publicly available execution logs hardly cover data flow. Therefore, a baseline algorithm is introduced to provide a comparison point.

---

[1] https://github.com/nico-ru/BAnDIT.

4.1 Data Sets

FINANCE: The data set was conducted over a time frame of several months from individual financial institutions. Anomalous data requests and process cases are produced with the consultation of expert knowledge. Point anomalies of each type are induced in three data sets from financial institutions. Data set one (**point-1**) consists of a total of 3868 samples. Data set two (**point-2**) consists of a total of 2570 samples. And data set three (**point-3**) consists of a total of 5716 samples. Contextual anomalies were induced in the data set (**sequence-1**), which consists of a total of 101 samples (one sample constitutes of one day of requests). The use case is discussed in [23].

MICRO: The *MICRO* data set is generated by the prototype implementation of a micro-service online shop system. The (**micro-1**) data set is used for inducing point and contextual anomalies. It is generated by 1000 executions of the implemented process choreography. In total, 4979 message events are produced by this simulation. The message content is generated in a JSON serialization and transformed into a flat dotlist format to better fit the message definition, cf. Sect. 2.

Anomalies are inserted randomized in both data sets with a ratio of 1–2% for point anomaly detection and 5–10% for contextual anomaly detection. The rates chosen for this evaluation align with the assumption of anomalies being rare as opposed to normal samples, cf. [4, 18].

4.2 Baseline Solution

To contextualize the results from the proposed anomaly detection, a baseline algorithm is introduced to address the same anomaly detection task. For point anomaly detection, skip-grams are generated from message content. These skip-grams exclude one term at a time. The probabilities for each term's absence is calculated, by counting all possible missing terms. Message occurrence probability is computed by multiplying term probabilities for every term in the message. Contextual anomaly detection employs the same technique, but with skip-grams of activities across cases instead of terms. The skip-gram and probability algorithms are available online (See footnote 1). In both cases, anomalies arise when a sequence's probability falls outside one standard deviation from the data set's probability distribution. Context anomaly results solely consider activity order, not message event content. This approach for the baseline solution draws inspiration from [3, 15, 16].

4.3 Evaluation Results

As detecting anomalies poses a binary classification problem, we use commonly accepted metrics for classification to report the performance of the proposed solution [10]. In particular, these are precision, recall, and F-scores. This aligns with [5], where all metrics are described. We consider the detection of all present anomalies as the most relevant, as any anomaly can cause serious errors. The results reported in Table 1 show the evaluation metrics for the individual data sets as an average over all anomaly types. For training the neural networks the data was split into train (75%), validation (5%) and test (20%) data.

Table 1. Evaluation results for the proposed solution as well as baseline solution.

	Point Anomalies				Context Anomalies (classifier-setting)		Context Anomalies (encoder-setting)
	point-1	point-2	point-3	micro-1	sequence-1	micro-1	sequence-1
Precision	1.00	0.75	0.83	**0.17**	0.83	0.85	**0.22**
Recall	0.95	0.90	0.98	0.80	0.91	0.85	0.54
F-score	0.97	0.82	0.90	0.28	0.87	0.85	0.31
F2-score	**0.96**	**0.87**	**0.94**	**0.36**	**0.91**	**0.85**	0.42
Baseline Results							
Precision	0.60	0.06	0.57	0.01	0.15	0.87	–
Recall	0.92	0.60	0.85	0.17	0.23	0.72	–
F-score	0.75	0.11	0.69	0.02	0.18	0.79	–
F2-score	0.84	0.21	0.78	0.04	0.21	0.75	–

Interpretation. Results show that the proposed model effectively learns the overall distribution of message events and successfully detects rare anomalies. While precision scores of the proposed solution may be sub-optimal in some cases, this can be attributed to the low number of real anomalous samples, making a single false positive significantly impact precision. Overall, the proposed solution outperforms the baseline, particularly with notable improvements in the F-scores, as observed in the point-2 data set.

Regarding contextual anomaly detection in the classifier-setting, similar performance is achieved compared to point anomaly detection. Performance variations can be attributed to variances in the accuracy of the message event classifier and the complexity of the monitored process.

Compared to related work on anomaly detection using deep neural networks [11,18], the proposed approach demonstrates comparable performance. However, direct comparison is possible only in a limited way due to the absence of message content evaluation in related research.

Detecting anomalies in the sequence of encoded message events poses the most challenging problem. Consequently, the results for contextual anomaly detection in the encoder-setting are less satisfying. Accurately predicting the next encoded message event proves difficult for the sequence RNN. This limitation may stem from a sub-optimal choice of loss function, as RNNs are generally capable of learning sequential patterns. It is likely that quantifying the distance between encoded message events is the main issue. Various loss functions were tested, with the cosine embedding loss yielding the best results.

5 Related Work

The general problem of anomaly detection is a well-explored topic; For an extensive discussion of this domain, we refer to a survey by Chandola et al. [6]. We and existing work make the assumption that anomalous samples occur far less frequently than normal ones, enabling training on uncleaned data. With this we align with other publications [6,8,18].

In the area of business processes, anomaly detection approaches have been proposed in the control flow of processes [3–5,11,18], in the temporal behavior of process executions [14,21], or also in activity attributes of processes [11,19]. While the detection performance of some of the proposed solutions is quite sophisticated, none of them provides the possibility of detecting anomalies in the exchanged message data of multiple process instances. Merely [11,19] are considering the data-flow of single process instances, by feeding activity attributes into the model abstracting the normal behavior of the process. Both methods are extensible towards a higher number of activity attributes, however, the highly versatile and complex message data can not be represented by either of the solutions. Predictive monitoring techniques are highly related to anomaly detection, as they also involve building a model of the normal behavior of a process [13,20]. However, the proposed solutions do not consider distributed process choreographies nor incorporate message data.

6 Conclusion

This paper introduces a novel method for identifying anomalies in distributed process instances engaged in a process choreography. The focus is on analyzing message data exchanged between these instances. The approach involves defining message events, creating process logs, and using a neural network-based process model. This model employs a two-step process to detect both point anomalies and contextual anomalies. By abstracting service compounds into profiles, the approach allows for detailed monitoring. The method's performance was evaluated on a real financial data and a synthetic data set of an e-commerce shop system. In the encoder-setting, where the complexity was considerably higher than in the decoder-setting and the loss function potentially unfitting, the results for contextual anomalies were less convincing. Overall, results showed effective abstraction of communication between process instances and adaptability to dynamic changes. For future work, we aim to refine the approach to enhance contextual anomaly detection and explore other anomaly detection techniques for process choreography message data. These efforts promise to advance anomaly detection methods and provide insights into analyzing message data in process choreography.

References

1. Aalst, W.: Data science in action. In: Process Mining, pp. 3–23. Springer, Heidelberg (2016). https://doi.org/10.1007/978-3-662-49851-4_1
2. Bahdanau, D., Cho, K., Bengio, Y.: Neural machine translation by jointly learning to align and translate (2014)
3. Böhmer, K., Rinderle-Ma, S.: Multi-perspective anomaly detection in business process execution events. In: Debruyne, C., et al. (eds.) OTM 2016. LNCS, vol. 10033, pp. 80–98. Springer, Cham (2016). https://doi.org/10.1007/978-3-319-48472-3_5
4. Böhmer, K., Rinderle-Ma, S.: Multi instance anomaly detection in business process executions. In: Carmona, J., Engels, G., Kumar, A. (eds.) BPM 2017. LNCS, vol. 10445, pp. 77–93. Springer, Cham (2017). https://doi.org/10.1007/978-3-319-65000-5_5
5. Böhmer, K., Rinderle-Ma, S.: Association rules for anomaly detection and root cause analysis in process executions. In: Krogstie, J., Reijers, H.A. (eds.) CAiSE 2018. LNCS, vol. 10816, pp. 3–18. Springer, Cham (2018). https://doi.org/10.1007/978-3-319-91563-0_1
6. Chandola, V., Banerjee, A., Kumar, V.: Anomaly detection: a survey. ACM Comput. Surv. **41**(3), 1–58 (2009)
7. Chung, J., Gulcehre, C., Cho, K., Bengio, Y.: Empirical evaluation of gated recurrent neural networks on sequence modeling (2014)
8. Eskin, E.: Anomaly detection over noisy data using learned probability distributions (2000)
9. Holtzman, A., Buys, J., Forbes, M., Choi, Y.: The curious case of neural text degeneration. CoRR abs/1904.09751 (2019). http://arxiv.org/abs/1904.09751
10. Hossin, M., Sulaiman, M.N.: A review on evaluation metrics for data classification evaluations. IJDKP **5**(2), 1 (2015)
11. Huo, S., Völzer, H., Reddy, P., Agarwal, P., Isahagian, V., Muthusamy, V.: Graph autoencoders for business process anomaly detection. In: Polyvyanyy, A., Wynn, M.T., Van Looy, A., Reichert, M. (eds.) BPM 2021. LNCS, vol. 12875, pp. 417–433. Springer, Cham (2021). https://doi.org/10.1007/978-3-030-85469-0_26
12. Leitner, M., Rinderle-Ma, S.: A systematic review on security in process-aware information systems - constitution, challenges, and future directions. Inf. Softw. Technol. **56**(3), 273–293 (2014). https://doi.org/10.1016/j.infsof.2013.12.004
13. Maggi, F.M., Di Francescomarino, C., Dumas, M., Ghidini, C.: Predictive monitoring of business processes. In: Jarke, M., et al. (eds.) CAiSE 2014. LNCS, vol. 8484, pp. 457–472. Springer, Cham (2014). https://doi.org/10.1007/978-3-319-07881-6_31
14. Mavroudopoulos, I., Gounaris, A.: Detecting temporal anomalies in business processes using distance-based methods. In: Appice, A., Tsoumakas, G., Manolopoulos, Y., Matwin, S. (eds.) DS 2020. LNCS (LNAI), vol. 12323, pp. 615–629. Springer, Cham (2020). https://doi.org/10.1007/978-3-030-61527-7_40
15. Meng, W., et al.: Device-agnostic log anomaly classification with partial labels. In: IWQoS 2018, pp. 1–6 (2018)
16. Mikolov, T., Chen, K., Corrado, G., Dean, J.: Efficient estimation of word representations in vector space (2013)
17. Nedelkoski, S., Cardoso, J.S., Kao, O.: Anomaly detection and classification using distributed tracing and deep learning. In: CCGRID 2019, pp. 241–250. IEEE (2019)
18. Nolle, T., Luettgen, S., Seeliger, A., Mühlhäuser, M.: Analyzing business process anomalies using autoencoders. Mach. Learn. **107**(11), 1875–1893 (2018)

19. Nolle, T., Seeliger, A., Mühlhäuser, M.: BINet: multivariate business process anomaly detection using deep learning. In: Weske, M., Montali, M., Weber, I., vom Brocke, J. (eds.) BPM 2018. LNCS, vol. 11080, pp. 271–287. Springer, Cham (2018). https://doi.org/10.1007/978-3-319-98648-7_16
20. Pauwels, S., Calders, T.: Incremental predictive process monitoring: the next activity case. In: Polyvyanyy, A., Wynn, M.T., Van Looy, A., Reichert, M. (eds.) BPM 2021. LNCS, vol. 12875, pp. 123–140. Springer, Cham (2021). https://doi.org/10.1007/978-3-030-85469-0_10
21. Rogge-Solti, A., Kasneci, G.: Temporal anomaly detection in business processes. In: Sadiq, S., Soffer, P., Völzer, H. (eds.) BPM 2014. LNCS, vol. 8659, pp. 234–249. Springer, Cham (2014). https://doi.org/10.1007/978-3-319-10172-9_15
22. Rud, D., Schmietendorf, A., Dumke, R.R.: Product metrics for service-oriented infrastructures. In: IWSM/MetriKon 2006 (2006)
23. Rudolf, N.: Profile-based Anomaly Detection in Service Oriented Business Processes. master thesis, University of Vienna (2023)
24. Sutskever, I., Vinyals, O., Le, Q.V.: Sequence to sequence learning with neural networks. CoRR abs/1409.3215 (2014). http://arxiv.org/abs/1409.3215

Resource-Driven Process Manipulation: Modeling Concepts and Valid Allocations

Felix Schumann[✉][iD] and Stefanie Rinderle-Ma[iD]

Technical University of Munich, TUM School of Computation,
Information and Technology, Garching, Germany
{felix.schumann,stefanie.rinderle-ma}@tum.de

Abstract. In situations of scarce resource availability, flexibility on
which resources execute which tasks is key to process and system performance. Tightly coupled control flow and resource modeling hampers
flexible resource allocation. Hence, in this work, we propose resource-
driven process manipulation (RDPM) to enable the separation between
the business and resource requirements for a process. RDPM enables
process modelers to specify resource-specific requirements for the control flow as part of resource profiles, e.g., a machine (resource) requires
configuration (task) before execution. Moreover, the resource is promoted
to a first-class citizen in process-aware information systems and enabled
to impact the execution. The basic concepts of RDPM are defined and
an algorithm is provided to find valid resource allocations for a task.
The approach is prototypically implemented and compared to existing modeling approaches w.r.t. complexity for the modeler and process
participant.

Keywords: Process-Aware Information Systems · Resource
Perspective · Resource Modeling · Process Changes · Resource
Allocation

1 Introduction

*"The resources of an organization are valuable assets, often cost-intensive,
and limited"* [7]. Especially in cooperative environments, processes and their
instances utilize resources in a shared manner [8,9]. Hence, modeling, assigning,
and allocating resources to process tasks is of utmost importance. Although existing approaches address the resource perspective of processes, often resources and
their assignments are only modeled as part of the control flow, e.g., as swimlanes
in BPMN. This "mixed modeling" approach results in unclear effects, especially
when resources change. Moreover, process and resource owner are not necessarily
the same person, hampering the modeling of both views and their requirements
(e.g., a resource demanding for an extra step or temporal requirement).

Hence, we propose the *separation of concerns* between control flow and
resource requirements in process-aware information systems (PAIS) as depicted
in Fig. 1, i.e., to model resources as objects at design time, which can manipulate the control flow of an instance at run-time to integrate its own process

M. Sellami et al. (Eds.): CoopIS 2023, LNCS 14353, pp. 416–426, 2024.
https://doi.org/10.1007/978-3-031-46846-9_23

requirements into it. With this resource-driven process manipulation (RDPM) approach, the process models are simplified, task modeling becomes easier for process and resource owners, and resources can be flexibly added/deleted and linked to the process. The latter particularly contributes to the adaptability of processes to varying resource availability.

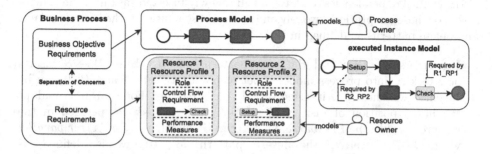

Fig. 1. Separation of process and resource requirements in RDPM

The core modeling concept of RDPM is the resource profile as depicted in Fig. 1 specifying resources, their linkage to the processes, and the manipulation of process instances required by this resource. Manipulation of process instances must not result in undesired side effects by introducing correctness issues into the instances. Hence, we have to provide means to check the validity of resource allocation in RDPM based on allocation trees.

In Sects. 2 and 3, we will introduce the basic concepts of RDPM and an algorithm for valid allocations. In Sect. 4 we present a first prototype, identified use cases for RDPM and a visual representation on how RDPM simplifies the models. Section 5 presents related work, Sect. 6 discusses the approach and gives an outline of further planned development of the approach.

2   Modeling Concepts of RDPM

The core concept of RDPM is the *resource profile*. In order to enable the separation of control flow and resource requirements, a resource profile contains all necessary information on the resource plus the linkage to the process and how the resource will manipulate the process instances it is allocated to. Equation 1 defines a resource profile *rp* as follows: it contains the resource *r* and its role *role*. Moreover, task *task* that the resource can perform is specified. Additional attributes *Attr* can be specified to, e.g., measure performance. Finally, the manipulation of a process instance, the resource is allocated to, is captured via a set of change patterns *CP*.

$$rp := (res, role, task, Attr, CP) \qquad (1)$$

Change patterns have been chosen as they are a well-defined concept for the evolution and adaptation of processes and process instances [18]. In this work, we focus on the insert, replace and delete pattern w.r.t. tasks. In the following, we will provide the RDPM change patterns which are either adapted from the change patterns in [18] (insert) or can be directly used as defined in [18] (replace, delete). Note that inserting, deleting, and replacing tasks require an adaptation of the control dependencies, e.g., to embed a newly inserted task into the control flow. For these adaptations, we rely on the formal semantics of the insert, replace, and delete patterns as defined in [14].

- **Insert:** As defined in [18], the *insert* pattern $Insert(S, X, A, B) \mapsto S'$ inserts new task X into process model S between activity sets A and B. It can be specified whether X is inserted serially or in parallel. For RDPM, we adapt the insert position of task X in relation to task $task$ as specified in the resource profile rp of $resource$, i.e., X can be inserted $before|after|parallel$ w.r.t. $task$. Overall, the insert pattern for RDPM is defined as $op_{RDPM} := Insert(S, X, before|after|parallel)$.
- **Replace:** $op_{RDPM} = Replace(S, X, Y) \mapsto S'$ is concerned with the replacement of a task with a new task. Although this operation can be expressed by delete and insert patterns, we follow the argumentation of [18] that the higher level of abstraction is favorable for users.
- **Delete:** The change pattern $op_{RDPM} = Delete(S, X) \mapsto S'$ deletes task X from process model S.

3   Finding Valid Resource Allocations

In general, when exposing a process model to change patterns, the risk of undermining the soundness of the model arises [18]. The previously refined change operations of RDPM (cf. Sect. 2) might not only affect control flow soundness, but also the validity of resource allocation and of the data objects.

Guarantee of Soundness and Executability of the Instance Process Model: RDPM manipulates the instance model of a process and might affect the successful execution of this instance. The successful execution depends on the structural and behavioral soundness of the instance process model. Structural soundness depends on the meta model and behavioral soundness demands for being able to reach desired final states and the absence of tasks that can never be executed (cf., e.g., [2]). Note that we assume the process model of interest to be structurally and behaviorally sound before instance manipulation takes place.

As process meta model, we rely on refined process structure trees (RPST) [17] as the RPST model of structuring processes in fragments enables to check the soundness of each fragment independently. Each fragment follows the single entry point, single endpoint (SESE) structure. The leaves of the tree represent the tasks. The RPST structure ensures the soundness of a node, iff all subfragments of the node are also sound SESE fragments. For more description of the RPST and how to compose other representations see [11,17]. Thus the soundness of the resulting process model after the application of a change pattern is sound, iff the original process model and the change patterns are sound.

Validity of Resource Allocation: An approach that deals with resources having a direct impact on the execution of a process instance requires checking that the execution is possible from the point of view of the resources. For RDPM, soundness from this perspective means that a change pattern can only be applied if there exist resources so that all tasks of the resulting instance model can be successfully allocated. Thus after allocating the first task and applying the connected change patterns, it must be checked if newly inserted tasks can also be allocated. For finding valid allocations, an *allocation tree* is built with the task to be allocated as its root node (cf. Algorithm 1). The tree consists of task nodes, and resource nodes and is created in a recursive way by building one branch after the other.

Algorithm 1: build_allocation_tree

---

input : root: task_node to allocate, ar: available resources, ex_tasks: excluded
         tasks, task_parent, res_parent
output: root: tree with all valid allocation branches for one task
for *resource in ar* **do**
    for *profile in resource.resourceprofiles* **do**
        if *root.label = profile.task and root.role = profile.role* **then**
            root.add_child(resource) ;   //Add resources as Children
        end
    end
end
if *not root.children* **then**
    delete task_nodes with current resource profile from res_parent
    return root ;   //Prune Branch without resources
end
for *resource in root.children* **do**
    if *resource.profile.change_patterns* **then**
        for *cp in profile.change_patterns* **do**
            tasks ← cp.get_tasks
            if *any task of tasks in ex_tasks* **then**
                delete resource from root.children
                break ;   //Prevent cycle
            end
            for *task in tasks* **do**
                task_parent ← root
                res_parent ← resource
                resource.add_child(build_allocation_tree(task, ar, ex_tasks,
                task_parent, res_parent)) ;   //Recursive function call
            end
        end
        return root
    end
end

The children of each node must be of the opposite type than its parent. As depicted in Fig. 2, a task node's children are all resource profiles with a role that is part of the task's authorized roles (Role Based Access). Each of these resource nodes has the tasks defined in its change patterns as its children. As input, the algorithm requires the task that needs a resource allocated to it and the resources that are available for allocation. Excluded tasks, task parent, and resource parent are optional parameters that are needed for the recursive call of the algorithm. In order to prevent a cyclic allocation, a task that is already part of a branch can not become part of the same branch again.

While building the tree, the validity of each branch is checked as follows: For a branch to be valid, every task (main task and tasks introduced by change patterns) needs an authorized resource allocated to it. Therefore, a branch only represents a valid allocation if all its leaves are of type resource. A branch that ends with a task as leaf (invalid allocation) can be pruned back until a task node with a valid allocation is found (see Fig. 2, dashed box).

The pruning based on resource validity leads to a minimal tree of valid branches. Once the whole tree is built, it is used to find the optimal branch for the allocation. Each branch of the tree represents one valid allocation and can be compared to the other branches based on the attributes defined in the resource profiles. Since the role, performance attributes and change patterns are part of the resource profile, the best branch for the set objective can be identified.

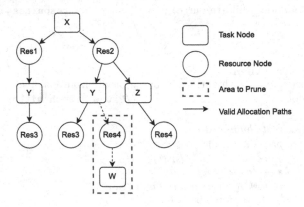

Fig. 2. Allocation tree, two valid allocation branches, one invalid branch to prune.

Validity Towards Data Objects: It is important to mention that also the data perspective can lead to invalid allocations. During the execution of a process, data objects are created, updated, and consumed. These data objects can be created by tasks that are deleted through RDPM or tasks inserted by RDPM need to consume data objects that are not yet created. Developing a concept of ensuring the validity of data objects poses an important task for future work, but is not in the scope of this paper.

4   Evaluation

The prototypical implementation of the RDPM approach is embedded in a service-oriented architecture. As evaluation, we identify fitting use cases where RDPM will improve quality and simplicity of the model, followed by a comparison of existing process and resource modeling approaches for a use case.

Prototypical Implementation: To realize RDPM, we propose to offer the allocation of tasks as an external service to the PAIS. Figure 3 shows how the RDPM service links the PAIS to a Resource Management System.

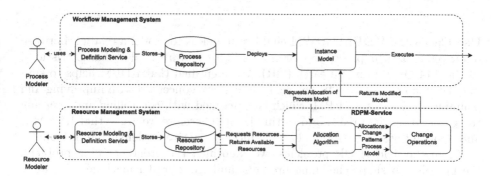

Fig. 3. Description of the system with RPDM as external service.

This service-oriented architecture enables a high level of flexibility towards the resource allocation task while realizing the separation between the business objective and the resource management as intended by RDPM by design.

For the implementation, we used the Cloud Process Execution Engine (CPEE)[1] as service-oriented PAIS. As resource repository, a description of the available resources, with resource profiles and change patterns, is given in an XML file. The creation of a complete Resource Management System is not in the scope of this work, but is considered for future development.

The allocation request is designed as a specific task in the CPEE at the beginning of the process model to call the RDPM service. Figure 4 shows this design in the CPEE. The "measure" and "operator" arguments set the objective for the best branch. A prototype with demo use cases is available.[2]

To generate the modified model, change operations are derived from the change patterns and applied to the model (cf. [3]). The modified instance model is returned to the CPEE and the execution of the instance is started. The returned instance model is a CPEE-Tree which is based on the RPST [10]. This modified CPEE-Tree is now augmented with the allocated resources.

---

[1] https://cpee.org/.
[2] https://github.com/Schlixmann/RDPM.

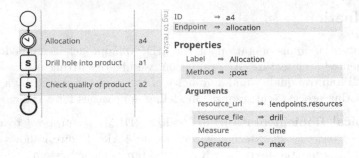

Fig. 4. Description of the allocation task and its connected parameters.

Use Cases for RDPM: RDPM enables modelers to model a relation between resources and their process requirements. This feature is also characteristic of the field of Operations Research (OR). We identified that RDPM helps to simplify the transition from OR problems, which are concerned with improving and planning operations, to BPM, which is concerned with controlling and enacting these operations in a real-world setting [1,5]. Therefore we argue that RDPM is an important step for BPM to become more proactive as demanded in [13].

From the field of OR problems, we identified the order batching problem, the flexible job shop scheduling problem and the parallel machine scheduling problem as problems that are well supported by RDPM. At the current state of RDPM, the parallel machine scheduling problem is best supported.

Comparison with Existing Modeling Approaches: Consider the following use case (cf. Fig. 5): In order to execute the task "drilling", the machine needs to be configured for "drilling". The task "configure machine for drilling" has to be inserted as predecessor (cf. setup time in yarn dyeing machines in [6]). In addition, assume that after drilling the hole, a quality check of the product is needed. Task "Check quality of product" can be done by three resources: manually by a technician or an inexperienced student technician, and automated by a 3D Measurement machine. The machine needs to be leveled before it can perform the measuring and the student needs supervision while checking the product. Figure 5(a) shows the use case modeled in traditional fashion.

The expectation of RDPM is a "clean" process model and an executable instance model. When using RDPM only the business objective must be modeled in the process model. Figure 5(b) shows this business objective-focused process. After applying RDPM to an instance of the process model, the allocated instance model of the use case is shown in Fig. 5(c) and is ready for execution.

Figure 5 shows that RDPM simplifies the process model as well as the instance model. Modelers and domain experts can profit from this visualization. Modeling multiple variants of a process is an important research field in BPM, where variants usually depend on data objects rather than the used resources. Process families (cf. [4]) model every possible trace in a separate process model and categorize these models into families. Another common approach is the def-

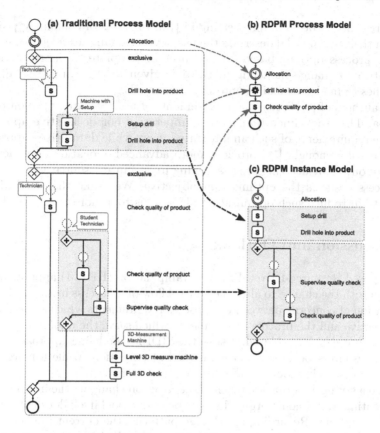

Fig. 5. (a) Process model designed traditionally for all resources; (b) process model designed following RDPM focused on the business objective of the process; (c) the instance model shows what will actually be executed.

inition of sub-processes in combination with late binding [18]. Both approaches lead to highly complex (sub-) process repositories. RDPM's advantage over these approaches is the simplicity of change patterns and the easy adjustment of these change patterns as part of the resource profile.

Resource-driven process manipulation generates a clean and easy-to-understand process model. After the allocation, the instance model is shown in a fully flattened way and can help users to understand the upcoming tasks. The flattened structure is considered more easily understandable [16]. If an adjustment of a change pattern is done, it is automatically applied to all related processes and thus the integrity of process models is ensured.

5 Related Work

Many approaches deal with flexibility or the usage of resources in BPM. The description of resource profiles was originally used to mine multiple attributes of resources in a process mining setting in [12]. In terms of combining processes based on their features, [4] describes the use of process families to enable multiple different process options based on one process template. A larger review on variability and change modeling in BPM is given in [15] comparing different approaches to model variability into process models.

The authors of [8] discuss the requirements of an integrated view on process and data. The study finds that neither imperative nor declarative approaches fulfill the requirements of such an integrated view, while data-driven approaches are not mature enough. [19] provides more advanced allocation approaches for human resources by utilizing process mining to optimize resource allocation with the process costs as the optimization objective. We argue that RDPM is an enabler to introduce such optimization algorithms to a more proactive BPM.

6   Discussion and Outlook

The proposed Resource-Driven Process Manipulation (RDPM) approach equips resources with the chance to alter the control flow of a process instance. This way a separation of concerns between the process requirements which serve the business objective and the process requirements which serve the underlying resource infrastructure can be achieved. Using the RDPM modeling approach, control flow and resources become closer connected at execution, while a more precise line can be drawn in modeling them.

While a strength of this approach is the focus on changing the instance model and executing it, one could argue that the process model itself does not represent all process options. Regarding the change patterns, the current implementation is not yet able to realize the change pattern concerned with deletion. To do so, we identified that dependencies are needed to further specify when a change pattern should be applied, e.g., only if the previous task is allocated to the same resource. The replace pattern in the current implementation is only applied to the task open for allocation, with the implementation of the delete pattern this will be enhanced to the full process. Lastly, the validity in terms of the data objects is not yet guaranteed. In future work, we plan to implement the delete pattern and to add the dependencies as a first step towards the data flow perspective.

Considering that one of RDPM's strengths is the identification of non-business-objective related processing times, the generated data can help to develop and integrate optimization algorithms, which realize an optimized resource allocation at run-time as described in [19]. To achieve this functionality, execution times or process performance could be predicted for the valid branches of the allocation tree. RDPM will help to enhance the flexibilty of PAIS w.r.t. resource allocation.

Acknowledgement. This work was funded by the Deutsche Forschungsgemeinschaft (DFG, German Research Foundation) - Project number 277991500.

References

1. van der Aalst, W.M.P.: Business process management: A comprehensive survey 2013, pp. 1–37 (2013). https://doi.org/10.1155/2013/507984
2. van Dongen, B.F., Mendling, J., van der Aalst, W.M.P.: Structural patterns for soundness of business process models. In: Enterprise Distributed Object Computing Conference, pp. 116–128 (2006). https://doi.org/10.1109/EDOC.2006.56
3. Fdhila, W., Indiono, C., Rinderle-Ma, S., Reichert, M.: Dealing with change in process choreographies: design and implementation of propagation algorithms. Inf. Syst. **49**, 1–24 (2015). https://doi.org/10.1016/j.is.2014.10.004
4. Gröner, G., Boskovic, M., Parreiras, F.S., Gasevic, D.: Modeling and validation of business process families. Inf. Syst. **38**(5), 709–726 (2013). https://doi.org/10.1016/j.is.2012.11.010
5. Hillier, F., Lieberman, G.: Introduction to Operations Research. McGraw-Hill Education (2021)
6. Hsu, H., Hsiung, Y., Chen, Y., Wu, M.: A GA methodology for the scheduling of yarn-dyed textile production. Expert Syst. Appl. **36**(10), 12095–12103 (2009). https://doi.org/10.1016/j.eswa.2009.04.075
7. Ihde, S., Pufahl, L., Völker, M., Goel, A., Weske, M.: A framework for modeling and executing task-specific resource allocations in business processes. Computing **104**(11), 2405–2429 (2022). https://doi.org/10.1007/s00607-022-01093-2
8. Künzle, V., Weber, B., Reichert, M.: Object-aware business processes: fundamental requirements and their support in existing approaches. Int. J. Inf. Syst. Model. Des. **2**(2), 19–46 (2011). https://doi.org/10.4018/jismd.2011040102
9. Leitner, M., Rinderle-Ma, S.: A systematic review on security in process-aware information systems - constitution, challenges, and future directions. Inf. Softw. Techn. **56**(3), 273–293 (2014). https://doi.org/10.1016/j.infsof.2013.12.004
10. Mangler, J., Rinderle-Ma, S.: Cloud process execution engine: architecture and interfaces. https://doi.org/10.48550/arXiv.2208.12214
11. Munoz-Gama, J., Carmona, J., Van Der Aalst, W.M.P.: Conformance checking in the large: partitioning and topology. In: Business Process Management, pp. 130–145 (2013). https://doi.org/10.1007/978-3-642-40176-3_11
12. Pika, A., Leyer, M., Wynn, M.T., Fidge, C.J., ter Hofstede, A.H.M., van der Aalst, W.M.P.: Mining resource profiles from event logs. ACM Trans. Manag. Inf. Syst. **8**(1), 1:1-1:30 (2017). https://doi.org/10.1145/3041218
13. Poll, R., Polyvyanyy, A., Rosemann, M., Röglinger, M., Rupprecht, L.: Process forecasting: towards proactive business process management. In: Business Process Management, pp. 496–512 (2018). https://doi.org/10.1007/978-3-319-98648-7_29
14. Rinderle-Ma, S., Reichert, M., Weber, B.: On the formal semantics of change patterns in process-aware information systems. In: Conceptual Modeling, pp. 279–293 (2008). https://doi.org/10.1007/978-3-540-87877-3_21
15. Rosa, M.L., Aalst, W.M.P.V.D., Dumas, M., Milani, F.P.: Business process variability modeling: a survey. ACM Comput. Surv. **50**(1), 2:1-2:45 (2017). https://doi.org/10.1145/3041957
16. Turetken, O., Dikici, A., Vanderfeesten, I., Rompen, T., Demirors, O.: The influence of using collapsed sub-processes and groups on the understandability of business process models. Bus. Inf. Syst. Eng. **62**(2), 121–141 (2019). https://doi.org/10.1007/s12599-019-00577-4
17. Vanhatalo, J., Völzer, H., Koehler, J.: The refined process structure tree. Data Knowl. Eng. **68**(9), 793–818 (2009). https://doi.org/10.1016/j.datak.2009.02.015

18. Weber, B., Reichert, M., Rinderle-Ma, S.: Change patterns and change support features - enhancing flexibility in process-aware information systems. Data Knowl. Eng. **66**(3), 438–466 (2008). https://doi.org/10.1016/j.datak.2008.05.001
19. Zhao, W., Yang, L., Liu, H., Wu, R.: The optimization of resource allocation based on process mining. In: Advanced Intelligent Computing Theories and Applications ICIC, pp. 341–353 (2015). https://doi.org/10.1007/978-3-319-22053-6_38

Graph Collaborative Filtering and Data Augmentation Strategies in Dual-Target CDR

Xiaowen Shao, Baisong Liu$^{(\boxtimes)}$, Xueyuan Zhang, Junru Li, Ercong Xu, and Shiqi Wu

Faculty of Electrical Engineering and Computer Science, NingBo University, Ningbo, China
{lbs,2211100090}@nbu.edu.cn

Abstract. Current dual-target recommendation methods focus on efficient feature fusion but neglect the inherent noise issues in the domains. However, noise negatively affects the fusion of domains. To tackle this issue, we introduce an improvement and noise reduction strategy named DA-DCDR(Data Augmentation-Dual Target Cross Domain Recommendation), for domain fusion. By refining and reducing noise in each domain's subgraphs, we not only enhance the accuracy of interaction data but also ensure consistency in data scales. To establish associations between distinct domains, we implement a graph co-training strategy. Key procedures of DA-DCDR include interaction refinement and noise reduction, domain fusion, and correlation expansion. We use graph encoders to acquire user/item embeddings for both domains before domain fusion, followed by enhancement and noise reduction in interactions via top-k sampling and re-prediction. Additionally, we amplify user-user and item-item correlation elements after the domain fusion. Experimental results validate the noteworthy performance enhancement of our proposed strategy in the dual-target recommendation, mitigating the noise effects and boosting the accuracy of the dual-target recommendation system.

Keywords: Recommendation System · Graph Collaborative Filtering · Augmentation · Denoising

1 Introduction

Cross-domain recommendation systems [1] address issues like data sparsity and cold-start by leveraging interaction information from a source domain to enhance recommendations in a target domain . Dual-target recommendation, a key aspect in this field, focuses on utilizing interactions from two domains to improve recommendations in both domains, catering to users' multi-domain needs. Methods like matrix factorization [2–4], mapping-based [5–7], entity representation combination [8–10], and graph neural network-based approaches [12,13] have been proposed for dual-target recommendation methods. Particularly, graph neural network-based methods in recommendation systems excel at capturing

M. Sellami et al. (Eds.): CoopIS 2023, LNCS 14353, pp. 427–437, 2024.
https://doi.org/10.1007/978-3-031-46846-9_24

high-order collaborative information. By using graph models to represent user-item relationships, graph collaborative filtering enhances data structure comprehension. Numerous studies confirm its strong performance and adaptability in dual-target recommendation.

Previous research on dual-target recommendation operated under the assumption of noise-free domain data. However, real-world cross-domain recommendation encounters challenges like noise, impacting model accuracy. Noise includes data missing (incomplete or lost interactions) incorrect labeling (users' errors in labeling items) and abnormal behavior (unusual interactions from some users like malicious actions or system errors), which disrupt model training.

Noise negatively affects dual-target crossx-domain recommendation models. Firstly, it introduces domain disparities, causing inconsistent data across domains, which harms recommendation performance. For example, one domain might have substantial missing data while another has more complete data. This could lead the recommendation model to rely heavily on complete data domain, diminishing the importance of incomplete data domain and affecting performance. Secondly, noise can spread during domain fusion, reducing overall model performance. For instance, in the movie domain, substantial noise could arise from fake ratings by certain users, providing inaccurate or malicious movie ratings. Conversely, the book domain generally has more accurate user ratings. Domain fusion might propagate movie domain noise to the book domain, leading to incorrect estimations of user preferences for books.

Our Approach and Contributions. This paper introduces a novel augmentation and denoising approach for dual-target CDR to tackle noise challenges. Our work's characteristics and contributions are as follows:

1. We propose DA-DCDR, an enhanced and denoising strategy designed to tackle the challenges of noise and data sparsity in dual-target cross-domain recommendation, with the ultimate goal of improving recommendation performance in both domains.
2. To mitigate the impact of noise during the domain fusion process, we introduce a domain-enhanced denoising module. This module enhances data accuracy and completeness by inferring missing user-item interactions and filtering out potentially erroneous noise data.
3. Extensive experimental validation demonstrates the significant effectiveness of the DA-DCDR method in reducing noise and improving recommendation performance. By leveraging the domain-enhanced denoising module, we successfully mitigate the adverse effects of noise on the model, leading to enhanced accuracy and reliability in the recommendation system.

2   Proposed Methods

In this section, we'll begin by introducing symbols for technical terms. Then, we'll outline the EA-DCDR model's structure, which consists of two core steps in the EA-DCDR framework: domain-specific enhancement and denoising, and correlation enhancement of the shared graph.

2.1   Notations and Definition

Given two domains D_A and D_B, users are common in both domains and represented by U (size $m = |U|$). Items in D_A and D_B are denoted as sets I_A (size $n_a = |D_A|$) and I_B (size $n_b = |D_B|$) respectively. The target of DA-DCDR is to simultaneously improve the recommendation performance in both domains. We denote the user-item interaction matrix in D_A as $R_A \in R^{m*n_a}$ (and in D_B as $R_B \in R^{m*n_b}$). Here, $r_{ui}^A \in \{0,1\}$ ($r_{uj}^B \in \{0,1\}$, respectively), indicating user u's interaction with item i (and item j, respectively). If there's an interaction, $r_{ui}^A = 1$ (and $r_{uj}^B = 1$), otherwise, it's 0.

In this paper, we aim to learn a function that predicts the level of user interest in unobserved items to rank the recommendation results. The predicted link scores for users and items in Domain A (Domain B) are represented by Eq. 1. Where f is the interaction function, θ are learnable parameters, and r signifies the predicted score.

$$\hat{r}_{ui}^A = f(u, i|\theta)(and \quad \hat{r}_{uj}^B = f(u, j|\theta)) \tag{1}$$

2.2   Interaction Enhancement and Denoising Module

The framework diagram of this module is shown in Fig. 1.

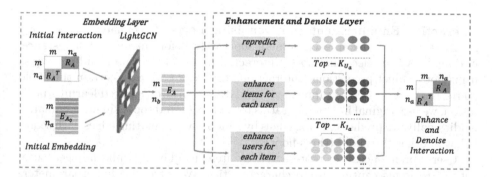

Fig. 1. The structure of enhancement and denoising module. On the EL, graphic convolution is performed on each domain using LightGCN to generate the initial user and project embeddings for both domains.In the IEDL, the initial embedding of the domain is used to obtain the enhanced interaction of each user and project in the two domains. In addition, interactive random denoising is performed by re-predicting existing user interactions.

Embedding Layer. We use LightGCN [15] as a pre-trained graph encoder to generate embeddings for entities in two domains, yielding user/item representations. For each domain, we leverage N graph convolutional layers to produce embeddings $E_A(u)$ and $E_A(i)$ (also $E_B(u)$ and $E_B(j)$ for domain B). LightGCN employs a straightforward weighted aggregator in its graph convolution, without feature transformation or non-linear activation, as defined by Eq. 3 and Eq. 4.

$$e_u^{k+1} = \sum_{i \in N_u} \frac{1}{\sqrt{|N_u||N_i|}} e_i^k, \tag{2}$$

$$e_i^{k+1} = \sum_{i \in N_i} \frac{1}{\sqrt{|N_u||N_i|}} e_u^k. \tag{3}$$

We optimize the pre-training step of the training data using the BPR (Bayesian Personalized Ranking) [17] loss, as shown in Eq. 4. Domain B as the same, show in Eq. 5.

$$\mathcal{L}_\mathcal{A} = \sum_{(u,i^+,i^- \in R)} log\sigma(e_u^T e_{i+} - e_u^T e_{i-}). \tag{4}$$

$$\mathcal{L}_\mathcal{B} = \sum_{(u,j^+,j^- \in R)} log\sigma(e_u^T e_{j+} - e_u^T e_{j-}), \tag{5}$$

where, i^+ (j^+) denotes interacting items for the user, while i^- (j^-) represents a randomly sampled non-interacting item. The resulting embeddings of the user (e_u) and items (e_i and e_j) are stored in matrix E_A for domain A, and equivalently in matrix E_B for domain B.

Interaction Enhancement and Denoising Layer. To enhance and denoise interactions, we focus on each domain separately before merging. For instance, in domain A, we select the top-k_a interacted items for each user and vice versa using dot product predictions. Interactions with scores above a certain threshold (thres-top) are treated as supplementary data. To ensure balanced learning post-fusion, we use original interaction ratios to set top-k_a and top-k_b in both domains. Additionally, we predict existing edges by randomly eliminating edges with scores below another threshold (thres-floor).

Users' preferences are represented by item neighbors, while adjacent user entities to items capture group characteristics. We introduce hyperparameters U_{k_a} and I_{K_a}, determining the maximum additional neighbors for users and items. To increase user interactions, we use Eq. 6 to identify the $top - k_a$ interacting items from the set of unknown interacted items for each user, adding interactions with prediction scores above the thres-top to the interaction matrix.

$$\underset{\{i_1,i_2,...,i_{U_k} \in I\}}{argmax} \quad e_u^T E_I^{\{N\}}, \tag{6}$$

Similarly, for the item side, we follow a similar process to generate top-K entities using Eq. 7. The enhanced E matrix combines user-item interactions generated from both user and item side.

$$\underset{\{u_1,u_2,...,u_{i_k} \in U\}}{argmax} \quad e_i^T E_U^{\{N\}}. \tag{7}$$

To mitigate the effect of random noise within each domain, we apply a random edge removal approach. We predict scores for all original interaction edges and filter out those below the threshold parameter thres-floor, reducing the impact of random noise.

And the same process should be applied to domain B.

2.3 Correlation Enhancement Module

The framework diagram of this module is shown in Fig. 2.

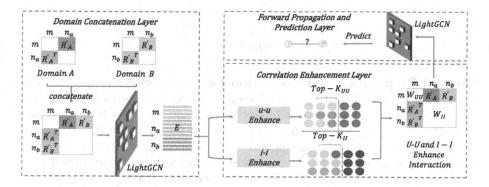

Fig. 2. The structure of correlation enhancement module. In the DCL, the interaction subgraphs of the two domains are joined and the graph convolution is applied to the new shared graph. In the CEL, the correlation enhancement is performed separately for each user and item based on dot product similarity. In FPPL, the probability of positive interaction of a given user-item pair is predicted after multilayer graph convolution.

Domain Concatenation Layer. The combined subgraphs of both domains create a shared graph for graph convolutional propagation. This strategy enhances feature correlation and integration, allowing the model to learn from both domains simultaneously. This shared space captures inter-domain associations, leveraging similarities and complementarities. This global perspective avoids subdomain limitations, ultimately enhancing cross-domain recommendation performance.

The user embeddings in the shared graph are obtained by taking the average of the user embeddings from both domains i.e. $E(u) : 1/2(E_a(u) + E_b(u))$; while the item embeddings are obtained from their respective domain-specific embeddings i.e. $E(i) : E_a(i)$ and $E(j) : E_b(j)$.

Correlation Enhancement Layer. After performing graph convolution on the shared graph, we extends $u - u$ (user-user) and $i - i$ (item-item) relationships, offering several advantages. It addresses interaction matrix sparsity by leveraging correlations between users and items to fill missing values, enhancing recommendation accuracy. Additionally, generating $u - u$ and $i - i$ interactions reveals similar user groups and item characteristics, enriching the recommendation system's information.

For users side, we control the number of neighboring entities with parameter UU_k, predicting top-k neighbors through Eq. 8. Similarly, for items, we use II_k to manage neighboring entities, shown as Eq. 9. Where, x denotes items in the shared domain. e_u^k signifies the user embedding after k convolution layers, while e_i^k represents the item embedding after k convolution layers. N_u refers to item neighbors of user u, and N_i denotes user neighbors of item i.

$$\underset{\{u_1,u_2,\ldots,u_{UU_k}\in U\}}{argmax} \quad e_u^T E_U^{\{N\}} \tag{8}$$

$$\underset{\{x_1,x_2,\ldots,x_{II_k}\in I\}}{argmax} \quad e_x^T E_I^{\{N\}} \tag{9}$$

Forward Propagation and Prediction Layer. In forward propagation, we employ the improved fused graph adjacency matrix and correlation-enhanced entity embeddings. These serve as inputs for the multi-layer graph convolutional network, facilitating information propagation and feature learning.

We concatenate the embeddings from each graph convolutional layer to create the final representation vectors for users and items, forming higher-dimensional representations that integrate information from multiple levels. This allows us to integrate feature information from multiple levels and capture a comprehensive and enriched representation of users and items.

Finally, these representation vectors enable us to predict the probability of positive interaction for a user-item pair, guiding our recommendation decisions using the formula in Eq. 10.

$$\hat{r}_{ui}^A = \hat{y}^A(u,i) = \sigma(e_u^T e_i) \tag{10}$$

2.4   Prediction and Training

DA-DCDR aims to enhance the predictive performance of both domains through joint training. One key advantage of joint training is the integration of data and tasks from different domains in a unified model. This eliminates the complexity of managing multiple independent models and allows training within a single framework, providing convenience and efficiency for recommendation system development. The loss function of DA-DCDR combines the joint BPR loss for recommendation predictions in both domains (represented as $L_a : -\sum_{(u,i+,i-\in R)} log\sigma(e_u^T r_{i+} - e_u^T e_{i-})$ and $L_b : -\sum_{(u,j+,j-\in R)} log\sigma(e_u^T r_{j+} - e_u^T e_{j-})$) with a regularization term ($L_{reg} : \lambda(||P^a||_F^2 + ||Q^b||_F^2)$), shown as Eq. 11. P and Q refer to all parameters of the two fields respectively

$$L = L_a + L_b + L_{reg} \tag{11}$$

3 Experiments, Results and Analysis

This section showcases our experiments to validate the efficacy of the DA-DCDR framework. Our experiment addresses three main research questions: Q1: Are the interaction enhancement and denoising modules effective? Q2: Does correlation enhancement work well? Q3: Does DA-DCDR outperform existing baselines in recommendation performance?

3.1 Setups

Datasets. Our evaluation utilized real-world cross-domain datasets from the publicly available Amazon dataset: Books and Movies [11]. We identified overlapping users, resulting in 15,120 users. The Books domain has 141,319 items (0.0142 % sparsity), and the Movies domain has 129,894 items (0.0382% sparsity). We employed a leave-one-out strategy for each user, using the last interaction item as the test item and the second-to-last item as validation. This approach rigorously tests our model's cross-domain recommendation performance while considering dataset sparsity.

Baseline Models. To demonstrate the effectiveness of DA-DCDR, we compared it with the following methods: NGCF [14], LightGCN [15], UltrGCN [16].

Evaluation Metrics. In the evaluation of all models, we used two metrics: Hit Ratio (HR@K) and Normalized Discounted Cumulative Gain (NDCG@K). The value of K ranged from [5,10,15,20,40].

Training Details. Across methods, we used a 32-dimensional initial embedding. In DA-DCDR, Light GCN was employed with 4 iterations. Coefficient: 0.0001 in all layers. Learning rate: 0.001. Hyperparameters: U_{k_a}, U_{k_b}: 1; I_{k_a}, I_{k_b}: 2; UU_k, II_k: 5; thres-top: 0.95; thres-floor: 0.5.

3.2 Performance Comparison and Analysis

Legend explanations: "LightGCN" is the baseline. "Noise" refers to the model without denoising and association enhancement. "Noise Enhance" has association enhancement without denoising. "Denoise" features denoising without association enhancement. "Denoise & Re Enhance" combines denoising and association enhancement.

Ablation Study (for Q1). To address Q1, we conducted ablation experiments using LightGCN as the baseline, comparing models with and without the interaction-enhanced denoising module. The LightGCN baseline was trained separately on each domain, and performance metrics like NDCG@N and HR@N were collected for fair comparison. Figure 3 shows experimental outcomes for Book and Movie domains with varying N values. Models lacking the denoising module exhibit substantial drops in NDCG@N and HR@N compared to the baseline, highlighting noise's detrimental effect on fusion and recommendation quality. However, the denoising enhancement module significantly boosts performance. Results indicate the model with denoising (removienoise) outperforms the module-free counterpart (withnoise) in NDCG@N and HR@N. This underscores noise handling's significance and validates our approach's effectiveness.

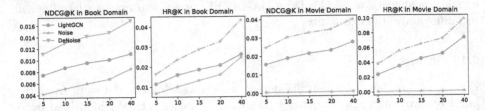

Fig. 3. Performance line plots of NDCG and HR metrics for the Movie and Book domains at different values of K. The experimental results of the removienoise module are significantly better than those without withnoise module under the indexes of NDCG@N and HR@N.

Ablation Study (for Q2). To address Q2, we designed two sets of experiments: (1) Compare the model performance with and without the inclusion of the correlation augmentation module, based on the absence of interactive enhancement and noise removal.(2) Compare the model performance with and without the inclusion of the correlation augmentation module, based on the presence of interactive enhancement and noise removal.

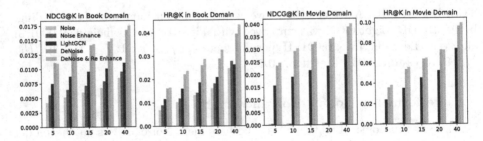

Fig. 4. Bar plots showing the NDCG and HR metrics for the Movie and Book domains at different values of K. (Color figure online)

We will display a bar chart to evaluate the performance of the five models in both experiment sets on a single plot. Figure 4 reveals that models with the association enhancement module (purple and red) consistently outperform models without it (red and blue) in both experiment sets. In the first set of experiments, due to prior unresolved noise, models fall short of optimal performance. Particularly in the Movie domain, with fewer interactions, after merging Movie and Book domains, models lean towards Book domain information, leading to limited learning in the Movie domain. In the second set of experiments, combining association enhancement with denoising demonstrates improved performance. This

Table 1. Performance comparison of different models in the Book domain.

Metric	H@5	H@10	H@15	H@20	H@40	N@5	N@10	N@15	N@20	N@40
LightGCN	0.0747	0.0872	0.0956	0.1008	0.1106	0.1157	0.1602	0.1869	0.2085	0.2619
UltarGCN	0.0427	0.0536	0.0626	0.0683	0.0799	0.0674	0.1081	0.1360	0.1640	0.2187
GTN	0.0401	0.0531	0.0710	0.0767	0.0846	0.0801	0.1208	0.1538	0.1767	0.2225
Enhanced-UI	**0.1111**	0.1299	0.1415	0.1475	0.1677	0.1615	0.2213	0.2607	0.2887	0.3943
DA-DCDR	0.1096	**0.1313**	**0.1435**	**0.1530**	**0.1753**	**0.1653**	**0.2366**	**0.2874**	**0.3268**	**0.4337**

Table 2. Performance comparison of different models in the Movie domain.

Metric	H@5	H@10	H@15	H@20	H@40	N@5	N@10	N@15	N@20	N@40
LightGCN	0.1562	0.1905	0.2162	0.2325	0.2770	0.2390	0.3522	0.4539	0.5238	0.7413
UltarGCN	0.1213	0.1463	0.1609	0.1707	0.1919	0.1818	0.2619	0.3128	0.3522	0.4628
GTN	0.1025	0.1315	0.1471	0.1591	0.1999	0.1577	0.2492	0.3204	0.3916	0.5772
Enhanced-UI	0.2355	0.2932	0.3196	0.3398	0.3880	0.3598	0.5366	0.6408	**0.7285**	0.9612
DA-DCDR	**0.2469**	**0.3044**	**0.3285**	**0.3458**	**0.4011**	**0.3827**	**0.5582**	**0.6497**	0.7260	**0.9943**

shows that denoising mitigates noise's impact, allowing association enhancement to positively influence the model more effectively.

Performance Comparison (for Q3). To answer Q3, we compared DA-DCDR with baseline models in Tables 1 and 2. These tables present performance metrics such as HR@N and NDCG@N for the Book and Movie domains. Please note that the values in the table have been multiplied by 10 for better readability. DA-DCDR consistently outperforms baseline models across various metrics, particularly excelling in H@5, N@5, N@40 for the Book domain, and H@5, H@10, N@40 for the Movie domain.

These findings underscore DA-DCDR's superior recommendation accuracy and effectiveness, driven by our novel graphical and attentional approach.

4 Conclusion

We introduce DA-DCDR, a dual-target recommendation approach that employs graph collaborative filtering and data augmentation techniques to tackle noise issues in domain fusion. By enhancing interaction integrity and filtering out erroneous interactions, we enhance data accuracy and maintain data consistency. We also extend user-user and item-item associations to leverage shared domain interaction data. Our approach is simple, effective, and validated through experiments, demonstrating improved recommendation performance in dual-target scenarios.

References

1. Berkovsky, S., Kuflik, T., Ricci, F.: Cross-domain mediation in collaborative filtering. In: Conati, C., McCoy, K., Paliouras, G. (eds.) UM 2007. LNCS (LNAI), vol. 4511, pp. 355–359. Springer, Heidelberg (2007). https://doi.org/10.1007/978-3-540-73078-1_44
2. Jiang, M., Cui, P., Yuan, N.J., Xie, X., Yang, S.: Little is much: bridging cross-platform behaviors through overlapped crowds. In: Proceedings of the Thirtieth AAAI Conference on Artificial Intelligence, 12–17 February 2016, Phoenix, Arizona, USA, pp. 13–19. AAAI Press (2016)
3. Rafailidis, D., Crestani, F.: Top-N recommendation via joint cross-domain user clustering and similarity learning. In: Frasconi, P., Landwehr, N., Manco, G., Vreeken, J. (eds.) ECML PKDD 2016. LNCS (LNAI), vol. 9852, pp. 426–441. Springer, Cham (2016). https://doi.org/10.1007/978-3-319-46227-1_27
4. Yang, C., Yan, H., Yu, D., Li, Y., Chiu, D.M.: Multi-site user behavior modeling and its application in video recommendation. In: Proceedings of the 40th International ACM SIGIR Conference on Research and Development in Information Retrieval, Shinjuku, Tokyo, Japan, 7–11 August 2017, pp. 175–184. ACM (2017)
5. Zhang, Y., et al.: Learning personalized itemset mapping for cross-domain recommendation. In: Proceedings of the Twenty-Ninth International Joint Conference on Artificial Intelligence, IJCAI 2020, pp. 2561–2567 (2020). https://www.ijcai.org/Proceedings/2020/354
6. Zhu, Y., et al.: Transfer-meta framework for cross-domain recommendation to cold-start users. In: SIGIR 2021: The 44th International ACM SIGIR Conference on Research and Development in Information Retrieval, Virtual Event, Canada, 11–15 July 2021, pp. 1813–1817. ACM (2021)
7. Wang, T., Zhuang, F., Zhang, Z., Wang, D., Zhou, J., He, Q.: Low-dimensional alignment for cross-domain recommendation. In: CIKM 2021: The 30th ACM International Conference on Information and Knowledge Management, Virtual Event, Queensland, Australia, 1–5 November 2021, pp. 3508–3512. ACM (2021)
8. Perera, D., Zimmermann, R.: Exploring the use of time-dependent cross-network information for personalized recommendations. In: Proceedings of the 2017 ACM on Multimedia Conference, MM 2017, Mountain View, CA, USA, 23–27 October 2017, pp. 1780–1788. ACM (2017)
9. Zhu, F., Chen, C., Wang, Y., Liu, G., Zheng, X.: DTCDR: a framework for dual-target cross-domain recommendation. In: Proceedings of the 28th ACM International Conference on Information and Knowledge Management, CIKM 2019, Beijing, China, 3–7 November 2019, pp. 1533–1542. ACM (2019)
10. Zhu, F., Wang, Y., Chen, C., Liu, G., Zheng, X.: A graphical and attentional framework for dual-target cross-domain recommendation (2020)
11. Liu, M., Li, J., G., Pan, P.: Cross domain recommendation via bi-directional transfer graph collaborative filtering networks. In: Proceedings of the 29th ACM International Conference on Information & Knowledge Management (2020). https://dx.doi.org/10.1145/3340531.3412012
12. Li, J., Peng, Z., Wang, S., Xu, X., Yu, P.S., Hao, Z.: Heterogeneous graph embedding for cross-domain recommendation through adversarial learning. In: Nah, Y., Cui, B., Lee, S.-W., Yu, J.X., Moon, Y.-S., Whang, S.E. (eds.) DASFAA 2020. LNCS, vol. 12114, pp. 507–522. Springer, Cham (2020). https://doi.org/10.1007/978-3-030-59419-0_31

13. Xu, K., Xie, Y., Chen, L., Zheng, Z.: Expanding relationship for cross domain recommendation. In: CIKM 2021: The 30th ACM International Conference on Information and Knowledge Management, Virtual Event, Queensland, Australia, 1–5 November 2021, pp. 2251–2260. ACM (2021)
14. Wang, X., He, X., Wang, M., Feng, F., Chua, T.-S. : Neural graph collaborative filtering. In: Proceedings of the 42nd International ACM SIGIR Conference on Research and Development in Information Retrieval, SIGIR 2019 (2019)
15. He, X., Deng, K., Wang, X., Li, Y., Zhang, Y., Wang, M.: LightGCN: simplifying and powering graph convolution network for recommendation. In: Proceedings of the 43rd International ACM SIGIR Conference on Research and Development in Information Retrieval, SIGIR 2020 (2020)
16. Mao, K., Zhu, J., Xiao, X., Lu, B., Wang, Z., He, X.: UltraGCN: ultra simplification of graph convolutional networks for recommendation. In: Proceedings of the 30th ACM International Conference on Information & Knowledge Management (2021). https://dx.doi.org/10.1145/3459637.3482291
17. Rendle, S., Freudenthaler, C., Gantner, Z., Schmidt-Thieme, L.: BPR: Bayesian personalized ranking from implicit feedback. In: Proceedings of the Uncertainty in Artificial Intelligence (2009)

Clustering Raw Sensor Data in Process Logs to Detect Data Streams

Matthias Ehrendorfer[✉][iD], Juergen Mangler[iD], and Stefanie Rinderle-Ma[iD]

Technical University of Munich, TUM School of Computation, Information and Technology, Garching, Germany
{matthias.ehrendorfer,juergen.mangler,stefanie.rinderle-ma}@tum.de

Abstract. The execution and analysis of processes is strongly influenced by sensor streams, e.g., temperature, that are measured in parallel to the process execution and stored in process event logs. This holds particularly true for application domains such as logistics and manufacturing. However, currently, these sensor streams are collected and stored in an arbitrary and unsystematic way. Hence, this work proposes an approach that prepares sensor streams into individual data streams that can be annotated to process tasks and used for process analysis and prediction.

Keywords: Process Models · Process Model Enhancement · Annotation of Context Data · Process Logs

1 Introduction

Data is paramount to drive and optimize process execution, i.e., at decision points in the process model and as input/output for services, application programs, and human actors invoked by the process tasks [1,13]. In addition to this *intrinsic data*, *extrinsic data* might affect the process execution, as well, for example the process outcome [4] or the prediction of concept drift [15]. Extrinsic data comprises raw data available in a machine participating in the process, or sensor data monitoring the environment in which the process is enacted. Recently, the DataStream XES extension (cf. [11]) has been proposed in order to enable the recording of sensor streams in process event logs.

Consider the realistic transportation scenario [10] depicted in Fig. 1. The process model shown in Fig. 1d collects multiple measurements relevant to an underlying public transport process, i.e., delay, weather, traffic, and construction sites, as response of one service call. The resulting data is logged in the XES SensorStream format. The raw sensor streams for weather and traffic are depicted in Fig. 1a and Fig. 1b respectively. As can be seen from the weather sensor stream,

This work has been partly funded by the Austrian Research Promotion Agency (FFG) via the "Austrian Competence Center for Digital Production" (CDP) under the contract number 881843. This work has been supported by the Pilot Factory Industry 4.0, Seestadtstrasse 27, Vienna, Austria.

M. Sellami et al. (Eds.): CoopIS 2023, LNCS 14353, pp. 438–447, 2024.
https://doi.org/10.1007/978-3-031-46846-9_25

multiple measurements are contained, e.g., temperature, wind, or pressure, in an arbitrary and hence unsystematic way. In order to utilize the sensor streams for process analysis and predictive process monitoring, the sensor streams are to be prepared, i.e., relevant sensor information is to be extracted from the raw stream and clustered into individual data streams. These data streams can then be annotated to process tasks such that, in the sequel, the data streams can be already collected in a systematic way.

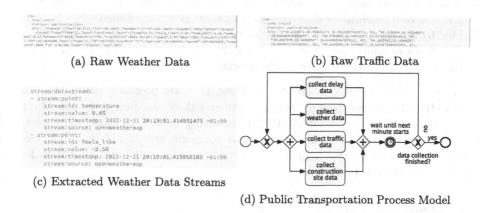

(a) Raw Weather Data   (b) Raw Traffic Data

(c) Extracted Weather Data Streams

(d) Public Transportation Process Model

Fig. 1. Public Transportation - External Service Log Data and Process Model

Explicitly annotating information about how and which data is collected in individual tasks of a process model is necessary for "Placing Sensors in a Process-Aware Way" [6]. However, as doing so manually is time-consuming, cumbersome, and error-prone, this paper provides a sensor stream extraction and fusion approach that constitutes the prerequisite for future task annotation. The approach (1) breaks down raw sensor streams in process event logs into comparable components, (2) describes how to determine a distance between these components in order to enable clustering and (3) explores different methods of clustering the collected context data to find individual data streams (sensor stream fusion).

The approach is evaluated using a synthetically created data set which portrays weather data and is used to demonstrate the applicability of the approach and a real-world data set from the manufacturing domain which contains context data from the machine tool and measuring machine used in the process.

Section 2 describes the approach presented in this paper, Sect. 3 contains the evaluation of the approach and Sect. 4 discusses the results. Furthermore, Sect. 5 gives an overview over related work and the paper is concluded in Sect. 6.

2   Context Data Clustering Approach

As motivated in the introduction and the transportation use case (cf. Fig. 1), sensor data streams collected as context data during process execution, currently, cannot be directly processed for process analysis and prediction due to the following reasons:

1. Sensor data might occur at "random" times from the point of view of the process as machines and sensors might not always send the same data or external endpoints are not under the control of the process.
2. Endpoints might provide different data depending on their implementation or be changed over time leading to inhomogeneous sensor data.
3. Sensor streams might contain multiple measurements, e.g., different data streams of a machine or different sensor readings are combined.
4. Due to the inhomogeneity, the raw sensor data does not have any schema.
5. It is unclear which sensor streams or parts of sensor streams are connected to the process instance or to single process tasks.

The proposed approach aims at tackling 1.–4. by breaking down the raw sensor streams into comparable components and then based on a structural (cf. Sect. 2.1) and value-based (cf. Sect. 2.2) clustering as well as based on a combination of both (cf. Sect. 2.3), fusing these components into individual, homogeneous data streams that can be connected to tasks and build the basis for process analysis and prediction.

2.1 Structural Analysis

The goal of the structural analysis is to find components of the raw sensor streams which are similar regarding their structure, i.e., they provide a value/timestamp pair with a certain label, they contain the same types of measurements (e.g., numerical temperature reading or textual description of the noise level), or any other structural similarity. Structural similarity is calculated using the JSON edit distance (JEDI) [5] that quantifies how similar two JSON documents are considering their structure. More precisely, the JEDI distance is calculated based on the number of edit operations (add, delete, rename) necessary to transform one structure into the other.

2.2 Value-Based Analysis

Even when data is structurally similar, it might still belong to different data streams based on its values (e.g., different measuring units are used or measurements are taken at completely different times). Calculating the distance between two sensor stream components regarding their values is not straightforward as multiple types of data values might occur. We compare the values of two sensor stream components as follows: Each value of the first component is compared to all values of the other component. Depending on the type of the values we use (1) Levenshtein distance [9] for strings, (2) time period between two values for timestamps, and (3) difference for numbers. The result is a $m x n$ matrix of distances between all data values. For each value the lowest distance to the other component is then added to the overall distance for this type of value. As a result a distance from one component to another is generated for each value type.

Distances of different value types might not be comparable to each other. Hence, they are scaled by dividing the value calculated in the first place by the maximum distance between all context data components for the respective value type. The results for each data type are then combined - weights can be chosen based on the scenario. Other types of values and other distance measures for the presented data types (string, timestamp, number) can be added easily.

2.3 Combining Structural and Value-Based Analysis

This section describes the steps of the overall approach based on the two analysis methods described in Sects. 2.1 and 2.2.

Step 0 - Extract Raw Sensor Stream Data From Event Logs: The extraction results in a list of sensor data elements collected at different points in time and by different events.

Step 1 - Break Down Sensor Stream Data Into Components: The extracted data is broken down into its components by using the whole raw data as starting point and then recursively adding available children (e.g., sensor measurement consists of temperature and humidity) to the components. This allows to compare different components of the sensor data as for some scenarios bigger parts of the original raw data are comparable while for other scenarios only lower level components (e.g., single value/timestamp pairs) can be compared.

Step 2 - Choose Strategy: When using **Strategy A** first structural analysis (cf. Sect. 2.1) is performed and afterwards the clusters are refined using value-based analysis (cf. Sect. 2.2). If **Strategy B** is used the order is reversed: first value-based analysis (cf. Sect. 2.1) is used and then clusters are refined using structural analysis (cf. Sect. 2.2). **Strategy C** only uses one kind of analysis, i.e., represents Strategy A or B but stopping after Step 3.

Strategy A: Initially use Structural Analysis and Afterwards Refine Using Value-Based Analysis:

- **Step 3A - Cluster Components Based on Structural Analysis:** The distance between components is found using structural analysis (cf. Sect. 2.1) and then used for clustering. We opt for using DBSCAN for clustering as the number of clusters does not have to be defined. We will experiment with other clustering approaches such as k-means in the future.
- **Step 4A - Refine Individual Clusters Based on Value-Based Analysis:** Afterwards, (value-based) distances (cf. Sect. 2.2) between components within structural clusters are used to build refined clusters (again using DBSCAN).

Strategy B: Initially use Value-Based Analysis and Afterwards Refine Using Structural Analysis:

- **Step 3B - Cluster Components Based on Value-Based Analysis:** The distance between components is found using value-based analysis (cf. Sect. 2.2) and then used for clustering (using DBSCAN).

- **Step 4B - Refine Individual Clusters Based on Structural Analysis:** Afterwards, (structural) distances (cf. Sect. 2.1) between components within value-based clusters are used to refine clusters (again using DBSCAN).

Strategy C: Only Consider Structural or Value-Based Analysis
This strategy considers either structural (C1) or value-based (C2) aspects of the components. Therefore, it is a modification of Strategy A (for C1) or B (for C2) where refinement is skipped (i.e., steps 4A and 4B are omitted).

3   Evaluation

The evaluation is performed on an artificial data set as well as on a real-world data set from the manufacturing domain. Code, data and instructions on how to run the code are available at gitlab[1].

Methodology: For both data sets, we first apply Strategy C in both variants, i.e., C1 based on structure and C2 based on values. C1 is then refined into Strategy A, i.e., structure-based clusters are refined into value-based ones, and C2 is refined into Strategy B, i.e., value-based clusters are again clustered based on the structure. The results can be shown in tables (see Table 1): the leftmost column represents the firstly built clusters (in this case structural), the second column represents the (in this case value-based) refinement. A "*" denotes that the original cluster before refinement is described. Entries in the following columns show that data components of this data stream can be found in this cluster. Apart from Table 1 only summarized results are reported by giving information about "Clusters per Data Stream" (CpDS) and "Data Streams per Cluster" (DSpC) for structural (Struct) and value-based (VB) clusters which allow to estimate the effectiveness of a strategy. A perfect result would be one where CpDS and DSpC are 1 for all clusters and data streams because then one cluster represents exactly one data stream and one data stream is represented by exactly one cluster.

For structural clustering an epsilon of 0.1 is used which means that components in a cluster have the exact same structure. A higher epsilon would lead to less similar components being in the same cluster and thus more imprecise results. Weights for the value-based analysis have been set so that all data types are considered with equal weight. The remaining parameters are explained in the relevant sections. For all results only clusters with >1 elements are considered.

3.1   Artificial Data Set

The following sensor measurements being "measured" in two different time slots on subsequent days are included in the artificial data:

- Temperature: **value in degree Celsius** (between −5 and 20), **value in degree Fahrenheit** (between 268 and 295), **short textual description** (e.g., "hot", "cold"), and **long textual description** (e.g., "Today the weather is very hot and it is expected that ...")

---

[1] https://gitlab.com/me33551/semi_automatic_context_data_extraction.

– Humidity: value providing **relative humidity** (between 40 and 90), **short textual description** (e.g., "high", "low"), **long textual description** (e.g., "We expect tropical weather with a high humidity for today.")

Strategy C1 and A: Using only structural analysis (Strategy C1) the results show that the clusters already provide some grouping regarding data streams contained in the data components of a cluster (cf. rows with "*" in column "VB" in Tab. 1 where cluster 2 contains textual data streams and cluster 5 contains all other data streams). Furthermore, some structural clusters (e.g., 3, 4, 6, ...) are already identified as not containing information representing any data stream i.e., they just contain single values or components including data from multiple streams. Looking at the "CpDS Struct" and "DSpC Struct" values it can be seen that each stream is contained in only one cluster (all CpDS Struct values are 1) but the problem is that for a component in a cluster it cannot be clearly decided to which data stream they belong (DSpC Struct values are 8 and 6).

When refining the structural clusters as described in Sect. 2.3 the results reported in Table 1 show that the refined clusters represent nearly all data streams available in the data set. This can be seen because all apart from 3 "CpDS VB" values are greater than 0. Also all but one "DSpC VB" values are 1 (and one is 2). This means that all but one of the refined clusters contain only one data stream. This is a good result because overall it means that all components can be assigned to a data stream based on the cluster in which they are.

Table 1. Artificial Data Set Results for Strategy C1 and A

Clusters		Temperature								Humidity						DSpC Struct	DSpC VB
Struct	VB	Celsius		Fahrenheit		Short Text		Long Text		Relative		Short Text		Long Text			
		Day 1	Day 2	D1	D2	D1	D2	D1	D2	D1	D2	D1	D2	D1	D2		
2	*					x	x	x	x			x	x	x	x	8	
	0						x										1
	2						x						x				2
	3					x											1
	5														x		1
	6											x					1
	7						x										1
	9					x											1
	11														x		1
3		N/A															N/A	
4		N/A															N/A	
5	*	x	x	x	x					x	x					6	
	0			x													1
	1	x															1
	3									x							1
	5										x						1
	6									x							1
	7				x												1
	8										x						1
	9		x														1
6		N/A															N/A	
8		N/A															N/A	
9		N/A															N/A	
12		N/A															N/A	
CpDS Struct		1	1	1	1	1	1	1	1	1	1	1	1	1	1		
CpDS VB		1	0	2	1	1	2	2	0	2	2	1	1	0	2		

Strategy C2 And B: When applying Strategy C2 (using only value-based analysis) only one cluster is found because all components are connected (distance of 0) via the root component. This is because values contained in lower level components (containing one or two values) are also included in higher level components (as well as the root). Therefore, the results shown in the "Artificial" section for Strategy B of Tab. 2 are only based on components which contain exactly two values (i.e., a value/timestamp pair). This results in "CpDS VB - B" values being the same values as for Strategy A. DSpC values are 1 for all but one data stream (where it is 2) meaning that in one of the clusters components from 2 data streams is included (components in other clusters can be easily allocated as their "DSpC VB" is 1 and therefore each cluster represents only one data stream).

Refinement using structural analysis (cf. Sect. 2.3) does not lead to new clusters because the exclusion as described in the paragraph above where only components with two values are used leads to structurally similar components. Even if refinements could be made this would not make sense because the clusters found using only value-based analysis already lead to a nearly perfect result with only one "DSpC VB" value not being 1. However, extensive domain knowledge about the internal structure of collected data is needed in order to select the components when starting with value-based analysis as in Strategy C2 and B while the results presented in Sect. 3.1 (using Strategy A) lead to comparable results without any prior knowledge.

Table 2. Summarized Results for Artificial and Real-World Data Sets

Artificial	Temperature								Humidity					
	Celsius		Fahrenheit		Short Text		Long Text		Relative		Short Text		Long Text	
	Day 1	Day 2	D1	D2	D1	D2	D1	D2	D1	D2	D1	D2	D1	D2
CpDS Struct - A	1	1	1	1	1	1	1	1	1	1	1	1	1	1
CpDS VB - A	1	0	2	1	1	2	2	0	2	2	1	1	0	2
CpDS VB - B	1	0	2	1	1	2	2	0	2	2	1	1	0	2

Real-World	Active Power				Spindle													
	A	B	C	keyence	act	drive	aaLeadP			aaTorque			aaVactB			aaLoad		
					Speed	Load	X	Y	Z	X	Y	Z	X	Y	Z	X	Y	Z
CpDS Struct - A	1	1	1	1	1	1	1	0	0	1	1	1	1	0	0	1	1	1
CpDS VB - A	4	4	4	6	2	2	2	0	0	2	2	1	2	0	0	2	2	1
CpDS VB - B	4	4	4	5	1	1	1	0	0	1	1	1	1	0	0	1	1	1

3.2 Real-World Data Set

The real-world data set[2] contains log files from a manufacturing process including data from (1) a robot handling transportation of the part between stations (2) the machine tool producing a part, and (3) measuring data from quality control of a part. Only part of the data available in the data set is used for the evaluation. Due to the high number of context data we focused on 3 different log events within one process instance and used the first 151 components of each event for the analysis. This already includes most of the data streams (i.e., only aaLeadP Y and Z and aaTorque Y and Z are not present in any cluster (see results).

---

[2] https://cpee.org/~demo/DaSH/batch14.zip [Online; accessed 15-Jul-2023].

Strategy C1 And A: Considering only structural analysis (Strategy C1) the results show that most of the data streams are included in the clusters (only 4 "CpDS Struct - A" values in Table 2 are 0). The "DSpC Struct" values are 4 and 10 meaning that the two structural clusters found contain this number of data streams. Root and high-level components are excluded from this structural analysis because a distance measure based on edit distance on such big data structures is very costly. Furthermore, these components would be in their own clusters because the epsilon with 0.1 allows only structurally equal components in the same cluster.

Refining the results described above (Strategy A) leads to "CpDS VB - A" values between 1 and 6 (apart from the 4 data streams with 0). The "DSpC VB" values are all 1 in one of the original structural clusters and between 2 and 4 in the other one. Therefore, refined clusters with a "DSpC" of 1 only contain components belonging to one data stream while for the ones with higher values it at least restricts the number of data streams to which components in this cluster belong.

Strategy C2 and B: As for the artificial data set (see Sect. 3.1) it is necessary to limit the number of values in the examined components to prevent one big cluster - therefore, only components with a minimum of 2 values and a maximum of 15 values are used. All but 4 of the data streams are found in one of the clusters ("CpDS VB - B" in Table 2 bigger than 0 for all but 4 data streams). The "DSpC VB" values are 1 for all clusters containing components with "keyence" or "Active Power" measurements. However, the other cluster has a "DSpC VB - B" value of 10 which means that it cannot be decided to which of these data streams a component in this cluster belongs. Furthermore, as in Sect. 3.1 refinement for Strategy B is not possible and finding the right parameters for the minimum and maximum number of values again requires in-depth domain knowledge.

4   Discussion

The evaluation shows that detecting data streams based on raw data included in logged events is possible. However, because the approach deconstructs all data received into its components and calculates distances between each of them for clustering this leads to a long calculation time. A run-time version needs to either reduce the amount of data or to not compare every component to each of the others. Another limitation is that some parameters need to be set (depending on the strategy used). This requires knowledge about the domain and collected data. For future work a user interface to inspect different combinations of parameters would be an option. However, for a fully automated approach another solution would be needed. Overall, the presented approach builds clusters representing different data streams collected in a process. This information can be used to create data schemas over all components in a cluster and use them for automatic extraction of data from raw event data loads. However, generating a schema which fits a cluster structurally and value-wise needs to be further investigated.

5   Related Work

Recent process mining papers such as [12] introduce the importance of the data perspective. [16,17] exploit textual information as additional source of unstructured data to improve process analysis results. Other examples include exploiting the sentiment for news data for remaining time prediction in [18] and [15] describing an approach to identify concept drifts based on sensor data. [2] proposes to predict process performance indicators based on identification of relevant context information through domain knowledge and expert feedback. [8] and [14] use sensor data as basis to identify process activities and discover a process model.

Another related area is Complex Event Processing (cf. [3]) where rules for events are defined to filter events and perform analysis. In contrast, our approach tries to find information about data streams in the process from the context data contained within events without prior definition of rules.

Our approach uses JSON edit distance (cf. [5]) which is an adoption of the well-known edit distance for XML documents to calculate the distance between two components. Other works in the context of NoSQL data stores deal with providing schemas for semi-structured JSON data as well as structural similarity measures (cf. [7]) or data handling in more specific cases (e.g., considering hidden data available as meta data or conceptual schema extraction).

6   Conclusion

This paper describes how to identify data streams appearing in a process by analyzing the raw data load contained in logged events. This includes making raw sensor streams comparable by breaking them down into components and calculating a distance between them based on structure or included values. Afterwards, different strategies to find clusters representing data streams occurring in the process are compared and discussed. The evaluation shows that using the presented approach the data stream to which a component belongs can be narrowed down based on its assigned cluster. Furthermore, it is discussed that when value-based analysis is performed without prior structural analysis (i.e., Strategy C2 and B) some components have to be excluded to still achieve meaningful results. However, this filtering requires domain knowledge which is not needed for Strategy C1 and A. Future work will further investigate how the components contained in a cluster can be used to create a schema for the data stream represented by it so that this information can be used to annotate data streams to process tasks to be used for process analysis and prediction.

References

1. Brunk, J., Stierle, M., Papke, L., Revoredo, K., Matzner, M., Becker, J.: Cause vs. effect in context-sensitive prediction of business process instances. Inf. Syst. **95**, 101635 (2021)

2. Chamorro, A.E.M., Revoredo, K., Resinas, M., del-Río-Ortega, A., Santoro, F.M., Ruiz-Cortés, A.: Context-aware process performance indicator prediction. IEEE Access **8**, 222050–222063 (2020)
3. Cugola, G., Margara, A.: Processing flows of information: from data stream to complex event processing. ACM Comput. Surv. **44**(3), 1–62 (2012)
4. Ehrendorfer, M., Mangler, J., Rinderle-Ma, S.: Assessing the impact of context data on process outcomes during runtime. In: Hacid, H., Kao, O., Mecella, M., Moha, N., Paik, H. (eds.) ICSOC 2021. LNCS, vol. 13121, pp. 3–18. Springer, Cham (2021). https://doi.org/10.1007/978-3-030-91431-8_1
5. Hütter, T., Augsten, N., Kirsch, C.M., Carey, M.J., Li, C.: JEDI: these aren't the JSON documents you're looking for? In: Management of Data, pp. 1584–1597 (2022)
6. Janiesch, C., et al.: The internet of things meets business process management: a manifesto. IEEE Syst. Man Cybern. Mag. **6**(4), 34–44 (2020)
7. Klettke, M., Störl, U., Scherzinger, S.: Schema extraction and structural outlier detection for JSON-based NoSQL data stores. In: Datenbanksysteme für Business, Technologie und Web, pp. 425–444 (2015)
8. Koschmider, A., Janssen, D., Mannhardt, F.: Framework for process discovery from sensor data. In: Enterprise Modeling and Information Systems Architectures. CEUR Workshop Proceedings, vol. 2628, pp. 32–38 (2020)
9. Levenshtein, V.I., et al.: Binary codes capable of correcting deletions, insertions, and reversals. In: Soviet Physics Doklady, pp. 707–710, no. 8. Soviet Union (1966)
10. Mangler, J., Kunkler, M.: XES logistics and transportation dataset - large (19 days) (2023). https://doi.org/10.5281/zenodo.7528638
11. Mangler, J., et al.: Datastream XES extension: embedding IoT sensor data into extensible event stream logs (2023). https://doi.org/10.3390/fi15030109
12. Mannhardt, F.: Multi-perspective process mining. In: BPM (Dissertation/Demos/Industry), pp. 41–45 (2018)
13. Park, G., Benzin, J., van der Aalst, W.M.P.: Detecting context-aware deviations in process executions. In: Di Ciccio, C., Dijkman, R., del Río Ortega, A., Rinderle-Ma, S. (eds.) BPM 2022. LNBIS, vol. 458, pp. 190–206. Springer, Cham (2022). https://doi.org/10.1007/978-3-031-16171-1_12
14. Seiger, R., Franceschetti, M., Weber, B.: An interactive method for detection of process activity executions from IoT data. Future Internet **15**(2), 77 (2023)
15. Stertz, F., Rinderle-Ma, S., Mangler, J.: Analyzing process concept drifts based on sensor event streams during runtime. In: Fahland, D., Ghidini, C., Becker, J., Dumas, M. (eds.) BPM 2020. LNCS, vol. 12168, pp. 202–219. Springer, Cham (2020). https://doi.org/10.1007/978-3-030-58666-9_12
16. Teinemaa, I., Dumas, M., Maggi, F.M., Di Francescomarino, C.: Predictive business process monitoring with structured and unstructured data. In: La Rosa, M., Loos, P., Pastor, O. (eds.) BPM 2016. LNCS, vol. 9850, pp. 401–417. Springer, Cham (2016). https://doi.org/10.1007/978-3-319-45348-4_23
17. Weinzierl, S., Revoredo, K., Matzner, M.: Predictive business process monitoring with context information from documents. In: European Conference on Information Systems (2019)
18. Yeshchenko, A., Durier, F., Revoredo, K., Mendling, J., Santoro, F.: Context-aware predictive process monitoring: the impact of news sentiment. In: Panetto, H., Debruyne, C., Proper, H.A., Ardagna, C.A., Roman, D., Meersman, R. (eds.) OTM 2018. LNCS, vol. 11229, pp. 586–603. Springer, Cham (2018). https://doi.org/10.1007/978-3-030-02610-3_33

Comparing the Performance of GPT-3 with BERT for Decision Requirements Modeling

Alexandre Goossens$^{(\boxtimes)}$, Johannes De Smedt , and Jan Vanthienen

Leuven Institute for Research on Information Systems (LIRIS), KU Leuven,
Leuven, Belgium
{Alexandre.Goossens,Johannes.Smedt,Jan.Vanthienen}@kuleuven.be

Abstract. Operational decisions such as loan or subsidy allocation are taken with high frequency and require a consistent decision quality which decision models can ensure. Decision models can be derived from textual descriptions describing both the decision logic and decision dependencies. Whilst decision models already help with modeling, implementing and automating decisions, the modelling step would still benefit from a (semi)-automated approach. The introduction of ChatGPT and GPT-3 offers opportunities to automatically discover decision dependencies from a given text. This paper evaluates the performance of two approaches that automatically extract decision dependencies from text, namely the best performing version of GPT-3 with a BERT-based approach. An evaluation with 36 experiments with a dataset of real-life cases and various levels of creativity allowed for GPT-3 concludes that theBERT BERT-based approach outperforms GPT-3 on the real-life dataset but that GPT-3 has promising results and requires further investigation.

Keywords: Decision Modeling · NLP · DMN · Decision Requirements

1 Introduction

High decision quality is crucial for certain daily and automatable operational decisions such as loan approvals or grant allocations [19]. To automate such decisions, the Object Management Group (OMG) introduced the Decision Model and Notation (DMN) standard allowing to model, communicate and execute these decisions [16]. A DMN model consists of two parts, one part models the structure of a decision with decision dependencies in so-called Decision Requirement Diagrams (DRD), the other part represents the decision logic behind each decision. One of the ways to represent decision logic are decision tables as they facilitate completeness, consistency and correctness [20].

This work was supported by the Fund for Scientific Research Flanders (project G079519N) and KU Leuven Internal Funds (project C14/19/082).

Understanding the decision structure improves decision comprehension as it simplifies modeling by breaking large decisions into smaller parts, but it involves gathering and analyzing data from regulations, guidelines, and internal documents. Automating this analysis can alleviate its intensity and complexity if information loss is minimized [19].

The recent introduction of Generative Pretrained Transformer (GPT)-3 [2] and ChatGPT[1] and their impressive capabilities raises the question whether these technologies could automatically discover decision structures from a given text without too much loss of decision model quality. Existing efforts in automatic extraction of DRDs from texts fall into pattern-based methods [7,18] and deep learning approaches [9]. Given the limitations of pattern-based techniques and their scalability issues [13,22], this study compares GPT-3 with a single deep learning method. This study investigates the quality of decision dependencies identified by GPT-3 using textual descriptions, addressing the following questions:

1. Can GPT-3 generate DRDs given a textual description?
2. What is the quality of these generated DRDs?
3. How does GPT-3 perform compared to the BERT-based approach that automatically extracts DRDs from texts [9]?

The rest of the paper is structured as follows: Sect. 2 deals with related work about the automatic discovery of DMN models from texts. Next, Sect. 3 deals with the methodology and set-up of the experiment followed by Sect. 4 reporting the results. Sections 5 and 6 respectively discuss the results, the limitations and future work together. Finally, Sect. 7 concludes this paper.

2   Related Work

The automatic extraction of DMN models from texts consists of two sub-tasks where one task is to extract decision dependencies from text and the other is to extract decision logic from text which is considered out of scope for this paper. The authors of [14] propose a pattern-based approach to extract decision tables from structured text in a Semantics Of Business Vocabulary And Rules (SBVR) format [17]. A pattern-based approach to extract decision logic from single unstructured sentences is investigated in [1]. The automatic extraction of DRDs and DMN models with pattern-based approaches with unstructured texts has been studied in [7] and [18] respectively. The use of deep learning approaches for the extraction of DRDs and decision logic has only been studied in [9] where it is concluded that finetuned BERT models perform better compared to fine-tuned Bidirectional LSTM with a Conditional Random Field (Bi-LSTM-CRF) [10] models on Named Entity Recognition (NER) tasks. However, a performance analysis on decision dependency extraction with GPT-3 is still lacking despite having comparable performances on various Natural Language Processing (NLP)

---

[1] https://openai.com/blog/chatgpt.

tasks compared to BERT [2]. GPT-3 models have already been used to generate common sense models outperforming human common sense models [11] and generate conceptual models such Unified Modeling Language (UML) models or Business Process Model and Notation (BPMN) models [8]. In [3], challenges and opportunities of using large language models to extract process models from text are explained.

3   Methodology

The aim is to assess the quality of predicted decision dependencies using GPT-3 and the BERT approach on a dataset of real-life cases gathered from the internet. In this section, Subsect. 3.1 outlines GPT-3's hyperparameters and experimental setup, while Subsect. 3.2 provides an overview of the BERT-based method for automatic DRD extraction from text

3.1   GPT-3 for DRD Extraction from Text

GPT-3 is part of a series large language models trained on a large textual corpus crawled from the internet which performs very well for various NLP tasks [2]. This subsection first explains the chosen hyperparameter values for the experiments with GPT-3 and then explains the experimental set-up with GPT-3. There exist multiple models of GPT-3, some of which are better at having user conversations, completing texts or code[2]. Secondly, the performance of GPT-3 is also determined by parameters which need to be set prior execution. The choice of these hyperparameter values will therefore influence the output that GPT-3 generates.

GPT-3 Hyperparameters. GPT-3 can be considered a more fitting choice regarding decision dependency extraction over ChatGPT since GPT-3 performs better at complex NLP tasks such as text summarization and generation.

According to OpenAI[3] the *da-vinci-003* model is the most capable and best performing GPT-3 model (actually GPT-3.5 model). The temperature parameter adjusts 'creativity'; low values provide stability and fidelity to the text, while higher values introduce randomness and freedom in output. GPT-3 predicts the next word based on assigned probabilities to each word in a set. Low temperature selects the most probable word, while higher values permit less probable words. This trade-off allows more relevant concepts but increases errors or hallucinations. Due to decision modeling's creative and interpretative nature, this parameter significantly affects outcomes. Hence, every text is tested with all temperature values in [0, 0.2, 0.4, 0.6, 0.8, 1]. Finally, the maximum amount of tokens in our experiment has been set to 3,015 tokens which fully covers the length of the provided queries and examples as well as the response of GPT-3.

---

[2] https://platform.openai.com/docs/models/overview.
[3] https://platform.openai.com/docs/models/gpt-3.

Prompt Engineering for DRD Construction With GPT-3. The following questions are asked to GPT-3:

1. *Do you know Decision Model and Notation and can you create a DRD?*
2. *Given a text description you are expected to provide a DRD in Graphviz code. Examples (4 examples):*
   Input: sample text
   Expected Graphviz Output: sample Graphviz output code.
3. *Only provide the expected Decision Requirements Diagram in formatted graphviz code with inputs as ovals and decision as rectangles and arrows going bottom-up from inputs to decisions as shown in the examples. Do not write anything else. Analyze the following text:* insert textual description.

Given GPT-3's increase performance with few-shot learning [2], we offer 4 examples related to pollution, vaccination policies, and Body Mass Index (BMI) risk assessment. GPT-3 can be expected to generate visualization code of a DRD in Graph Visualization Software (Graphviz[4]) well since other works have also produced UML or BPMN models in visual code using GPT-3 [8].

Manual prompt engineering for question 3.1 has been performed following the guidelines laid out in [12,21] ensuring consistently desirable and usable DRD graphs. Note that question 3.1 further specifies the semantics of a DRD, e.g., that inputs should be ovals which is in line with the idea of chain of thought reasoning [21]. GPT-3 was also specified to only provide a Graphviz code as otherwise it tends to provide a long explanation about what the decision is about. The complete prompt can be found in the footnote[5].

3.2   BERT for DRD Extraction from Text

The other approach to extract DRDs from text uses BERT [9]. It involves taking a decision's textual description as input, followed by preprocessing and analysis steps. The outcome includes a DRD and the logical statements in the text. Unlike GPT-3, BERT does not produce Graphviz code here; instead, it is designed for NER tasks. A complete overview of this approach can be found in [9] and the results of the BERT approach are included in Table 2. In short, the approach encompasses these steps:

1. Identify which words refer to the same concepts, e.g., *street* and *road* mean the same and as such *road* is replaced by *street* or the other way around.
2. For each sentence, a fine-tuned BERT classifier automatically determines whether the sentence describes decision dependencies, decision logic or both.
3. A finetuned BERT model predicts for each predicted decision logic sentence, the logical statements present in the sentence. Basically, it returns the IF-THEN parts of a logical statement.

---

[4] https://graphviz.org.
[5] Github link.

4. A finetuned BERT model predicts for each predicted decision dependency sentence what the decisions and inputs are and returns these.
5. Lastly, a tool was developed to correctly build a DRD graph based on this information.

4   Empirical Evaluation

This section is structured as follows: Subsect. 4.1 introduces a dataset of real life decision descriptions. Followed by Subsect. 4.2 explaining the evaluation metrics used to compare the performance of both approaches. Lastly, Subsect. 4.3 reports the results.

4.1   Real Life Decision Dependency Dataset

We use the dataset described in [9] containing six real textual descriptions directly collected from various university and governmental websites such as the Decision Management Community challenges[6], universities and official government websites. These texts describe decision dependencies dealing with various topics such as grant and health support allocation (**Housing Loan Eligibility, Personal Loan Eligibility and Obama Care**), student support eligibility (**Student AID US, Student Support VUB**) and a **Fraud Rating Score** problem. These texts have undergone no changes, except for the removal and replacement of bullet points with "and". The number of words in a textual description varies between 38 and 101 words. An example of such a text is the following dealing with financial student support at a Belgian university:

International students are generally self-supporting or supported by a scholarship. Our financial support is generally limited to Belgian nationals, although there are some exceptions. In order to be eligible for most types of support, you need to meet our general conditions. Our general conditions consist of nationality and academic requirements. We advise all international students to take a close look at the nationality requirements before applying. There may also be additional specific conditions per type of support.

4.2   Evaluation Metrics

Next to the 6 best experiments of [9], 36 experiments are performed (6 texts × 6 temperatures). To evaluate the performance, the same evaluation procedure and metrics, adapted for DRDs, as introduced in [9,18] are used. The golden standard, modeled by an expert, (#gold) is taken directly from [9] and represents the number of input elements and decisions. Next, the predicted and the correctly predicted number of input elements and decisions for each model are respectively reported with *#pred* and *#ok*. This evaluation is performed manually by comparing the predicted DRD with the golden standard modeled by the expert. An

---

[6] https://dmcommunity.org/challenge/.

input element or decision is only deemed correct if the label correctly captures the underlying concept and if the correct shape was given to the element. Finally, the classical classification metrics are reported with Precision ($P = \#ok/\#pred$), Recall ($R = \#ok/\#gold$), and F1-score ($F1 = 2PR/(P + R)$). For decision dependencies, the same evaluation metrics are used. A decision dependency is only deemed correct if the input and decision elements are correctly identified (label and shape) as well as the relation connecting the two.

4.3   Results

When looking at Table 1 with the detailed results, it is interesting to note that BERT is not clearly performing better than the GPT-3 models. However, GPT-3 is regularly performing on par with BERT or even better in the case of **Obama Care** where the BERT approach wrongly classified an input element as a decision which the GPT-3 models did not. The only case in which GPT-3 really performed poorly is the **Fraud Rating Score** which is a technical description of how to calculate a fraud rating score. None of the GPT-3 models were able to correctly identify the relevant concepts, but instead identified a lot of concepts (high number of *#pred* values) and linked them together without a clear reasoning behind it. Regarding the **Student AID US** example, the main reason why the GPT-3 models are not performing on par with the BERT approach is because the golden standard identified *legal resident* and *US Citizen* as two separate input elements whilst GPT-3 merged these two together.

Figures 1 and 2 show the predicted DRDs of the **Student Support VUB example**. Figure 1 is interesting as GPT-3 with a temperature of 0.2 identifies two extra concepts being *International Students* and *Belgian Nationals* and connects it to *Nationality Requirements*. However, it did not make *Nationality Requirements* a rectangle which in that case it should be. The predicted DRD by the BERT approach (see Fig. 2) correctly identified all the decisions, intermediary decisions, and inputs and correctly linked them together in this case.

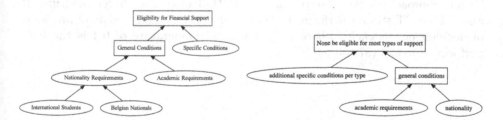

Fig. 1. Predicted DRD by GPT_0.2 for the student support VUB example

Fig. 2. Predicted DRD by BERT for the student support VUB example

Table 2 reports the averages for each analyzed temperature of GPT-3 over all cases as well as the average of the BERT-based approach. When only looking

Table 1. Detailed Results

Source	Model	#words	Decision and Input Data						Decision Dependencies					
			#gold	#pred	#ok	P	R	F1	#gold	#pred	#ok	P	R	F1
Fraud Rating Score	GPT_0	101	5	10	4	40%	80%	53%	4	9	0	0%	0%	0%
	GPT-3_0.2			10	4	40%	80%	53%		9	0	0%	0%	0%
	GPT-3_0.4			10	4	40%	80%	53%		9	3	33%	75%	46%
	GPT-3_0.6			10	4	40%	80%	53%		9	0	0%	0%	0%
	GPT-3_0.8			10	3	30%	60%	40%		8	0	0%	0%	0%
	GPT-3_1			9	2	22%	40%	29%		7	0	0%	0%	0%
	BERT			5	5	100%	100%	100%		4	4	100%	100%	100%
Housing Loan Eligibility	GPT_0	38	8	8	8	100%	100%	100%	7	7	7	100%	100%	100%
	GPT-3_0.2			8	8	100%	100%	100%		7	7	100%	100%	100%
	GPT-3_0.4			8	8	100%	100%	100%		7	7	100%	100%	100%
	GPT-3_0.6			8	8	100%	100%	100%		7	7	100%	100%	100%
	GPT-3_0.8			8	8	100%	100%	100%		7	7	100%	100%	100%
	GPT-3_1			8	8	100%	100%	100%		7	7	100%	100%	100%
	BERT			8	8	100%	100%	100%		7	7	100%	100%	100%
Obama Care	GPT_0	51	6	5	5	100%	83%	91%	5	4	4	100%	80%	89%
	GPT-3_0.2			5	5	100%	83%	91%		4	4	100%	80%	89%
	GPT-3_0.4			5	5	100%	83%	91%		4	4	100%	80%	89%
	GPT-3_0.6			5	5	100%	83%	91%		4	4	100%	80%	89%
	GPT-3_0.8			5	5	100%	83%	91%		4	4	100%	80%	89%
	GPT-3_1			7	5	71%	83%	77%		6	4	67%	80%	73%
	BERT			6	5	83%	83%	83%		8	4	50%	80%	62%
Personal Loan Eligibility	GPT_0	44	8	7	7	100%	88%	93%	7	6	6	100%	86%	92%
	GPT-3_0.2			7	7	100%	88%	93%		6	6	100%	86%	92%
	GPT-3_0.4			7	7	100%	88%	93%		6	6	100%	86%	92%
	GPT-3_0.6			7	7	100%	88%	93%		6	6	100%	86%	92%
	GPT-3_0.8			7	7	100%	88%	93%		6	6	100%	86%	92%
	GPT-3_1			7	7	100%	88%	93%		6	6	100%	86%	92%
	BERT			9	8	89%	100%	94%		8	7	88%	100%	93%
Student AID US	GPT_0	59	6	5	4	80%	67%	73%	5	4	4	100%	80%	89%
	GPT-3_0.2			5	4	80%	67%	73%		4	4	100%	80%	89%
	GPT-3_0.4			5	4	80%	67%	73%		4	4	100%	80%	89%
	GPT-3_0.6			6	4	67%	67%	67%		5	4	80%	80%	80%
	GPT-3_0.8			5	4	80%	67%	73%		4	4	100%	80%	89%
	GPT-3_1			5	4	80%	67%	73%		4	4	100%	80%	89%
	BERT			7	6	86%	100%	92%		6	5	83%	100%	91%
Student support VUB	GPT_0	85	5	5	5	100%	100%	100%	4	4	4	100%	100%	100%
	GPT-3_0.2			7	5	71%	100%	83%		6	4	67%	100%	80%
	GPT-3_0.4			5	5	100%	100%	100%		4	4	100%	100%	100%
	GPT-3_0.6			3	3	100%	60%	75%		2	2	100%	50%	67%
	GPT-3_0.8			4	4	100%	80%	89%		3	3	100%	75%	86%
	GPT-3_1			5	5	100%	100%	100%		4	3	75%	75%	75%
	BERT			5	5	100%	100%	100%		4	4	100%	100%	100%

at the GPT-3 models a temperature of 0.4 yields the best overall results both for decision and input data and decision dependencies. When comparing the BERT approach to the best performing GPT-3 models with temperatures 0 and 0.4, BERT still outperforms GPT-3 in all but one metric namely precision of decision dependencies where GPT-3 with a temperature of 0.4 is the best performing model (87% vs 89 %).

Table 2. Averages of GPT-3 and BERT models over all cases

Model	Decision and Input Data						Decision Dependencies					
	#gold	#pred	#ok	P	R	F1	#gold	#pred	#ok	P	R	F1
Total_GPT-3_0	38	40	33	87%	86%	86%	32	34	25	83%	74%	79%
Total_GPT-3_0.2		42	33	82%	86%	84%		36	25	78%	74%	76%
Total_GPT-3_0.4		40	33	87%	86%	86%		34	28	89%	87%	88%
Total_GPT-3_0.6		39	31	84%	80%	82%		33	23	80%	66%	72%
Total_GPT-3_0.8		39	31	85%	80%	82%		32	24	83%	70%	76%
Total_GPT-3_1		41	31	79%	80%	79%		34	24	74%	70%	72%
Average_BERT		40	37	93%	97%	95%		37	31	87%	97%	91%

5 Discussion

From the results, it is interesting to note that the predicted decision elements by GPT-3 are often correctly identified as relevant elements within a decision context, but GPT-3 still struggles with predicting the decision dependencies which is challenging for humans as well. Despite the query specifically asking GPT-3 to make the decision elements oval, i.e., *Nationality Requirements*, this is not always performed correctly (see *Nationality Requirements* in Fig. 1). Moreover, GPT-3 sometimes exchanges the input elements and decision elements causing it too perform very poorly in the case of **Fraud Rating Score**.

Another interesting result of this experiment is that with higher temperatures, GPT-3 gives itself more creativity resulting in the wrong identification of concepts and returning DRDs where the elements are wrongly connected between one another. In fact, temperatures of 0.4 and lower are, according to the results in Table 2, just the right amount of creativity GPT-3 should be allowed to have to achieve the best results for DRD construction.

A few things need to be remarked about GPT-3 itself. GPT-3 is more likely to understand and link concepts to one another as it has been trained on much more data (approximately 470 times more data compared to BERT) [2,5]. Moreover, the BERT-based approach makes use of a neural net scoring model [4] for coreference resolution which is no longer considered state of the art in contrast to large scale pre-trained language models [15]. In case similar patterns can quickly be learned with the provided examples and a certain leniency is allowed, large language models are recommended [6]. In this case, a human modeler can always provide the final modifications to the discovered DRD. Finally, because there is no way of knowing the exact full knowledge GPT-3 has on a topic, there is also no systematic way of knowing which question formulation and provided examples will maximize the retrieval of the whole knowledge which makes manual prompt engineering needs to be performed [12,21].

In short, it can be concluded that GPT-3 can generate DRDs given a textual description however using higher temperatures (above 0.4) sporadically resulted in the creation of semantically wrong DRDs. The quality of generated DRDs is dependent on the temperature values with the best temperature being 0.4. In this study, all GPT-3 models are outperformed in all but one metric by the BERT-based approach for automatic DRD extraction from texts.

6   Limitations and Future Work

A first limitation is that the evaluation is performed on a rather small dataset of real life cases. We plan to address this in the future by collecting a larger dataset of various real life cases describing decisions. Secondly, given that providing more context and reasoning logic to GPT-3 could improve the results [21], a future study will investigate whether fine-tuning GPT-3 even further can improve the results. As said earlier, it is difficult to know for sure whether a prompt formulation is actually the best possible formulation possible. Also, the examples have been chosen to deal with a variety of topics so that GPT-3 can learn as much as possible from them, however here as well it is difficult to know whether the provided examples are the best possible examples for the expected task. Both previous observations will be investigated further in future work. Next, this study did not include a comparison with GPT-4 as at the time of writing the access to its API was not public yet. The expectations are that GPT-4 will perform even better given that it is trained on more data compared to GPT-3 allowing for multimodal inputs such as pictures which could directly be provided DRD figures instead of Graphviz code and allows for more context and thus more examples. Therefore, an interesting next study would be to investigate whether GPT-4 is better at producing DRDs by only providing Graphviz code, only providing DRD figures or a combination of the two. Lastly, this paper takes the assumption that is better to first model a decision with its structure and logic based on the relevant texts and to automate the execution of a decision using this DMN model next. However, what if the textual descriptions are directly given to GPT-3 and reasoning is done directly with these?

7   Conclusion

Since decisions are described in various textual documents such as regulations and guidelines, the construction of decision models and more specifically decision dependencies is a time-consuming activity. Therefore, this research studied whether GPT-3 can be used for the automatic construction of decision dependency graphs with various levels of 'creativity' or temperatures. A first conclusion is that GPT-3 with low temperatures actually perform well, even though not as good as the BERT-based approach, and as such it seems that GPT-3 or more likely GPT-4 could potentially be used to automatically extract decision dependencies from texts in the future.

References

1. Arco, L., Nápoles, G., Vanhoenshoven, F., Lara, A.L., Casas, G., Vanhoof, K.: Natural language techniques supporting decision modelers. Data Min. Knowl. Disc. **35**(1), 290–320 (2021)
2. Brown, T., et al.: Language models are few-shot learners. Adv. Neural. Inf. Process. Syst. **33**, 1877–1901 (2020)

3. Busch, K., Rochlitzer, A., Sola, D., Leopold, H.: Just tell me: prompt engineering in business process management. In: van der Aa, H., Bork, D., Proper, H.A., Schmidt, R. (eds.) BPMDS EMMSAD 2023. LNBIP, vol. 479, pp. 3–11. Springer, Cham (2023). https://doi.org/10.1007/978-3-031-34241-7_1

4. Clark, K., Manning, C.D.: Deep reinforcement learning for mention-ranking coreference models. arXiv preprint arXiv:1609.08667 (2016)

5. Devlin, J., Chang, M.W., Lee, K., Toutanova, K.: BERT: pre-training of deep bidirectional transformers for language understanding. arXiv preprint arXiv:1810.04805 (2018)

6. Dziri, N., et al.: Faith and fate: limits of transformers on compositionality. arXiv preprint arXiv:2305.18654 (2023)

7. Etikala, V., Van Veldhoven, Z., Vanthienen, J.: Text2Dec: extracting decision dependencies from natural language text for automated DMN decision modelling. In: Del Río Ortega, A., Leopold, H., Santoro, F.M. (eds.) BPM 2020. LNBIP, vol. 397, pp. 367–379. Springer, Cham (2020). https://doi.org/10.1007/978-3-030-66498-5_27

8. Fill, H.G., Fettke, P., Köpke, J.: Conceptual modeling and large language models: impressions from first experiments With ChatGPT. Enterp. Modell. Inf. Syst. Archit. (EMISAJ) Int. J. Conceptual Model. 18, 1–15 (2023). https://doi.org/10.18417/emisa.18.3

9. Goossens, A., De Smedt, J., Vanthienen, J.: Extracting decision model and notation models from text using deep learning techniques. Expert Syst. Appl. 211, 118667 (2023)

10. Huang, Z., Xu, W., Yu, K.: Bidirectional LSTM-CRF models for sequence tagging. arXiv preprint arXiv:1508.01991 (2015)

11. Hwang, J.D., et al.: (Comet-) atomic 2020: on symbolic and neural commonsense knowledge graphs. In: Proceedings of the AAAI Conference on Artificial Intelligence, vol. 35, pp. 6384–6392 (2021)

12. Jojic, A., Wang, Z., Jojic, N.: GPT is becoming a turing machine: here are some ways to program it. arXiv preprint arXiv:2303.14310 (2023)

13. Khurana, D., Koli, A., Khatter, K., Singh, S.: Natural language processing: state of the art, current trends and challenges. Multimed. Tools Appl. 1–32 (2022)

14. Kluza, K., Honkisz, K.: From SBVR to BPMN and DMN models. Proposal of translation from rules to process and decision models. In: Rutkowski, L., Korytkowski, M., Scherer, R., Tadeusiewicz, R., Zadeh, L.A., Zurada, J.M. (eds.) ICAISC 2016. LNCS (LNAI), vol. 9693, pp. 453–462. Springer, Cham (2016). https://doi.org/10.1007/978-3-319-39384-1_39

15. Liu, R., Mao, R., Luu, A.T., Cambria, E.: A brief survey on recent advances in coreference resolution. Artif. Intell. Rev. 1–43 (2023)

16. OMG: Omg: Decision model and notation 1.0 (2015) (2008). https://www.omg.org/spec/DMN/1.0/. Accessed 08 Jan 2022

17. OMG: Omg: Semantics of business vocabulary and rules (2008) (2008). https://www.omg.org/spec/SBVR/1.0. Accessed 13 Mar 2023

18. Quishpi, L., Carmona, J., Padró, L.: Extracting decision models from textual descriptions of processes. In: Polyvyanyy, A., Wynn, M.T., Van Looy, A., Reichert, M. (eds.) BPM 2021. LNCS, vol. 12875, pp. 85–102. Springer, Cham (2021). https://doi.org/10.1007/978-3-030-85469-0_8

19. Vanthienen, J.: Decisions, advice and explanation: an overview and research agenda. In: A Research Agenda for Knowledge Management and Analytics, pp. 149–169. Edward Elgar Publishing (2021)

20. Vanthienen, J., Mues, C., Aerts, A.: An illustration of verification and validation in the modelling phase of KBS development. Data Knowl. Eng. **27**(3), 337–352 (1998)
21. Wei, J., et al.: Chain of thought prompting elicits reasoning in large language models. arXiv preprint arXiv:2201.11903 (2022)
22. Wolf, T., et al.: Transformers: state-of-the-art natural language processing. In: Proceedings of the 2020 Conference on Empirical Methods in Natural Language Processing: System Demonstrations, pp. 38–45 (2020)

A Requirements Study on Model Repositories for Digital Twins in Construction Engineering

Philipp Zech[1]([⊠])(iD), Georg Fröch[2], and Ruth Breu[1]

[1] Department of Computer Science, University of Innsbruck, Tyrol, Austria
{philipp.zech,ruth.breu}@uibk.ac.at
[2] University of Innsbruck, Unit of Construction Management and Tunneling, Tyrol, Austria
georg.froech@uibk.ac.at

Abstract. Building information modeling is becoming the preferred tool-assisted methodology in civil and construction engineering for the design, management, and creation of digital replicas of buildings. However, current tool support for creating and managing these *twins* is limited as of lacking interoperability at the model level. Yet, the Industry foundation classes describe a standardized format for exchanging models and data of buildings and bears a strong resemblance to the class- and object-based nature of the Unified modeling language. From this resemblance, we postulate the application of model-driven engineering for establishing a model repository as an open collaboration platform in Building information modeling. Based on our experience from ongoing and concluded interdisciplinary research projects in civil and construction engineering and computer science, in this paper, we seminally elicit requirements for such a model repository.

Keywords: Model repositories · Digital twins · Building information modeling (BIM) · BIM repository

1 Introduction

Building information modeling (BIM), the holistic modeling of a building and its assets has attracted a lot of attention recently. BIM postulates to move away from plain 2D/3D CAD models for the benefit of introducing a tool-supported process for the creation and management of digital representations of physical and functional characteristics of built assets along their life cycle. This vision of BIM exhibits a strong resemblance to the notion of a digital twin (DT) [22], a model-based, virtual replica of a cyber-physical system (CPS) with bidirectional data exchange among both [13]. A fractured delivery landscape in civil and construction engineering, however, drastically stymies the successful implementation of BIM along multiple dimensions [6]. This stymie palpably epitomizes in a lack of model federation, and hence, tool interoperability as of repeated media disruptions at the model level [6]. In this context, the Industry foundation classes (IFC) [15] serves as a universally accepted standard for the exchange and sharing of models and data. Hence, BIM and IFC are crucial in fostering model-based collaboration for information exchange. To attain this benefit, repositories for collaborative model federation are vital. However, at present, such repositories are absent which we attribute to the absence of dedicated requirements in this regard.

Model repositories facilitate collaborative work in model-driven engineering [8] (c.f. Eclipse CDO [27], Neo4EMF [4], MONDO [12], Collabora [16], or Chronsphere [14]). These repositories either provide generic, yet limited, modeling support [4,16,27] or are tailored toward specific industry requirements and are thus not *DT-ready* as they only consider a DT's manifestation by its design models but no runtime models or data [31]. According to Grieves and Vickers, DTs comprise [13] (i) a *virtual instance*, i.e., the models which replicate the CPS, (ii) a *physical* (or product) *instance*, i.e., the CPS, and (iii) *interchanged data and connections*, or *twinning*, between the virtual and physical instance. Per Grieves and Vickers' definition and our introductory discussion, we define *DT-readiness* for a model repository against Bordeleau et al.'s challenges in model-driven DT engineering [7] as:

1. The integration of heterogeneous models that address the different aspects and domains of the CPS.
2. The synchronization of virtual and physical replicas by bidirectional data exchange.
3. The co-development, management, and evolution of the virtual replica alongside the physical asset by teams of domain engineers.

A model repository for DTs has to consider both static *and* dynamic models, i.e., design *and* runtime models, and accompanying data. Conquering this fundamental limitation of only federating design models is the central challenge in conceptualizing model-based DT repositories [7].

We investigate model repositories that address models and data [31] as architectural backbones for BIM-based DTs. Specifically, we identify *essential requirements* that a model repository must meet to be DT-ready. These requirements are derived from the underlying problem context of our study, namely the construction and operation of DTs in civil and construction engineering. Given these requirements, we then infer the necessary *technical features*. Our study is based on our experience gathered through completed and ongoing interdisciplinary research projects in civil and construction engineering and computer science over the last years. In these projects, we collaborate with construction industry stakeholders throughout all phases of the building's life cycle, including prime operators, energy and lighting planners, subsurface engineers, building contractors, and building operators. Numerous project-*internal* and -*external* requirements engineering and analysis workshops, e.g., under the auspices of "Digital findet Stadt" [25], were conducted over the last years (late 2021 until early 2023) to investigate and confirm the elicited requirements.

Organization. Section 2 outlines the problem context of our study. Sect. 3 infers necessary requirements and features for a model repository for BIM-based DTs. Sect. 4 discusses our contributions and positions it concerning related work. We conclude in Sect. 5.

2   Problem Context

The following interdisciplinary projects in civil and construction engineering and computer science constitute the basis for eliciting the proposed requirements (c.f. Sect. 3).

BIM2BEM-Flow [5] (B2BF) establishes integrated Building energy modeling (BEM) workflows using a property server to add energy-efficiency features to BIM models. Incompatibilities between BIM and BEM tools require model transformations given tool mappings. MTBim [21] (MTB) unifies building and medicinal technology planning by integrating medical device attributes into BIM models. Tool mappings translate the model to IFC to establish a single source of truth for construction and Computer-aided facility management (CAFM). SensorBIM [23] (SBIM) integrated modeling and optimization of building design and control by instantiating a DT from IFC models. Energy simulations during early planning and design phases were used to optimize the design (c.f., variability modeling and product line engineering (PLE)). During operation, the DT governs the monitoring and control of the building. TeamBuilding [28] (TB) provided a monitoring and decision-support infrastructure regarding the energy efficiency of shared buildings. BIM models function as operational models for CAFM, necessitating model transformations to accommodate CAFM software. TIM [29] develops computerized technologies for underground construction on a vast scale. Integration and federation of geology, construction, subsurface infrastructure, design, control and monitoring models is required calling for property management, analogous to BIM2BEM-Flow [5] and MTBim [21]. *As-is* modeling must optimize design, monitoring, and control models in response to changing soil conditions. TwinLight [30] (TL) aims to enhance the workflow of BIM2BEM-Flow [5] by incorporating artificial lighting and shading planning thereby enabling the preconfiguration of building systems from BIM models. Table 1 summarizes these projects by grouping use-cases (UCX) and associated actors in correlation with motivating projects. Common to all projects is their dependence on a unified digital model of the building as the common unit of collaboration.

2.1   Model Repository Landscape

From a model repository perspective, DT engineering is both novel and unique by comprising (i) a heterogeneous design scenario, (ii) a data warehouse scenario, and (iii) a runtime scenario where models meet data [31] as outlined in Fig. 1. These aspects yield distinct context characteristics (CX) as elaborated in the following.

Table 1. Use cases from the AECO perspective as motivated by projects.

Use case		B2BF	MTB	SBIM	TB	TIM	TL	Actor(s)
UC1	Building system control			×	×	×	×	Operator(s), control engineers
UC2	Building design modeling and evolution	×	×	×	×	×	×	Planner(s), designer(s)
UC3	Energy flow modeling and simulation	×			×		×	Designer(s), building physicist(s), data and control engineer(s)
UC4	Asset life cycle management		×		×	×	×	Planner(s) and operator(s)
UC5	Lighting modeling and simulation	×					×	Designer(s), data and control engineer(s)
UC6	Building operation and maintenance		×	×	×	×	×	Operator(s)
UC7	Establishing a unified digital model and model views	×	×	×	×	×	×	Designer(s) and control engineer(s)
UC8	Building system monitoring			×	×	×	×	Operator(s)
UC9	Building operation optimization	×		×	×	×	×	Operator(s), building physicist(s), control and data engineers
UC10	Property management	×	×			×	×	Planner(s), designer(s), control engineer(s)
UC11	PLE and variability modeling	×		×		×	×	Planner(s), designer(s), control engineer(s)
UC12	Tool mappings	×	×			×	×	Planner(s) and designer(s)

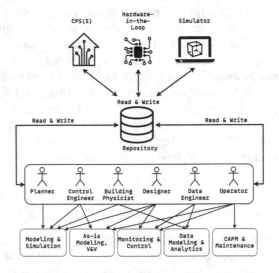

Fig. 1. Repository landscape in the context of BIM-based DTs.

The amount and quality of aggregated data [C6] for monitoring [C11] during building operations depends on the available data sources in the building. The heterogeneity of the design scenario [C1] results from different tools and modeling formalisms on the part of involved stakeholders [C3]. The repository has to abstract this heterogeneity away by supporting multi-paradigm modeling [32].

The life cycle of modern buildings nowadays spans decades, introducing *long-living* models [C10] that perambulate technological shifts [C2]. During planning and design, use cases comprise product variability modeling [C7], and simulating and optimizing [C5] potential manifestations under different conditions. During construction, the repository serves to update models from data using *as-is* modeling [C4]. By describing the ideal of the CPS, the DT further is used for verification and validation (V&V) [C8] of the CPS late during the construction and throughout the operation phase.

Finally, during operation, the repository enables the integration of models and data [C9] for monitoring, optimizing, and controlling [C5] building systems [C11] from accumulated data. The repository thus provides element history traces for root-cause and impact analysis, and auditing [C8]. Eventually, the DT represents the operating model for the physical instance with *models controlling the CPS at runtime* [C12] (c.f. [3, 24]).

Table 2 summarizes the just discussed model repository landscape by a list of its characteristics [C1-C12] as motivated from Table 1 and depicted in Fig. 1.

Table 2. Application context with associated use cases.

Context		Use case(s)
C1	Heterogeneous Model Federation	Model conversions to establish a unified model and model views [UC7]; Tool mappings to establish integrated workflows [UC12]
C2	Technology Shifts of a CPS	Building operation and maintenance [UC6]; Building model and physical asset life cycle management [UC4]
C3	Multiple Stakeholders	Model conversions to establish a unified model and model views [UC7]; Property management for building model extension [UC10]
C4	As-is Modeling	Building design modeling and evolution [UC2]; Building model and physical asset life cycle management [UC4]
C5	Simulation, HiL, and Optimization	Energy flow and usage modeling and simulation [UC3]; Artificial and natural building lighting modeling and simulation [UC5]; Building operation optimization [UC9]
C6	Data Aggregation, Integration, and Provisioning	Building system control [UC1]; Building system monitoring [UC8]; Building operation optimization [UC9]
C7	Variability Modeling of a CPS	Building design modeling and evolution [UC2]; Product line engineering and variability modeling [UC11]
C8	Traceability and Auditing	Building design modeling and evolution [UC2]; Building model and physical asset life cycle management [UC4]
C9	Models and Data	Energy flow and usage modeling and simulation [UC3]; Artificial and natural building lighting modeling and simulation [UC5]; Building operation and maintenance [UC6]; Building operation optimization [UC9]
C10	Longevity of Models	Building model and physical asset life cycle management [UC4]; Building operation and maintenance [UC6]
C11	Monitoring and Control of a CPS	Building system control [UC1]; Building system monitoring [UC8]
C12	Models@runtime	Energy flow and usage modeling and simulation [UC3]; Artificial and natural building lighting modeling and simulation [UC5]; Building system control [UC1]; Building system monitoring [UC8]; Building design modeling and evolution [UC2]

3   Requirements and Features from Context

This section is devoted to eliciting requirements (FX) for a model repository for engineering and operating DTs in the AECO community. Sect. 3.2 establishes corresponding technical features. Our discussion focuses on domain-specific, functional requirements that are necessary to deliver the aforesaid use-cases (c.f., Sect. 2 and Table 1) thus leaving out any non-functional requirements, e.g., data granularity, access, or performance.

3.1   Requirements from Context

We tackle model heterogeneity [C1] with a homogenous metamodel [R1] and a *single unified model* (SUM; c.f. Atkinson et al. [1]) which supports the definition of views and tool mappings [R10]. The use of a homogenous metamodel further allows for capturing technological shifts [C2]. The SUM which evolves and grows during the lifetime of the DT entails the repository to offer the necessary scalability to handle large models [R11].

Being built with a claim for longevity [C10], over the lifetime of a DT, multiple stakeholders [C3] require changing and comparing different manifestations during variability modeling and PLE [C7]. Model versioning and evolution [R2] with model branching and merging [R3] allow for this. Since merging requires the comparison of model states, evaluating a query on any model version on any branch [R5] is crucial. As to concurrent access [R12] (c.f. [C3]), model and model query consistency guarantees [R13] are imperative [10]. Furthermore, versioning models and their elements yields element history traces [R6] for traceability and auditing [C8].

DTs use for simulation and optimization [C5], model-based monitoring and control [C11], and model-driven data analysis [C9] demands aggregation and integration of external data about the CPS in the repository [C6]. This allows for *as-is* model curation [C4] by tracking deviations from the initial design. The repository addresses this by bidirectional communication with the CPS [R7] for aggregating and integrating data with models in the repository [R4] by manipulating models [R9] at runtime [C12].

To maintain a complete representation of the virtual instance (c.f. Sect. 1), the repository additionally requires means for versioning simulation and optimization models, and other documents, e.g., BIM issues. The code- and text-based nature of such artifacts renders them incompatible with our model-based approach, yet also requires nothing more than file-based versioning [R8].

Table 3 summarizes the requirements for the proposed model repository alongside the relevant application context. Intriguingly, for the AECO domain, the requirements from Table 3 subsume key requirements for dedicated BIM repositories [11].

3.2   Features from Requirements

We tackle model heterogeneity using semantic modeling as the modeling backbone [F1] of our repository. This readily yields a SUM by linking different seman-

Table 3. Requirements as prompted by the application context (c.f. Table 2).

Requirement		Context
R1	Homogenous Metamodel	C1-C3, C10
R2	Model Versioning and Evolution	C10, C8
R3	Model Branching and Merging	C7
R4	Integration of Models and Data	C4-C6, C9, C11
R5	Branch- and Version-independent Queries	C8
R6	Per-Element History Traces	C8
R7	Bidirectional Communication APIs	C9, C11
R8	File-based Versioning	C5
R9	Model Manipulation and Execution	C4, C11, C12
R10	Single Unified Model, Model Views and Model Mappings	C1, C8
R11	Scalability in Model Size	C10, C12
R12	Concurrent Access to Models and Data	C3, C9
R13	Consistency of Models and Query Results	C3, C8, C9

tic models into one large model. As to the considerable size of a SUM, the repository provides a model view engine [F14] to enable the configuration of viewpoints on the SUM. In addition, it offers a model mapping engine [F15] for model-based tool integration (MBTI) [17] to connect incompatible tools. The graph-based nature of semantic models naturally leads to a per-element persistency solution [F2]. In-memory model management [F5] further merits performance and scalability.

Element versioning and as-is modeling require model evolution and alignment [F3] which is implemented by a model execution engine [F13] for (i) auto-updating models, and (ii) model-based monitoring and control. Product variability modeling and PLE require branching [F4] and semi-automated merging [F6]. Model agility and independence are guaranteed with a full branching approach where a complete copy of the model is created.

Consistency and integrity mechanisms [F7] are necessary to assure the provisioning of consistent views on both static and dynamic and historical data [F9] for change-tracking, auditing, and data analysis. By linking runtime data with the SUM we deliver a knowledge base that is accessed via a dedicated API [F8] to provision both historic and real-time as well as static and dynamic data about the physical instance. The therefore necessary bidirectional connection to a physical asset dictates the need for an IoT API [F11]. Along with this API, the repository embeds a data warehouse to provide data-as-a-service [F10] for efficiently aggregating integrating, and provisioning large quantities of data.

As for building models, also the aforesaid code- and text-based artifacts require versioning along the life cycle of the DT. Our repository delivers this requirement by embedding an off-the-shelf, versioning file system [F12].

Figure 2 summarizes our overall process of inferring (i) requirements (c.f. Table 3) from the problem context (c.f. Sect. 2) and (ii) technical features that deliver these very requirements.

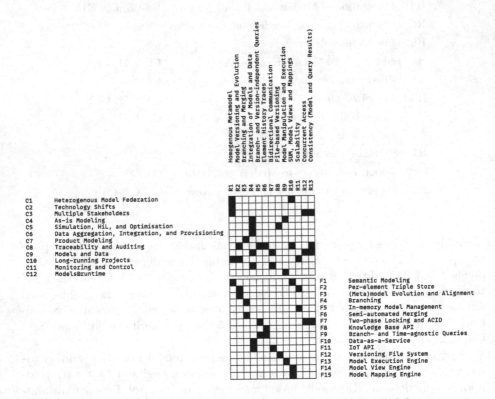

Fig. 2. Traceability matrices between context, requirements, and features.

4   Discussion and Positioning Concerning Related Work

To the best of our knowledge, our work is the first to empirically investigate requirements and features for a model repository for engineering and operating DTs. Although there already exist multiple model repositories [4,12,16,27], none of these solutions is DT-ready as they all lack the integration of models and data. This also applies to Lehner et al.'s recent proposal for a reference architecture for leveraging model repositories for DTs [19].

Recently, two BIM-specific repositories have been proposed. bimserver.org [2] provides an EMF-based model repository for IFC, LBDServer [20] implements a hub for linking building data. Yet, none of these proposals is DT-ready as of not addressing the conflation of models and data [31].

In face of existing requirements studies for engineering and operating DTs [9,18,26], we can identify a somewhat overlap. Durão et al. similarly mention real-time data integration or data warehousing efficiency [9]. Lehner et al. mention bidirectional synchronization, real-time behavior, or convergence between the virtual and physical instance [18]. Steindl and Kastner identify data heterogeneity, semantic richness, or data warehousing [26]. However, none of these studies eventually identifies the need for a platform to enable multi-domain *and* -stakeholder collaboration along the complete life cycle of the CPS.

4.1   Threats to Validity of Identified Requirements

Our study is subject to issues that threaten its validity, specifically, the internal and external validity of identified requirements, resulting features, and a general threat of bias by our requirements. We argue however that these threats are properly tackled as

1. our experience does not rely on a single project only but instead multiple projects [5,21,23,28–30],
2. all projects are interdisciplinary by tightly collaborating with civil and construction engineers from both academia and industry over all phases of a building, and
3. apart from numerous project-*internal*, we held multiple project-*external* requirements engineering and analysis workshops from late 2021 to early 2023, e.g., under the auspices of "Digital findet Stadt" [25], with non-project-affiliated members, to assure the validity of our results.

The tight interaction and communication with civil and construction engineers, and industry stakeholders establishes valid cause-effect relationships for inferring practically relevant requirements, motivated from joint projects [5,21,23,28–30].

5   Conclusion

We presented a requirements' elicitation study for a model repository for engineering and operating DTs in the AECO domain. Crucially, our analysis is founded on multiple years of experience from finished and ongoing interdisciplinary research projects in civil and construction engineering, and computer science. Given these requirements, we further identified necessary technical features. By capitalizing on semantic modeling and linked data our repository however is not limited to the AECO domain only. Given that the models of a virtual replica can be formalized using a semantic model which usually is the case our repository can manage this very virtual replica.

Our next steps comprise the prototypical implementation of our proposed model repository for engineering and operating DTs along the established requirements.

Acknowledgments. This research has received funding from the FFG [5,21,29,30], Interreg [23], and the Office for Economic Development Tyrol [28].

References

1. Atkinson, C., Tunjic, C.: A deep view-point language and framework for projective modeling. Inf. Syst. **101**, 101440 (2021)
2. Beetz, J., van Berlo, L., de Laat, R., van den Helm, P.: Bimserver.org-an open source IFC model server. In: Proceedings of the CIP W78 Conference, p. 8 (2010)
3. Bencomo, N., Götz, S., Song, H.: Models@run.time: a guided tour of the state of the art and research challenges. Softw. Syst. Model. **18**(5), 3049–3082 (2019)
4. Benelallam, A., Gómez, A., Sunyé, G., Tisi, M., Launay, D.: Neo4EMF, a scalable persistence layer for EMF models. In: Cabot, J., Rubin, J. (eds.) ECMFA 2014. LNCS, vol. 8569, pp. 230–241. Springer, Cham (2014). https://doi.org/10.1007/978-3-319-09195-2_15
5. BIM2BEM-Flow (2021). https://projekte.ffg.at/projekt/4396767. Accessed 20 June 2023
6. Boje, C., Guerriero, A., Kubicki, S., Rezgui, Y.: Towards a semantic construction digital twin: directions for future research. Autom. Constr. **114**, 103179 (2020)
7. Bordeleau, F., Combemale, B., Eramo, R., van den Brand, M., Wimmer, M.: Towards model-driven digital twin engineering: current opportunities and future challenges. In: Babur, Ö., Denil, J., Vogel-Heuser, B. (eds.) ICSMM 2020. CCIS, vol. 1262, pp. 43–54. Springer, Cham (2020). https://doi.org/10.1007/978-3-030-58167-1_4
8. Di Rocco, J., Di Ruscio, D., Iovino, L., Pierantonio, A.: Collaborative repositories in model-driven engineering [software technology]. IEEE Softw. **32**(3), 28–34 (2015)
9. Durão, L.F.C.S., Haag, S., Anderl, R., Schützer, K., Zancul, E.: Digital twin requirements in the context of industry 4.0. In: Chiabert, P., Bouras, A., Noël, F., Ríos, J. (eds.) PLM 2018. IAICT, vol. 540, pp. 204–214. Springer, Cham (2018). https://doi.org/10.1007/978-3-030-01614-2_19
10. Eswaran, K.P., Gray, J.N., Lorie, R.A., Traiger, I.L.: The notions of consistency and predicate locks in a database system. Commun. ACM **19**(11), 624–633 (1976)
11. Fadeyi, M.O.: The role of building information modeling (BIM) in delivering the sustainable building value (2017)
12. Gómez, A., et al.: Scalable modeling technologies in the wild: an experience report on wind turbines control applications development. Softw. Syst. Model. **19**(5), 1229–1261 (2020)
13. Grieves, M., Vickers, J.: Digital twin: mitigating unpredictable, undesirable emergent behavior in complex systems. In: Kahlen, F.-J., Flumerfelt, S., Alves, A. (eds.) Transdisciplinary Perspectives on Complex Systems, pp. 85–113. Springer, Cham (2017). https://doi.org/10.1007/978-3-319-38756-7_4
14. Haeusler, M., Trojer, T., Kessler, J., Farwick, M., Nowakowski, E., Breu, R.: Chronosphere: a graph-based EMF model repository for it landscape models. Softw. Syst. Model. **18**(6), 3487–3526 (2019)
15. Industry Foundation Classes (IFC) for data sharing in the construction and facility management industries - Part 1: Data schema. Standard, International Organization for Standardization, Geneva, CH (2018)
16. Izquierdo, J.L.C., Cabot, J.: Collaboro: a collaborative (meta) modeling tool. PeerJ Comput. Sci. **2**, e84 (2016)

17. Kapsammer, E., Reiter, T., Schwinger, W.: Model-based tool integration-state of the art and future perspectives. In: Proceedings of the 3rd International Conference on Cybernetics and Information Technologies, Systems and Applications (CITSA 2006) (2006)
18. Lehner, D., et al.: Digital twin platforms: requirements, capabilities, and future prospects. IEEE Softw. **39**(2), 53–61 (2022)
19. Lehner, D., Wolny, S., Mazak-Huemer, A., Wimmer, M.: Towards a reference architecture for leveraging model repositories for digital twins. In: 2020 25th IEEE International Conference on Emerging Technologies and Factory Automation (ETFA), pp. 1077–1080. IEEE (2020)
20. Malcolm, A., Werbrouck, J., Pauwels, P.: LBD server: visualising building graphs in web-based environments using semantic graphs and GlTF-models. In: Eloy, S., Leite Viana, D., Morais, F., Vieira Vaz, J. (eds.) Formal Methods in Architecture. ASTI, pp. 287–293. Springer, Cham (2021). https://doi.org/10.1007/978-3-030-57509-0_26
21. MTBim (2022)
22. Ozturk, G.B.: Digital twin research in the AECO-FM industry. J. Build. Eng. **40**, 102730 (2021)
23. SensorBIM (2014). https://www.sensorbim.eud. Accessed 20 June 2023
24. Seybold, D., Domaschka, J., Rossini, A., Hauser, C.B., Griesinger, F., Tsitsipas, A.: Experiences of models@run-time with EMF and CDO. In: Proceedings of the 2016 ACM SIGPLAN International Conference on Software Language Engineering, pp. 46–56. ACM (2016)
25. findet Stadt, D.: (2020). https://www.digitalfindetstadt.at. Accessed 20 June 2023
26. Steindl, G., Kastner, W.: Semantic microservice framework for digital twins. Appl. Sci. **11**(12), 5633 (2021)
27. Stepper, E.: CDO model repository (2010)
28. TeamBuilding (2020). https://team-building.tirol. Accessed 20 June 2023
29. TIM (2021). https://projekte.ffg.at/projekt/3368110. Accessed 20 June 2023
30. TwinLight (2022). https://nachhaltigwirtschaften.at/de/sdz/projekte/twinlight.php. Accessed 20 June 2023
31. Van Den Brand, M., Cleophas, L., Gunasekaran, R., Haverkort, B., Negrin, D.A.M., Muctadir, H.M.: Models meet data: Challenges to create virtual entities for digital twins. In: 2021 ACM/IEEE International Conference on Model Driven Engineering Languages and Systems Companion (MODELS-C), pp. 225–228. IEEE (2021)
32. Vangheluwe, H., De Lara, J., Mosterman, P.J.: An introduction to multi-paradigm modelling and simulation. In: Proceedings of the AIS 2002 conference (AI, Simulation and Planning in High Autonomy Systems), Lisboa, Portugal, pp. 9–20 (2002)

Joint Dynamic Resource Allocation and Trajectory Optimization for UAV-Assisted Mobile Edge Computing in Internet of Vehicles

Runji Li and Haifeng Sun[(✉)] [iD]

School of Computer Science and Technology, Southwest University of Science and Technology, Mianyang 621010, China
dr_hfsun@163.com

Abstract. Computation offloading in Mobile Edge Computing (MEC) represents a key technology for the future of the Internet of Vehicles (IoV), reducing the time and energy consumption of vehicles for computation tasks, while Unmanned Aerial Vehicles (UAVs) equipped with computation resources can act as aerial based stations to provide computation offloading services to vehicles moving on the road. In this paper, a joint dynamic resource allocation and UAV trajectory optimization scheme is proposed. In the scheme, an UAV is deployed with an edge server to execute the partially offloaded computation tasks from multiple vehicles. The goal of the problem is to maximize the total computation workload while minimizing the energy consumption of all vehicles by jointly optimizing the computation frequency, the wireless transmission power, the task offloading decisions of vehicles, as well as the flight angle of the UAV in each time slot. Since the problem is non-convex in continuous action space, we consider the Twin Delayed Deep Deterministic (TD3) policy gradient algorithm to solve the problem. Experimental results demonstrate the effectiveness of the TD3 policy gradient algorithm in the proposed optimization scheme in terms of the convergence speed and the system reward.

Keywords: Mobile Edge Computing · computation offloading · unmanned aerial vehicles · dynamic resource allocation · trajectory optimization

1 Introduction

Mobile Edge Computing (MEC) is an energy-efficient method to enhance the computation capability in proximity to mobile devices [1,2]. MEC integrates functions such as collection, computation and storage, and sinks these functions to the edge of networks, making server nodes closer to users [8]. Offloading tasks

This work was supported in part by NSFC of China under Grant 62261051.

M. Sellami et al. (Eds.): CoopIS 2023, LNCS 14353, pp. 470–479, 2024.
https://doi.org/10.1007/978-3-031-46846-9_28

from vehicles to edge nodes is a promising scheme to improve vehicle network performance and quality of experience (QoE) of applications [6]. In recent years, unmanned aerial vehicles (UAVs) with computation equipment is more used as mobile edge computing servers. [5]. When the UAV assists the vehicle to complete the computation task, it will cause the extra costs of delay and energy for transmitting the task to the UAV [4].

Recently, some existing literature has studied dynamic resource allocation and trajectory optimization problems in UAV-assisted mobile edge computing networks. Zhao *et al.* established a computation offloading scenario supporting Software Defined Network (SDN) and deployed the SDN controller to obtain the real-time positions of vehicles and the UAV [13]. Wang *et al.* considered using the Road Side Unit (RSU) as a collector of global information [9]. Zhang *et al.* considered the load balancing of the computation resources at the edge servers, with the objective to minimize the processing delay of all the computation tasks [12]. But these works only considered the instantaneous changing positions of vehicles. Yang *et al.* proposed a vehicle motion-aware task offloading scheme, which jointly optimized the task offloading decision and the computation resource allocation [11]. Wang *et al.* considered the time-varying channel state in an UAV-assisted MEC system, and jointly optimized the user scheduling, the UAV trajectory and the resource allocation [10]. But in these works, the MEC server only serves one user at the same time and the flight trajectory of the UAV is only affected by the mobility of the current service user. Peng *et al.* formulated a path planning problem to optimize the weighted amount of offloading task bits and the energy consumption [7]. But these works only optimized the fixed hovering point of the UAV, without considering the flight trajectory of the UAV.

In this paper, a joint dynamic resource allocation and trajectory optimization scheme for UAV-assisted computation task offloading is proposed. The main contributions of this paper are as follows:

1) An MEC system model of multi-vehicle and a single UAV is investigated. The UAV equipped with an MEC server is employed to assist partial task offloading of vehicles. During the offloading period, the time-varying channel influence caused by the mobility of multiple vehicles and the UAV is considered.
2) A joint dynamic resource allocation and UAV flight trajectory scheme is proposed for the optimization problem by maximizing the amount of total system computing workload while minimizing the energy consumption of all vehicles. The non-convex problem is then expressed as a Markov decision process (MDP) problem.
3) Due to the high complexity and the continuous action space of the MDP problem, a computation offloading algorithm based on TD3 policy gradient algorithm is designed to solve the problem.

The rest of this paper is described as follows. Section 2 describes the system model. Section 3 describes the employment of the TD3 policy gradient algorithm for solving the proposed problem. Section 4 performs the numerical experiments. We conclude our work in Sect. 5.

2   System Model

In this section, a dynamic application scenario consisting of multiple vehicles moving on the ground and an UAV equipped with an MEC server is established. As shown in Fig. 1, an UAV is deployed with an edge server, and can provide offloading services for multiple vehicles traveling on the road at a constant speed and each of which generate computation tasks in each time slot.

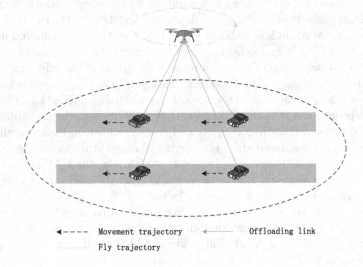

Fig. 1. System model.

Let the amount of vehicles is K, $k \in \mathcal{K} = \{1, 2, ..., K\}$. Suppose each vehicle is traveling on a straight road at a constant velocity V_v, and the time is assumed to be discretized into T time slots, indexed by $t \in \mathcal{T} = \{1, 2, ..., T\}$ with a time slot length τ. Since each time slot is small, the position of the vehicle and the UAV in each time slot is assumed to be unchanged. We consider a three-dimensional Cartesian coordinate system to describe the positions of the vehicles and the UAV. The UAV flies at a constant altitude H and a constant speed V_u. Therefore, in the time slot t, the position of the UAV can be denoted as $q_u[t] = (x_u[t], y_u[t], H)$, and the position of the vehicle k can be recorded as $q_k[t] = (x_k[t], y_k[t], 0)$. Assuming that the flight angle of the UAV is $\beta[t]$ in the time slot t, the horizontal and vertical coordinates of the UAV after a flight with a time slot τ can be expressed respectively as:

$$x_u[t + 1] = \tau v_u \cos(\beta[t]) + x_u[t], \tag{1}$$

$$y_u[t + 1] = \tau v_u \sin(\beta[t]) + y_u[t]. \tag{2}$$

Supposing in each time slot, each vehicle generates only one computation task. Denote $\lambda_k[t]$ as the amount of task bits of the task k and $c_k[t] \in [0, 1]$ as the task partition ratio, then each computation task will be divided into two disjoint parts. One part $c_k[t]\lambda_k[t]$ is executed locally, and the other part $(1 - c_k[t])\lambda_k[t]$ is offloaded to the UAV for computation.

2.1 Queuing Model

Consider establishing two task buffers at each vehicle, where Q_k^{loc} stores task bits for local processing and Q_k^{off} stores task bits for offloading. Denote $B_k^{loc}[t]$ as the amount of task bits which have been completed locally by the vehicle k and $B_k^{off}[t]$ as the amount of task bits which have been offloaded to the UAV in the time slot t. The corresponding evolution equations of Q_k^{loc} and Q_k^{off} can be represented as:

$$Q_k^{loc}[t+1] = [Q_k^{loc}[t] - B_k^{loc}[t]]^+ + c_k[t]\lambda_k[t], \tag{3}$$

$$Q_k^{off}[t+1] = [Q_k^{off}[t] - B_k^{off}[t]]^+ + (1 - c_k[t])\lambda_k[t], \tag{4}$$

where $[x]^+ = \max\{x, 0\}$.

2.2 Computation Model

For each time slot, the vehicle keeps computing the task bits at a constant computation frequency throughout the time slot. Denote $f_k[t]$ as the computation frequency of the vehicle k in the time slot t, and F_k be the maximum computation frequency of the vehicle k. In addition, the amount of CPU cycles required by the on-board unit to compute a primitive bit is expressed as w. Therefore, the amount of task bits completed locally at the vehicle k in the time slot t can be expressed as:

$$B_k^{loc}[t] = \frac{\tau f_k[t]}{w}. \tag{5}$$

The energy consumption of the vehicle k to compute these task bits can be expressed as:

$$E_k^{loc}[t] = \tau \gamma_u [f_k[t]]^3, \tag{6}$$

where γ_u is the effective capacitance coefficient.

2.3 Communication Model

In our model, we use the frequency division multiple access (FDMA) scheme for communication between the UAV and the vehicles on the road. The distance between the vehicle k and the UAV in the time slot t is expressed as:

$$d_k[t] = \sqrt{(x_k[t] - x_u[t])^2 + (y_k[t] - y_u[t])^2 + H^2}. \tag{7}$$

The channel power gain from the vehicle k to the UAV in the time slot t is expressed as [3]:

$$g_k[t] = h_k[t]g_0\left(\frac{d_0}{d_k[t]}\right)^\theta, \tag{8}$$

where g_0 is the path loss coefficient, θ is the path loss index, $h_k[t]$ is the small scale Rayleigh fading coefficient between the vehicle k and the UAV in the time slot t, and d_0 is the reference distance.

For each time slot, the vehicle offloads computation task bits to the UAV with constant wireless transmission power in the whole time slot. Set $p_k[t]$ as the transmission power of the vehicle k in the time slot t, and P_k is the maximum transmission power of the vehicle k. Due to the mobility of vehicles and the UAV, the channel gain will change with time, and the data transmission rate will also change accordingly. The time-varying transmission rate can be expressed as:

$$r_k[t] = \frac{W}{K} \log_2(1 + \frac{p_k[t]g_k[t]}{\sigma_0^2}), \tag{9}$$

where W is the bandwidth, σ_0^2 is the noise power of the UAV. Then the amount of task bits offloaded by the vehicle to the UAV within a time slot can be expressed as:

$$B_k^{off}[t] = \tau \cdot r_k[t] = \tau \cdot \frac{W}{K} \log_2(1 + \frac{p_k[t]g_k[t]}{\sigma_0^2}). \tag{10}$$

The energy consumption generated by the vehicle transmitting these task bits can be expressed as:

$$E_k^{off}[t] = \tau p_k[t]. \tag{11}$$

Thus, the total computation workload and energy consumption of the vehicle k in the time slot t can be expressed respectively as:

$$B_k[t] = B_k^{loc}[t] + B_k^{off}[t], \tag{12}$$

$$E_k[t] = E_k^{loc}[t] + E_k^{off}[t]. \tag{13}$$

2.4   Problem Formulation

In the scheme, the goal of the problem is to maximize the amount of total computation workload while minimizing the energy consumption for all vehicles, with jointly optimizing the computation frequency, the wireless transmission power, the task partition ratio of vehicles and the flight angle of the UAV in each time slot. Therefore, the problem can be defined as:

$$\max_{\{c_k[t], f_k[t], p_k[t], \beta[t]\}} \frac{1}{T} \sum_{t=1}^{T} \sum_{k=1}^{K} (aB_k[t] - bE_k[t]) \tag{14a}$$

$$s.t. \quad \lim_{t \to +\infty} \frac{\mathbb{E}\{Q_k^{loc}[t]\}}{t} = 0, \forall k \in \mathcal{K}, t \in \mathcal{T}, \tag{14b}$$

$$\lim_{t \to +\infty} \frac{\mathbb{E}\{Q_k^{off}[t]\}}{t} = 0, \forall k \in \mathcal{K}, t \in \mathcal{T}, \tag{14c}$$

where the weight coefficient a, b is to balance the order of magnitude. Equations (14b) and (14c) guarantee the task buffers Q_k^{loc} and Q_k^{off} to be mean rate stable.

3 Problem Solving

In this section, the problem presented can be expressed as a Markov Decision Process (MDP). The problem is considered to be solved using the TD3 policy gradient algorithm, a deep reinforcement learning algorithm supporting continuous action space. The state space, the action space and the reward in the MDP are represented as follows:

1) State: The state space consists of the coordinates of all vehicles and the UAV and two task queues for each vehicle, with a vector of $4K + 2$ dimensions in total. Then, the state space can be expressed as:

$$s_t = \{(x_k[t], y_k[t], x_u[t], y_u[t], Q_k^{loc}[t], Q_k^{off}[t]), \\ \forall k \in \mathcal{K}, t \in \mathcal{T}\}. \tag{15}$$

2) Action: Set the computation frequency, the wireless transmission power, the task partition ratio of vehicles and the flight angle of the UAV in each time slot, with a total amount of $3K + 1$ dimensions vector as the action space, which is expressed as:

$$a_t = \{(f_k[t], p_k[t], c_k[t], \beta[t]), \forall k \in \mathcal{K}, t \in \mathcal{T}\}. \tag{16}$$

3) Reward: Our goal is to maximize the amount of total computation workload while minimizing the energy consumption of all vehicles defined in Eq. (14a), then the reward at each step can be defined as follow:

$$R_t = \{\sum_{k=1}^{K} (aB_k[t] - bE_k[t]), \forall t \in \mathcal{T}\}. \tag{17}$$

We describe the pseudo code of the algorithm in Algorithm 1, in which G is the maximum amount of episodes. Line 1 denotes the initializing parameters of the critic network and the actor network. Line 3 denotes initializing the state at the beginning of each episode. Lines 4–17 mean that each episode contains T time slots. In each time slot t, line 5 means that the action is obtained through the actor network, and the noise ϵ is added to the output action to target policy smoothing. Then observe the new state s_{t+1}. Line 6 means that the transition tuple (s_t, a_t, R_t, s_{t+1}) will be stored in the replay buffer. Lines 7–16 estimate if t is greater than or equal to M, then the agent samples a random mini-batch of M transitions from $\mathcal{D}$ to train the actor and critics. Line 9 means that the output action a_{t+1} is updated through $\pi_{\varphi'}(s_{t+1})$, properly smoothing the target policy through the noise addition to the target action. Line 10 means to select the minimum Q value in both critic networks to calculate the target value y. Line 11 means to update the critic network parameters θ_i. Lines 12–15 denote update the actor network parameter

φ, the critic network is updated d times, the actor network is updated once.

Algorithm 1: TD3-based policy gradient algorithm

Input : $\lambda_k[t]$, $q_u[t]$, $q_k[t]$
Output: $p_k[t]$, $f_k[t]$, $\beta[t]$, $c_k[t]$

1 Initialize critic networks $Q(s, a|\theta_i)$, the actor network $\pi(s|\varphi)$, the target network $\theta_i' \leftarrow \theta_i$, $\varphi' \leftarrow \varphi$ and the replay buffer $\mathcal{D}$;

2 **for** *episode* = 1 **to** G **do**

3   Initialize s_0;

4   **for** $t = 1$ **to** T **do**

5   Select the action by $a_t \sim \pi(s_t|\varphi) + \epsilon$, where $\epsilon \sim \text{clip}(\mathcal{N}(0, \sigma))$ is the exploration noise, and observe the reward R_t from equation (17) and the next state s_{t+1};

6   Store the transition tuple (s_t, a_t, R_t, s_{t+1}) in $\mathcal{D}$;

7   **if** $t \geq M$ **then**

8   Sample the mini-batch of M transitions tuples from $\mathcal{D}$;

9              $\tilde{a}_{t+1} \leftarrow \pi(s_{t+1}|\varphi') + \epsilon$, $\epsilon \sim \text{clip}(\mathcal{N}(0, \sigma), -c, c)$;

10             $y \leftarrow R_t + \gamma \min_{i=1,2} Q(s_{t+1}, \tilde{a}_{t+1})$;

11   Update the critics network:

                $\theta_i \leftarrow \min_{\theta_i} \frac{1}{M} \sum_{j=1}^{M} (y - Q(s_j, a_j|\theta_i))^2$;

12   **if** $t \bmod d$ **then**

13   Update the actor network:

                    $\nabla J_\varphi \leftarrow \frac{1}{M} \sum_{j=1}^{M} \nabla_a Q(s_j, a_j|\varphi)|_{a_j = \pi(s_j|\varphi)} \nabla_\varphi \pi(s_j|\varphi)$;

14   Update target network: $\theta_i' \leftarrow \rho\theta_i + (1-\rho)\theta_i'$,

                  $\varphi' \leftarrow \rho\varphi + (1-\rho)\varphi'$;

15   **end**

16   **end**

17   **end**

18 **end**

---

4 Results and Analysis

In this section, we illustrate the numerical simulations for the proposed computation offloading scheme.

4.1 Simulation Setup

In the proposed MEC scenario, it is assumed that the offloading scheme is set in a $400\,\text{m} \times 400\,\text{m}$ rectangular map, with the map center as the origin of the three-dimensional Cartesian coordinate system, and the starting position of the UAV is $(200, 200, 50)$. Suppose $\lambda_k[t]$ is randomly generated within $[5, 7] \times 10^4$ bits, and channel power gain $g_k[t]$ is exponentially distributed with the mean of $g_0 \cdot (d_k[t]/d_0)^{-3}$, where the reference distance $d_0 = 1\,\text{m}$ and $g_0 = -40$ dB. The replay buffer size of $\mathcal{D}$ is 10^6, then other detailed parameters are set in Table 1.

Table 1. Simulation parameters

Parameter	Value	Parameter	Value
K	10	F_k	[0.5, 1]GHz
V_v	10m/s	G	10000
V_u	25m/s	σ	0.04
T	100	c	0.05
τ	0.1	d	2
W	1MHz	α_{Actor}	0.00002
$\sigma_0{}^2$	-90dbm	α_{Critic}	0.00004
γ_u	1×10^{-27}	γ	0.999
w	10^3 cycles/bit	M	128
P_k	[0.5, 1.5]W	ρ	0.005

4.2 Performance Analysis

According to the general experimental research method, the optimization objective designed in this paper is also applied to the following three benchmark schemes which are all solved by the TD3 policy gradient algorithm.

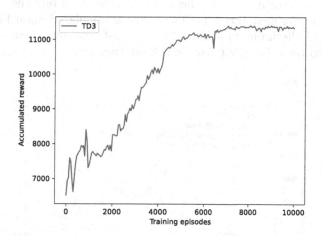

Fig. 2. Accumulated reward under the number of episodes.

Figure 2 displays the convergence of the TD3 policy gradient algorithm applied for the optimization problem in the proposed scheme. A total number of 10000 episodes of experiments were conducted. The TD3 policy gradient algorithm reaches convergence in about 6500 episodes.

As shown in Fig. 3, the relationship between the total amount of time slots and the accumulated reward is revealed. With the increase of the total amount of time slots, the accumulated rewards of all the four schemes increase obviously. Compared with the benchmark schemes, which suggests that our proposed scheme has excellent performance when time evolves.

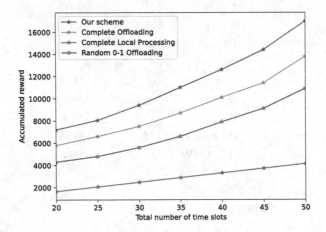

Fig. 3. Comparison of accumulated reward by total amount of the time slots.

Figure 4 shows the relationship between the input task bits and the accumulated reward. Experimental results show as the accumulated reward is positively proportional to the input task bits. As the input task bits increases, the disparity between the other three benchmark schemes and our proposed scheme is exaggerated.

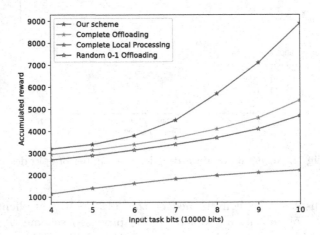

Fig. 4. Comparison of accumulated rewards by the input task bits.

5 Conclusions

In this paper, we have studied the problem of dynamic resource allocation and trajectory optimization for UAV-assisted vehicle computation offloading, where the mobility of vehicles and the UAV are all taken into account. A dynamic resource allocation and UAV flight trajectory optimization scheme is proposed to satisfy maximizing the amount of total system computing workload while minimizing the energy consumption. Extensive simulation results have validated the effectiveness of the proposed scheme.

References

1. Abbas, N., Zhang, Y., Taherkordi, A., Skeie, T.: Mobile edge computing: a survey. IEEE Internet Things J. **5**(1), 450–465 (2017)
2. Cao, Z., Sun, H., Zhang, N., Lv, X.: Energy-efficient cooperative offloading for Multi-AP MEC in IoT networks. In: Gao, H., Wang, X. (eds.) CollaborateCom 2021. LNICST, vol. 407, pp. 3–17. Springer, Cham (2021). https://doi.org/10.1007/978-3-030-92638-0_1
3. Hu, H., Song, W., Wang, Q., Hu, R.Q., Zhu, H.: Energy efficiency and delay tradeoff in an MEC-enabled mobile IoT network. IEEE Internet Things J. **9**(17), 15942–15956 (2022)
4. Jeong, S., Simeone, O., Kang, J.: Mobile edge computing via a UAV-mounted cloudlet: optimization of bit allocation and path planning. IEEE Trans. Veh. Technol. **67**(3), 2049–2063 (2017)
5. Kawamoto, Y., Nishiyama, H., Kato, N., Ono, F., Miura, R.: Toward future unmanned aerial vehicle networks: architecture, resource allocation and field experiments. IEEE Wirel. Commun. **26**(1), 94–99 (2018)
6. Liu, J., et al.: RL/DRL meets vehicular task offloading using edge and vehicular cloudlet: a survey. IEEE Internet Things J. **9**(11), 8315–8338 (2022)
7. Peng, Y., Liu, Y., Zhang, H.: Deep reinforcement learning based path planning for UAV-assisted edge computing networks, pp. 1–6. IEEE (2021)
8. Sun, H., Wang, J., Peng, H., Song, L., Qin, M.: Delay constraint energy efficient cooperative offloading in MEC for IoT. In: Gao, H., Wang, X., Iqbal, M., Yin, Y., Yin, J., Gu, N. (eds.) CollaborateCom 2020. LNICST, vol. 349, pp. 671–685. Springer, Cham (2021). https://doi.org/10.1007/978-3-030-67537-0_40
9. Wang, X., Ning, Z., Guo, S., Wang, L.: Imitation learning enabled task scheduling for online vehicular edge computing. IEEE Trans. Mob. Comput. **21**(2), 598–611 (2020)
10. Wang, Y., Fang, W., Ding, Y., Xiong, N.: Computation offloading optimization for UAV-assisted mobile edge computing: a deep deterministic policy gradient approach. Wirel. Netw. **27**(4), 2991–3006 (2021)
11. Yang, C., Liu, Y., Chen, X., Zhong, W., Xie, S.: Efficient mobility-aware task offloading for vehicular edge computing networks. IEEE Access **7**, 26652–26664 (2019)
12. Zhang, J., Guo, H., Liu, J., Zhang, Y.: Task offloading in vehicular edge computing networks: a load-balancing solution. IEEE Trans. Veh. Technol. **69**(2), 2092–2104 (2019)
13. Zhao, L., Yang, K., Tan, Z., Li, X., Sharma, S., Liu, Z.: A novel cost optimization strategy for SDN-enabled UAV-assisted vehicular computation offloading. IEEE Trans. Intell. Transp. Syst. **22**(6), 3664–3674 (2020)

Towards an Improved Unsupervised Graph-Based MRI Brain Segmentation Method

Maria Popa$^{(\boxtimes)}$ and Anca Andreica

Department of Computer Science, Babe-Bolyai University, Mihail Kogalniceanu 1,
400084 Cluj-Napoca, Romania
{maria.popa,anca.andreica}@ubbcluj.ro

Abstract. Brain disorders are becoming more prevalent, and accurate brain segmentation is a vital component of identifying the appropriate treatment. This study introduces an enhanced graph-based image segmentation technique. The node selection process involves creating an ellipsoid centered at the image's center of mass. The proposed approach is evaluated using the NFBS dataset and demonstrates superior visual and numerical outcomes compared to some of existing approaches.

Keywords: Brain segmentation · Unsupervised segmentation · Graph-based segmentation

1 Introduction

Brain segmentation is a commonly used technique in the analysis of various neurological diseases and represents the preliminary step in neurosurgical operations and in finding an appropriate treatment.

Recently, there has been a significant surge in the number of individuals experiencing various brain disorders. Developmental delay, cerebral palsy, epilepsy, cortical dysplasia, brain malformation (hemimegalencephaly) are just a few of the problems where an accurate segmentation is crucial. According to the World Health Organisation (WHO) over 50 million people across the world develop epilepsy.

Fortunately, early examination could lead to a treatment. MRI, being a quick, painless, and precise diagnostic tool that generates 3D volumetric data, is extensively utilized for screening purposes. However, as various brain disorders necessitate periodic screening and the process of manual analysis is time-intensive, the creation of precise computer-aided tools is inevitable.

Brain segmentation, also referred to as skull stripping, is the process of separating the brain from the skull. There are numerous studies in the literature that employ both supervised and unsupervised techniques to achieve this segmentation. Recent literature has shifted towards unsupervised methods to extract the brain, as supervised approaches are time-consuming and require more effort and input from doctors.

Brain extraction tool (BET) [7] is a widely used unsupervised brain segmentation method due to its speed and robustness. This technique uses surface tessellation to extract the brain in 1000 iterations. However this approach fails to segment the top and the bottom of the brain, by including non-brain tissue in the segmentation. Improved BET (BET*) [9] tries to overcome those problems, by using an ellipsoid to approximate the brain. Although the number of iterations is reduced to 50 and BET* achieves more accurate segmentation of the top and middle portions of the brain, it still fails to include non-brain tissue in the bottom region of the brain.

Graph-Based Unsupervised Brain Segmentation (GUBS) [2] is another segmentation method that relies on graph-based techniques to extract the brain. This approach utilizes a minimal spanning tree (MST) to accomplish the segmentation. However, one limitation of GUBS is its reliance on the user to define specific parameters for each dataset. Sphere-GUBS [3] improves upon GUBS by eliminating the need for user interaction and reducing the time complexity. This is achieved by introducing a sphere-based approach for selecting brain nodes during the segmentation process. While Sphere-GUBS achieves a higher level of accuracy in brain segmentation, it still encounters difficulties in accurately segmenting the top and bottom regions of the brain.

This paper presents an enhanced unsupervised graph-based method for brain extraction, which addresses the limitations of Sphere-GUBS while maintaining a user intervention-free approach and achieving improved segmentation accuracy. The proposed method is evaluated on the NFBS dataset [4] and the results are compared with those obtained using Sphere-GUBS and the original GUBS.

The rest of the paper is structured as follows: Sect. 2 presents the related work; in Sect. 3 the novel approach is detailed; in Sect. 4 the obtained results are described and Sect. 5 refers to the conclusion and future work.

2 Related Work

Among all the available approaches, BET is commonly utilized for brain segmentation. BET* differs from the initial BET by using an ellipsoid to approximate the brain surface. It improves BET by reducing the iterations to 50 and removing the false positives by using fuzzy C-Means and morphological operations.

Graph-CUTS [5] is another popular method for skull stripping, as it involves segmenting the brain using morphological operations and then representing the MRI as a graph, followed by the use of graph-cuts to eliminate narrow connections. One drawback of this method is that it relies on the region growth of the white matter, which can be time-consuming.

GUBS is an unsupervised brain segmentation method that utilizes a minimal spanning tree (MST) approach. The process of constructing the weighted graph involves edge detection within the MRI data, as well as calculating the weights between the nodes. In this method, node selection is influenced by dataset-specific parameters and requires human intervention to determine the selection threshold for nodes. These nodes are chosen from three distinct categories: voxels within the brain tissue, nodes from the skull, and nodes outside the skull.

The weights assigned to edges are determined based on the intensity difference between adjacent voxels. However, GUBS necessitates the initialization of parameters for each dataset and fails to accurately segment the brain without incorporating non-brain tissue into the segmentation.

In a previous study [3], a method called Sphere-GUBS was introduced. Even though it uses a minimal spanning tree to segment the brain, as presented in [2], it eliminates the need for parameter setting and human intervention by selecting nodes within a sphere with the center in the center of mass for the MRI and the radius equal to $\frac{r}{3}$, where r is computed by taking into consideration the volume of all voxels greater then the multi-otsu threshold. While this method improves segmentation compared to GUBS, it is not without flaws. To enhance the Sphere-GUBS method, the proposed method considers more slices in the node selection process. The use of a sphere results in the removal of some slices from the MRI, which means missegmentation of the brain.

The paper [6] presents a graph-based neural network (GNN) approach for the segmentation of brain tumors. This technique involves representing the 3D MRI data as a graph, with supervoxels serving as the nodes. These supervoxels are generated using the Simple Linear Iterative Clustering (SLIC) algorithm [1], with the cluster number set to 15,000. While this deep learning approach delivers promising results, it needs a considerable training duration, often spanning several hours, and relies on robust hardware resources.

3   Proposed Approach

The proposed approach is based on the main idea of Sphere-GUBS. In this method, an MRI is represented using a weighted graph, and a minimum spanning tree (MST) is applied to segment the brain. The construction of the MST follows the same process as Sphere-GUBS, where voxels are selected only from two regions: inside and outside the brain, in contrast to GUBS, which selects nodes from three categories. Unlike the method mentioned in [3] but similar to [2], the novel approach eliminates the need for parameters and human intervention in node selection. The main point of distinction from Sphere-GUBS lies in the way voxels are selected. The method can be devided in three steps: Preprocessing, Nodes selection, MST construction & Brain segmentation.

3.1   Preprocessing

The preprocessing part consists of resizing the images to $128 \times 128 \times 128$ and scaling the intensities to the range 0–1.

3.2   Nodes Selection

Nodes are sampled from two regions, brain and background. Unlike the Sphere-GUBS method where the brain nodes are selected within a sphere, the proposed approach selects the nodes within an ellipsoid.

The idea of using an ellipsoid was inspired by [9], which utilized an ellipsoid to approximate the brain surface instead of a sphere in the tessellation model.

Although the Sphere-GUBS method, which uses a sphere, enhances results compared to GUBS, it includes non-brain tissue into the segmentation for certain planes or missegments the brain. This is because a sphere includes the same number of slices in all three planes, whereas an ellipsoid varies in three dimensions.

$$9 \cdot \frac{x^2}{r^2} + 9 \cdot \frac{y^2}{r^2} + \frac{9}{16} \cdot \frac{z^2}{r^2} \leq 1 \tag{1}$$

The brain's nodes are chosen from the ellipsoid, as outlined in Eq. 1, where x, y, z represent the voxel coordinates and r is determined by considering the volume of voxels that surpass the multi-otsu threshold. Increasing the dimensions of the ellipsoid axes results in a growth in the number of the selected nodes, which denotes a more complex graph. On the other hand, reducing the size for the dimensions results in a too small graph.

The center of the ellipsoid is calculated in the same manner as for the Sphere-GUBS, by calculating the center of mass for the image.

The selection of nodes from the background follows the same approach as presented in [2] and Sphere-GUBS, randomly choosing 20000 nodes from the all six faces.

3.3 MST Construction and Brain Segmentation

Because of the complexity of the graph, similar to [2] and [3] the nodes are collapsed in such a way that a minimal spanning tree is built. When encountering node collapse, the method follows specific constraints. Firstly, any edge that connects two nodes located in the same region is discarded. Then, for any remaining edges, the node found in the selected seeds is replaced by the first seed in that region. Finally, all remaining selected nodes, except the first, are discarded. The segmentation process involves a final step, which entails dividing the image into two regions - brain and background - by eliminating the edge with the highest weight from the MST path [3].

We call the proposed method Ellipsoid-GUBS.

4 Results

To conduct the testing, the Neurofeedback Skull-stripped repository (NFBS) [4] was utilized. This repository comprises T1W MRI images from 125 subjects between the ages of 21 to 45, with varying clinical and subclinical psychiatric symptoms. The images are manually skull-stripped, and have a resolution of 256 × 256 × 192 with isotropic voxels of 1.00 mm. For testing purposes the images were resized to 128 × 128 × 128 and the intensities were scaled in the range 0 to 1.

To effectively evaluate and highlight the advancements of the novel approach, Ellipsoid GUBS is compared against other MST-based methods, namely the original GUBS and Sphere-GUBS. This comparative analysis aims to showcase the improvements achieved by Ellipsoid-GUBS in brain segmentation.

4.1 Evaluation Metrics

To assess the performance of the proposed approach, six metrics were used: accuracy, precision, sensitivity, specificity, Jaccard Index, and Dice Coefficient. These similarity measures were calculated between the predicted and ground truth MRI images. TP represents the voxels that have been correctly identified as brain tissue, TN represents the voxels inaccurately identified as non-brain tissues, FP represents the voxels that are inaccurately identified as brain tissues, FN refers to the voxels within the brain region that are inaccurately identified as non-brain tissues.

Voxel accuracy [10] is defined as $\frac{TP+TN}{TP+TN+FP+FN}$ and denotes the proportion of accurately classified voxels.

Precision [8] is computed with the formula $\frac{TP}{TP+FP}$ and denotes the percentage of the accurately classified voxels in the brain tissue.

Sensitivity [8], calculated as $\frac{TP}{TP+FN}$ measures the percentage of brain tissue voxels in the ground truth that are accurately detected as brain tissue in the prediction.

Specificity [8], determined with $\frac{TN}{TN+FN}$ represents the ratio of non-brain tissue voxel in the ground truth that are correctly identified as non-brain in the prediction.

Jaccard Index [8], defined as $\frac{TP}{TP+FP+FN}$ presents the overlap between the ground truth and segmentation results, divided by the union between the ground truth and segmentation results.

Dice Coefficient [8], having the formula $\frac{2TP}{2TP+FP+FN}$ quantifies the resemblance between the two sets of labels.

4.2 Visual and Numerical Results

Ellipsoid-GUBS demonstrates considerable improvements compared to Sphere-GUBS and significant enhancements compared to GUBS. Figure 1 illustrates the visual comparison. In Slice 80 of the coronal plane, the segmentation results for Ellipsoid-GUBS, Sphere-GUBS, the original GUBS, and the Ground Truth are presented. GUBS failed to segment the brain, while Sphere-GUBS closely approximated the ground truth. However, Sphere-GUBS included non-brain tissue at the bottom of the segmentation and mis-segmented the top.

Ellipsoid-GUBS achieved enhanced segmentation results. It no longer includes non-brain tissue from the bottom, as seen in Sphere-GUBS. Additionally, Ellipsoid-GUBS slightly improved the segmentation at the top of the image, particularly in the left-top region.

It can be seen that even though there is still room for improvements, Sphere-GUBS fails by including non-brain tissue into segmentation, while Ellipsoid-GUBS not. In addition to this, at the top of the brain, the proposed method better segments the brain compared to Sphere-GUBS, where the tissues is missed.

The numerical comparison is presented in Table 1. The novel method presents improved results for all six metrics. There is an increased with 3% in the precision for Ellipsoid-GUBS compared to Sphere-GUBS, while a 28% compared to initial GUBS, meaning that the method identifies better the voxels inside the brain. This can be also observed at the top of Fig. 1, as indicated in the visual comparison. The Jaccard Index and Dice coefficient, which represent the percentage of the overlapping between the prediction and ground truth are increased with 2% compared to Sphere-GUBS. The improvements to the other metrics underline an overall better segmentation.

Visual comparison for MRI A00056097, slice 80 - Coronal plane

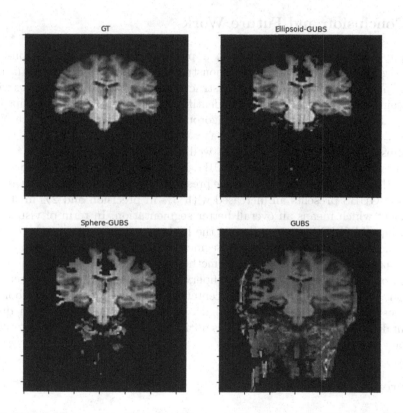

Fig. 1. Visual Comparison for slice 80, coronal plane for GUBS, Sphere-GUBS, Ellipsoid-GUBS and ground truth (GT)

Table 1. Numerical results on all six metrics for GUBS, Sphere-GUBS and Ellipsoid-GUBS

	GUBS	Sphere-GUBS	Ellipsoid-GUBS
Accuracy	0.9041 ± 0.0138	0.9401 ± 0.0198	$\mathbf{0.9432 \pm 0.0206}$
Precision	0.5200 ± 0.0498	0.7732 ± 0.1223	$\mathbf{0.8077 \pm 0.1242}$
Jaccard Index	0.4568 ± 0.0594	0.5024 ± 0.1520	$\mathbf{0.5214 \pm 0.1613}$
Dice coefficient	0.6245 ± 0.0670	0.6523 ± 0.1577	$\mathbf{0.6681 \pm 0.1649}$
Specificity	0.9163 ± 0.0157	0.9781 ± 0.0189	$\mathbf{0.9797 \pm 0.0222}$
Sensitivity	0.7975 ± 0.0903	0.6015 ± 0.1997	$\mathbf{0.6167 \pm 0.2088}$

5   Conclusion and Future Work

The paper presents Ellipsoid-GUBS, a pioneering unsupervised graph-based brain segmentation method that demonstrates enhanced performance in brain extraction. This approach involves constructing a graph by selecting nodes within the brain and the background. To identify brain tissue nodes, an ellipsoid is employed. The method underwent rigorous testing using the complete NFBS dataset, which comprises 125 MRI images.

Ellipsoid-GUBS presents visual as well as numerical improvements in brain segmentation, compared to Sphere-GUBS. In the previous study the nodes selection method used a sphere, while in the presented approach an ellipsoid was used. Ellipsoid-GUBS presents an increased with 3% in precision and 2% in the dice coefficient which means an overall better segmentation. In term of visual analysis, Ellipsoid-GUBS segments better the brain in comparison to Sphere-GUBS which includes non-brain tissue into segmentation.

Future work involves testing the method on more datasets and comparing it with other approaches, including supervised methods. Exploring alternative methods for defining the ellipsoid's center is another objective. Collaboration with hospitals to gather doctor feedback and creating a dataset with diverse patient disorders are also planned. This initiative aims to enhance the algorithm's accuracy through rigorous evaluation.

References

1. Achanta, R., Shaji, A., Smith, K., Lucchi, A., Fua, P., Süsstrunk, S.: Slic superpixels compared to state-of-the-art superpixel methods. IEEE Trans. Pattern Anal. Mach. Intell. **34**(11), 2274–2282 (2012). https://doi.org/10.1109/TPAMI.2012.120
2. Mayala, S., et al.: GUBS: graph-based unsupervised brain segmentation in MRI images. J. Imaging **8**(10) (2022). https://doi.org/10.3390/jimaging8100262
3. Popa, M.: An 3D MRI unsupervised graph-based skull stripping algorithm. Procedia Computer Science, KES 2023, Accepted (2023)
4. Puccio, B., Pooley, J.P., Pellman, J.S., Taverna, E.C., Craddock, R.C.: The preprocessed connectomes project repository of manually corrected skull-stripped

T1-weighted anatomical MRI data. GigaScience **5**(1), s13742–016-0150-5 (2016). https://doi.org/10.1186/s13742-016-0150-5

5. Sadananthan, S.A., Zheng, W., Chee, M.W., Zagorodnov, V.: Skull stripping using graph cuts. Neuroimage **49**(1), 225–239 (2010). https://doi.org/10.1016/j. neuroimage.2009.08.050

6. Saueressig, C., Berkley, A., Kang, E., Munbodh, R., Singh, R.: Exploring graph-based neural networks for automatic brain tumor segmentation. In: Bowles, J., Broccia, G., Nanni, M. (eds.) DataMod 2020. LNCS, vol. 12611, pp. 18–37. Springer, Cham (2021). https://doi.org/10.1007/978-3-030-70650-0_2

7. Smith, S.M.: Fast robust automated brain extraction. Hum. Brain Mapp. **17**(3), 143–155 (2002)

8. Taha, A.A., Hanbury, A.: Metrics for evaluating 3d medical image segmentation: analysis, selection, and tool. BMC Med. Imaging **15** (2015)

9. Wang, L., Zeng, Z., Zwiggelaar, R.: An improved bet method for brain segmentation. In: 2014 22nd International Conference on Pattern Recognition, pp. 3221–3226 (2014). https://doi.org/10.1109/ICPR.2014.555

10. Zhang, H., Fritts, J.E., Goldman, S.A.: Image segmentation evaluation: a survey of unsupervised methods. Comput. Vis. Image Underst. **110**(2), 260–280 (2008). https://doi.org/10.1016/j.cviu.2007.08.003

User-Friendly Exploration of Highly Heterogeneous Data Lakes

Nelly Barret[✉][iD], Simon Ebel, Théo Galizzi, Ioana Manolescu[iD], and Madhulika Mohanty[iD]

Inria and Institut Polytechnique de Paris, Paris, France
{nelly.barret,simo.ebel,theo.galizzi,ioana.manolescu,
madhulika.mohanty}@inria.fr

Abstract. The proliferation of digital data sources and formats has led to the apparition of *data lakes*, systems where numerous data sources coexist, with less (or no) control and coordination among the sources, than previously practised in enterprise databases and data warehouses. While most data lakes are designed for very large number of *tables*, ConnectionLens [2,3] is a data lake system for structured, semi-structured, and unstructured data, which it integrates into a single *graph*; the graph can be explored via graph queries with keyword search [4] and entity path enumeration [5]. In this paper, we describe ConnectionStudio, a user-friendly platform leveraging ConnectionLens, and integrating feedback from non-expert users, in particular, journalists. Our main insights are: (*i*) improve and entice exploration by giving a *first global view*; (*ii*) facilitate tabular exports from the integrated graph; (*iii*) provide interactive means to improve the graph constructions. The insights can be used to further advance the exploration and usage of data lakes for non-IT users.

Keywords: Heterogeneous data · Data lake · Data exploration

1 Outline: Highly Heterogeneous Data Lakes

The past few decades have seen an important rise in the production of digital data. This data spans across multiple domains, e.g., healthcare, environment, finance, administration; it is owned and used by many actors other than the data producers, notably data journalists and researchers for crucial data journalism applications. The heterogeneity poses multiple challenges for data integration, its exploration and understanding of the data. **Data lakes** [7,9,10,12] are centralized repositories designed to store, process, and secure large amounts of structured, semi-structured, and unstructured data. A data lake stores data in its native format and supports various styles of data processing; the data model most often considered in such settings is relational, e.g., [6,8,11]. ConnectionLens [2,3] is a data lake system integrating such heterogeneous data in a *graph* format, capturing the fine-granularity structure that (semi-)structured data sources may have. Further, ConnectionLens applies Information Extraction

M. Sellami et al. (Eds.): CoopIS 2023, LNCS 14353, pp. 488–496, 2024.
https://doi.org/10.1007/978-3-031-46846-9_30

techniques to identify, from any value (leaf) node encountered in the data, entities such as people, places, organizations, emails, URIs, dates, etc. Such entities are very appealing in particular to data journalists, because they are at the heart of their work: analyzing the activity of entities of particular interest, e.g., political leaders, or companies, and finding how those entities may be connected. ConnectionStudio supports querying this integrated graph using keyword search [4] and entity path enumeration [5]. Using keyword search, users submit keywords that interest them, and ConnectionLens returns *connecting trees*, showing how, in the graph, nodes matching the keywords are connected. When the users know the types of entities of interest (which is the case with data journalists), an efficient *entity path enumeration algorithm* enumerates and allows visualizing paths that connect entities of interest, e.g., a politician owns shares in a company, or a politician's wife serves in the governing board of a company, etc.

New Requirements for Non-expert Users. Working with journalists, we found that heterogeneous graphs produced by ConnectionLens were still hard for them to comprehend. They found it difficult (α) relating the documents they added to the data lake, to the resulting data graphs; (β) figuring out what keywords to use when searching; (γ) generally, working with the data graph paradigm. It turns out that in their profession, those with digital skills are especially at ease with spreadsheet tools, thus data tables are appealing to them, while data graphs are not. Further, (δ) ConnectionLens graphs interconnect data through extracted entities; like any trained model, our extractors introduce some errors (false positives, false negatives, wrongly typed entities). In some cases, especially when a dataset has some regularity, users can provide guidance on what entities are to be expected in certain parts of the data, thus contribute to increasing the graph quality. To articulate such guidance, they need to be able to inspect the data, and to formulate extraction hints. Moreover, (ϵ) journalists formulated the need for tangible, intuitive data analysis results (diagrams, graphs, tables) that they can download from our graph data lake and share, for instance, within newsrooms, to convince colleagues or managers of the interest of spending time to analyze complex data.

Based on these requirements, we built **ConnectionStudio**, a new platform based on ConnectionLens and extending it in several ways in order to address (α) to (ϵ) above. Below, after recalling basic information about ConnectionLens to make this paper self-contained, we detail ConnectionStudio's novel extensions, which are the contributions of this work. We believe they may help others devising similar heterogeneous data lakes. ConnectionStudio is available online, together with examples and tutorials at https://connectionstudio.inria.fr/.

2   Background: Graph Integration of Heterogeneous Data

ConnectionLens ingests any structured, semi-structured or unstructured data as follows. When ingesting an XML document, each element, attribute, or text node becomes a graph node; parent-child relationships in the XML document lead to corresponding edges in the graph. A JSON document is similarly converted: each map, array, and (leaf) value is converted into a graph node. RDF graphs are most easily ingested: each triple of the form s, p, o leads to two nodes labelled "s" and "o" connected through an p-labelled edge. For CSV and relational data, each tuple and value lead to a node, edges labelled with the column names are connecting those (if the column name is empty, so the edge label). Text documents are segmented into paragraph, each of which is a node, child of a common root. Office and PDF documents are converted into JSON then ingested as above.

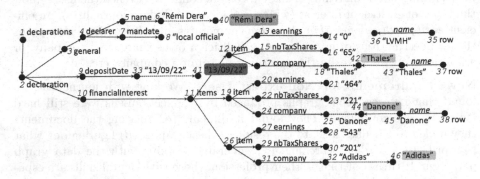

Fig. 1. Sample data graph built from HATVP declarations and CAC40 companies.

NER (Named Entity Recognition) is applied on every leaf node of the graph, leading to (new) extracted entity nodes. Each entity node is labelled with the recognised named entity (NE, in short) and connected to the leaf value from which it has been extract through an edge (dashed edges in Fig. 1). Moreover, when two NE nodes are identical, i.e. they have the exact same label, they are fused and only one is kept in the integrated graph. This allows to easily find connections *across sources*, that are (much) harder to find manually. For instance, there is only one node "Thales", extracted from N18 and N43.

Figure 1 shows the data graph obtained from (*i*) an XML sample of the large HATVP French transparency dataset (ministers' declarations about their wealth, stocks they own, business interests, etc.), on the left; and (*ii*) a CSV file listing the 40 most influential French companies (known as CAC40), on the right. Each (black) circle is a data node in the integrated data graph, edges are connecting them accordingly to their relationships in the datasets. Value data nodes are quoted; named entities are highlighted (blue for people, purple for dates and yellow for organizations).

3   Novel ConnectionStudio Modules

Built on top of ConnectionLens, ConnectionStudio allows users to import datasets into an integrated graph, search the graph via keywords, and find paths connecting entities. Further, ConnectionStudio includes new modules, to answer the requirements stated at the end of Sect. 1. We describe them below.

3.1   Global View of the Data Lake: Entity (Dataset) Statistics

Users are familiar with the data files they brought (PDF, Office formats, JSON, CSV, etc.), but told us they felt "lost" once the system ingested their data, especially if the latter is large and/or complex. To help them get a first global view of the data lake (or graph, requirement (α)), we present them a set of *entity* and *entity-dataset statistics*, as follows:

- The total numbers of entities of each type (Person, Location, Organization, date, URI, email, hashtag, mention), overall in the graph;
- The total number of entities per type and per dataset in which they appear;
- A tag cloud of the most frequent entities in the whole graph.
- A summary of the *entity-dataset associations*: we show the entity type, label, and datasets where it appears, starting with the entities present in the highest number of datasets. These entities are more interesting, because they allow making connections *across datasets* (potentially heterogeneous files), saving important manual efforts to journalists combining such data sources for their investigations.

The above statistics give a first idea of what the datasets contain, and also suggest entity names to use as search keywords (requirement (β)). For instance, Fig. 2a shows the number of different types of extracted entities and the tag cloud in the dataset of Fig. 1. Figure 2b shows the frequent common entities in the two datasets.

3.2   From the Integrated Graph to Data Tables

In a prior ConnectionLens application [3], based on PubMed biomedical literature data, journalists were interested in the paths that connect medical experts with companies that fund their research. We expressed this path as a query over the graph, and exposed its results as a table through an ad-hoc Web interface manually built just for this scenario. In a more general manner, in [5], users select a pair of entity types (τ_1, τ_2) of interest to them, e.g., people and organizations, and the system automatically finds and computes the paths connecting such entities in the ConnectionLens graph. Each path leads to a data table, where entities of types τ_1, τ_2 are in the first, resp., last column, and the other columns are the nodes along the path.

As stated in requirement (γ), *users requested more support in extracting tabular data from the graph*. For instance, in the HATVP dataset, they may want to extract: for each elected politician, their name, elected office, election date, and companies they have stocks in; note that this query is not a path, since it returns many values. Users view the first three fields as required, but the last one is optional, i.e., a politician should be part of the result even if they have no stocks. Optional query fragments correspond to *outerjoins* in database terms.

To allow users to *easily and intuitively express a much larger set of queries*, we proceed as follows.

(a) Count of entities and tag cloud

Label	Type	Freq...	Datasets ↑
2017	Date	452	Cac40.csv, hatvp-cleaned.xml
Legrand	Organization	7	Cac40.csv, hatvp-cleaned.xml
Engie	Organization	20	Cac40.csv, hatvp-cleaned.xml
2000	Date	63	Cac40.csv, hatvp-cleaned.xml
2009	Date	29	Cac40.csv, hatvp-cleaned.xml
Pernod Ricard	Organization	6	Cac40.csv, hatvp-cleaned.xml
Alsace	Location	8	Cac40.csv, hatvp-cleaned.xml

(b) Frequent entities

Fig. 2. Statistics for the sample dataset.

(1) Upon loading, ConnectionStudiocomputes, from each dataset, a set of *elementary paths* that can be seen as "query building blocks". Each path reflects one or more consecutive edges in the data graph. The source of a path is always an internal node, while its destination is either an internal node, a value, or an extracted entity. For instance, in the above example, elementary paths include: `declarations`, `declarations.declaration`, `declarations.declaration.general.de-clarer.name#val` (this ends in strings comprising politicians' names), `declarations.declaration.general.declarer.name#val.extract:p` (ending in person entities extracted from the strings), etc.

(2) Users can select paths from a drop-down list, and add them one by one to compose a query. The first selected path is required; the others can be either optional or required. To each path are associated two variables: one for the source

node, and the other for the destination (internal node, value, or entity). Users can edit the paths, and the variables, to adjust them, and specify how they connect. For instance, in the HATVP scenario, a user may:

- Start by selecting a path ending in `declaration`; name its starting point (source variable) `decls` and its end point (target variable) `decl`.
- Select `declarations.declaration.general.mandat.label#val` as the second elementary path;
- Edit (shorten) it into `declaration.general.mandat.label#val`, going from the variable `decl` to the variable `position`. Reusing `decl` is intuitive since in both paths, this variable denotes the graph nodes labeled `declaration`.
- Similarly, edit other elementary paths to obtain `declaration.general.dateDe-butMandat#val.extract:d` going from `decl` to `startDate`, etc.

(3) When the user has finished specifying the paths to combine in a query, they can trigger the evaluation of this query on the underlying graph. This leads to tabular results, with a column for each user-specified variable and a line for each result; users can download results in CSV to be further processed, shared etc.

For instance, Fig. 3 shows the result of joining three paths and renaming the variables to obtain the declaration number, the start date, the position and the name of the person.

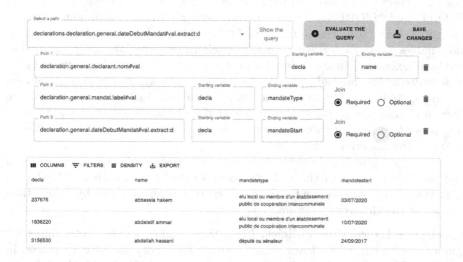

Fig. 3. The data view for HATVP declarations and CAC40 companies samples.

Generating Elementary Paths. As explained above, users can compose queries by "cutting & pasting" elementary paths; here is how ConnectionStudio extracts these from the data. From an XML or JSON document, each path starting from the document root, and ending in an internal node, text node, or extracted entity (child of a text node) is proposed to the user. From CSV data, we propose paths of the form `row`, `row.att#val`, `row.att#val.extract:`τ where `row` is the label of each node created out of a CSV row (tuple), `att` is an attribute name, and `extract:`τ denotes an extraction edge for some entity type τ (such as person, location, email etc., recall Sect. 2). From RDF, for each property `p` encountered in an `s, p, o` triple, we propose simply `p` as an elementary path, with two variables for the subject and object of the triple; similarly, for each `s, rdf:type, c` triple, we propose `rdf:type c` as an elementary path with one variable for the subject.

3.3 Correcting and Improving the Graph Through a Table View

The paradigm of path querying also gives us two ways to improve and correct the graph (requirement (δ)).

Editing Value and Entity Labels. As stated above, an elementary path ending in `#val` returns the set of values encountered in the data in certain positions, while a path ending in `#val.extract:`τ, for some entity type τ, shows entities extracted by ConnectionLens from the data, using trained language models [3]. When visualising the result of such a query, users can *edit* entity or values shown in the query result, and *propagate* their modifications to the underlying database, thus updating the graph. ConnectionLens implements a set of similarity functions and (very conservatively) unifies entities whose labels are very similar, e.g., "L'Oral" and "L'OREAL", once they are both recognized as organizations by the entity extractor. The ability to edit the data, offered by ConnectionStudio enables users to further normalize (uniformize) the label of value nodes, and/or of extracted entity nodes. This corresponds to a carefully restricted case of *database update through views* [1]. As well known, such updates cannot always be propagated correctly to the underlying database. In ConnectionStudio, we allow updates only on values or entities at the destination end of a path. It is easy to see that such updates can always be propagated to the graph persistently stored in the underlying database.

For instance, in Fig. 4a, while inspecting the results of a query, when users find multiple versions of the same organization "Alstom", such as "Alsthom", "Als thom" or "Alstom grid", they can correct each of them by hand, then propagate the changes to the underlying database.

Specifying Extraction Policies. Inspecting results of entity-returning path queries may help users learn what entities are (not) in specific places in the data. Thus, a user noticing the extracted names "Bertrand Martin" and "Julie Dupont" under `declaration.general.declarer.name#val.extract:p` may conclude that every `declaration.general.declarer.name#val` contains people, and formulate an *extraction policy* of the form $\boxed{path\ \tau}$, specifying that all values found under *path* are to be interpreted as entities of the given entity type τ. This helps circumvent extractor misses, e.g., for a less usual name such as "Xin Jong" which does not fit the extractor's trained model. Users can also

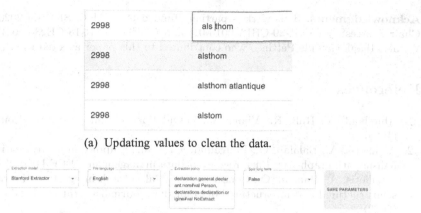

(a) Updating values to clean the data.

(b) Specify extraction policies before loading data.

Fig. 4. Correcting and improving the graph.

specify that extraction should *not* be performed on values on some path(s), $\boxed{path\ NoExtract}$, if they are not interested in the entities that may be found there. Extraction policies, both negative and positive, speed up the graph construction, by avoiding the (costly) entity extraction effort during graph loading.

Extraction policies were first mentioned in [3]. However, only now, via ConnectionStudio's path query features, our tool helps non-expert users formulate them. For instance, in Fig. 4b, the user specified that: declarers' names should always be recognized as person entities, and that no extraction should be applied on the values found on the path `origine#val`. Users can decide this after seeing that all these values are equal (probably a code introduced by anonymization), thus there is no point in searching for entities in them.

4 Perspectives and Conclusion

Data lakes such as [7,9,10,12] and ConnectionLens [2,3] aim to help users explore many heterogeneous data sources. ConnectionLens adopts a graph paradigm for integrating the sources, and extracts entities leading to inter-dataset connection opportunities. In this work, we describe novel data exploration and discovery paradigms we implemented in ConnectionStudio, following requirements expressed by journalists; they allow users to *discover* the graph, *simplify querying* for connections across sources, and *as-you-go* cleaning of the graph. We believe these features are useful additions to next-generation heterogeneous data lakes. Going forward, we plan to conduct an elaborate user-study in order to understand better how ConnectionStudio helps novice users explore graphs and also inculcate the feedback to further improve upon the features provided by ConnectionStudio.

Acknowledgments. This work is partially funded by DIM RFSI PHD 2020-01, AI Chair SourcesSay (ANR-20-CHIA-0015-01) and CQFD (ANR-18-CE23-0003) grants. We also thank Camille Pettineo who contributed to this paper as a data journalist.

References

1. Abiteboul, S., Hull, R., Vianu, V.: Foundations of databases. Addison-Wesley (1995)
2. Anadiotis, A., Balalau, O., Bouganim, T., et al.: Empowering investigative journalism with graph-based heterogeneous data management. IEEE DEBull (2021)
3. Anadiotis, A., Balalau, O., Conceicao, C., et al.: Graph integration of structured, semistructured and unstructured data for data journalism. Inf. Syst. **104**, 101846 (2022)
4. Anadiotis, A.C., Manolescu, I., Mohanty, M.: Integrating connection search in graph queries. In: ICDE (2023)
5. Barret, N., Gauquier, A., Law, J.J., Manolescu, I.: Exploring heterogeneous data graphs through their entity paths. In: Abelló, A., Vassiliadis, P., Romero, O., Wrembel, R. (eds.) ADBIS 2023. LNCS, vol. 13985, pp. 163–179. Springer, Cham (2023). https://doi.org/10.1007/978-3-031-42914-9_12
6. Fan, G., Wang, J., Li, Y., Zhang, D., Miller, R.J.: Semantics-aware dataset discovery from data lakes with contextualized column-based representation learning. PVLDB **16**(7) (2023)
7. Giebler, C., Gröger, C., Hoos, E., Schwarz, H., Mitschang, B.: Leveraging the data lake: current state and challenges. In: Ordonez, C., Song, I.-Y., Anderst-Kotsis, G., Tjoa, A.M., Khalil, I. (eds.) DaWaK 2019. LNCS, vol. 11708, pp. 179–188. Springer, Cham (2019). https://doi.org/10.1007/978-3-030-27520-4_13
8. Giebler, C., Gröger, C., Hoos, E., Schwarz, H., Mitschang, B.: Modeling data lakes with data vault: practical experiences, assessment, and lessons learned. In: Laender, A.H.F., Pernici, B., Lim, E.-P., de Oliveira, J.P.M. (eds.) ER 2019. LNCS, vol. 11788, pp. 63–77. Springer, Cham (2019). https://doi.org/10.1007/978-3-030-33223-5_7
9. Hai, R., Geisler, S., Quix, C.: Constance: an intelligent data lake system. In: SIGMOD. New York, NY, USA (2016)
10. Hai, R., Koutras, C., Quix, C., Jarke, M.: Data lakes: A survey of functions and systems. IEEE Trans. Knowl. Data Eng. (2023)
11. Kuschewski, M., Sauerwein, D., Alhomssi, A., Leis, V.: BtrBlocks: efficient columnar compression for data lakes. Proc. ACM Manag. Data **1**(2), 1–26 (2023)
12. Nargesian, F., Zhu, E., Miller, R.J., Pu, K.Q., Arocena, P.C.: Data lake management: challenges and opportunities. Proc. VLDB Endowment **12**(12), 1986–1989 (2019)

Optimizing Hospital Patient Flow by Predicting Aftercare Requests from Fuzzy Time Series

Renata M. de Carvalho[1]([✉]) [iD], Stef van der Sommen[1],
and Danilo F. de Carvalho[2] [iD]

[1] Department of Mathematics and Computer Science, Eindhoven University
of Technology, Eindhoven, The Netherlands
r.carvalho@tue.nl
[2] Jheronimus Academy of Data Science, Eindhoven University of Technology,
Eindhoven, The Netherlands
d.ferreira.de.carvalho@tue.nl

Abstract. Predictive modelling can be a huge benefit when it comes to optimizing patient flows in a hospital. Hospital beds are considered critical resources, thus the need for optimizing patient flow is evident. This paper focuses on predicting the out-flow of hospital patients to external aftercare facilities, to mitigate the waiting times that currently dominate this flow and have a negative influence on the patient recovery process. In order to achieve this, we analyze hospital patient time series data in the form of aftercare requests. Such predictions allow hospital and aftercare facilities to be aligned such that, as soon as a patient is medically ready for discharge, the aftercare facility can immediately allocate the patient, avoiding for such patient to stay longer in the hospital occupying a bed while waiting for a place in the aftercare facility.

Keywords: Optimization of patient flow · Prediction model · Fuzzy time series · Healthcare

1 Introduction

Every day, it can be challenging for a hospital to match the available resources to the daily patient flow whilst keeping all patients satisfied and providing proper patient care. Amongst the most important resources are the amount of available beds each day. When a hospital reaches its capacity, and no more patients can be admitted, this is detrimental to the level of care that can be provided by said hospital. Therefore, it is important for hospitals to optimise patient flow as much as possible, to be able to keep providing the best care they can.

A Dutch hospital observed that one of the processes diminishing the patient flow is found with patients that must go to an aftercare facility after their treatment is completed. However, as with hospital beds, places at such facilities are scarce. Ideally, we would like to notify such a facility in advance, so that when a

M. Sellami et al. (Eds.): CoopIS 2023, LNCS 14353, pp. 497–505, 2024.
https://doi.org/10.1007/978-3-031-46846-9_31

patient treatment is finalised, they can immediately be transferred, thus optimising the flow of this patient. However, most cases do not fit this ideal situation. Often, the request can only be made towards the end of the treatment, resulting in a lack of places at any aftercare facility. Thus, the patient remains in the hospital, not able to go home due to their condition. Furthermore, the patient recovery is delayed, and a hospital bed is occupied while it should not be.

To mitigate this, the goal of this project is to support the hospital by attempting to predict the outflow of hospital patients to the aftercare facilities in advance. If successful, this will allow them to communicate the expected number of patients and thus allow the aftercare facilities to prepare in advance, ensuring enough available spaces, ultimately optimising the patient flow and care process.

Predictive modelling with hospital data as the subject is a well studied field, likely because the importance of predictive ability in a medical sense is self explanatory. However, we often see that modelling is done based on patient features [3,4]. Proper feature selection often requires domain specific knowledge and a thorough understanding of all related data, thus being a very intensive process. On the contrary, this work aims at providing a more statistical approach towards the predictive task at hand by abstracting from the patient level.

Also, we see time series forecasting related works relying heavily on artificial neural networks [4,5]. However, downsides to such an approach are that ANNs often are very resource intensive to train and retrain, and offer only a black box approach with limited interpretability. In [10], a more statistical approach is provided. They used a SARIMA model on time series data to provide improvement over the existing predictive method used by the hospital. However, the accuracy provided in the paper would not suffice in our setting, where every bed is important and the problem can only be solved by a high accuracy result.

The remainder of the paper is organized as follows. We introduce predictive models in Sect. 2. The data used in the proposed analysis comes in Sect. 3, followed by results in Sect. 4. Finally, the paper is concluded in Sect. 5.

2   Predictive Modeling

After collecting the time series data and performing initial analysis, one can attempt to capture the behaviour of the data in models in order to make predictions of future values of observations. Therefore, this section will focus on predictive techniques that can be used for time series based predictions.

2.1   Seasonal Autoregressive Integrated Moving Average

The Seasonal Autoregressive Integrated Moving Average model (SARIMA) is generally noted as $SARIMA(p, d, q)(P, D, Q, s)$, where the seasonal component repeats every s observations. The p, d, q and P, D, Q variables represent the autoregressive order, difference order, and moving average order of the trend and seasonality respectively.

2.2   Fuzzy Models

Using fuzzy logic for time series purposes was first introduced by Song and Chisson [8] and developed further by Chen [2]. For them, each time series has its own Universe of Discourse, which we can divide into partitions, or fuzzy sets. From these sets we can learn patterns from the time series and extract rules.

As described before, it can be the case that looking at a single variable of a time series does not suffice for predictive modelling. If that is the case, we can make use of multiple variables to provide us with extra information regarding the behaviour of the series. Thus, in such a multivariate approach, we see multiple explanatory variables (or exogenous variables) and a target variable (the endogenous variable). A model capable of using the information provided by such exogenous variables is the Multivariate FTS model. Essentially, the model builds on the conventional FTS model explained. It allows for model building and fuzzyfication of multiple variables simultaneously, so as to generate a rule set consisting of the different variables inserted into the model.

Granular Weighted Multivariate FTS. Fuzzy Time Series literature often features approaches where fuzzy clustering is used as a way of partitioning multivariate time series so that a univariate problem is obtained and can be solved [1]. In more recent years, fuzzy information granules have become more popular [9]. The goal of the fuzzy information granules is the same as using clustering: bringing back a multivariate problem to a univariate one. This is important, as the increase in dimensionality also increases model complexity. Whereas most implementations of a fuzzy information granule based approach are still computationally expensive, Silva [7] proposes a new approach that should even allow for multivariate predictions with multiple outputs, showing promising results.

3   Data Description and Analysis

The timeseries data used is created based on all aftercare requests made by a Dutch hospital from 2018 to 2021 to different aftercare institutions using the mentioned platform. It contains 16526 requests in total. There are five types of aftercare that might be requested: **ELV** "Eerstelijnsverblijf (Primary care residence)"; **GRZ** "Geriatrische revalidatiezorg (Geriatric rehabilitation care)"; **WLZ** "Wet langdurige zorg (Long-term care)"; **Extramuraal** "Extramurale zorg (Extramural care)"; and **Terminaal** "Terminale zorg (Terminal care)".

Besides the type of aftercare needed, the time series data is created based on the date the request was made. For that, the requests will be aggregated both in a daily and a weekly basis. Other features available are considered in this study but will be considered for future development of the proposed approach.

3.1   Data Distribution

As discussed, we are interested in predicting the amount of future requests for aftercare per care type. To identify whether or not we should create multiple models for each type of care, we can check their distributions. Figure 1 shows the distribution of the number of daily requests per care type. From the figure, one can clearly see that the daily request distribution differs for the different care types. Thus, it is likely to need uniquely configured models for each of them.

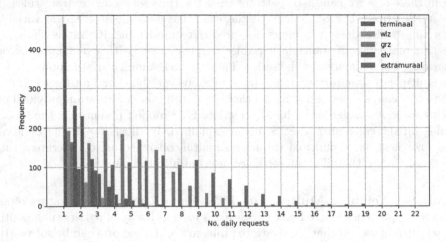

Fig. 1. Histograms per care type showing the frequency of daily requests

4   Predicting Aftercare Requests

This section will focus on the experiments that have been performed towards the objective of predicting aftercare requests. Each of the methods discussed here have been optimised by testing multiple configurations and reviewing how well they perform on the data. To ensure that we do not overfit the data, an 80–20 split is used, where 80% of the data is used as training data to learn from and obtain an optimal configuration, and 20% of the data has been used to verify the effectiveness of the optimised models.

4.1   SARIMA

To assert the necessity of a more complex approach towards forecasting, we will first assess the effectiveness of the classical time series forecasting methods. We define a SARIMA model as $SARIMA(p, d, q)(P, D, Q, S)$, where p, d, q and P, D, Q represent the autoregressive order, difference order, and moving average order of the trend and seasonality respectively. Finally, S denotes the seasonal value. To optimise performance, the parameters of the SARIMA model were tuned. This was done using the SARIMA auto configuration module, which finds the best SARIMA model based on minimising the Akaike Information Criterion (AIC [6]). The SARIMA models have been fitted and tested for each type of

Table 1. Resulting configurations of the optimal SARIMA models and their MSE

	Daily		Weekly	
	SARIMA configuration	MSE	SARIMA configuration	MSE
ELV	(0, 1, 3)(0, 0, 2, 7)	1.1706	(1, 0, 0)(1, 0, 1, 5)	7.3150
Extramural	(6, 1, 0)(0, 0, 1, 7)	7.1695	(2, 0, 2)(0, 0, 1, 32)	69.7958
GRZ	(6, 1, 0)(1, 0, 1, 7)	4.8076	(3, 0, 0)(1, 0, 0, 35)	41.8868
Terminal	(6, 1, 1)(2, 0, 0, 7)	1.1974	(1, 1, 2)(0, 0, 1, 14)	7.2607
WLZ	(6, 1, 1)(2, 0, 1, 7)	1.0686	(2, 1, 1)(1, 0, 0, 13)	7.5374

care, both on a day and week level. The resulting optimal configurations and the corresponding MSE for the daily and weekly data can be found in Table 1.

Based solely on the MSE, some of the results seem promising. However, further analysis indicate that the SARIMA models are not capable of handling the variations in the data. From the MSE values for the weekly series in Table 1 we can immediately see that the predictive capacity of the model on a week level is not better than that of the day level. Although further investigation shows that the same repetitiveness of the prediction values of the SARIMA model for daily values is not observed: the predicted values are not accurate enough to be considered usable.

4.2 Fuzzy Approaches

In the previous section we have determined that the classical time series approach in the form of SARIMA models is not suitable for the problem of predicting the number of care requests per care type on a daily or weekly basis. This section focuses on exploring fuzzy time series (FTS) as a predictive model for the given problem. Our goal is to achieve reasonably accurate predictions whilst maintaining a high level of explainability for the model.

Conventional FTS. The first fuzzy logic based model tested is the Conventional FTS model. As with the SARIMA model, the Conventional FTS model aims at forecasting future values based on a single time series and is therefore a univariate timeseries model. Table 2 depicts the quantitative results provided by the Conventional FTS model after optimisation.

When observing the MSE in Table 2 and comparing it to the results denoted in Table 1, the model would be classified as performing worse than the SARIMA model. However, further analysis reveals an interesting development. Although the predictions are very conservative, we do see a pattern which seemingly follows the actual values.

Multivariate FTS. It was expected that a univariate model would give moderate results, as the model is limited to past information of the series on which

Table 2. Conventional FTS results for each type of care on the daily time series.

Care type	Configuration	MSE
ELV	mf = triangular, npart = 20	0.925111
Extramural	mf = trapezoidal, npart = 20	9.453497
GRZ	mf = gaussian, npart = 28	9.101146
Terminal	mf = gaussian, npart = 3	2.792941
WLZ	mf = triangular, npart = 3	3.028980

it is trying to make a prediction. To aid in this task, introducing relevant contextual information and converting the problem to a multivariate problem can be useful.

To determine to what degree a multivariate model can actually learn from the proposed approach, three types of multivariate models have been tested: the classical Multivariate FTS model, the Exponentially Weighted Multivariate FTS model (WMVFTS), and the Grannular WMVFTS model. Each of the multivariate models takes as an input a set of variables, which are represented by the separate time series per care type, as well as the newly created time series for the total amount of care requests.

Table 3 shows the resulting optimised models for each type of care on the daily time series. Note that the 'configuration' column now features an array of numbers. These denote the number of partitions for each of the variables introduced to the model, in the order ['ELV', 'Extramural', 'GRZ', 'Terminal', 'Total', 'WLZ']. Interesting to note is that based on the MSE, we see that the Granular approach suggested by Silva [7] does indeed provide much better results than the other tested multivariate models. This is likely partially due to the model being higher order, and thus able to exploit more past information for the next prediction. The quantitative results appear promising, which is confirmed by the plots that can be found in Fig. 2.

Table 3. The quantitative results for the optimised versions of each model per care type for the daily time series

	MVFTS		WMVFTS		GWMVFTS	
	configuration	MSE	configuration	MSE	configuration	MSE
ELV	[7, 19, 17, 5, 32, 6]	1.013	[7, 17, 15, 4, 33, 5]	0.827	[7, 18, 16, 5, 31, 4]	0.123
Extramural	[5, 19, 17, 5, 25, 6]	5.935	[6, 19, 17, 6, 33, 6]	4.888	[7, 17, 16, 6, 30, 6]	0.734
GRZ	[5, 19, 17, 5, 34, 4]	6.183	[7, 10, 16, 6, 4, 6]	5.800	[7, 18, 17, 6, 30, 4]	0.875
Terminal	[7, 19, 12, 6, 26, 6]	0.947	[7, 19, 11, 6, 27, 5]	0.430	[6, 17, 17, 5, 28, 4]	0.124
WLZ	[7, 19, 17, 6, 23, 6]	0.853	[6, 17, 14, 5, 26, 6]	0.500	[4, 17, 17, 4, 19, 6]	0.072

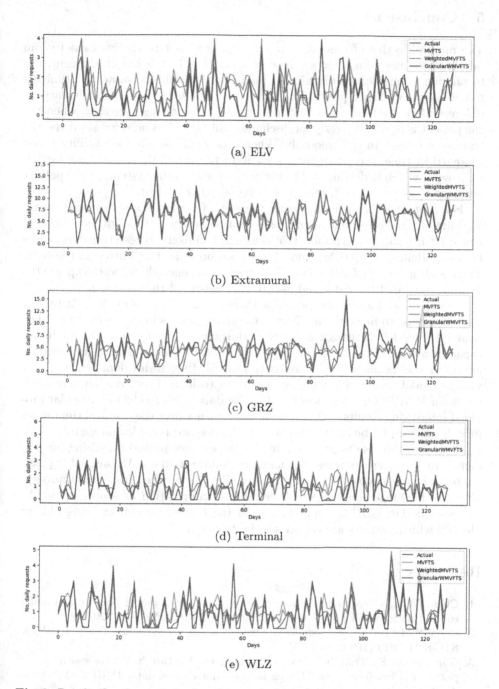

(a) ELV

(b) Extramural

(c) GRZ

(d) Terminal

(e) WLZ

Fig. 2. Results for the optimised multivariate fuzzy timeseries models per care type for the daily data

5   Conclusions

The main objective of this paper was to explore what predictive capacity can be obtained based on aftercare request data of a Dutch hospital. Being able to provide a reliable and explainable prediction aids the hospital in optimizing patient flow. With such prediction, the hospital is able to ensure enough places in different aftercare facilities (of different types). This makes sure that, whenever the patient is medically ready for discharge, but there is a need for aftercare, the transfer process can run smoothly. When a place in an aftercare facility is not arranged in time, the patient waits for it in the hospital, without any further treatment, which is detrimental to the patient and to the system, as the patient occupies a bed that could, otherwise, serve another patient.

For that, we aimed at analyzing the data from a time series perspective, focusing on predicting the amount of each aftercare type that will be needed in a near future. After ascertaining that the data is unlikely to need transformations before modelling, a SARIMA model has been optimised and fitted to the data. The resulting models for the daily timeseries data generally failed to capture the variable nature of the data, and mostly only captured the seasonality.

Moreover, we have experimented with Fuzzy Time Series models. At first, it was attempted to fit univariate fuzzy time series models in the form of the Classical FTS model. Although a better performance was noticed, the predictive capacity was again not enough to provide useful results. Thus, a multivariate approach was evaluated. We have combined all time series data into a multivariate model, to provide more context data to learn from. A relatively novel Granular WMVFTS model was fitted to the data. This model in particular provided interesting results with drastic improvements over the classical time series models, and would be accurate enough to be deemed reliable and useful.

Although the results presented in this paper have proved promising for predicting future aftercare requests, many possibilities remain. Although it is possible to make arrangements based on the predictions resulted from this approach, aftercare facilities would like to have patient information as soon as possible, to accommodate his/her requirements. In the future, we aim at being able to identify which patients are the ones to be transferred.

References

1. Chen, M.Y., Chen, B.T.: A hybrid fuzzy time series model based on granular computing for stock price forecasting. Inf. Sci. **294**(C), 227–241 (2015)
2. Chen, S.M.: Forecasting enrollments based on fuzzy time series. Fuzzy Sets Syst. **81**(3), 311–319 (1996)
3. Gopakumar, S., Tran, T., Luo, W., Phung, D., Venkatesh, S.: Forecasting daily patient outflow from a ward having no real-time clinical data. JMIR Med. Inform. **4**, e25 (2016)
4. Gül, M., Guneri, A.: Forecasting patient length of stay in an emergency department by artificial neural networks. J. Aeronaut. Space Technol. (Havacilik ve Uzay Teknolojileri Dergisi) **8**, 43–48 (2015)

5. Kaushik, S., et al.: AI in healthcare: time-series forecasting using statistical, neural, and ensemble architectures. Frontiers Big Data **3**, 4 (2020)
6. Lord, D., Qin, X., Geedipally, S.R.: Chapter 2 - fundamentals and data collection. In: Lord, D., Qin, X., Geedipally, S.R. (eds.) Highway Safety Analytics and Modeling, pp. 17–57. Elsevier (2021)
7. Silva, P.: Scalable Models for Probabilistic Forecasting with Fuzzy Time Series. Ph.D. thesis (09 2019)
8. Song, Q., Chissom, B.S.: Fuzzy time series and its models. Fuzzy Sets Syst. **54**(3), 269–277 (1993)
9. Yang, X., Yu, F., Pedrycz, W.: Long-term forecasting of time series based on linear fuzzy information granules and fuzzy inference system. Int. J. Approximate Reasoning **81**, 1–27 (2017)
10. Zinouri, N., Taaffe, K.M., Neyens, D.M.: Modelling and forecasting daily surgical case volume using time series analysis. Health Syst. **7**, 111–119 (2018)

Author Index

M. Sellami et al. (Eds.): CoopIS 2023, LNCS 14353, pp. 507–508, 2024.
https://doi.org/10.1007/978-3-031-46846-9

Printed in the United States
by Baker & Taylor Publisher Services